The Firebird Book

Second Edition

by Helen Borrie

Vol. 1: Firebird Fundamentals

IBP Publications

The Firebird Book (Second Edition): A Reference for Database Developers

Volume 1: Firebird Fundamentals

ISBN (paperback): 1-48274-497-X

Reviewers were Aage Johansen, Dimitry Sibiryakov, Thomas Steinmaurer, Calin Pirtea

Design of the cover and Part headers is by Stella Damaschin.

Body text is 10pt Garamond.

AUTHOR'S FOREWORD

This, the second edition of The Firebird Book, has been gestating for more than seven years, since the first edition in August, 2004. The first book's milestone was Firebird 1.5. Its objective was to to provide an up-to-date working reference for developers, whether coming to Firebird from another database management system or moving into it with past experience in its closed source cousin, InterBase.

The Firebird Book Second Edition became too large to distribute as a paper book. Its initial distribution has been as an electronic book in PDF format with a number of navigation aids. A few months on from its release, when it became clear that many of you still like having a paper book at hand, I proceeded to split up the content into three companion printed volumes:

Volume 1: ***Firebird Fundamentals*** (this book) describes and illustrates the architectures of the client/server models and introduces basic procedures for installing Firebird, configuring it for "plain Jane" network use and beginning to work with databases. It works through the essential lexicon for creating databases and the objects within them, using the Data Definition Language (DDL) subset of Firebird's SQL language. It also provides the information needed to use the command-line tool *isql* and to understand and work with transactions.

Volume 2: ***Developing with Firebird Data*** picks up the story with a focus on the Data Manipulation Language (DML) and programming (PSQL) lexicons that have expanded so much in the years since Firebird 1.5.

Volume 3: ***Administering Firebird Servers and Databases*** packages the issues of concern to the administrator, including installation, configuration, database management, backup and monitoring and all of the tools.

In the years since the first book, Firebird has evolved through three further major versions: 2.0, 2.1 and 2.5. At the time of this writing, all three are still under maintenance and the re-architected version 3.0 is in alpha development. Maintenance of version 1.5 ceased in 2009.

The energy and dedication of Firebird's development team continue to be a source of wonder and inspiration to me and, I'm sure, to anyone else who works with Firebird. The polyglot Core team—Dmitry Yemanov, Vlad Khorsun, Alex Peshkov and Adriano dos Santos Fernandes—works closely and tirelessly under Dmitry's chieftainship. Pavel Cisar and Philippe Makowski lead quality assurance testing and Claudio Valderrama is responsible for scrutinising incoming code changes. Claudio's hand is often seen in improvements to the command-line tools, as well.

Because Firebird is distributed free, in all senses of the word, it produces no revenue to pay salaries to the code workers. Many of these volunteers depend on Firebird Foundation grants to supplement their incomes to make space for their Firebird work.

The Firebird Foundation is funded by donations, cash sponsorships and membership subscriptions from individuals and companies that perceive and acknowledge the benefits of using Firebird and keeping it under active development. You can view the current list of sponsors at *http://www.firebirdsql.org/en/sponsors/*. Bless 'em all!

Some sponsors contribute much more than cash. IBPhoenix, for example, contributes the manpower for QA, binary builds and basic documentation. Neither this book nor its predecessor would have come to fruition without IBPhoenix funding. Broadview Software hosts the issue tracker, pre-release and build servers while IBSurgeon funds the hosting and development of the Firebird web site at *www.firebirdsql.org*.

Amongst the volunteers who contribute their time and expertise to the Firebird Project without grants I must name Paul Vinkenoog, who has been almost single-handedly responsible for filling the free documentation gap between the legacy InterBase manuals and the release notes that are distributed with the binary kits. It is a vast and ongoing task that is often thankless. At the time of writing this, Paul is working with Dmitry Yemanov to produce comprehensive on-line SQL documentation that will not be inhibited by the copyright issues that still prohibit reuse of the legacy InterBase material.

Under the Firebird Project umbrella, volunteers also develop and maintain several of the drivers and language interfaces for Firebird—Jaybird (for Java), the Firebird .NET providers, the ODBC driver and the interfaces for PHP and Python.

If you are coming to Firebird as a newcomer, welcome! I wish you a long and happy experience with our software. To you and to those devotees who are freshening up your Firebird experience, I wish you great satisfaction from your use of this Second Edition of ***The Firebird Book***.

Helen Borrie (author) December 2012

About the Author

Helen Borrie is a contracting software engineer who doubles as a writer and technical editor. She has been involved with database development for 30 years and with Firebird and its ancestors since 1996.

Helen is an active member of the Firebird online support community and a founding member of the Firebird Foundation, incorporated as a non-profit organisation in New South Wales, Australia, in 2002.

Sparky

Approximately once a year, the Firebird community has an international conference in a European city. Each time there's a conference, Helen makes a Sparky, which is auctioned at an outrageous price to help with the fund-raising for the Firebird Foundation. Thus it is that, to the date of this publication, ten of these fierce creatures are living somewhere in the world.

INTRODUCTION

What Is Firebird?

Firebird is a powerful, compact client/server SQL relational database management system (RDBMS) that can run on a variety of server and client operating system platforms, including Windows, Linux, MacOSX and several other UNIX platforms. It is an industrial-strength RDBMS that features a high level of compliance with SQL standards, while implementing some powerful language features in the vendor-specific sphere of procedure programming.

Who Needs This Book?

Developers with some database experience, who may be moving to client/server for the first time, will discover all of the basics they need to become productive with Firebird in this book. Although not a primary tutorial on SQL or database design, this guide emphasizes good client/server RDBMS design practice and documents Firebird's SQL definition, manipulation, and programming language sets with plenty of detail, insider tips, and examples.

Firebird is serious software designed for deployment on networks small and large, including some useful capabilities for stand-alone configurations. Its small footprint makes it easy for sole developers to do large enterprise development from a home office. For the database administrator or system designer, the book is a basic installation, configuration, tuning, security, and tools resource. Firebird's strengths and high compliance with standards make it an attractive medium for university-level IT study. The book will serve amply as a resource for second- and third-year computer science students using Firebird for assignment work.

For those who have been using older Firebird versions or InterBase until now, the Firebird Book introduces the security, language, and optimizer enhancements that were added with the "2-series" releases: 2.0.x, 2.1.x and 2.5.x.

Where to Find What You Need

Part One is a "101 course" for those who are new to Firebird. There, you will find the basics for understanding the client/server architecture, installing the software, getting a network client up and running, and for essential operations.

In ***Part Two***, you will find a detailed reference to each of the SQL data types supported in Firebird. There is a chapter for each class of data type—numbers, date/time types, character types, and so on—with plenty of tips for using them.

Part Three examines the database and the various objects and relationships in detail. The SQL language subset for creating, modifying and removing objects is data definition language (DDL). Its statement syntaxes and usages are covered in this section. It also includes an introductrion to some useful features of the administrative command-line toolset, *gfix*. The part ends with a detailed chapter on using the command-line *isql* tool to perform batch operations, query databases interactively and get information about them.

Part Four addresses transactions: how they work, how to configure them.

Appendices and Glossary

All of the Appendices and the Glossary appear in ***The Firebird Book (Second Edition)*** which is distributed through IBPhoenix on its Developer DVD. In the paperback volumes, the selection varies. The identifier Vol. 1 refers to ***Firebird Fundamentals***; Vol. 2 refers to ***Developing with Firebird Data***; while Vol. 3 refers to ***Administering Firebird Servers and Databases***. Details of materials available in the appendices and glossary are as follows:

I: Internal and External Functions contains names, descriptions and examples for the internal functions, as well as external functions (UDFs) in the shipped `fb_udf` and `ib_udf` libraries.

II: Reserved and Non-Reserved Keywords tabulates all of the keywords, both reserved and non-reserved, that are applicable to the various versions of Firebird.

III: Context Variables lists the context variables available by version and explains their usage.

IV: Firebird Limits enumerates the various physical limits applicable to Firebird, by version.

V: System Tables and Views provides the data description specifications for the schema and monitoring tables[1] maintained by the Firebird server inside every database. It includes source code listings for some useful views you can create to interrogate the system tables.

VI: Character Sets and Collations is a full reference to the international character sets and language-specific collation sequences distributed with Firebird versions.

VII: Error Codes (Vol. 2: Appx VII, Vol. 3: Appx IV) is a full, tabulated listing of the exception codes (SQLCODE and GDSCODE) defined in Firebird versions along with the associated symbolic constants and the message texts in English.

VIII: SQLSTATE Codes (Vol. 2: Appx VIII, Vol. 3: Appx V) lists the SQL-standard status and error codes that were introduced in v.2.1.

IX: Database Repair How-To (Vol. 3: Appx VI) is a step-by-step procedure you can follow, using Firebird's own tools, when a database seems to be logically corrupted.

X: Default Disk Locations (Vol. 3: Appx VII) indicates where you could expect to find all of the components of a Firebird installation, by operating system platform.

XI: Healthcare for Databases (Vol. 3: Appx VIII) describes good practices for keeping databases in good shape.

XII: Upgrade Scripts (Vol. 3: Appx IX) contains the scripts referred to in Vol. 3, Chapter 4, ***Migration Notes***.

XIII: Application Interfaces (Vol. 2: Appx IX) contains notes regarding some of the host language interface layers that are available to programmers writing applications with Firebird back-ends.

XIV: Resources (Vol. 1: Appx VII, Vol. 2 & Vol. 3: Appx X) is a compilation of resources available to Firebird users. It includes book and other documentary recommendations, along with links to some software tool and support offerings.

The ***Glossary*** provides summary descriptions of terminology and concepts you are likely to encounter on your journey into Firebird.

Firebird's Origins

Developed as an ongoing open source project, Firebird was the first new-generation descendant of Borland's InterBase 6.0 Open Edition code, which was released for open source development in July 2000 under the InterBase Public License (IPL).

1. Monitoring tables do not exist in databases of ODS 11.0 or lower.

The Firebird source code tree is maintained in a *Subversion* repository and developed on the international open source code foundry, SourceForge.net (http://sourceforge.net), by a stable team of professional developers, comprising both volunteers and others in specialist roles that are partly funded by grants from community and commercial contributions.

The Firebird RDBMS products and several associated modules are distributed completely free of registration or deployment fees under a variety of open source licenses.

The Firebird Project

The developers, designers, and testers who gave you Firebird and several of the drivers are members of the Firebird open source project at SourceForge, an amazing virtual community that is home to thousands of open source software teams. The Firebird project's address there is *http://sourceforge.net/projects/firebird*. At that site are the *Subversion* (SVN) source code tree and a number of technical files that can be downloaded for various purposes related to the development and testing of the codebases.

The Firebird Project developers and testers use an e-mail list forum, *firebird-devel@lists.sourceforge.net*, as their "virtual laboratory" for communicating with one another about their work on enhancements, bug fixing, and producing new versions of Firebird.

Anyone who is interested in watching the progress and feedback on beta development can join this forum.

Support for Application Developers and DBAs

Firebird has a powerful community of willing helpers, including a large body of active developers with many years of experience developing with and deploying Firebird and its InterBase ancestors. The esprit de corps among this large group is such that, having acquired the skills and learned the "inside tricks" from the advice of others, its members stay around the lists as mentors to new users. The mainstream free support channel is the *Firebird-support* forum.

More specialized groups within the project's arena conduct specific forums—Java, Delphi and C++Builder, tools, Visual Basic, ADO.NET provider, PHP, and more. The groups run as e-mail lists, and many are mirrored to a news server. The latest links to these forums can always be found at the main community website at *www.firebirdsql.org/en/support/*.

The *IBPhoenix* site also hosts an enormous volume of technical and user documentation, links to third-party tools, and a running news board of events happening throughout the Firebird community.

The Firebird Foundation

The Firebird Foundation (Inc.) is a non-profit foundation incorporated in New South Wales, Australia, that raises funds around the world for grants to developers working on general and special projects for extending, testing, and enhancing Firebird. Funds come in through private and corporate sponsorships, donations, and membership subscriptions. It provides a way for appreciative Firebird users to return a contribution for the free use of software and community support. Look it up at *www.firebirdsql.org/en/firebird-foundation/*.

Overview of Firebird

Firebird is a true client/server software, designed especially for use in local and wide-area networks. Accordingly, its core consists of two main software programs: the database server, which runs on a network host computer, and the client library, through which users on remote workstations connect to and communicate with databases managed by the server.

Administering and developing with a full-blooded SQL client/server RDBMS may be new territory for you. It can present a steep learning curve if this is your first venture into data management software that is purpose-built for multiple concurrent writers. Chapter 1 of this book provides an introduction to client/server concepts.

Firebird Versions

The original Firebird version 1.0.x binaries were developed by correcting and enhancing the modules, written in the C language, that the open source community inherited from InterBase 6.0. Firebird 1.5 and all subsequent versions were completely rewritten in C++, with a high degree of standardization across compilers.

*At the beginning of Chapter 5 in **The Firebird Book Second Edition** or Chapter 4 in the companion volume to this, Vol. 3: **Administering Firebird Servers and Databases**, you can review the various major releases in the topic Version Lineage.*

Network Access

A Firebird server running on any platform accepts TCP/IP client attachments from any client platform that can implement the Firebird API.

Clients cannot attach to a Firebird server through any medium of filesystem sharing (NFS shares, Samba client connections, Windows shares or mapped drives, etc.).

A client must attach through an absolute physical path. However, from Firebird 1.5 onward, a database aliasing feature allows applications to "soft-connect" through named aliases, whose absolute paths are configured specifically on each deployed server.

A Firebird server running on a services-capable Windows host can accept attachments from Windows clients through the *Named Pipes* network protocol (sometimes wrongly referred to as "NetBEUI").

Multi-generational Architecture

Firebird's model for isolating and controlling the work of multiple users revolves around an architecture that is able to store more than one version of a record in the database concurrently. Multiple generations of a record can exist simultaneously—hence the term "multi-generational." Each user task holds its own contextual view of database state (see the next section) and, when ready, writes its own versions of records on the server's disk. At that point, the new version (or a deletion) cannot be accessed by other user tasks.

The most recently committed record version is the only one visible outside the user task that successfully posted a new version, and it continues to be the version seen by other tasks. Others will be aware that something has happened to the record because they will be blocked from updating or deleting the same record until the new version becomes "official" by being committed.

Because of its multi-generational architecture (known as MGA), Firebird has no need for the two-phase locking used by other DBMSs to control multi-user concurrency.

Transactions

All user tasks in Firebird are enclosed within transactions. A task begins with a START TRANSACTION statement and ends when work posted by the user task is committed or rolled back. A user task can make multiple requests for operations to be performed within a single transaction, including operations in more than one database.

Work is saved to the database in two stages. In the first stage, changes are stored to disk, without changing database state. In the second stage, changes are committed or rolled back by the client process. Clients can "unpost" parts of work inside an uncommitted transaction by tagging stages in a process as *savepoints* and rolling back to a savepoint without rolling back an entire transaction.

Firebird transactions are atomic, which means that all work posted in a transaction will succeed or all will fail.[2]

Every transaction is configurable, with three levels of isolation and a variety of strategies for fine-tuning concurrency and read-write conditions.

Stored Procedures and Triggers

Firebird has a rich language of procedural extensions, PSQL, for writing stored proceduresand triggers. It is a structured language with support for FOR looping through sets, conditional branching, exception handling, and event triggering. PSQL code is compiled at creation and stored in binary form.

In the "2" series and higher, blocks of procedural code can be submitted dynamically by a client application, using the EXECUTE BLOCK syntax.

Trigger support is strong, with a Before and After phase for each DML event.

Multiple triggers may be stored for each phase/event and optionally numbered in an execution sequence. Before or After triggers that comprise behaviors for all three DML events, with conditional branching per event, are supported.[3]

Referential Integrity

Firebird has full support for formal, SQL-standard referential integrity—sometimes known as *declarative* referential integrity—including optional cascading updates and deletes with a number of RI trigger action options.

Database Shadowing

Firebird servers can optionally maintain database shadows. A shadow is a real-time copy of the database with some extra attributes that make it unavailable for reading until it is made available by the server. Shadows can be "kicked in" if required, either manually or automatically. The purpose of shadowing is to enable the database to become available very quickly if a disk crash occurs.

Shadowing is not replication.

Security

At host level, Firebird provides user access to the server by means of user IDs and encrypted passwords. Like any database server, it relies on adequate physical, network access, and filesystem security being in place. Firebird can store encrypted data but, except for password encryption, it provides no capability to encrypt data itself.

While an embedded server application has its uses for single-user, stand-alone applications, on Windows it bypasses the host's security gateway altogether. SQL

2. From v.2.5 onward, autonomous transactions within procedural (PSQL) modules are supported. Under certain conditions, an autonomous transaction can be configured to "stick", even if the transaction in which the module is running is rolled back.

3. Not in Firebird 1.0.x.

privileges defined at database level still apply, but an embedded application can get password-free access to any database on its host machine.

SQL Privileges

Although a user must be authorized to access a Firebird server, no user except the SYSDBA and the database owner has automatic rights to anything within an individual database. Database-level security is supported on an "opt-in" basis, by means of SQL privileges. Users must be granted privileges to any object explicitly.

SQL Roles allow sets of privileges to be aggregated and granted as a "package" to individual users. A single user may have privileges under several roles, although only one may be selected when logging into the database.

Operating Modes

Firebird server can be installed to run in one of four modes: Superserver, Classic server, Superclassic or Embedded Server. The distinction is largely a question of architecture. Any client application written to attach to the Superserver can attach in exactly the same way to the Classic or Superclassic[4] server and perform exactly the same tasks. The reverse is also true, except that Superserver has more exacting thread-safety requirements for external function modules (user-defined functions, character set libraries, and BLOB filters).

The Embedded Server is a variant of Superserver.

Classic and Superclassic Servers

The Classic server[5] preceded Superserver historically. It was designed late in the 1980s, when machine resources on servers were scarce and programs used them with great economy. The Classic server model continued for operating systems whose threading capabilities were non-existent or too limited to support the Superserver. Classic server remains the best option for environments where high performance is important and system resources are adequate to accommodate linear growth of usage as each new connection is added.

When a client connects to a Classic server, the server spawns a dedicated process for that attachment. Superclassic, introduced in Firebird 2.5, is like Classic except that it spawns threads for attachments.

Classic or Superclassic are the recommended options where utilisation of multiple CPUs is desirable.

Superserver

In 1996, Firebird's ancestor, InterBase 4.1, introduced the multi-threaded Superserver for the then-new Windows 32-bit platforms. It promised to make better use of the advancing capabilities of servers and networks. Superserver's abilities to spin off process threads and to allocate cache memory dynamically make it more capable than Classic server where the number of interactive read/write users is high and system resources are limited.

With the explosion of the GNU/Linux operating system on Intel toward the end of the 1990s, a Superserver became a realizable goal for some POSIX platforms.

A Superserver skeleton for Linux was released with the InterBase 6.0 beta open source code and was fully realized in Firebird.

Superserver does not play well with multiple CPUs, especially on Windows, where CPU affinity must be set to a single CPU.

4. Superclassic is not available prior to v.2.5.
5. Not available on Windows in Firebird 1.0.x.

Embedded Server

The embedded variant is a fully functional Firebird rserver compiled with an embedded client that connects directly and exclusively to its database. This single dynamic library (`libfbembed.so` on POSIX, `fbembed.dll` on Windows) uses inter-process communication space to transport client requests and server responses. The API is identical to that presented by a regular Firebird client. Nothing special is required in application code to implement an Embedded Server application.

Embedded Server caters to the extreme "low end" of scalability requirements for a Firebird server, enabling a stand-alone, fast-performing, single-machine database application to be packaged and deployed with a small footprint. Since the database can be accessed by a regular server performing a replication service when the embedded application is offline, Embedded Server is particularly suitable for "briefcase" deployment—for example, on a notebook computer, or even on a flash disk.

The Sample Database

Throughout this guide, the language examples use the sample database that can be found in the examples directory beneath the Firebird installation root. In all versions except v.1.0.x its name is `employee.fdb`. In Firebird 1.0.x, it is `employee.gdb`. It can be found in the `examples/empbuild` sub-directory of a standard Firebird installation.

Document Conventions

General body text is in this font.

```
Passages in this font are code, scripts, or command-line examples.
```

Passages highlighted like this are to draw your attention to something important that might affect your decision to use the feature under discussion.

Passages highlighted like this contain tips, bright ideas, or special recommendations.

Pay special attention to passages like this.

Passages like this provide a bit more information or tell you where to find it.

Passages like this signal something you need to remember.

Syntax Patterns

Some code passages present syntax patterns—that is, code models that demonstrate the optional and mandatory elements of statement and command-line syntax. Certain symbol conventions apply to syntax patterns. To illustrate the conventions, the following extract shows a syntax pattern for the SQL SELECT statement:

```
SELECT
  [FIRST (m)] [SKIP (n)] [[ALL] | DISTINCT]
  <list of columns> [, [column-name] | expression |constant ] AS alias-name]
FROM <table-or-procedure-or-view>
```

```
  [{[[INNER] | [{LEFT | RIGHT | FULL} [OUTER]] JOIN}] <table-or-procedure-or-view>
ON <join-conditions [{JOIN..]]
  [WHERE <search-conditions>]
[GROUP BY <grouped-column-list>]
[HAVING <search-condition>]
[UNION <select-expression> [ALL]]
[PLAN <plan-expression>]
[ORDER BY <column-list>]
[FOR UPDATE [OF col1 [,col2..]] [WITH LOCK]]
```

Special Symbols

Elements (keywords, parameters) that are mandatory in all cases appear without any markings. In the preceding example, the keywords SELECT and FROM are mandatory for every SELECT statement.

Certain characters that never occur in SQL statements or command-line commands are used in syntax patterns to indicate specific rules about usage. These symbols are [ ], { }, | , <string>, and . . . . None of them is valid in the actual command syntax. They are used in the patterns, as follows:

Square brackets [ ] indicate that the element(s) within the brackets are optional. When square brackets are nested, it means that the nesting, or the nested element, is optional.

Curly braces { } indicate that the elements within the braces are mandatory. The usual usage of curly braces is seen within an optional (square-bracketed) element, meaning "If the optional element is used, the curly-braced portion is mandatory." In the preceding example, if the optional explicit JOIN clause is used

```
[{[[INNER] | [{LEFT | RIGHT | FULL} [OUTER]] JOIN}]
```

the outer pair of curly braces indicates that the keyword JOIN is mandatory. The inner pair of curly braces indicates that, if an OUTER join is specified, it must be qualified as either LEFT, RIGHT, or FULL, with optional use of the keyword OUTER.

The *pipe symbol* | is used to separate mutually exclusive elements. In the preceding example, LEFT, RIGHT, and FULL are mutually exclusive, and inner join and any outer join are mutually exclusive. The first option of a set of choices is normally the default.

Parameters are indicated with a string representing the parameter, enclosed angle brackets <>. For example, `[WHERE <search-conditions>]` indicates that one or more search conditions are required as parameters to the optional WHERE clause in the SELECT syntax.

In some cases, the <string> convention may be a shorthand for more complex options, that subsequent lines in the syntax pattern would "explode," level by level, to provide finer details. For example, you might see an expansion line like this:

```
<search-conditions> := <column-expression> := <constant> | <expression>
```

Pairs or triplets of dots ... may be used in some syntax patterns to indicate that the current element is repeatable.

The Firebird Book
A Reference for Database Developers

SECOND EDITION

Volume 1: Firebird Fundamentals

Contents

PART I

Firing Up with Firebird

CHAPTER

1

Firebird Servers and Clients

The Firebird server is a program that runs on a host node in a network and listens for clients on a communication port. It serves requests from multiple clients to multiple databases simultaneously.

SuperServer is a multi-threaded process that starts a new thread for each attached client. In Classic, a new process is started for each connection. Firebird 2.5 introduced Superclassic, a modification of the Classic model that launches threads to attach clients from a single parent process.

Firebird servers can run on a wide spectrum of hardware and accept client connections from applications running on incompatible systems. Small-footprint server installations can be done on outdated equipment, even old boxes running 32-bit Windows XP or a minimal Linux. At the other end of the scale, Firebird servers are running in distributed environments, managing databases in the Terabyte range.

Of course, it is not realistic to plan an enterprise information system to run on a 32-bit Windows box. However, it is a simple matter to start with a minimally configured server and scale both vertically and horizontally as need arises.

The Role of the Server

The server's jobs include

- managing database storage and disk space allocation
- regulating all transactions started by clients, ensuring that each gets and keeps a consistent view of the permanently stored data that it has requested through the client
- managing commits, data and housekeeping
- maintaining locks and statistics for each database
- handling requests to insert, modify or delete rows and maintain the currency and obsolescence of record versions
- maintaining the metadata for each database and servicing client requests to create new databases and database objects, alter structures, validate and compile stored procedures and triggers
- servicing client requests for result sets and procedure execution
- routing messages to clients
- maintaining cached data to keep frequently-used data sets and indexes in the foreground

- maintaining a separate security database for verifying user access

Operating System Platforms

Firebird server platforms include, but are not limited to

- Linux, FreeBSD and several UNIX operating systems
- Microsoft Windows service-capable platforms NT 4.0 and Windows 2000 (Server or Workstation editions), XP Professional and Server 2003. Windows 9x, ME and XP Home can support servers listening on TCP ports but not Named Pipes protocols such as NetBEUI
- MacOS X (Darwin)
- Sun Solaris Sparc and Intel
- HP-UX

Databases

Each database exists in one or more files, which grow dynamically as need arises. Database files must be stored on disk storage that is under the physical control of the machine on which the server is hosted. Only a server process can perform direct I/O on the database files.

A Firebird database file consists of blocks of storage known as pages. The size of one database page can be 1, 2, 4, 8 or 16 Kb and it is set at database creation time. It can be changed only by restoring a backed-up database and specifying a new size. Different databases on the same server can have different page sizes.

The server maintains a number of different page types in each database—data pages, several levels of index pages, BLOB pages, inventory pages for various accounting purposes, and so on. It lays out pages in a geography known only to itself and a handful of gifted wizards. Unlike file-served database management systems, Firebird does not store tables in physical rows and columns but in a continuous stream, on pages. When a page is nearing full capacity and more rows are to be written, the server requests disk space from the operating system and allocates a new page. Pages from a single table are not stored in any contiguous sequence. In fact, pages belonging to a single table could be distributed across several database files on several disks.

Server-side Programming

Among Firebird's powerful features for dynamic client/server application programming is its capability to comple source code on the server into a binary form for run-time interpretation. Such procedures and functions are executed completely on the server, optionally returning values or data sets to the client application. Firebird provides two styles of server-side programming capability: stored procedures and triggers. In addition, external functions, also known as "user-defined functions" (UDFs) can be written in a high-level language and made available to the server for use in SQL expressions.

Stored procedures

Firebird's procedure language (PSQL) implements extensions to its SQL language, providing conditional logic, flow control structures, exception handling (both built-in and user-defined), local variables, an event mechanism and the capability to accept input arguments of almost any type supported by Firebird. It implements a powerful flow control structure for processing cursors which can output a dataset directly to client memory without the need to create temporary tables. Such procedures are called from the client with a SELECT statement and are known to developers as "selectable stored procedures".

Stored procedures can embed other stored procedures and can be recursive. All stored procedure execution, including selection of data sets from procedures and embedded calls to other procedures, is under the control of the single transaction that calls it. Accordingly, the work of a stored procedure call will be cancelled totally if the client rolls back the transaction.

Autonomous Transactions

In the normal workflow of a stored procedure, it is not possible to start and commit a transaction autonomously from within a stored procedure, as it breaks the consistency model whereby the client application maintains full control over what, when and how database state changes.

However, in v.2.5 the capability was introduced to execute autonomous transactions in a limited way, using the IN AUTONOMOUS TRANSACTION DO.. construct or an enhanced implementation of EXECUTE STATEMENT in Firebird's procedural language (PSQL) that provides a WITH AUTONOMOUS TRANSACTION attribute. The latter route can be used to enable the updating of data in another database.

Triggers

Triggers are special procedures you can create for specific events in a database, for automatic execution at some appointed phase of the event.

Row-level triggers

During the process of posting the insertion, update or deletion of a row to the server, you can write triggers for the table that "fire" before or after that event. A trigger fires for every row in its parent table that is affected by the event. Any table can have any number of triggers to be executed before or after inserts, updates and deletions. Execution order is determined by a position parameter in the trigger's declaration. Row-level triggers have some language extensions not available to regular stored procedures or to dynamic sql, notably the context variables OLD and NEW which, when prefixed to a column identifier, provide references to the existing and requested new values of the column.

Triggers can call stored procedures but not other triggers.

Work performed by table-level triggers will be rolled back if the transaction that prompted them is rolled back.

"Database-level" triggers

The v.2.1 release introduced triggers whose scope is broader than the table-level trigger. The term "database-level" is not really appropriate, since these higher-level triggers are written with an explicit duration in view. A "connection-level" trigger takes effect when a client session begins and its effects last until the session ends. A "transaction-level" trigger takes effect when a transaction begins and its effects end when the transaction is committed or rolled back.

Such triggers have several uses, including the ability to restrict connections to specific users and the ability to block specified actions if some criteria are not met. They can be used to set and get context variables, a feature that was also enhanced at v.2.1 to enable user-defined context variables.

User-defined functions

By design, in order to preserve its small footprint, Firebird in many of its older versions comes with a very modest arsenal of internally-defined (native) data transformation functions. Developers can write their own very precise functions in familiar host-language code such as C/C++, Pascal or Object Pascal to accept arguments and return a single result. Once an external function—UDF—is declared to a database, it becomes available as a valid SQL function to applications, stored procedures and triggers.

Firebird supplies two libraries of ready-to-use UDFs: `ib_udf` and and `fbudf`, available for both Windows and POSIX.

Many of the functions in these libraries have been superseded in v.2.1 and higher by a substantial collection of internal functions. Where both an internal implementation and an external version of the same function exist, the internal function is preferred, both to reduce the vulnerability of the engine to outside interference and to make use of the greater standards compliance of the internal versions.

UDF functions are adjuncts to the Firebird engine, not to the client libraries. Firebird looks for UDFs in libraries stored in the `/udf` directory of its installation or in other directories configured in firebird.conf by the ***UdfAccess*** parameter.

v.1.0.x *In the v.1.0.x configuration file, the name of the parameter is* ***external_function_directory****.*

Multi-database Applications

Firebird applications can be connected to more than one database simultaneously, with . any number of databases open and accessible to the client application at the same time. Tables from separate databases can not be joined to return linked sets, but cursors can be used to combine information.

If consistency across database boundaries is required, Firebird can manage output sets from querying multiple databases inside a single transaction. Firebird implements automatic two-phase commit when data changes occur, to ensure that changes cannot be committed in one database if changes in another database, within the same transaction context, are rolled back or lost through a network failure.

From v.2.5 forward, external databases can be updated from within a single database connection, using autonomous transactions in procedural SQL.

Server Security

For controlling user access to the server, the Firebird server creates and maintains the security database, a database of users known to the server. For Firebird 2.0 and higher server versions, the name of this database is `security2.fdb`. For v.1.5, it is `security.fdb`, whilst its name in v.1.0.x is `isc4.gdb`. At installation time, this database contains one user: SYSDBA.

- In Windows installations, the SYSDBA password is *masterkey*. It is strongly recommended that you run the program gsec.exe (in the installation /bin directory) immediately after installing and change this password. This is one of the best-known passwords in the database world!
- From v.1.5 forward, the Linux RPM installers generate a random password for SYSDBA and update the database to replace *masterkey*. This password is stored in the installation root in a text file named `SYSDBA.password`. If you want to keep using the password, delete this file!

The SYSDBA has full privileges to every database on the server and, in the current security model, this can not be changed. The root user on Linux/UNIX gets SYSDBA privileges automatically in all versions. A parallel policy was introduced for Windows in v.2.1 for network administrators and was modified in v.2.5. The database Owner (the user which created the database) has full privileges to that database.

For all other users, access to objects in a database is by "opt-in" SQL privileges only—mentioned next.

At v.2.5, some mechanisms were introduced to make it possible for the SYSDBA to confer administrative rights on ordinary users via a privileged SQL role, RDB$ADMIN.

Database Security

All users except those with full privileges must be granted rights to each object to which they are to be allowed access. The SQL GRANT statement is used for assigning privileges.

Firebird supports the SQL ROLE. A user-defined role must first be created using a CREATE ROLE statement, and committing it. Groups of privileges can be granted to a role and then the role can be granted to a user. In order to use those privileges, the user must log in to the database using both user name and role name.

Databases created under Firebird 2.5+ (ODS 11.2 or higher) come with an inbuilt role, RDB$ADMIN, which the SYSDBA can grant to any user, to confer SYSDBA rights to that user in the current database.

This topic is discussed in detail in Chapter 37 of ***The Firebird Book Second Edition*** and in the companion volume to this, ***Volume 3: Administering Firebird Servers and Databases***.

The Firebird Server Models

Firebird servers come in three flavours—Superserver, Classic server and Superclassic—to cater for differing user demand. Any can be scaled up or down to handle the simplest to the most complex configurations.

Resource Usage

Firebird server software makes efficient use of system resources on the host computer.

- The Superserver process uses approximately 2MB of memory. Each Superserver client connection is likely to add about 200KB to server memory consumption, more or less, according to the characteristics of the client applications and the database design.
- Each Classic connection starts its own server process—or server thread in Superclassic mode—consuming about 2 Mb.
- Superclassic, introduced with Firebird 2.5, runs as a parent process that launches a thread for each connection. Each thread will consume approximately the same amount of RAM as a single Classic process.

Server cache memory consumed depends on database page size, configuration and the process model chosen. Cache is configured in database pages, so memory usage by the cache is calculated by multiplying the number of pages by the page size. The default page size is 4 Mb (4096 bytes) for v.2.0+, 2Mb for v.1.5 and 1 Mb for v.1.0.

- On Superserver, a common cache configuration for a network of 20-40 concurrent users is likely to be in the range of 8 to 64 Mb per database. For each database, the cache is shared as a pool by all connections.
- Each Classic server process or Superclassic thread is assigned a static cache—the default is 75 pages per user. Multiply this by the page size to calculate the amount of RAM allocated for each attachment.
- Like a Classic process, each Superclassic attachment uses an individual database cache..

Servers other than v.1.0.x will also use RAM to speed up sorting, if it is available.

Don't overlook the memory limitations of 32-bit processes: a 32-bit process cannot use more than 2 Gb of RAM, even on a 64-bit machine, regardless of how much is installed.

Disk space for a minimal Firebird installation ranges from 9MB to 12MB, depending on platform. Additional disk space is required for temporary storage during operation and additional memory could be needed for database page caching. Both are configurable according to performance demands and the likely volume and type of data to be handled.

Running Superserver as an application on Windows

On Windows server platforms the normal mode of operation for a Firebird server is to run as a service. One advantage of this is that nobody needs to be logged in to the host machine in order to make the service available to remote clients.

It is possible on Windows to run the server executable as an application. The executable runs in the user's application space, which means that the user must be logged in with the fbserver application running. The implications for physical security are obvious.

Older versions of Firebird can run on very old Windows versions, viz., Windows 9x, ME, NT4, Windows 2000. Whilst the last two provide service capabability, the others do not. Running Firebird as an application is the only option on Windows 9x and ME hosts.

It is a mistake to assume that Firebird will continue to support obsolete operating systems for ever. Support for Windows 9x and NT4 was dropped at v.2.0 and for Windows 2000 at v.2.1. It does not imply that newer versions will not run on those platforms, but it does mean that no QA testing is performed on them.

Comparing Superserver, Superclassic and Classic Architectures

While Superserver and Classic/Superclassic share many common characteristics—indeed, they are built from the same code-base—they present quite distinct models of operation "under the hood".

Executable and processes

Classic—Runs one server process per connection, on demand. When a client attempts to connect to a Firebird database, an instance of the *fb_inet_server* process is initiated and remains dedicated to that client connection for the duration of the connection. When the client detaches from the database, the server process instance ends.

- On POSIX, the the *[x]inetd* daemon monitors the network for attachment requests and starts each *fb_inet_server* process
- On Windows, a parent instance of the *fb_inet_server* service monitors for attachment requests.

Figure 1.1 The Classic network and process model

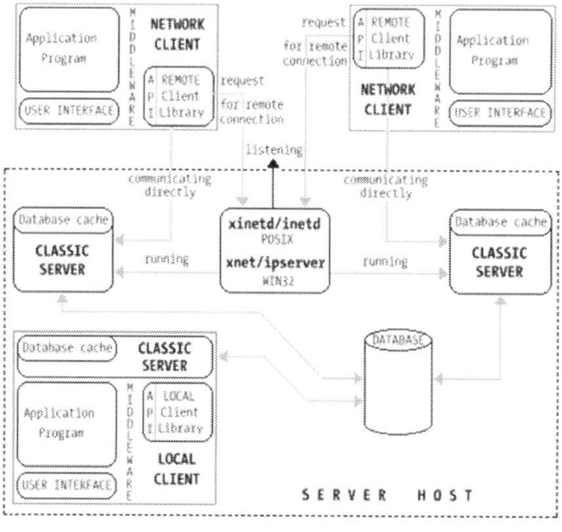

Superclassic—Similar to Classic except that, to attach clients, the listening process launches threads, rather than separate processes.

- On POSIX, the Superclassic listener is the executable *fb_smp_server*, a special build of *fb_inet_server* that does not use *[x]inetd* at all.

Superserver—Runs as a single invocation of the *fbserver* executable. The *fbserver* process is started once, by a system boot script or by the system administrator, and stays running, waiting for connection requests. Threads are created or re-used for attachments. The process is terminated by an explicit shutdown.

Figure 1.2 The Superserver network and process model

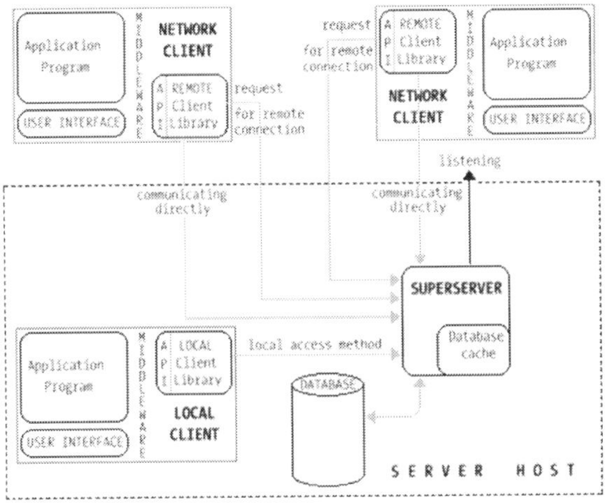

Lock management

Classic/Superclassic—Each client's server process has its own, dedicated database cache and multiple processes contend for access to the database. A Lock Manager subsystem—*fb_lock_mgr*—uses inter-process communication (IPC) methods to arbitrate and synchronize concurrent page access among the processes.

SuperServer—The lock manager is implemented as a thread within the *fbserver* process and uses inter-thread communication mechanisms instead of POSIX signaling.

Resource use

Classic/Superclassic—Each instance of *fb_inet_server* is allocated a static cache of database pages in its memory space. Resource growth per additional client connection is therefore linear. However, when the number of concurrent connections is relatively low, Classic uses fewer overall resources than Superserver.

Superclassic—Makes better use of resources overall than Classic on a well-provisioned 64-bit system, since it is cheaper to thread process instances than to fork them. When a Superclassic server is serving clients to multiple databases, the resource load can be spread across multiple CPUs on multi-core systems.

Deploying Superclassic on 32-bit servers is not recommended.

Superserver—Employs one single cache space which is shared by client attachments, allowing more efficient use and management of cache memory when the number of simultaneous connections grows larger.

Multiple processors

Although Firebird does not support splitting the load from one process or thread across multiple CPUs or cores, its Classic and Superclassic models can make use of the capabilities of multi-processor host machines for load distribution.

SMP with Superserver on Windows

On Windows, SMP machines often exhibit problems with Superserver, specifically a "see-saw" effect, whereby Windows will shift the entire process from one CPU or core to another. For this reason, Superserver for Windows uses only the first processor or core in your computer, by default.. The ***CpuAffinityMask*** parameter in `firebird.conf` allows you to change it so Firebird affines to a different CPU or so that you can test whether your particular Windows/hardware combination suffers from the "see-saw" effect. Unfortunately, most do.

For the v.2.5 release, Superserver was improved to the extent that the process is able to utilise multiple CPUs or cores if it is accessing multiple databases concurrently. To enable SMP support for Superserver for a multi-database host environment, adjust ***CpuAffinityMask*** and test thoroughly for both good and (known) bad effects.

For a single-database system, the situation is unchanged—CPU affinity should be restricted to one CPU or core.

*All other servers (including Superserver for POSIX platforms) ignore **CpuAffinityMask**.*

Crash behaviour

Both Superserver and Superclassic use a single process and launch threads for client sessions. A server crash therefore takes out all client sessions with it. If a Classic server process crashes, the other connections continue unaffected.

Firebird Guardian—fbguard

If the optional Guardian service is used with Superserver (any platform) or Superclassic (POSIX only) it will attempt to restart the *fbserver* or *fb_smp_server* process if it should terminate abnormally.

The Guardian gives some extra reliabilty because it automatically restarts a crashed Superserver. On Windows server platforms, services can be configured at OS level to behave this way, which means the Guardian can be regarded as superfluous for that environment.

The obsolete Windows 9x and ME platforms do not provide services capability. There and on other Windows platforms where Firebird must run as an application, Superserver gains a benefit from running under the Guardian.

The Guardian should not be used with Classic as it can cause the untoward side effect of starting "ghost processes" after abnormal termination of a bona fide Classic process.

Local access method

Superserver—Expects applications to use a network method for I/O requests and satisfies those requests by proxy.

- On POSIX, SuperServer does not support direct local access—local connections to Superserver are made through the localhost server (at IP address 127.0.0.1, by convention).
- A Windows server and local client can simulate a network connection in the shared inter-process communication (IPC) space. This mechanism—referred to as the "local protocol" and *ipserver*—can not handle multiple connections safely. Beyond Firebird 1.5, an improved local access method for *ipserver* uses the XNET subsystem.

Classic/Superclassic—On POSIX, application processes that are running on the same machine as the server and databases can perform I/O on database files directly, using the integrated client/server library `libfbembed.so`.

- On Windows, in versions prior to v.2.0, "Windows local protocol" is not available on Classic.

Performance

As a general observation, the three models perform equally well on equivalent hardware. However, no deployment scenario is exactly like another. Classic uses fewer resources if the number of connections is low. On well-resourced 32-bit hosts it is most recommended for environments that would gain from being able to use multiple CPUs and have adequate resources to support the private database caches. Superclassic may perform better than Classic on larger sites running 64-bit servers.

Superclassic and Superserver use system resources more efficiently than Classic when the number of simultaneous connections grows into the hundreds. Superserver is the most efficient of the three, because all connections share the same cache. However, Superserver does not support SMP and is more limited than Classic/Superserver in the number of simultaneous connections it can carry.

If you are unsure which model is going to perform best for your conditions, you might consider starting with Superclassic for your 64-bit host machine or Classic if you are constrained to 32-bit. You can always switch to another model later: the internal differences are in the server, not in your databases.

Page Cache size differences

The page cache is a dedicated block of RAM where a Firebird process accumulates an image of the database pages it visits. When properly configured, the cache progressively reduces the amount of disk reads it has to do, particularly on frequently accessed tables.

The different server models use cache differently. If you are swapping back and forth between Superserver and Classic/Superclassic, it is essential to get acquainted with the page cache size differences and to understand how page size affects the amount of RAM reserved for the cache.

The default 2048 pages assigned for Superserver's shared cache is far too large for a Classic/Superclassic setup, where each client connection uses a private cache, whilst the default Classic cache of 75 pages is of little use to Superserver's cache sharers. Inattention to this one detail of difference accounts for the majority of "performance problems" that appear in the support lists!

You should also bear in mind that, if you are running a 32-bit Firebird server process, the entire RAM usage of the process is limited to 2GB, regardless of how much RAM is installed.

Events

Firebird servers can capture events in the execution of stored procedures and triggers and, on committal of the transaction, return messages to client applications that are listening for specified events. A TCP/IP network channel is created for event traffic.

The traditional architectural differences between the models has meant that the full features of the event mechanism are not available in some topographies where Classic is the model of choice. As versions progress, the conditions improve but only in v 2.5 and higher versions are events available to all topographies regardless of which model is in use.

Events port

By default, the server chooses an available TCP/IP port at random for event traffic. If the server is behind a firewall or if connections are made through a secure tunnel, a specific events port must be assigned and the tunnel or firewall configured to enable traffic. On the Firebird side, the firebird.conf configuration parameter for configuring the port is ***RemoteAuxPort***.

Embedded Server

An embedded server comprises a single-user server folded together with a client instance, providing direct, stand-alone access to databases directly from applications. On Linux, it was always available by attaching using the "direct local" client for Classic, named `libfbembed.so`. On Windows, a functionally similar option was introduced in Firebird 1.5, but embedding Superserver with a single client.

In v.2.5, the architectures of the embedded servers on all platforms were unified so that all use the Superclassic model, enabling multi-threading for the embedded client.

The embedded servers are described in more detail later in this chapter, on page 17, in the topic ***Typical Deployment Topologies***.

Introduction to Client/Server

Generically, a client/server system is a pair of software modules designed to communicate with each other across a network using an agreed protocol. The client module makes requests across the network to a listening server program and the server responds to the requests.

If you are new to client/server systems, the rest of this chapter may help you to understand the concept behind the architecture and how radically different it is to desktop or file-served data storage systems.

Servers and Clients

To take an example of a client/server arrangement that is not primarily a database management system, an e-mail client dispatches a message across a network to an e-mail server, with a request directing the server to send the message to an address on a server somewhere. If the request complies with the agreed protocol and the destination address is valid, the server responds by repackaging the message and dispatching it, returning an acknowledgment to the client.

The key principle is that the task is split—or distributed—between two separate software components that are running independently on physically separate computers. The model does not even require that the components be running on compatible operating or file systems. The e-mail client could be any email client program that runs on a Windows, Mac or any other system and the e-mail server is often running on a UNIX or Linux system. The client and the server programs are able to cooperate successfully because they have been designed to be *interoperable*.

In a client/server database system the model is no different. A host machine in a network is running a program that manages databases and client connections—a database server. It occupies a node that is known to client programs running on machines at other nodes in the network. It listens for requests from the network, from clients that want to attach to a database and from other clients that are already attached to databases.

As with the e-mail example, the protocol for communication is at two levels. Like the e-mail system, it uses a standard network protocol and overlays it with other, purpose-specific protocols. For e-mail the overlay will be POP3, IMAP, SMTP; for the database system, it takes form at several levels, as protocols for database connection, security, database transfer and language.

Client/Server vs File-Served Databases

File-sharing systems could be cited as another example of client/server systems. File servers and filesystem servers serve client requests for access to files and file systems, sometimes in very sophisticated ways. NFS, SMB and the Windows native networking services are examples. The file server gives clients access to files that the client machine can read into its own memory and write to, as though it were performing I/O on its own, local storage system.

A desktop-based data management system, lacking its own, internal provisions to manage I/O requests from a network, is itself a client of the file-server. When it receives I/O requests from its own clients, it depends on operating system controls to provide the central locking and queuing system necessary to manage conflicting requests.

These file-served DBM systems are not client/server database systems. Both the client and the DBMS software are clients to a file-sharing server. Whilst the flow of input and, often, output are to some extent managed by the DBMS program, physical data integrity is under the control of the filesystem services.

In a client/server database relationship, clients—even if located on the same machine as the server—never get closer to the physical data than sending messages to the server about what they want to do. The server processes the messages and executes the requests using its own code and, in advanced systems like Firebird, its own disk management and accounting system. The server program performs all of the physical changes to metadata and data storage structures within a physical on-disk structure that is independent of the host's filesystem-level I/O layer and inaccessible to it.

Characteristics of a Client/Server DBMS

A fully-featured client/server database management system is realised by the degree to which it meets the five recognised reliability criteria for robust data storage and retrieval systems, viz., scalability, interoperability, data protection, distribution of function and standardization.

Scalability

The advent of comparatively inexpensive PC networks throughout the 1980s and '90s provoked an increasing demand for scalable information systems with user-friendly human interfaces. Spreadsheet and desktop database software and graphical interfaces gave non-technical users a taste for the power of desktop computing. Once the sharing of files across networks and amongst different types of software became standard practice in large enterprises, the customers demanded more. Desktop and LAN-based data management also came within reach of the smallest businesses. Today, it is almost unthinkable to design an enterprise information system under the monolithic model of the mainframe and the text terminal.

Scalability is judged in two dimensions: horizontal and vertical. Horizontal scalability is the capacity of the system to accommodate additional users without impact on the capability of the software or resources. Vertical scalability corresponds with what it takes to reproduce the system on simpler or more complex platforms and hardware configurations in response to variations in load and access requirements. It ranges from the low end—making the system available to users of mobile devices, for example—to a high end that has no conceptual limit.

Interoperability

Client/server architecture for database systems evolved as a response to the fragility, low load capacity and speed limitations of the file-sharing database model in PC networks as multi-user demand increased. Its emergence coincided with the parallel development of the SQL language. Both were, in part, strategies to neutralize the dependency on mainframe hardware and software that prevailed in the 1980s. True client/server architecture for databases is heterogeneous and interoperable: it is not restricted to a single hardware platform or a single operating system. This model allows clients and servers to be placed independently on nodes in a network, on hardware and operating systems appropriate to their function. Client applications can communicate simultaneously with multiple servers running on disparate operating systems.

Data protection

The great flaw with file-served database systems is the vulnerability of data to error, damage and corruption when they are physically accessible to file-sharing clients and placed under the direct control of humans. In the client/server database model, client applications never touch the physical data. When clients request changes to data state, the server subjects the requests to rigorous validation. It rejects requests that fail to comply with internal rules or metadata rules. When a write request is successful, the actual change of database state is executed entirely by code resident in the server module and within disk structures that are under the server's control.

Distribution of function

The client/server model allows the areas of work in the system to be distributed appropriately and effectively amongst hardware and software components. The database server takes care of storing, managing and retrieving data and, through stored procedures, triggers or other callable processes, provides the bulk of data processing capacity for the system. The client process manages the "sharp end" for applications by translating their requests into the communication structures that form the protocols for database and data access.

Applications are the dynamic layer in the model. They provide a potentially infinite variety of interfaces through which humans, machines and external software processes interact with the client process. For its part, the client module exposes itself to applications via a comprehensive, preferably standardized, language-neutral application programming interface (API).

In some systems, it is possible for applications to act almost entirely as deliverers of information and receptors of input, delegating virtually all data manipulation to the server's processing engine. This is an ideal for client/server systems because it locates CPU-intensive tasks where processing power is concentrated and leaves applications to utilize the capacity of the workstation to deliver the best-performing user interfaces.

At the other end of the scale are systems in which, through poor design or an impractical concern for interoperability, virtually all data processing is performed on client workstations. Such systems are often characterized by poorly performing user interfaces, delays in synchronizing database state and unresponsive networks.

Between heaven and hell are well-performing client/server database systems that make good use of processing capacity on servers while retaining some data processing functions on workstations where it is justified to reduce network traffic or improve the flexibility of task implementations.

The two-tier model

The following diagram conceptualizes the classic two-tier client/server model. The middleware layer, which may or may not be present, represents a driver, such as ODBC, JDBC or PHP, or a data access component layer that is integrated with the application program code. Other layerings at the client side are possible. Applications may also be written to access the API directly, with no middleware.

Figure 1.3 Client/server: the two-tier model

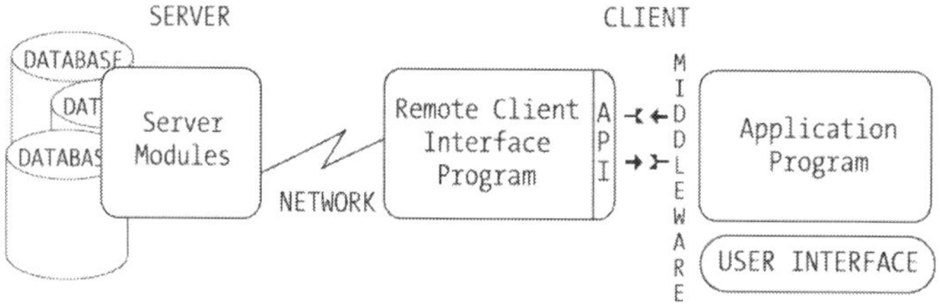

The n-tier model

Upscaling and requirements for greater interoperability give rise to a model with more layers. The client interface moves to the center of the model and is joined by one or more application server layers. In this central complex will be located middleware and network modules. The application layer becomes a kind of database superclient—being served by multiple database servers sometimes—and itself becomes a proxy server for database requests from applications. It may be located on the same hardware as the database server but it could just as well be running on its own hardware.

Figure 1.4 Client/server: an n-tier model

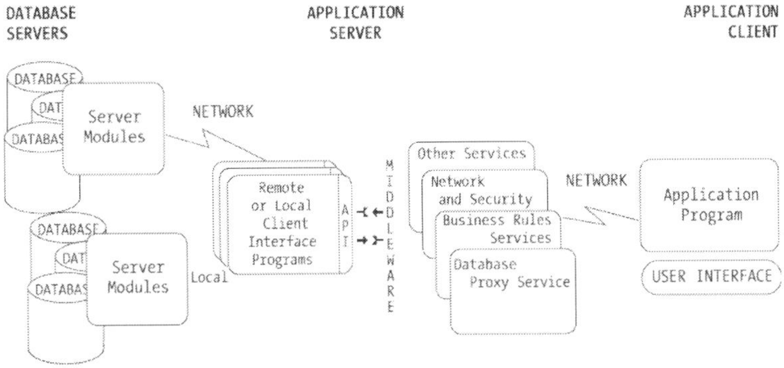

Standardization

Acknowledged standards for hardware and software interopability and, especially, for metadata and query language are characteristic of client/server database systems. The rise of the relational database systems and the consolidation of SQL standards over two decades have been and remain inseparable. The abstract nature of well-designed relational database systems, along with their relative neutrality with respect to choice of application language for "front ends", ensure that RDBMS continues to hold its place as the preferred database architecture for client/server back-ends.

That is not to dismiss other architectures, however. While, for the time being, object database systems continue to be closely bound to application languages, object-relational architectures are making significant inroads into the relational tradition. The most recent SQL standards make several provisions for standardizing O-R methods and syntaxes. When people start demanding standards for technologies, it's generally a good indication that the technology is expected to be around for a while.

Typical Deployment Topologies

The Firebird server comes in several "models", providing a variety of scaling options, ranging from the single-user, stand-alone desktop to the server farm.

Figure 1.5, below, depicts a flexible system, where multiple Firebird servers are running on different operating and filesystem platforms. There is a mix of workstations, each running remote clients appropriate to its local platform. There are gateways to other networks. The Windows server here happens to be serving the day-to-day data processing of the business and is commanding a lot of disk capacity. It is possible for the Windows clients to be conversing with the Windows server using the Named Pipes protocol—commonly called NetBEUI—although it should be avoided in favor of TCP/IP, if possible.

The Linux server may be serving firewalls, gateways, ancillary databases and other client/server systems, including company e-mail, Internet and file services such as NFS and Samba.

Figure 1.5 Two-tier Firebird client/server topology

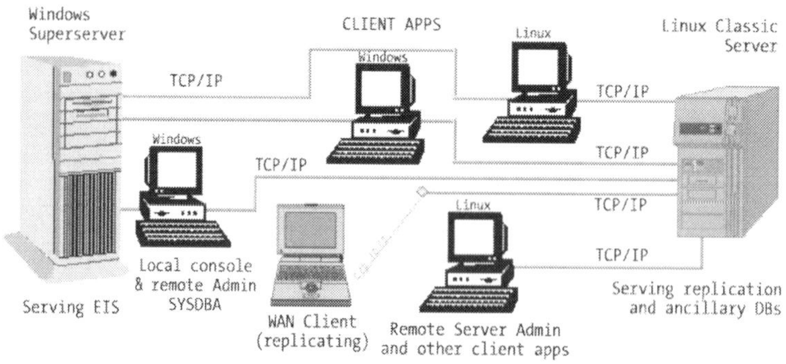

Heterogeneous database-serving networks are a common environment for Firebird. In small, single-server networks where an on-site administrator may not be part of the permanent staff, the trend is away from running the database server on a single, high-specification, multi-purpose Windows host, toward low-cost, dedicated Linux machines, well-supplied with RAM and fast storage. Maintenance is low, making it realistic to outsource most of the administrative functions. Systems like this have capacity for growth without major upheaval.

The single-user model

All Firebird servers can accept local clients. The connection protocols and options vary according to the server model you choose. Single-user installations fall into two categories:

Stand-alone server: in this model, the server is installed and running on the machine. Local attachments are made via network-style protocols, using the normal client libraries.

Embedded server: no server is installed. The client and server programs are rolled into a single dynamic library or shared object that is invoked by the application and starts a single, exclusive server process on attachment. When the application program terminates, the server process is unloaded.

Stand-alone server

In the stand-alone client/server model, the localized client attaches to the running server using a local protocol. The server can listen for connections from remote clients whilst a local client is attached. Figure 1.6 illustrates the options.

Figure 1.6 Stand-alone servers

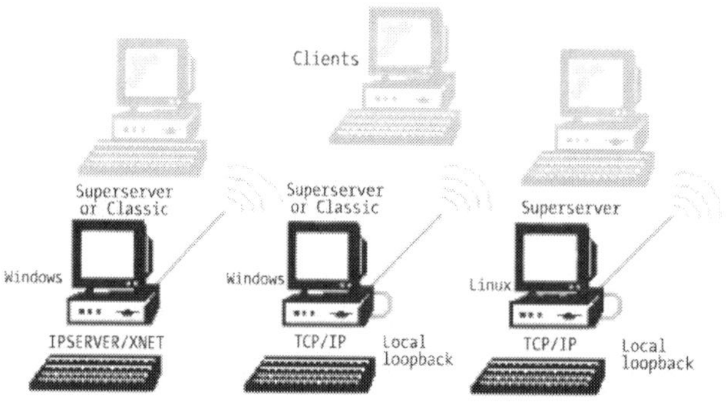

The first example shows the "local connect" model. Up to and including Firebird 1.5, the *ipserver* subsystem simulates a network connection within the same block of inter-process communication space. Beyond v.1.5, the local protocol uses the faster, more robust, native XNET subsystem. A "local connect" is supported for Classic on POSIX, in the form of a client embedded with a single-client server instance.

In the other two, on Windows, Linux or any other supported platform, the TCP/IP local loopback protocol is used with the Superserver. It is a regular TCP/IP attachment to the special IP address 127.0.0.1 which most TCP/IP subsystems install by default as `localhost`. On Linux, the v.1.5 Classic server can be used in this mode, provided the client library `libfbclient.so` is used.

Embedded server

Embedded servers are supported on both Windows and Linux/UNIX platforms, although, prior to v.2.5, the implementation models are different. In v.2.5, the platforms are more integrated with one another architecturally, with the embedded server implemented as a flavour of Superclassic and the embedded client being threadable. It also became possible to attach to the same database simultanously using both embedded and a Classic thread.

For the the older versions, the Windows library, `fbembed.dll`, embeds a single-client Superserver, which runs an exclusive Superserver process, while on Linux, the `libfembed.so` client referred to in the previous sub-topic embeds a Classic server that connects directly to databases. On Linux it is not exclusive: remote clients using `fbclient.so`, another `libfbembed.so` instance or `fbclient.dll` can connect concurrently to *fb_inet_server* instances through the [*x*]*inetd* network daemon. (*launchd*, in the case of MacOSX).

Embedded servers are a deployment option, intended for single-user, stand-alone use on a single workstation. As such, they have some limitations that will get in your way, especially if you are developing applications on Windows.

- The embedded client/server arrangement on Windows can use only the "Windows local" access method.
- In versions prior to v.2.5, the embedded server engine, being Superserver, employs a write lock on a database after the initial attachment, to protect it from a Windows path anomaly that can cause corruption. The older `fbembed.ll` supports one and only one connection to each local database.
- Client applications connect to the embedded servers without the degree of authentication that challenges remote clients. Prior to v.2.5, server-level authentication on Windows is bypassed completely. It is always essential to protect servers from unauthorised physical access, of course, but workstations are often running embedded applications in public areas, making them especially vulnerable.

The Embedded Client as a Network Client

Besides its ability to connect to and access one or more local databases exclusively through the embedded server, the embedded client in `fbembed.dll` or `libfbembed.so` can also connect as a regular network client to databases on other servers.

Firebird servers in distributed environments

A detailed discussion of distributed transaction processing (DTP) environments is beyond the scope of this guide. However, suffice it to say, the Firebird full servers sit well in a variety of DTP scenarios.

The Open Group defined the X/Open standard for DTP, envisioning three software components in a DTP system. The XA specification defines the interface between two of them, the transaction manager and the resource manager (RM). The system has one RM module for each server and each RM is required to register with the transaction manager.

Figure 1.7 illustrates how a Firebird server could be slotted into an XA-compliant DTP environment. The database application server module provides a bridge between high-level user applications and the resource manager, encapsulating the XA connection. The resource manager (RM) performs a client-like role to negotiate with the database server for access to data storage.

The encapsulation of the XA connection enables the application developer to build and execute SQL statements against the resource manager. Transaction demarcation—which requires two-phase commit capability on the part of all servers—is moderated by the global transaction processing monitor (TPM). Cross-database transactions under the management of a transaction manager are made through a two-phase commit process. In the first phase, transactions are prepared to commit; in the second, the transaction is either fully committed or rolled back. The TPM will alert the calling module when a transaction does not complete for some reason.

The TPM coordinates distributed transactions in multiple database systems so that, for example, one transaction can involve one or more processes and update one or more databases. It keeps account of which resource managers are available and involved in transactions.

Figure 1.7 Firebird in distributed transaction processing environments

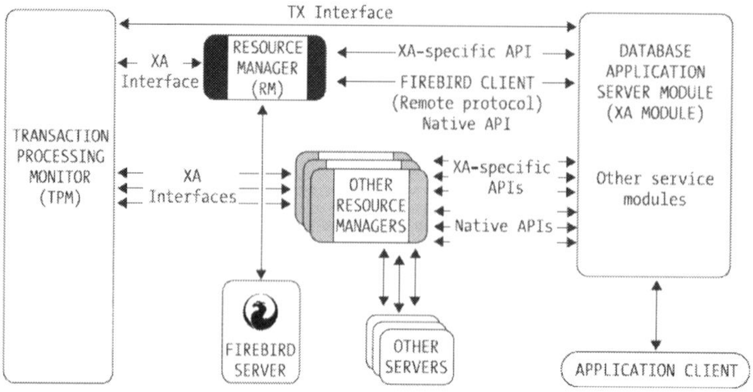

The framework supports multiple databases per server and multiple servers, which need not be all Firebird. Up to and including Version 2.5.x, Firebird does not support spanning a single database across multiple servers or serving a database that is not controlled by its host machine.

Transaction Server frameworks

Microsoft Transaction Server (MTS) with COM+ is one such scenario. MTS/COM+ provides a process-pooling environment that encompasses the deployment and management of business logic components, including auditing control, security and performance monitoring. One of its most significant features is declarative transaction management. Transactions initiated by MTS/COM+ are controlled by the Microsoft DTC (Distributed Transactions Coordinator), an XA resource manager. The native Firebird interface requires an ODBC or OLE-DB provider that both supports both Firebird's two-phase commit capability and the MTS/COM+ call context.

Terminal Servers

Firebird is successfully deployed in Citrix and Microsoft Terminal Server frameworks. Protocol is TCP/IP with attachments connecting to network IP addresses in all cases.

It is strongly inadvisable to install the terminal server and the database server on the same node. However, in any situation where the application server is running on the same physical node as the database server, the connection must be to the IP address of the node. TCP/IP local loopback (localhost as server) is not possible.

Firebird Clients

A client on a remote workstation requires a client library and an application program that can interact with the application programming interface published in the library.

A client library provides the wire protocol and the transport layer that your client application uses to communicate with the server. The standard shared library for Windows clients is a Windows DLL. For POSIX clients, it is a shared object (.so library) or, for MacOSX, a .dylib library. The size of the standard client library is approximately 350 Kb.

Some access layers, such as the Firebird .NET provider and the JayBird Java drivers, replace the standard client library and implement the Firebird wire protocol directly. Another option is an embedded server—a library that merges both a client and a server instance—for single-user use.

A client workstation can also, optionally, have a copy of the current `firebird.msg` file, or a localized version, to ensure that correct server messages are displayed when applications include calls to the Services API.

Generally, you would install a copy of the client library on the host server, for use with several of the Firebird command-line utilities and/or any server-based management programs you might wish to use locally. Many of these utilities can be run remotely, however. A remote system administrator can manage some of the essential services provided by these utilities by accessing them through a host service controller interface.

A host-based client application, such as a web application, needs the client layers present.

What is a Firebird Client?

A Firebird client is an application, usually written in a high-level language, that provides end-user access to the features and tools of the Firebird database management system and to data stored in databases. The *isql* interactive SQL utility and the other command-line utilities in your `$firebird$/bin` directory are examples of client applications.

Firebird clients typically reside on remote workstations and connect to a Firebird server running on a host node in a network. Firebird also supports a stand-alone model allowing client applications, the Firebird client library and the Firebird server to execute on the same physical box.

Client applications need not involve end-users at all. Daemons, scripts and services can be clients.

Firebird is designed for heterogeneous networks. Clients running under one operating system can access a server on a different operating system platform. A common arrangement is to have Windows XP/7 and Linux workstations concurrently accessing a departmental server running Windows Server 20xx, or any of several flavors of UNIX or Linux.

In the client/server model, applications never touch the database directly. Any application process converses with the server through the Firebird client library, a copy of which must be installed on each client workstation. The Firebird client library provides the application programming interface (API) through which programs make function calls to retrieve, store and manipulate data and metadata. Generally, other layers are also involved in the interface between the application program and the Firebird client, that surface generic or application-language-specific mechanisms for populating and calling the API functions.

For Java development, Firebird's stable of supported drivers includes the Jaybird JDBC/JCA-compliant Java driver for flexible, platform-independent application interfacing between many open source and commercial Java development systems and Firebird databases.

Open source and third-party interfacing components and drivers for many other development platforms, including Embarcadero Delphi®, Kylix® and C++Builder®, commercial and open source C++ variants, Python, PHP and DBI::Perl are available. For .NET development, a Firebird NET provider is under constant development, keeping pace with Microsoft's rapid scene changes. Contact and other information can be found in Appendix XIII, Application Interfaces.

The Firebird Client Libraries

The Firebird client library comes in a number of variants, all of which surface an identical API to applications, for the server release version to which they apply.

The client library uses—in most cases—the operating system's client network protocols to communicate with one or more Firebird servers, implementing a special Firebird client/server application-layer interface on top of the network protocol.

It is important not to mismatch the client library release version with the release version of the server. Use a v.2.5 client with a v.2.5 server. It is normally fine to use a higher client with a server of a lower version. A mismatch is likely to occur when a lower client accesses a higher server, owing to potential API enhancements as major versions rise.

Realize too that the client for one version may or may not be installed to the same location as the client for another. When redeploying with a new version, be sure to study the readme and installation documents—located in the Firebird root directory and /doc subdirectory of the server—for information that may outdate the information in this guide.

The Firebird API

All client applications and middleware must use the API in some way to access Firebird databases. The Firebird API is backwardly compatible with the API from old InterBase versions. The ***InterBase 6.0 API Guide*** (ApiGuide.pdf) is downloadable from many places on the Web, including the InterBase archives on the IBPhoenix website, http://www.ibphoenix.com. It provides reference documentation and guidelines for using the API to develop language interfaces and even applications, if you want to do things the hard way.

Enhancements made to the API since the Firebird fork are documented in the Firebird release notes and, to a limited extent, in the header files distributed with Firebird.

More About Clients

Client-only installs—next chapter, *Performing a Client-Only Install*

Further information about the client side of Firebird can be found in ***The Firebird Book Second Edition*** and in the companion volume to this, Volume 2: ***Developing with Firebird Data***.

CHAPTER

2

INSTALLATION

This chapter describes how to obtain an installation kit for the platform and version of Firebird server that you want to install on your server machine. The full installers install both the server and the client on a single machine.

Remote clients do not require the server at all. The procedure for installing the Firebird client varies somewhat, according to platform. For instructions, refer to the topic *Performing a Client-Only Install* in this chapter.

If you are new to Firebird, do not attempt a client-only install until you have worked out how all the pieces fit together in the default installation.

System Requirements

- Server memory
- Installation drives and disk space (*Installation Drives*)
- *Minimum Machine Specifications*
- *Operating System*

Server Memory (All Platforms)

Estimating server memory involves a number of factors:

- Firebird server process: The Firebird server process makes efficient use of the server's resources. The Superserver utilizes around 2MB of memory. On POSIX, the Classic server uses no memory until a client connection is made. On Classic for Windows, a small utility service is listening for connection requests.
- Client connections: Each connection to the Superserver adds approximately 115KB, more or less, according to the style and characteristics of client applications and the design of the database schema. Each connection to the Classic server uses about 2MB.
- Database cache: The default is configurable, in database pages. The Superserver shares a single cache (with a default size of 2,048 pages) among all connections and increases cache automatically when required. The Classic server creates an individual cache (with a default of 75 pages) per connection.

Databases with large page sizes consume resources in larger chunks than do those with smaller page sizes. Resource usage on the Classic server grows by a fixed amount per client attachment; on Superserver, resources are shared and will grow dynamically as needed. Extra available RAM will be used for sorting if enough is available to accommodate one or more of the intermediate sets; otherwise those sets are written to temporary disk space.

Installation Drives

Firebird server—and any databases you create or connect to—must reside on a hard drive that is physically connected to the host machine. You cannot locate components of the server, or any database, on a mapped drive, a filesystem share, or a network filesystem.

Disk Space

When estimating the disk space required for an installation, consider the sizes of the following executables. Disk space, over and above these minimum estimates, must also be available for database files, shadows (if used), sort files, logs, backups.

- Server: A minimal server installation requires disk space ranging from 9MB to 12MB, depending on platform and architecture.
- Client library: Allow 350KB (embedded: 1.4MB–2MB).
- Command-line tools: Allow ~900KB.
- DB administration utility: Allow 1MB–6MB, depending on the utility selected. For a list of free and commercial utilities available, refer to Appendix XIV, ***Resources***.

CD-ROM

You cannot run a Firebird server from a CD-ROM. However, you can attach to a read-only database on a CD-ROM drive that is physically attached to the server.

Default Disk Locations

Default disk locations for the standard Firebird installations are listed in an Appendix in ***The Firebird Book Second Edition*** and in the companion volume to this, Vol 3: ***Administering Firebird Servers and Databases***.

Minimum Machine Specifications

Minimum specifications depend on how you plan to use the system. You can run a server and develop database schemas on a minimally-configured PC—for v.1.5 and later, a 586 with 128MB should be regarded as minimum. Windows is more demanding on CPU and memory than a Linux server running at the console level. Operating system versions will influence the requirements: some UNIX platforms are expected to demand more resources at both server and client, and the requirements of some Windows versions push the baseline out, independent of any software requirements.

SMP and Hyperthreading Support

Firebird Superserver, Superclassicand Classic can use shared memory multiprocessors on Linux. On Windows, SMP support is available only for Classic.

Hyperthreading is uncertain and seems to depend on several variables, including operating system platform, hardware vendor, and server version. Some users have reported success; others have had problems. If you have a machine with this feature, try your selected server with it enabled initially, and be prepared to disable it at the BIOS level if performance appears slow or unstable.

On Windows, for Superserver and Superclassic, processor affinity can be configured at the server level in `firebird.conf` (v.1.5 and above) or `ibconfig/isc_config` (v.1.0.x). The

CPU affinity mask should be set to a single CPU on a SMP machine. For instructions, refer to the entry *CpuAffinityMask* in Chapter 34, ***Configuration Parameters in Detail*** .

Operating System

Table 2.1 shows the minimum operating system requirements for running Firebird servers. However, always check the README files in the /doc/ directory of your kit for late-breaking information about operating system issues.

Table 2.1 Firebird Minimum Operating System Requirements

Operating System	Version	Requirements/Recommendations
Microsoft Windows	All	Visual C++ Runtime libraries
		–msvcp60.dll or higher required for v.1.5 (or C Runtime library msvcrt.dll v.6. or higher required for v.1.0)
		–msvcp70.dll or higher required for v.2.0
		–msvcp80.dll or higher required for v.2.1 and 2.5
		Database files should not use the extension ".gdb".
	Server 2003 and 2008 versions and spin-offs, 64-bit	Recommended for deploying Firebird to medium to large enterprise sites, if Windows is a requirement.
		Databases should be on partitions that have the VSS (volume shadowing) feature disabled.
	Server 2003 and 2008 versions and spin-offs, 32-bit	Usually suitable for deploying any Firebird version [1] to small enterprise sites of up to 200 users.
		Databases should be on partitions that have the VSS (volume shadowing) feature disabled.
	Win 7 64-bit	Should be suitable as a server for small to medium sites, any Firebird version 2.1 or higher
	XP 64-bit, Vista 64-bit	Fully patched installation may be suitable as a server for small sites, any Firebird version 2.1 or higher.
		Databases should be on partitions that have System Restore disabled.
	XP 32-bit, Vista 32-bit, Win 7 32-bit	OK for single-user and very small workgroups, using any version in Classic or Superserver models; not suitable as a server otherwise. Service pack 3 required.
		Databases should be on partitions that have System Restore disabled.
	Windows 2000	Service pack 4. OS not recommended for Firebird versions higher than v.1.5.x
	NT 4.0	Requires Service Pack 6a. OS not recommended for Firebird versions higher than v.1.5.x
	95/98/ME	Not recommended for Firebird versions higher than v.1.5.x.

Operating System	Version	Requirements/Recommendations
Linux	Any	Many Linuxen now have their own Firebird package maintainers with most or all released versions available from distro repositories Firebird 2.5 Classic and Superclassic may not run satisfactorily with glibc runtimes 2.7 or lower. Use glibc 2.9 or higher. Kernels that do not support the New POSIX Threading model (NPTL) will not work with Superserver Firebird 2.1 and higher or Superclassic (Firebird 2.5 and higher).
	OpenSuse & family	v.10.1 or higher for Firebird 2 and above, v.8.10 or higher for Firebird 1.5, v.7.2 or higher for Firebird 1.0.
	Fedora & Family	
	Debian, Ubuntu and Family	
	Mandriva & Family	
MacOSX/Darwin		Firebird 2.5 will run only on MacOSX 10.6 (Snow Leopard) or higher versions.
Other platforms	Solaris (Intel, Sparc), FreeBSD, HP-UX 10+	Refer to the relevant Firebird distribution kits for details

1. Because of the memory-addressing limitations on 32-bit systems, Superclassic may be unsuitable if demand for resources becomes sufficent to terminate the server process. Classic will be more robust under these conditions. On the other hand, one over-demanding Classic process could bring the host to its knees with continual swapping.

32-bit or 64-bit

An application compiled as 32-bit can be installed on either a 32-bit or a 64-bit operating system. A 64-bit application cannot be installed on a 32-bit operating system.

A 32-bit Firebird client can connect to a 64-bit Firebird server and a 64-bit client can connect to a 32-bit server. It is the application environment that determines which client library must be used.

- if the application is 32-bit, the 32-bit client and any driver layers (ODBC, .NET provider, et al.) must be 32-bit versions
- if the application is 64-bit, the 64-bit Firebird client library and drivers must be 64-bit
- If the application (32-bit or 64-bit) calls external functions ("UDFs") and the Firebird server is 64-bit, then the UDF library must be compiled as 64-bit.

Citrix or other terminal server installations are themselves client applications. The client you install in this environment is governed by the architecture of that tier, even if it is running on the same host machine as the server. For example, a 32-bit tier running on a 64-bit operating system that is hosting 64-bit Firebird must use the 32-bit versions of all connecting layers, including the Firebird client.

How to Get an Installation Kit

The main download area for Firebird release kits can be linked from the main Firebird website, *http://firebirdsql.org*. Links on the download pages will take you to *http://sourceforge.net/projects/firebird/files/*.

The main page of the Firebird site usually displays a list of links to the latest releases for Linux and Windows. Other links will point you to distributions for other platforms, that may be in repositories other than Firebird's Sourceforge repository.

If a file has "src" in its name, it is buildable source code, not an installable binary kit.

Kit Contents

All of the kits contain all of the components needed to install the Firebird server:

- The Firebird server executable
- A number of other executables needed during installation and/or runtime
- Shell scripts or batch files needed during installation, which may also be available as server utilities
- The security database (`security2.fdb` for "2" series versions, `security.fdb` for v.1.5.x or `isc4.gdb` for v.1.0.x;)
- One or more versions of the client library for installing on both the server and the client workstations
- The command-line tools
- The standard external function libraries and their declaration scripts (*.sql)
- A sample database
- The C header files (not needed by beginners!)
- Text files containing up-to-the-minute notes for use during installation and configuration
- Release notes, Quick Start Guide and various README files (these are essential reading)

Kit Naming Conventions

File naming of kits across platforms is not consistent. Alas, it is not even "consistently inconsistent," with builders often needing to conform to platform-specific conventions or simply making their own rules. However, certain elements in the file names will help you to identify the kit you want.

Classic or Superserver?

In general, the first part of the name string is "Firebird."

- If a Windows release supports the Classic server (fb_inet_server.exe), it will be included in the same kit as the Superserver (fbserver.exe). Both 64-bit and 32-bit kits are available as either executable installers or zip archives.
- For POSIX platforms that support both models, separate installers are provided for the Classic/Superclassic server and Superserver in x86 and AMD64 flavours. The kit name will begin with "FirebirdCS" (for Classic/Superclassic server) or "FirebirdSS" (for Superserver).
- For MacOSX, there are different packages for Classic/Superclassic and for Superserver. Recent releases have followed the same convention as the other POSIX kits, of prefacing the package name with "FirebirdCS" and "FirebirdSS", respectively. Each has at least an Intel x86 platform package, while some versions come in 64-bit flavours. Some versions of Firebird come with PowerPC packages and "lipo" fat client packages as well.
- For minor platforms, the architecture might be less obvious and the first part of the name might be that of the OS or hardware platform.

Version Numbers

All release kit names should contain a dot-separated string of numbers in the following order: version number, release number, subrelease number. For example, "2.0.6" is the seventh subrelease of the "Firebird 2.0" series, while "2.5" or "2.5.0" is the initial release of the "Firebird 2.5" series. Most kits also include the absolute build number (e.g., "2.5.0.26074". For some Linuxen and some minor platforms, especially those that impose their own naming rules and build on different compilers, version numbers may be less obvious.

Architecture Designators

Where builds are offered for both 32-bit and 64-bit platforms, the infix varies according to chipset:

- Windows: ***Win32*** and ***x64***
- Linux: ***i686*** and ***amd64***
- MacOSX and Darwin: ***i386*** and ***x86-64*** (for Intel platforms); ***ppc*** for PowerPC. The "fat client" packs for x86-64 have the infix ***lipo***.
- In the past, some platforms that required a special build to support 64-bit I/O carried the infix "64IO" somewhere in the name string.
- Assume Solaris kits are for Intel unless the "SPARC" tag is present in the kit name.

The download page at http://firebirdsql.org, for the particular version you are interested in, is generally the most useful indicator of the minimum chipset supported by the distribution and of any "gotchas" regarding OS and hardware with a specific build.

Do not try to install a 64-bit kit on a version of that OS or hardware that does not support 64-bit I/O.

Installing a Server

Where practicable, executable installers have been provided for all binaries distributed by the Firebird Project. Where there are issues that need your attention, you will find detailed instructions in the release notes, README files, and distribution notes.

The kits install a running Firebird server. "Newbies" take note that there is no visible interface—"GUI"—that pops up when installation is complete. A later topic in this chapter explains how to test that your installation worked.

*If you need the release notes before installing your kit, go to the Downloads > Firebird Database Engine page at the Firebird website at http://firebirdsql.org and read or download a copy from there. The **Documentation Index** at the Firebird site also gives access to these downloads.*

The FIREBIRD Variable

FIREBIRD is an optional environment variable that provides a system-level pointer to the root directory of the Firebird installation. If it exists, it is available everywhere in the scope for which the variable was defined.

The FIREBIRD variable is not removed by scripted uninstalls and it is not updated by the installer scripts. If you leave it defined to point to the root directory of a different installation, there will be situations where the Firebird engine, command-line tools, cron scripts, batch files, installers, etc., will not work as expected.

Unless you are very clear about the effects of having a wrong value in this variable, you should remove or update it before you begin installing Firebird 2.1. After doing so, you should also check that the old value is no longer visible in the workspace where you are installing Firebird--use the SET FIREBIRD command in a Windowsshell or printenv FIREBIRD in a POSIX shell.

Finalise your Server Choice

Before you begin your installation, you must finalise your choice of which model of the Firebird server you want. If you are still unclear about it, refer back to Chapter 1, ***Choosing a Server***.

Reminder: Superclassic is for 64-bit systems

Superclassic was introduced at Firebird 2.5 as a precursor to a new, SMP-aware architecture proposed for Firebird 3. It is not an option with any lower versions.

Superclassic is intended to improve the utilisation of resources on 64-bit servers with high loads, especially those with multiple CPUs and large amounts of RAM. It consumes considerably more machine resource than multiple Classic processes.

Superclassic may be an unsuitable choice if you are installing Firebird on a 32-bit production server.

Uninstall and remove other Firebird servers

If your new installation is to replace an existing version, uninstall and remove the artefacts of the existing server before you begin installing this one.

- If you are unsure about how to do a clean uninstall, see the topic ***Uninstalling Firebird*** on *page 42* of this chapter.

If you intend to run this server concurrently with another Firebird server or an InterBase server, your task will not be quite so straightforward. Visit the topic *Configuring the TCP/IP Port Service* in Chapter 33, ***Configuring Firebird and Its Environment***, before proceeding with a zip kit installation.

- Before you start, make sure that any application or server instance of Firebird running on the host machine is shut down.

The Firebird Variable

If the Windows installer program finds a value for the optional `%FIREBIRD%` variable, it will make that path the default location that it offers, instead of `c:\Program Files\Firebird\Firebird_2_5`. Take care about this: it may or may not be what you desire!

Windows

The official kits for Windows are distributed both as executable installers and as compressed (.zip) ready-built filesystem frameworks. If you are new to Firebird, it is strongly recommended that you use the installer in preference to dealing with the subsequent scripting required for a manual installation from a .zip kit.

The Windows install kits include executables and associated files for both server models: Superserver and Classic/Superclassic. The installer sets default parameters with a number of option fields. A dialog box in the installer will prompt you for the model you want to install (Superserver or Classic) and the other one will not be copied to your disk. If you choose Classic you will be given the option to enable Superclassic.

Do not try to install a Classic or Superclassic server if you already have a Superserver installed, or vice versa. You should be logged in as an Administrator for a normal installation.

V.1.0.x For Firebird 1.0.x, the only model supported on Windows is Superserver.

Windows Platforms

On service-capable platforms—Windows 7, Vista, XP, 2000 and NT—the installer installs Firebird, by default, to run as a service. The service will be installed and started automatically at the end of the installation process and, subsequently, each time you boot up your server machine. To find out how to stop and start the server manually, see Chapter 4, ***Operating Basics***.

The very old low-end Windows platforms—Windows 95, 98, and ME—do not support services. The installation will start Superserver as an application, protected by the Guardian program. If the server application should terminate abnormally for some reason, the Guardian will attempt to restart it.

If you are installing Superserver on a services-capable system, it is up to you whether you take the option to use the Guardian. On those platforms you have the option to configure services, including the Firebird service, to have the operating system attempt to restart on failure.

Do not try to install the Guardian with a Firebird Classic server.

Running the Installer

If you are running Windows XP/Server 2003 or an older version of Windows, check the version of the Windows installer installed on your machine by running *msiexec.exe* from a command prompt. A help screen will be displayed that shows the version. If it is earlier than v.3.0 you must update.

To start the Firebird installer, double-click on the ".exe" file for your chosen version and follow the prompts. If you are studious in following the advice given so far, taking care that the server model you select (Classic/Superclassic/Superserver) is the one you really want, the install should be a walk in the park.

- Make sure the Guardian option is unselected if you choose Classic.

Installing from a 'zip' kit

To use a ".zip" kit, you will require a utility, such as 7zip, WinZip, PKZip or WinRAR, to inspect and/or extract the contents before you begin.

Extract the contents to the root location where you want to install Firebird. Let's suppose you have decided to create a folder for it called C:\Programs. You should end up with a file structure along these lines:

```
C:\Programs\Firebird\Firebird_2_5
C:\Programs\Firebird\Firebird_2_5\bin
C:\Programs\Firebird\Firebird_2_5\doc
C:\Programs\Firebird\Firebird_2_5\include
```

..and so on.

If the kit you are installing is v.2.5 then the Firebird root directory will be `C:\Programs\Firebird\Firebird_2_5;` similarly, `..\Firebird_2_1`, `..\Firebird_2_0` or `..\Firebird_1_5` if you are installing an older version. From here on, we'll refer to your equivalent of `C:\Programs\Firebird\Firebird_2_5` as `$firebird$`.

The Microsoft C and C++ Runtimes

Neither the Firebird server nor a Firebird client will run without (as a minimum) the Microsoft C and C++ runtimes that were present in Microsoft Visual Studio on the computer the binary was built on. The Firebird installer programs for versions 2.1.3 and higher take care of installing the appropriate run-time assemblies—MSVCRT8 at the time of this writing.

By default, the v.2.5 installer and possibly the latter sub-releases of v.2.1 will create a "global assembly" in your $system$\winSXS folder, in a sub-folder with a name of the patttern xnn_Microsoft.VC80.CRT_1fc8b3b9a1e18e3b_8.0.50727.6195_x-ww_44262b86. The characters represented by "nn" will be either "86" for a 32-bit installation or "64" for 64-bit. The sequence after the "_" character in the folder name will be unique on your machine. The folder contains the files msvcm80.dll, mscvp80.dll and msvcr80.dll.

Manual install of the MSVCRT runtime assemblies

For your zip-kit install and for older versions, you must take care of installing the run time librariess yourself. The Microsoft redistributable packs are distributed in all of the zip kits (including the ones for Firebird Embedded). In the server installation kits, you will find them here:

- For 32-bit: `$firebird$\system32\vccrt8_Win32.msi`
- For 64-bit: `$firebird$\system32\vccrt8_x64.msi`

In the older v.2.1.x kits, you may find the equivalent installers in your zip kit as executables with the names `vcredist_x86.exe` *and* `vcredist_x64.exe`*, respectively.*

The runtimes for v.2.0 and v.1.5 are `msvcp70.dll` and `msvcrt.dll`. The latter, which is the C runtime, may have a numeric infix. They are usually present in established Windows systems but may be found in the `$firebird$\bin` directory if needed.

Running the Setup Programs

Unzipping the kit does not install Firebird.

After checking and, if necessary, installing the runtimes, you still have some programs to run from the command window. Run them in the order indicated in Table 2.2, Commands for Installing Firebird Manually on Windows.

All commands must be run from the `$firebird$\bin\` *directory.*

Table 2.2 Commands for Installing Firebird Manually on Windows

Program	Switches	Comments
instreg.exe	install	Optional command, causes the installation path of the directory above the current directory to be written into the registry (HKLM\Software\Firebird Project\Firebird Server\Instances\DefaultInstance)
instsvc.exe	install	Installs Superserver (fbserver.exe) to run as a service
	-d[emand]	Use this switch if you don't want the service to start automatically.
	-g[uardian]	Use if you want the Guardian to start the service and restart it in the event of failure.
instsvc.exe	install -c[lassic]	Installs the Classic listener (fb_inet_server.exe) to run as a service
	-d[emand]	Use this switch if you don't want the service to start automatically

Program	Switches	Comments
instsvc.exe	install -m[ultithreaded]	Installs the Classic listener (fb_inet_server.exe) to run in multi-threaded mode ("Superclassic") as a service. Not always an optimal choice for 32-bit servers and not available in versions prior to Firebird 2.5.
	-d[emand]	Use this switch if you don't want the service to start automatically.
instclient.exe	install f[bclient] | g[ds32]	Generates a copy of the client library in Windows\system32 using the library name you specify—it can only be fbclient or gds32.
	-force	-force switch can optionally precede the library argument to force overwriting existing library of the same name

Be sure to configure the firebird.conf parameter DefaultDbCachePages appropriately for the server model you have chosen to install.

Installing Superserver to run as an application

It is possible to install Superserver to run as an application, either on demand or automatically at startup. In that case, do not run the *instsvc.exe* command at all.

Be aware that, when Firebird runs as an application, the Windows user who started it must be logged in to make remote connections to databases possible.

If you want to make a Windows shortcut to start Superserver as an application, the "run" command is

```
$firebird$\bin\fbserver.exe -a
```

where (as before) $firebird$ is the entire path of your firebird root directory. You can copy this shortcut to wherever you like, including the Startup folder of the user who will use it.

Linux and Many Other POSIX

Both RPM installers and tarballs are available for the "main line" Linux distributions of Firebird versions up to v.2.5.0. Many distributions also have custom, distro-specific packages available in their repositories.

RPM (Red Hat Package Manager)

If your Linux distribution supports RPM installers, you may prefer to choose an RPM kit. Running *rpm* with `--i` switch will create the directories and install everything required, prompt you to set a password for the SYSDBA user, and start your chosen server.

Do not try to use `rpm --update` to bring any existing Firebird package installation up to date. The Firebird RPM packages do not support it.

Note that not all AMD chipsets are recognised by all Linuxen as compatible with Firebird's i686 RPM installers. For example, the Firebird RPM kits will not install on a 32-bit Mandriva that is running on AMD Athlon 64. However, the tarballs install flawlessly.

RPM installer packages are to be discontinued at some point during the v.2.5.x series. The reason? Distribution-specific rules have become so diverse over the years that it has become virtually impossible to produce a RPM package that is sufficiently generic to avoid bumping into them.

glibc Issues (and libstdc++.so.5)

Installation of Firebird versions prior to v.2.1.4 on Linux requires a *glibc* package installed that is equal to or greater than glibc-2.2.5. However, to enable support for some older distros, the generic binaries are built in a compiler environment that will ensure compatibility with the v.2.2.5 kernel. For this reason, the runtime library `libstdc++.so.5` must be present in your system before you attempt to install those older versions of Firebird.

It can be achieved in various ways, viz.,

- by installing a *compat-glibc* package (RedHat, CentOs, OpenSuse, Debian) or a *libstdc++5* package (Mandriva)
- by using a Firebird RPM kit (or other, appropriate package type) provided by your distro instead of the generic one provided by the Firebird Project
- by compiling Firebird yourself, on the same system that you are going to run it on!

Distribution-specific builds

In recent years, much effort has gone into assisting Firebird into the package management systems of a variety of Linux distributions. These days, it is very likely that the PM system of your Linux installation will be able to find and install a distro-specific package of a version of Firebird that you want. Don't overlook the benefits of this method of installation, particularly the automated installation of other packages that Firebird depends on and the relocation of Firebird file assets to comply with the rules of the particular distro.

The instructions here do not necessarily apply to installations from distro repositories, although they might be helpful as a troubleshooting aid if things fail at some point.

Compressed Files (Tarballs)

For Linux distributions that cannot process RPM packages, and for the various UNIX flavors, use the tarball kit (usually .tar.gz or .bz2), as it will give the experienced Linux hand more control over the installation process. The appropriate decompression utility will be needed on your server for decompressing and "untarring" the kit into the filesystem.

Shell scripts have been provided in the `/bin/` directory of the tarball. In some cases, the distribution notes may instruct you to modify the scripts and make some manual adjustments. Skilled users can also study and adjust the installation scripts to make structures that work on less common distros.

Where possible, the build engineers for each Firebird version and sub-release attempt to document, in release notes and ReadMe texts, any known issues with various kernel versions and distributions. In all cases, read any distributed text files, along with any specific topics in the official release notes that pertain to the version of Firebird that you are going to install.

SYSDBA Password

During the install, a temporary SYSDBA password will be created in `/opt/firebird/SYSDBA.password`, a plain text file. You will need a SYSDBA password in order to attach to any database initially, so write it down somewhere as soon as your install completes. You can change it later, using the script `changeDBAPassword.sh` that is stored in `/opt/firebird/bin/`.

Installing a Tarball

Download the compressed tarball you want to install, e.g., FirebirdCS-2.5.0.26074-0.i686.tar.gz, into your home directory, say, ~/Downloads. The extraction and untarring procedure is the same for either a Classic or Superserver tarball kit, viz.,

```
$ cd ~/Downloads
$ tar -xzf FirebirdCS-2.5.0.26074-0.i686.tar.gz
```

The new directory FirebirdCS-2.5.0.26074-0.i686 will appear.

It is fine to simplify the name of the directory, e.g.,

```
$ mv FirebirdCS-2.5.0.26074-0.i686 fireball
```

Classic or Superclassic

Firebird Classic is installed so that the *[x]inetd* daemon listens for remote connection requests and operates one instance of the *fb_inet_server* process for each connection. Each connection therefore has its own copy of the database cache.

Ensure that you have the appropriate daemon installed and running before you install your Firebird Classic kit.

Now, you can run the install script, which will take care of everything to complete the install. You need root privileges to run the script:

```
$ sudo fireball/install.sh
```

Installing and Configuring Superclassic

Superclassic is an alternative mode of operation of the Firebird Classic model that was introduced with the v.2.5 Classic servers. Older versions do not have Superclassic.

In this mode, a specialised process called *fb_smp_server* becomes the listener that is responsible for spawning threaded instances of *fb_inet_server* for each successful connection request. The *[x]inetd* daemon is not required at all for Superclassic.

Although Superclassic is available as a 32-bit application, it is not recommended to try to run it on 32-bit production installations of more than a few users, due to the resource limitations that apply to 32-bit applications. Classic remains the recommended model to use on well-resourced 32-bit servers.

The Superclassic Enabling Script

Do not try to do this while any *fb_smp_server* or *fb_inet_server* process is running.

The interactive script `changeMultiConnectMode.sh` is provided in the `/bin/` directory beneath the Firebird root directory. To complete the installation of the Superclassic server requires running this script, regardless of whether you installed the Classic package from the RPM kit or the tarball.

In the $firebird-root$/bin directory, run the script as follows and you will be prompted to choose the mode:

```
$ ./changeMultiConnectMode.sh
Which option would you like to choose: multi-(process|thread) [process] ?
```

- To select Superclassic, enter "m" (without the quotes)
- If Superclassic is already enabled and you are running this script to revert to Classic, enter "p" (without the quotes)

Configuration

Several parameters in the firebird.conf configuration file in Firebird's root directory will affect the way the server runs in Superclassic mode.

Pay particular attention to ***DefaultDbCachePages***. Unlike Superserver, Superclassic does NOT provide a shared cache for all its process threads. Each thread has an individual cache so it will be important to allocate cache wisely, just as one would for Classic.

Parameters pertaining to locking and shared memory (names starting with ***Lock--***) may also prove to be of interest as you test Superclassic under production conditions.

Restart the Superclassic server after changing parameters in `firebird.conf`.

Superserver

The Superserver binary is called *fbserver*. You can set it up to run with or without the Guardian, which is enabled on POSIX by supply the the -f[orever] switch when starting the executable.

NPTL Implementation

The so-called "new" Native POSIX Thread Library (NPTL), that replaced *pthreads*, has been around for much of Firebird's life. Buggy kernel implementations can cause problems for Firebird Superserver and locally-compiled programs in old versions of Red Hat (9.x and below) and possibly some laterLinux distributions. The *gbak* utility was reported to throw a "broken pipe" error in these conditions. If you cannot avoid using the old or buggy kernel version, you will be limited to using a version of Firebird that supports the old *pthreads* threading model (search the Firebird download pages for a "non-NPTL" kit).

Follow these steps if you need to enforce the use of *pthreads* on a Linux that has a buggy implementation of NPTL:

1 Take care of the server instance. In `/etc/init.d/firebird`,

```
LD_ASSUME_KERNEL=2.2.5
export LD_ASSUME_KERNEL
```

2 You need to have the environment variable set up within the local environment as well, so add the following to `/etc/profile`, to ensure every user picks it up for the command line utilities. After

```
HISTSIZE=1000
```

add

```
LD_ASSUME_KERNEL=2.25
```

On the following line, export it:

```
export PATH USER LOGNAME MAIL HOSTNAME HISTSIZE INPUT_RC LD_ASSUME_KERNEL
```

Firebird 2.0.5 was the last build that supported the option to use the old pthreads threading model. V.2.0.6 and all successive "2 series" Firebird Superserver versions do not come with kits capable of running on systems where the NPTL is disabled.

MacOSX/Darwin

The official kits for MacOSX are distributed as zipped .pkg (package) installer files that create a framework. To unzip the package contents, double click the file icon to unzip automatically. Using *unzip* is also an option.

From the operator's point of view, all the kits install in the same way. Just double click on the package icon in the Finder window and the installer will take care of everything, including permissions, environment variables and so on.

Alternatively, run the *installer* utility as from the command line, e.g.

```
sudo installer -verbose -dumplog -pkg nameofpkg -target /
```

The root for Firebird (any model) will be `/Library/Frameworks/Firebird.framework/`.

In order for multi-threading conditions to work properly, the Firebird 2.5 engine uses Grand Central Dispatch, which was first released in MacOSX 10.6 (Snow Leopard). If you want to use an earlier version of OSX you will need to use an earlier version of Firebird.

Classic or Superclassic

Classic (*fb_inet_server* in Classic mode) runs by way of a daemon—*launchd* if the MacOSX version is 10.5 or higher, *inetd* or *xinetd* on lower versions. Ensure that you have the appropriate daemon installed and running. Once the framework is in place, simply connecting to a database will start an instance of *fb_inet_server* for the requesting client.

Do not try to install the Guardian with a Classic server..

Enabling Superclassic

Superclassic is *fb_inet_server* in threaded mode. On this platform, as with other POSIX, it uses a binary named *fb_smp_server*. It does not use *launchd*/ *[x]inetd* but runs as a self-contained "listener" daemon itself, that is started by way of *StartupItems*.

To convert from *fb_inet_server* to *fb_smp_server*, change to `/Library/Frameworks/Firebird.framework/Resources/bin/` and find the script named `ChangeMultiConnectionMode.sh`. Run this script. Your *fb_smp_server* daemon will start listening for connections.

Superserver

The installation procedure for Superserver is the same as for Classic.

SuperServer (*fbserver*) starts via StartupItems. If the `-forever` option is used, the Guardian (*fbguard*) will start first and kick off the *fbserver* process.

The Start and Stop commands are the same as for Superclassic.

"lipo" Packages

The "lipo" packages provide both 32-bit and 64-bit client libraries ("fat-libs"), useful if you want to be able to use a 32-bit client—such as the open source Flamerobin database management toolset—locally with a 64-bit server.

Install a "lipo" package in just the same way as before. The installation will be the same as its regular 64-bit counterpart except that your Mac will accept either 64-bit or 32-bit client requests in accord with the requesting application.

Other Host Platforms

If you are installing Firebird on a POSIX platform that is not covered here, be sure to study any README and other information texts that are in the root of the tarball or in the documentation (/doc/) directory of the installation.

Testing Your Installation

If everything works as designed, the Firebird server process will be running on your server when the installation finishes. You can run some tests to verify the installation and work out any adjustments you might need in your configuration.

Network Protocol

At this point, it is assumed that you will use the recommended TCP/IP protocol for your Firebird client/server network, to take advantage of the benefits of platform-independent networking.

In an all-Windows environment, you also have the alternative of using Named Pipes protocol (wrongly referred to as "NetBEUI" in Delphi programming environments), although it is not recommended except possibly within a very small office LAN. For more information, refer to the Network Protocols topic at the beginning of the next chapter.

Pinging the Server

Usually, the first thing you will want to do once installation is complete is ping the server. This just gives you a reality check, to ensure that your client machine is able to see the host machine in your network. For example, if your server's IP address in the domain that is visible to your client is 192.13.14.1, go to a command shell and type the following command:

```
ping 192.13.14.1
```

Substitute this example IP address for the IP address that your server is broadcasting.

*If you get a timeout message, refer the next chapter, **Network Setup and Initial Configuration**, for further instructions. If you need more information about how to set up or find out your server's IP address, see the topic A Network Address for the Server in the next chapter.*

TCP/IP Local Loopback

If you are connecting to the server from a local client—that is, a client running on the same machine as the server—you can ping the virtual TCP/IP loopback server:

```
ping localhost
```

or

```
ping 127.0.0.1
```

Checking That the Firebird Server Is Running

Techniques for checking whether the server is running vary according to the operating system and Firebird model.

Classic Server on POSIX, including MacOSX

Use the ps command in a command shell to inspect the running processes. If any clients are connected to a Firebird Classic process, you should see one process named fb_inet_server for each connected client. The ps command has several switches, but the following will provide a satisfactory list. The grep command will filter the output so you only see the Firebird processes. Look for processes named *fb_inet_server*.

On Linux:

```
[xxx]$  ps aux | grep fb
```

On MacOSX:

```
ps ax | grep fb
```

V.1.0.x The "fb" prefix belongs to Firebird versions 1.5 and higher, while "gds" and "ib" belong to Firebird 1.0.x. If you are running v.1.0.x use ps aux | grep gds.

Superserver on POSIX, including MacOSX

Because Superserver forks off a thread for each connection, it is interesting to throw the -f[ork] switch into the mix for examining its processes and threads. You get a formatted display of the forking processes.

```
[xxx]$ ps auxf | grep fb
```

The same ps command should show one process named *fbguard* if the server was started with the –f[orever] switch, and one main process named *fbserver*. There will be at least one child process thread named *fbserver* forking off one more such process thread. This first group is "the running server," sans any client connections except those that the server uses for listening on ports and for garbage collection. Beyond that will be a group of threads for each connection.

Windows Server Platforms

For the Windows server platforms, start the Firebird Server Control applet from the Control Panel.

Server Control Applet

Figure 2.1 shows the Firebird Server Control applet display on a Windows Server. If you used the installer, this applet will have been installed to your Control Panel. Its appearance may vary from one Windows server edition to another.

Figure 2.1 Server Control applet

You can use the applet to start and stop the service and to modify the start and run options. It is not recommended to change to "Run as an application" for multi-user use, for security reasons—you have to leave the server logged in to keep the server running.

Services Applet

If you have no Control Panel applet, you can inspect the Services applet (see Figure 2.2) in the Administration Tools display. On most Windows platforms, you can access this applet from the Control Panel, under Administrative Tools.

Figure 2.2 Services applet on Windows server platforms

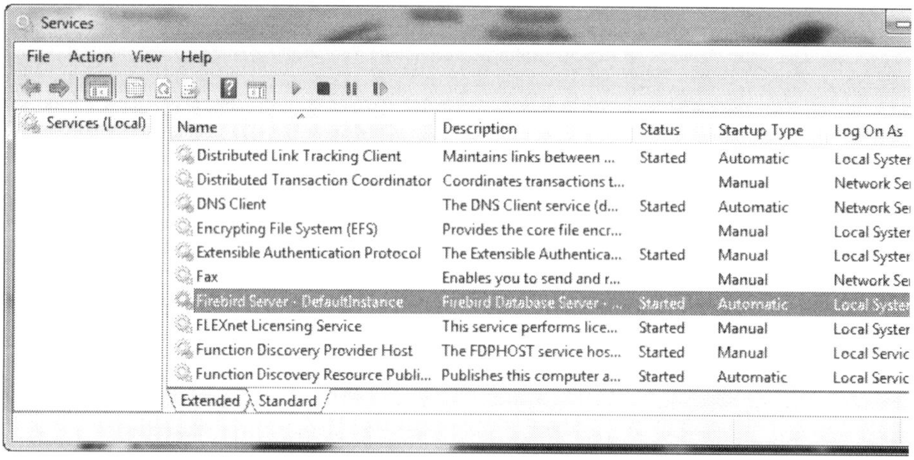

Figure 2.2 shows the service names for for the Guardian and the Superserver. They may have different service names because of version changes; the Guardian may not appear at all. A user with Administrator privileges can right-click the service name to stop or restart the service. If you are using the Guardian, stop that service to stop both Guardian and server.

On the Windows server platforms, the Guardian is a convenience rather than a necessity, since these operating systems have the facility to watch and restart services.

Windows 9x, ME, and XP Home

Windows 9x and ME do not support services. Firebird server should be running as an application, monitored by the Guardian. If you used an installation kit that installed but did not automatically start the Guardian and the Firebird server, you can set it up manually, as follows:

1. Locate the executable file for the Guardian program (ibguard.exe) and create a shortcut for it in the Startup area of your machine's Start menu.
2. Open the Properties dialog box of the shortcut and go to the field where the command line is.
3. Edit the command line so it reads as follows:
   `fbguard.exe -a`
4. Save and close the Properties dialog box.
5. Double-click the shortcut to start the Guardian. The Guardian will proceed to start *fbserver.exe*.

The Guardian should start up automatically the next time you boot your machine.

The Client Libraries

All installation kits are distributed with the client libraries included. Since the principal use of a client library is to provide the programming interface between remote client applications and the server, its presence is required as a component of any remote client application.

Of course, some applications live on the server. A copy of one or more of the client libraries native to the server platform is installed in an appropriate location for use by server-local applications such as the command-line tools, database management or monitoring applications and server-based components of n-tier applications.

Windows

On Windows, the client is named `fbclient.dll` and it is installed by default into the `\bin\`directory beneath the Firebird root directory. By default, the command-line utilities load the client from there, not the System directory.

The installer gives you the option of placing fbclient.dll in the system directory, if you need it there for compatibility with application code.

An option exists also to generate a version of the client library that is named `gds32.dll` and contains an identity string that will make the Embarcadero "InterBase Express" components recognise it.

V.1.0.x For Firebird 1.0.x, the name of the client library is `gds32.dll` and it is installed into the system directory. Command-line utilities load the client from there.

MacOSX/Darwin

On MacOSX/Darwin the client libraries are `libfbclient.dylib` (the remote client) and `libfbembed.dylib` (the embedded server, used for direct access to databases).

After installation, the embedded server library—which works only on the host machine—moves into `/Library/Frameworks/Firebird.framework/Firebird Classic`, while the remote client will be in `/Library/Frameworks/Firebird.framework/Libraries`.

Performing a Client-Only Install

Installing remote clients is an essential part of deploying your database applications in a client/server network.

Each remote client machine needs to have the client library that matches the release version of the Firebird server it will attach to. In general, it will be safe to use a client library from a different build of a release, as long as the version numbers match. However, when upgrading the server, do read any readme documents that come with a point release, to determine whether any "gotchas" exist regarding lower client versions.

Search carefully in the system path of any client workstation on which you want to deploy a Firebird client, to find and, if necessary, disable existing client installations for InterBase® or older Firebird versions.

Newer client versions should be able to connect to databases running under an old server. Firebird 1.0.x and 1.5 client applications usually have no problem with legacy applications written for Interbase databases running under the very ancient InterBase 6.0 or lower. The exception is applications built with Embarcadero's InterBaseXpress (IBX) components, which are hard-wired to look for a certain version string in the file. All of the Firebird installers, along with the executable instclient.exe, provide the option to generate a Firebird client named gds32.dll that has a version string that IBX likes.

Firebird 1.5 and later versions on Windows can co-exist with InterBase® or Firebird 1.0.x on both server and client. It is still a matter of setting things up manually, however, and tools are available to assist with the task.

Installing a Linux/UNIX client

POSIX operating system layouts are famously idiosyncratic. The suggestions below should be helpful as a guide to installing clients on many common Linux and UNIX flavors but this is an area where uncertainty is the only certainty!

Log into the client machine as root and look for the client library in the server installation.

The binary for remote clients is `libfbclient.so.n.n.n`, where "n's" are numbers corresponding to the major and minor release numbers of the server. The RPM and tarball scripts install it by default in `/opt/firebird/lib` and symlink it (see below).

v.1.0.x The client libraries for Firebird 1.0.x inherit from the InterBase ancestor the confusing habit of distributing both the local client (the embedded version, that comes with the Classic package) and the remote client, that comes with the Superserver package, with the same name, `libgds.so.n.n.n`, where the "n's" might be a variety of numbers. Installation symlinks either client with `libgds.so.0`. The default location is `/usr/lib`.

Step 1: Symbolic linking

Copy the library to `/usr/lib` on the client and create symbolic links for it, using the following commands:

```
ln -s /usr/lib/libfbclient.so.1.5 /usr/lib/libfbclient.so.0
ln -s /usr/lib/libfbclient.so.0 /usr/lib/libfbclient.so
```

v.1.0.x:

```
ln -s /usr/lib/libgds.so.0 /usr/lib/libgds.so
```

The embedded library, `libfbembed.so`, has the capability to connect to a remote server, as well as to the embedded server. The client component in it will work just as the regular `libfbclient.so` does and will connect client applications to databases on either Classic/Superclassic or Superserver servers.

Step 2: Position other Firebird components

Create a directory `/opt/firebird` on the client for the message file (firebird.msg) and copy the file into it from the firebird root on server to the client.

v.1.0.x Create /opt/interbase on the client and copy the file interbase.msg into it.

Step 3: Set the FIREBIRD environment variable

In system-wide default shell profile, or using `setenv()` from a shell, create the environment variable that will enable the API routines to find the messages:

```
setenv FIREBIRD "/opt/firebird/"
```

v.1.0.x

```
setenv INTERBASE "/opt/interbase/"
```

Installing a Windows client

You can install a Windows client using the same installer that you use for installing a server or you can extract the files from the matching ZIP kit and install the client manually. The latter method may suit you if you want to script a client install for use on multiple workstations.

The recommended way to install a client is to use the installer program.

Although you are not going to install the server, allowing the installer to install to a root location will ensure that optional pieces—including the Registry key—that are needed by some software products are available on the client machine. Later, you can customize the setup manually, if necessary.

If you are installing the command-line tools for remote use, a properly installed root location is essential.

Choosing a root location for the client components

The first choice you need to make is where the root of the client installation is to be located. It is recommended that you take the default (`c:\Program Files\Firebird\Firebird_n_n`), since it will simplify future upgrades. The "n_n" part here should be replaced by the "major version" numbers of your server version, e.g. "_2_5" if your server is v.2.5.

However, you can specify a custom location if necessary.

Microsoft run-time libraries

The client libraries, like the server, are compiled on a specific version of Microsoft Visual Studio. This means that, also like the server, they need to have the correct Microsoft C and C++ run-time libraries available. Newer versions of the runtimes should work satisfactorily with older Firebird binaries but, sadly, it does not always work that way. To review the information about the runtimes, see ***The Microsoft C++ Run-times*** on page 28.

Using the Firebird Installer

The simplest way to install a Firebird Windows client is to copy the Firebird installer to a portable storage device and run it on the client machine, selecting a "Client-only" install option when prompted by the installer dialog. You can choose whether to install the client with or without the command-line tools.

Most clients will not need the tools and it is not recommended to install them on client workstations that do not need admin access to the server.

The installer will create the default root directory in `c:\Program Files\Firebird`, which you can vary when it prompts for a location. Here, it will write the message file—`firebird.msg`—and, if you selected to install the tools, it will create a `\bin\` directory beneath the root and install the tools there.

If you have asked it to, it writes `fbclient.dll` or `gds32.dll` to the system directory, provided it is valid to do so for your Windows version. If the Microsoft C/C++ run-time libraries are too old, or absent, it may write the correct ones there also.

Finally, it runs a program named `instreg.exe` to install the Registry key, whose value is the absolute path to where `firebird.msg` is. If you chose the default installation directory, the key is HKLM\Software\Firebird Project\Instances. If any running DLLs were overwritten during the installation, you will be prompted to reboot the machine.

v.1.0.x The old InterBase client library was always installed by default in the system directory, c:\windows\system32 on WindowsXP and Server 2003, for example. Firebird 1.0.x followed suit, retaining the old names and locations. The library is `gds32.dll`.

Installing a client manually

Installing a client manually requires all of the above steps.

You will need to copy the following files from your server installation, or extract them from the ZIP kit, to portable storage or a shared folder:

firebird.msg

bin\fbclient.dll

bin\{Microsoft Visual C run-time DLL} (if needed)

bin\{Microsoft Visual C++ run-time DLL} (if needed)

bin\{Manifest file for the local assembly} (if present and if needed)

bin\instreg.exe

bin\instclient.exe

For Firebird 2.1.x and 2.5.x clients, the whole Microsoft Visual C/C++ run-time assembly comprises `msvcr80.dll`, `msvcp80.dll` *and* `Microsoft.VC80.CRT.manifest`.

For older versions, check the names and versions of the run-times that are present in the \bin\ folder of the server install structure for that version of the server. In the v.2.1 and 2.0 kits, you may find there is a ".msi" redistributable installer present.

Once you have created your Firebird "root" directory on the client machine, copy `firebird.msg` there.

Create a `\bin\` folder beneath the "root" directory and copy into it all of the files from the `\bin\` folder on your storage device.

In a command window, change to the\bin\ folder that you created and run `instreg.exe` from there:

```
c:\Program Files\Firebird\Firebird_2_5\bin>instreg.exe
```

Alternatively, you could run `instreg.exe` from your portable storage device, e.g., from a flash drive assigned as drive K:

```
K:\> instreg.exe 'C:\Program Files\Firebird\Firebird_2_5'
```

If you placed the root directory for your Firebird client installation somewhere different, use that path as the root directory argument.

Running instclient.exe

The program instclient.exe can be run when you need a client version that can be accessed and used by existing software, drivers or components that expect the client to be named gds32.dll and/or to be located in the Windows system path.

Still in the command window, from the \bin\ location, run the command according to the following syntax:

```
instclient.exe {i[nstall]} [-f[orce]] {fbclient | gds32}
```

The parameters `i` (or install) and either `fbclient` or `gds32` are required.

If the program finds there is already file in the system directory with the name of the file you are trying to install (fbclient.dll or gds32.dll) it will not proceed. To have the program write the file even if it finds a pre-existing copy, use the –f (or –force) switch.

Your operating system may require you to reboot the machine to complete the installation.

Querying the installed client

The `instclient.exe` program can be used for querying about Firebird running on the machine. The syntax for querying about the client is

```
instclient.exe {q[uery] fbclient | gds32}
```

For example,

```
instclient.exe q fbclient
```

returns

```
Installed FBCLIENT.DLL version : 2.5.0.26074 (shared DLL count 1)
```

Using instclient.exe to uninstall a client DLL

To remove a Firebird client that is installed in the system directory, use the following syntax:

```
instclient.exe {r[emove] fbclient | gds32}
```

For example, the following command removes the client reported in the query example above:

```
instclient.exe r fbclient
```

Installing an Embedded Server

Embedded Server on Windows

If you have not used Firebird before, it is strongly recommended that you bypass this option until you have gained some experience of working with one of the server versions and the "regular" client. You will not lose anything by attempting your first applications under the normal client/server model; they will work just fine with the embedded server.

Download Kit

The files for the embedded server are distributed in a separate kit from the server models. Look for downloads with the infix "embed".

V.1.0.x There is no embedded server version for v.1.0.x.

The merged server and client are in the dynamic link library `fbembed.dll`, which you will find in the `\bin\` directory of your regular Firebird server installation. You can install an embedded server if you already have a full server or other embedded servers installed.

For each embedded server application, the home directory of your application executable becomes the root directory for that embedded server application. To set up an embedded Firebird server installation with your application, do as follows:

- Copy `fbembed.dll` to the home directory and rename it to either `fbclient.dll` or `gds32.dll`, according to the client file name your database connectivity software expects.
- Copy the files `firebird.msg` and `firebird.conf` to the home directory.
- If you want to use the database aliasing feature (recommended), copy `aliases.conf` to the home directory and configure it for any databases this particular application will connect to.
- If external libraries are required for your application, such as international language support (`fbintl.dll` and the `icu*.dll` files), UDF libraries, or blob filter libraries, create folders for them (`../intl`, `../UDF`) directly beneath your application home directory and copy them to these locations.
- If you want any of the command-line tools available to the application user, place the required executables in the home directory, alongside your own executable.

Example of an Embedded Installation Structure

The following is an example of the directory structure and configuration for an installed embedded server application:

```
home = D:\my_app
D:\my_app\MyApp.exe
D:\my_app\fbclient.dll
D:\my_app\firebird.conf
```

```
D:\my_app\aliases.conf
D:\my_app\firebird.msg
D:\my_app\firebird.conf
D:\my_app\gbak.exe
D:\my_app\intl\fbintl.dll
D:\my_app\UDF\fbudf.dll
MyDatabase = D:\databases\MyDB.fdb
```

Uninstalling Firebird

As with installation, uninstalling Firebird is specific to the operating system platform and the integration of the original installation with the software inventory tools of the platform.

Linux

If you need to uninstall Firebird, you must do so as root. How you go about it depends on how it was installed, viz.

- from a RPM kit
- from a tarball
- by a distribution-specific method

The following examples use the context of a Classic installation, but the same holds true for Superserver by replacing the 'CS' in the package name with 'SS'.

Uninstalling a RPM package

As root, query the list of installed RPM packages to verify the correct name of the package that was installed, if indeed the installation was performed by RPM:

```
rpm -qa Firebird
```

Once you have veriified the correct package name, e.g., `FirebirdCS-2.5.0.26074-0`, use the -e switch to remove (erase) the package:

```
$rpm -e FirebirdCS-2.5.0.26074-0
```

If the RPM query does not return any package names, that should tell you that Firebird was installed on your server by another means.

Uninstalling a tarball installation

The tarball installations come with an uninstall script in the /bin/ directory. As root, simply do

```
$/opt/firebird/bin/uninstall.sh
```

Check any symlinks that you might have created yourself and remove them.

Uninstalling a distribution-specific installation

If you installed Firebird from a repository for your Linux distribution using apt or some like tool, use the same tool to uninstall it.

Windows

When Firebird was installed on your Windows host, it would have been done either by running the installer executable or by unzipping the zip kit and completing the installation manually.

Uninstalling Using Windows Native Tools

If you used the installer program to install Firebird there should be a record of it in the Registry and it will appear in the pick list when you run Add/Remove Progams applet from the Control Panel.

First, get all connections off-line, if possible, before shutting down each database that is potentially being served by the Firebird server that you want to uninstall.

Next, shut down the Guardian (if running) and Firebird services from the Services applet in the Administrative Tools section of the Control Panel. If the server and/or Guardian are running as applications, use the Firebird Server Manager Control Panel applet to stop them, if it is available.

Now, use the Add/Remove Programs applet to remove Firebird.

What is left after an uninstall

The uninstall routine preserves some files that you may need, in case you intend to install an upgrade or to reinstall on another machine:

`security.fdb` or `security2.fdb` (depends on version)

`firebird.log`

`firebird.conf`

`aliases.conf`

Any files that were added to the server's directory structure after the original installation are left untouched.

Shared files such as fbclient.dll (or gds32.dll) and the icu* libraries are deleted only if the share count would become 0 by their removal.

The Registry keys are removed.

Uninstalling a zip kit install

To remove Firebird without a Windows Uninstaller profile in the Registry database, do the following steps in order:

1. get all users off-line if possible and shut down all databases
2. stop the server as described in the previous section
3. open a command window and cd to the Firebird installation's \bin\ folder, then run
   a. `instreg.exe remove`
   b. `instsvc.exe remove`
   c. `instclient.exe remove fbclient.dll`
   d. `instclient.exe remove gds32.dll`

Finally, backup any files you want to preserve and delete the Firebird installation directory.

Do not delete the client libraries from system locations, such as the system32 directory, manually, because it is likely to make the system's shared library count inaccurate. An important task of instclient.exe is to enable the installation and removal of the client library into and from system locations without breaking the shared library count.

MacOSX/Darwin

To remove Firebird from a Mac system cleanly, use the following shell script:

```
#!/bin/sh
echo "Clean User"
dscl localhost -delete /Local/Default/Users/firebird echo "Clean Group"
dscl localhost -delete /Local/Default/Groups/firebird if [ -f
"/Library/StartupItems/Firebird" ]; then echo "Remove Superserver StartupItem"
rm -fr /Library/StartupItems/Firebird
fi
if [ -f "/Library/LaunchDemons/org.firebird.gds.plist" ]; then echo "Remove Launchd"
launchctl unload /Library/LaunchDemons/org.firebird.gds.plist rm
/Library/LaunchDemons/org.firebird.gds.plist fi
echo "Remove Framework"
rm -fr /Library/Frameworks/Firebird.framework echo "Remove Receipt"
rm -fr /Library/Receipts/Firebird*.pkg
echo "Remove /tmp/firebird"
rm -fr /tmp/firebird
```

Other Things You Need to Know

We finish this chapter with a few items that you will need to know if you are new to Firebird.

Default User Name and Password

The SYSDBA user has all privileges on the server. The installation program will install the SYSDBA user into the security database (`security2.fdb`, or `security.fdb` if you are installing Firebird 1.5).

V.1.0.x *In Firebird 1.0, the security database is named* `isc4.gdb`.

On Windows and in the v.1.0.x Linux versions, the password is ***masterkey***. Actually, the password is ***masterke***, since all characters after the eighth one are ignored.

On the v.1.5 and higher Linux versions, the installer generates a random password during installation, sets it in the security database, and stores it in clear in the text file `SYSDBA.password`. Either memorize it or use it to get access to the security database and change it to something easier to remember.

If your server is exposed to the Internet at all, you should change this password immediately.

How to Change the SYSDBA Password

If you are on a Linux or other system that can run a bash script, cd to the `/bin/` directory of your installation and find the script named `changeDBAPassword.sh`. All you need to do is run this script and respond to the prompts. The first time you run the script, you will need to enter the password that the installer wrote in `SYSDBA.password`—it is in the Firebird root directory:

```
[bin]# sh changeDBAPassword.sh
```

or

```
[bin]# ./changeDBAPassword.sh
```

Using *gsec* directly

The command-line and shell utility *gsec* exists solely for maintaining login credentials for Firebird users. The following procedure will work on both Windows and Linux.

On Linux, you need to be logged into the operating system as Superuser (root) to run *gsec*. Let's say you decide to change the SYSDBA password from ***masterkey*** to ***icuryy4me*** (although, on Linux, the installed password will not be "masterkey", but something much more obscure!). You would need to follow these steps to do so:

1 Go to a command shell on your server and change to the directory where the command-line utilities are located. Refer to Appendix X to find this location.

2 Type the following on Windows, treating it as case-sensitive:

```
gsec -user sysdba -password masterkey
```

On POSIX platforms type as follows:

```
./gsec -user sysdba -password masterkey ()
```

You should now see the shell prompt for the gsec utility:

```
GSEC>
```

3 Type this command:

```
GSEC> modify sysdba -pw icuryy4me
```

4 Press Enter. The new password ***icuryy4m*** (note, 8 characters!) is now encrypted and saved, and ***masterke***[y] is no longer valid.

5 Now quit the *gsec* shell:

```
GSEC> quit
```

Because Firebird ignores all characters in a password past the eighth character, icuryy4m will work, as will icuryy4monkeys.

Full instructions for using *gsec* are in Chapter 36, <u>*Protecting the Server and its Environment*</u>.

Linux/UNIX Users and Groups

From Firebird 1.5, the ***firebird*** user is the default user that runs the server software. This means you need to put non-root users into the ***firebird*** group to enable them to access databases using the embedded model.

To add a user (for example, "sparky") to the firebird group, the root user needs to enter:

```
$ usermod -G firebird sparky
```

The next time sparky logs on, s/he can start working with Firebird databases.

To list the groups that a user belongs to, type the following at the command line:

```
$ groups
```

*The **firebird** user will also need read-write privileges to all databases and read-write-execute privileges to all directories where databases are located.*

Admin Tools

The Firebird kits do not come with GUI admin tools. The excellent third-party GUI tools available for use with a Windows client machine are too numerous to describe here. Readers are recommended to look at the cross-platform, open source GUI toolset named FlameRobin, at its project website http://www.flamerobin.org.

Firebird does have a set of multi-platform command-line tools, executable programs that are located in the `/bin/` directory of your Firebird installation. They are summarised in Chapter 4, ***Operating Basics***, in <u>*Summary of Command-line Tools*</u>, where you will find links to detailed usage instructions in later chapters.

A list of the better-known third-party database administration tools for Firebird appears in Appendix 14, ***Resources***, in <u>*Third-Party Tools*</u>. For up-to-date and more comprehensive listings, visit *http://www.ibphoenix.com*, select the Contributed link from the Downloads area, and then choose the Administration Tools link.

Because of the heterogenous nature of Firebird, you can use a Windows admin client to access a Linux or MacOSX server and all permutations of mixed platforms.

CHAPTER

3

NETWORK SETUP AND INITIAL CONFIGURATION

As a relational database management system (RDBMS) purposely built for client/server deployment, Firebird is designed to allow remote and local clients to connect concurrently to the server using a small range of network protocols.

The default installers will set up a default TCP/IP configuration for connecting the server-based client to your server and for receiving connections from clients using a default TCP port. Unless there is some external reason to use a custom network configuration, it should not be necessary to configure anything in order to get your first installation of Firebird up and running.

Network Protocols

Firebird supports TCP/IP as the protocol of choice for client/server communications. Support for Novell was dropped early in Firebird's life, reflecting lack of demand for it. It continues to support the deprecated "Named Pipes" transport on Windows, although it will go the same way as Novell eventually.

The Firebird API, or its implementation in driver layers, deduces the protocol to use by interpreting the connection string passed to it by the client application.

TCP/IP

Firebird supports TCP/IP for all combinations of client and server platforms. The default port is 3050. In the event that the host network is already using port 3050, the Firebird server, the client application, or both, can be configured to use another port.

Make sure that port 3050 (or whatever port Firebird is configured to listen on) is opened with the appropriate sub-net scope in the firewall.

Named Pipes

Firebird supports the deprecated Microsoft WNet Named Pipes protocol for Windows server platforms and Windows clients. The default pipe name is `interbas`.

As noted earlier, this protocol is often wrongly referred to as "NetBEUI", especially by the documentation and property sheets for Delphi driver products. NetBEUI is actually not a protocol but an old transport layer used for networking in Windows 3.1 and 9X.

Windows 9x and ME do not have the capability to be WNet servers.

Local Access

Although Firebird is designed to be a database server for remote clients, it offers a number of options for local access.

Client/server

TCP/IP local loopback: For n-tier server application layers and other clients accessing a local server on any supported platform using TCP/IP, even without a network card, connection can be made through the special localhost server at IP address 127.0.0.1.

The localhost connection is not possible for embedded server applications.

"Windows local" connection mode: For Windows clients running the Firebird Superserver on the same physical machine, Firebird supports a local connection mode involving inter-process communication to simulate a network connection without a physical network interface or wire protocol. It is useful for access to a database during development, for embedded server applications and for console-tool clients, but it does not support Firebird's event mechanism.

- From the "2" series onward, the subsystem that provides this "Windows local connect" is XNET. The name of the shared memory area used for this transport channel is FIREBIRD. If the host operating system is Windows 7 or Vista, or you are running Windows Server 2003 or XP with terminal services enabled, you will probably need to configure this namespace explicitly to get "Windows local" to work. The entry in firebird.conf is ***IpcName*** and you should change it to

  ```
  Global\FIREBIRD
  ```

The prefix `Global` is case-sensitive.

- In versions 1.X, it is a less functional transport channel referred to as "IPServer" or "IPCServer". XNET and IPCServer are not compatible.

  In Firebird 1.5.x, the default value of ***IpcName*** is `FirebirdIPI`. In Firebird 1.0.x, it is `InterbaseIPI`.

Direct local connect on POSIX: Whether a local client can connect to a database on Linux and some other POSIX systems depends primarily on the server mode you have installed (Classic or Superserver) and, secondarily, on the type of client connection.

- Superserver on POSIX does not accept local connections through the normal API clients at all. The connection path must always include the TCP/IP host name. However, it does accept local connections from "embedded applications", i.e. applications written using embedded SQL (ESQL). The command-line tools, *gsec*, *gfix*, *gbak* and *gstat*, which are embedded applications, can make local connections to a Superserver.

- If you are running the Classic server, direct connection is possible from a local client.

Embedded server

On Linux, the client library *libfbembed.so* that is a component of a Classic installation is a fully functional embedded server (client and server merged as a dynamic library) that dates back to pre-Firebird times. A client application running on the host machine in this environment can connect directly to a database. The client/server connection is entirely self-contained: no network resources are involved and no daemon intercedes in the client attachment. Normal server-level authentication applies.

From Firebird 1.5 onward, the Firebird Windows offerings have included a functionally similar embedded library, named *fbembed.dll*. For application development, its features are identical to those of the normal client/server model except that there is no network protocol support: connection must be via the "Windows local" style of emulated network connection.

On Windows, connections between the embedded client and the embedded server bypass server authentication.

Mixed Platforms

Firebird's design enables clients running one operating system to access a Firebird server that is running on a different platform and operating system to the client. A common arrangement, for example, is to run several inexpensive Windows workstations concurrently accessing a departmental server running on a host that might be Windows, Linux, or any of several brands of UNIX.

A database that was built for access by one server model can be served by any of them. For example, when an embedded server application is off-line, its database can be under the control of a different embedded server application or a full Firebird server serving remote clients.

Porting a Database

The same database can be ported from platform to platform without modification. It is strongly recommended that the database be backed up with *gbak* on the old platform and restored with *gbak* on the new. File-copying databases is not recommended, especially with databases that were created using a Firebird version lower than 2.0.x and still have an old on-disk structure ("ODS").

ODS 11.1 and 11.2 databases should be completely portable between Intel platforms, even when porting from i86 to i64 operating systems. Still, if a gbak backup/restore is practicable for such migrations, it should be in the plan. If not, be certain to test and verify copies thoroughly.

Never file-copy a database that has active connections. This warning applies, even if the copy is not going to be used. File-copying applications can be aggressive about overriding locks that databases rely on for data integrity.

Besides the Windows and Linux platforms, current server implementations of Firebird (Classic, Superclassic, Superserver) are available also for Mac OSX (Darwin). Older versions of Classic and, in some cases, Superserver, are available for FreeBSD, Sun Solaris (Intel and Sparc), HP-UX and potentially AIX, and can be built for a number of additional UNIX platforms.

Old Netware

Firebird does not currently have platform support for any version of Netware by Novell, nor for any other species of networking that accords to the largely obsolete IPX/SPX protocol. With the demise of Novell support for this protocol, sites often operate Firebird server on a Linux system, with network clients connecting to this subsystem via TCP/IP.

A Network Address for the Server

The host on which the Firebird server is running needs a network address in order for network clients to connect to it.

- If you are on a managed network, get the server's IP address from your system administrator
- If you have a simple network of two machines linked by a crossover cable, or a small, switched network, you can set up your server with any suitable unique IP address you like except 127.0.0.1 (which is reserved for a local loopback server)
- If you know the "native" IP addresses of your network cards, and they are different, you can simply use one of those that the remote Firebird client applications can "see"
- If you know the TCP/IP host name of the server, you can use that. On POSIX, the host name must be resolved in /etc/hosts. Note that the network name of a Windows server will resolve automatically to both its TCP/IP host name and its NetBIOS destination name.
- If you are intending to try out a single-machine installation of both client and server, you should use the local loopback server address—localhost, or its IP address 127.0.0.1

It is possible for a single user to connect locally to a server, without using a local TCP/IP loopback, either as an or embedded client or, on Windows, as an ipServer client ("Windows local" protocol). A server address is neither required nor valid for such a connection and cannot be used to verify that TCP/IP is working properly in your setup.

Hosts File

When setting up Firebird nodes for TCP/IP networking, it is recommended that you configure the host name files on clients and use these, rather than the IP addresses directly, for attaching to the server. Whilst most up-to-date operating systems can use the host's IP address in your client connection string in lieu of the host name, connection through a host name ensures that the server's address remains static, regardless of dynamic address changes in the network.

If your TCP/IP network is not running a domain name service (DNS), or your network's dynamic host addressing is sometimes unreliable, it may be advisable to inform each node individually of the mappings of IP addresses to host names in your network. To enable this, update the HOSTS file of each node (server and client).

Locating the HOSTS file

on Linux and many UNIX versions, the `hosts` file is normally located in `/etc/`. Note that a file name is case-sensitive on the Unix family of platfoms.

- on Windows server platforms the `HOSTS` file is located in `c:\windows\system32\drivers\etc\` (or `c:\winnt\system32\drivers\etc\` on Windows 2000 or a host that was upgraded from Windows 2000)
- on Windows 95/98/ME it is located in `c:\windows\`

If HOSTS is not present, a file named `Hosts.SAM` will be found in the same location. Copy this file and rename it to `HOSTS`. On Windows, a file name is not case-sensitive.

Examples of hosts file entries

```
10.12.13.2 db_server # Firebird server (in your LAN)
216.34.181.60 sourceforge.net # (server on a WAN)
127.0.0.1 localhost # local loopback server (on Windows)
127.0.0.1 localhost.localdomain # local loopback server (on Linux)
```

Open and edit the hosts file with a plain text editor.

- The IP address, if not 127.0.0.1 (localhost) must be the valid one configured for the host in your network.
- Server_name can be any unique name in your network.
- The comments following the hash (#) symbol are optional, but recommended

- The text format is identical, regardless of whether the host is running on Windows or a POSIX operating system. However, if you are copying a hosts file around a mixed network, be aware of the differences in end-of-line characters used on Windows, MacOSX and Linux/other POSIX.

After editing, check that your editor saves HOSTS with no file extension. If necessary, remove any extension by renaming the file.

On Windows 95 and early Windows 98 the network support does not recognize an IP address in the connection string at all because they were installed with Winsock 1. Installing Winsock 2 is effectively a requirement for current Firebird versions. Free upgrade packs may still be available from Microsoft customer support sites.

Server Name and Database Path

When you create or relocate a database, ensure that it is on a hard disk that is physically attached to your server machine. Database files located on shares, mapped drives or (on Unix) mounted as SMB (Samba) or NFS filesystems can not be seen by the server.[1]

SAN (storage area network) devices and NAS/iSCSI boxes (network-attached storage with iSCSI control) are seen as locally attached.

From Firebird 1.5 forward, you have the option of storing the paths to databases on your server as database path aliases. This not only simplifies the business of setting up portable connection strings in your applications, but adds an extra layer of security to your remote connections. Database path aliasing prevents sniffer programs determining where your databases are located and using that information to compromise your files.

Refer to Database aliasing in Chapter 4, ***Operating Basics***, for information.

Connection string syntax

These are the "in-clear" connection strings for each platform, which you need for configuring aliases and for attaching clients to databases running on Firebird 1.0, which does not support database aliasing.

TCP/IP

A TCP/IP connection string has two elements: the server name and the absolute disk/filesystem path as seen from the server. It may optionally include a third element, the TCP port number, only necessary if the server is listening on a port other than 3050. Its format is as follows:

For connecting to a Linux server

```
hostname:/filesystem-path/database-file
```

or, with the optional TCP port number included:

```
hostname/port-number:/filesystem-path/database-file
```

Examples

Examples for connecting to a Linux or other Unix-family server named "hotchicken":

```
hotchicken:/opt/firebird15/examples/LeisureStore.fdb
hotchicken/103050:/opt/firebird15/examples/LeisureStore.fdb
```

All file names are case-sensitive on these platforms.

1. Unless the database is read-only and *RemoteFileOpenAbility* is confgured "on" in firebird.conf. For normal, read-write databases, here be dragons!

For connecting to a Windows server

```
hostname:Drive:\filesystem-path\database-file
```

or, with the optional TCP port number included:

```
hostname/port-number:Drive:\filesystem-path\database-file
```

Examples

Examples for connecting to a Windows server named "winserver":

```
winserver:C:\Program Files\Firebird15\examples\LeisureStore.fdb
winserver/103050:C:\Program Files\Firebird15\examples\LeisureStore.fdb
```

Forward slashes are also valid on Windows:

```
winserver:C:/Program Files/Firebird15/examples/LeisureStore.fdb
```

Windows Networking (Named Pipes/WNet)

For connecting a remote client to a Windows server using the Named Pipes protocol, an UNC-style notation is used:

```
\\servername\filesystem-path\database-file
```

where `\\Servername` must be the properly-identified node name of the server machine on the Windows network, not a share or a mapped drive.

For example,

```
\\winserver\c:\databases\LeisureStore.fdb
```

Windows local connection

For connecting an embedded client or a local external client in Windows local mode:

```
C:\Program Files\Firebird15\examples\LeisureStore.fdb
```

Inconsistent connection strings for Windows connections

To protect databases from a long-standing bug in Windows, Superserver or Superclassic on Windows establishes an exclusive lock on the database file when the first client connection is activated.

The connection path bug

Windows will accept two forms of the absolute local path to a file: one (correct according to the DOS standard) being `Drive:\path-to-database` and the other, optionally omitting the backslash following the drive designator, `Drive:path-to-database`.

If the server were to receive two client connection requests, the first using the standard path form and the subsequent one using the optional form, it would treat the two attachments as though they were connected to two different databases. The effects of any concurrent DML operations would cause destructive corruption the database.

For connections to Superserver or Superclassic, the exclusive lock pre-empts the problem by requiring all connections to use the same path format as was used by the first connection.

Classic

The same solution cannot be applied to Classic server process because each connection works with its own instance of the server. Take care to ensure that your application always passes consistent path strings.

It is highly recommended that you use the database aliasing feature for all connections and also ensure that aliases.conf contains one and only one alias for each database. See the topic <u>Database aliasing</u> in the next chapter.

Testing Connections

All things being equal, the last reality check is to make sure your client machine is communicating with the server host. You can quickly test whether a TCP/IP client can reach the server, using the ping command in the command shell. Usage is:

```
ping server_name
```

substituting the name you entered in the `hosts` file, of course.

If the connection is good and everything is properly configured, you should see something like this:

```
Pinging hotchicken [10.10.0.2] with 32 bytes of data
reply from 10.10.0.2: bytes=32 time<10ms TTL=128
reply from 10.10.0.2: bytes=32 time<10ms TTL=128
reply from 10.10.0.2: bytes=32 time<10ms TTL=128
reply from 10.10.0.2: bytes=32 time<10ms TTL=128
```

Press Ctrl–C to stop the ping responses.

If ping fails

If you get something like

```
Bad IP address hotchicken
```

then your host name file entry for the server_name (in this example, *hotchicken*, may be missing or wrongly spelt. For example, all identifiers on Linux/UNIX are case sensitive. Another cause might be simply that your server machine's host name has not been configured.

If you see

```
Request timed out
```

it means that the IP address referred to in your host name file cannot be found in the subnet. Check that—

- there are no typos in the host name file entry, remembering that a Linux host name is case-sensitive
- the network cable is plugged in and the wires and contacts are free from damage and corrosion
- the network configuration allows you to route network traffic between the client and server in question. Subnet or firewall restrictions may be preventing the host server from receiving the ping from the client.

Another possibility is that the host machine may be firewalled against ICMP requests, in which case ping will be blocked.

Use the *netstat* tool

netstat (network statistics) is a command-line tool that displays both incoming and outgoing network connections, routing tables, and a number of network interface statistics. It is available on both POSIX and Windows.

A useful netstat call is *netstat -a* which shows all sockets from all connections. If the Firebird server is listening for connections, it will be listed with the local port address it is configured to listen on (3050 by default).

On Windows the output of *netstat -a* might look something like this:

```
Active Connections

  Proto  Local Address          Foreign Address        State
```

```
TCP    dev1:http              dev1:0            LISTENING
TCP    dev1:epmap             dev1:0            LISTENING
TCP    dev1:https             dev1:0            LISTENING
TCP    dev1:microsoft-ds      dev1:0            LISTENING
TCP    dev1:2869              dev1:0            LISTENING
TCP    dev1:3050              dev1:0            LISTENING
TCP    dev1:17500             dev1:0            LISTENING
```

On POSIX

```
Active Internet Connections
Proto Recv-Q Send-Q Local Address    Foreign Address    (State)
tcp        0      0 *:domain         *:*                LISTEN
tcp        0      0 *:time           *:*                LISTEN
tcp        0      0 *:3050           *:*                LISTEN
tcp        0      0 *:telnet         *:*                LISTEN
tcp        0      0 *:chargen        *:*                LISTEN
tcp        0      0 *:daytime        *:*                LISTEN
tcp        0      0 *:discard        *:*                LISTEN
tcp        0      0 *:echo           *:*                LISTEN
tcp        0      0 *:shell          *:*                LISTEN
tcp        0      0 *:login          *:*                LISTEN
```

For more information about the command switches available for *netstat* on your platform, refer to the on-line documentation (`man netstat` on POSIX, `netstat /?` on Windows).

Try Telnet

If ping is not working and you know, from running *netstat*, that Firebird's service port is open, you can try using Telnet to test the connection. In a command shell, type:

```
telnet [hostname|IPaddress] <service-port>
```

For example,

```
telnet dbhost 3050
```

If the screen goes blank, with no messages, then Telnet has found the port.

Firewalls

Your connection test might fail if the database server is behind a software or hardware firewall that blocks port 3050 or your reconfigured port.

Subnet restrictions

TCP/IP can be configured to restrict traffic between subnets. If your client machine is part of a complex network of subnets, check with the network adminstrator that it has unrestricted access to the host server.

WNet cannot route network traffic between subnets.

Problems with events

Although each client connects with the server through a single pipe, Firebird events—a callback mechanism that can channel event notifications back to clients from triggers and stored procedures—use *random* available ports. On static, self-contained networks without internal firewalls, this usually causes no problems. On networks where there are multiple subnets, dynamic IP addressing and tightly configured firewalls, the event channels can fail.

It is possible to configure an IP address in the network explicitly for events traffic. Use the `firebird.conf` parameter ***RemoteAuxPort*** to set statically a port number on the server that is available for event routing.

v.1.0.x In Firebird 1.0.x, the network administrator needs to configure some way to ensure that a port is available that is always free, open and static. It can be solved in one way or another on most networks.

For more information about Firebird events, refer to Chapter 32, ***Error Handling and Events***.

Initial Configuration

Firebird does not require the intense and constant reconfiguration that many other heavy-duty RDBMS systems do. To begin with—and possibly, for all time—you can go with the defaults and operate Firebird effectively.

A range of configuration options is available for customizing a Firebird server and the host system on which it runs for your particular needs. We will not look at most of them here: they are described in detail in Part VII, ***Configuring Firebird***. This topic serves just as an introduction to a few of the parameters that may affect the particular conditions you encounter with your hardware or network.

The Firebird Root Directory

The root directory of your Firebird installation is used in many ways, both during installation and as an attribute that server routines, configuration parameters and clients depend on. If you installed Firebird with all defaults, everything should be where Firebird's components expect it to be. If something about your installation is different, it will be helpful to know about the different ways the location can be configured and the precedence trail that the server follows at startup, to determine it correctly. It is described in detail in Chapter 33 of ***The Firebird Book Second Edition*** and in the companion volume to this, Volume 3: ***Administering Firebird Servers and Databases***.

The Firebird Configuration File

When a Firebird server process starts up, it reads the configuration file and adjusts its runtime flags to any non-default values contained in the configuration file. The file will not be read again until next time the server is restarted. The default configuration parameters and their values are listed in the configuration file, commented out by "#" comment markers. It is not necessary to uncomment the defaults in order to make them visible to the server's startup procedure.

The Firebird configuration file is named `firebird.conf` on all platforms and models since Firebird 1.5.

v.1.0.x In Firebird 1.0.x, the configuration file's format and the names of the parameters are different, more restrictive and there are fewer of them. The name of the old configuration file depends on the operating system:

- On Linux/UNIX the name is `isc_config`
- On Windows, the name is `ibconfig`.

Changing configuration parameters

It should be unnecessary to change any defaults until and unless you need to customize something. It is not recommended to do so if you lack a clear understanding of the effects.

A handful of default configuration settings that may be showstoppers for some legacy applications or non-default installations are discussed briefly here in case you suspect you cannot proceed without looking at them. The configuration file can be edited with any plain text editor, e.g. *vim* or *nano* (Linux or MacOSX) or *Notepad* (Windows).

Do not copy the file between platforms without being aware of the conversions you need to do to address the differences in the ways line breaks are stored on each platform! The free, open source editor ***Notepad++*** *enables cross-platform text conversions and is available on both POSIX and Windows.*

Parameter entries in firebird.conf are in the form:

```
parameter_name = value
```

- `parameter_name` is a string that contains no whitespace and names a property of the server being configured.
- `value` is a number, Boolean (1=True, 0=False) or string that specifies the value for the parameter

To set any parameter to a non-default setting, delete the comment (#) marker and edit the value. You can edit the configuration file while the server is running.

You might prefer to retain the default value beside the '#' marker as documentation and insert a fresh line below it to set your non-default value.

To activate configuration changes, it is necessary to stop and restart the service.

On Linux, you should assume that parameter names are case-sensitive.

v.1.0.x The *ibconfig*/*isc_config* format is

```
parameter_name    value
```

where the white space between the name and the value can be tabs or spaces, as desired, to please the eye. Each line of the file is limited to 80 characters. Unused parameters and installation defaults are commented with '#'.

Parameters relating to file access

Firebird has several parameters for protecting its files and databases from accidents and unauthorized access. If you are porting an old database application or admin tool to Firebird 1.5 or higher, it may be important for you to refer to Chapter 34 for detailed information about these parameters:

- ***RootDirectory*** can be used to configure the absolute path to a directory root on the local filesystem. It should remain commented unless you want to force the startup procedure to override the path to the root directory of the Firebird server installation, that it would otherwise detect for itself.
- ***DatabaseAccess*** parameter can be used to provide tighter security controls on access to database files and to support the database-aliasing feature. The default installation configures this to Full—the server can attach to any database in its local filesystem and is always accessed by applications passing the file's absolute filesystem path. Alternative options can restrict the server's access to aliased databases only, or to databases located in specified filesystem trees.

  From v.2.5 forward, if Restrict is configured, Firebird uses the first tree root in the list as the default location for creating a database.

  It is strongly recommended that you set this option and make use of the database-aliasing feature. For information about database aliasing, refer to the next chapter.

  See also ***UdfAccess*** and ***ExternalFileAccess*** in Chapter 34, ***Configuration Parameters in Detail***, if your new installation will be using an existing database that relies on external functions ("UDFs") or has database tables defining external text files as the source of data.

TempDirectories (***tmp_directory*** in v.1.0.x) can be configured as one of the ways to allocate temporary sort space for the server in a specific disk location.

Other parameters of interest

- ***CpuAffinityMask*** (***cpu_affinity*** in v.1.0.x) solves a problem affecting many, if not most, SMP host machines running Firebird on Windows. The operating system continually swaps the entire Superserver process back and forth between processors, resulting in a system stall whenever CPU usage becomes heavy. It is known as "the see-saw effect" and, if manifest on your system, requires the CPU affinity of the Superserver process to be restricted to a single CPU.

  By default, the affinity mask is set to use the first CPU in the array. Refer to the instructions in Chapter 34, ***Configuration Parameters in Detail*** if you need to change it to a different CPU.
- ***LockMemSize*** is specific to Classic servers and represents the number of bytes of shared memory allocated to the memory table used by the lock manager. You may need to adjust this if you encounter the error "Lock manager is out of room" on Classic. Refer also to the ***LockHashSlots*** parameter in relation to this problem.
- ***TempBlockSize*** and ***TempCacheLimit*** (***SortMemBlockSize*** and ***SortMemUpperLimit***, respectively, in v.1.5 and v.2.0) are two parameters that enable you to set and limit the amount of RAM the server uses for in-memory sorting. For Classic servers on hosts with low resources, the default settings may be too large to sustain more than a few connections.
- ***DummyPacketInterval*** (***dummy_packet_interval*** on v.1.0.x) is a relic from 16-bit systems that causes problems on all Windows systems. It should be kept at the default setting of zero on all platforms, to disable it.
- ***RemoteBindAddress***: By default, clients may connect from any network interface through which the host server accepts traffic. This parameter allows you to bind the Firebird Superserver or Superclassic service, or Classic on Windows, to incoming requests through one single IP address (e.g. network card) and to reject connection requests from any other network interfaces. This helps to solve problems in some networks when the server is hosting multiple subnets.

  For Classic on a POSIX platform, you can include the optional "bind" parameter in `[x]inetd.conf`:

```
service gds_db
  {
          disable          = no
          bind             = 192.150.22.1
          ...
  }
```

v.1.0.x ***RemoteBindAddress*** is not supported on v.1.0.x.

Environment Variables

A number of environment variables can be set, as required, to configure a variety of non-default conditions. Their effects are discussed in detail in Chapter 33 of ***The Firebird Book Second Edition*** and in the companion volume to this, Volume 3: ***Administering Firebird Servers and Databases***.

CHAPTER

4

OPERATING BASICS

Once you have Firebird server installed on your host server machine, what then?

The server you installed should be running when the installation completes. In this chapter you will find enough to get you going on the basics.

Looking for a User Interface

If you are a complete newcomer to client/server systems, you might expect to see some kind of graphical user interface ("GUI") that indicates the server is running and offers you ways to do things with databases. The Firebird servers do not interface directly with humans at all. All of their interaction with the world is through the application programming interface—API—that is realised in the client libraries.

Several excellent utility client programs are available in the marketplace for accessing Firebird databases. Many are commercial products, with or without stripped-down free versions. One open source product whose developers work closely with the Firebird Project is FlameRobin—see *http://www.flamerobin.org* for details and downloads. It is available for multiple client platforms, including Linux, Windows and MacOSX.

All Firebird versions are distributed with a command-line SQL query and general database information tool named *isql*. You will find this program in the `/bin/` directory of your Firebird installation. Near the end of this chapter is a brief introduction to *isql*. Full coverage of this tool can be found in Chapter 24.

Running Firebird on POSIX

The adminstration differences between the Super* servers (Superserver, Superclassic) are much more distinct on POSIX platforms than on Windows. Hence, it avoids confusion to introduce their operating basics separately. However, the newcomer may rest assured that the internals of databases running under different Firebird models are not affected by the architectural differences.

Superserver and Superclassic

The default installation directory for either Superserver (executable: *fbserver*) or Superclassic (*fb_smp_server*) is `/opt/firebird`. The binary itself, found in the `/bin` subdirectory, runs as a daemon process on Linux/UNIX. It is started automatically at the end of a RPM or script installation and whenever the host server is rebooted, by running the daemon script `firebird`, residing in /etc/rc.d/init.d in most distributions. This script calls the command-line Firebird Manager utility `fbmgr.bin`. Firebird Manager is surfaced as *fbmgr*, which can be used from a shell to start and stop the process manually.

Superclassic, offered from v.2.5 forward, is designed to improve the utilisation of resources, especially large RAM configurations and multiple processors, on well-resourced 64-bit operating systems. It is not recommended for production deployment on a 32-bit server.

v.1.0 The default installation directory is `/usr/firebird`. The executable is named *ibserver*, whilst the Firebird Manager is *ibmgr*.

Starting the server: *fbmgr*

If you have to start the Firebird server manually for some reason, log in as root or as the `firebird` user. Take care about which account you use when starting *fbserver* because, once it has been started, all of the objects created belong to that account. If another user later starts the process using one of the other special user accounts, those objects will be inaccessible.

It is strongly recommended to create a system user named `firebird` and run the Firebird server process under that account.

To start the process, execute the following command from a shell:

```
./fbmgr -start -forever
```

v.1.0

```
./ibmgr -start -forever
```

The `-forever` switch causes the Guardian monitor process (*fbguard*) to start. Under Guardian, if the *fbserver* process should terminate for some reason, it will be restarted automatically.

To start the server without the Guardian, enter

```
./fbmgr -start -once
```

v.1.0

```
./ibmgr -start -once
```

The `-once` switch makes it so that, if the server crashes, it stays down until manually restarted.

Stopping the server

For safety, if possible, ensure that all attachments to databases have been disconnected before you stop the server.

The `-shut` switch rolls back all current transactions and shuts down the server immediately.

You do not need to be logged in as root to stop the Firebird server with *fbmgr*, but you do need SYSDBA authority. Execute the following command:

```
./fbmgr -shut -password <SYSDBA password>
```

v.1.0

```
./ibmgr -shut -password <SYSDBA password>
```

Controlled shutdown

If you need to allow clients an interval to complete work and detach gracefully, shut down individual databases using the *gfix* tool with `-shut` and one of a range of available arguments to control detachment. See the topic <u>*Shutting Down a Database*</u> in the companion volume to this, Vol. 3: ***Administering Firebird Servers and Databases*** or in ***The Firebird Book Second Edition***, the chapter entitled ***Configuring and Managing Databases***.

In versions 1.x on this platform, Firebird does not provide a utility for counting users connected to a database on the Superserver

Other *fbmgr* commands

The general syntax for invoking *fbmgr* from a command shell is:

```
./fbmgr -command [-option [parameter] ...]
```

Alternatively, you can start an interactive *fbmgr* shell session, i.e. go into "prompt mode".

Type:

```
./fbmgr <press Return/Enter>
```

to bring up the prompt:

```
FBMGR>
```

In prompt mode, the syntax for commands is:

```
FBMGR> command [-option [parameter] ...]
```

For example, you can start the server in either of the following ways:

From the command shell:

```
./fbmgr -start -password password
```

In prompt mode:

```
FBMGR> start -password password
```

Switches for use with fbmgr

Following is a summary of the switches available for *fbmgr* and *ibmgr* in either shell or prompt mode.

Table 4.1 Switches for fbmgr/ibmgr

Switch	Argument	Other switches	Description
–start	–forever | –once	–user, –password	Starts the fbserver process if it is not already running
–shut	-	–user, –password	Stops the fbserver process
–show	-	-	Shows host and user
–user	*user-name* (Recommended: use SYSDBA)	-	Used with –start and –stop switches if system user is not root or equivalent
–password	SYSDBA password, or password of *user-name* if not SYSDBA	-	Used with –start and –stop switches if system user is not root or equivalent
–help	-	-	Prints brief help text for *fbmgr*
–quit	-	-	Use to quit Prompt mode

Classic server

Firebird Classic uses the *xinetd* or *inetd* process to handle incoming requests. (The process it uses depends which is in your Linux version.) There is no need to start the server explicitly. Provided *xinetd/inetd* is installed and running, the process runs automatically. When it accepts a request from a Firebird client to attach, it forks off a process named *fb_inet_server* for that client.

How the server listens for connection requests

If Firebird Classic was installed using a scripted or RPM installer, a startup configuration file for *fb_inet_server*, named `firebird`, should have been added to the services that *[x]inetd* knows about. On most Linux distributions, the location of this file is the directory `/etc/xinetd.d`. To have *[x]inetd* "listen" for connection requests from clients to your Firebird Classic server, the firebird script must be in this directory when the *[x]inetd* process starts.

If *[x]inetd* is running and no client connection requests succeed at all, check whether the firebird script is actually where it is supposed to be. If not, the script `firebird.xinetd` may be extracted from the compressed install kit, copied to the correct location and renamed to firebird. To make *[x]inetd* "see" the Firebird service:

```
~ $ service xinetd status
xinetd start/running, process nnnn
~ $ sudo service xinetd reload
```

If you see a message indicating that *[x]inetd* is stopped, just start it:

```
~ $ service xinetd start
```

*Substitute **inetd** for **xinetd** if your system does not support xinetd.*

Stopping and starting [x]inetd and its services

The *[x]inetd* daemon is itself a service which manages on-demand services like the Firebird Classic attachments. Stopping *[x]inetd* will cause each of the processes which it manages to stop also. Starting or restarting it will cause it to resume listening for requests to start any of its managed processes.

If all of the services in the `../rc.d` root (see above) are safe to shut down, log in as root and stop *x[inetd]* with the following shell command:

```
#  service xinetd stop
```

or, as appropriate,

```
#  service xinetd stop
```

If *x[inetd]* has not been configured to restart automatically when shut down, restart it with

```
#  service xinetd restart
```

Stopping a Firebird process

If you need stop a runaway Firebird process, in Classic you can do it for any version. Find the offending process by running the `top` command from a shell. This utility displays a list of the most CPU-intensive running processes and updates it constantly. Any *fb_inet_server* instances with extraordinary resource usage should appear in this list.

Get the PID (process ID) of the offending *fb_inet_server* process from the leftmost column of the display. You can use this PID with the **kill** command to send a signal to an errant process. For example, for a PID of 12345, you can attempt a controlled shutdown with

```
#  kill 12345
```

If the process remains visible in the top display, you can attempt a forced shutdown with

```
#  kill -9 12345
```

Exercise great care with kill, especially if you are logged in as root.

Running Firebird on Windows

The notes in this section refer to all models of Firebird for Windows hosts—Superserver, Superclassic and Classic—except where differences are noted.

Servers and the Guardian

On Windows, a Firebird server can run as a stand-alone program or it can be monitored by the Guardian program, *fbguard.exe*. The Guardian provides a capability that emulates the auto-restart capabilities of Windows services and those of POSIX services running with the `-forever` switch. If the *fbserver.exe* (Superserver) or *fb_inet_server.exe* (Superclassic) application should terminate abnormally, the Guardian will attempt to restart it.

It is recommended that you use the Guardian option on hosts running Firebird Superserver as an application. When running Superserver as a service, it is not really necessary, since services can be configured to restart automatically.

- On the services-capable Windows versions, the Superserver program or the Classic listener program can run as a service or as an application. The default installation on a services-capable Windows installs the Firebird server—and the Guardian, if selected—to run automatically as services. Both can be changed to run instead as applications.
- On Windows 95/98, ME and XP Home Edition, Firebird can run only as an application.

When Firebird runs as an application, an icon appears in the system tray. Limited administration tasks can be done manually by right-clicking on the tray icon.

Classic and the Guardian

Do not try to use the Guardian if you have installed the Classic server. Apart from the fact that it is redundant to the architecture of Classic, it can cause "ghost processes" to be created when clients have lost connections through network faults or have terminated their sessions abnormally. These ghosts can accumulate progressively, appropriating resources but doing nothing.

Running as a service

Unless you have a special contrary requirement, it is strongly recommended to keep Firebird server running as a service on a services-capable host.

Stopping and starting the service manually

To stop the service manually, first open a command shell window. Because the NET commands return messages to the command shell, do not try to run them directly using the Run.. option on the Start Menu.

The example here uses the default service name that is installed by the Firebird installers. If you are using v.2.5 or higher, the service might have been installed using a custom service name. If so, use that name instead as the argument to these commands.

Start the shell first by invoking *cmd.exe*.

In the shell, enter the command

```
NET STOP FirebirdServerDefaultInstance
```

To start or restart the server manally:

```
NET START FirebirdServerDefaultInstance
```

The NET STOP and NET START commands do not work on a Firebird server running as (or to be run as) an application.

Stopping and restarting the service using instsvc

The alternative, "native Firebird" way to start and stop the Firebird and Guardian services is to use the *instsvc.exe* utility, which is located in the `/bin` folder beneath the Firebird root directory. *Instsvc.exe* is used by the system to install the Firebird service—and Guardian, if selected—when the host server is booted up. Because it was not originally intended for general use by humans, it is a DOS-style command with switches.

Open a command shell and navigate to the rootdirectory/bin folder.

To stop the Firebird service:

```
C:\Program Files\Firebird\Firebird_2_5\bin> instsvc stop
```

To (re)start the Firebird service:

```
C:\Program Files\Firebird\Firebird_2_5\bin> instsvc start
```

Using instsvc with these switches does not respectively unload and reinstall the service.

Firebird Manager applets

When Firebird runs as a service, a small degree of administration, including stopping and restarting, can be done through the Firebird Manager Control Panel applet that is optionally installed by the installer into the system folder appropriate to the host machine's Windows version. The name of the applet in Firebird 2 and higher installations is `Firebird2Control.cpl`.

On older versions, the name of the "official" applet was FBControl.cpl.Several third-party applets were in circulation in those days, too, so it would not be unusual to find an older Firebird installation with a differently named applet.

Be aware that old control panel applets will not work on Vista or Windows 7. They may actually break the Control Panel altogether.In reality, the Control Panel applet is superfluous if you are not intending to run Firebird as an application. Administrators usually find it quicker to manage Firebird directly from the Services applet.

Running as an application

If Superserver or the Classic listener is running as an application, you should see an icon in the system tray of the server machine. You won't see a tray icon if the server has not been started. Unless you checked the installation option to start the server automatically, you will need to start it manually.

The appearance of the tray icon depends on whether you are running the server "stand-alone" or you have it under the Guardian's control.

It is recommended to use the Guardian when running Superserver as an application and to avoid it when running Classic.

Figure 4.1 Application tray icon

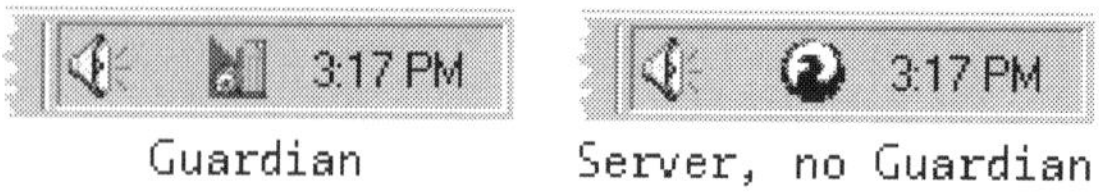

Starting the server as an application manually

If the Superserver is not running, it can be started or restarted manually by selecting it from the Start | Programs | Firebird menu.

Alternatively, Guardian or the server can be started from the command prompt: Invoke the command shell window and change to the `\bin` folder of your Firebird installation.

Superserver

The Guardian program is called *fbguard.exe* (*ibguard.exe* on v.1.0.x). Use the following command to start it:

```
fbguard.exe -a
```

v1.0

```
ibguard.exe -a
```

The Guardian places its icon in the tray and automatically starts the Superserver.

The name of the Superserver program is *fbserver.exe* (*ibserver.exe* on v.1.0.x). To start the Superserver directly yourself, without Guardian protection, use this command instead:

```
fbserver.exe -a
```

v.1.0

```
ibserver.exe -a
```

The server starts and places its own icon in the tray.

Classic server

These notes apply to Firebird 1.5 and later. Classic on Windows is not supported in older versions.

The process that is the "ears" for clients requesting attachment to a Classic server is an initial instance of a program named *fb_inet_server.exe*. If this initial instance of *fb_inet_server* is not running, it will not be possible for a client/server connection to be made and you will get the error "Unable to connect to server. Database cannot be found."

To start the initializing instance of the Classic server manually as an application, go to a command window, cd to your Firebird\bin directory and type:

```
fb_inet_server.exe -a
```

The server icon should appear in the tray and your server is ready to start receiving connections.

Stopping the server

If you need to stop a server that is running as an application, it is an operation that affects Superserver and Classic differently.

Superserver

Right-click the Firebird Guardian or server icon and choose Shutdown from the context menu. If Guardian is running, it first stops the server and then shuts down itself. Users currently logged on will lose any uncommitted work.

Classic

Taking the Shutdown option from the Server tray icon will prevent any further connections to the server but it does not affect any processes that are currently connected. Under most conditions, it should be unnecessary to "stop" the Classic server.

It is rarely, if ever, necessary to shut down Classic processes manually, since closing a client connection terminates its process instance cleanly and correctly. The only way to stop a Classic process that is running as an application is by applying brute force, via the Task List.

Running Firebird on MacOSX

Operating basics for Firebird on MacOSX are very similar to those on any other POSIX platform. Some variations that are due to vernacular differences should be noted.

The Super* Models

The Start and Stop commands for Superserver and Superclassic are:

```
/Library/StartupItems/Firebird/Firebird start
/Library/StartupItems/Firebird/Firebird stop
```

Classic

Classic on MacOSX uses the *launchd* daemon, which is similar to *[x]inetd* on Linux and related daemons on some other POSIX (described above). As with processes launched by *[x]inted* on those platforms, you can stop (unload) and [re]start (load) the Classic listener from the command shell.

To disable the listener:

```
$sudo launchctl unload /Library/LaunchDemons/org.firebird.gds.plist
```

To enable (or re-enable) it:

```
$sudo launchctl load  /Library/LaunchDemons/org.firebird.gds.plist
```

Mixed Platforms

If your Firebird server is running on Linux, databases must be on Linux, too, on storage devices that are under the direct physical control of the host machine. The same host-database relationship goes for a host running Windows, MacOSX or any other operating system.

A Firebird server cannot serve requests for operations on a database that resides on another box, or even on a VM that is running on the same box. This rules out databases that are located on logical devices in the host's file system that are physically located on another box.

SAN (storage area network) devices and NAS/iSCSI boxes (network-attached storage with iSCSI control) that are visible to the server are seen as locally attached.

On all POSIX versions and on Windows from v.2.5, it is possible to configure the Firebird server to enable reading a database that is on a networked partition. The mechanism that enables this is the configuration parameter RemoteFileOpenAbility. Be strictly warned that such a facility should be restricted to databases that have the "read-only" attribute set in the header by SYSDBA or the database owner, using the gfix utility or a Services API call.

On the other hand, Firebird is neutral about the client application platform. You can run a client application on Windows workstation, for example, that connects to a database on a Mac OSX host across a TCP/IP network. The client needs a copy of the client library that is built for the platform that the application runs on and, usually, one or more translation layers that "hook up" the application to the client library.

Database aliasing

The concept of database aliasing is not just to relieve keyboard-weary developers. It improves the portability of applications and tightens up control of both internal and external database file access.

Aliases.conf

With database aliasing comes the configuration file `aliases.conf`. It is located in the root directory of your Firebird server installation and should not be moved from there.

Portability

Client applications connect to the server using a connection string which includes the absolute path to the server. The format of the absolute path varies according to whether the server is running on Windows or a POSIX-compliant platform (Linux, Unix, etc.) and, with a Windows server, whether the clients are using TCP/IP or NetBeui for network connectivity.

For example, suppose we have a server named "hotchicken".

With the server running on a POSIX-compliant platform, TCP/IP clients would connect to databases using a string of this format:

```
hotchicken:/opt/databases/Employee.fdb
```

With the server running on Windows, TCP/IP clients would connect with a different path format:

```
hotchicken:D:\databases\Employee.fdb
```

Database aliasing makes it so that, for TCP/IP clients, these differences become transparent. The absolute path portion of the connection string goes into the alias file, associated with a simple alias name. For example, in `aliases.conf` on a Linux server, the example could be stored as

```
db1 = /opt/databases/Employee.fdb
```

On a Windows server installation with TCP/IP or NetBEUI (Named Pipes) clients, it could be

```
db1 = D:\databases\Employee.fdb
```

Regardless of whether the server is POSIX or Windows, the TCP/IP connection string becomes

```
hotchicken:db1
```

It is not quite so neat if you want to make it so your application's connection string to a Windows host is transparent across either a TCP/IP or a NetBEUI connection, however. The UNC notation for a Windows host server to NetBEUI clients means that, although the database alias would be identical, the server portion is not portable:

`\\hotchicken\db1` versus `hotchicken:db1`

Make sure that all of the entries in aliases.conf point to local paths. If you port a database from Windows to POSIX, or vice versa, don't forget to edit the alias entries.

Access control

The principal benefit of the aliasing option is that it can be used, in combination with the `firebird.conf` parameter ***DatabaseAccess = NONE***, to restrict the server to opening only a specific set of named database files, viz. those which are identified in `aliases.conf`.

To implement database aliasing, edit the file `aliases.conf` in the root directory of your Firebird installation, using a plain text editor such as Notepad (on Windows) or vi (on Linux).

aliases.conf

The installed aliases.conf looks similar to this:

```
#
# List of known database aliases
# ------------------------------
#
# Examples:
#
#   dummy = c:\data\dummy.fdb
#
```

As in all of Firebird's configuration files, the '#' symbols are comment markers. To configure an alias, simply delete the '#' and change the dummy line to the appropriate database path:

```
# fbdb1 is on a Windows server:
fbdb1 = c:\Programs\Firebird\Firebird_2_5\examples\empbuild\Employee.fdb
# fbdb2 is on a Linux server
fbdb2 = /opt/databases/killergames.fdb
#
```

These examples would not be in the same aliases.conf file! The first would be in a file on a Windows server, while the second would be on a Linux server.

Each connection request containing a path using the alias format causes the server to read `aliases.conf`. You can edit `aliases.conf` whilst the server is running. The server does not have to be restarted for a new entry to take effect: just make sure you save the edits.

Changing the alias for a database will not affect current connections but future connections will use the new or modified alias. Thus, if you change the alias during a process that makes multiple connections—such as gbak—you are likely to cause the process to end with errors.

Connecting using an aliased database path

For TCP/IP connections, using the `alias.conf` examples above, the modified connection string in your application looks like this:

```
Server_name:aliasname
```

For example,

```
hotchicken:fbdb2
```

For Windows Named Pipes connections:

```
\\hotchicken\fbdb2
```

For a local connection, simply use the alias on its own.

The SYSDBA User and Password

The SYSDBA user is the only Firebird user installed in the security database at installation. The SYSDBA can access any database with full, destructive[1] privileges. At installation time, Windows and MacOSX platform versions have a password assigned that is known to everyone who ever used Firebird or InterBase. It is `masterke`. (or masterkey, if you prefer: only the first eight characters are significant).

It is imperative that you change the password at the earliest opportunity, using the *gsec* utility that is in Firebird's \bin\ directory:

```
..\BIN> gsec -modify SYSDBA -pw newpassw -user SYSDBA -password masterke
```

1. "Destructive" in the sense that SYSDBA or a user with equivalent privileges can alter or delete objects owned by anyone—including the database itself.

*Notice that this command contains two password switches: **-pw**, which takes the new password as its argument, and **-password**, which takes the current SYSDBA password for authentication.*

Linux

On Linux, the SYSDBA password that is stored in the security database is generated during the installation process and stored in a text file in Firebird's root directory. If your installation used the default file structure, you can find this password in the file `/opt/firebird/SYSDBA.password`.

- If you would like to keep the generated password, write it down somewhere, then delete the file
- If you want to change it to something else, either use *gsec* as above, or run the script `/opt/firebird/bin/changeDBAPassword.sh` and follow the prompts.

Administering Databases

The command-line utility *isql* incorporates tools and techniques for using SQL to maintain database objects, manage transactions, display metadata and manage database definition scripts. A shell interface is available that is consistent across all platforms. This brief introduction will get you started on the basics of connecting (attaching) to a database and creating your first database.

The employee.fdb Database

You can begin practising your Firebird SQL skills right away, using the "old faithful" `employee.fdb` database that is installed in the `../examples/empbuild` subdirectory of your Firebird installation. This database predates Firebird by many years: in InterBase installations its name was employee.gdb. While the employee database will never win any prizes for excellence in database design, it is a useful sampler for getting started with Firebird's SQL language.

You might like to create an alias for employee.fdb if you plan to use it for experimenting with the language features of Firebird. For example, you might add an entry like this to aliases.conf on a Windows installation in a folder called Programs:

```
emp25 = c:\Programs\Firebird\Firebird_2_5\examples\empbuild\employee.fdb
```

Starting isql

There are several different ways to connect to a database using *isql*. One way is to start its interactive shell. To begin, in a command shell, go to the `/bin` directory of your Firebird installation, where the *isql* program is installed, and start *isql* as follows:

For a POSIX server:

```
[chick@hotchicken]# ./isql
```

For a Windows server:

```
C:\Program Files\Firebird\Firebird_2_5\bin>isql
```

Press Return/Enter to open the program. The *isql* interactive shell should now open, displaying this message:

```
Use CONNECT or CREATE DATABASE to specify a database
```

Using isql

The characters 'isql' stand for Interactive SQL [utility]. Once connected to a database, you can query its data and metadata by entering regular dynamic SQL statements as well as a special subset of statements that work only in the isql environment.

Semi-colon terminators

Each statement you want to execute in isql must be terminated with a designated character. The default terminator is the semi-colon (;). This terminator is not a syntax element of the SQL but a convention that is specific to the usage of this application.

Make sure you terminate each SQL command with a semi-colon. If you forget, the next thing you will see is isql's continuation prompt:

```
CON>
```

The actual purpose of `CON>` (continuation) is to enable the convenient entry of long commands, phrase by phrase. *isql* will just keep filling the command buffer until it encounters a terminator. Thus, if you see the continuation prompt and have already completed your command, simply type a semi-colon and press Enter/Return.

You can change the designated terminator character. In certain isql tasks there is a compelling reason why you would need to. If you are preparing to run a sequence of commands, interactively or as a script, that will contain procedural SQL (PSQL) you might consider changing it at the beginning of the work. For more information, look up SET TERM in Chapter 24.

The CONNECT statement

The CONNECT statement is a standard SQL command statement for connecting to a database. Here it's assumed you haven't changed the SYSDBA password yet. If you have done so (recommended!) then use your own password.

For connecting to a Linux/Unix server

All in one line:

```
SQL> CONNECT 'hotchicken:/opt/firebird/examples/empbuild/employee.fdb' user 'sysdba'
password 'masterkey';
```

For connecting to a Windows server

All in one line:

```
SQL> CONNECT 'WINSERVER:C:\Program
Files\Firebird\Firebird_2_5\examples\empbuild\employee.fdb' user 'SYSDBA' password
'masterkey';
```

On Linux Classic and Windows Superserver it is possible to connect to a database locally, e.g. CONNECT '/opt/firebird/examples/employee.fdb' on Linux Classic or CONNECT 'c:\Program Files\Firebird\Firebird_1_5\examples\employee.fdb' on Windows Superserver.

At this point, isql will inform you that you are connected:

```
DATABASE 'hotchicken:/opt/firebird/examples/empbuild/employee.fdb', User: sysdba
SQL>
```

If the server is on Windows:

```
DATABASE "WINSERVER:C:\Program
Files\Firebird\Firebird_2_5\examples\empbuild\employee.fdb", User: sysdba
SQL>
```

Continue to play about with the `employee.fdb` database. You can use isql for querying data, getting information about the metadata, creating database objects, running data definition scripts and much more.

To get back to the command prompt type

```
SQL> QUIT;
```

Creating a database using isql

There is more than one way to create a database using isql. Here, we will look at one simple way to create a database interactively—although, for your serious database definition work, you should create and maintain your metadata objects using data definition scripts (also known as DDL scripts, SQL scripts, metadata scripts, schema scripts). This topic is covered in detail in Chapter 24

If you are currently logged into a database through the isql shell, leave it now with the following command:

```
SQL> QUIT;
```

Next, restart it, without connecting to a database:

For a Linux server:

```
[chick@hotchicken]# ./isql
Use CONNECT or CREATE DATABASE to specify a database
```

For a Windows server:

```
C:\Program Files\Firebird\Firebird_2_5\bin>isql
Use CONNECT or CREATE DATABASE to specify a database
```

The CREATE DATABASE statement

Now, you can create your new database interactively. Let's suppose that you want to create a database named test.fdb on your Windows server and store it a directory named "data" on your D drive:

```
SQL> CREATE DATABASE 'D:\data\test.fdb' user 'SYSDBA' password 'masterkey';
```

Press Enter. The database will be created and, after a few moments, the SQL prompt will reappear. You are now connected to the new database and can proceed to create some test objects in it.

To verify that there really is a database there, type in this query and press Enter:

```
SQL> SELECT * FROM RDB$RELATIONS;
```

The screen will fill up with a large amount of data! This query selects all of the rows in the system table where Firebird stores the metadata for tables. An "empty" database is not empty—it contains a set of system tables which will become populated with metadata as you begin creating objects in your database.

Almost all metadata objects in Firebird databases have identifiers prefixed with "RDB$". From v.2.1 forward, another series of system tables, for database monitoring, have the prefix "MON$".

To get back to the command prompt type

```
SQL> QUIT;
```

For full information about using *isql*, refer to Chapter 24.

Summary of Command-line Tools

The command-line tools that are built from the Firebird sources and distributed with the official binary kits are summarised in Table 4.1, below.

Table 4.2 Summary of Command-line Tools

Tool	Purpose	Details
isql	SQL client. Comprises an interactive interface with some internal language extensions and shell access and a command-only mode for use in a shell or for automation scripting.	In Chapter 17, ***Interactive SQL Utility*** on *page 253*
gfix	Utility toolset for configuring database attributes and for analysing and repairing some corruptions.	In V3, TFB2E, chapter entitled Configuring Databases, ***The gfix Toolset***
gsec	Utility comprising an interactive shell and a command-only mode for use in a shell, for maintaining server users in the authentication database.	In V3, TFB2E, chapter entitled Protecting the Server and Its Environment, ***The gsec Utility***
fbtracemgr	Utility for working interactively with trace services.	In V3, TFB2E, Monitoring and Logging Features, ***Command-line Utility fbtracemgr***
gstat	Statistics-gathering tool for collecting statistics about the transaction inventory, index distribution and behaviour—can output reports to display screen or files.	In V3, TFB2E, Monitoring and Logging Features, ***Collecting Database Statistics—gstat***
fb_lock_print	Utility that extracts the lock table statistics as either static reports or samplings done interactively at specified intervals.	In V3, TFB2E, Monitoring and Logging Features, ***The Lock Print Utility***
gbak	Backup and restore utility, used for regular backups, for on-disk structure (ODS) upgrades and also, with *gfix,* in database repair procedures.	In V3, TFB2E,Backing Up Databases, ***The gbak Utility***
nBackup	Increcremental backup facility for scheduled or ad hoc backups of database page images as the page inventory grows. Comprises both command-line and SQL interfaces.	In V3, TFB2E,Backing Up Databases, ***Incremental Backup***
fbsvcmgr	Simple utility for accessing Services API functions from a shell.	In V3, TFB2E, The Services Manager, ***The fbsvcmgr Utility***

V2=Companion Vol. 3: Administering Firebird Servers and Databases;TFB2E=The Firebird Book Second Edition

The Firebird Book
A Reference for Database Developers
SECOND EDITION

PART II

Firebird Data Types & Domains

CHAPTER

5

About Firebird Data Types

Data type is the primary attribute that must be defined for each column in a Firebird table. It establishes and constrains the characteristics of the set of data that the column can store and the operations that can be performed on the data. It also determines how much space each data item occupies on the disk. Choosing an optimum size for data values is an important consideration for network traffic, disk economy and index size.

The Basics

Firebird supports most SQL data types. In addition, it supports dynamically-sizeable typed and untyped binary large objects (BLOBs) and multi-dimensional, homogeneous arrays of most data types.

Where to Specify Data Types

A data type is defined for data items in the following situations:

- specifying column definitions in a CREATE TABLE specification
- creating a re-usable global column template using CREATE DOMAIN
- modifying a global column template using ALTER DOMAIN
- adding a new column to a table or altering a column using ALTER TABLE
- declaring arguments and local variables in stored procedures and triggers
- declaring arguments and return values for external (user-defined) functions

Supported Data Types

- Number types (Chapter 7)
  - BIGINT, INTEGER and SMALLINT
  - NUMERIC and DECIMAL
  - FLOAT and DOUBLE PRECISION
- Date and time types (Chapter 8)

    - DATE, TIME, and TIMESTAMP
- Character types (Chapter 9)
    - CHARACTER, VARYING CHARACTER, and NATIONAL CHARACTER
- BLOB and ARRAY types (Chapter 10)
    - BLOB, typed and untyped
    - ARRAY

Booleans

Up to and including release 2.5, Firebird does not provide a Boolean ("logical") type. The usual practice is to define a 1-char or SMALLINT domain for generic use whenever the design calls for a Boolean.

For tips about defining Boolean domains, refer to Chapter 11.

SQL "Dialects"

Firebird supports three SQL "dialects" which have no practical use except to facilitate conversion of an ancient InterBase v.5 (or older) database to Firebird. Firebird's "native" dialect is currently known as "dialect 3". By default, a Firebird server creates databases in this native dialect. If your Firebird experience brings with it no cargo of existing assumptions nor any legacy databases that you want to upgrade to Firebird, you can safely "go native" and ignore all of the notes and warnings about dialect 1.

If you are an ex-InterBase user, or you have used outdated migration tools to convert another RDBMS to InterBase, then SQL dialects will be an issue for you in one way or another.

As you work your way through this book, issues that are affected by SQL dialect are annnotated appropriately for your attention. However, some of the more serious effects arise from the dialectal differences between data types. For this reason, the question of dialects gets space in the chapter ***Migration Notes*** in the companion volume to this, Volume 3: ***Administering Firebird Servers and Databases*** and in ***The Firebird Book Second Edition***.

Quick check for SQL dialect

If you have a legacy database and you don't know which dialect your database speaks, you can do a quick check with the *gstat* tool, located in the ../bin/ directory of your Firebird installation. You don't need any special privileges for this. Go to that directory and type

for POSIX:

```
./gstat -h yourserver:/path/to/your/database
```

for Windows:

```
gstat -h yourserver:d:\path\to\your\database
```

You will see a list of useful information about your database, which gstat has read from the database header page. The dialect and on-disk structure (ODS) are included in the list.

- If you are using the isql interactive tool, you can get a similar summary using SHOW DATABASE.
- The SHOW SQL DIALECT command displays both the client and database dialects.

Any database that has an ODS lower than 10 will always be dialect 1.

Context Variables

Firebird makes available a number of system-maintained variable values in the context of the current client connection and its activity. These context variables are available for use in SQL, including the trigger and stored procedure language, PSQL. Some are available only in PSQL and most are available only in Dialect 3 databases.

The context variables are fully listed and described in Appendix III, *Context Variables*. Table 6.1 is a sampling of some commonly used context variables.

Table 5.1 A Sampling of Available Context Variables

Context variable	Data type	Description	Availability
CURRENT_CONNECTION	INTEGER	System ID of the connection that is making this query	Firebird 1.5 onward, DSQL and PSQL
CURRENT_TRANSACTION	INTEGER	System ID of the transaction in which this query is being requested	Firebird 1.5 onward, DSQL and PSQL
CURRENT_TIMESTAMP	TIMESTAMP	Current date and time on the host server's clock to the nearest millisecond	Prior to v.2.0, milliseconds were not returned. The UDF *GetExactTimestamp()* could be used with the older versions to return server time to nearest ten-thousandths of a second.
CURRENT_TIME	TIME	Current time on the server's clock, expressed as seconds since midnight	All versions, all SQL environments, Dialect 3 only
CURRENT_USER	VARCHAR(128)	User name that is communicating through this instance of the client library	All versions, all SQL environments

Points about Usage

Remember that these are transient values.

- CURRENT_CONNECTION and CURRENT_TRANSACTION have no meaning outside the current connection and transaction contexts respectively. Do not treat them as perpetually unique, since the Firebird engine stores these identifiers on the database header page. After a restore, their series will be re-initialized to zero.
- CURRENT_TIMESTAMP records the server time at the start of the operation and should not be relied upon as the sole sequencer of a batch of rows inserted or updated by a single statement.
- Even though CURRENT_TIME is stored as the time elapsed since midnight on the server's clock, it is a TIME value, not an interval of time. To achieve a time interval, use timestamps for start and finish times and subtract the start time from the finish time. The result will be a time interval in days.
- The date/time context variables are based on server time, which may be different to the internal clock time on clients.

Examples using context variables

This statement returns the server time at the moment the server serves the request of the Firebird client:

```
SELECT CURRENT_TIME AS TIME_FINISHED FROM RDB$DATABASE;
```

In this insert statement, current transaction ID, the current server timestamp and the system user name will be written to a table:

```
INSERT INTO TRANSACTIONLOG (TRANS_ID, USERNAME, DATESTAMP)
  VALUES (
    CURRENT_TRANSACTION,
    CURRENT_USER,
    CURRENT_TIMESTAMP);
```

Pre-defined Date Literals

A number of date literals—single-quoted strings which Firebird SQL will accept in lieu of certain special dates—are available to both Dialect 1 and Dialect 3 databases. In Dialect 1, the strings can be used directly; in Dialect 3, they must be cast to type. Table 6.2 shows the usage in each dialect.

Table 5.2 List of predefined date literals

Date literal	Date substituted	Dialect 3 Type	Dialect 1 Type
'NOW'	Current date and time	TIMESTAMP	DATE (equivalent to Dialect 3 Timestamp)
'TODAY'	Current date	DATE (date-only type)	DATE (TIMESTAMP) with zero time part
'YESTERDAY'	Current date – 1	DATE	DATE (TIMESTAMP) with zero time part
'TOMORROW'	Current date + 1	DATE	DATE (TIMESTAMP) with zero time part

The Dialect 1 DATE type is equivalent to a Dialect 3 TIMESTAMP. In Dialect 3, the DATE type is date only. Dialect 1 has no equivalent type.

Examples using predefined date literals

In a Dialect 1 database, this statement returns exact server time:

```
SELECT 'NOW' AS TIME_FINISHED FROM RDB$DATABASE;
```

In a Dialect 3 database the date literal must be cast as a timestamp type:

```
SELECT CAST('NOW' AS TIMESTAMP) AS TIME_FINISHED FROM RDB$DATABASE;
```

This update statement sets a date column to server time plus one day in Dialect 1:

```
UPDATE TABLE_A
  SET UPDATE_DATE = 'TOMORROW'
  WHERE KEY_ID = 144;
```

The same operation in Dialect 3, with casting:

```
UPDATE TABLE_A
  SET UPDATE_DATE = CAST('TOMORROW' AS DATE)
  WHERE KEY_ID = 144;
```

Optional SQL-92 Delimited Identifiers

In Dialect 3 databases, Firebird supports the ANSI SQL convention for optionally delimiting identifiers. To use reserved words, case-sensitive strings, or embedded spaces in an object name, enclose the name in double quotes. It is then a delimited identifier. Delimited identifiers must always be referenced in double quotes.

For more details, follow up this topic in Chapter ??, Database object naming conventions and constraints.

For more information about naming database objects with CREATE or DECLARE statements, refer to Part Three, ***A Database and its Objects***. Refer to Appendix II for the list of keywords that are reserved for SQL.

Columns

Data in a relational database system such as Firebird are arranged logically in sets consisting of rows and columns. A column holds one piece of data with defining attributes which are identical for every row in the set. A column definition has two required attributes—an identifier (or column name) and a data type. Certain other attributes can be included in a column definition, such as a CHARACTER SET and constraints like NOT NULL and UNIQUE.

Sets that are defined for storing data are known as tables. The row structure of a table is defined by declaring a table identifier and listing the column identifiers, their data types and any other attributes needed, on a column-by-column basis.

A simple example of a table definition is:

```
CREATE TABLE SIMPLE (
    COLUMN1 INTEGER,
    COLUMN2 CHAR(3),
    COLUMN3 DATE);
```

For full details about defining tables and columns, refer to the relevant chapters in Part Three, ***A Database and its Objects***.

Domains

In Firebird you can pre-package a column definition, with a data type and a "template set" of attributes, as a ***domain***. Once a domain is defined and committed, it is available for use in any table in your database, just as if it were a data type in its own right. In Firebird 2.5+, a domain can be used to declare the data type of a variable in a PSQL module, although it is not possible in older versions.

Columns based on a domain definition inherit all attributes of the domain—its data type, along with any number of optional, extra attributes, including a default value for inserts, validation constraints, character set and collation order.

Any attribute except the data type can be overridden when the domain is used to define a column in a table definition, by replacing an attribute with a different, compatible attribute or by adding an attribute. Thus, for example, it is possible to define a domain with a complex set of attributes, not including NOT NULL, which can be made nullable in some usages and NOT NULL in others.

For full details about defining, maintaining and using domains, refer to Chapter 11, *Domains*, later in this part.

Converting Data Types

Normally, you must use compatible data types to perform arithmetic operations, or to compare data in search conditions. If you need to perform operations on mixed data types, or if your programming language uses a data type that is not supported by Firebird, then data type conversions must be performed before the database operation can proceed.

Implicit type conversion

Dialects 1 and 3 behave differently with regard to implicit type conversion. This will be an issue if you wish to convert an existing database to Dialect 3 and update its supporting applications.

- In dialect 1, for some expressions, Firebird automatically converts the data to an equivalent data type (an implicit type conversion). The CAST() function can also be used, although it is optional in most cases.
- In dialect 3, the CAST() function is required in search conditions to explicitly translate one data type into another for comparison purposes.

For example, comparing a DATE or TIMESTAMP column to `'12/31/2012'` in Dialect 1 causes the string literal `'12/31/2012'` to be converted implicitly to a DATE entity.

```
SELECT * FROM TABLE_A
WHERE START_DATE < '12/31/2012';
```

In Dialect 3:

```
SELECT * FROM TABLE_A
WHERE START_DATE < CAST('12/31/2012' AS DATE);
```

An expression mixing integers with string digits in Dialect 1 implicitly converts the string to an integer if it can. In the following expression:

```
3 + '1'
```

Dialect 1 automatically converts the character '1' to a smallint for the addition whereas Firebird dialect 3 returns an error. It requires an explicit type conversion:

```
3 + CAST('1' AS SMALLINT)
```

Both dialects will return an error on the next statement, because Firebird cannot convert the character "a" to an integer:

```
3 + 'a'
```

Both dialects will happily perform an explicit type conversion for concatenating:

```
SQL> select 1||'3' from rdb$database;

CONCATENATION
=============
13
```

Explicit type conversion: CAST()

When Firebird cannot do an implicit type conversion, you must perform an explicit type conversion using the CAST() function. Use CAST() to convert one data type to another inside a SELECT statement, typically, in the WHERE clause to compare different data types. The syntax is:

```
CAST (value | NULL AS data type)
```

You can use CAST() to compare columns with different data types in the same table, or across tables. For example, you can cast between properly formed strings and date/time types and between various number types. For detailed information about casting between specific types, refer to the chapter in this part of the guide that deals with the data types in question.

Changing column and domain definitions

In both dialects, you can change the data type of a column in tables and domains. If you are migrating a database from another RDMBS, this can be useful. Certain restrictions apply when altering the data type:

1 Firebird does not allow the data type of a column or domain to be altered in a way that might result in data loss. For example the number of characters in a column is not allowed to be smaller than the largest value in the column.

2 Converting a numeric data type to a character type requires a minimum length for the character type as listed in Table 6.3, below.

Table 5.3 Minimum character lengths for numeric conversions

Data type	Minimum length for character type
BigInt	19 (or 20 for signed numbers)
Decimal	20
Double precision	22
Float	13
Integer	10 (11 for signed numbers)
Numeric	20 (or 21 for signed numbers)
SmallInt	6

Altering data type of a column

Use the ALTER COLUMN clause of the ALTER TABLE statement with the TYPE keyword. For example:

```
ALTER TABLE table1 ALTER COLUMN field1 TYPE char(20);
```

For more information about altering columns in a table, refer to the topic *Altering Tables* in Chapter 14.

Altering data type of a domain

Use the TYPE clauselet of the ALTER DOMAIN statement to change the data type of a domain. For example:

```
ALTER DOMAIN MyDomain TYPE VARCHAR(40);
```

For more information about altering the attributes of a domain, refer to *Changing a Domain Definition* in Chapter 10.

Valid Conversions

Table 6.4 shows the data type conversions that are possible.

Table 5.4 Valid data type conversions using ALTER COLUMN and ALTER DOMAIN

Convert TO ► / FROM ▼	ARRAY	BIGINT	BLOB	CHAR	DATE	DECIMAL	DOUBLE	FLOAT	INTEGER	NUMERIC	TIMESTAMP	TIME	SMALLINT	VARCHAR
Array														
BigInt				■		■	■							■
BLOB														
Char				■										■
Date				■	■									
Decimal				■		■				■				■
Double				■			■	■						■
Float				■			■	■						■
Integer		■		■		■				■				■
Numeric				■						■				■
Timestamp				■	■						■	■		
Time				■										
Smallint		■		■		■	■	■	■	■			■	■
Varchar				■										■

Keywords Used for Specifying Data Type

The keywords for specifying the data type in DDL statements is provided here for quick reference. For exact syntax, refer to the relevant chapter in this part of the guide for the data type in question and to Chapters 11, *Domains* and 15, *Tables*.

```
--
{SMALLINT | INTEGER | FLOAT | DOUBLE PRECISION} [<array_dim>]
| {DATE | TIME | TIMESTAMP} [<array_dim>]
|{DECIMAL |NUMERIC} [ (precision [, scale])] [<array_dim>]
| {CHAR | CHARACTER | CHARACTER VARYING | VARCHAR} [(int)]
[<array_dim>] [CHARACTER SET charname]
| {NCHAR | NATIONAL CHARACTER | NATIONAL CHAR}
[VARYING] [(int)] [<array_dim>]
| BLOB [SUB_TYPE int | subtype_name} ] [SEGMENT SIZE int]
[CHARACTER SET charname]
| BLOB [(seglen [, subtype])]
```

also supported, from v.2.1 onward:

```
| TYPE OF <domain-name>
```

and, from v.2.5 on:

```
| TYPE OF COLUMN <table-name.column-name>
```

More detail can be found in the companion volume to this, Volume 2: ***Developing with Firebird Data*** and in ***The Firebird Book Second Edition***, in the chapter entitled ***Expressions and Predicates***.

Demystifying NULL

NULL can be quite a mystery for folk who have previously worked with desktop database systems that conveniently swallow NULLs by storing them as "zero values": empty strings, 0 for numerics, false for logicals, and so on. In SQL, any data item in a nullable column—that is, a column that does not have the NOT NULL constraint—will be stored with a NULL token if no value is ever provided for it in a DML statement or through a column default.

All column definitions in Firebird default to being nullable. In triggers, procedures and procedural blocks, variables contain NULL until a value is assigned to them. Unless your database has been consciously designed to prevent NULLs from being stored, all of your data manipulation work needs to be prepared to encounter and manage them.

If you are reading this chapter as a newcomer to SQL, then some terminology in this topic might baffle you. Don't worry—you will meet them all again. For now, the important thing is to know and understand how NULL works.

NULL in expressions

NULL is not a value, so it cannot be "equal to" any value. For example, a predicate such as

```
WHERE (COL1 = NULL)
```

will return an error because the equivalence operator ("=") is not valid for NULLs. NULL is a *state* and the correct predicator for a NULL test is *IS NULL*. The corrected predicate for the failed test above would be

```
WHERE (COL1 IS NULL)
```

You can also test for NOT NULL:

```
WHERE (COL1 IS NOT NULL)
```

Two NULLs are not equal to each other, either. When constructing expressions, be mindful of the cases when a predicate might resolve to

```
WHERE <NULL result> = <NULL result>
```

because false is always the result when two NULLs are compared.

An expression like

```
WHERE COL1 > NULL
```

will fail because an arithmetic operator is not valid for NULL.

NULL in calculations

In an expression where a column identifier "stands in" for the current value of a data item, a NULL operand in a calculation will produce NULL as the result of the calculation, e.g.

```
UPDATE TABLEA
  SET COL4 = COL4 + COL5;
```

will set COL4 to NULL if COL5 is NULL.

In aggregate expressions using operators like SUM( ) and AVG( ) and COUNT(<specific_column_name>), rows containing NULL in the targeted column are ignored for the aggregation. AVG( ) forms the numerator by aggregating the non-null values and the denominator by counting the rows containing non-null values.

Gotchas with True and False

Semantically, if a result is neither false nor true, it should be returned as "unknown". However, in SQL, assertions resolve as either "true" or "false"— an assertion that does not evaluate as "true" shakes out as "false".

The "IF" condition implicit in search predicates can trip you up when the NOT predicator is used on an embedded assertion, i.e.

NOT <condition evaluating to false> evaluates to TRUE

whereas

NOT <condition evaluating to null> evaluates to NULL

To take an example of where our assumptions can bite, consider

```
WHERE NOT (COLUMNA = COLUMNB)
```

If both COLUMNA and COLUMNB have values and they are not equal, the inner predicate evaluates to false. The assertion NOT(FALSE) returns true—the flip-side of false.

However, if either of the columns is NULL, the inner predicate evaluates to NULL, standing for the semantic meaning "unknown" ("not proven", "unknowable"). The assertion that is finally tested is NOT(NULL) and the result returns NULL. Take note also that NOT(NULL) is not the same as IS NOT NULL—a pure binary predicate that never returns "unknown".

The lesson in this is to be careful with SQL logic and always to test your expressions hard. Cover the null conditions and, if you can do so, avoid NOT assertions altogether in nested predicates.

Setting a value to NULL

A data item can be made NULL only in a column that is not subject to the NOT NULL constraint—refer to the topic <u>*The NOT NULL Constraint*</u> in Chapter 15, ***Tables***.

In an UPDATE statement the assignment operator is "=":

```
UPDATE FOO SET COL1= NULL
    WHERE COL2 = 4;
```

In an INSERT statement, pass the keyword NULL in place of a value:

```
INSERT INTO FOO (COL1, COL2, COL3)
  VALUES (1, 2, NULL);
```

In this case, NULL overrides any default set for COL3, because the data content for it is set explicitly.

Columns defaulting to NULL

In Firebird, all columns are created nullable by default. What this means is that, unless you apply a NOT NULL constraint to a column, NULL is treated as valid content.

If you came from MS SQLServer or another system that has low compliance with standards, you might expect things to be the other way around, where all columns are constrained as NOT NULL unless explicitly defined as NULLABLE.

This characteristic provides another way to cause NULL to be stored by an INSERT statement since, if the nullable column is omitted from the input list, the engine will set it to NULL.

For example, the following statement has the same effect as the previous example, as long as no default is defined for the column COL3:

```
INSERT INTO FOO (COL1, COL2)
  VALUES (1, 2);
```

Assigning NULL to variables

In PSQL (procedural language), use the "=" symbol as the assignment operator when assigning NULL to a variable and use IS [NOT] NULL in the predicate of an IF test:

```
...
DECLARE VARIABLE foobar integer;
...
IF (COL1 IS NOT NULL) THEN
  FOOBAR = NULL;
...
```

CHAPTER

6

NUMBER TYPES

Firebird supports both fixed (exact precision) decimal and floating-point (approximate precision) number types. Fixed decimal types are the zero-scaled integer types SMALLINT, INTEGER and, in dialect 3, BIGINT, and two nearly identical scaled numeric types, NUMERIC and DECIMAL. The two floating-point types are FLOAT (single precision) and DOUBLE PRECISION.

Firebird does not support an unsigned integer type.

Numerical Limits

Table 7.1 below shows the numerical limits of each number type in Firebird:

Table 6.1 Limits of Firebird number types

Number type	Minimum	Maximum
SMALLINT	–32,768	32,767
INTEGER	–2,147,483,648	2,147,483,647
BIGINT	-2^{63}	$2^{63}-1$
(for masochists)	-9223372036854775808	9223372036854775807
NUMERIC †	varies	varies
DECIMAL †	varies	varies
FLOAT		
Positive	1.175×10^{-38}	3.402×10^{38}
Negative	-3.402×10^{38}	
DOUBLE PRECISION[1]		
Positive	2.225×10^{-308}	1.797×10^{308}
Negative	-1.797×10^{308}	

† Limits for NUMERIC and DECIMAL types vary according to storage type and scale. The limits will always fall within the range for the internal type in which they are stored.[2]

[1] Precision describes the number of significant digits, ignoring trailing or leading zeroes, that can be stored in the data type with overflow or loss of information.

[2] Stored type is SMALLINT, INTEGER or BIGINT, according to the declared precision.

Points About Points

In SQL, the decimal point symbol is always a full-stop (a.k.a. "period", "punkt", "point", etc.). Using a comma or any other character to represent a decimal point will cause a type exception.

If you are in a country where the convention is to group numerals to the left of the decimal point using full-stops, e.g., 2.100 representing "two thousand one hundred", be aware of the risk of exponential errors if you fail to protect your applications from inputs that allow this convention.

Operations on Number Types

Operations supported include

Comparisons using the standard relational operators (=, <, >, >=, <=, <> or !=).

String comparisons using SQL operators such as CONTAINING, STARTING WITH, and LIKE are possible. In these operations, the numbers are treated as strings. For more information about these operators, refer to the Chapter 21, Expressions and Predicates.

Arithmetic operations The standard dyadic arithmetic operators (+, - * and /) can be applied.

Conversions Firebird automatically converts between fixed numeric, floating point and character types when performing operations on mixed data types. When an operation involves a comparison or arithmetical operation between numeric data and non-numeric data types, data are first converted to a numeric type, then operated on.

Sorts By default, a query retrieves rows in the exact order that it finds them in the table, which is likely to be unordered. You can sort rows on integer columns using the ORDER BY clause of a SELECT statement in descending or ascending order. If numbers are stored or cast as character types, the sort order will be alphanumeric, not numeric, e.g. 1 – 10 – 11 ... 19 - 2

Integer Types

All integer types are *signed exact numerics* having a scale of zero.

Notation

In all versions, integer values are submitted in decimal notation. From v.2.5 onwards, you have the option of submitting them in either decimal or hexadecimal notation.

Numbers with 1–8 hex digits are interpreted as 32-bits, while numbers with 9–16 hex digits as interpreted as 64 bits.

For example, the following two statements are equivalent:

```
INSERT INTO ATABLE (ID, PASSPHRASE)
VALUES (1273, 'ELEPHANT IN THE ROOM');
--
INSERT INTO ATABLE (ID, PASSPHRASE)
VALUES (0x4F9, 'ELEPHANT IN THE ROOM');
```

Also, the A-F digits are case-insensitive:

```
INSERT INTO ATABLE (ID, PASSPHRASE)
VALUES (0X4f9, 'ELEPHANT IN THE ROOM');
```

Types

Firebird supports three named ranges of precision as integer data types: SMALLINT, INTEGER and BIGINT.

- SMALLINT is a signed short integer with a range from –32,768 to 32,767
- INTEGER is a signed long integer with a range from –2,147,483,648 to 2,147,483,647
- BIGINT is a signed 64-bit integer with a range from 2-63 to 263 -1. Not available in Dialect 1.

v.1.0.x For Firebird 1.0.x, dialect 3, you need to declare a 64-bit integer as NUMERIC(18,0) or DECIMAL(18,0). It is always valid to use this syntax for the integer types, optionally omitting the second (scale) argument.

Scale, precision and the operations that can be performed on fixed types are discussed in more detail in the next section, ***Fixed decimal (scaled) types***.

The next two statements create a domain and a column with the SMALLINT and INTEGER data types respectively:

```
CREATE DOMAIN RGB_RED_VALUE AS SMALLINT;
/**/
CREATE TABLE STUDENT_ROLL (
    STUDENT_ID INTEGER,
    ...);
```

Each of these statements creates a domain which is a 64-bit integer:

```
CREATE DOMAIN IDENTITY BIGINT CHECK (VALUE >=0); /* Firebird 1.5 and higher */
CREATE DOMAIN IDENTITY NUMERIC(18,0) CHECK (VALUE >=0);
```

SMALLINT

A two-byte integer providing compact storage for whole numbers with a limited range. For example, SMALLINT would be suitable for storing the value of colors in the RGB scale, as in the domain example above.

SMALLINT is often used to define a two-state Boolean, usually 0=False, 1=True. An example of this usage can be found in Chapter 11, ***Domains***, in the topic *Defining a BOOLEAN Domain*.

INTEGER

A four byte integer. You can store integers in BigInt columns without casting.

In Dialect 1, generators (see below) generate integers.

BIGINT, NUMERIC(18,0)

Available in Dialect 3 only, this is an 8-byte integer, useful for storing whole numbers with very low and high ranges. In Dialect 3, generators or sequences (see below) generate BigInt numbers.

In a Dialect 1 database, Firebird rejects any attempt to define a domain or column as BIGINT. It will not raise an exception if you try to define a NUMERIC(18,0) domain or column, but will silently define a DOUBLE PRECISION column instead. Because of precision problems with matching floating point numbers, be careful to avoid accidentally using NUMERIC(18,0) in a Dialect 1 database to define a column which is going to be used as a key for searches or joins.

Autoincrement or Identity type

Firebird has no autoincrement or identity type such as you find in some other database management systems. What it does have is a number-generator engine and the ability to maintain independent, named series of BIGINT numbers. Each series is known as a ***generator*** or ***sequence***.

Generators are ideal for populating an automatically incrementing unique key or a stepping serial number column or other series. The benefit of generator values is that they are guaranteed to be unique and they operate outside transaction control. This absolutely assures the integrity of number sequences, provided the generators are not tampered with by humans!

Details about creating and working with generators (sequences) are in Chapter 11, ***Designing and Defining a Database***, in the topic Generators (Sequences).

Integer/integer division

Using the example above, the following query in dialect 3 returns the integer 0 because each operand has a scale of 0, so the sum of the scales is 0:

```
SELECT i1/i2 FROM t1
```

In dialect 1, in line with many desktop-style data management products, dividing one integer by another produces a floating-point result of DOUBLE PRECISION type:

```
SELECT 1/3 AS RESULT FROM RDB$DATABASE
```

yields `.3333333333333333`

Although this dialect 1 rule is intuitive for language programmers and calculator users, it does not conform with the SQL-92 standard. Integer types have a scale of 0 which, for consistency, requires that the result (quotient) of any integer/integer operation conform with the scaling rules for fixed numerics and produce an integer.

Dialect 3 conforms with the standard and truncates the quotient of integer/integer division operations to integer. Hence, it can trap the unwary:

```
SELECT 1/3 AS RESULT FROM RDB$DATABASE
```

yields `0`

When you need to preserve sub-integer parts in the result (quotient) of integer/integer divisions in dialect 3, be sure that you either scale one of the operands or include a "factor" in the expression which will guarantee a scaled result.

Examples

```
SELECT (1 + 0.00)/3 AS RESULT FROM RDB$DATABASE
```

yields `.33`

```
SELECT (5 * 1.00)/2 AS RESULT FROM RDB$DATABASE
```

yields `2.50`

Fixed Decimal (Scaled) Types

Fixed decimal types allow the management of numbers which need to be expressed with a fractional portion that is exact to a specific number of decimal places, or scale. Typically, you need scaled types for money values and any other numbers that result from counting or performing arithmetic on whole units and parts of units.

Firebird provides two fixed decimal or scaled data types: NUMERIC and DECIMAL. Broadly, either scaled type is declared as TYPE(P, S) with P indicating precision (number of significant digits) and S indicating scale (number of decimal places, i.e. digits to the right of the decimal point symbol).

According to the SQL-92 standard, both NUMERIC and DECIMAL constrain the stored number to be within the declared scale. The difference between the two types is in the way the precision is constrained. Precision is exactly "as declared" for a column of type NUMERIC, whereas a DECIMAL column can accept a number whose precision is at least equal to that which was declared, up to the implementation limit.

NUMERIC and DECIMAL types, as implemented in Firebird, are identical except when precision is less than 5. Both types effectively conform with the standard DECIMAL type. NUMERIC is thus not compliant with SQL-92.

The predictability of results from multiplying and dividing fixed-point numbers favors choosing them for storing money values. However, because fixed-point types have a finite "window" in which numbers may be accommodated, they become prone to overflow/underflow exceptions near their upper and lower limits.

In countries where the unit of currency represents a small value, number limits should be considered carefully with regard to huge totals. For example, the following statement applies a tax rate (DECIMAL(5,4)) to a net profit (NUMERIC(18,2):

```
UPDATE ATABLE
  SET INCOME_AFTER_TAX = NET_PROFIT  - (NET_PROFIT * TAX_RATE);
```

Let the tax rate be 0.3333

Let the net profit be 1234567890123456.78

Result:

```
ISC ERROR CODE:335544779
Integer overflow.  The result of an integer operation caused the most significant bit of
the result to carry.
```

Internal Storage

Internally, Firebird stores the scaled number as a SmallInt (16 bits), Integer (32 bits) or BigInt (64 bits) type, according to the size of precision declared. Its declared precision is stored, along with the declared scale negated to a sub-zero scale-factor , representing an exponent of 10. When the number is referred to for output or a calculation, it is produced by multiplying the stored integer by 10^{scale_factor}.

For example, for a column defined as NUMERIC(4,3), Firebird stores the number internally as a SMALLINT. If you insert the number 7.2345, Firebird silently rounds the rightmost digit (4) and stores a 16-bit integer 7235 and a scale_factor of –3. The number is retrieved as 7. 235 ($7235 * 10^{-3}$).

Numeric data type

Format:

```
NUMERIC(p,s)
```

For example, NUMERIC(4,2) formally defines a number consisting of up to 4 digits, including two digits to the right of the decimal point. Thus, the numbers 89.12 and 4.321 will be stored in a NUMERIC(4,2) column as 89.12 and 4.32 respectively. In the second example, the final 1-3 is out of scale and is simply dropped.

It is possible to store in this column a number of greater precision than that declared. The maximum here would be 327.67, i.e. a number with a precison of 5. Because the database stores the actual number as a SMALLINT, numbers will not begin to cause overflow errors until the internally-stored number is more than 32,767 or less than -32,768.

Decimal data type

Format:

```
DECIMAL(p,s)
```

Similarly to Numeric, DECIMAL(4,2) formally defines a number consisting of at least 4 digits, including two digits to the right of the decimal point. However, because Firebird stores DECIMAL of precision 4 and below as INTEGER, this type could, in a DECIMAL(4,1) column, potentially store a number as high as 214,748,364.7 or as low as -214,748,364.8 without causing an overflow error.

Dialect 1 Databases

Exact numerics can be confusing because of the slightness of difference between the two types. If you have the misfortune to be still dealing with a dialect 1 database, the confusion is worse the dialect of the database affects the range of precision available. The following Table 7.2 may assist as a summary guide for the precision and scale you need to specify for your various exact numeric requirements.

Table 6.2 Range and storage type of Firebird NUMERIC and DECIMAL types

Precision	Type	Dialect 3	Dialect 1
1 to 4	NUMERIC	SMALLINT	SMALLINT
	DECIMAL	INTEGER	INTEGER
5 to 9	NUMERIC and DECIMAL	INTEGER	INTEGER
10 to 18	NUMERIC and DECIMAL	BIGINT	DOUBLE PRECISION†

† Exact numerics with precision higher than 9 can be declared in a dialect 1 database without an exception occurring. However, numbers will be stored as DOUBLE PRECISION and be subject to the same precision restrictions as any floating point numbers.

Converted databases

If a dialect 1 database is restored using *gbak*, numeric fields defined with precision higher than 9 will remain implemented as DOUBLE PRECISION. Although they will still appear as they were originally defined, e.g. NUMERIC(15,2), they will continue to be stored and used in calculations as DOUBLE PRECISION.

For information about converting dialect 1 databases to dialect 3, refer to the topic *Dialect 1 Databases* in the companion volume to this, Vol. 3: ***Administering Firebird Servers and Databases***, or in ***The Firebird Book Second Edition***, the chapter entitled *Migration Notes*.

Special restrictions in static SQL

The host languages of embedded applications cannot use or recognize small precision NUMERIC or DECIMAL data types with fractional portions when they are stored internally as SMALLINT or INTEGER types. To avoid this problem, in any database that is going to be accessed via embedded applications (ESQL):

1. Do not define NUMERIC or DECIMAL columns or domains of small precision in a dialect 1 database. Either store an integer and have your application code deal with scale; or use DOUBLE PRECISION and apply a suitable rounding algorithm for calculations.
2. In a dialect 3 database, define NUMERIC and DECIMAL columns or domains of any size using a precision of at least 10, to force them to be stored internally as BIGINT.

Specify a scale if you want to control the precision and scale. Apply CHECK constraints if you need to control the ranges.

Behaviour of fixed types in operations

It may be helpful to know how fixed types are treated during arithmetic operations. As before, some dialectal differences do exist that may affect your choice of data type.

Division

When performing division on fixed types, dialects 1 and 3 behave differently.

In dialect 3, where both operands are of a fixed numeric type, Firebird adds together the scales of both operands to determine the scale of the result (quotient). The quotient has a precision of 18. When designing queries with division expressions, therefore, be aware that quotients will always have more precision than either of the operands and take precautions where precision could potentially overflow the maximum of 18.

Dialect 1 In dialect 1, division always produces a quotient of DOUBLE PRECISION type.

Examples

In dialect 3, the quotient of dividing a DECIMAL(12,3) by a DECIMAL(9,2) is a DECIMAL(18,5). The scales are added together:

```
SELECT 11223344.556/1234567.89 FROM RDB$DATABASE
```

yields `9.09090`

Compare the difference in the quotient when the same query is run in dialect 1. The first operand is treated as a DOUBLE PRECISION number because its precision (12) is higher than the maximum for a dialect 1 scaled type. The quotient is also a double. The result is `9.09090917308727` because of the errors inherent in floating-point types.

From the following table defined in dialect 3, division operations produce a variety of results:

```
CREATE TABLE t1 (
    i1 INTEGER,
    i2 INTEGER,
    n1 NUMERIC(16,2),
    n2 NUMERIC(16,2));
COMMIT;
INSERT INTO t1 VALUES (1, 3, 1.00, 3.00);
COMMIT;
```

The following query returns the NUMERIC(18,2) value 0.33, since the sum of the scales 0 (operand 1) and 2 (operand 2) is 2:

```
SELECT i1/n2 from t1
```

The following query returns the NUMERIC(18,4) value 0.3333, since the sum of the two operand scales is 4.

```
SELECT n1/n2 FROM t1
```

Dialect 1 database with dialect 3 client

A dialect 1 database that is opened with a dialect 3 client may cause some surprises with respect to integer division. When an operation does something that causes a CHECK condition to be checked, or a stored procedure to be executed, or a trigger to fire, the processing that takes place is based on the dialect under which the check, stored procedure, or trigger was defined, not the dialect in effect when the application causes the check, stored procedure, or trigger to be executed.

For example, suppose that a dialect 1 database has a table MYCOL1 INTEGER and MYCOL2 INTEGER with a table definition includes the following CHECK condition that was defined when the database was dialect 1:

```
CHECK(MYCOL1 / MYCOL2 > 0.5)
```

Now suppose that a user starts *isql*, or another application, and sets the dialect to 3. It tries to insert a row into the converted database:

```
INSERT INTO MYTABLE (COL1, COL2) VALUES (2,3);
```

Because the CHECK constraint was defined in dialect 1, it returns a quotient of `0.666666666666667`, and the row passes the check condition.

The reverse is also true. If the same CHECK constraint were added to the dialect 1 database through a dialect 3 client, dialect 3 arithmetic is stored for the constraint. The INSERT statement above would fail because the check would return a quotient of 0, violating the constraint.

There's a moral to this: use dialect 3 databases and always connect as dialect 3. If you intend to use Firebird then upgrade any existing databases to dialect 3—then rest easy and avoid a raft of nasty surprises.

Multiplication

As with division, if both multiplier operands are exact numeric, multiplying the operands produces an exact numeric with a scale equal to the sum of the scales of the operands. For example:

```
CREATE TABLE t1 (
    n1 NUMERIC(9,2),
    n2 NUMERIC(9,3));
COMMIT;
INSERT INTO t1 VALUES (12.12, 123.123);
COMMIT;
```

The following query returns the number `1492.25076` because n1 has a scale of 2 and n2 has a scale of 3. The sum of the scales is 5.

```
SELECT n1*n2 FROM t1 as product
```

In Dialect 3, the precision of the result of multiplying a fixed numeric by a fixed numeric is 18. Precautions must be taken to ensure that potential overflows will not result from the propagation of scale in multiplication.

In Dialect 1, if the propagation of scale caused by the calculation would produce a result with precision higher than 9, the result will be DOUBLE PRECISION.

Addition and subtraction

If all operands are exact numeric, adding or subtracting the operands produces an exact numeric with a scale equal to that of the largest operand. For example:

```
  CREATE TABLE t1 (
    n1 NUMERIC(9,2),
    n2 NUMERIC(9,3));
COMMIT;
INSERT INTO t1 VALUES (12.12, 123.123);
COMMIT;
SELECT n1 + n2 FROM t1;
```

The query returns `135.243`, taking the scale of the operand with the larger scale.

Similarly, the following query returns the numeric `-111.003`:

```
SELECT n1 - n2 FROM t1;
```

In dialect 3, the result of any addition or subtraction is a NUMERIC(18,3). In dialect 1, it is a NUMERIC(9,3).

Numeric input and exponents

Any numeric string in dynamic SQL (DSQL) that can be stored as a DECIMAL(18,S) is evaluated exactly, without the loss of precision that might result from intermediate storage as a DOUBLE PRECISION. The DSQL parser can be forced to recognize a numeric string as floating point by the use of scientific notation, i.e. appending the character "e" or "E" followed by an exponent, which can be zero.

For example, DSQL will recognize `16.92` as a scaled exact numeric and passes it to the engine in that form. On the other hand, it will treat `16.92E0` as a floating-point value.

Floating Point Types

Floating-point types employ a sort of "sliding window" of precision appropriate to the scale of the number. By the nature of "float" types, the placement of the decimal point is not a restriction—it is valid to store, in the same column, one value as 25.33333, and another as 25.333. The values are different and both are acceptable.

Define a floating-point column when you need to store numbers of *varying scale*. The general rule of thumb for choosing a floating-point, rather than a fixed decimal type, is "use them for values you measure, not for values you count". If a floating-point column or variable must be used to store money, you should pay careful attention both to rounding issues and to testing the results of calculations.

Floating point numbers can be used to represent a value over a much larger range than is possible with plain or scaled integers. For example, the FLOAT type can carry values with a magnitude as large as 3.4E38 (that's 34 followed by 37 zeros), and as small as 1.1E-38 (that's 11 preceded by 37 zeros and a then a decimal point).

The breadth of range is achieved by a loss in exactness. A floating-point carries an approximate representation of its value that is accurate for a specific number of digits (its precision), according to the current magnitude (scale). It can not carry a value close to either extreme of its range.

The floating-point value carries more information than the stated number digits of precision. The FLOAT type, for example, is said to have a precision of 7 digits but its "assumed accurate" precision is 6 digits. The last part is an approximation providing additional information about the number, such as an indicator for rounding and some more things that are important when arithmetic is performed on the number.

For example, a FLOAT can carry the value 1000000000 (1,000,000,000, or 10^9). The FLOAT "container" sees this value as (effectively) 100000*E4. (This is illustrative only—an authoritative exposition of floating point implementation is beyond the scope of this book and seriously beyond the author's reach!) If you add 1 to the value of the FLOAT, the additional information carried in the seventh digit is ignored because it is not significant in terms of the number's current magnitude and the precision available. If you add 10,000—a value that is significant to the magnitude of the number currently stored in the FLOAT—it can represent the result as 100001*E4.

Even values within the available precision of the float may not always store an exact representation. Values such as 1.93, or even 123 may be represented in storage as a value that is very close to the specific number. It is close enough that, when the floating point number is rounded for output, it will display the value expected and, when it is used in calculations, the result is a very close approximation to the expected result.

The effect is that, when you perform some calculation that should result in the value 123, it may only be a very close approximation to 123. Exact comparisons (equality, greater than, less than, and so on) between two floating-point numbers, or between a floating-point number and zero, or a floating-point number and a fixed type, thus can not be depended on to produce the expected results.

For this reason, do not consider using floating-point columns in keys or applying uniqueness constraints to them. They will not work predictably for foreign key relationships or joins.

For comparisons, test floating-point values as being BETWEEN some acceptable range rather than testing for an exact match. The same advice applies when testing for 0—choose a range appropriate to the magnitude and signing of your data that between zero and a near-zero value, or between two suitable near-zero values.

Dialect 1 In a dialect 1 database, the need to store numeric data values having a wider range than the limits of a 32-bit integer may force the choice of a DOUBLE PRECISION type. Dialect 1 limitations also require the use of floating-point numbers for all reals if the database is going to be accessed by an embedded (ESQL) application.

Supported Float Types

Firebird provides two floating-point or approximate numeric data types, FLOAT and DOUBLE PRECISION, differing only in the limit of precision.

FLOAT

FLOAT is a 32-bit floating-point data type with a limit of approximately 7 digits of precision—assume 6 digits for reliability. A 10-digit number 25.33333312 inserted into a FLOAT column is stored as 25.33333. Range from -3.402 x 1038 to 3.402 x 1038. The smallest positive number it can store is 1.175 x 10 –38.

DOUBLE PRECISION

DOUBLE PRECISION is a 64-bit floating-point data type with a limit of approximately 15 digits of precision. Range from -1.797×10^{308} to 1.797×10^{308}. The smallest positive number it can store is 2.225×10^{-308}.

Arithmetic mixing fixed and floating-point types

When a dyadic operation (addition, subtraction, multiplication, division) involves an exact numeric operand and a floating-point operand, the result will be a DOUBLE PRECISION type.

The next statement creates a column, PERCENT_CHANGE, using a DOUBLE PRECISION type:

```
CREATE TABLE SALARY_HISTORY (
  ...
    PERCENT_CHANGE DOUBLE PRECISION
    DEFAULT 0 NOT NULL
    CHECK (PERCENT_CHANGE BETWEEN -50 AND 50),
    ...
);
```

The following CREATE TABLE statement provides an example of how the different numeric types can be used: an INTEGER for the total number of orders, a fixed DECIMAL for the dollar value of total sales, and a FLOAT for a discount rate applied to the sale.

```
CREATE TABLE SALES (
  ...
  QTY_ORDERED INTEGER
    DEFAULT 1
    CHECK (QTY_ORDERED >= 1),
  TOTAL_VALUE DECIMAL (9,2)
```

```
DISCOUNT FLOAT
    DEFAULT 0
    CHECK (DISCOUNT >= 0 AND DISCOUNT <= 1)
  );
```

CHAPTER

7

DATE AND TIME TYPES

Firebird supports SQL standard DATE, TIME, and TIMESTAMP data types.

Dialect 1 In dialect 1, only one date type is supported, a timestamp-like implementation which, although named DATE, is not interchangeable with the dialect 3 DATE type.

Choices for Date and Time Values

Each of the three options for storing date and time values has its own, distinct usages.

DATE

DATE stores the date alone, with no time portion – "date-only". Storage is a 32-bit signed longword. Storable dates range from January 1, 0001 to December 31, 9999. SQLTYPE is *isc_date.*

Choose DATE only if you are certain that nobody will ever want to use the date in a context narrower than a day. Examples are birthdays—as long as the time of birth is not significant—and publication dates. If a more granualr record is not in the current requirements but might be needed in future, choose TIMESTAMP instead.

Dialect 1 There is no "date-only" type in dialect 1. To store a "date-only" value, pass a valid date and time literal with "00:00:00.0000" in the time portion. For more information about date and time literals, keep reading.

If you are using isql to examine dialect 1 dates, you can toggle on/off the display of the time-part of date output using the isql command SET TIME; "Off" is the default.

TIMESTAMP

The TIMESTAMP data type is made of two 32-bit longword portions, storing a date and a time. It is stored as two 32-bit longwords, equivalent to the DATE type in dialect 1. SQLTYPE is *isc_timestamp.*

TIMESTAMP is the general purpose type for recording both dates and times. It is the recommended type for usages where one of the following possibilities applies:

- either the date or the time of the record, or both, are likely to be relevant
- intervals of time might need to be calculated
- dates or times might need to be compared across different time zones

Fractions of seconds

Fractions of seconds, if stored, are in ten-thousandths of a second for all date and time types.

TIME

A column or variable of type TIME stores the time of day, with no date portion – "time-only". Storage is a 32-bit unsigned longword. Storable times range `00:00` to `23:59:59.9999`. SQLTYPE is *isc_time.*

Dialect 1 If time of day needs to be stored, extract the hours, minutes and seconds elements from the DATE data and convert it to a string. A suggested technique follows later in this chapter—refer to the topic Combining EXTRACT(..) with other functions.

Interval of time (time elapsed)

It is a common mistake to think that a TIME type can store an interval of time (time elapsed). It cannot. To calculate an interval of time, subtract the later of two date or time types from the earlier. The result will be a DOUBLE PRECISION number expressing the interval (time elapsed) in days for TIMESTAMP and DATE arguments or in seconds for TIME arguments.

Use regular arithmetic operations to convert days to hours, minutes or seconds, as required.

Suppose, for example, that the columns STARTED and FINISHED are both TIMESTAMP. To calculate and store the time elapsed in minutes into a DOUBLE PRECISION column TIME_ELAPSED:

```
UPDATE ATABLE
  SET TIME_ELAPSED = (FINISHED - STARTED) * 24 * 60
  WHERE ((FINISHED IS NOT NULL) AND (STARTED IS NOT NULL));
```

Calculating intervals between two TIME types has traps because a TIME value has no "day" context. Think about a time-clock that records the start time and end time of a worker's shift. How would you handle the situation where a worker started the night shift at 10 p.m. and worked an eight-hour shift?

Date/Time Literals

Date literals are "human-readable" strings, enclosed in single quotation marks, that a Firebird server recognises as date or date-and-time constants for EXTRACT and other expressions, INSERT, and UPDATE operations and in the WHERE clause of a SELECT statement.

Specifically, date literals are used when supplying date constants to

- SELECT, UPDATE and DELETE statements, in the search condition of a WHERE clause
- INSERT and UPDATE statements, to enter date and time constants
- the FROM argument of the EXTRACT function.

Recognised Date/Time Literal Formats

The formats of the strings recognized as date literals are restricted. These formats are discussed below, using placeholders for the elements of the strings. Table 8.1 provides a key to the conventions used.

Table 7.1 Elements of date literals

Element	Representing
CC	Century - first two digits of a year segment, e.g. '20' for the twenty-first century
YY	Year in century. Firebird always stores the full year value if the year is entered without the 'CC' segment, using a "sliding window" algorithm (see below) to determine which century to store.
MM	Month, evaluating to an integer in the range 1 to 12. In some formats, two digits are required.
MMM	Month, one of [JAN, FEB, MAR, APR, MAY, JUN, JUL, AUG, SEP, OCT, NOV, DEC]. English month names fully spelt out (correctly) are also valid.
DD	Day of the month, evaluating to an integer in the range 1 to 31. In some formats, two digits are required. An invalid day-of-month number for the given month will cause an error.
HH	Hours, evaluating to an integer in the range 00 to 23. Two digits are required when storing a time portion.
NN	Minutes, evaluating to an integer in the range 00 to 59. Two digits are required when storing a time portion.
SS	Whole seconds, evaluating to an integer in the range 00 to 59. Two digits are required when storing a time portion.
[.]nnnn	Ten-thousandths of a second in the range zero to 9999. Optional for time portions, defaults to 0000. If used, four digits are required.

The recognised formats are shown in Table 8.2:

Table 7.2 Recognised date and time literal formats

Format	Dialect 3 DATE	Dialect 3 TIMESTAMP	Dialect 1 DATE
'CCYY-MM-DD' or 'YY-MM-DD'	Stores date only	Stores date and a time portion of 00:00:00	Stores date and a time portion of 00:00:00
'MM/DD/CCYY' or 'MM/DD/YY'	As above	As above	As above
'DD.MM.CCYY' or 'DD.MM.YY'	As above	As above	As above
'DD-MMM-CCYY' or 'DD-MMM-YY'	As above	As above	As above
'DD,MMM,CCYY' or 'DD,MMM,YY'	As above	As above	As above
'DD MMM CCYY' or 'DD MMM YY'	As above	As above	As above
'DDMMMCCYY' or 'DDMMMYY'	As above	As above	As above

Case-insensitive English month names fully spelt out are also valid in the MMM element. Correct spelling is shown in Table 8.3, below.

Format	Dialect 3 DATE	Dialect 3 TIMESTAMP	Dialect 1 DATE
'CCYY-MM-DD HH:NN:SS.nnnn' or 'YY-MM-DD HH:NN:SS.nnnn' (".nnnn" element is optional)	Stores date only: may need to be CAST as date. Time portion is not stored	Stores date and time.	Stores date and time.
'MM/DD/CCYYHH: NN:SS.nnnn'or 'MM/DD/YY HH:NN:SS.nnnn'	As above	As above	As above
'MM/DD/CCYYHH: NN:SS.nnnn'or 'MM/DD/YY HH:NN:SS.nnnn'	As above	As above	As above
'DD.MM.CCYYHH: NN:SS.nnnn'or 'DD.MM.YY HH:NN:SS.nnnn'	As above	As above	As above
'DD-MMM-CCYY HH:NN:SS.nnnn' or 'DD-MMM-YY HH:NN:SS.nnnn'	As above	As above	As above

The TIMESTAMP type accepts both date and time parts in a date literal. A date literal submitted without a time part will be stored with a time part equivalent to '00:00:00'.

The DATE type accepts only the date part. The TIME data type accepts only the time part.

Firebird's "sliding century window"

Whether the year part of a DATE or TIMESTAMP literal is submitted in SQL as 'CCYY' or 'YY', Firebird always stores the full year value. It applies an algorithm in order to deduce the 'CC' (century) part and it always includes the century part when it retrieves date types. Client applications are responsible for displaying the year as two or four digits.

To deduce the century, Firebird uses a sliding window algorithm. Its effect is to interpret a two-digit year value as the nearest year to the current year, in a range spanning the preceding 50 years and the succeeding 50 years.

For example, if the current year were 2012, two-digit year values would be interpreted thus:

Table 7.3 Deduction of year from two-digit year if current year is 2012

taking 2012 as an example of current year

Two-digit year	becomes year	Deduced from
98	1998	(2012 – 1998 = 14) < (2098 – 2012 = 86)
00	2000	(2012 – 2000 = 12) < (2100 – 2012 = 88)
45	2045	(2012 – 1945 = 67) > (2045 – 2012 = 33)
50	2050	(2012 – 1950 = 62) > (2050 – 2012 = 38)
62	1962	(2012 – 1962 = 50) = (2062 – 2012 = 50) ‡
63	1963	(2012 – 1963 = 49) < (2063 – 2012 = 51)

‡ The apparent equivalence of this comparison could be misleading. However, 1962 is closer to 2012 than is 2062 because all dates between 1962 and 1963 are closer to 2012 than all dates between 2062 and 2063.

Separators in non-US dates

Nothing causes more confusion for international users than Firebird's restricting the use of the forward slash date-part separator character ("/") to only the US 'MM/DD/CCYY' format. Although almost all other countries use 'DD/MM/CCYY', Firebird will either record the wrong date or throw an exception with date literal using the 'DD/MM/CCYY' convention.

For example, the date literal `'12/01/2012'` will always be stored with meaning 'December 1, 2012' and `'14/01/2012'` will cause an out-of-range exception because there is no month 14.

Note that Firebird does not honor the Windows or Linux date locale format when interpreting date literals. Its interpretation of all-number date formats is decided by the separator character. When dot (.) is used as separator, Firebird interprets it as the non-US notation DD.MM, whereas with any other separator its assumes the US MM/DD notation. Outside the US date locale, your applications should enforce or convert locale-specific DD/MM/CCYY date input to a literal that replaces the forward slash with a period (dot) as the separator. `'DD.MM.CCYY'` is valid. Other date literal formats may be substituted.

White space in date literals

Spaces or tabs can appear between elements. A date part must be separated from a time part by at least one space.

Quoting of date literals

Date literals must be enclosed in apostrophes (single-quotes) (ASCII 39/Unicode U+0027). Only single-quotes are valid.

Month literals

Month literals with correct English spellings

Cardinal Number	Abbreviated form	Full Month Name
	Case-insensitive	*Case-insensitive*
01	JAN	January
02	FEB	February
03	MAR	March
04	APR	April
05	MAY	May
06	JUN	June
07	JUL	July
08	AUG	August
09	SEP	September
10	OCT	October
11	NOV	November
12	DEC	December

Examples of date literals

The 25th day of the sixth month (June) in the year 2012 can be represented in all of the following ways:

'25.6.2012'	'06/25/2012'	'June 25, 2012'	'25.jun.2012'
'6,25,2012'	'25,jun,2012'	'25jun2012'	'6-25-12'

'Jun 25 12'	'25 jun 2012'	'2012 June 25'	'20120625'
'25-jun-2012'	' '2012-jun-25'	'20120625'	'25 JUN 12'
'2012-06-25'	'2012,25,06'		

Pre-defined Date Literals

Firebird supports a group of pre-defined date literals: single-quoted English words that Firebird captures or calculates and interprets in the context of an appropriate date/time type. The literals `'TODAY'`, `'NOW'`, `'TOMORROW'` and `'YESTERDAY'` are interpreted according to Table 8.4 below.

Table 7.4 Predefined date literals

Date Literal	Dialect 3 type	Dialect 1 type	Meaning
`'NOW'`	TIMESTAMP	DATE	Server date and time that was current at the start of the DML operation. 'NOW' will be cast and stored correctly in dialect 3 DATE, TIME, and TIMESTAMP fields and in dialect 1 DATE fields. In versions prior to v.2.0,, the sub-second portion is always stored as '.0000'. †
`'TODAY'`	DATE	DATE stored with a time part equivalent to '00:00:00'	Server date that was current at the start of the operation. If midnight is passed during the operation, the date does not change. Equivalent to the dialect 3 CURRENT_DATE context variable. Not valid in fields of TIME type.
`'TOMORROW'`	DATE	DATE stored with a time part equivalent to '00:00:00'	Server date that was current at start of the operation, plus one day. If midnight is passed during the operation, the date from which the 'TOMORROW' date is calculated does not change. Not valid in fields of TIME type.
`'YESTERDAY'`	DATE	DATE stored with a time part equivalent to '00:00:00'	Server date that was current at start of the operation, minus one day. If midnight is passed during the operation, the date from which the 'YESTERDAY ' date is calculated does not change. Not valid in fields of TIME type.

† All is not lost, however. You can get the server timestamp to 1/10,000th of a second by using instead the external function *GetExactTimestamp(..)* from the Firebird UDF library, *fbudf*. For more information, refer to the entry GetExactTimestamp (fbudf) in Appendix I, ***Internal and External Functions***.

Type-casting of Date/Time Literals

Whenever date literals—whether regular or pre-defined—are used in SQL in the context of corresponding date/time type columns or variables, the SQL parser can interpret them correctly without casting. However, in a small number of cases, where there is no typed value to which the parser can map the date literal, it treats any date literal as a string.

For example, it is perfectly valid to ask a SELECT query to return a constant that is unrelated to any database column. A common "hack" in Firebird to use the system table RDB$DATABASE for just such a query—since this table has one and only one row and thus can always be relied upon to return a scalar set—to pick up a single context value from the server. The next two examples illustrate a typical use of this hack:

```
SELECT 'NOW' FROM RDB$DATABASE;
```

Because the query returns a constant, not a column value, its data type is interpreted as a char(3), 'NOW'.

```
SELECT '2.09.2012' FROM RDB$DATABASE;
```

returns a CHAR(9), `'2.09.2012'`.

To have the parser correctly interpret a date literal in conditions where the parser cannot determine the data type, use the CAST(..) function:

```
SELECT CAST('NOW' AS TIMESTAMP) FROM RDB$DATABASE;
SELECT CAST('2.09.2012' AS TIMESTAMP) FROM RDB$DATABASE;
```

We take a more detailed look at casting later, in the topic *Operations Using Date and Time Values*.

Date and Time Context Variables

Date and time context variables CURRENT_DATE, CURRENT_TIME, and CURRENT_TIMESTAMP return date and time values capturing the server time at the moment execution of the containing SQL statement begins.

Table 7.5 Date and time context variables

Variable	Dialect 3 type	Dialect 1 type	Meaning
CURRENT_TIMESTAMP	TIMESTAMP	DATE	Current date and time to the nearest millisecond (default).
CURRENT_DATE	DATE	Not supported	Current date on the server.
CURRENT_TIME	TIME	Not supported	Current time, expressed as hours, minutes and seconds since midnight, to the nearest millisecond (default).

Specifying Sub-seconds Precision

From v.2.0 forward, the sub-second part of CURRENT_TIMESTAMP and CURRENT_TIME is returned by default as milliseconds. It may be overridden to hundredths of seconds, tenths of seconds or to the v.1.X behaviour by the inclusion of an optional argument of the form

```
CONTEXT_VAR(n)
```

where n signals the sub-seconds precision as follows:

(3) for milliseconds. It is the default and need not be specified.	(2) for hundredths of second	(1) for tenths of seconds	(0) for legacy behaviour, returning subseconds as `'.0000'`

Operations Using Date and Time Values

The use of an arithmetic operation to manipulate, calculate, set or condition the relationships between two dates has already been visited in the topic earlier in this chapter, Interval of time (time elapsed). The capability to subtract an earlier date, time or timestamp value from a later one is possible because of the way Firebird stores date/time types. It uses one or two integers to store timestamps, date-only dates or time of day, respectively. The units represented by these numbers are days in the date-part integer and fractions of days in the time-part integer. The date part represents the number of days since "date zero"—November 17, 1898. The time part represents the portion of one day elapsed since midnight.

Dialect 3 DATE stores only the date part. Dialect 3 TIME stores only the fractional part. TIMESTAMP and dialect 1 DATE store both parts.

Quite simply, these number structures can be operated on, using simple addition and subtraction expressions, to calculate time differences (intervals), increment or decrement dates and set date and time ranges. Table 8.6 explains which operations are valid and the results to be achieved.

Table 7.6 Arithmetic involving date/time data types

Operand 1	Operator	Operand 2	Result
DATE	+	TIME	TIMESTAMP (arithmetic concatenation)
DATE	+	Numeric value *n* ‡	Advances DATE value by *n* whole days (ignoring any fractional part supplied for *n*)
TIME	+	DATE	TIMESTAMP (arithmetic concatenation)
TIME	+	Numeric value n‡	Advances TIME value by *n* seconds †
TIMESTAMP	+	Numeric value n‡	Advances the time part of TIMESTAMP value by fraction part of *n* (if present) in seconds and date part by the whole-number part of *n* in days
DATE	–	DATE	DECIMAL(9,0) days of interval
DATE	–	Numeric value n‡	Reduces DATE value by *n* whole days (ignoring any fractional part supplied for *n*)
TIME	–	TIME	DECIMAL(9,4) seconds of interval
TIME	–	Numeric value n‡	Reduces TIME value by n seconds †
TIMESTAMP	–	TIMESTAMP	DECIMAL(18,9) days and part-day of interval
TIMESTAMP	–	Numeric value n‡	Reduces the time part of TIMESTAMP value by fraction part of n (if present) in seconds and date part by the whole-number part of n in days

† If necessary, repeats (result=modulo(result, (24 * 60 * 60))) until resultant day-part is eliminated.

‡ For dialect 3 DATE type, n is an integer, representing days. For TIMESTAMP and dialect 1 DATE types, n can be a numeric representing days to the left of the decimal point and a part-day to the right. For TIME type, n is an integer representing seconds.

General rules for operations

One date/time value can be subtracted from another, provided

- both values are of the same date/time type

- the first operand is later than the second

A valid subtraction involving date/time types produces a scaled DECIMAL result in dialect 3 and a DOUBLE PRECISION result in dialect 1.

Date/time types cannot be added together. However, a date-part can be concatenated to a time-part using

- dyadic[1] addition syntax to concatenate a pair of fields or variables
- string concatenation to concatenate a date/time literal with another date/time literal or with a date/time field or variable

Multiplication and division operations involving date/time types are not valid.

[1]Dyadic: in or by groups of two

Expressions as operands

The operand to advance or reduce a TIMESTAMP, TIME or DATE value can be a constant or an expression. An expression may be especially useful in your applications when you want to advance or reduce the value specifically in seconds, minutes or hours or, for example, half-days, rather than directly by days.

When using expressions in dialect 3, ensure that one of the operands is a real number to avoid the possibility of a division-by-zero error resulting from SQL-92 integer division.

The following table 8.7 provides some examples of operand expressions that could be used to resolve input values to days or part-days for date/time additions to and subtractions from date/time values in calculations.

Table 7.7 Examples of operands using expressions

Input n	Add or subtract	Alternative
in seconds	n/86400.0	n * 1.0/(60 * 60 * 24)
in minutes	n/1440.0	n * 1.0/(60 * 24)
in hours	n/24.0	
in half days	n/2	Depends on the result you want. For example, if n=3 and the divisor for half-days is 2, the result will be 1, not 1.5, according to the rules for SQL integer/integer division.

Because years, months and quarters are not constant, more complex algorithms are needed for handling them in date/time operations. It may be worth your while to seek out user-defined functions (UDFs) that you can use in operand expressions to suit these requirements.

Expressions can involve functions, as we have already noted when we touched on CAST(..). The next topics look at the use of some date/time compatible functions.

Using CAST( ) with Date/Time Types

We have encountered the CAST(..) function in expressions involving date literals and date parts. This topic explores the various aspects of date and time casting in more depth and breadth.

Casting between date/time types

Generally, casting from one date/time type to another is possible wherever the source date/time type provides the right kind of data to reconstruct as the destination date/time type. For example, a TIMESTAMP can provide the date part to cast on to a date-only

DATE type or a time-only TIME type, whereas a TIME type cannot provides enough data to cast on to a DATE type. Firebird allows a DATE type to be cast to TIMESTAMP by casting on a time part of midnight; and it allows a TIME type to be cast to TIMESTAMP by concatenating it on to the context variable CURRENT_DATE (the server date).

Table 7.8 Dialect 3 casting between date/time types

Cast source type	AS TIMESTAMP	AS DATE	AS TIME
TIMESTAMP	n/a	YES: casts on date part, ignores time part	YES: casts on time part, ignores date part
DATE	YES: time part is set to midnight	n/a	NO
TIME	YES: date part is set to CURRENT_DATE	NO	n/a
DATE + TIME	YES: CAST((DATEFIELD + TIMEFIELD AS TIMESTAMP)	NO	NO

Casting from date types to CHAR(n) and VARCHAR(n)

Use the SQL CAST() function in statements to translate between date and time data types and character-based data types.

Firebird casts date/time types to formatted strings where the date (if present) is in a set format—dependent on dialect—and the time part (if present) is in the standard Firebird HH:NN:SS.nnnn time format. It is necessary to prepare a CHAR or VARCHAR column or variable of a suitable size to accommodate the output you want.

Both fixed length CHAR and variable-length VARCHAR types can be cast to and from date/time types. Because the size of a cast date/time string is known and predictable, CHAR has a slight advantage over VARCHAR where date and time castings are concerned: using char will save you transmitting over the wire the two bytes that are added to varchars to store their length.

The "right size" depends on dialect, so care is needed here. VARCHAR may be more suitable to use in application code that may need to handle both dialects.

If the character field is too small for the output, an overflow exception will occur. Suppose you want a cast string to contain only the date part of a TIMESTAMP. Preparing a character container of smaller size will not work: CAST(..) does not truncate the output string to fit. It is necessary to perform a double cast, first casting the timestamp as DATE and then casting that date to the correctly-sized character type—refer to examples below.

Dialect 3

Casting DATE or TIMESTAMP outputs the date part in ISO format (CCYY-MM-DD). To get the full length of the output, allow 10 characters for DATE and 11 for TIMESTAMP (date part plus one for the blank preceding the time part). Allow 13 characters for TIME or the time part of TIMESTAMP.

For example:

```
SELECT CAST(timestamp_col as CHAR(24)) AS TstampTxt
  FROM ..
```

produces a string like this:

```
2012-06-25 12:15:45.2345
```

This produces an overflow exception:

```
SELECT CAST(timestamp_col as CHAR(20)) AS TstampTxt
  FROM ..
```

A double-cast will produce the right string:

```
SELECT FIRST 1 CAST (CAST (timestamp_col AS DATE) AS CHAR(10))
  FROM ..
2012-06-25
```

Unfortunately, it is not possible by direct casting to return a cast date + time string without the sub-second portion. It can be done using a complex expression involving both CAST(..) and EXTRACT(..). For an example, refer below to the topic *The EXTRACT() Function*, below.

Dialect 1

The date part of a Dialect 1 DATE type is converted to the format DD-MMM-CCYY, not the ISO format as in Dialect 3. So, for example,

```
SELECT CAST(d1date_col as CHAR(25)) AS DateTimeTxt
    ...
```

produces

```
26-JUN-2012 12:15:45.2345
```

Consequently, casting dialect 1 dates requires 11 characters instead of 10 for the date part, plus one for the blank space, plus 13 for the time part, 25 in all.

More complex expressions

CAST(..) can be used in more complex expressions, in combination with other expression operators. For example:

```
select cast (10 + cast(('today') as date) as char(25)) texttime
  from rdb$database;
```

or

```
select cast (10 + current_timestamp) as date) as char(25)) texttime
    from rdb$database;
```

produces a text string showing a date 10 days advanced from today's date.

Casting between date/time types and other types

Any character type or expression whose content can be evaluated to a valid date literal can be cast to the appropriate date/time type.

Date and time types cannot be cast to or from SMALLINT, INTEGER, FLOAT, DOUBLE PRECISION, NUMERIC, DECIMAL or BLOB types.

Uses for casting

- Exchanging date/time data with other applications
  - Importing date/time data created elsewhere—by another database system, host language or data-capture device, for example—often involves some degree of "massaging" before it can become valid date/time data for storing in a Firebird database.
  - Most host languages do not support the DATE, TIME, and TIMESTAMP types, representing them internally as strings or structures.
  - Data capture devices usually store dates and times in a variety of string formats and styles.
  - Date/time types are often incompatible between different database hosts.

Conversion generally requires evaluating and decoding the date-element content of the source data. The second part of the process is to reconstruct the decoded elements and pass them in Firebird SQL by some means. For a host language that has no means to pass native Firebird date/time types, the use of CAST(..) in combination with valid text strings for Firebird to process as date literals can be invaluable.

In some cases, external data stored into text files in date literal formats may be the best solution. Firebird can open such files as input tables in a server-side code module—stored procedure or trigger—and use CAST(..) and other functions to process data into date/time columns in native tables. Refer to *Using External Files as Tables* in Chapter 15 for more information.

CAST(..) can equally be used to prepare internal data for export.

- In search condition expressions

  Situations arise where using CAST(..) in the WHERE clause with a date/time type will solve logical problems inherent in comparing a column of one type with a column of a different type.

  Suppose, for example, we want to join a customer account table, which contains a DATE column BALANCE_DATE, with a customer transaction table which has a TIMESTAMP column TRANS_DATE. We want to make a WHERE clause that returns a set containing all of the unbilled transactions for this customer that occurred on or before the BALANCE_DATE. We might try:

```
SELECT...
  WHERE CUST_TRANS.TRANSDATE <= CUSTOMER.BALANCE_DATE;
```

  This criterion does not give us what we want! It will find all of the transaction rows up to midnight of the BALANCE_DATE, because it evaluates BALANCE_DATE with a time part of 00:00:00. Any transactions after midnight on that date will fail the search criterion.

  What we really want is to include all of the transactions where the date part of TRANS_DATE matches BALANCE_DATE. Casting TRANS_DATE to a DATE type saves the day:

```
SELECT...
  WHERE CAST(CUST_TRANS.TRANSDATE AS DATE) <= CUSTOMER.BALANCE_DATE;
```

- In a dialect conversion

  Dialect 3 provides richer date/time support than dialect 1. One task that is likely to catch your attention if you do such a conversion is to replace or enhance existing dialect 1 DATE type columns (which are equivalent to TIMESTAMP in dialect 3) by converting them to the dialect 3 DATE (date-only) or TIME types. CAST(..) makes this job a no-brainer.

For an example of one style of conversion using cast, refer to *A sample date/time type conversion task* at the end of this chapter.

Quick Date/Time Casts

An SQL-compliant short expression syntax—sometimes referred to as "hints"—is available for casting both the predefined date/time literals and the regular constant date/time literals. It takes the form

```
<data type> <date literal>
```

Taking the CAST example above, the short syntax would be as follows:

```
select TIMESTAMP 'NOW'
  FROM RDB$DATABASE
```

With a regular date/time literal:

```
SELECT TIME '15:05:45.345' FROM RDB$DATABASE
```

This short syntax can participate in other expressions. The following example illustrates a date/time arithmetic operation on a predefined literal:

```
update mytable
    set OVERDUE = 'T'
  where DATE 'YESTERDAY' - DATE_DUE > 10
```

The EXTRACT( ) Function

EXTRACT (..) decodes fields of date/time types and returns a variety of elements. It can operate on all dialect 3 and dialect 1 date/time fields.

Syntax

```
EXTRACT (element FROM field)
```

- `element` must be a defined element that is valid for the data type of field. Not all elements are valid for all date/time types. The data type of element varies according to the element extracted. Table 10-10 below enumerates the elements available for each date/time type.
- `field` can be a column, a variable or an expression that evaluates to a date/time field.

Table 8.9 shows thetypes, the arguments and the rules on their usage with EXTRACT (..).

Table 7.9 EXTRACT(..) arguments, types and rules

Element	Data type	Limits	TIMESTAMP[1]	DATE	TIME
YEAR	SMALLINT	0-5400	valid	valid	not valid
YEARDAY	SMALLINT	0-365	valid	valid	not valid
MONTH	SMALLINT	1-12	valid	valid	not valid
WEEK[2, 3]	SMALLINT	1-53	valid	valid	not valid
DAY	SMALLINT	1-31	valid	valid	not valid
WEEKDAY	SMALLINT	0-6[4]	valid	valid	not valid
HOUR	SMALLINT	1-23	valid	not valid	valid
MINUTE	SMALLINT	1-59	valid	not valid	valid
SECOND	DECIMAL(6,4)	0-59.9999	valid	not valid	valid

[1] Also dialect 1 DATE type

[2] Under the ISO 8601 standards, dates may not overlap weeks in adjoining years and no date can fall into a gap between weeks. Hence, the ISO year starts at the first Monday of Week 1 and ends at the Sunday before the new ISO year.

- If 1 January is on a Monday, Tuesday, Wednesday or Thursday, it is in week 01.
- If 1 January is on a Friday, Saturday or Sunday, it is in week 52 or 53 of the previous year. You can identify the years that have a "Week 53" by counting the number of Thursdays in the calendar year.

[3] The WEEK element is not supported in any 1.X versions.

[4](0 = Sunday...6 = Saturday)

Combining EXTRACT(..) with other functions

Following are two examples where EXTRACT(..) is used with CAST(..) to obtain date representations not available with either function.

To cast date + time without sub-seconds

Although it is not possible by direct casting to return a cast date + time string without the sub-second portion, it can be done using a complex expression involving both CAST(..) and EXTRACT(..).

To extract a TIME string

This technique has more meaning for dialect 1 than for dialect 3. However, it can be extrapolated to any dialect 3 date or time type if you need to store time of day as a string, such as when writing to an external file for sharing with another application.

The EXTRACT(..) function makes it possible to extract the individual elements of date and time types to SMALLINT values. The following trigger extracts the time elements from a dialect 1 DATE column named CAPTURE_DATE and converts them into a CHAR(13) mimicking the Firebird standard time literal `'HH:NN:SS.nnnn'`:

```
SET TERM ^;
CREATE TRIGGER BI_ATABLE FOR ATABLE
ACTIVE BEFORE INSERT POSITION 1
AS
BEGIN
  IF (NEW.CAPTURE_DATE IS NOT NULL) THEN
  BEGIN
    NEW.CAPTURE_TIME =
    CAST(EXTRACT (HOUR FROM NEW.CAPTURE_DATE) AS CHAR(2))|| ':' ||
    CAST(EXTRACT (MINUTE FROM NEW.CAPTURE_DATE) AS CHAR(2))|| ':' ||
    CAST(EXTRACT (SECOND FROM NEW.CAPTURE_DATE) AS CHAR(2))|| '.0000';
  END
END ^
SET TERM ;^
```

Other Date/Time Functions

Until v.2.1, only a small set of in-built functions was available. That is not as tough as it might appear to be: Firebird travels with two large libraries of external functions ("UDFs") and a great many more are available in third-party libraries.

From v.2.1, the majority of the functions in the Firebird external libraries were integrated into Firebird's data manipulation language (DML), many with improvements and SQL standards conformance. The internal date/time functions and their descriptions are grouped together for convenience, under *Date and Time Functions* in Appendix I. In the same Appendix, on *page 335*, you will find also the external date/time functions.

A sample date/time type conversion task

The CHAR(13) string stored by the trigger in the example above (*To extract a TIME string*) does not behave like a dialect 3 TIME type. However, by simple casting, it can be converted in a subsequent upgrade to dialect 3, to a dialect 3 TIME type.

First, we add a temporary new column to the table to store the converted time string:

```
ALTER TABLE ATABLE
  ADD TIME_CAPTURE TIME;
COMMIT;
```

Next, populate the temporary column by casting the dialect 1 time string:

```
UPDATE ATABLE
  SET TIME_CAPTURE = CAST(CAPTURE_TIME AS TIME)
  WHERE CAPTURE_TIME IS NOT NULL;
COMMIT;
```

The next thing we need to do is temporarily alter our trigger to remove the reference to the dialect 1 time string. This is needed to prevent dependency problems when we want to change and alter the old time string:

```
SET TERM ^;
RECREATE TRIGGER BI_ATABLE FOR ATABLE
ACTIVE BEFORE INSERT POSITION 1
AS
BEGIN
  /* do nothing */
END ^
SET TERM ;^
COMMIT;
```

Now, we can drop the old CAPTURE_TIME column:

```
ALTER TABLE ATABLE DROP CAPTURE_TIME;
COMMIT;
```

Now, we just rename the temporary column to CAPTURE_TIME:

Create it again, this time as a TIME type:

```
ALTER TABLE ATABLE
  ALTER COLUMN TIME_CAPTURE CAPTURE_TIME;
COMMIT;
```

Finally, fix up the trigger so that it now writes the CAPTURE_TIME value as a TIME type:

```
SET TERM ^;
RECREATE TRIGGER BI_ATABLE FOR ATABLE
ACTIVE BEFORE INSERT POSITION 1
AS
BEGIN
  IF (NEW.CAPTURE_DATE IS NOT NULL) THEN
  BEGIN
    NEW.CAPTURE_TIME = CAST(NEW.CAPTURE_DATE AS TIME);
  END
END ^
SET TERM ;^
COMMIT;
```

All of these steps can be written as an SQL script. For details about SQL scripting, refer to the topic Creating and Running Scripts in Chapter 24, ***Interactive SQL Utility (isql)***.

CHAPTER

8

CHARACTER TYPES

Firebird supports both fixed length and variable-length character (string) data types. They can be defined for local usage in any one of a large collection of character sets. Fixed-length character types cannot exceed 32,767 bytes in absolute length; for variable-length types, the limit is reduced by two bytes to accommodate storing a character-count with each string stored.

String Essentials

Firebird stores strings very economically, using a simple run-length encoding algorithm to compress the data, even if it is a fixed-length CHAR or NCHAR type. In case that tempts you to define very large string columns, be aware that there are compelling reasons to avoid very long strings—client memory limitations and index size limits, to name two.

V.1.0 If you are still using Firebird 1.0.x, it is also important to know that strings, whether fixed or variable length types, are decompressed and padded to full declared length before they leave the server.

The CHARACTER SET attribute of character types is important not only for compatibility with localized application interfaces but also, in some cases, for deciding the size of the column. Certain character sets use multiple bytes—typically two, three or four bytes— to store a single character. When such character sets are used, the maximum size is reduced by a factor of the byte size. Over-length input for Firebird character columns incurs an overflow exception.

Note *The CHARACTER SET attribute is optional in a declaration. If no character set is defined at column level, the character set attribute is taken to be the default character set of the database. The mechanism for determining the character set of columns and variables is discussed in more detail later in this chapter.*

String Delimiter

Firebird's string delimiter is ASCII 39/U+0027, the single-quote or apostrophe character, for example:

```
StringVar = 'This is a string.';
```

Double-quotes are not permitted at all for delimiting strings. You should remember this if you are connecting to Firebird using application code written for ancient InterBase 5 databases, which permitted double-quoted strings. Strings should also be corrected in the source code of stored procedures and triggers in these old databases if you plan to recompile them in Firebird.

Concatenation

Firebird uses the SQL standard symbol for concatenating strings: a doublet of the single-pipe character, ASCII code 124/U+01C0, known as double-pipe: "||".

Do not confuse this pair of pipe characters with the Unicode "double-pipe", U+01C1. They are not interchangeable.

The pipe-pair can be used to concatenate string constants, string expressions and/or column values. For example:

```
MyBiggerString = 'You are my sunshine,' || FirstName || ' my only sunshine.';
```

Character elements can be concatenated to numbers and number expressions to produce an alphanumeric string result. For example, to concatenate the character '#' to an integer:

```
NEW.TICKET_NUMBER = '#' || NEW.PK_INTEGER;
```

Concatenation and NULL

Avoid using concatenation expressions where one or more of the elements might be null. If any part of a concatenation contains a NULL, the result of the concatenation will be NULL. That is not usually the desired result.

An "empty string", represented as two apostrophe (single-quote) characters, is not the same as NULL.

Escape Characters

As a rule, Firebird does not support escape characters as a means to embed non-printable codes or sequences in character fields. The single exception is the "doubling" of the apostrophe character (ASCII 39/U+0027) to enable the apostrophe to be included as a stored character and prevent its being interpreted as the end-delimiter of the string:

```
...
SET HOSTELRY = 'O''Flaherty''s Pub'
...
```

Non-printable characters

It is possible to store non-printable characters in strings. Use the function `AsciiChar(asciivalue)` to pass such characters in strings. Declare and use the corresponding external function of the same name in the `ib_udf` if you are using a Firebird version older than v.2.1.

The following statement outputs a set of text fields—to an external file, for example—with a carriage return and line feed in the last one:

```
INSERT INTO EXTFILE(DATA1, DATA1, DATA3, CRLF)
VALUES ('String1', 'String2', 'String3', AsciiChar(13)||AsciiChar(10));
```

String Functions

Functions can be applied to the character types in expressions to modify string input or output in many different ways. For v.2.1 and beyond, a wide range of useful functions is implemented internally. In the older versions, many of the same (or comparable) functions are available to the Firebird engine as external functions in the dynamic libraries ib_udf and fbudf, the default location of which is the sub-directory ../UDF beneath the root of your installation.

Prior to v.2.1, for the declaration of AsciiChar(..) that is used in the example above, and other external functions in the `ib_udf` library, look in the `../UDF` subdirectory beneath the root of your Firebird installation for the script named `ib_udf.sql`. You can copy and paste the declaration into your own script or database administration tool.

Case

Strings can be "upper-cased" (converted to all upper case or "capitalised") in any version of Firebird, using the internal function UPPER(). The internal function LOWER(), to convert strings to all lower case characters, is available from the "2" series onward. In older versions, use the external function LOWER() in the `../UDF/fbudf` library or an equivalent function from a third-party library that works correctly with your character sets.

String length

The length of a string can be measured in different ways by counting different aspects of its existence.

For the "2" series and onward, the ISO-compliant internal functions CHAR_LENGTH (or CHARACTER_LENGTH), OCTET_LENGTH and BIT_LENGTH each returns an integer value that counts, respectively, characters, bytes (octets) or bits.

For older versions, you are less well-served by the Firebird UDF libraries. The ib_udf libary has STRLEN(), which is equivalent to CHARACTER_LENGTH().

Substrings

The internal function SUBSTRING() is available in all Firebird versions except v.1.0.x. TRIM(), for trimming leading and/or trailing white space, is available from the "2" series onward. Other functions (LEFT(), RIGHT() internal functions for v.2.1+, or various external functions in the fbudf library, such as SRIGHT() and SUBSTRLEN()) can return substrings from specified start and/or end positions in strings.

NULL Inputs

Before Firebird 2.0, the string functions in the *ib_udf* library would not accept NULL as input. From the "2" series onward, the external functions ASCII_CHAR, LOWER, "LOWER", LPAD, LTRIM, RPAD, RTRIM, SUBSTR and SUBSTRLEN can accept a NULL input, if those functions are declared correctly in the database.

For example, using ASCII_CHAR() again:

```
DECLARE EXTERNAL FUNCTION ascii_char
INTEGER NULL
RETURNS CSTRING(1) FREE_IT
ENTRY_POINT 'IB_UDF_ascii_char' MODULE_NAME 'ib_udf';
```

Finding a suitable function

Appendix I, *Internal and External Functions*, has full details, with examples, of the string functions available, both internally and through the UDFs that are distributed in the Firebird kits.

If you cannot find what you need, you might like to check out some of the better-known third party external function libraries. The IBPhoenix web site maintains *summaries and links* for several of these.

Limitations with Character Types

If you are planning to store data in large character columns, it is important to be aware of factors that might have impact on your design.

Multi-byte character sets

Multi-byte character sets reduce the potential sizes of text items, especially those with variable length. In UTF8, for example, even a 256-character column will be relatively large—potentially a Kilobyte or more—both to store and to retrieve. More is said later in this chapter regarding the caution you need to observe when considering text storage for multi-byte character data.

Index restrictions

When deciding on the length, character set and collation sequence for a character column, you need to be aware that indexing character columns is limited to 25% of the database page size. Multi-byte and many of the more complex 1-byte character sets use up many more bytes than the simpler character sets. Multi-segment indexes consume extra bytes, as do collation sequences. Do the byte calculations at design-time!

v.1.X For server versions 1.0.x and 1.5.x and databases whose on-disk structure (ODS) is less than 11, the total width of any index can not exceed 253 bytes—note bytes, not characters.

At the time of this writing, a useful on-line calculator for the index sizes, that takes into account the character set, collation and number of index keys, is free to use at the website of my long-time friend and colleague, Ivan Prenosil. Try this URL: http://www.volny.cz/iprenosil/interbase/ip_ib_indexcalculator.htm If it fails, Google Ivan's name to find a new link.

For more details, see Chapter 16, *Indexes*, and study the topics later in this chapter about character sets and collation sequences.

Client Memory Consumption

Clients programs will allocate memory to store copies of rows that they read from the database. Many interface layers allocate sufficient resources to accommodate the maximum (i.e. defined) size of a fixed- or variable-length column value, even if none of the actual data stored is that large. Buffering large numbers of rows at a time may consume a large amount of memory and users will complain about slow screen refreshes and lost connections!

Consider, for example, the impact on the workstation if a query returns 1024 rows consisting of just one column declared as VARCHAR(1024). Even with the "leanest" character set, this column would cost at least1Mb of client memory. For a Unicode column, multiply that cost by three (UNICODE_FSS) or four (UTF8). Some Unicode collations may even consume five, six or even more bytes per character in index keys.

Fixed-length Character Data

Firebird's fixed-length string data types are provided for storing strings whose length is consistently the same or very similar or where the format or relative positions of characters might convey semantic content . Typical uses are for items such as identification codes, telecom numbers, character-based numbering systems and for defining fields to store pre-formatted fixed-length strings for conversion to other data types—Firebird date literals, for example—or for exporting to other data systems that require fixed-length text records.

Leading spaces characters (ASCII character 32) in fixed-length string input are significant, whereas trailing spaces are not. When storing fixed-length strings, Firebird strips trailing space characters. The strings are retrieved with right-padding out to the full declared length.

Using fixed-length types is not recommended for data which might contain significant trailing space characters, or items whose actual lengths are expected to vary widely.

Transport across the network

Fixed-length string types are padded to their full declared width for transport to the client.

CHAR(n), alias CHARACTER(n)

CHAR(*n*), alias CHARACTER (*n*) is the base fixed-length character type. *n* represents the exact number of characters stored. CHAR and CHARACTER are completely synonymous. It will store strings in any of the supported character sets.

If the length argument, n, is omitted from the declaration, a CHAR(1) is assumed. It is acceptable to declare single-character CHAR fields simply as CHAR.

NCHAR(n), alias NATIONAL CHARACTER(n)

NCHAR(*n*), alias NATIONAL CHAR(*n*) is a specialized implementation of CHAR(*n*) that is pre-defined with ISO8859_1 as its character set attribute. Of course, it is not valid to define a character set attribute for an NCHAR column, although a collation sequence—the sequence in which the sorting of characters is arranged for searches and ordered output—can be defined for a column or domain that uses this type.

Variable-length Character Data

Firebird's variable-length string data types are provided for storing strings which may vary in length. The mandatory size argument *n* limits the number of discrete characters that may be stored in the column to a maximum of *n* characters. The size of a varchar cannot exceed 32,765 bytes because Firebird adds a two-byte size element to each varchar item.

Important *Counting bytes is not necessarily the same as counting characters. For two-byte character sets the maximum length of a VARCHAR is 16,382 characters; for UTF8 it is 8,191 characters.*

Choosing, storing and retrieving variable-length text

A variable-length character type is the workhorse for storing text because the size of the stored structure is the size of the actual data plus two bytes. All characters submitted as input to a field of a variable-length type are treated as significant, including both leading and trailing space characters ("blanks").

Transport across the network

Variable-length string types are not padded for transport to the client.

V.1.0.x Before Firebird 1.5, retrieved variable-length text data items were padded at the server to the full, declared size before being returned to the client, a "gotcha" that might influence your choice of column size and type if you are writing applications for remote clients connecting to a 1.0.x server on a slow network.

Although variable-length types can store strings of almost 32Kb, in practice it is not recommended to use them for defining data items longer than about 250 bytes, especially if their tables will become large or will be subject to frequent SELECT queries. BLOBs of SUB_TYPE 1 (text) are usually more suitable for storing large string data. Text BLOBs are discussed in detail in the next chapter.

VARCHAR(n), alias CHARACTER VARYING(n)

VARCHAR(*n*), alias CHARACTER VARYING(*n*), is the base variable-length character type. *n* represents the maximum number of characters that can be stored in the column. It will store strings in any of the supported character sets. If no character set is defined, the character set attribute defaults to the one defined during CREATE DATABASE as DEFAULT CHARACTER SET. If there is no default character set, the column default is CHARACTER SET NONE.

NCHAR VARYING(n), alias NATIONAL CHAR VARYING(n)

also aliased as NATIONAL CHARACTER VARYING(*n*)

NCHAR VARYING(n), alias NATIONAL CHAR VARYING(n), alias NATIONAL CHARACTER VARYING(n), is a specialized implementation of VARCHAR(n) that is pre-defined with ISO8859_1 as its character set attribute. It is not valid to define a character set attribute for an NVARCHAR column, although a collation sequence—the sequence in which the sorting of characters is arranged for searches and ordered output—can be defined for a column or domain that uses this type.

Character Sets and Collation Sequences

A character set is a collection of symbols that includes at least one *character repertoire*.. A character repertoire is a set of characters used by a particular culture for its publications, written communication and—in the context of a database—for computer input and output.

For example, ISO Latin_1 is a character set that encompasses the English repertoire (A, B, C … Z) and the French repertoire (A, Á, À, B, C, Ç, D … Z), making it useful for systems that span both cultural communities.

The character set chosen for storing text data determines:

- the characters that can be used in CHAR, VARCHAR, and BLOB SUB_TYPE 1 (text) columns.
- the number of bytes allocated to each character
- the default collation sequence ("alphabetical order") to be used when sorting CHAR and VARCHAR columns.

Firebird allows character sets and collations to be defined for any character field or variable declaration.

BLOBs cannot be sorted–so collation sequence is not relevant to text BLOBs from that point of view. However, because they can be upper-cased and searched case-insensitively, that aspect of a collation is likely to be relevant wherever the character set contains characters of more than 7 bits.

Character Sets

Text input from keyboards and other input devices such as bar code readers—potentially for all characters—is encoded specifically according to a certain standard *code page* that may be linked to the locale that the input device is set up for.

In one code page, the numeric code that maps to a certain character image may be quite different to its mapping in another. Broadly, a character set reflects a certain code page or group of related code pages. Some character sets work with more than one code page; in some cases, a code page will work with more than one character set. Different languages may share one overall character set but map different upper-case/lower-case pairs, currency symbols, and so on.

The server needs to know what character set is to be stored, in order to compute the storage space and to assess the collation characteristics for proper ordering, comparison, upper-casing, and so on. Other than those requirements, it is unconcerned about the content of text input.

Default Character Set

The keyword triplet DEFAULT CHARACTER SET can be used as a parameter on the CREATE DATABASE statement. In Firebird 2.5+, you can use the optional

COLLATION keyword to extend the DEFAULT CHARACTER SET parameter amd specify a *default collation order* to be used with that character set.

If no default character set is defined for the database, the default is CHARACTER SET NONE.

Character Set Overrides

The default character set and collation are overridden by any CHARACTER SET or COLLATE clause, respectively, in column, domain or index definitions. Hence, having set the global default for the database, you can override it further down the food chain, if required. You can include a character set attribute when you create a domain. You can override either the database default or a domain setting in an individual column definition.

Overriding the database's default character set on a column or domain definition propagates the change only to rows added subsequently. Existing data retains the characteristics that were formerly stored. Great care should be taken to avoid having columns containing data that might be incompatible from one row to another.

Character set NONE

Character set NONE will accept any characters without complaining. It does not "know" about multi-byte characters and it does not recognise any single-byte characters other than the 7-bit unaccented "US ASCII" ones that are common to all character sets. Problems start when—in a non-US-English or mixed-language environment—you find that you are getting transliteration errors when you SELECT your text data. What comes out isn't always what goes in!

If your database is for use in an English-only language environment, you can be tempted to ignore character sets and just let Firebird go ahead and use NONE for everything. Don't be tempted unless you are certain that no text data will ever contain data that depends on interpretation of characters of eight bits or more.

Client Character Set

What really matters with regard to character set is the interaction between server and client. The Firebird client library must be passed a character set attribute as part of the structure of a connection request.

The client application specifies its character set before it connects to the database. Connecting applications must pass the character set of the database to the API via the database parameter block (DPB) in the parameter *isc_dpb_lc_ctype*.

If the engine detects a difference between the client's character set setting and the character set of the target storage destination, it performs "transliteration"—automatically substituting the character codes according to the mapping it assumes from the information about the two character sets. It assumes that the incoming codes are correct for the client's code page.

That makes it possible to store text in different target columns having character sets that are not the same as the default character set of the database.

If the client and target character sets are the same, the engine assumes that the input it is receiving really is encoded for the defined character set and stores the input unmodified. Troubles ensue if the input was not what the client said it was. When the data are selected, searched or restored after a backup, they cause transliteration errors.

Database connection classes for Delphi, Java, et al., generally surface the *isc_dpb_lc_ctype* parameter as an attribute or property of the class that implements the API function call *isc_attach_database()*. An ESQL application—such as the *isql* utility—must execute a SET NAMES statement immediately before the CONNECT statement.

For example, the following ISQL command specifies that *isql* is using the ISO8859_1 character set. The next command connects to the `authors.fdb` database of our earlier example:

```
SET NAMES ISO8859_1;
CONNECT 'lserver:/data/authors.fdb' USER 'ALICE' PASSWORD 'XINEOHP';
```

GUI admin tools usually provide an input field of some sort for selecting the client character set. Host-language drivers and components often use the symbol lc_ctype as the name of a property or method for setting the client character set.

If you need to cater for a non-English language, spend some time studying the character sets available and choose the one which is most appropriate for most of your text input storage and output requirements. Remember to include that character set in the database attributes when you create the database.

- Refer to the relevant topic under *Database Attributes* in Chapter 14 for the syntax.
- For a list of character sets recognized by Firebird, refer to Appendix VI, *Character Sets and Collations*.

Firebird character sets

Firebird supports an increasingly broad variety of international character sets, including a number of two-byte sets and the (potentially) four-byte UTF8 subset of Unicode.

v.1.X In the old versions 1.5.x and 1.0.x the only Unicode support is in the form of the three-byte UNICODE_FSS character set, an outdated version of UTF8 that accepts malformed strings and does not enforce maximum string length correctly. A character set named "UTF8" is available in v.1.5 but it is merely an alias to UNICODE_FSS.

For many character sets, choices of collation sequence are available.

Naming of character sets

Most Firebird character sets are defined by standards and their names closely reflect the standards that define them. For example Microsoft defines Windows 1252 and Firebird implements it as WIN1252. Character set ISO8859_1 is "the set of characters defined by ISO Standard 8859-1, encoded by the values defined in ISO standard 8859-1, having each value represented by a single 8-bit byte."

Aliases

Character-set alias names support differences in the naming standards between different platforms. For example, if you find yourself on an operating system that uses the identifier WIN_1252 for the WIN1252 character set, you can use an alias that is defined in the system table RDB$TYPES (see *Adding an Alias for a Character Set*, below).

Storage of character sets and aliases

A catalogue of character sets is "hard-wired" in a database at creation time, when the system table RDB$CHARACTER_SETS is built and populated. For a listing by character set name, including the name of the default collation sequence in each case, execute this query:

```
SELECT
  RDB$CHARACTER_SET_NAME,
  RDB$DEFAULT_COLLATE_NAME,
  RDB$BYTES_PER_CHARACTER
FROM RDB$CHARACTER_SETS
  ORDER BY 1 ;
```

Aliases are added as required to RDB$TYPES, another system table which stores enumerated sets of various kinds used by the database engine. To see all of the aliases which are set up at database-creation time, run this query, filtering RDB$TYPES to see just the enumerated set of character set names:

```
SELECT
```

```
    C.RDB$CHARACTER_SET_NAME,
    T.RDB$TYPE_NAME
  FROM RDB$TYPES T
    JOIN RDB$CHARACTER_SETS C
    ON C.RDB$CHARACTER_SET_ID = T.RDB$TYPE
  WHERE T.RDB$FIELD_NAME = 'RDB$CHARACTER_SET_NAME'
    ORDER BY 1 ;
```

If an alias you want is not present, you can add one. Later in this chapter, the topic Adding character sets shows how to do it.

In order to use any character set other than NONE, ASCII, OCTETS and UNICODE_FSS, it is necessary to have the fbintl library present in the /intl directory beneath the root directory. (For Windows embedded server, the \intl directory should be a sub-folder of the folder where the fbembed.dll is located).

Well-formedness

Some character sets (especially multi-byte ones) do not accept "just any string". In the "2" series and beyond, the engine verifies that strings are well-formed when assigning from NONE/OCTETS and when processing statement strings and text parameters sent by a client application.

Versions1.X *In the 1.X versions there are no well-formedness checks.*

Storage restrictions

It is really important to understand how your choice of character set affects the storage boundaries for the data you plan to accommodate. In the case of CHAR and VARCHAR columns, the maximum amount of storage in any column to 32,767 bytes and 32,765 bytes, respectively. Yes, BYTES, not characters.

In versions prior to Firebird 2, the engine does not verify the logical length of multi-byte character set strings. Hence, for example, a UNICODE_FSS field takes three times as many characters as the declared field size, three being the maximum length of one UNICODE_FSS character. The three-byte rule applies, even if the actual character is only one or two bytes. That rule is retained for the pre-existing multi-byte character sets to maintain compatibility.

Character sets added since Firebird 2, UTF8 for example, do not inherit that limitation. Under the newer rules, the byte length of characters is counted on the actual data.

The actual number of characters that can be stored might be severely limited by a number of factors:

Non-indexed columns using the default collation sequence can store (number of characters) * (number of bytes per character) up to the byte limit for the data type. For example, a VARCHAR(32765) in character set ISO_8859_1 can store up to 32,765 characters, while in character set UTF8 (which uses up to four bytes per character) the upper limit may be as little as 8,191 characters.

If a column is to be indexed and/or modified with a COLLATE clause, a significant number of "spare" bytes must be allowed. Even the least demanding index—on a single VARCHAR column using a single-byte character set and the default collation sequence—is limited to 25 per cent of the database page size. In the old 1.X versions, the limit is 252 bytes.

For multi-byte character set columns, the character limit for an index is less than (252/(number of bytes per character). Multi-column indexes consume more bytes than do single-column indexes; those using a non-default collation sequence consume still more. For more detail about these effects, refer to the topic Collation sequence and index size later in this chapter.

Tip *When designing columns, always consider likely needs with regard to character set, indexing and key usage. Keep a special "scratch-pad" table in your development database just for testing the limits of indexes and keys.*

The storage size for BLOB columns, which are non-indexable, is not formally restricted by the limits on string sizes.

Field-level character set overrides

A character set attribute can be added to the individual definition of a domain, table column or PSQL variable of type CHAR, VARCHAR or BLOB SUB_TYPE 1 to override the default character set of the database.

For example, the following script fragment creates a database with a default character set of ISO8859_1 and a table containing different language versions of similar data in separate columns:

```
CREATE DATABASE '/data/authors.fdb' DEFAULT CHARACTER SET ISO8859_1;
...
CREATE TABLE COUNTRY_INTL(
  CNTRYCODE INTEGER NOT NULL,
  NOM_FR VARCHAR(30) NOT NULL,  /* uses default charset */
  NOM_EN VARCHAR(30), /* uses default charset */
  NOM_RU VARCHAR(30) CHARACTER SET CYRL,
  NOM_JP VARCHAR(30) CHARACTER SET SJIS_0208
);
```

Another fragment from the same script creates a domain for storing BLOB data in the Cyrillic character set:

```
CREATE DOMAIN MEMO_RU AS BLOB SUB_TYPE 1 CHARACTER SET CYRL;
```

Later in the script, we define a table that stores some text in Cyrillic:

```
CREATE TABLE NOTES_RU (
  DOC_ID BIGINT NOT NULL,
  NOTES MEMO_RU
);
```

Creating domains is explained in Chapter 11, *Domains*. Complete syntax for CREATE TABLE is in Chapter 15, *Tables*.

Statement-level character set overrides

The character set for text values in a statement is interpreted according to the connection's character set at run-time (not according to the character set defined for the column when it was created) unless you specify a character set marker (or "introducer") to indicate a different character set.

Character set marker—INTRODUCER

A character set marker—also known as an INTRODUCER—consists of the character set name prefixed by an underscore character. It is required to "introduce" an input string when the client application is connected to the database using a character set that is different to that of the destination column in the database.

Position the marker directly to the left of the text value being marked. For example, the introducer for input to a UNICODE_FSS field is `_UNICODE_FSS`:

```
INSERT INTO CONTRACTOR(Contractor_ID, Contractor_Name)
  values(1234, _UNICODE_FSS'Smith, John Joseph');
```

For clarity, you may leave white space between the introducer and the string without affecting the way the input is parsed.

Use the name of the character set for the introducer, not an alias. Thus, for example, use _ISO8859_1, not any of (_ANSI, _ISO88591, _LATIN1), which will just return character set errors.

String literals

A string literal in a test or search condition, for example, in a WHERE clause, is interpreted according to the character set of the client's connection at the time the condition is tested. An introducer will be required if the database column being searched has a character set which is different to that of the client connection:

```
... WHERE name = _ISO8859_1 'joe';
```

When you are developing with mixed character sets, it is good practice to use introducers as a matter of form, especially if your application will cross the boundaries of multiple databases and/or it will be deployed internationally.

sqlsubtype of an XSQLVAR

An XSQLVAR is a structure that applications pass across the interface when describing columns or parameters supplied in statements. Usually, the *sqlsubtype* member of an XSQLVAR pertaining to a column contains the identifying number of the column's character set.

In Firebird 2 and higher, when the character set of a CHAR or VARCHAR column is anything but NONE or OCTETS and the attachment character set is other than NONE, the *sqlsubtype* contains the identifier of the client character set instead.

The scope of this book does not reach the API. It is assumed that you will be using an existing API wrapper or driver for your application development. The change is mentioned here because it could present a compatibility issue with legacy applications that have been built using an API wrapper for an older Firebird, or for InterBase.

Special Character Sets

The general rule for character sets is that every byte (or pair or trio, in the case of multi-byte sets) is specifically defined by the standard it implements. There are four special exceptions—NONE, OCTETS, ASCII and UNICODE_FSS. The following table explains the special qualities of these three sets.

Table 8.1 Special character sets

Name	Qualities
NONE	Each byte is part of a string but no assumption is made about which character set it belongs to. Client-side or user-defined server code is responsible for character fidelity.
OCTETS | BINARY	Bytes which will not be interpreted as characters. Useful for storing binary data, GUID strings, hexidecimal numbers and for correcting string data that is causing transliteration errors. Aliased as BINARY from the "2" series onward.
ASCII	Values 0..127 are defined by ASCII; values outside that range are not characters, but are preserved. Firebird is fairly liberal about transliterating bytes in the 0..127 range of ASCII characters.
UNICODE_FSS	A limited UTF8 implementation that was superseded by a more proper UTF8 implementation from the "2" series onward. In v.1.X it is aliased as UTF8. Firebird still uses this character set to store metadata text. No collation sequence other than the default binary one is available

Two special character sets, NONE and OCTETS, can be used in declarations. However, OCTETS cannot be used as a connection character set. The two sets are similar, except that the space character of NONE is ASCII 0x20, whereas the space character of OCTETS is 0x00.

Conversion Rules

NONE and OCTETS follow different conversion rules to those that apply to other character sets. With other character sets, conversion is performed as

```
CHARACTER_SET1->UNICODE->CHARACTER_SET2,
```

With NONE and OCTETS, the bytes are just copied verbatim:

```
NONE/OCTETS->CHARACTER_SET2 and CHARACTER_SET1->NONE/OCTETS
```

Binary Strings

You can use either NONE or OCTETS to store binary strings, such as GUIDs, hexadecimal numbers or bit arrays. Both are locale-neutral. OCTETS is recommended over NONE because of its special treatment of trailing blanks in equality comparisons: they are stored as the NUL character (hex 0), instead of the SPACE character (hex 20), and will not be ignored.

In isql, from the "2" series onward, columns in OCTETS are displayed in hexadecimal format.

Hexadecimal input

From v.2.5 onward, you have the option to enter "binary string" literals in hexadecimal notation, i.e., as pairs of hex digits (0..9, a..f, A..F), each pair representing one byte. The input syntax has the pattern:

```
{X|x}'<hex-pairs>'
```

The letter "X" signals that the ensuing strings are to be interpreted as hex pairs. It can be lower or upper case. The string of hex pairs itself must not contain spaces and will cause an exception if the digit count is an odd number.

For example, to input a hex string and return a string in character set NONE:

```
select x'44756c63696d6572' from rdb$database
```

—returns the "binary string" '44756c63696d6572'

If we want the hex string returned as a character string, we can apply the "introducer" syntax to tell the engine to interpret the hex string according to a specific character set, e.g.,

```
select _UTF8 x'44756c63696d6572' from rdb$database
```

—returns 'Dulcimer'

The next hex input contains a Norwegian character:

```
select x'76696e646dc3a5bc6572' from rdb$database
```

—returns the "binary string" '76696e646dc3a5bc6572'

```
select _utf8 x'76696e646dc3a5bc6572' from rdb$database
```

—returns 'vindmåler'

Notice how the hex string contains an "extra" byte: it has 10 hex pairs for nine characters. All of the characters in 'vindmåler' are single-byte except the sixth (å), which has two. This feature will have its uses where you might want to store data from multiple character sets in the same column. You could define the column with character set OCTETS and input the data as hex strings.

ISO8859_1 (LATIN_1) and WIN1252

The Firebird ISO8859_1 character set is often specified to support European languages. ISO8859_1, also known as LATIN_1, is a proper subset of WIN1252: Microsoft added characters in positions that ISO specifically defines as Not a character (not "undefined", but specifically "not a character"). Firebird supports both WIN1252 and ISO8859_1. You can always transliterate ISO8859_1 to WIN1252, but transliterating WIN1252 to ISO8859_1 can result in errors.

Character sets for Microsoft Windows

Five character sets support Windows client applications, such as Paradox for Windows. These character sets are WIN1250, WIN1251, WIN1252, WIN1253, and WIN1254.

The names of collation sequences for these character sets that are specific to Paradox for Windows begin "PXW" and correspond to the Paradox/DBase language drivers supplied in the now-obsolete BDE (Borland Database Engine).

A "Gotcha"

The PXW collation sequences really implement collations from Paradox and DBase, including ALL BUGS. One exception, PXW_CSY was fixed in Firebird 1.0. Thus, legacy InterBase® databases that use it, for example in indexes, are not binary-compatible with Firebird.

For a list of the international character sets and collation sequences that Firebird supports "out-of-the-box" at the time of this writing, see Appendix VI.

Transliteration

Converting characters from one Firebird character set to another—for example, converting from DOS437 to ISO8859_1—is transliteration. Firebird's transliterations preserve character fidelity: By design, they will not substitute any kind of "placeholder" character for an input character that is not represented in the output character set. The purpose of this restriction is to guarantee that it will be possible to transliterate the same passage of text from one character set to another, in either direction, without losing any characters in the process.

Transliteration errors

Firebird reports a transliteration error if a character in the source set does not have an exact representation in the destination set (error code 335544565):

```
Cannot transliterate character between character sets
```

An example of where a transliteration error may occur is when an application passes input of some unspecified character set into a column defined with NONE and later tries to select that data for input to another column that has been defined with a different character set. Even though you thought it should work because the character images looked as though they belonged to the character set of the destination column, the entire transliteration fails because a character is encountered which is not represented in the destination character set.

Fixing transliteration errors

How can you deal with a bunch of character data that you have stored using the wrong character set? One trick is to use character set OCTETS as a staging post between the wrong and the right encoding. Because OCTETS is a special character set that blindly stores only what you poke into it—without transliteration—it is ideal for making the character codes neutral with respect to code page.

For example, suppose your problem table has a column COL_ORIGINAL that you accidentally created in character set NONE, when you meant it to be CHARACTER SET ISO8859_2. You've been loading this column with Hungarian data but, every time you try to select from it, you get that wretched transliteration error!

Here's what you can do:

```
ALTER TABLE TABLEA
  ADD COL_ISO8859_2 VARCHAR(30) CHARACTER SET ISO8859_2;
COMMIT;
```

```
UPDATE TABLEA
  SET COL_ISO8859_2 = CAST(COL_ORIGINAL AS CHAR(30) CHARACTER SET OCTETS);
```

Now you have a temporary column designed to store Hungarian text—and it is storing all of your "lost" text from the unusable COL_ORIGINAL.

It would be wise to view the data in column COL_IS08859_2 now! Of course, we assume that you are on a computer than can display Hungarian characters. If it looks good, you can proceed to drop COL_ORIGINAL:

```
ALTER TABLE TABLEA
  DROP COL_ORIGINAL;
COMMIT;
```

Now, all that is left to do is to rename the temporary column to the name of the dropped column:

```
ALTER TABLE TABLEA
ALTER COLUMN COL_ISO8859_2 TO COL_ORIGINAL;
COMMIT;
```

Collation Sequence

Beyond character sets, different countries, languages, or even cultural groups using the same character mappings, use different sequences to determine "alphabetical order" for sorting and comparisons. Hence, for most character sets, Firebird provides a variety of collation sequences. Some collation sequences also take in upper/lower case pairings to resolve case-insensitive orderings. The COLLATE clause is used in several contexts where collation sequence is important.

Each character set has a default collation sequence that specifies how its symbols are sorted and ordered. Collation sequence determines the rules of precedence that Firebird uses to sort, compare, and transliterate character data.

Because each character set has its own subset of possible collation sequences, the character set that you choose when you define the column limits your choice. You must choose a collation sequence that is supported for the column's character set.

Collation sequence for a column is specified when the column is created or altered. When set at the column level, it overrides any collation sequence set at the domain level.

Default collation sequence

Each character set in the catalogue comes with a default collation with the same name as the character set. The sort order for this default collation is binary, the sort sequence reflecting the binary codes of the characters. In versions older than v. 2.5, it is not possible to specify a default collation sequence at database level.

As mentioned already, when creating a database of on-disk structure (ODS) 11. 2 or higher, you can use the optional COLLATION keyword to extend the DEFAULT CHARACTER SET parameter amd specify a default collation sequence to be used with that character set.

Uppercasing in the default collations

The default collations of character sets in Firebird versions prior to the "2" series provided lower/upper case mappings only for the 7-bit characters—that group of characters traditionally referred to as "ASCII characters". In the 1.X versions, the binary collations cannot handlet mappings for accented characters at all.

Adriano dos Santos Fernandes, who implemented the international interface for the "2" series releases, provided an illustrative example of how the differences in upper-casing between old and new in the binary collations manifest themselves.

```
isql -q -ch dos850
SQL> create database 'test.fdb';
```

```
SQL> create table t (c char(1) character set dos850);
SQL> insert into t values ('a');
SQL> insert into t values ('e');
SQL> insert into t values ('á');
SQL> insert into t values ('é');

SQL> select c, upper(c) from t;
```

This is the result in versions 1.X:

```
C      UPPER
====== ======
a      A
e      E
á      á
é      é
```

In Firebird 2.0 the result is:

```
C      UPPER
====== ======
a      A
e      E
á      Á
é      É
```

Listing available collation sequences

The following query yields a list of character sets with the available collation sequences:

```
SELECT
  C.RDB$CHARACTER_SET_NAME,
  CO.RDB$COLLATION_NAME,
  CO.RDB$COLLATION_ID,
  CO.RDB$CHARACTER_SET_ID,
  CO.RDB$COLLATION_ID * 256 + CO.RDB$CHARACTER_SET_ID AS TEXTTYPEID
FROM RDB$COLLATIONS CO
JOIN RDB$CHARACTER_SETS C
  ON CO.RDB$CHARACTER_SET_ID = C.RDB$CHARACTER_SET_ID;
```

Naming of collation sequences

Many Firebird collation names use the naming convention XX_YY, where XX is a two-letter language code, and YY is a two-letter country code. For example, DE_DE is the collation name for German as used in Germany; FR_FR is for French as used in France; and FR_CA is for French as used in Canada.

Where a character set offers a choice of collations, the one with the name matching the character set is the default collation sequence, which implements binary collation for the character set. Binary collation sorts a character set by the numeric codes used to represent the characters. Some character sets support alternative collation sequences using different rules for determining precedence.

This topic explains how to specify collation sequence for character sets in domains and table columns, in string comparisons, and in ORDER BY and GROUP BY clauses.

Collation sequence for a column

When a CHAR or VARCHAR column is created for a table, with either CREATE TABLE or ALTER TABLE, the collation sequence for the column can be specified using the COLLATE clause. COLLATE is especially useful for multi-language character sets such as ISO8859_1 or DOS437 that support many different collation sequences.

For example, the following dynamic ALTER TABLE statement adds a new column to a table, and specifies both a character set and a collation sequence:

```
ALTER TABLE 'EMP_CANADIEN'
  ADD ADDRESS VARCHAR(40)
    CHARACTER SET ISO8859_1 NOT NULL COLLATE FR_CA;
```

Refer to Chapter 15 for complete syntax for *Altering Columns in a Table* (ALTER TABLE, et al).

Collation sequence for string comparisons

It can be necessary to specify a collation sequence when CHAR or VARCHAR values are compared in a WHERE clause, if the values being compared use different collation sequences and it matters to the result.

To specify the collation sequence to use for a value during a comparison, include a COLLATE clause after the value. For example, the following WHERE clause fragment forces the column value to the left of the equivalence operator to be compared with the input parameter using a specific collation sequence:

```
...
WHERE SURNAME COLLATE FR_CA >= :surname;
```

In this case, without matching collation sequences, the candidates for "greater than" might be different for each collation sequence.

Collation sequence in sorting criteria

When CHAR or VARCHAR columns are ordered in a SELECT statement, it can be necessary to specify a collation order for the ordering, especially if columns used for ordering use different collation sequences.

To specify the collation sequence to use for ordering a column in the ORDER BY clause, include a COLLATE clause after the column name. For example, in the following ORDER BY clause, the collation sequences for two columns are specified:

```
...
ORDER BY SURNAME COLLATE FR_CA, FIRST_NAME COLLATE FR_CA;
```

For the complete syntax of the ORDER BY clause, see Chapter 22, ***Ordered and Aggregated Sets***.

Collation sequence in a GROUP BY clause

When CHAR or VARCHAR columns are grouped in a SELECT statement, it can be necessary to specify a collation order for the grouping, especially if columns used for grouping use different collation sequences.

To specify the collation sequence to use for grouping columns in the GROUP BY clause, include a COLLATE clause after the column name. For example, in the following GROUP BY clause, the collation sequences for multiple columns are specified:

```
...
GROUP BY ADDR_3 COLLATE CA_CA, SURNAME COLLATE FR_CA, FIRST_NAME COLLATE FR_CA;
```

For the complete syntax of the GROUP BY clause, see Chapter 22, ***Ordered and Aggregated Sets***.

Collation sequence and index size

If you specify a non-binary collation (one other than the default collation) for a character set, the index key can become larger than the stored string if the collation includes precedence rules of second-, third-, or fourth-order.

Non-binary collations for ISO8859_1, for example, use full dictionary sorts, with spaces and punctuation of fourth-order importance:

- First order: A is different from B

- Second order: A is different from À
- Third order: A is different from a
- Fourth order: the type of punctuation symbol (hyphen, space, apostrophe) is important

Example

```
Greenfly
Green fly
Green-fly
Greensleeves
Green sleeves
Green spot
```

If spaces and punctuation marks are treated instead as a first-order difference, the same list would be sorted as follows:

```
Greenfly
Greensleeves
Green fly
Green sleeves
Green spot
Green-fly
```

How non-binary collations can limit index size

When an index is created, it uses the collation sequence defined for each text segment in the index. Using ISO8859_1, a single-byte character set, with the default collation, the index structure in a database with a page size of 4Kb can hold about 1020 (252 in Firebird 1.X) characters (fewer, if it is a multi-segment index). However, if you choose a non-binary collation for ISO8859_1, the index structure might accommodate only 340 characters (84 in v.1.X), despite the fact that the characters in the column being indexed occupy only one byte each.

Some ISO8859_1 collations, DE_DE for example, require an average of three bytes per character for an indexed column.

Adding an Alias for a Character Set

If you need to add a custom alias for a character set that is available on your server, all that is required is to add a member to the Firebird enumerated type identified as 'RDB$CHARACTER_SET_NAME' in the table of symbolic constants, RDB$TYPES.

The following stored procedure takes as arguments the name of the character set you want to alias, the alias name you want to use and an optional user description.

```
SET TERM ^;
CREATE PROCEDURE LOAD_CHAR_ALIAS (
  CHARSET CHAR(31) CHARACTER SET UNICODE_FSS,
  ALIAS_NAME CHAR(31) CHARACTER SET UNICODE_FSS,
  USER_DESCRIPTION VARCHAR(200) CHARACTER SET UNICODE_FSS)
AS
DECLARE VARIABLE TYPE_ID SMALLINT;
BEGIN
  TYPE_ID = 0;
  SELECT RDB$CHARACTER_SET_ID FROM RDB$CHARACTER_SETS
  WHERE RDB$CHARACTER_SET_NAME = UPPER(:CHARSET)
  INTO :TYPE_ID;
  IF (TYPE_ID > 0 AND TYPE_ID IS NOT NULL) THEN
```

```
      INSERT INTO RDB$TYPES (
        RDB$FIELD_NAME,
        RDB$TYPE,
        RDB$TYPE_NAME,
        RDB$DESCRIPTION,
        RDB$SYSTEM_FLAG)
      VALUES (
        'RDB$CHARACTER_SET_NAME',
        :TYPE_ID,
        UPPER(:ALIAS_NAME),
        :USER_DESCRIPTION,
        0) ;
END ^
COMMIT ^
SET TERM ;^
```

Now, to load your new alias—let's say it is to be ' x-sjis' as an alias for the character set SJIS_0208—execute the procedure as follows:

```
EXECUTE PROCEDURE LOAD_CHAR_ALIAS
  ('SJIS_0208', 'x-sjis', 'This is a description');
COMMIT;
```

Although metadata are stored in UNICODE_FSS, the system identifiers are constrained to permit only the 7-bit alphanumeric characters.

Custom character sets and collations

From the "2" series forward, Firebird comes with plug-in support for the open source "International Components for Unicode" (ICU) libraries.

New character sets and collations are implemented through dynamic libraries and installed in the server with a manifest file, which acts like an index or catalogue of available character sets and their implementations. Not all implemented character sets and collations need to be listed in the manifest file but only those listed are available. If duplications are present in the manifest, only the first-occurring entry is loaded. An error is reported in `firebird.log` if a subsequent duplicate entry is detected but no exception occurs.

The manifest file should be put in the $rootdir/intl with a ".conf" extension. For an example, see `fbintl.conf` *in the* `/intl` *folder of your Firebird server installation.*

Dynamic Libraries

For Windows, the dynamic libraries for the plug-in language support are located in the `\bin` directory of your Firebird installation, with names starting with "icu", e.g., Firebird 2.5 ships with `icudt130.dll`, `icuin30.dll` and `icuuc30.dll`.

For Linux, the shared objects and symlinks are installed in the `/lib` subdirectory with names starting with "libicu".

You must deploy the ICU libraries with the "2" series and higher servers. This applies to the Windows Embedded Server model as well, in which the libraries are deployed in the emulated Firebird <root> directory.

Adding More Character Sets to a Database

For installing additional character sets and collations into a database, the character sets and collations should be registered in the database's system tables (RDB$CHARACTER_SETS and RDB$COLLATIONS). Don't try to update the metadata tables manually: the file

/misc/intl.sql, in your Firebird 2.X installation, is a script of stored procedures for registering and unregistering them.

Example The following is an example of a section from fbintl.conf.The symbol $(this) is used to indicate the same directory as the manifest file. The library extension should be omitted.

```
<intl_module fbintl>
    filename $(this)/fbintl
</intl_module>
<charset ISO8859_1>
    intl_module fbintl
    collation ISO8859_1
    collation DA_DA
    collation DE_DE
    collation EN_UK
    collation EN_US
    collation ES_ES
    collation PT_BR
    collation PT_PT
</charset>
<charset WIN1250>
    intl_module fbintl
    collation WIN1250
    collation PXW_CSY
    collation PXW_HUN
    collation PXW_HUNDC
</charset>
```

Using ICU Character Sets

All non-wide and ASCII-based character sets present in ICU can be used by Firebird 2.1 and higher versions. To reduce the size of the distribution kit, Firebird's ICU distribution is customised to include only essential character sets and any for which there was a specific feature request.

If the character set you need is not included, you can replace the ICU libraries with another complete module, provided it is installed in your operating system.

A good place to start looking for the libraries is http://site.icu-project.org/download.

Registering an ICU Character Set Module

To use an alternative character set module, you need to register it in two places:

1 in the server's language configuration file, intl/fbintl.conf

2 in each database that is going to use it

You should prepare and register the module in the server before you register the character set[s] in the database.

Registering a Character Set on the Server

Using a text editor, register the module in intl/fbintl.conf, as follows.-

```
<charset        NAME>
    intl_module     fbintl
    collation       NAME [REAL-NAME]
</charset>
```

For example, to register a new character set and two of its collations, add the following to fbintl.conf:

```
<charset        GB>
        intl_module     fbintl
        collation       GB
        collation       GB18030
</charset>
```

Registering a Character Set in a Database

It takes two steps to make the character set and your required collation available in a database:

1. Run the procedure sp_register_character_set, the source for which can be found in misc/intl.sql beneath your Firebird 2.1 root, AND—
2. Use a CREATE COLLATION statement to register each collation

Step 1

Using the Stored Procedure

The stored procedure takes two arguments: a string that is the character set's identifier as declared in the configuration file and a smallint that is the maximum number of bytes a single character can occupy in the encoding. For the example (above) that we registered on the server:

```
execute procedure sp_register_character_set ('GB', 4);
```

Step 2

Registering the Collations

For the purpose of our example, the syntax for registering the two collations in a database is very simple:

```
CREATE COLLATION GB FOR GB;
CREATE COLLATION GB18030 FOR GB;
```

More complex directives can be used in CREATE COLLATION, as we discover next.

The CREATE COLLATION Statement

If you are using a server version 2.1 or higher and the ODS of your database is 11.1 or higher, the new CREATE COLLATION statement provides a way for you to register your collation to your database through dynamic SQL. The syntax pattern is:

```
CREATE COLLATION <name>
  FOR <charset>
  [ FROM <base> | FROM EXTERNAL ('<name>') ]
  [ NO PAD | PAD SPACE ]
  [ CASE SENSITIVE | CASE INSENSITIVE ]
  [ ACCENT SENSITIVE | ACCENT INSENSITIVE ]
  [ '<specific-attributes>' ]
```

Attributes are presented as a string that consists of a list of specfic attributes separated by semi-colons. The attributes are case-sensitive.

The new collation should be declared in a `.conf` file in the `<root>/intl` directory before you prepare and execute the CREATE COLLATION statement.

Examples

```
CREATE COLLATION UNICODE_ENUS_CI
  FOR UTF8
  FROM UNICODE
  CASE INSENSITIVE
  'LOCALE=en_US';
--
CREATE COLLATION MY_COLLATION
  FOR WIN1252
  PAD SPACE;
```

More examples follow in the next section, illustrating use of specific attributes.

Conventions and Attributes

Attributes are stored at database creation time and only into databases having an on-disk structure of 11.1 or higher. Hence, these files can be utilised if you are creating a new database under Firebird 2.1+ or if you are restoring an older database in a server version that is newer than Firebird 2.0.

It is strongly recommended that you follow the naming convention as modelled in `fbintl.conf`, using the character set name followed by the collation name, with the two name parts joined by an underscore character, viz.:

```
<characterset>_<collation>
```

Examples

```
CREATE COLLATION WIN1252_UNICODE
    FOR WIN1252;
  --
CREATE COLLATION WIN1252_UNICODE_CI
    FOR WIN1252
    FROM WIN1252_UNICODE
    CASE INSENSITIVE;
```

Specific Attributes for Collations

Some attributes may notbe applicable to some collations. If that is the case, no error is reported.

`DISABLE-COMPRESSIONS`

Prevents compressions (otherwise referred to as "contractions") from changing the order of a group of characters. It is not valid for collations of multi-byte character sets.

Format: `DISABLE-COMPRESSIONS={0 | 1}`

Example

```
DISABLE-COMPRESSIONS=1
```

`DISABLE-EXPANSIONS`

Prevents expansions from changing the order of a character to sort as a group of characters. It is not valid for collations of multi-byte character sets.

Format: `DISABLE-EXPANSIONS={0 | 1}`

Example

```
DISABLE-EXPANSIONS=1
```

`ICU-VERSION`

Specifies the version of the ICU library to be used for UNICODE and UNICODE_CI.

Valid values are the ones defined in the configuration file (`intl/fbintl.conf`) in the entry `intl_module/icu_versions`.

Format: `ICU-VERSION={default | major.minor}`

Example

```
ICU-VERSION=3.0
```

`LOCALE`

Specifies the collation locale for UNICODE and UNICODE_CI.

To use this attribute you need the complete version of the ICU libraries.

Format: LOCALE=xx_XX

Example

```
LOCALE=en_US
```

`MULTI-LEVEL`

Registers that the collation uses more than one level for ordering purposes. It is not valid for collations of multi-byte character sets.

Format: `MULTI-LEVEL={0 | 1}`

Example `MULTI-LEVEL=1`

`SPECIALS-FIRST`

Specifies that special characters (spaces, symbols, etc) precede alphanumeric characters. It is not valid for collations of multi-byte character sets.

```
Format:   SPECIALS-FIRST={0 | 1}
```

Example `SPECIALS-FIRST=1`

`NUMERIC-SORT`

For UNICODE collations only, available from v.2.5 onward, specifies the sorting order for numeral characters.

Format & usage

```
Format:   NUMERIC-SORT={0 | 1}
```

Examples The default, 0, sorts numerals in alphabetical order, e.g.

```
1
10
100
2
20
...
```

1 sorts numerals in numerical order, e.g:

```
1
2
10
20
100
create collation sort_numeral for UTF8
  from UNICODE 'NUMERIC-SORT=1';
```

Checking attributes

In *isql*, use SHOW COLLATION <characterset>_<collation> to display the attributes.

Unregistering a collation

To unregister an unwanted collation, use the DDL statement

```
DROP COLLATION <collation-name)
```

Rolling Your Own

It is possible to write your own character sets and collations and have the Firebird engine load them from a shared library, which should be named `fbintl2` in order to be recognised and linked.

It is also possible to implement custom character sets or collations using user-defined functions (UDFs) to transliterate input. The Firebird engine automatically uses functions that have names specially formatted to be recognized as character sets and collations. The name "USER_CHARSET_nnn" indicates a character set, while "USER_TRANSLATE_nnn_nnn" and "USER_TEXTTYPE_nnn" indicate character set + collation sequence. (*nnn* represents 3-digit numbers, usually in the range 128 to 254).

It is an advanced topic, beyond the scope of this book. The developer of the original *fbintl2* plug-in for custom character sets, David Brookestone Schnepper, makes a do-it-yourself kit freely available, containing sample C code, mappings and instructions. These days, it is archived at several locations around the Web, including http://www.ibphoenix.com/resources/documents/attic/doc_39. Because the kit includes lucid instructions for creating character sets, it is also a useful reference if you plan to use the UDF approach to implement a custom character set.

Metadata Text Conversion

Firebird versions 2.0.x had two problems related to character sets and metadata extraction. You will know you have at least one of these problems if one of the first things you see on connecting to your newly upgraded database is a "Malformed string" error.

Problem 1: "raw" text in metadata

When creating or altering objects, text associated with metadata was not transliterated from the client character set to the system (UNICODE_FSS) character set of these BLOB columns. Instead, raw bytes were stored there. The database will have to be repaired in order to read the metadata correctly.

The types of text affected were PSQL sources, descriptions, text associated with constraints and defaults, and so on.

The problem can still occur if CREATE or ALTER operations are performed with the connection character set as NONE or UNICODE_FSS and you are using non-UNICODE_FSS data or if you process scripts containing strings that were written in an external editor and stored in ASCII or ANSI encoding.

Problem 2: malformed strings returned from text BLOBs

In reads from text BLOBs, transliteration from the BLOB character set to the client character set was not being performed.

Solutions

If your metadata and/or user BLOB text was created with encoding that was consistently wrong, it can be repaired using scripts distributed in the v.2.1 and 2.5 kits. The repair script for metadata is installed beneath your Firebird root directory in

```
/misc/upgrade/metadata/metadata_charset_create.sql
```

If you have user text BLOBs that are affected by Problem 2, you can use the same script as a model for writing another script to repair them. For more details, refer to the section Metadata Repair in the companion volume to this, Vol. 3: ***Administering Firebird Servers and Databases*** and in ***The Firebird Book Second Edition***, in the chapter entitled Migration Notes.

For v.2.5, the conversion for both problems was simplified with the addition of two new restore switches in the *gbak* utility. For details, refer to the topic The gbak method in the reference cited above.

CHAPTER

9

BLOBS AND ARRAYS

BLOB types—Binary Large OBjects—are complex structures used for storing discrete data objects of variable size, which may be very large. They are "complex" in the sense that Firebird stores these types in two parts: a kind of hyperlink—referred to as a BLOB_ID—is stored with the owning row, while the actual data are stored apart from the row, often on one or many different database pages, keyed to the BLOB_ID.

Almost any sort of storable data can be stored in a BLOB: bit-mapped graphics images, vector drawings, sound files, video segments, chapter or book-length documents, or any other kind of multimedia information. Because a blob can hold different kinds of information, it requires special processing at the client for reading and writing.

BLOB types can, where practicable , store data files generated by other applications such as word processors, CAD software or XML editors. The gains can be the benefit of transaction control for dynamic data, protection from external interference, control of versions and the ability to access externally-created data through the medium of SQL statements.

BLOB types can not be indexed.

Array Types, discussed separately after BLOBs, are implemented in Firebird as a specially-formatted, system-managed BLOB subtype.

BLOBs and Subtypes

A BLOB *subtype* is a positive or negative integer that identifies the nature of the data contained in the column. Besides the two subtypes predefined for general use, Firebird has a number of subtypes that it uses internally. All of these internal subtypes have positive numbers.

Subtypes with positive numbers greater than 1 have specific purposes for storing and converting metadata.They should never be declared for user data. T

Supported User Subtypes

Out-of-the-box, Firebird makes two pre-defined BLOB types available for use in user tables, distinguished by the sub_type attribute (SQL keyword SUB_TYPE):

Table 9.1 Pre-defined BLOB subtypes

Definition	SQL Alias	Purpose
BLOB SUB_TYPE 0	BINARY	Generic BLOB type for storing any sort of data, including text. Commonly referred to as "an untyped binary BLOB". Firebird is unaware of the contents. This is the default subtype.
BLOB SUB_TYPE 1	TEXT	More specialized sub-type for storing plain text. Equivalent to CLOB and MEMO types implemented by some other DBMSs. Recommended for use with application interfaces such as RAD components or search engines that provide special treatment for such types.

Custom Subtypes

Negative subtype numbers—from –1 to –32,768—are reserved for assigning to custom subtypes. Custom subtypes with negative numbers can be added to distinguish, identify and document special types of data objects that you want to store in BLOBs, such as HTML, XML or word-processor documents, JPEG, PNG images, etc.—the choice is up to you.

Firebird is unaware of what is stored in any BLOB and thus cannot perform any kind of validation on the streams that are written to BLOBs of a custom subtype.

BLOB Filters

Blob sub-typing also allows specific conversion from one subtype to another. Firebird has extensible support for automatic conversion between a given pair of blob sub-types in the form of *blob filters*. Blob filters are special kind of external function with a single purpose: to take a BLOB object in one format and convert it to a BLOB object in another format.

It is possible to create a blob filter that converts between a custom (negative) subtype and a predefined subtype, commonly the TEXT one.

A BLOB filter is like an external function (UDF) in most respects. The object code for blob filters is placed in shared object libraries. The filter, which is invoked dynamically when required, is recognized at database (not server) level by way of a declaration in metadata, of the form:

```
DECLARE FILTER <filter-name>
  INPUT_TYPE <sub-type> /* identifies type of object to be converted */
  OUTPUT_TYPE <sub-type> /* identifies type of object to be created */
  ENTRY_POINT '<entry-point-name>' /* name of exported function */
  MODULE_NAME '<external-library-name>'; /* name of BLOB filter library */
```

The writing and usage of BLOB filters are beyond the scope of this book. More information on the topic can be found by searching the Firebird knowledgebases.

Declaration Syntax

A BLOB is declared as a regular column for a table in a CREATE TABLE or ALTER TABLE statement. The following example defines two BLOB columns: BLOB1 with subtype 0 (the default), BLOB2 with Firebird subtype 1 (TEXT):

```
CREATE TABLE TABLE2 (
  .., /* other columns */
  BLOB1 BLOB, /* SUB_TYPE 0 */
  BLOB2 BLOB SUB_TYPE 1,
  ..);
```

The next defines a domain which is a text BLOB to store text in character set ISO_8859_1:

```
CREATE DOMAIN MEMO
  BLOB SUB_TYPE TEXT /*BLOB SUB_TYPE 1 */
  CHARACTER  SET ISO_8859_1;
```

This SQL snippet shows how a local BLOB variable is declared in a PSQL module:

```
CREATE PROCEDURE ...
...
DECLARE VARIABLE AMEMO BLOB SUB_TYPE 1;
...
```

BLOB Segments

BLOB data are stored in a different format to regular column data and, usually but not always, apart from them. They are stored in blocks known as *segments* in one or more database pages, in a distinct row version that is unlike the format of a row of regular data. Segments are discrete chunks of unformatted data that are usually streamed by the application and passed to the API to be packaged for transmission across the network, one chunk at a time, in contiguous order.

In the regular row structure of the parent row, the BLOB is linked through a BLOB ID that is stored with the regular row data. A BLOB ID is a unique hexadecimal value that provides a cross-reference between a BLOB and the table it belongs to. On arrival at the server, segments are laid down in the same order as they are received, although not necessarily in chunks of the same size in which they were transported.

Where possible, the BLOB row versions are stored on the same page as parent row. However, large BLOBs can extend across many pages and this initial "blob row" may not contain actual data but an array of pointers to a data pages that are specialised as blob pages.

It is sometimes the case that the actual BLOB data will fit on the same data page as the record that owns the BLOB. Thus, it is not uncommon for Firebird to store small BLOBs on the same page as the record data.

Segment Size

When a BLOB column is defined in a table, the definition can optionally include the expected size of segments that are written to the column. The default—80 bytes—is really quite arbitrary. Mythology says it was chosen because it was exactly the length of one line on a text terminal display!

The segment size setting does not affect Firebird's performance in processing BLOBs on the server: the server does not use it at all. For DSQL applications—which is what most people write—you can simply ignore it or, if relevant, set it to some size that suits some local storage buffer in which your application stores BLOB data.

For DML operations—SELECT, INSERT and UPDATE— the length of the segment is specified in an API structure when it is written and can be any size, up to a maximum

65,535 bytes. Reusable classes for development environments such as FreePascal/Delphi, C++ and Java usually take care of BLOB segmentation in their internal functions and procedures if they have uses for it. If you are programming directly to the API, you might need to develop your own routines for constructing segments.

ESQL Applications

In databases for use with ESQL apps written for pre-processing by the *gpre* pre-processor—today a highly esoteric genre for Firebird development!—the segment size must be declared to indicate the maximum number of bytes that an application is expected to write to any segment in the column. Normally, an ESQL application should not attempt to write segments larger than the segment length defined in the table; doing so overflows the internal segment buffer, corrupting memory in the process. It may be advantageous to specify a relatively large segment, to reduce the number of calls to retrieve BLOB data.

The following statement creates two BLOB columns, BLOB1, with a default segment size of 80, and BLOB2, with a specified segment length of 1024:

```
CREATE TABLE TABLE2 (
  BLOB1 BLOB SUB_TYPE 0,
  BLOB2 BLOB SEGMENT SUB_TYPE TEXT SEGMENT SIZE 1024);
```

In this ESQL code fragment, an application inserts a BLOB segment. The segment length is specified in a host variable, segment_length:

```
INSERT CURSOR BCINS VALUES (:write_segment_buffer :segment_length);
```

When to Use BLOB Types

The BLOB is preferred to character types for storing text data of infinitely variable length. Because it is transported in "mindless chunks", it is not subject to the 32 Kb length limit of strings, as long as the client application implements the appropriate techniques to pass it in the format required by the server for segmenting it.

Because the BLOB is likely to be stored apart from regular row data, it is not fetched automatically when row data are selected. Rather, the client requests the data on demand, by way of the BLOB_ID. Consequently, there is big "win" in the time taken to begin fetching rows from a SELECT, compared to the traffic involved when character types are used for storing large text items. On the other hand, some developers may consider it a disadvantage to have to implement "fetch-on-demand".

When considering whether to use BLOB for non-text data, other issues arise. The convenience of being able to store images, sound files and compiled documents has to be balanced against the overhead it adds to backups. It may be an unreasonable design objective to store large numbers of huge objects that are never going to change.

Security

The idea that large binary and text objects are more secure when stored in BLOBs than when stored in filesystem files is largely an illusion. Certainly, they are more difficult to access from end-user tools. However, database privileges currently do not apply to BLOB and array types beyond the context of the tables to which they are linked by indirection. It is not absurd to suppose that a malicious hacker who gained access to open the database file could write application code that scanned the file for BLOB_IDs and read the data directly from storage, as external BLOB functions do.

Operations on BLOBs

A BLOB is never updated. Every update which "changes" a blob causes a new BLOB to be constructed, complete with a new BLOB_ID. The original BLOB becomes obsolete once the update is committed.

A BLOB column can be tested for NULL/NOT NULL and, from the "2" series forward, one text BLOB can be compared with another for equality. A BLOB cannot be compared with a string.

V.1.X No internal function exists to compare one BLOB with another in the older versions. Several BLOB UDFs are available from community download sites, including some that compare two BLOBs for equality.

String input to BLOB columns

As a broad rule, the writing of the contents of a BLOB is manipulated by client applications. Firebird does not update the contents of a BLOB: it is up to the client application to provide new contents for assignment to a BLOB when a statement updates a row and to package it using the specialised structures that are declared in the API for the purpose.

However, when accepting data for input to text BLOB columns by way of an INSERT or UPDATE operation, Firebird can take a string as input and transform it into a BLOB. For example:

```
INSERT INTO ATABLE (PK, ABLOB)
  VALUES (99, 'This is some text.');
```

Note that passing a string to a stored procedure for an input argument that was defined as BLOB will cause an exception. The following, for example, will fail:

```
CREATE PROCEDURE DEMO
  (INPUTARG BLOB SUB_TYPE 1)
AS
BEGIN
  ...
END ^
COMMIT ^
EXECUTE PROCEDURE DEMO('Show us what you can do with this!') ^
```

Instead, either

- define the input argument as a VARCHAR and have your procedure submit the string to the INSERT or UPDATE statement itself; or
- have your client program take care of converting the string to a text BLOB. This will be the preferred solution if the length of the string is unknown.

Character set conversion

Conversion from one character set to another, when assigning either a string to a BLOB or the contents of a BLOB to another BLOB, is supported from the "2" series onward.

Manipulating output

For retrieving output from text BLOBs, the situation has improved with successive versions. For the "2" series and beyond, the manipulations at the server side that are available for strings have been progressively extended to work with text BLOBs, too.

Collations

Whilst Firebird always provided the means to specify the character set for a text BLOB, older versions cannot apply a collation sequence to the output. That changed with the"2" series, when something like the following became a valid way to retrieve BLOB text, in this case from a UTF8 BLOB:

```
select a_blob_column from table1
  where a_blob_column COLLATE UNICODE STARTING WITH 'Étu';
```

String functions

When the SUBSTRING() internal function was implemented in Firebird 1.5, it was also implemented for text BLOBs. Up to and including v.2.0, the substring returned is a string and is thus limited to the maximum size, in bytes, of the character type that receives the result.

In Firebird versions 2.1 and higher, most of the internal functions that apply to strings will also work with text BLOBs. Those that return strings as their result when operating on string input will return a text BLOB when operating on text BLOB input.

> *These enhancements mean that the SUBSTRING() function returns a BLOB, whereas it returns a string in versions 2.0 and 1.5. Legacy client and PSQL code written for the older server versions will present a migration issue for developers.*

Concatenation

From v.2.1 onward, BLOBs can be concatenated together or to strings, producing a BLOB as the result. In versions 2.0.x and below, attempting this operation will result in a conversion error.

Upper-casing

From v.2.1 onward, BLOBs can be upper-cased in search expressions and query output, using the internal function UPPER(). In versions 2.0.x and below, attempting this operation will result in a conversion error.

External functions

Very few external functions exist for operating on BLOBs. The `fbudf` library includes just one: the function STRING2BLOB(), which takes a string or string expression as input and returns a BLOB of subtype TEXT. Its purpose was largely superseded when it became possible to pass a string argument to insert into or update text BLOB columns or variables.

Nevertheless, with careful attention to the byte-length limits for strings, it might have its uses in expressions that concatenate strings for storage into a BLOB column or variable.

Finding a suitable function

Appendix I, *Internal and External Functions*, has full details, with examples, of the functions available for BLOB inputs, both internally and through the UDFs that are distributed in the Firebird kits.

Some third-party UDF libraries have external functions that operate on BLOBs. You might like to check out some of the better-known third party external function libraries. The IBPhoenix web site maintains *summaries and links* for several of these.

Array Types

Firebird allows you to create homogeneous arrays of most data types. Using an array can enable multiple data items to be stored as discrete, multi-dimensional elements in a single column. At certain levels, Firebird can perform operations on an entire array, effectively treating it as a single element, or it can operate on an array slice, a subset of array elements. An array slice can consist of a single element, or a set of many contiguous elements.

ARRAY Types and SQL

Arrays are not a "natural" feature for a relational database. The relational model's approach to packaging multi-dimensional data is to store it in rows of columns and retrieve it dynamically as sets. It has been well argued that arrays belong in client-side dynamic structures and have no place in relational databases. It has certainly remained an area of minimal attention and low demand during Firebird's life to date.

Because Firebird does not implement any dynamic SQL syntax for operating on ARRAY types, performing DML and searches on them from a dynamic SQL (DSQL) interface is not simple. The Firebird API surfaces structures and functions to enable dynamic applications to work with them directly. Some RAD data access components—for example, IBObjects, a popular suite of components for use with Object Pascal (Delphi) and FreePascal language environments—provide classes encapsulating this area of API functionality.

Arrays are stored in a specialised BLOB structure. Multi-dimensional arrays are stored in row-major order.[1]

Embedded SQL (ESQL)—which does not use the API structures and function calls—supports several static SQL syntaxes for operating on ARRAY types and integrating them with arrays declared in the host language. Like ESQL, arrays have remained an area of mild esoteric interest without engendering any remarkable interest in their existence.

For both dynamic and static applications, it is feasible—albeit not very practicable—to read array data into a stored procedure and return values that the client application can use. An example appears later in the topic entitled *Limited DSQL Access*.

When to Use an Array Type

Using an array may be appropriate when:

- The data items naturally form a set of the same data type.
- The entire set of data items in a single database column must be represented and controlled as a unit, as opposed to storing each item in a separate column.
- Each item must also be identified and accessed individually.
- There is no requirement to access the values individually in triggers or stored procedures, or you have external functions that enable such access

Eligible Element Types

An array can contain elements of any Firebird data type except BLOB. Arrays of ARRAY are not supported. All of the elements of a particular array are of the same data type.

Defining Arrays

An array can be defined as a domain (using CREATE DOMAIN) or as a column, in a CREATE TABLE or ALTER TABLE ADD COLUMN statement. Defining an array domain or column is similar to defining any other, with the additional inclusion of the array dimensions. Array dimensions are enclosed in square brackets following data type specification.

Example The following statement defines both a regular character column, and a one-dimensional character array column containing eight elements:

```
CREATE TABLE ATABLE (
```

1. A flag exists in the API array descriptor that is said to enable m-d arrays to be stored in column-major order. It has never been properly documented and it is unknown whether it ever worked.

```
ID BIGINT,
ARR_CHAR(14)[8] CHARACTER SET OCTETS
); /* stores 1 row * 8 elements */
```

Multi-dimensional Arrays

Firebird supports multi-dimensional arrays, arrays with 1 to 16 dimensions. For example, the following statement defines three INTEGER array columns with two, three, and four dimensions respectively:

```
CREATE TABLE BTABLE (
/* stores 4 rows X 5 elements = 20 elements */
  ARR_INT2 INTEGER[4,5],
/* 6 layers, each 4 rows X 5 elements = 120 elements */
  ARR_INT3 INTEGER[4,5,6],
/* 7 storeys, each 6 layers of 4 rows * 5 elements = 840 elements */
  ARR_INT6 INTEGER[4,5,6,7]
);
```

Firebird stores multi-dimensional arrays in row-major order. Some host languages, such as FORTRAN, expect arrays to be in column-major order. In these cases, care must be taken to translate element ordering correctly between Firebird and the host language.

Specifying Subscript Ranges for Dimensions

Firebird's array dimensions have a specific range of upper and lower boundaries, called *subscripts*. Dimensions are 1-based by default, i.e. the first element of the dimension array of *n* elements has subscript 1, the second element, 2, and the last element, *n*. For example, the following statement creates a table with a column that is an array of four integers:

```
CREATE TABLE TABLEC (
  ARR_INT INTEGER[4]
  );
```

The subscripts for this array are 1, 2, 3, and 4.

Custom (explicit) subscript boundaries

A custom set of upper and lower boundaries can be defined explicitly for each array dimension when an array column is created. For example, C and Pascal programmers, familiar with zero-based arrays, might want to create array columns with a lower boundary of zero to map transparently to array structures in application code.

Both the lower and upper boundaries of the dimension are required when defining custom boundaries, using the following syntax pattern:

```
[lower:upper]
```

The following example creates a table with a single-dimension, zero-based array column:

```
CREATE TABLE TABLED (
  ARR_INT INTEGER[0:3]
  ); /* subscripts are 0, 1, 2, and 3. */
```

Each dimension's set of subscripts is separated from the next with commas. For example, the following statement creates a table with a two-dimensional array column where both dimensions are zero-based:

```
CREATE TABLE TABLEE (
  ARR_INT INTEGER[0:3, 0:3]
  );
```

Storage of ARRAY Columns

As with other types implemented as BLOB, Firebird stores an array ID with the non-BLOB column data of the database table, that points to the page(s) containing the actual data .

Updates

As with other BLOB types, the Firebird engine cannot course through the data seeking successive individual target elements for conditional or selective update. However, in a single DML operation, it is possible to isolate one element or a set of contiguous elements—known as a *slice*—and target that slice for update.

Inserts

INSERT cannot operate on a slice. When a row is inserted in a table containing ARRAY columns, it is necessary to construct and populate the array entirely, before passing it in the INSERT statement.

Accessing Array Data

Some application interfaces do provide encapsulation of the API functions and descriptors and limited read access is possible from stored procedures.

The array descriptor

The API exposes the array descriptor structure for describing to the server the array or array slice to be read from or written to the database. It is presented to programmers in the C language API header file, `ibase.h`, located in the `../include` sub-directory of your Firebird installation.

Documentation

- The ***InterBase® 6 API Guide*** (ApiGuide.pdf), published by Borland Software Corp, provides detailed instructions for manipulating arrays through the API structures.
- More information about using arrays in embedded applications can be obtained from the ***Embedded SQL Guide*** (EmbedSql.pdf), a companion volume in the Borland set.

These documents can be downloaded from the archives at the IBPhoenix web site, at the URL *http://www.ibphoenix.com/resources/documents/attic*.

Limited DSQL Access

The following example is a simple demonstration of how a dynamic SQL application might get limited read access to an array slice through a stored procedure:

```
create procedure getcharslice(
  low_elem smallint, high_elem smallint)
returns (id integer, list varchar(50))
as
declare variable i smallint;
declare variable string varchar(10);
begin
    for select a1.ID from ARRAYS a1 into :id do
    begin
        i= low_elem;
        list = '';
```

```
            while (i <= high_elem) do
            begin
                select a2.CHARARRAY[:i] from arrays a2
                where  a2.ID = :id
                into :string;
                list = list||string;
                if (i < high_elem) then
                  list = list||',';
                i = i + 1;
            end
            suspend;
        end
    end
```

CHAPTER

10

DOMAINS

Domains in Firebird are akin to the concept of "user-defined data types". Although it is not possible to create a new data type, with a domain you can package a set of attributes with those of an existing data type, give it an identifier and, thereafter, use it in place of the data type parameter to define columns for any table.

Domain definitions are global to the database—all columns in any table which are defined with a particular domain will have completely identical attributes unless modified in the table definition by overrides.

Column-level overrides to domain attributes are discussed later in this chapter.

Columns based on a domain definition inherit all attributes of the domain, which can be:

- data type (required)
- a default value for inserts
- NULL status
- CHECK constraints
- character set (for character and text BLOB columns only)
- collation sequence (for character columns only)

You cannot apply referential integrity constraints to a domain.

Benefits of Using Domains

The benefits for encapsulating a data definition are obvious. For a simple but common example, suppose your design calls for a number of small tables where you want to store the text descriptions of enumerated sets—"type" tables—account types, product types, subscriptions types, etc. You have decided that each member of each of these sets will be keyed on a three-character upper-case identifier which points to a character field having a maximum of 25 characters.

All that is required is to create two domains:

- the domain for the pointer will be a CHAR(3) with two attributes added—a NOT NULL constraint because you are going to use it for primary and lookup keys and a CHECK constraint to enforce upper-case. For example,

```
CREATE DOMAIN Type_Key AS CHAR(3) NOT NULL
  CHECK (VALUE = UPPER(VALUE));
```

- the description domain will be a VARCHAR(25). You want it to be non-nullable because the tables you want to use it in are control tables:

```
CREATE DOMAIN Type_Description AS VARCHAR(25) NOT NULL
```

Once you have these domains defined, all of your type-lookup tables can have similar definitions; and all tables which store lookup keys to these tables will use the matching domain for the key column:

```
CREATE TABLE TRANSAC_TYPE (
  TRANSAC_TYPE TYPE_KEY,
  DESCRIPTION TYPE_DESCRIPTION
);
CREATE TABLE CURRENCY (
  CURRENCY_CODE TYPE_KEY,
  DESCRIPTION TYPE_DESCRIPTION,
  EXCHANGE_FACTOR DECIMAL(6,4)
);
```

Creating a Domain

The data definition language (DDL) syntax patternfor creating a domain is:

```
CREATE DOMAIN <domain-identifier> [AS] <data-type>
  [DEFAULT literal |NULL |USER}]
  [NOT NULL] [CHECK (<dom-search-condition>)]
  [CHARACTER SET {<character-set> | NONE}]
  [COLLATE collation];
```

Domain identifier

When you create a domain in the database, you must specify an identifier for the domain which is globally unique in the database. Developers often use a special prefix or subscript in domain identifiers, to facilitate self-documentation—the characters "D_" are suggested. For example,

```
CREATE DOMAIN D_TYPE_IDENTIFIER...
CREATE DOMAIN D_TYPE_DESCRIPTION...
```

Data type for the domain

The data type is the only other required attribute that must be set for the domain—all other attributes are optional. It specifies the SQL data type that will apply to column defined using the domain. Any Firebird native data type can be used.

The following statement creates a domain that defines an array of CHARACTER type:

```
CREATE DOMAIN DEPTARRAY AS CHAR(31) [4:5];
```

The next statement creates a BLOB domain with a text subtype that has an assigned character set: overriding the default character set of the database. It effectively creates a specialized memo type for storing Japanese text:

```
CREATE DOMAIN DESCRIPT_JP AS BLOB SUB_TYPE TEXT
  CHARACTER SET SJIS;
```

The DEFAULT attribute

A domain can define a default value that the server will use when inserting a new row if the INSERT statement does not include the column in its specification list. Defaults can save time and error during data entry. For example, a possible default for a DATE column could be today's date, or to write the CURRENT_USER context variable into a UserName column.

Values for DEFAULT can be:

a constant (literal): The default value is a user-specified string, numeric value, or date value—often used for placing a "zero value" into a non-nullable column

- CURRENT_TIMESTAMP, CURRENT_DATE, CURRENT_TIME or a Firebird predefined date literal—see Chapter 8, *Date and Time Types*
- USER, CURRENT_USER or CURRENT_ROLE (if roles are applicable)
- CURRENT_CONNECTION, CURRENT_TRANSACTION

It is possible to specify NULL as a default, but it is redundant, since nullable columns are initialized as NULL by default anyway. Furthermore, an explicit NULL default can cause conflicts when a column using the domain needs to be defined with a NOT NULL constraint (see below).

The following statement creates a domain that must have a positive value greater than 1,000. If the INSERT statement does not present a VALUE, the column will be assigned the default value of 9,999:

```
CREATE DOMAIN CUSTNO AS INTEGER
  DEFAULT 9999
  CHECK (VALUE > 1000);
```

If your operating system supports the use of multi-byte characters in user names, or you have used a multi-byte character set when defining roles, then any column into which these defaults will be stored must be defined using a compatible character set.

When defaults won't work

It is a common mistake to assume that a default value will be used whenever Firebird receives NULL in a defaulted column. When relying on defaults, it must be understood that a default will be applied

- only upon insertion of a new row AND
- only if the INSERT statement does not include the defaulted column in its column list

If your application includes the defaulted column in the INSERT statement and sends NULL in the values list, then NULL will be stored—or cause an exception in a non-nullable column—regardless of any default defined.

The NOT NULL attribute

Include this attribute in the domain if you want to force all columns created with this domain to contain a value.

NULL—which is not a *value*, but a *state*—will always be disallowed on any column bearing the NOT NULL attribute.

You cannot override the NOT NULL attribute on a domain but you can override a nullable domain definition when using it for a column definition. Consider the benefit of not including it in the domain's attributes, thereby leaving it as an option to add the attribute when columns are defined.

CHECK data conditions

The CHECK constraint provides wide scope for providing domain attributes that restrict the content of data which can be stored in columns using the domain. The CHECK constraint sets a search condition (dom-search-condition) that must be true before data can be accepted into these columns.

Syntax patterns for CHECK constraints

```
<dom-search-condition> =
  VALUE <operator> <val>
  | VALUE [NOT] BETWEEN <val> AND <val>
```

```
    | VALUE [NOT] LIKE <val> [ESCAPE <val>]
    | VALUE [NOT] IN (<val> [, <val> ...])
    | VALUE IS [NOT] NULL
    | VALUE [NOT] CONTAINING <val>
    | VALUE [NOT] STARTING [WITH] <val>
    |(<dom-search-condition>)
    |NOT <dom-search-condition>
    | <dom-search-condition> OR <dom-search-condition>
    | <dom-search-condition> AND <dom-search-condition>
<operator> ={=|<|>|<=|>=|!<|!>|<>|!=}
```

The VALUE keyword

VALUE is a placeholder for any constant or variable value or expression which would be submitted through SQL for storing in a column defined using the domain. The CHECK constraint causes VALUE to be validated against the restrictions defined in the conditions. If validation fails, an exception is raised.

If NULL is allowed in lieu of a value, it must be accommodated in the CHECK constraint. For example:

```
CHECK ((VALUE IS NULL) OR (VALUE > 1000));
```

The next statement creates a domain that disallows any input value of 1000 or less:

```
CREATE DOMAIN CUSTNO AS INTEGER
  CHECK (VALUE > 1000);
```

The next statement restricts VALUE to being one of four specific values:

```
CREATE DOMAIN PRODTYPE AS VARCHAR(8) NOT NULL
  CHECK (VALUE IN ('software', 'hardware', 'other', 'N/A'));
```

A validation condition can be made to search for a specific pattern in a string input. For example, the next validation check enforces a rule that requires a bracketed area code to precede telecom numbers, e.g. (02)43889474:

```
CREATE DOMAIN TEL_NUMBER AS VARCHAR(18)
  CHECK (VALUE LIKE '(0%)%');
```

Multiple CHECK conditions

A domain can have only one CHECK clause but multiple conditions can be ANDed or ORed within this single clause. Care is needed with bracketing the condition expressions to avoid getting logical exceptions when the DDL statement is prepared.

For example, this statement fails:

```
create domain rhubarb as varchar(20)
  check (value is not null) and (value starting with 'J');
```

It excepts with a "oken unknown" error upon the word "and". The corrected statement encloses the entire list of conditions within outer brackets and succeeds:

```
create domain rhubarb as varchar(20)
  check ((value is not null) and (value starting with 'J'));
```

The example above checks that the incoming value is not null. This is fine, but using the NOT NULL constraint directly is more powerful for application interfaces. The API can inform the client application at Prepare time of a NOT NULL constraint, whereas CHECK validation triggers do not fire until a DML request is actually posted to the server.

A domain's CHECK constraint cannot be overridden by one declared during column definition. However, a column can extend its use of the domain's CHECK constraint by adding its own CHECK conditions.

Dependencies in CHECK constraints

In tables, CHECK constraints can be defined legally with expressions referring to other columns in the same table or, less desirably, referring to columns in other database objects (tables, stored procedures).

Domains, of course, cannot refer to other domains. It is possible, although almost always unwise, to define a domain that refers to a column in an existing table. For example:

```
create domain rather_silly as char(3)
  check (value in (select substring(registration from 1 for 3)
  from aircraft));
```

Conceptually, it's not such a wild concept to use select expression in domains. Firebird allows it but it really does not follow through and implement it as an integrated design. It is an accidental by-product, not a feature.

As a database design approach, it integrates poorly with the referential integrity features that are purposefully implemented. Foreign key relationships enforce existence rules in all areas, whereas the scope of a CHECK constraint is limited to data entry.

CHECK constraints with inter-table dependencies would be disabled on restoring the database from a backup. They would silently fail to compile because the dependent tables had not yet been recreated. To put them back into effect, they would have to be reinstated manually, by some means. Implementing such checks at domain level has mind-boggling implications.

In some situations, where the dependency applies to a highly static table whose name is low in alphabetical sequence (*gbak* restores tables in alphabetical order), such a CHECK condition might be faintly arguable. The problem remains, that the domain has no control over what happens to data stored in tables beyond the event of checking the data coming into columns that use it.

There is also the possible future situation of wishing to extract SQL metadata scripts directly from the database (perhaps you lost the scripts used to create the database, or they have gone out of synch with the current database structure). In such situations it is very difficult for any automated extract procedure to produce a script with the correct sequence to rebuild the database structure.

If you absolutely need to use this kind of check condition, apply it as an extra condition when you declare the column. Preferably, evaluate all of the alternatives—including the hand-coding of referential triggers in cases where foreign keys on lookup fields would cause recognized problems with index selectivity.

The CHARSET/CHARACTER SET attribute

For systems that need to be concerned about multiple character sets inside a single database, declaring character-set-specific domains for all of your text columns (CHAR, VARCHAR, BLOB SUB_TYPE 1 and arrays of character types) can be a very elegant way to deal with it. Refer to Chapter 9, ***Character Types***, for character set definition syntax.

The COLLATE attribute

A COLLATE clause in a domain creation statement specifies an explicit collation sequence for CHAR or VARCHAR domains. You must choose a collation that is supported for the domain's declared, inherited or implied character set.

Refer to the previous chapter for COLLATE definition syntax. For a list of the collation sequences available for each character set, see Appendix VI, *Character Sets and Collations*.

Using a Domain

A domain can be used in place of a native data type in any column definition and it is the recommended way to design your data. From v.2.1 forward, you can also apply domain definitions to the declaration of variables in procedural SQL (PSQL) modules.

Domains in Column Definitions

The best way to illustrate the use of a domain in a column definition is with an example. In a certain database, SYSUSER is a domain of up to 31 characters, having a DEFAULT value which is to be obtained by reading the context variable CURRENT_USER:

```
CREATE DOMAIN SYSUSER AS VARCHAR(31) DEFAULT CURRENT_USER;
```

A table is defined, having a column UPDATED_BY which uses this SYSUSER domain:

```
CREATE TABLE LOANS (
  LOAN_DATE DATE,
  UPDATED_BY SYSUSER,
  LOAN_FEE DECIMAL(15,2)
);
```

A client submits an INSERT statement for the LOANS table:

```
INSERT INTO ORDERS (LOAN_DATE, LOAN_FEE)
    VALUES ('16-MAY-2014', 10.75);
```

Because the statement does not name the UPDATED_BY column in its column list, Firebird automatically inserts the user name of the current user, ALICEFBIRD:

```
SELECT * FROM LOANS;
```

returns

```
16-MAY-2014 ALICEFBIRD    10.75
```

Domain overrides

Columns defined using a domain can override some attributes inherited from the domain, by replacing an inherited attribute with an equivalent attribute clause. The column definition can also be extended by adding further attributes.

Table 11.1 shows which domain attributes can be overridden.

Table 10.1 Domain attributes and column overrides

Attribute	Override?	Notes
Data type	No	
DEFAULT	Yes	
CHARACTER SET	Yes	Can also be used to revert a column to database default
COLLATE	Yes	
CHECK	No	Use a regular CHECK clause in CREATE or ALTER TABLE statement to extend CHECK clause with more conditions
NOT NULL	No	If you want to be able to have a domain nullable in some usages and non-nullable in others, let the domain default to nullable and apply NOT NULL as a column override during CREATE or ALTER TABLE

The following example shows how to extend the attributes of a column that is being defined to use a domain, using an earlier domain definition example:

```
CREATE DOMAIN TEL_NUMBER AS VARCHAR(18)
  CHECK (VALUE LIKE '(0%)%');
```

Let's say we want to define a table having a telecom number column in it. We want the domain's attributes but we also want to allow for telephone numbers where keypad mnemonics have been used to express some numerals as alphabetic characters. For this usage we want to ensure that any non-numeral characters are input in upper case:

```
CREATE TABLE LIBRARY_USER (
    USER_ID INTEGER NOT NULL.
    ... <other columns>,
    PHONE_NO TEL_NUMBER,
    CONSTRAINT CHK_TELNUM_UPPER
        CHECK (PHONE_NO = UPPER(PHONE_NO))
  );
```

Now, we have an extra CHECK validation on this particular column. This statement

```
INSERT INTO LIBRARY_USER (USER_ID, PHONE_NO)
  VALUES (99, '(02) 4388 wish');
```

fails, because the extra CHECK constraint requires the phone number to be '(02) 4388 WISH'.

Domains in PSQL Variable Declarations

From Firebird 2.0 onward you can a domain in place of a native data type when declaring arguments and variables in procedural language (PSQL)—stored procedures, triggers and code blocks for use in EXECUTE BLOCK passages. The argument can be declared one of two ways. According to your requirements, you can declare the argument or variable using either

—the domain identifier alone, in lieu of the native data type identifier, to have the variable inherit all of the attributes of the domain; or

—the data type of the domain, without inheriting any CHECK constraints or DEFAULT value defined in the domain, by including the TYPE OF keyword in the declaration

The syntax pattern for declarations is:

```
data-type ::= <native-data-type> | <domain-name> | TYPE OF <domain_name>
```

Examples

Using our TEL_NUMBER domain from previous examples:

```
CREATE DOMAIN TEL_NUMBER AS VARCHAR(18)
  CHECK (VALUE LIKE '(0%)%');
```

Our (somewhat fatuous!) example shows how to declare two input variables, TEL_NO1 and TEL_NO2, two local variables, V1 and V2, and two output variables, OUT1 and OUT2, using both options. TEL_NO1 and V1 use the complete domain definition and expect the input variable to include the bracketed area prefix, while TEL_NO2 and V2 expect nothing other than a string of up to 18 characters:

```
CREATE PROCEDURE MYPROC (
  TEL_NO1 TEL_NUMBER,
  TEL_NO2 TYPE OF TEL_NUMBER)
RETURNS (
  OUT1 TEL_NUMBER,
  OUT2 TYPE OF TEL_NUMBER)
AS
DECLARE VARIABLE V1 TEL_NUMBER;
DECLARE VARIABLE V2 TYPE OF TEL_NUMBER;
BEGIN
...
END
```

The feature is not supported if you are operating on a database whose on-disk structure is less than 11.1.

Databases of ODS 11.1 or more include a column named RDB$VALID_BLR in the system tables RDB$PROCEDURES and RDB$TRIGGERS to indicate whether the module's stored binary language representation is valid after an ALTER DOMAIN operation. Its value is displayed in the SHOW PROCEDURE and SHOW TRIGGER outputs in isql versions 2.1 and higher.

Using Domains with CAST()

In the "2" series and onward, you can use a CAST() expression to convert a column or an expression to the data type of a domain, in lieu of a native data type.

The syntax pattern is:

```
CAST (<expression> AS TYPE OF <domain-name>)
```

As with its application to PSQL variable declarations, conversion to TYPE OF applies just the underlying data type. Casting using the singular TYPE keyword is not supported in current versions.

Example Using our TEL_NUMBER domain again:

```
CAST :Input_Number as TYPE OF TEL_NUMBER
```

will take a parameter of up to 18 characters or digits.

Where domains won't work

A domain cannot be used

- with the CAST (aValue AS <another type>) function in versions prior to the '2' series
- to define the data type of the elements of an ARRAY. A domain can itself be an ARRAY type, however.
- to declare the type of an argument or variable in a trigger or stored procedure in Firebird servers older than v.2.1 and databases with on-disk structure version lower than 11.1.

Defining a BOOLEAN Domain

Up to and including release 2.5, Firebird does not provide a Boolean type. A Boolean-styled domain is ideal, because you can define attributes that will be consistent across all tables. It is recommended to use the smallest possible data type: a CHAR for T[rue]/F[alse] or Y[es]/N[o] switches or a SMALLINT 1/0 pairing. The following examples suggest ways you might implement your Booleans.

Example 1: a two-phase switch that defaults to `'F'` (false):

```
CREATE DOMAIN D_BOOLEAN AS CHAR
  DEFAULT 'F' NOT NULL
  CHECK(VALUE IN ('T', 'F'));
```

Example 2: a three-phase switch that allows UNKNOWN (i.e. NULL):

```
CREATE DOMAIN D_LOGICAL AS SMALLINT
  CHECK (VALUE IS NULL OR VALUE IN (1,0));
```

Example 3: a three-phase switch that represents UNKNOWN as a value:

```
CREATE DOMAIN D_GENDER AS CHAR(4)
  DEFAULT 'N/K' NOT NULL
  CHECK (VALUE IN ('FEM', 'MASC', 'N/K'));
```

Don't use BOOLEAN, UNKNOWN, TRUE or FALSE as names for your Boolean domains. They are either already reserved words in Firebird or are likely to become so in a future version.

Changing a Domain Definition

The DDL statement ALTER DOMAIN can be used to change any aspect of an existing domain except its NOT NULL setting. Changes that you make to a domain definition affect all column definitions based on the domain that have not been overridden at the table level.

Whether altering a domain is a desirable thing to do is your decision. However, keep in mind that every definition or declaration in the database that uses that domain is a dependency on it. It may much more of a major work to remove the dependencies than to define an entirely new domain and use ALTER TABLE ALTER COLUMN statements to switch the columns to the new domain.

Existing data are not changed by ALTER DOMAIN. For some changes, it is often essential to run an update over the tables afterwards to update the existing data so that it will be consistent with new data that will be created under the new rules.

A domain can be altered by its creator, the SYSDBA user or any user with operating system root privileges.

*On Windows, "users with operating system root privileges" refers to Windows users with the optional escalated privileges (RDB$ADMIN role) granted on the database, on a server that is configured, via `firebird.conf`, for trusted or mixed **Authentication**. It is applicable only to versions 2.1+ and needs to be explicitly provisioned.*

Using ALTER DOMAIN you can:

- Rename the domain (if it has no dependencies)
- Modify the data type
- Drop an existing default value.
- Set a new default value.
- Drop an existing CHECK constraint.
- Add a new CHECK constraint.

The only way to "change" the NOT NULL setting of a domain is to drop the domain and recreate it with the desired combination of features.

The syntax pattern is:

```
ALTER DOMAIN { name | old_name TO new_name }{
[SET DEFAULT {literal | NULL | USER | etc.}]
| [DROP DEFAULT]
| [ADD [CONSTRAINT] CHECK (<match_conditions>)]
| [DROP CONSTRAINT]
|TYPE data_type
};
```

Examples of valid changes to domains

This statement sets a new default value for the BOOK_GROUP domain:

```
ALTER DOMAIN BOOK_GROUP SET DEFAULT -1;
```

In this statement, the name of the BOOK_GROUP domain is changed to PUBL_GROUP:

```
ALTER DOMAIN BOOK_GROUP TO PUBL_GROUP;
```

Constraints on altering data types

The TYPE clause of ALTER DOMAIN allows the data type to be changed to another, permitted data type. For permitted type conversions, refer to the topic *Changing column and domain definitions* in Chapter 6, especially the table *Valid data type conversions using ALTER COLUMN and ALTER DOMAIN*.

Any type conversion that could result in data loss is disallowed. For example, the number of characters in a domain could not be made smaller than the size of the largest value in any column that uses it.

Converting a numeric data type to a character type requires a minimum length for the character type that can accommodate all of the characters "created" by conversion of the highest possible number. For example, The following statement changes the data type of a BIGINT domain, BOOK_ISBN, to VARCHAR(19), in order to accommodate the maximum number of digits in a BIGINT:

```
ALTER DOMAIN BOOK_ISBN TYPE VARCHAR(19);
```

Dropping a Domain

DROP DOMAIN removes an existing domain definition from a database, provided the domain is not currently used for any column definition in the database.

To avoid exceptions, use ALTER TABLE to drop any table columns using the domain before executing DROP DOMAIN. The best way to do this in a single task is with a DDL script. You can read more about DDL scripts in Chapter 24..

A domain can be dropped by its creator, the SYSDBA user or (on Linux/UNIX) any user with operating system root privileges. The syntax pattern is:

```
DROP DOMAIN <domain-name>
```

The following statement deletes an unwanted domain:

```
DROP DOMAIN rather_silly;
```

PART III

A Database & Its Objects

CHAPTER

11

DESIGNING AND DEFINING A DATABASE

A database, of course, stores data. However, data alone have no use unless they are stored according to some rules that, first, capture their meaning and value and, next, allow them to be retrieved consistently. A database having an existence within the context of a database management system (DBMS), such as Firebird, comprises a lot of "things" besides data.

Firebird is a *relational* database management system. As such, it is intended to support the creation and maintenance of abstract data structures, not just to store data but also to maintain relationships and to optimize the speed and consistency with which requested data can be retrieved and returned to SQL client applications.

Designing a Database

Although relational databases are very flexible, the only way to guarantee data integrity and satisfactory database performance is a solid database design—there is no built-in protection against poor design decisions. A good database design:

Satisfies the users' content requirements for the database. Before you can design the database, you must do extensive research on the requirements of the users and how the database will be used. The most flexible database designs today evolve during a well-managed process of analysis, prototyping and testing that involves all of the people who will use it.

Ensures the consistency and integrity of the data. When you design a table, you define certain attributes and constraints that restrict what a user or an application can enter into the table and its columns. By validating the data before it is stored in the table, the database enforces the rules of the data model and preserves data integrity.

Provides a natural, easy-to-understand structuring of information. Good design makes queries easier to understand, so users are less likely to introduce inconsistencies into the data, or to be forced to enter redundant data. .

Satisfies the users' performance requirements. Good database design ensures better performance. If tables are allowed to be too large (wide), or if there are too many (or too few) indexes, long waits can result. If the database is very large with a high volume of transactions, performance problems resulting from poor design are magnified.

Insulates the system from design mistakes in subsequent development cycles.

Description and analysis

A database abstractly represents a world of organization, relationships, rules and processes. Before reaching the point of being capable of designing the structures and rules for the database, the analyst-designer has much to do, working with people involved to identify the real-life structures, rules and requirements from which the database design will be rendered. The importance of scrupulous description and analysis can not be over-emphasized.

Logical data analysis is an iterative process of refining and distilling the world of inputs, tasks and outputs whose scope is to be encompassed by the database. Large, haphazard structures of information are reduced progressively to smaller, more specialized data objects and are gradually mapped to a data model.

An important part of this reduction process involves ***normalization***—splitting out groups of data items with the goal of establishing essential relationships, eliminating redundancies and associating connected items of data in structures that can be manipulated efficiently.

This phase can be one of the most challenging tasks for the database designer, especially in environments where the business has been attuned to operating with spreadsheets and desktop databases. Regrettably, even in established client/server environments, too many poorly-performing, corruption-prone databases are found to have been "designed" using reports and spreadsheets as the basis.

Data model <> database

The "world" which evolves during description and analysis provides a logical blueprint for your data structures. It is a "given" that the logical model should discover every relationship and set. It is usually a mistake—and a trap inherent in many CASE tools—to translate the data model blindly into a database schema. In sophisticated data management systems like Firebird, a table structure does not always represent the optimal object from which data should be retrieved. Queries, views, global temporary tables (GTTs), calculated columns and "selectable" stored procedures are just a few of the retrieval and storage mechanisms available that will influence how you implement the model in the physical design.

Even an excellent data model will lack flexibility and will under-perform if it does not take into account the power and economy of the server's dynamic capabilities. Dynamic structures for the selection and manipulation of data are the arteries of a client/server database.

One database or many?

A single Firebird server can control multiple databases within the physical filesystem that is its host. It is not unusual in large enterprises to run multiple databases serving separated divisional subsystems. Because one database is not aware of the objects and dependencies in another, it takes careful design, planning and balancing of system resources and network services to integrate these independent systems. Typically, such databases are synchronized periodically by a replication system.

When designing, bear in mind that Firebird does not support queries that join or union tables across database boundaries. However, it does support simultaneous queries across multiple databases within one single transaction, with two-phase commit. It is thus possible for applications to accomplish tasks that work with data images from two or more databases and perform DML on one database using data read from another. For more details about cross-database transactions and two-phase commit, refer to Chapter 27, ***Programming with Transactions***.

The Physical Objects

The time to start thinking about the physical design is when—and only when—the business of describing the requirements and identifying the data required and the processes they will be subject to is done.

Tables

A database table is usually visualized as a two-dimensional block consisting of columns (the vertical dimension) and rows (the horizontal dimension). The storage attributes of individual items of data are specified in columns—usually related to or dependent upon one another in some way—and rows. A table can have any number of rows (limit to 2^{32} for databases with and ODS lower than 11), or even no rows at all. Although every row in one table shares the specification of its columns with every other row, rows do not depend on other rows in the same table.

Firebird does support techniques for implementing self-referencing tables—row structures which enforce dependencies between rows within the same table. For details, refer to the topic Tree Structures in Chapter 15.

Files and pages

If you are moving to Firebird from a database system that implements tables by physically tabulating columns and rows in the file system, Firebird may bring some surprises. In Firebird, all data belonging to a single database are stored in one file, or set of linked files that is logically one file. In multi-file databases, there is no correlation between any specific database object and a particular member of the database file-set.

Within the boundaries of the file, the Firebird server engine manages evenly-sized blocks of disk known as ***database pages***. It manages several different page "types", according to the types of data it needs to store: regular columns for tables (data pages), BLOBs (blob pages) and indexes (index pages), for example. The engine allocates fresh blocks to itself from the host filesystem as required. All pages are the same size, regardless of type. ***Page size*** can be specified in the CREATE DATABASE statement, if you want a size larger or smaller than the default 4KB. It cannot be altered except by backing up the database and reconstructing it with a new page size, using the *gbak* utility.

Unlike the file-based data management systems, Firebird does not maintain table data in a tabulated format at all. Rows from one table may not be stored contiguously with other rows from the same table. Indeed, row data for a single table may be distributed among several files and several disks. The engine uses various types of ***inventory pages*** to store information about the physical locations of rows belonging to each table.

Columns and fields

Abstractly, a column is a constellation of attributes, defining the data item that can be stored in one specific cell location in the left-to-right structure of a table's row. However, columns don't just exist in tables in the database. Each time a query is submitted to the database engine for processing, that query specifies a set of columns and one or more operations to be carried out on those columns. The columns do not have to be in the same left-to-right order as is defined for them in the table. For example, the statement

```
SELECT FIELD3, FIELD1, FIELD2 FROM ATABLE;
```

will output a set in the column order specified in the query. The query may specify columns from multiple tables, through joins, subqueries and unions. It may define columns that do not exist in the database at all, by computing them or even just by specifying them as named constants.

Some people use the term *field* when referring to a column, e.g. "I have a table TABLE1 which has three fields." Relational database textbooks often discourage the use of "field" as a substitute for "column", some preferring to use "field" to mean "the value in the column" or "the reference to a column".

In this book, "field" is used only as a term to generalize the concepts of column, argument and local variable; and to refer to output items that are constructed at run-time. "Column" is used to refer to the physical columns defined for tables.

Keys

Keys are the "glue" of relationships between tables.

The primary key

An essential part of the database design process is to abstract the logical model of the database to the point where, for each table, there is a single, unique column or composite column structure that distinguishes each row from every other row in the table. This unique column or column combination is the logical primary key. When you implement your physical model, you use the PRIMARY KEY constraint to tell the data management system which column or columns form this unique identifying structure. You may define only one PRIMARY KEY constraint per table. Syntax is discussed in Chapter 15, in the topic *Constraints*.

Other unique keys

It can happen in your data modeling process that, for various reasons, you end up with more than one unique column or structure in a table. For enforcing the required uniqueness on such columns or structures, Firebird provides the optional UNIQUE key constraint. It is effectively an alternative primary key and can be used in lieu of the primary key at times, if required.

Foreign keys

The "glue" that makes a relational database "relational" is foreign keys. This is the column or column structure that shows up in your data model on the "many" side of a one-to-many relationship. In the physical design, a foreign key matches up with the column or column structure of the primary key of the table on the "one" side of the relationship.

For example, in the following simple model, the detail lines of an order are linked to the order header by the ORDER NUMBER key.

Figure 11.1 Simple relational link

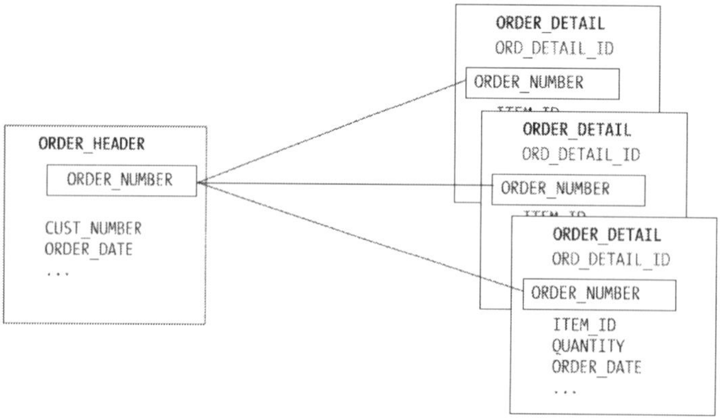

This model requires that each header row have a unique ORDER_NUMBER and that at least one order detail row exists for each order header row. Other rules may apply to the existence and linking. Firebird provides powerful trigger procedure capabilities for setting, conditioning and applying rules to relationships. Additionally, it can automate many of the typical rules governing relationships, using the FOREIGN KEY constraint with its optional action arguments. Underlying this constraint are system-generated referential integrity triggers. Firebird's referential integrity support is discussed briefly below and in detail in Chapter 17, *Referential Integrity*.

Making keys atomic

An important tenet of good relational database design is ***keys atomicity***. In the context of primary and foreign keys, atomicity means that no key should have any meaning as data: it should have no other role or function except to be a key.

The column that your analysis determines to be the primary key, or an element of the primary key, almost always stores a data item that has some meaning. Take, for example, a table storing personal details:

```
CREATE TABLE PERSON (
    FIRST_NAME VARCHAR(30) NOT NULL,
    LAST_NAME VARCHAR(50) NOT NULL,
    PHONE_NUMBER VARCHAR(18) NOT NULL,
    ADDRESS_1 VARCHAR(50),
  ...);
```

The designer decides that the combination (FIRST_NAME, LAST_NAME, PHONE_NUMBER) is a good candidate for the primary key. People do share phone numbers but it is extremely unlikely that two people with identical first and last names would share the same number, right? So, the designer does this:

```
ALTER TABLE PERSON
    ADD CONSTRAINT PK_PERSON(LAST_NAME, FIRST_NAME, PHONE_NUMBER);
```

The first problem with this primary key is that every element of the primary has meaning. Every element is maintained by humans and may change or be misspelt. The two keys ('Smith', 'Mary', '43889474') and ('SMITH', 'Mary', '43889474') are not the same and will both be capable of being stored in this table. Which record gets changed if Mary gets married or changes her phone number?

The second problem is that this complex key has to be propagated, as a foreign key, to any tables that are dependent on PERSON. Not only is the integrity of the relationship at risk through alterations or errors in the data, it is a broad channel—potentially 98 characters—across which to implement the foreign key relationship.

Mandatory indexes are created to enforce keys. The real showstopper may occur if index key columns use multi-byte character sets or non-binary collations. Index widths are limited to one quarter of the database page size, or even to as little as 253 bytes if you are still using an old ODS 10 or 10.1 database. It is possible that such a key will be impossible because it is simply too wide.

Surrogate keys

The solution is to add an extra column to tables to accommodate an artificial or surrogate primary key: a unique, narrow column, preferably system-generated, that replaces (surrogates) the function of the theoretical primary key. Firebird provides GENERATOR objects, which can be implemented to maintain the required unique series of BIGINT numbers—a primary key of a mere 8 bytes or less.

A common technique for using generators to implement an auto-incrementing primary key, untouched by human hand, is described in the chapter entitled ***Triggers*** in ***The Firebird Book Second Edition*** and in the companion volume to this, Volume 2: ***Developing with Firebird Data***.

The atomicity of keys should be enforced in applications by hiding them from users or, at least, making them read-only.

Surrogate keys vs natural keys – summary

Database developers tend to take strong positions in the arguments for and against using artificial keys. The author's position in favour of atomicity is probably evident. However, in the interest of fairness, the arguments are summarized here in Table 12.1.

Table 11.1 Surrogate (artificial) keys vs natural keys

Feature	Pro	Con
Atomicity	Surrogate keys carry no meaning as data and never change	Natural keys are inherently unstable because they are subject to human error and externally-imposed changes
Convenience	Natural keys carry information, reducing the necessity to perform joins or follow-up reads to retrieve data in context Natural keys are easier to use with interactive query tools	Surrogate keys carry no information beyond their linking function, necessitating joins or subqueries to retrieve the associated "meaningful" data
Key size	Surrogate keys are compact	Natural keys are characteristically large and often escalate into compound keys that complicate querying and schema
Navigation	Surrogate keys provide clean, fast-tracking "navigation by code"	Natural keys are generally unsuitable for code-style navigation because of case, collation, denormalization and size issues
Normalization	Surrogate keys can be normalized throughout the database	Natural keys tend toward complexity, propagating denormalized data to foreign keys

Should you design databases with a mix of natural and artificial keys? The extreme view is to advise a consistent design approach—choose natural or artificial and apply the rule without exception. Yet a more moderate approach may offer the best of both worlds. It may be realistic to use a natural key for stable lookup or "control" tables that rarely change, are never required to participate in compound key structures and appear often in output.

When designing keys for a Firebird database, be reminded that keys are enforced by indexes and indexes have a size limit. Be aware that compounding, collation sequences and multi-byte international character sets reduce the number of characters of actual data that can be accommodated in an index.

Keys are not indexes

Keys are table-level constraints. The database engine responds to constraint declarations by creating a number of metadata objects for enforcing them. For primary keys and unique constraints, it creates a unique index on the column(s) assigned to the constraint. For foreign keys, it creates a non-unique index on the assigned columns, stores records for the dependency and creates triggers to implement the actions.

- The keys are the constraints
- The indexes are required to enforce the constraints

You should not create indexes of your own that duplicate the indexes created by the system to enforce constraints. This is such an important precaution from the performance perspective that it is reiterated in several places in this book. The topic Dropping an Index in Chapter 16 explains why duplicating these indexes can wreck the performance of queries.

Referential integrity

Accidental altering or deletion of rows that have dependencies will corrupt the integrity of your data. Referential integrity, generally, is a qualitative expression that describes the degree to which dependencies in a database are protected from corruption. However, in the context of this book, it refers to the inbuilt mechanisms for enforcing foreign key relationships and performing the desired actions when the primary key of a master row is changed or the row is deleted.

The syntax and implications of Firebird's formal referential integrity constraints are discussed in detail in Chapter 17.

Indexes and query plans

Indexes provide the database with navigational aids for searching large amounts of data and quickly assessing the best way to retrieve the sets requested by clients. Good indexing speeds things up, missing or bad indexes will slow down searches, joins and sorting.

As a relational database management engine, Firebird can link almost any column object to almost any other column object—the exceptions being the various BLOB types, including ARRAYS—by reference to their identifiers. However, as the numbers of rows, linking columns and tables in a query increase, so performance tends to slow down.

When columns that are searched, joined or sorted are indexed in useful ways, performance in terms of execution time and resource usage can be dramatically improved. It must also be said that poor indexing can hurt performance!

Firebird uses optimization algorithms that are largely cost-based. In preparing a submitted query, the optimizer calculates the relative costs of choosing or ignoring available indexes and returns a query plan to the client, reporting its choices. Although it is possible to design and submit your own plan to the optimizer—an important feature in RDBMS engines that use rule-based optimization—as a general rule the Firebird optimizer knows best. Custom plans tend to be most useful in detecting and eliminating problem indexes.

Index design and creation are discussed in Chapter 16.

Views

Firebird provides the capability to create and store pre-defined query specifications, known as views, which can be treated in most ways just as though they were tables. A view is a class of derived table that stores no data. For many tasks—especially those where access to certain columns in the underlying tables needs to be denied or where a single query specification cannot deliver the required degree of abstraction—views solve difficult problems.

Views and other types of run-time sets are discussed in Chapter 23.

Stored procedures and triggers

Stored procedures and triggers are modules of compiled, executable code that are executed on the server. The source code is a set of SQL language extensions known as procedural SQL, or PSQL.

Stored procedures can be executable or selectable. They can take input arguments and return output sets. Executable procedures execute completely on the server and optionally return a single-row set (a "singleton") of constants on completion. Selectable procedures generate multiple-row sets of zero or more rows, which can be used by client applications in most ways like any other output set.

Triggers are a specialized form of PSQL module, which can be declared to execute at one or more of six stage/operation phases—before and after inserting, updating and deleting—during a data manipulation (DML) operation on the table that owns them. Clusters of triggers can be defined for each phase, to execute in a defined sequence. From release 1.5 forward, the behavior for any or all DML operations can be combined, with conditions, in a single "before" or "after" trigger module. Triggers do not accept input arguments nor return output sets.

Stored procedures can call other stored procedures. Triggers can call stored procedures that, in turn, can call other stored procedures. Triggers cannot be called from a client application nor from a stored procedure.

PSQL provides mechanisms for exception handling and callback events. Any number of exception messages can be defined as objects in the database using CREATE EXCEPTION statements. Callback events are created inside the PSQL module and applications can set up structures to "listen" for them.

For detailed discussion of writing and using PSQL modules, exceptions and events, refer to Part Six, ***Programming on the Server***.

Generators (Sequences)

Generators—also known as sequences—are ideal for using to populate an automatically incrementing unique key or a stepping serial number column or other series. When Firebird generates a value in a series from a generator or sequence, that number can never be generated again in the same series.

Generators are declared in a database using a CREATE statement, just like any other database object.

```
CREATE GENERATOR AGenerator;
```

or

```
CREATE SEQUENCE ASequence;
```

A generator is a sequence is a generator—they are fully interchangeable. However, the syntaxes from this point on are not parallel. Using the SEQUENCE syntax is preferred because its compliance with standards should provide a benefit in interoperability with other database engines.

Generators can be set to any starting value:

```
SET GENERATOR AGenerator TO 1;
```

or

```
ALTER SEQUENCE Asequence RESTART WITH <new-value>
```

There are strong caveats against resetting generators once a series is in use—see below.

Calling for the next value

To call for the next value, either

- invoke the SQL function `GEN_ID(GeneratorName, n)`, where GeneratorName is the name of the generator and n is BIGINT (or, in dialect 1, an integer), specifying the size of the step. The query

  ```
  SELECT GEN_ID(AGenerator, 2) from RDB$DATABASE;
  ```

  returns a number that is two greater than the last generated number and increments the current value of the generator to the value it just generated.

- use a NEXT VALUE FOR operation on the sequence. For example, the following snippet from a trigger pulls the next value from the same generator used in the first method:

  ```
  new.thing_id = NEXT VALUE FOR AGenerator;
  ```

NEXT VALUE FOR does not support a step (increment) other than 1. If your requirement calls for a different step increment, use the GEN_ID function.

Current value of a generator

```
SELECT GEN_ID(AGenerator, 0) from RDB$DATABASE;
```

returns the current value of the generator, without incrementing it. Since NEXT VALUE FOR does not allow a step value, there is no parallel SEQUENCE syntax to obtain this information.

Populating a variable

PSQL, Firebird's programming language, allows a value to be generated directly into a variable:

```
...
DECLARE VARIABLE MyVar BIGINT;
...
MyVar = GEN_ID(AGenerator, 1);
```

or

```
MyVar = NEXT VALUE FOR AGenerator'
```

More details about using generators in PSQL modules—especially triggers—can be found in Chapters 29 and 30.

Using GEN_ID() for negative stepping

The step argument of GEN_ID(..) can be negative. Thus, it is possible to set or reset a generator's current value by passing a negative argument as either an integer constant or an integer expression. This capability is sometimes used as a "trick" for meddling with generator values in PSQL, since PSQL does not allow DDL commands such as SET GENERATOR.

For example, the statement

```
SELECT
  GEN_ID(AGenerator,
  ((SELECT GEN_ID(AGenerator, 0) from RDB$DATABASE) * -1)
from RDB$DATABASE;
```

causes the generator to be reset to zero.

Caveats about resetting generator values

The general rule of thumb about resetting generator values in production databases—whether through SQL, PSQL or some Admin interface—is DON'T.

The benefit of generator values is that they are guaranteed to be unique. Unlike any other user-accessible operation in Firebird, generators operate outside transaction control. Once generated, a number is "gone" and cannot be reverted by transaction rollback. This absolutely assures the integrity of number sequences, provided the generators are not tampered with.

Reserve the resetting of generators in a production database for the rare circumstances where a design requirement calls for it. For example, some older-style accounting systems pass journals into history tables with new primary keys, empty the journal table and reset the primary key sequence to zero; or, in multi-site organizations, separated ranges of key values are allocated to each site in "chunks" to ensure key integrity on replication.

Never reset generators in an attempt to correct bugs or input errors or to "fill gaps" in a sequence.

Object Naming Conventions

The following conventions and associated limitations on naming database objects must be observed:

- Start each name with an alphabetic character (A–Z or a–z).
- Restrict object names to 31 characters. Some objects, such as constraint names, are restricted to 27 bytes in length when the on-disk structure is lower than 11.
- Allowable characters for database file names—as with all metadata objects in Firebird—include dollar signs ($), underscores (_), 0 to 9, A to Z, and a to z..
- Observe uniqueness requirements within a database:
- In all cases, objects of the same type—all tables, for example—must be unique.
- Column identifiers must be unique within a table. All other object identifiers must be unique within the database.
- Avoid the use of reserved words, spaces, diacritic characters and any characters that fall beyond the 7-bit range:
  - In dialect 1, they cannot be used at all.
  - In dialect 3 you can delimit "illegal" identifiers using pairs of double-quote symbols. Details follow.

A full list of reserved words, version by version, is in Appendix II.

Optional SQL-92 delimited identifiers

In Dialect 3 databases, Firebird supports the ANSI SQL convention for optionally delimiting identifiers. To use reserved words, diacritic characters, case-sensitive strings, or embedded spaces in an object name, enclose the name in double quotes. It is then a delimited identifier. Delimited identifiers must always be referenced in double quotes.

Names enclosed in double quotes are case sensitive. For example:

```
SELECT "CodAR" FROM "MyTable"
```

is different from:

```
SELECT "CODAR" FROM "MYTABLE"
```

To quote or not to quote

The double-quoting convention for object identifiers was introduced in dialect 3 for compliance with standards. To those who have been used to the global case-insensitivity of other database systems, the feature is at best confusing and at worst exasperating.

If you define objects with double-quotes, you must use them everywhere and every time with double-quotes and perfect case-matching. Most experienced Firebird developers recommend avoiding them, except in the occasional cases where you are stuck with using an "illegal" identifier. The choice is yours.

The case-matching exception

If you have double-quoted identifiers in all-uppercase, you can use them in SQL without the quotes and treat them as case-insensitive. The ability to do this comes from the way identifiers are stored in the internal schema tables and the sequence that the engine follows to resolve them during retrieval.

Most GUI database administration tools for Firebird provide the option to apply quoted identifiers automatically to all identifiers. One or two of these tools actually apply quoted identifiers by default to all database objects. Unless you have a strong reason to do this, it is recommended that you look for the 'OFF switch' and avoid quoted identifiers.

Dialect 1 In a dialect 1 database, reserved words, diacritic characters and embedded spaces in an object name are not permitted. You will get an exception if you try to use the double-quoting convention and case-sensitive identifiers are not supported.

File-naming Conventions for Databases

The established convention for naming Firebird database files on any platform is to apply the three-character suffix ".fdb" to the primary file and to name secondary files ".f01", ".f02", etc. This is only a convention—a Firebird database file can have any extension, or no extension at all.

Because of known problems on Windows servers, involving the SystemRestore feature actively targeting files with the suffix ".gdb", developers are advised to change the traditional InterBase file suffix when migrating these databases to Firebird.

The name of the security database—`security2.fdb` since v.2.0, `security.fdb` in v.1.5.x and `isc4.gdb` in release 1.0.x—must not be changed. Unfortunately, Firebird 1.0.x requires the ".gdb" suffix and there is no workaround for it.

Metadata

Collectively, objects defined within a database are known as its metadata or, more traditionally, its schema. The process of creating and modifying metadata is referred to as data definition. The term "data definition" is often also applied to the description of a single object and its attributes.

The system tables

Firebird stores metadata in a set of tables which it creates right inside the database—the system tables. All system tables have identifiers beginning with "RDB$". For example, the table which stores the definitions and other information about all of the table structures in your database is called RDB$RELATIONS. A related table, RDB$RELATION_FIELDS, stores information and definitions for the columns of each table.

This "database within a database" is highly normalized. DDL statements are designed to perform operations on the metadata tables safely and in full cognisance of the cascading effects.

It is possible to alter the data in the system tables by performing regular SQL operations on them. Some admin tools, such as *isql* and *gfix*, do internally change data in the system tables. However, as a sophisticated database management system, Firebird was not designed with raw end-user manipulation of the system tables in mind.

Any human intervention is likely to cause unpredictable types of damage. It cannot be stressed enough how important it is to treat DML on the system tables as a minefield. From Firebird 3 onward, the tables will be read-only.

SELECT queries on the system tables are fine and can be very useful for listing out things like character sets, dependencies and so on. For full schema of the system tables, refer to Appendix V.

Firebird's SQL Language

An SQL statement is used to submit a query to the database. The language of the query is expressed in statements that specify purpose: what is to be done (an operation), the objects to which it is to be done and the details of how it is to be done.. In theory, every possible interaction between the outside world and a database is surfaced through an SQL statement of some kind.

Statement syntaxes are grouped according to two broad purposes:

1. Those that CREATE, ALTER or DROP metadata objects (also known as schema objects or schema elements). Such queries are referred to as data definition language, or DDL.
2. Those that operate on data. They provide language for defining sets of data in columns and rows and specifying operations to
   - retrieve and transform (SELECT) images of those sets from storage for reading by applications
   - change the state of the database by adding, modifying or deleting the specified sets (INSERT, UPDATE and DELETE operations).

   These statements that operate on data are referred to as data manipulation language, or DML.

The Firebird implementation of the SQL language falls into a number of overlapping subsets, each used for a specific purpose and incorporating its own language elements:

Dynamic SQL (DSQL)—the subset in most common use today, it is used by all database interface layers that communicate with the server through the Application Programming Interface (API). It comprises all DDL and DML statements and their syntaxes.

Procedural SQL (PSQL)—consists of all DML statements, with the addition of a number of procedural extensions.

Embedded SQL (ESQL)—the "base" SQL implementation, consisting of DDL and DML syntax that the other subsets incorporate, where possible. It was the original implementation of SQL in the InterBase predecessors, designed to be embedded in client applications and pre-compiled. It is rarely used today and we do not cover it in this book.

Interactive (ISQL)—the language implemented for the command-line *isql* utility. It is based on DSQL with extensions for viewing metadata and some system statistics and to control *isql* sessions.

SQL "Dialects"

The concept of "dialect" arose in Firebird's long-ago predecessor, InterBase 6, as a transition feature allowing the database engine to recognise, accept and correctly process the features and elements of legacy InterBase 5 and older databases (Dialect 1), to access these older data for conversion to the new features and elements (Dialect 2) or to apply the full Firebird set of features, elements and rules to converted or newly created databases (Dialect 3).

Firebird creates a database in Dialect 3 by default. It is actually possible to create a new database in Firebird as Dialect 1 but it is strongly recommended to avoid doing so. Dialect 1, to which newer language features are unavailable, it will be deprecated eventually.

It is not possible to create a Dialect 2 database, since Dialect 2 is a client attribute intended for converting Dialect 1 databases to Dialect 3. The implementation of Dialect 2 is fairly imperfect and it will never be improved.

Firebird and the ISO Standards

SQL (pronounced "ess cue ell") is a data sub-language for accessing relational database management systems. Its elements, syntax and behavior became standardized under ANSI and ISO in 1986.

The standard SQL query language is non-procedural; that is, it is oriented toward the results of operations rather than toward the means of getting the results. It is intended to be a generic sub-language, to be used alongside a host language. The purpose of standards is to prescribe a surface-level mechanism whereby a specified query request returns a predictable result, regardless of how database engines manipulate input internally.

Since its introduction, the SQL standard has undergone three major reviews: SQL-89 (published in 1989), SQL-92 (1992 or thereabouts) and more recently "SQL 3", an ongoing work published in part as "SQL-99". While the standards prescribe in great detail how the elements of the language shall be expressed and how the logic of operations is to be interpreted, it makes no rules about how a vendor should implement it.

Conformance with the standard is a matter of degree, rather than an absolute. Vendors may freely implement language features that the standard does not prescribe. Conformance is about the ways that features recognised and described by the standards are implemented, if they are present. Conformance varies inversely with the number of standard features that are implemented in an idiosyncratic fashion.

A "conforming" implementation is expected to provide the basic set of features and may include other features, grouped and standardized at levels above "entry level". Firebird's SQL language adheres closely to the SQL-92 and SQL-3 standards at entry level.

Data Definition Language (DDL)

The underlying structures of a database—its tables, views, and indexes—are created using a subset of the Firebird SQL language known as Data Definition Language (DDL). A DDL statement begins with one of the keywords CREATE, ALTER, RECREATE or DROP, causing a single object to be created, modified, reconstructed or destroyed, respectively. The database and, thereafter, its objects, rules and relationships interlock to form the structure of a relational database.

The next six chapters cover the creation and maintenance of databases and the objects in them, using DDL.

Data Manipulation Language (DML)

Data manipulation language (DML) comprises the syntaxes for statements and expressions that store, modify and retrieve data. DML statements begin with a verb—either INSERT, UPDATE, DELETE, EXECUTE or SELECT. Along the way are functions and operations that can group, sort and limit output sets.

Dynamic vs Static SQL

SQL statements embedded and precompiled in code are sometimes referred to as static SQL. By contrast, statements that are generated by a client program and submitted through the API to the server for execution during run-time are known as dynamic SQL (DSQL).

Unless you are writing code for ESQL applications, you are using DSQL. Statements executed by the interactive SQL utility (isql), or other interactive desktop utility programs are DSQL, as are those processed through client applications that use the API directly or indirectly (through database access drivers like ODBC, JDBC and the BDE).

In ESQL applications, static SQL allows queries to bypass the Firebird API, instead being pre-compiled to use macro calls to the API structures. ESQL is rarely used these days and is not covered in this book.

Chapters 18 to 23 cover the many aspects of DML.

Procedural language (PSQL)

The standard does not prescribe procedural language features since, in principle, it assumes that general programming tasks will be accomplished using the host language. There is no specification for language constructs to manipulate, calculate or create data programmatically inside the database management system.

Those RDBMS engines which support server-based programming usually provide SQL-like statement formats and syntaxes to extend SQL. Each vendor's implementation freely provides its own variants of these constructs. Typically, such code modules in the database are called ***stored procedures***.

Firebird provides them as procedure language (sometimes referred to as PSQL), a set of SQL extensions which programmers use, along with a variant of the ESQL language set, to write the source code for stored procedures and triggers. PSQL is extended to include flow control, conditional expressions, and error handling. It has the unique ability to generate multi-row output sets that can be directly accessed using SELECT statements.

Certain SQL constructs, including all DDL statements, are excluded from PSQL workflow. However, the EXECUTE STATEMENT syntax of PSQL enables the execution of DSQL commands, including some DDL for those willing to take the risk.

PSQL for stored procedures and triggers is described in detail in Part Six, ***Programming on the Server***.

Interactive SQL (ISQL)

The interactive query tool *isql* uses DSQL statements, along with a two subsets of extension commands (the SET XXX and SHOW XXX groups) which allow certain settings and schema queries, respectively, to be performed interactively. Certain SET commands can also be included in data definition scripts for batch execution in isql.

The isql language set also includes other specific commands for use in scripting, such as INPUT, OUTPUT, EDIT and more.

The isql utility, including its command set and scripting, is fully covered in Chapter 24, *Interactive SQL Utility (isql)*.

Schemas and Scripts

It is very good practice to use DDL scripts to create your database and its objects. Some of the reasons include

- Self-documentation. A script is a plain text file, easily handled in any development system, both for updating and reference. Scripts can—and should—include detailed comment text. Alterations to metadata can be signed and dated manually.
- Control of database development and change. Scripting all database definitions allows schema creation to be integrated closely with design tasks and code review cycles.
- Repeatable and traceable creation of metadata. A completely reconstructable schema is a requirement in the quality assurance and disaster recovery systems of many organizations.
- Orderly construction and reconstruction of database metadata. Experienced Firebird programmers often create a set of DDL scripts, designed to run and commit in a specific order, to make debugging easy and ensure that objects will exist when later, dependent objects refer to them.

Using isql to run scripts

A large section of Chapter 24 describes how you can use *isql* to create and run scripts of DDL statements and more, both interactively and as a "job" using command-line (console) mode. Refer to the topic *Creating and Running Scripts*.

Scripts created for use with isql can be used with many of the more sophisticated third-party administration software products available out there in the Firebird tools market.

Resources

For a list of resources to help you on your Firebird journey, refer to Appendix XIV, *Resources*.

CHAPTER

12

DATA DEFINITION LANGUAGE—DDL

When defining metadata for use in a Firebird database, we use a lexicon of standard SQL statements and parameters that provide for the creation of an object by its type and name—or identifier—and for specifying and modifying its attributes. Also in this lexicon, known as data definition language (DDL), are statements for removing objects.

Queries using DDL are reserved for the purpose of metadata definition—so

- control them carefully if implementing them in end-user applications
- expect compiler exceptions if you attempt to use them directly in stored procedures or to pass their names as input parameters

Firebird's DDL is described in the next five chapters. View definitions, other run-time predfined set structures and the granting and revoking of SQL permissions are also DDL. Views, which incorporate both DDL and DML, are discussed in ***The Firebird Book Second Edition*** and in the companion volume to this, Volume 2: ***Developing with Firebird Data***, in the chapter enititled *Views and Other Runtime Set Objects*. Defining and manipulating SQL permissions is described in ***The Firebird Book Second Edition*** and in the companion volume to this, Volume 3: ***Administering Firebird Servers and Databases***, in the chapter entitled *Database-Level Security*.

SQL Data Definition Statements

Following is a round-up of the verbs that comprise the DDL lexicon.

CREATE

```
CREATE <object>
```

All objects you create in a database come into being by way of a CREATE statement, including the database itself, of course.

The object's owner

Every object has an owner. The owner is the user who creates the object, regardless of which user owns the database. Whilst a database's owner can change (by being restored from a backup by a different user), all of the objects within the database retain their original owner, even after a restore.

Many objects require you to be logged in as the owner of an object in order to create associate objects, e.g., indexes or triggers for a table. You also need to be the owner of an object to change its metadata or to delete it.

SYSDBA and other privileged users

A user logged in as SYSDBA (or another with SYSDBA-like privileges in the database) can perform the owner's tasks without incurring exceptions. It is important to keep in mind that "ownership sticks". If SYSDBA creates an index for a table owned by another user, SYSDBA is the owner of the index but not of the table. This is not a desirable situation.

RECREATE

```
RECREATE <object>
```

The RECREATE verb is available for some types of objects but not others. The implementation of RECREATE syntax for the different object types has been a progressive process across versions—whether it is available depends on server version.

RECREATE is exactly like its CREATE counterpart except that, if the object already exists, the old object will be dropped (removed) before the new one is created from scratch.

If there is an existing object of the same type and name,

- RECREATE will fail if it has other objects dependent on it. For example, you could not RECREATE a table if another table has a FOREIGN KEY or a CHECK constraint defined that references it.
- All existing related objects and data will be lost.

ALTER

also CREATE OR ALTER

```
ALTER <object>
CREATE OR ALTER <object>
```

ALTERand its near relative, CREATE OR ALTER, are the less "aggressive" than RECREATE. The ALTER syntax will make the metadata changes without requiring the dissociation of dependent objects. Data, indexes and triggers for tables are preserved.

CREATE OR ALTER works exactly like ALTER if an existing object of the same name or type exists; otherwise, it works exactly like CREATE.

In some cases, ALTER syntax is provided for objects whose definition you cannot actually alter. For example, ALTER INDEX can only activate or deactivate the index, which sets a flag on its metadata record in the system table RDB$INDICES to ACTIVE | INACTIVE. A similar trick is at work with ALTER TRIGGER, which can be used with nothing but the ACTIVE | INACTIVE parameter to enable and disable the trigger.

DECLARE

Some object "types" are actually declarations of external pieces that are for optional usage in databases. External functions (UDFs) and BLOB filters are declared in a database, not created, because they live in separate shared libraries, in locations known to the engine by way of parameters in `firebird.conf`. If they are not declared, they are not available.

Example

```
DECLARE EXTERNAL FUNCTION getExactTimestampUTC
TIMESTAMP
RETURNS PARAMETER 1
ENTRY_POINT 'getExactTimestampUTC' MODULE_NAME 'fbudf';
```

Other, unrelated parts of the wider lexicon use the DECLARE verb. For example, in procedural SQL (PSQL), the same verb is used for declaring variables and cursors.

DROP

```
DROP <object>
```

DROP is the universal verb for killing objects permanently. It is the easiest statement to type in SQL—it takes no arguments other than the name of the object you want to remove.

Dropped objects are gone for ever!

Storing Descriptive Text

Firebird does not come with a formal data dictionary tool but the metadata of every metadata object, including the database itself, has a TEXT BLOB column named RDB$DESCRIPTION. Any amount of descriptive text can be stored there.

Objects with RDB$DESCRIPTION columns

The object types that have RDB$DESCRIPTION columns are

The database itself (in RDB$DATABASE)		Tables	Views
Tables	Views	Domains	Columns
Indexes	Triggers	Stored Procedures	Parameters
Character sets	Collations	Exceptions	Roles
Generators (Sequences)		External functions (UDFs)	
BLOB Filters			

Many graphical administration tools enable viewing and editing of this description text. The open source *FlameRobin* displays them with table properties and provides an editing interface. Mario Zimmerman developed a free tool, called *IBDesc*, that produces reports containing the information stored in RDB$DESCRIPTION.

Without dedicated tools, this column can be queried interactively by applications for any of the object types that have this column.

It is in the development plans for Firebird to make the system tables read-only in future versions. If you intend developing your own tools for maintaining a data dictionary for your databases, keep in mind that writing and updating these BLOBs by direct DML has a limited life expectancy.

The COMMENT statement

From the "2" series onward, you can populate the RDB$DESCRIPTION column using the explicit DSQL verb COMMENT. It takes as its argument a string expression that will be converted to a BLOB and stored persistently.

While implementing the COMMENT verb is a step in the right direction towards including provision for documenting databases without recourse to performing DML on the system tables, it is a small step. BLOBs cannot be updated: if you need to "change" the content of the descriptive text, you have to start over. Once the system tables become read-only, application tools that currently provide a direct BLOB editing interface will not work, unless the Firebird developers implement some special exclusion, perhaps by providing a system view to enable privileged users write access to RDB$DESCRIPTION. The 32Kb limit on string size (bytes, not characters) is a limitation, given that metadata text is stored in the 3-byte UNICODE_FSS character set.

Syntax

```
COMMENT ON <object> IS {'Supply text here' | NULL}
```

```
<object> ::= DATABASE | <basic-type> objectname |
  COLUMN relationname.fieldname | PARAMETER procname.paramname
<basic-type> ::= CHARACTER SET | COLLATION | DOMAIN | EXCEPTION |
  EXTERNAL FUNCTION | FILTER | GENERATOR | INDEX |
  PROCEDURE | ROLE | SEQUENCE | TABLE | TRIGGER | VIEW
```

The text

The text can be anything you want, as long as it does not exceed 32,767 bytes. It will be transliterated to UNICODE_FSS for storage. For retrieval, it will be transliterated to the character set of the client.

NULL is the default content when a row is created in the relevant system table. If you supply an empty string (' ') it will be stored as NULL.

Examples

```
COMMENT ON DATABASE IS 'I am valuable: please back me up regularly'
COMMENT ON TABLE EMPLOYEE IS 'If you work here we know who you are.'
COMMENT ON COLUMN EMPLOYEE.FULL_NAME IS
  'Read-only: concatenates LAST_NAME and FIRST_NAME'
```

Comments in scripts

Writing DDL for a database in a script for input to the *isql* utility is highly recommended. The subject is covered in Chapter 24, *Interactive SQL Utility (isql)*.

In scripts—and anywhere you store SQL statements—you have two ways to include comments.

- the C-style comment marker-pair /* comment */ can be used to enclose one or more lines of comment, as in

```
/* This is a line of useful information:
   Make sure you read it! */
```

  This method can also be used for in-line comments, such as "commenting out" code that you don't want to delete, as in

```
ALTER TABLE VEGETABLES
ADD SEASON VARCHAR(10) /* , SUGAR_CONTENT DOUBLE PRECISION, */
```

- the one-line comment marker, consisting of two hyphens '--' at the beginning of a line. Everything following that marker will be ignored. For example,

```
-- This is one line of useful information
```

Object Dependencies

In a relational database management system like Firebird, many kinds of objects have dependencies on other objects. For example, when a FOREIGN KEY constraint references a PRIMARY KEY or UNIQUE constraint in another table, the referenced table acquires the referencing table as a dependency.

Dependencies occur when you place a CHECK constraint on a table, column or domain that refer to another object in the database. The object referred to by the CHECK constraint acquires that constraint as a dependency.

It is also possible—although a very bad idea unless it is a self-referencing relationship protected by referential integrity—to cause dependencies between rows within the same table. An example would be a CHECK constraint that validates an incoming value by checking a value in another row in the same table.

Generators (a.k.a. sequences) live an independent life. When created, they owe nothing to any other database object. It is not unusual for the same generator to serve multiple purposes in a database.

However, generators (sequences) are widely used in triggers to automate the creation of keys for tables. (For details of that technique, refer to the Triggers chapter in the companion volume to this, Volume 2: ***Developing with Firebird Data*** and in ***The Firebird Book Second Edition.)*** Thus, a generator is usually a dependency for a trigger somewhere.

The engine is very thorough about protecting dependencies. You will get exceptions if you try to change or delete any object that another object depends on. When you must do that change or deletion, you must always remove the dependencies first—drop a constraint that depends on an unwanted object, for example.

Using DDL to Manage User Accounts

Firebird 2.5 introduced DDL syntax to enable user accounts on the server to be managed by submitting SQL statements when logged in to a regular database.

CREATE/ALTER/DROP USER

The CREATE USER, ALTER USER and DROP USER statements can be used by the SYSDBA or another privileged user as a direct alternative to using the gsec utility for managing the global user table in the security database. CREATE USER and ALTER USER also include the optional parameters GRANT ADMIN ROLE and REVOKE ADMIN ROLE to enable a privileged user to grant the RDB$ADMIN role in the security database to an ordinary user.

For the full overview of the RDB$ADMIN role, refer to Chapter 36, ***Protecting the Server***.

Syntax Patterns

The SYSDBA, or a user with SYSDBA privileges in both the current database and the security database, can add a new user:

```
CREATE USER <username> {PASSWORD 'password'} [FIRSTNAME 'firstname']
  [MIDDLENAME 'middlename'] [LASTNAME 'lastname'] [GRANT ADMIN ROLE];
```

The PASSWORD clause is required when creating a new user. It should be the initial password for that new user. The user can change it later, using ALTER USER.

The SYSDBA, or a user with SYSDBA privileges in both the current database and the security database, can change one or more of the password and proper name attributes of an existing user. Non-privileged users can use this statement to alter only their own attributes.

```
ALTER USER <username> [PASSWORD 'password'] [FIRSTNAME 'firstname']
  [MIDDLENAME 'middlename'] [LASTNAME 'lastname'] [{GRANT | REVOKE} ADMIN ROLE];
```

At least one of PASSWORD, FIRSTNAME, MIDDLENAME or LASTNAME must be present.

ALTER USER does not enable the changing of user names. If a different user name is required, the old one should be dropped and a new one created.

The GRANT/REVOKE ADMIN ROLE arguments

GRANT ADMIN ROLE and REVOKE ADMIN ROLE are optional arguments to the CREATE USER and ALTER USER statements. These arguments provide a way to elevate the privileges of an ordinary user.

See also ALTER ROLE, discussed in detail in Chapters 36, ***Managing Users***, and 37, ***Database-level Security***.

The SYSDBA, or a user with SYSDBA privileges in both the current database and the security database, can delete a user:

```
DROP USER <username>;
```

Restrictions

CREATE USER and DROP USER statements and the arguments GRANT | REVOKE ADMIN ROLE are available only for the SYSDBA, or a user that has acquired the RDB$ADMIN role in both the current database and the security database.

An ordinary user can ALTER his own password and elements of his proper name. An attempt to modify another user will fail.

Examples

SYSDBA, or a user with equivalent privileges in both the current database and the security database, can do:

```
CREATE USER fluffy PASSWORD 'test';
..
ALTER USER fluffy FIRSTNAME 'Foufou' LASTNAME 'Curlychops';
ALTER USER fluffy PASSWORD 'MePOOdle';
```

The following statement escalates the privileges of user 'FLUFFY' globally, i.e., gives it SYSDBA-equivalent rights over all objects in all databases:

```
ALTER USER fluffy GRANT ADMIN ROLE;
```

To drop user FLUFFY:

```
DROP USER fluffy;
```

Reference Material

When the first edition of this book was published in 2004, the Firebird Project had virtually no reference material of its own for SQL. Users relied heavily on two volumes of the beta documentation that had been written for the InterBase 6 code that was subsequently released as open source: the Data Definition Guide and the Language Reference, along with the detailed release notes produced for each release and sub-release of Firebird.

The Firebird Project has been inhibited in producing its own updated documentation by the fact that the proprietors of InterBase have never permitted the content of that beta documentation to be re-used without threat of legal action. However, copies of the original PDF books are available in numerous locations on the Web and links can be found at the Firebird website, in the Documentation section.

Since 2004, the coordinator of Firebird's documentation project, Paul Vinkenoog, has dedicated hundreds of voluntary hours and much talent to producing the "Firebird Language Reference Update" books for each major Firebird version, starting with v.1.5. They merge both the Data Definition and the Language Reference changes in a cumulative series. They are mind-bogglingly good in their detail.

The latest, at the time of this writing, is the ***Firebird 2.5 Language Reference Update***, comprehending all of the changes in DDL, DML and PSQL since the InterBase 6 beta was forked to become Firebird at the end of July, 2000. It is authoritative and is updated frequently, always after the publication of release notes—which means its content at any point can be counted more reliable than the release notes it was sourced from.

Since 2010, the language reference update PDFs have been distributed in the binary kits and scripted to install in the /doc/ subdirectory beneath the Firebird root.

If you need to download any of these volumes, you can find the links at the Firebird website:

Firebird Language Reference Updates: *http://www.firebirdsql.org/en/reference-manuals/*, scroll down to "Reference Material"

Latest Release Notes for all versions: *http://www.firebirdsql.org/en/release-notes/*

InterBase 6 Beta Manuals, including Data Definition Guide and Language Reference: *http://www.firebirdsql.org/en/reference-manuals/*, scroll down to "InterBase 6.0 Manuals"

CHAPTER

13

CREATING AND MAINTAINING A DATABASE

A Firebird database is, first and foremost, a filesystem file under the control of the I/O subsystem of the host machine on which the Firebird server runs. Once the server has created this file, its management system takes control of managing the space, using a low-level protocol to communicate with the I/O subsystem.

Because of this protocol, a Firebird database must exist on the same physical machine as the Firebird server. It cannot be located on any sort of storage device whose physical I/O system is not directly controlled by server's host.

A new, "empty" database occupies about 540-600 Kb of disk. The database file is not empty at all, in fact, because the act of creation—the CREATE DATABASE statement—causes more than 40 system tables to be created. These tables will store every detail of the metadata as database objects are added and altered. Because the system tables are regular Firebird database objects, they already contain the metadata records for themselves. The server has already allocated database pages from disk for these data and has set up inventory pages for various types of object—tables, indexes, BLOBs—as well as for transactions and for the pages themselves.

Amongst the tables created in versions 2.1 and above are the monitoring tables, the suite of tables designed to be populated with the transient information about the running database, whenever requested by a client.

The schemata of the system and monitoring tables can be found in Appendix V.

Physical Storage for a Database

Before creating the database, you should know where you are going to create it! This is not as silly as it sounds. The CREATE DATABASE—alias CREATE SCHEMA—statement will create the file or files you name, but it cannot create directories and it cannot change filesystem permissions. These details must be attended to first.

Additionally, a Firebird server may be configured to restrict the locations where databases may be accessed. Check the ***DatabaseAccess*** parameter in the `firebird.conf` file to discover whether your server is restricting access. If the setting is the default *Full* then you can create the database anywhere. Otherwise:

Restrict will indicate the filesystem tree-roots under which database access is permitted. Ensure that the user that starts your server has sufficient permissions to create a file there (or, in the case of the Windows embedded server, the user under which you are logged in).

Note *In Firebird 2.5 and above, if **DatabaseAccess** is Restrict then new databases, by default, are created in the first location listed in the arguments for that parameter. Supplying a path or alias in the CREATE DATABASE statement overrides it.*

None permits the server to attach only databases that are listed in `aliases.conf`. You can create a database anywhere but, except at creation, no client will be able to attach to it unless its alias and its absolute path are present in `aliases.conf`..

Full is the default setting when Firebird is installed. It is strongly recommend that you change this option and make use of the database-aliasing feature. For more information, refer to the topic Database aliasing in Chapter 4.

About Security Access

It is not always obvious to newcomers that there is a distinction between server access and database security. When you "log in" to a Firebird database using *isql* or your favorite admin tool you always supply a user name and password, along with server, port (sometimes) and path parameters. Whenever you do this, you are logging in to the *server* and opening an attachment to a database.

If the database doesn't exist yet and you have started *isql* from the command line with no parameters, then two things are "givens":

1. you are logged in to the server
2. until you submit a CONNECT or CREATE DATABASE request to the server, the program is not attached to a database

Password access *in some form* is always required to log in to the server unless the user has root or Administrator privileges from the operating system. Once in, you can attach to any database. What you can do, once attached, depends on SQL privileges, which are stored within the database.

The SYSDBA user has full destructive rights to every database and every object within it. The owner—the user that created the database—has automatic rights to the database, although not to any objects within it that were created by other users. SQL privileges are "opt-in". That means that, although any user with server access can attach to any database, it will have no rights to do anything to anything, other than what has been explicitly or implicitly granted to it as access privileges, using GRANT statements.

Detailed information about server access can be found in the companion volume to this, Volume 3: ***Administering Firebird Servers and Databases*** and in Chapters 36 and 37 of ***The Firebird Book Second Edition***.

ISC_USER and ISC_PASSWORD

It is possible to set up the two environment variables ISC_USER and ISC_PASSWORD on the server, to avoid the need to log in when working with databases locally. You will be able do everything that the named user is allowed to do, without needing to supply credentials each time. This feature is handy for administrative tasks but it must be used with a high level of caution because it leaves your database access open to any local user who happens upon your command shell.

If you want to play with fire, set these two variables permanently. If you want to have that extra level of convenience and script security, set them temporarily each time you want them and be certain to reset them whenever you leave your console:

On Linux, in the same shell from which you will launch the application:

```
]# setenv ISC_USER=SYSDBA
]# setenv ISC_PASSWORD=masterkey
```

To unset, either

```
]# setenv ISC_USER=
]# setenv ISC_PASSWORD=
```

or simply close the shell.

On Windows, go to the command prompt and type:

```
set ISC_USER=SYSDBA
set ISC_PASSWORD=masterkey
```

To unset:

```
set ISC_USER=
set ISC_PASSWORD=
```

Creating a Database

You can create a database interactively in isql. Some other database administration tools can meet the API requirements (see below) and let you create databases interactively, while others require a script.

In any case, it is preferable to use a data definition file (DDL script) because it provides an easy way to "replay" your statements if a statement fails—it is easier to start over from a corrected source file than to retype interactive SQL statements.

Refer to Chapter 24, *Interactive SQL Utility (isql)* for usage instructions.

Dialect — default dialect 3

Firebird creates a dialect 3 database by default. You should retain the default unless you have a genuine reason to create the database in dialect 1.

If you wish to create a dialect 1 database, the first statement in the script (or the prior action in your admin tool) should be

```
SET SQL DIALECT 1;
```

If isql is currently attached to a database, it will prompt you to commit the current transaction. Answer Yes to proceed with creating the new database. Some third-party tools may require that you disconnect from any existing attachment first.

CREATE DATABASE Statement

The next statement—or the first, for a dialect 3 database—must be the CREATE DATABASE or CREATE SCHEMA statement, using the prescribed syntax. First, we consider the syntax for a single-file database. We look at the extra syntax for a multi-file database a little later.

The database created will have the on-disk structure (ODS) associated with the version of the Firebird server that is running. The lineage of the ODS versions is chronicled in the companion volume to this, Vol. 3: ***Administering Firebird Servers and Databases*** and in ***The Firebird Book Second Edition***, in the chapter entitled *Migration Notes*.

Syntax

```
CREATE {DATABASE | SCHEMA} 'file-specification'
  [USER 'username' [PASSWORD 'password']]
  [PAGE_SIZE [=] int]
  [LENGTH [=] int [PAGE[S]]]
```

```
[DEFAULT CHARACTER SET character-set [COLLATION collation]]
[DIFFERENCE FILE 'difference-file-path']
```

Use single quotes to delimit strings such as file names, user names, and passwords.

'DATABASE' or 'SCHEMA'?

CREATE DATABASE and CREATE SCHEMA are the same statement. It is merely a question of preference which you use.

Mandatory and optional parameters

The only mandatory parameter for the CREATE statement is the file-specification—the name of the primary database file and the filesystem path to its location, or its alias.

Database path and name

The file-specification must be one of the following:

- the fully-qualified, absolute path to the file, in a valid format for the operating system platform, for example:

  POSIX

  ```
  CREATE DATABASE '/opt/databases/mydatabase.fdb'
  ```

  Win32

  ```
  CREATE SCHEMA 'd:\databases\mydatabase.fdb'
  ```

  You can use either forward slashes (/) or backslashes (\ ) as directory separators. Firebird automatically converts either type of slash to the appropriate type for the server operating system.

  The enclosing single-quotes for file_specification are not optional. All elements of the file specification are case-sensitive on POSIX platforms.

- an alias that has already been registered in aliases.conf, that complies with the rules above and points to a valid location
- under Firebird 2.5 or higher, a file name alone, provided the ***DatabaseAccess*** parameter in `firebird.conf` is configured to *Restrict* and designates at least one valid directory path. This option does not work if you are creating the database remotely.

  If you use an unqualified file name in lower versions, the database file will be created in the current working directory if ***DatabaseAccess*** is configured to Full; otherwise, an exception is thrown.

If creating the database remotely, i.e., from a client workstation, or locally on Linux Superserver, either interactively or using a script, you must include the host name. For example:

POSIX Classic or Superclassic

```
CREATE DATABASE 'myserver:/opt/databases/mydatabase.fdb'
```

POSIX SS local, as above, or

```
CREATE DATABASE 'localhost:/opt/databases/mydatabase.fdb'
```

Windows, TCP/IP protocol:

```
CREATE SCHEMA 'WinServer:d:\databases\mydatabase.fdb'
```

Windows, Named Pipes (NetBEUI) protocol:

```
CREATE SCHEMA '\\WinServer\d:\databases\mydatabase.fdb'
```

Ownership

If you are logged in as SYSDBA then SYSDBA will own the new database unless you include the clause specifying the USER and PASSWORD. Although it is optional to designate an owner, it is highly desirable to do so. However, for security reasons, you will probably wish to remove the user's password from the script before archiving it with other system documentation.

```
CREATE DATABASE '/opt/databases/mydatabase.fdb'
  USER 'ADMINUSR' PASSWORD 'yyuryyub';
```

Page size

The option PAGE_SIZE attribute is expressed in bytes. If you omit it, it will default to 4096 bytes with *isql*. Some other tools apply their own defaults, so there is a strong argument for specifying it explicitly in the script The page size can be 4096, 8192 or 16384. Any other numbers will be resolved back to the next lowest number in this range. For example, if you specify 5000, Firebird will create a database with a page size of 4096.

If the size specified is smaller than 4096, it will be silently converted to 4096.

Example

```
CREATE DATABASE '/opt/databases/mydatabase.fdb'
  USER 'ADMINUSR' PASSWORD 'yyuryyub'
  PAGE_SIZE 8192
  ...
```

V.1.X 1024 and 2048 are valid page sizes under the v.1.0.x servers and 2048 is valid under v.1.5.x.

Factors influencing choice of page size

Choosing a page size is not a question of applying some rule. It will do no harm to begin with the default size of 4 Kb. When the time comes to tune the database for performance improvements, you can experiment by backing up the database and restoring it with different page sizes. For instructions, refer to the section *The gbak Utility* in the companion volume to this, Vol. 3: ***Administering Firebird Servers and Databases*** or in ***The Firebird Book Second Edition***, the chapter entitled *Backing Up Databases*.

The page size you choose can benefit performance or affect it adversely, according to a number of factors having mostly to do with the structures and usage of the most frequently accessed tables. Each database page will be filled to about 80 per cent of its capacity, so think in terms of an actual page size that is around 125 percent of the size you determine to be the minimum.

The row size of the most-frequently accessed tables may have an effect. A record structure that is too large to fit on a single page requires more than one page fetch to read or write to it, so access can be optimized by choosing a page size that can comfortably accommodate one row or simple row multiples of these high-volume tables.

The number of rows that your main tables can be predicted to accommodate over time may have an influence. If multiple rows can be accommodated in a single page, a larger page size may reduce the overall tally of data and index pages that need to be read for an operation.

Default character set

Strongly recommended unless all—or nearly all—of your text data will be in US ASCII. From v.2.5 onward, you can also specify the default COLLATION sequence for character columns that use the default character set.

If you are not sure about the availability of the character set and/or collation that you want to be the default, check the manifest file fbintl.conf in the /intl/ sub-directory of your Firebird 2.1 or higher installation. (COLLATION is not available under v.2.1.)

```
CREATE DATABASE '/opt/databases/mydatabase.fdb'
  USER 'ADMINUSR' PASSWORD 'yyuryyub'
  PAGE_SIZE 8192
  DEFAULT CHARACTER SET ISO8859_1
    COLLATION FR_CA;
```

For details regarding character sets refer to the topic *Character Sets and Collation Sequences* in Chapter 9, ***Character Types***.

Difference file

If you are planning to use the *nBackup* incremental backup tool, you have the option of specifying the full path to the file that will be used to store "delta" files whilst *nBackup* has the database in a LOCKED (i.e., read-only) state for a copy operation. For more information, see the topic *Incremental Backup Tool (nBackup)* in Chapter 39 of ***The Firebird Book Second Edition*** or Chapter 12 of the companion volume to this, Vol. 3: ***Administering Firebird Servers and Databases***.

Getting information about the database

Once you have created and committed the database, you can display its details in *isql* using the SHOW DATABASE command:

```
SQL> SHOW DATABASE;
Database: /opt/databases/mydatabase.fdb
        Owner: ADMINUSR
PAGE_SIZE 8192
Number of DB pages allocated = 176
Sweep interval = 20000
Forced Writes are ON
Transaction - oldest = 5
Transaction - oldest active = 6
Transaction - oldest snapshot = 6
Transaction - Next = 9
Default character set: ISO8859_1
Default collation: FR_CA
ODS = 11.2
```

Database Attributes

The list of database attributes in the output comes from the database header page of the database. You can get almost exactly the same information from calling *gstat -h*. Some of those attributes have come from the CREATE DATABASE specification; others are installed as defaults at creation time.

Sweep interval and transactions

For information about sweeping and sweep interval refer to the topic *Keeping a Clean Database* later in this chapter.

The values of the oldest ("oldest interesting"), oldest active and next transactions are important for performance and server behavior. For details, refer to the chapters in Part Five, ***Transactions***.

Forced writes

Forced Writes is synonymous with synchronous writes. On platforms that support asynchronous writes, Firebird databases are created with Forced Writes enabled by default. The term "disabling Forced Writes" means switching the write mode from synchronous to asynchronous, an action that should only be done by a privileged user with exclusive access.

- With forced (synchronous) writes enabled, new records, new record versions and deletions are physically written to disk immediately upon posting or, at the latest, upon committing..

- Asynchronous writes cause new and changed data to be withheld in the filesystem cache, relying on the flushing behavior of the operating system to make them permanent on disk.

For discussion of the implications of disabling Forced Writes and instructions for setting it using *gfix*, see the topic Forced Writes in the companion volume to this, Vol. 3: ***Administering Firebird Servers and Databases*** or ***The Firebird Book Second Edition,*** the chapter entitled ***Confguring Databases***.

The Windows 95 platform does not support asynchronous writes. The same applies to Linux for the following versions of Firebird, due to a previously undiscovered bug in the Linux kernel:

- *all 1.X versions*
- *all 2.0.x versions prior to v.2.0.6*
- *all 2.1.x versions prior to v.2.1.4*

Single and Multi-file Databases

Any Firebird database can be multi-file. You don't have to decide between single and multiple at the beginning. A single file database can be converted to multi-file at any time, using ALTER DATABASE (see below) or the *gbak* tool.

Specifying file size for a single-file database

You can optionally specify a file length, in pages, for the primary file, following the PAGE_SIZE attribute. For example, the following statement creates a database that is stored in one 10,000-page-long file:

```
CREATE DATABASE '/opt/databases/mydatabase.fdb'
  USER 'ADMINUSR' PASSWORD 'yyuryyub'
  PAGE_SIZE 8192
  LENGTH 10000 PAGES  /* the PAGES keyword is optional */
  DEFAULT CHARACTER SET ISO8859_1
  COLLATION FR_CA;
```

If the database grows larger than the specified file length, Firebird extends the primary file beyond the LENGTH limit until the filesystem size limit for shared access file is reached or disk space runs out. To avoid this, you can store a database in more than one file, called secondary files. The files can be on separate disks.

Creating a Multi-file Database

Multi-file databases are more of an issue on older filesystems where the absolute limit for a shared-write file is 2 Gb (FAT32, ext2) or 4 Gb (NTFS systems with 32-bit I/O). A Firebird database cannot be corrupted by "blowing the limit" of its primary or secondary file's capacity—it simply denies all writes when the last file hits the limit. Any outstanding writes will be lost.

In the following example, a database is created consisting of three files, each potentially of 2 Gb. If the filesystem supports a larger shared-access file, the last file will continue to grow until the filesystem limit (if any) is reached.

```
CREATE DATABASE 'LOCALHOST:/data/sample.fdb'
  PAGE_SIZE 8192
  DEFAULT CHARACTER SET ISO8859_1
  LENGTH 250000 PAGES
  FILE '/data/sample.fd1'
  FILE '/data/sample.fd2'
  STARTING AT 250001;
```

You must specify a range of pages for each file either by providing the *number of pages* in each file, or by providing the *starting page number* for the file. For the last file, you don't need a length, because Firebird always dynamically sizes the last file and will increase the file size as necessary until all the available space is used or until it reaches the filesystem limit.

In the example, the first secondary file will "kick in" when the first primary file is nearing the 2 Gb limit. The next file in the chain comes into use when a requested operation is likely to need more pages allocated than the previous files could satisfy without exceeding their specified limits.

It is the responsibility of the database administrator to monitor database growth and ensure that a database always has ample capacity for extension. Deciding if and when to split a database file depends on how large you expect the database to grow and how quickly. More files can be added at any time using the ALTER DATABASE statement (below).

With multi-file databases you can avoid confining databases to the size of a single disk if the system does not support spanning a single, huge file across multiple disks. There will be no problems installing a RAID array and distributing a multi-file Firebird database across several disks on any supported platform.

Important *All files must be located on disks that are under the direct physical control of the Firebird server's host machine.*

The Database Cache

Database cache is a chunk of memory reserved for each database running on the server. Its purpose is to cache all of the database pages (sometimes referred to as "page buffers") that have been most recently used. It is configured as a default for new databases and for all databases that are not individually configured. You can check this default setting by looking up the parameter ***DefaultDbCachePages*** in `firebird.conf`.

The value constitutes a number of blocks of memory, or "buffers", each the size of one database page. It follows, then, that databases with large page sizes will use more cache memory than those will smaller page sizes.

V.1.0.x For v.1.0.x, check ***database_cache_pages*** in `isc_config` (POSIX) or ***ibconfig*** (Win32).

It should be emphasized that configuring the cache is not a "must-do". The default configuration for Superserver fits most normal needs and server level reconfiguration might never be necessary. On Classic, the default is more worthy of attention, since it may be too high for a system with more than a few concurrent users.

Pay special attention to the cache sizes if you are likely to be swapping from Classic to Superserver, or vice versa.

Database-level setting

A newly created database has a database-level cache size of zero pages. If the cache setting is left at zero, connections to that database will use the ***DefaultDbCachePages*** setting from `firebird.conf`.

Cache size can be configured individually and permanently, per database. It can be changed again, if required. Other databases that retain (or are changed to) zero-cache will use the server default.

Sizing the cache

The number of cache buffers required is approximate—there no one "thing" that dictates what size you should choose. It needs to be large enough to cater for the page requirements of databases but not so large as to consume memory that is needed for other operations. Up to a point, the more activity that can be handled in the cache, the better the overall performance. The axiom "Database servers love RAM" is true for Firebird. But Firebird uses RAM for other activities that are at least as important as caching. Transaction inventory and index bitmaps are maintained in RAM; sorting and merging are done in memory, if it is available, in all versions except v.1.0.x.

It is important to realize that every system has a critical point where a too-large cache configuration will consume more memory resources than the system can spare. Beyond this point, enlarging the cache will cause performance to degrade.

Limits and defaults

The minimum cache size is 50 pages. There is no maximum, as long as the allocation in total does not exceed the RAM available.

Default cache allocation is

- Superserver 2048 pages for each running database. All users share this common cache pool.

  As an indication of how resources can be consumed, a single database running at the default settings for PAGE_SIZE (4Kb) and DefaultDbCachePages (2 Kb) requires 8Mb of memory. Two databases running with the same settings require 16Mb, and so on. Default cache usage is calculated by:

  ```
  PAGE_SIZE * DefaultDbCachePages * number of databases
  ```

- Classic Server 75 cache pages per client attachment. Each attachment is allocated its own cache. The amount of memory required is the total of the cache requirements of all client attachments to each database. Cache usage is calculated by:

  ```
  PAGE_SIZE * DefaultDbCachePages * number of attachments
  ```

Cache usage

When Firebird reads a page from the database from disk, it stores that page in the cache. Ordinarily, the default cache size is adequate. If your application includes joins of five or more tables, Firebird Superserver automatically increases the size of the cache. If your application is well localized, that is, it uses the same small part of the database repeatedly, you might want to consider increasing the cache size so that you never have to release one page from cache to make room for another.

Because the database cache is configured in pages, obviously a database with a larger page_size consumes more memory than one with a smaller page_size. When there are multiple databases running on the same server, it may be desirable to override the server-wide cache size at database level or, in some cases, at application level (details below).

An application that performs intensive indexed retrievals requires more buffers than one that performs mainly inserts.

Where many clients are accessing different tables, or different parts of a single table, the demand for cache memory is higher than where most clients are working with the same, or overlapping, sets of data.

Estimating the size requirement

Estimating the size of the cache is not a simple or precise science, especially if you have multiple databases that have to run concurrently. The likely server cache usage is driven by the database with the largest page size. Classic allocates a cache for each attachment, whereas Superserver pools cache for all attachments to a particular database. As a starting point, it will be useful to work with the numbers and needs for the database with the biggest page size. Actual usage conditions will determine whether any adjustments are needed.

It is not necessary to have a cache that will accommodate an entire database. Arrive at a reduction factor for each database by estimating the proportion that is likely to be accessed during normal usage. The estimation suggested here is just that—there is no "rule". Assume when we talk about DB cache pages here, or "buffers", we are talking about the size of the cache for a particular database but not necessarily the default server setting for new and unconfigured databases.

Reduction factor, *r*, should be a value between 0 and 1.

Size of database, in pages, (size) can be established as follows:

- For a single-file database, take the maximum file size allowed by the filesystem, minus 1 byte, and divide it by the page size.

  On operating systems which support huge files, use the database file size instead of the maximum file size.

- For a multi-file database, take the STARTING AT value of the first secondary file and add the LENGTH values of all of the secondary files.

Let DB cache pages = number of cache pages (buffers) required by this database.

For each database, calculate

DB cache pages = r * size

Calculate and record this figure for each individual database.

Keep these records with other database documentation for use when you need to tune the cache for an individual database.

It can happen that too many cache buffers are allocated for available RAM to accommodate. With many databases running simultaneously, a request could demand more RAM than was available on the system. The cache would be swapped back and forth between RAM and disk, defeating the benefits of caching. Other applications (including the server) could be starved of memory if the cache were too large.

It is important, therefore, to ensure that adequate RAM is installed on the system to accommodate the database server's memory requirements. If database performance is important for your users, then avoid creating competition for resources by running other applications on the server.

Calculating RAM requirements for caching

To calculate the amount of RAM required for database caching on your server, take the PAGE_SIZE of each database and multiply it by the ***DefaultDbCachePages*** value. These results for all databases, when added together, will approximate the minimum RAM required for database caching.

If you are running Firebird on a 32-bit system,or 32-bit Firebird on a 64-bit system, keep in mind that the total RAM available to a 32-bit process is limited 2 GB. Cache is only one of several ways that Firebird uses RAM.

Setting cache size at database level

There are several ways to configure the cache size for a specified database. Changes do not take effect until the next time a *first connection* is made to Firebird Superserver or the next client connects to the Classic server.

Only the SYSDBA or a user with equivalent privileges in the database can change the cache size.

Use gfix

The recommended way to set a database-level override to ***DefaultDbCachePages*** is to use the *gfix* utility with the following switches:

```
gfix -buffers n database_name
```

where *n* is the required number of database pages. This approach permits fine tuning to reduce the risk of under-using memory or working with a cache that is too small. The override is written permanently to the database header page and will remain in place until the next time it is changed with *gfix*.

For more information about using *gfix*, see *The gfix Tool Set* in Chapter 35, ***Configuring and Managing Databases***.

Use the *isql* command-line query tool

To increase the number of cache pages for the duration of one session of the command-line utility *isql*, logging in as a super user, you have two options:

Either:

- include the number of pages (*n*) as a switch when starting isql

  ```
  isql -c n database_name
  ```

  n is the number of cache pages to be used for the session and temporarily overrides any value set by the ***DefaultDBCachePages*** (server default) configuration or *gfix* (database default). It must be greater than 9.

or

- include CACHE n as an argument to the CONNECT statement once *isql* is running:

  ```
  SQL> connect database_name CACHE n
  ```

  The value *n* can be any positive integer number of database pages. For Superserver, if a database cache already exists because of another attachment to the database, the cache size is increased only if *n* is greater than current cache size.

Use the database parameter buffer (DPB)

In an application for use by a super user, the cache size can be set in a database parameter buffer (DPB) using either the *isc_dpb_num_buffers* or the *isc_dpb_set_page_buffers* parameter, according to your server's requirements.

isc_dpb_num_buffers sets the number of buffers (pages of cache memory) to be used for the current connection. It makes most sense in a Classic architecture, where each connection gets a static allocation of cache memory. In Superserver, it will set the number of buffers to be used for the specific database, if that database is not already open, but will not persist after the server closes the database.

isc_dpb_set_page_buffers is useful in both Classic and Superserver. It has the same effect as using *gfix* to perform a persistent override of ***DefaultDbCachePages***, for the cited database.

Be cautious about providing end-user applications with the ability to modify the cache. Although any request to change the cache size will be ignored on all connection requests except the first, many versions of Firebird allow non-technical users to change settings in the database header via the DPB. It is likely to have unpredictable effects on performance, besides exposing databases to ill-advised, ad hoc manipulations.

The vulnerable versions are:

- v.2.1 and 2.1.1
- all versions lower than v.2.0.5

Changing the server default

Setting the value for the server-level ***DefaultDBCachePages*** to be the largest of the DB Cache Pages values you have recorded may be overkill. When you change the server-level default setting in the configuration file, it becomes the default for every new and zero-configured database on the server.

To change it, open the configuration file in a text editor, find the parameter ***DefaultDBCachePages*** and change the number.. If it is commented with a '#' symbol, delete the '#' symbol.

V.1.0.x In the v.1.0.x config files, it is ***default_cache_pages***. Uncomment the line if necessary and make the entry `database_cache_pages=nnnn`, where *nnnn* is the new cache size.

For Superserver, the change will take effect the next time a first connection is made to the affected databases. For Classic, it will affect all connections made after the reconfiguration.

A pragmatic approach

Do not overrate the importance of the database cache. Any cache imposes its own overhead on the overall memory resources and the filesystem cache plays its own role in optimizing the system's read-write performance. There is always a point at which the real gain in overall server performance does not justify the cost of tying up resources for the "worst-case" demand scenario.

The best advice is: don't rush into cache size optimization as a "must-do" for Firebird. Work with the default settings during development and, for deployment, just verify that the amount of RAM available can accommodate the defaults.

Once into production conditions, use a monitoring tool to observe and record how reads and writes are satisfied from the cache for typical and extreme situations. If the statistics are not satisfactory, then begin considering optimization.

The first broad-brush optimization you can try is to increase the default cache to a size that will occupy approximately two-thirds of available free RAM. If there isn't enough RAM installed, install more.

At that point, start monitoring again. If it fails to improve things, repeat the exercise.

Verifying cache size

To verify the size of the database cache currently in use, execute the following commands in *isql*:

```
ISQL> CONNECT database_name;
ISQL> SET STATS ON;
ISQL> COMMIT;
Current memory = 415768
Delta memory = 2048
Max memory = 419840
Elapsed time = 0.03 sec
Buffers = 2048
Reads = 0
Writes 2
Fetches = 2
ISQL> QUIT;
```

After SET STATS ON, the empty COMMIT command prompts *isql* to display the information about memory and buffer usage. Read the `Buffers=` line to determine the current size of the cache, in pages.

Read-only Databases

By default, databases are in read-write mode when created. Read-write databases can not be on a read-only filesystem, even if they are used only for SELECT, because Firebird writes information about transaction states to a data structure in the database file.

A Firebird database can be deployed as a read-only file, providing the ability to distribute catalogs, albums of files and other non-maintained types of database on CDs and other read-only filesystems. Read-only databases can, of course, be accessed on read-write systems as well.

A read-only database is not the same thing as a database file that has its read-only attribute set on. File-copying a read-write database to a CD-ROM does not make it into a read-only database.

The application will need to be written so as to avoid requests that involve writing to the database or to trap the exceptions raised when they are attempted. The following will throw the error 335544765, "Attempted update on read-only database":

- UPDATE, INSERT or DELETE operations
- metadata changes.
- operations that try to increment generators

External files

Any accompanying files linked to the database by having been declared with CREATE TABLE tablename EXTERNAL FILE 'filename' will also be opened read-only, even if the file itself is not carrying the filesystem read-only attribute.

Making a database read-only

Exclusive access is required to switch a database between read-write and read-only modes—see the instructions in Chapter 35, ***Configuring Databases***, in the topic <u>*Using the Tools*</u>. The mode-switch can be performed by the database owner or a user with SYSDBA rights.

Either *gfix* or *gbak* can be used :

- Using *gbak*, back up the database and restore it in read-only mode using the –c[reate] option. For example,

  ```
  gbak -create -mode read_only db1.fbk db1.fdb
  ```

- Using *gfix*, issue a `-m[ode] read_only` command. For example,

  ```
  gfix -mode read_only db1.fdb
  ```

Restore read-only databases with full page usage—use the -use switch to specify "use all space". In a read-write database, pages are filled by default to 80% of page capacity because it can help to optimize the re-use of pages. Space reservation makes no sense in a read-only database and fully-filled pages are denser and faster.

Databases with ODS lower than 10, e.g., old InterBase 5 databases, cannot be made read-only.

Keeping a Clean Database

Firebird uses a ***multi-generational architecture***. This means that multiple versions of data rows are stored directly on the data pages. When a row is updated or deleted, Firebird keeps a copy of the old state of the record and creates a new version. This proliferation of record back versions can increase the size of a database.

Background garbage collection

To limit this growth, Firebird continually performs garbage collection (GC) in the background of normal database activity. In Superserver, GC is literally a background operation performed by threads during idle times. In Classic and Superclassic, GC is performed cooperatively: everyone cleans up after everyone else. Each time a Firebird process or thread touches a table, it collects garbage left from the committing of recent transactions.

Garbage collection does nothing to get row versions that are caught up in unresolved transactions into a state where they can be flagged obsolete—they will not be visited during normal housekeeping activity. To completely sanitize the database, Firebird can perform database sweeping.

Sweeping

Database sweeping is a systematic way of removing all outdated row versions and freeing the pages they occupied so that they can be reused. Periodic sweeping prevents a database from growing unnecessarily large. Not surprisingly, although sweeping occurs in an asynchronous background thread, it can impose some cost on system performance.

By default, a Firebird database performs a sweep when the sweep interval reaches 20,000 transactions. Sweeping behavior is configurable, however: it can be left to run automatically, the sweep interval can be altered, or automatic sweeping can be disabled, to be run manually on demand instead.

Sweep interval

The Firebird server maintains an inventory of transactions. Any transaction that is uncommitted is known as an interesting transaction. The oldest of these "interesting" transactions (Oldest Interesting Transaction—OIT) marks the starting point for the sweep interval. If the sweep interval setting is greater than zero, Firebird initiates a full sweep of the database when the difference between the OIT and the Oldest Snapshot transaction passes the threshold set by the sweep interval.

Aspects of configuring and running sweeps are discussed in detail in the companion volume to this, Vol. 3: ***Administering Firebird Servers and Databases*** and in ***The Firebird Book Second Edition***, in the chapter entitled Configuring and Managing Databases.

Garbage collection during backup

Sweeping a database is not the only way to perform systematic garbage collection. Backing up a database achieves the same result, because the Firebird server must read every record, an action that forces garbage collection throughout the database. As a result, regularly backing up a database can reduce the need to sweep and helps to maintain better application performance.

Backup is NOT a replacement for sweep. While backup performs full database garbage collection, it does not clean up the transaction accounting as sweep does. The effects of sweeping—or neglecting to do so—are discussed in several topics throughout Chapter 25, Overview of Firebird Transactions.

Objects and counters

The structures of objects that you create in a Firebird database can be modified, using ALTER statements. Firebird keeps a count of the ALTER statements for tables, views and stored procedures and bumps up the "format version" of the object each time an ALTER statement for it is committed. The allowed number of format versions per object is limited—currently 255, for all versions.

If *any one object* reaches the limit, the whole database is rendered unusable. A backup and restore with *gbak* will be required to make it serviceable.

Transaction counter

All operations in Firebird occur in transactions. Each transaction is uniquely numbered with a Transaction ID that is a 32-bit unsigned integer. When the integers "run out", the database will be rendered unusable. Again, backup and restore will be needed to fix the situation.

The highest 32-bit integer is 2,147,483,647.

Validation and repair

Firebird provides utilities for validating the logical structures in databases, identifying minor problems and, to a limited extent, repairing them. A variety of such errors may appear from time to time, particularly in environments where networks are unstable or noisy or the power supply is subject to fluctuation. User behavior and application or database design deficiencies are also frequent causes of logical corruption.

Abnormal termination of client connections does not affect database integrity, since the Firebird server will eventually detect the lost connection. It preserves committed data changes and rolls back any left pending. Cleanup is more of a housekeeping issue, since data pages that were assigned for uncommitted changes are left as "orphans". Validation will detect such pages and free them for reassignment.

The validation tools are capable of detecting and removing minor anomalies caused by operating system or hardware faults. Such faults usually cause database integrity problems, due to corrupt writes to or loss of data or index pages.

Data thus lost or damaged are not recoverable but their artefacts must be removed to restore database integrity. If a database containing these compromised structures is backed up, the database will not be capable of being restored. It is important, therefore, to follow a controlled course of action to detect errors, eliminate them if possible and get the database back into a stable state.

The issues of validation and repair and how the tools can help are discussed in detail in the topic *Analysing and Repairing Logical Corruption* in the chapter entitled *Configuring and Managing Databases* in the companion volume to this, Vol. 3: ***Administering Firebird Servers and Databases*** and in ***The Firebird Book Second Edition***.

If you suspect you have a corrupt database, it is important to follow a proper sequence of recovery steps in order to avoid further corruption. The first, most important thing to do is ask or, if necessary, force all users to cancel their work and log out.

An Appendix entitled *Database Repair How-To* in the companion volume to this, Vol. 3: ***Administering Firebird Servers and Databases*** and in ***The Firebird Book Second Edition*** provides a detailed procedure for attempting to repair a corrupt or suspect database.

How to corrupt a Firebird database

Firebird is famously tolerant of trauma that are fatal to other DBMS systems. However, experience has shown up a few techniques that have proven useful if destruction of your database is among your objectives. The author wishes to share these database-killers with the reader.

1 Modify the system tables[1]

Firebird stores and maintains all of the metadata for its own and your user-defined objects in—a Firebird database! More precisely, it stores them in relations (tables) right in the database itself. The identifiers for the system tables, their columns and several other types of system objects begin with the characters 'RDB$'.

Because these are ordinary database objects, they can be queried and manipulated just like your user-defined objects. However, just because you can does not say you should.

It cannot be recommended too strongly that you use DDL—not direct SQL operations on the system tables—whenever you need to alter or remove metadata.

2 Restore a backup to a running database

Two of the restore options in the *gbak* utility (`-r[ecreate_database]` and `-rep[lace_database]`) allow you to restore a *gbak* file over the top of an existing database by overwriting it. It is possible for this style of restore to proceed without warning while users are logged in to the database. Database corruption is almost certain to be the result.

Prior to v.2.0, the `-r` abbreviation was for `-replace_database;` from v.2.0 the `-r` abbreviation is applicable to `-r[ecreate_database],` which acts like the `-c[reate]` switch and stops if the named database already exists, unless the `OVERWRITE` argument is present. No extra arguments are required for `-replace_database`. For now, it remains, in a deprecated status.

1. In a future version, probably v.3, the system tables will be made read-only.

Your Admin tools and procedures must be designed to prevent any user (including SYSDBA) from overwriting your active database if any users are logged in.

If is practicable to do so, it is recommended to restore to spare disk space using the `gbak -c[reate]` option. Before making the restored database live, test it in the spare location using *isql* or your preferred admin tool.

3 Allow users to log in during a restore

If your organization likes living on the edge, then use the –restore switch and let users log in and perform updates. Restore recreates the database from scratch and, as soon as the tables are recreated, your users can, potentially at least, hit them with DML operations while referential integrity and other constraints are still in the pipeline. At best, they will cause exceptions and a stack of uncommitted transactions in the partly-constructed database. At worst, they will thoroughly break data integrity in divers irrecoverable ways.

4 Copy database files while users are logged in

Use any filesystem copying or archiving utility (DOS copy, xcopy, tar, gzip, WinZip, WinRAR, etc.) to copy files while any user (including SYSDBA) is logged in. The copy will be damaged but, worse, sector locking and/or caching by these programs can cause data loss and possibly corruption within the original file.

Backup and Stand-by

Firebird 2 and higher come with two backup utilities: *gbak* and *nBackup*. They achieve backup in entirely different ways:

- For a backup, *gbak* writes a text file in a compressed formant (XDR) that contains instructions for reconstructing the entire database, including all data. A *gbak* restore recreates the database with completely fresh metadata and uses DML to populate it with the data that has been compressed into the backup file. It also has roles in maintaining database health.

  gbak can back up single-file or multi-file databases and restore them as single-file or multi-file. It can enable changes on restore of attributes such as page size and Owner.

  For details and instructions, refer to *The gbak Utility* in the companion volume to this, Vol. 3: ***Administering Firebird Servers and Databases*** or T***he Firebird Book Second Edition***, the chapter entitled *Backing Up Databases*.

- *nBackup*, available from the "2" series onward, is an incremental backup utility that works by keeping images of database pages. Working from a base image of the full database, it makes incremental files of changed pages, according to a user-defined cycle that can be at multiple levels. A restore is achieved by tracing a path from the base file through the latest incremental files down the levels until the most recent images of all pages are reconstituted.

  nBackup does not have any capabilities to clear garbage or monitor data in any fashion. It does not support multi-file databases.

  For details and instructions, refer to *Incremental Backup Tool (nBackup)* in the companion volume to this, Vol. 3: ***Administering Firebird Servers and Databases*** or T***he Firebird Book Second Edition***, the chapter entitled *Backing Up Databases*.

Stand-by

Firebird has the ability to maintain a "database shadow" for each database under the purview of the server. A shadow is a file whose internal structure is almost identical to a database and whose data is an exact copy of the latest data and metadata in the database it shadows, including, unfortunately, any data that were corrupted in writing. Firebird has tools to create shadows and to activate them when needed. Shadowing is neither replication nor backup but it might have its uses in the event of a hard disk crash, provided it is being maintained on a physically separate hard disk, of course.

For details and instructions, refer to *Database Shadowing* in the companion volume to this, Vol. 3: ***Administering Firebird Servers and Databases*** or ***The Firebird Book Second Edition***, the chapter entitled *Backing Up Databases*.

Dropping a Database

When a database is no longer required, it can be deleted (dropped) from the server. Dropping a database deletes all files pertaining to the entire database—primary and secondary files, shadow files, log files—and with it, of course, all its data.

The command to delete a database is DROP DATABASE and it takes no parameters. In order to execute the command, you need to be logged in to the database as its owner, as SYSDBA or as a user with root or Administrator system root privileges.

Syntax

```
DROP DATABASE;
```

A dropped database cannot be recovered, so

1. be certain that you really want it to be gone forever
2. take a backup first if there is even a remote chance that you will need anything from it in future

CHAPTER

14

TABLES

In SQL terms Firebird tables are persistent base tables. The standards define several other types, including viewed tables, which Firebird implements as views (see chapter 23) and derived tables, which Firebird implements in more than one way.

About Firebird Physical Tables

Unlike desktop databases, such as Paradox and xBase databases, a Firebird database is not a series of "table files" physically organized in rows and columns. Firebird stores data, independently of their structure, in a compressed format, on database pages. It may store one or many records—or, correctly, rows—of a table's data on a single page. In cases where the data for one row are too large to fit on one page, a row may span multiple pages.

Although a page which stores table data (a *data page*) will always contain only data belonging to one table, there is no requirement to store pages contiguously. The data for a table may be scattered all around the disk and, in multi-file databases, may be dispersed across several directories or disks. BLOB data are stored apart from the rows that own them, in another style of database page (a *BLOB page*).

Firebird can access text files that have data arranged as fixed length records and can read from or insert into them as though they were tables. For more details, refer to the later topic, Using External Files as Tables in this chapter.

Structural descriptions

Metadata—the physical descriptions of tables and their columns and attributes, as well as those of all other objects—are themselves stored in ordinary Firebird tables inside the database. RDB$RELATIONS stores a row for each table, while RDB$RELATION_FIELDS stores descriptive data for columns and links to the domains—stored in RDB$FIELDS—that provide the technical details of their definitions.[1] The Firebird engine writes to these tables when database objects are created, modified or destroyed. It refers to them constantly when carrying out operations on rows. These tables are known as *system tables*. Schemata for the system tables are in Appendix V.

1. RDB$FIELDS stores a dedicated domain definition for every column created unless that column was defined using a user-defined domain.

Creating Tables

It is assumed that, having reached the point where you are ready to create tables, you have already prepared your data analysis and modeling and have very clear blueprint for the structures of your main tables and their relationships. In preparation for creating these tables, you need to have performed these steps:

- You have created a database to accommodate them. For instructions, refer to the previous chapter.
- You have connected to the database
- If you plan to use domains for the data type definitions of your tables' columns, you have already created the domains—refer to Chapter 11

Table ownership and privileges

When a table is created, Firebird automatically applies the default SQL security scheme to it. The person who creates the table (the owner), is assigned all SQL privileges for it, including the right to grant privileges to other users, triggers, and stored procedures. No other user, except the SYSDBA or equivalent, will have any access to the table until explicitly granted privileges.

This security is as good (or bad) as the security of access to your server. Anyone who can log in to your server can create a database. Anyone who can attach to a database can create tables in it. You can mitigate the inherent risks by limiting the locations where databases can be created and accessed. See the DatabaseAccess parameter in firebird.conf.

For information about SQL privileges, refer to the companion volume to this, Vol. 3: ***Administering Firebird Servers and Databases*** or to ***The Firebird Book Second Edition***, the chapter entitled *Database-Level Security*.

CREATE TABLE statements

The DDL for creating a table is the CREATE TABLE statement.

Syntax

```
CREATE TABLE table [EXTERNAL [FILE] 'filespec']
  (<col_def> [, <col_def> | <table-constraint> ...]);
```

The first essential argument to CREATE TABLE is the table identifier . It is required, and must be unique among all table, view and procedure names in the database, otherwise you will be unable to create the table. You must also supply at least one column definition.

Defining columns

When you create a table in the database, your main task is to define the various attributes and constraints for each of the columns in the table.

Syntax for defining a column:

```
<col_def> = col {datatype | COMPUTED [BY] (<expr>) | domain}
[DEFAULT {literal |NULL |USER}]
[NOT NULL] [<col_constraint>]
[COLLATE collation]
```

The next sections list the required and optional attributes that you can define for a column.

Required attributes

- a column identifier (name), unique among the columns in the table.
- one of the following:

- an SQL data type
- an expression (expr) for a computed column marked by the COMPUTED [BY] keyword
- a domain definition (domain) for a domain-based column

Columns are separated by commas.

Example

```
CREATE TABLE PERSON (
    PERSON_ID BIGINT NOT NULL,
    FIRST_NAME VARCHAR(35),
    LAST_NAMES VARCHAR (80),
    FULL_NAME COMPUTED BY FIRST_NAME ||' '|| LAST_NAMES,
    PHONE_NUMBER TEL_NUMBER);
```

The column FULL_NAME is a computed column, calculated by concatenating two other columns in the definition, FIRST_NAME and LAST_NAMES. We will come back to computed columns a little later. A NOT NULL constraint is applied to PERSON_ID because we want to make it a primary key—details later.

For the PHONE_NUMBER column we use the domain that was defined in our Chapter 11 example:

```
CREATE DOMAIN TEL_NUMBER AS VARCHAR(18)
  CHECK (VALUE LIKE '(0%)%');
```

Columns based on domains

If a column definition is based on a domain, it can include a new default value, additional CHECK constraints, or a COLLATE clause that overrides one already defined in the domain definition. It can also include additional attributes or column constraints. For example, you can add a NOT NULL constraint to the column if the domain does not already define one.

A domain that is configured as NOT NULL cannot be overridden at column-level to be nullable.

For example, the following statement creates a table, COUNTRY, referencing a domain called COUNTRYNAME, which doesn't have a NOT NULL constraint:

```
CREATE TABLE COUNTRY (
    COUNTRY COUNTRYNAME NOT NULL PRIMARY KEY,
    CURRENCY VARCHAR(10) NOT NULL);
```

We add the NOT NULL constraint to the column definition of COUNTRYNAME because we know it is going to be needed as the primary key of the COUNTRY table.

Optional attributes

One or more of the following optional attributes can be included in a column definition.

DEFAULT value

Defining a default value can save data entry time and prevent data entry errors when new rows are inserted into a table. If the row is inserted without including the column in the column list, a default value—if defined—can be automatically written into the column. In a column based on a domain, the column can include a default value that locally overrides any default defined for the domain.

For example, a possible default for a TIMESTAMP column could be the context variable CURRENT_TIMESTAMP (server date and time). In a (True/False) Boolean-style character column the default could be set to 'F' to ensure that a valid, non-null state was written on all new rows.

A default value must be compatible with the data type of the column and consistent with any other constraints on the column or its underlying domain. A default, as appropriate to data type, can be:

- a constant, e.g. some string, numeric or date value.
- a context variable, e.g. CURRENT_TIMESTAMP, CURRENT_USER , CURRENT_CONNECTION, etc.
- a predefined date literal such as 'NOW', 'TOMORROW', etc.
- NULL can be set as the default for any nullable column . Nullable columns default to NULL automatically but you may wish to override an unwanted domain-level default. Don't define this default on a column that has a NOT NULL constraint.

When relying on defaults, it must be understood that a default will be applied only upon insertion of a new row AND only if the INSERT statement does not include the defaulted column in its column list. If your application includes the defaulted column in the INSERT statement and sends NULL in the values list, then NULL will be stored, regardless of any default defined. If the column is not nullable, passing NULL will always cause an exception.

Example The following example defines a column CREATED_BY that defaults to the context variable CURRENT_USER:

```
CREATE TABLE ORDER (
    ORDER_DATE DATE,
    CREATED_BY VARCHAR(31) DEFAULT CURRENT_USER,
    ORDER_AMOUNT DECIMAL(15,2));
```

A new row is inserted by user JILLIBEE, omitting CREATED_BY from the column list:

```
INSERT INTO ORDER (ORDER_DATE, ORDER_AMT)
  VALUES ('15-SEP-2014', 1004.42);
```

The table is queried:

```
SELECT * FROM ORDER;
...
ORDER_DATE  CREATED_BY       ORDER_AMOUNT
=========== ==========  ================
...
15-SEP-2014  JILLIBEE             1004.42
...
```

CHARACTER SET

A CHARACTER SET can be specified for an individual character or text BLOB column when you define the column. If you do not specify a character set, the column assumes the character set of the domain, if applicable; otherwise, it takes the default.character set of the database.

Example

```
CREATE TABLE TITLES_RUSSIAN (
    TITLE_ID BIGINT NOT NULL,
    TITLE_EN VARCHAR(100),
    TITLE VARCHAR(100) CHARACTER SET WIN1251);
```

Refer to Chapter 9, *Character Types*, for details about character sets and to Appendix VI for a list of available character sets.

A COLLATE clause

A COLLATE clause can be added to a CHAR or VARCHAR column to override a collation sequence otherwise defined for the column's character set by the underlying domain, if applicable. Collation sequence is not applicable to BLOB types.

Extending the example above to include a COLLATE clause:

```
CREATE TABLE TITLES_RUSSIAN (
    TITLE_ID BIGINT NOT NULL,
    TITLE_EN VARCHAR(100),
```

```
TITLE VARCHAR(100) CHARACTER SET WIN1251 COLLATE PXW_CYRL);
```

Caution *Take care when applying COLLATE clauses to columns that need to be indexed. The index width limit of one-quarter of page size (or, worse, 253 bytes for an ODS 10.n database) can be drastically reduced by some collation sequences. Experiment first!*

Refer to Appendix VI for a list of available character sets and the collations for each.

You can get your own list, which may include more recently added collation sequences, by creating a new database and running the query listed in Chapter 9, under the topic Listing available collation sequences.

COMPUTED columns

A computed column is one whose value is calculated each time the column is accessed at run time. It can be a convenient way to access redundant data without the negative effects of actually storing it. Not surprisingly, such columns cannot perform like hard data—refer to the restrictions enumerated below.

Syntax 1

```
..,
<col_name> COMPUTED [BY] (<expr>)
..
```

Syntax 2 In versions 2.1 and higher:

```
..,
<col_name> GENERATED ALWAYS AS (<expr>)
...
```

There is no need to specify the data type—Firebird calculates an appropriate one. `<expr>` is any scalar expression that is valid for the data types of the columns involved in the calculation. External functions are fine to use, as long as you are sure that the libraries used by the functions will be available on all platforms where the database might be installed. (For more information about external functions, a.k.a. "UDF's", refer to the chapter entitled *Expressions and Predicates* in the companion volume to this, Vol. 2: ***Developing with Firebird Data***, or in ***The Firebird Book Second Edition***.

Other restrictions exist for computed columns:

- Any columns that the expression refers to must have been defined before the computed column is defined, so it is a sensible practice to place computed columns last.
- A computed column cannot be defined as an ARRAY type or return an array.
- You can define a computed BLOB column by using a SELECT statement on a BLOB in another table but it is strongly recommended that you don't do this.
- Computed columns cannot be indexed
- Constraints placed on computed columns will be ignored or, in some cases, cause exceptions.
- Computed columns are output-only and read-only: including them in INSERT, UPDATE or INSERT OR UPDATE statements will cause exceptions

It is possible to create a computed column using a SELECT statement into another table. It is a practice to be avoided because of the undesirable dependencies involved. A properly normalized database model should not require it. DML syntax is available to obtain such subqueries at run-time or in a view.

Examples The following statement creates a computed column, FULL_NAME, by concatenating the LAST_NAME and FIRST_NAME columns.

```
CREATE TABLE PERSON (
    PERSON_ID BIGINT NOT NULL,
    FIRST_NAME VARCHAR(35) NOT NULL,
    LAST_NAMES VARCHAR (80) NOT NULL,
    FULL_NAME COMPUTED BY FIRST_NAME ||' '|| LAST_NAMES);
/**/
```

```
SELECT FULL_NAME FROM PERSON
WHERE LAST_NAMES STARTING WITH 'Smi';
FULL_NAME
=============================
Arthur Smiley
John Smith
Mary Smits
```

Notice the NOT NULL constraints on the two names being concatenated for this computed column. It is important to attend to such details with computed columns, because NULL as an element in a concatentation will always cause the result to be NULL.

The next statement computes two columns using context variables. This can be useful for logging the particulars of row creation:

```
CREATE TABLE SNIFFIT
    (SNIFFID INTEGER NOT NULL,
    SNIFF COMPUTED BY (CURRENT_USER),
    SNIFFDATE COMPUTED BY (CURRENT_TIMESTAMP));
/**/
SELECT FIRST 1 FROM SNIFFIT;
SNIFFID  SNIFF      SNIFFDATE
==============================
      1  SYSDBA     2014-08-15 08:15:35.0000
```

The next example creates a table with a calculated column (NEW_PRICE) using the previously created OLD_PRICE and PERCENT_CHANGE definitions:

```
CREATE TABLE PRICE_HISTORY (
    PRODUCT_ID D_IDENTITY NOT NULL, /* uses a domain */
    CHANGE_DATE DATE DEFAULT CURRENT_TIMESTAMP NOT NULL,
    UPDATER_ID D_PERSON NOT NULL, /* uses a domain */
    OLD_PRICE DECIMAL(13,2) NOT NULL,
    PERCENT_CHANGE DECIMAL(4,2)
      DEFAULT 0
      NOT NULL
      CHECK (PERCENT_CHANGE BETWEEN -50.00 AND 50.00),
    NEW_PRICE COMPUTED BY
      (OLD_PRICE + (OLD_PRICE * PERCENT_CHANGE / 100)) );
```

Constraints

In the parlance of relational databases, any restriction imposed on the format, range, content or dependency of a data structure is known as a constraint. Firebird provides several ways to implement constraints, including both formal, standards-defined integrity and referential constraints and user-defined CHECK constraints.

Constraints are visible to all transactions that access the database and are automatically enforced by the server. They exist in their own right as objects in a Firebird database and can be assigned custom identifiers. Each constraint is uniquely represented in the metadata, with the rules and dependencies of each being defined through regular relationships between the system tables.

Scope of Constraints

Constraints vary in their scope of action. Some—such as NOT NULL, for example—are applied directly to a single column (*column constraints*) while others—such as PRIMARY

KEY and some CHECK constraints—take effect at table level (*table constraints*). The FOREIGN KEY constraint has table-to-table scope.

Integrity Constraints

Integrity constraints impose rules that govern the state of acceptable data items or a relationship between the column and the table as a whole—often both. Examples are NOT NULL (rejects input that has unknown value), UNIQUE (requires that an incoming item has no matching value in that column anywhere in the table) and PRIMARY KEY (combines both of the others and also "represents" the table for referential relationships with other tables).

Each of the integrity constraints is discussed individually in detail later in this chapter.

The referential constraint

The referential constraint is implemented as FOREIGN KEY. A foreign key constraint exists only in the context of another table and a unique key from that table, signalled implicitly or explicitly by the REFERENCES clause of its definition.

Tables that are linked in a foreign key relationship are said to be bound by a referential integrity constraint. Thus, any column or group of columns constrained by a PRIMARY KEY or UNIQUE constraint is also potentially subject to referential constraints.

The subject is discussed in detail in Chapter 17, *Referential Integrity*.

Named constraints

When declaring a table-level or a column-level constraint, you can optionally name the constraint using the CONSTRAINT clause. If you omit the CONSTRAINT clause, Firebird generates a unique system constraint name. Constraints are stored in the system table, RDB$RELATION_CONSTRAINTS.

Although naming a constraint is optional, assigning a meaningful name with the CONSTRAINT clause can make the constraint easier to find for changing or dropping or when its name appears in a constraint violation error message. Consider, for example, a constraint with the assigned name INTEG_99: you could spend a lot of time chasing around the system tables to find out what it belongs to and what might have caused a violation.

Apart from its benefits for self-documentation, this style is particularly useful for distinguishing the key definitions from the column definitions in scripts that will be kept as system documentation.

PRIMARY KEY and FOREIGN KEY names

Naming a constraint has special implications for PRIMARY KEY and FOREIGN KEY constraints, particularly from Firebird 1.5 forward. It is possible to override Firebird's native naming rules for keys:

In all versions, a supplied name will override the default name INTEG_nn and apply the supplied name to the constraint. The supporting indexes will, by default, have the same name as the named constraint, if the constraint is named; other wise they will be named RDB$PRIMARYnn and RDB$FOREIGNnn, respectively.

V.1.0.x In versions 1.0.x, the default index name (RDB$PRIMARYnn or RDB$FOREIGN_nn) is enforced

The constraint-naming behaviors are described in more detail below and in Chapter 17, *Referential Integrity*.

The NOT NULL Constraint

The optional NOT NULL constraint is a column-level constraint that can be applied to force the user to enter a value.

Because of its role in the formation of keys, you need to be aware of certain restrictions pertaining to the NOT NULL constraint:

- it must be applied to the definition of any column that will be involved in a PRIMARY KEY or UNIQUE constraint
- it cannot be removed from a domain or column by an ALTER DOMAIN or ALTER TABLE ALTER COLUMN statement nor by overriding a domain at column level—do not use a domain that is constrained NOT NULL to define a column that is allowed to be NULL
- it is recommended in the definition of any column that will be involved in a UNIQUE constraint or a unique index since one and only one NULL is allowed per key segment in such indexes and allowing NULLs in these structures is not good practice, normally.

V.1.0.x Firebird 1.0 versions do not permit any NULLs in UNIQUE constraints or UNIQUE indexes.

Firebird does not support a NULLABLE attribute, as some non-standard DBMS do. In compliance with standards, all columns in Firebird are nullable unless explicitly constrained to be NOT NULL. Null is not a value, so any attempt to input null to the column or set it to null will cause an exception.

For more insight into NULL, refer to the topics <u>*Demystifying NULL*</u> in Chapter 5 and <u>*Considering NULL*</u> in the chapter entitled <u>*Expressions and Predicates*</u> in the companion volume to this, Vol. 2: ***Developing with Firebird Data***, or in ***The Firebird Book Second Edition***.

The PRIMARY KEY constraint

PRIMARY KEY is a table-level integrity constraint—a set of enforceable rules—which formally earmarks a column or group of columns as the unique identifier of each row in the table. While the PRIMARY KEY constraint is not itself a *referential constraint*, it is usually a mandatory part of any referential constraint, being potentially the object of the REFERENCES clause of a FOREIGN KEY constraint.

A table can have only one primary key. When you define the constraint, Firebird automatically creates the required index, using a set of naming rules which cannot be overridden. The names of primary key indexes are discussed below.

Simply creating a unique index does not create a primary key. A primary key is not an index, but a constraint in its own right. Creating a PRIMARY KEY constraint does, however, create the required index using the columns enumerated in the constraint declaration.

Do not import an existing primary index from a file-based legacy system or create such an index in anticipation of declaring a primary key constraint. Firebird cannot piggy-back a primary key constraint onto an existing index—at least up to and including release 2.5—and the query optimizer does not perform properly if indexes are duplicated.

Choosing a primary key

Identifying candidate columns to be the primary key is a science in itself and beyond the scope of this Guide. Many worthy tomes have been written on the subject of normalization, the process of eliminating redundancy and repeating groups in sets of data and arriving at a correct identification of the element that uniquely represents one single row set in the table. If you are a newcomer to relational databases, the value of investing in a good book about data modeling cannot be stressed enough.

A primary key candidate—which may be one column or a group of columns—has two unbreakable requirements:

- The NOT NULL attribute must be declared for all columns in the group of one or more columns which will be used. The integrity of the key can be enforced only by comparing values and NULL is not a value.
- The column or group of columns has to be unique—that is, it cannot occur in more than one row in the table. A driver's licence or social security number might be considered, for example, because they are generated by systems that are presumed not to issue duplicate numbers.

To these theoretical "givens" must be added a third one:

- The total size (width) of the candidate key must be within the limit of one-quarter of the page size. In Firebird 1.X, the limit is even smaller: 253 bytes or less. This is not simply a matter of counting characters. The implementation limit will be reduced—in some cases, drastically—if there are multiple columns, non-binary collations or multi-byte character sets involved.

How real data can defeat you

Using the EMPLOYEE table from the `employee.fdb` database in the Firebird `root/examples/empbuild` directory (`employee.gdb` in the v.1.0.x kits), let's illustrate how real data can defeat your theoretical assumptions about uniqueness. Here is a declaration that shows, initially, the meaningful data stored in this table:

```
CREATE TABLE EMPLOYEE (
    FIRST_NAME VARCHAR(15) NOT NULL, /* assumption: an employee must have
                                                        a first name */
    LAST_NAME VARCHAR(20) NOT NULL, /* assumption:  an employee must have
                                                        a last name */
    PHONE_EXT VARCHAR(4),
    HIRE_DATE DATE DEFAULT CURRENT_DATE NOT NULL,
    DEPT_NO CHAR(3) NOT NULL,
    JOB_CODE VARCHAR(5) NOT NULL,
    JOB_GRADE SMALLINT NOT NULL,
    JOB_COUNTRY VARCHAR(15) NOT NULL,
    SALARY NUMERIC (15, 2) DEFAULT 0 NOT NULL,
    FULL_NAME COMPUTED BY FIRST_NAME ||' '||LAST_NAME
) ;
```

This structure in fact has no candidate key. It is not possible to identify a single employee row by using (FIRST_NAME, LAST_NAME) as the key, since the combination of both elements has a medium-to-high probability of being duplicated in the organization. We could not store records for two employees named "John Smith".

In order to get a key, it is necessary to invent something. That "something" is the mechanism known as a *surrogate key*.

Surrogate keys

We have already visited the surrogate key in the introductory topic on keys in Chapter 14. A surrogate primary key is a value of guaranteed uniqueness and no semantic content, that substitutes for the key in a table structure that cannot provide a candidate key from within its own structure. The EMPLOYEE table therefore introduces EMP_NO (declared from a domain) to take this surrogate role for it:

```
CREATE DOMAIN EMPNO SMALLINT ;
COMMIT;
ALTER TABLE EMPLOYEE
    ADD EMP_NO EMPNO NOT NULL,
    ADD CONSTRAINT PK_EMPLOYEE
```

```
PRIMARY KEY(EMP_NO) ;
```

This database also maintains a generator named EMP_NO_GEN and a Before Insert trigger named SET_EMP_NO on the EMPLOYEE table, to produce a value for this key whenever a new row is inserted. The topic *Implementing Auto-Incrementing Keys* in the *Triggers* chapter of the companion volume to ths, Vol. 2: ***Developing with Firebird Data***, or in ***The Firebird Book Second Edition***, describes this technique in detail. It is the recommended way to implement surrogate keys in Firebird.

You may wish to consider the benefits of using a surrogate primary key not just in cases where the table cannot supply candidates but also in cases where your candidate key is composite. Any columns containing data that are meaningful and/or editable are non-atomic. Using non-atomic columns for keys is poor practice in general. For more discussion, read on to the topic *Atomicity of PRIMARY KEY columns* later in this section.

Composite primary keys

During data analysis, it sometimes happens that no single unique column can be found in the data structure. Theory suggests that the next best thing is to look for two or more columns that, when grouped together as the key, will ensure a unique row. When multiple columns are conjoined to form a key, the key is called a *composite key* or, sometimes, a *compound key*.

If you come to Firebird with a cargo of background experience working with a DBMS such as Paradox, using composite keys to implement hierarchical relationships, it can be quite hard to part with the notion that you cannot live without them. Yet, in practice, composite keys should be considered with a high degree of restraint in a DBMS like Firebird, which does not track through disk-based physical index structures to implement relationships.

Firebird does not need composite indexes and, more to the point, they do impose some problems, both for development and, when large tables are involved, for performance:

- Composite keys are typically composed of non-atomic key elements—that is, the columns selected have semantic meaning (they are "significant as data") and are almost certainly vulnerable to external changes, redundancy, duplication and typographical errors.
- Any foreign keys in other tables that reference this table will have to propagate every element of the composite key. Referential integrity is at risk from the use of non-atomic keys. A combination of non-atomic elements compounds the risk.
- Keys—foreign, as well as primary—have mandatory indexes. Composite indexes have stricter size limits than single-column indexes.
- Composite indexes tend to be large. Large indexes use more database pages, causing indexed operations (sorts, joins, comparisons) to be slower than is necessary.

Atomicity of PRIMARY KEY columns

It is recommended practice to avoid involving in your primary and foreign keys any column which is meaningful as data. It violates one of the primary principles of relational database design, that of *atomicity*. The atomicity principle requires that each item of data exist completely in its own right, with a single, internal rule governing its existence.

For a primary key to be atomic, it should be beyond the reach of human decision. If a human has to spell it or type it, it is not atomic. If it is subject to any rule except the non-nullable, unique requirements, it is not atomic. Using the earlier example, even a systematic number such as a driver's licence or a social security number does not have the atomicity required for a primary key, because it is subject to an external system.

Syntaxes for declaring the primary key

Several syntaxes are available for assigning the PRIMARY KEY constraint to a column or group of columns. All columns that are elements in a PRIMARY KEY must be previously defined as NOT NULL. Since it is not possible to add a NOT NULL constraint to a column after it has been created, it is essential to take care of this constraint before applying the additional constraint.

The PRIMARY KEY constraint can be applied in any of the following phases of metadata creation:

- in the column definition, during CREATE TABLE or ALTER TABLE, as part of the column's definition set
- in the table definition, during CREATE TABLE or ALTER TABLE, as a separately-defined table constraint

Defining PRIMARY KEY as part of a column definition

In the following sequence, a non-nullable domain is defined and committed ahead; then the primary key column is defined using that domain and, simultaneously, the PRIMARY KEY constraint is applied to the table immediately:

```
CREATE DOMAIN D_IDENTITY AS BIGINT NOT NULL;
COMMIT;
CREATE TABLE PERSON (
      PERSON_ID D_IDENTITY PRIMARY KEY,
      ...
);
```

Firebird creates a table constraint with a name like INTEG_nn and an index with a name like RDB$PRIMARYnn. With this method, you cannot influence what these names will be, nor change them.

nn in each case is a number spun from a generator. The two numbers are unrelated.

The effect is similar if you use the same approach when adding a column using ALTER TABLE and make it the primary key:

```
ALTER TABLE BOOK
    ADD BOOK_ID D_IDENTITY PRIMARY KEY;
```

Defining PRIMARY KEY as a named constraint

Another way to define the primary key in the table definition is to add the constraint declaration at the end of the column definitions. The constraint declarations are placed last because they are dependent on the existence of the columns to which they apply. This method gives you the option of naming the constraint. The following declaration names the primary key constraint as PK_ATABLE:

```
CREATE TABLE ATABLE (
    ID BIGINT NOT NULL,
    ANOTHER_COLUMN VARCHAR(20),
    CONSTRAINT PK_ATABLE PRIMARY KEY(ID) );
```

Now, instead of the system-generated name RDB$PRIMARYnnn, Firebird stores PK_ATABLE as the name of the constraint. Except in Firebird 1.0.x, it also applies the user-defined constraint name to the enforcing unique index: in this example, the index will be named PK_ATABLE (but INTEG_nn in v.1.0.x).

Using a custom index

It is possible to ask Firebird to enforce the primary key with a descending index. For this, there is an optional syntax extension in the form of the USING clause, enabling constraint-supporting indexes to be defined as either ASC[ENDING] or DESC[ENDING] and to have a name that is different to that of the named constraint. It cannot be used as a way to utilise an index that already exists.

ASC and DESC determine the direction of the search order—lowest or highest first. The concept is discussed in more detail in the next chapter, *Indexes*.

If you specify a DESCENDING index for a primary or unique constraint, you must be sure to specify USING DESC INDEX when defining any foreign keys that reference it.

The following statement will create a primary key constraint named PK_ATEST and enforce it by creating a descending index named IDX_PK_ATEST:

```
CREATE TABLE ATEST (
      ID BIGINT NOT NULL,
      DATA VARCHAR(10));
COMMIT;

ALTER TABLE ATEST
    ADD CONSTRAINT PK_ATEST PRIMARY KEY(ID)
      USING DESC INDEX IDX_PK_ATEST;
COMMIT;
```

The create-time syntax will work, too:

```
CREATE TABLE ATEST (
    ID BIGINT NOT NULL,
    DATA VARCHAR(10),
    CONSTRAINT PK_ATEST PRIMARY KEY(ID)
      USING DESC INDEX IDX_PK_ATEST;
```

Adding a primary key to an existing table

The addition of table constraints can be deferred. It is a common practice for developers to define all of their tables without any table constraints and to add them subsequently, using a separate script. The rationale behind this practice is good: large scripts notoriously fail because the author overlooked some dependency. It simply causes fewer headaches to build databases in a sequence that eliminates the time and spleen spent on patching dependency errors and re-running scripts.

Typically, in the first script, we declare and commit the tables:

```
CREATE TABLE ATABLE (
      ID BIGINT NOT NULL,
      ANOTHER_COLUMN VARCHAR(20),
      < more columns > );
CREATE TABLE ANOTHERTABLE (
      ... );
...
COMMIT;
ALTER TABLE ATABLE
      ADD CONSTRAINT PK_ATABLE
      PRIMARY KEY(ID);
ALTER TABLE ANOTHERTABLE...
```

and so on.

In Chapter 17, when exploring FOREIGN KEY definitions, the benefits of building databases in a dependency-safe sequence will become obvious.

The UNIQUE constraint

A UNIQUE constraint, like a primary key, ensures that no two rows have the same value for a specified column or group of columns. You can have more than one UNIQUE constraint defined for a table, but it cannot be the applied to the same set of columns that is used for either the PRIMARY KEY or another UNIQUE constraint.

A unique constraint, in fact, actually creates a unique key that has virtually the same powers as the primary key. It can be selected as the controlling key for a referential integrity constraint. This makes it useful for situations where you define a thin, surrogate primary key for atomicity and to improve performance of join and search operations, but you want to keep the option to form an alternative FOREIGN KEY link on the unique key for occasional use.

Although a nullable field is allowed in a UNIQUE constraint, no more than one NULL is allowed in each segment of the supporting index. Unless you have a specific design requirement for certain records with NULLs in the segments, simplify your life and make all the key fields non-nullable.

V.1.0.x In Firebird 1.0.x, the NOT NULL attribute must be applied to all of the columns on which the UNIQUE constraint will operate.

Like the primary key constraint, UNIQUE creates its own mandatory, unique index to enforce its rules. Naming of both the constraint and the index follows the same rules of behavior applicable to other keys: you can customise the name and direction of the supporting index by naming the constraint and/or by applying the optional `USING <index-name>` clause

. The following example in *isql* illustrates the naming behavior:

```
SQL> CREATE TABLE TEST_UQ (
CON>  ID BIGINT NOT NULL,
CON>  DATA VARCHAR(10),
CON>  DATA_ID BIGINT NOT NULL);
SQL> COMMIT;
SQL> ALTER TABLE TEST_UQ
CON>ADD CONSTRAINT PK_TEST_UQ PRIMARY KEY(ID),
CON>ADD CONSTRAINT UQ1_DATA UNIQUE(DATA_ID) ;
SQL> COMMIT;
SQL> SHOW TABLE TEST_UQ;
ID          BIGINT          NOT NULL
DATA        VARCHAR(10)     NULLABLE
DATA_ID     BIGINT          NOT NULL
CONSTRAINT PK_TEST_UQ:
   Primary key (ID)
CONSTRAINT UQ1_DATA:
   Unique key (DATA_ID)
SQL> SHOW INDICES TEST_UQ;
PK_TEST_UQ UNIQUE INDEX ON TEST_UQ(ID)
UQ1_DATA UNIQUE INDEX ON TEST_UQ(DATA_ID)
SQL> /* optional USING clause sets a custom name for the supporting index
CON> and, if a for the supporting index
SQL> CREATE TABLE TEST2_UQ (
CON> ID BIGINT NOT NULL,
CON> DATA VARCHAR(10),
CON> DATA_ID BIGINT NOT NULL,
CON> CONSTRAINT PK_TEST2_UQ PRIMARY KEY
CON> USING INDEX IDX_PK_TEST2_UQ);
```

```
SQL> COMMIT;
```

Remember the mantra: "an index is not a key". You can define unique indexes—see the next chapter for details—but making a unique index does not create a unique key. If there is a chance that you might need to use a uniquely indexed column or structure as a key, consider defining the constraint instead.

CHECK constraints

A CHECK constraint is used for validating incoming data values—it enforces a match condition or requirement that a value must meet in order for an insert or update to succeed. It cannot change the incoming value—it will return a validation exception if the input fails the check.

CHECK constraints are applied after "Before" triggers have fired. Use a trigger when you need to perform a validation and conditionally change it to a valid one. "Before" and "After" triggers are discussed in detail in Chapter 30.

In a table definition, a CHECK constraint applies at table level. Unlike the CHECK constraints applied to domain definitions, its checked element is expressed as a column reference, not a generic value.

For example, on a domain, a CHECK clause might be

```
CHECK (VALUE > 10)
```

In a table definition, the same conditioning for a column named ACOLUMN would be expressed as

```
CHECK (ACOLUMN > 10)
```

CHECK activity

A CHECK constraint is active in both INSERT and UPDATE operations. Although it is a table-level constraint, its scope can range from column-level, through row-level and, although it is not recommended, to table-level and even beyond the boundaries of the table. It guarantees data integrity only when the values being verified are in the same row as the value being checked.

Beware of using expressions that compare the value with values in different rows of the same table or in different tables, since any row other than the current one is potentially in the process of being modified or deleted by another transaction. Especially, do not rely on a CHECK constraint to enforce a referential relationship!

.The search condition can

- verify that the value entered falls within a defined range
- match the value with a list of allowed values
- compare the value with a constant, an expression or with data values in other columns of the same row

Constraint restrictions

- A column can have only one CHECK constraint, although its logic can be expressed as a complex search condition—one constraint, many conditions.
- A CHECK constraint on a domain-based column cannot override the inherited domain-level check. The column definition can use a regular CHECK clause to add additional constraint logic to the inherited constraint. It will be ANDed to the inherited conditions.
- A CHECK constraint cannot refer to a domain.

Syntax of the CHECK constraint

A CHECK constraint can be written to support practically any validation rule—theoretically, almost any search condition will be accepted. It is important for the designer to choose conditions that are reasonable and safe, since they affect every insert and update operation on the table.

```
CHECK (<search condition>);
<search_condition> =
<val> <operator> {<val> |(<select_one>)}
| <val> [NOT] BETWEEN <val> AND <val>
| <val> [NOT] LIKE <val> [ESCAPE <val>]
| <val> [NOT] IN (<val> [, <val> ...] | <select_list>)
| <val> IS [NOT] NULL
| <val> {[NOT]{=|<|>}|>=|<=}
{ALL |SOME |ANY}(<select_list>)
| EXISTS (<select_expr>)
|SINGULAR (<select_expr>)
| <val> [NOT] CONTAINING <val>
| <val> [NOT] STARTING [WITH] <val>
|(<search_condition>)
|NOT<search_condition>
| <search_condition> OR <search_condition>
| <search_condition> AND <search_condition>
```

For syntaxes for setting the various styles of search condition consult the companion volume to this, Vol. 2: ***Developing with Firebird Data***, or ***The Firebird Book Second Edition***, the chapter entitled *Expressions and Predicates*.

Example

This constraint tests the values of two columns to ensure that one is greater than the other. Although it also implies NOT NULL conditioning on both columns—the check will fail if either column is null—it does not confer NOT NULL constraint on the column:

```
CHECK (VALUE (COL_1 > COL_2));
```

The check will fail if the arithmetic test fails or if either COL_1 or COL_2 is null. This succeeds:

```
INSERT INTO TABLE_1 (COL_1, COL_2) VALUES (6,5);
```

Using External Files as Tables

In the current SQL argot, Firebird supports the external virtual table, or EVT. File-system files in text format can be read and manipulated by Firebird as if they were tables—albeit with considerable limitations arising from the fact that they are not internal database objects. Other applications can thus exchange data with a Firebird database, independently of any special transforming mechanism. External tables can be converted to internal tables.

The EXTERNAL FILE clause enables a table to be defined with its row structure mapping to fixed length "fields"in "records" (usually delimited by line-feeds) that reside in an external file. Firebird can select from and insert into such a file as if it were a regular table. It cannot, however, perform update or delete operations on external tables.

The text file containing the data must be created on or copied to a storage device that is physically under the control of the server—as usual, no NFS devices, shares or mapped drives.

Shared access by Firebird and other applications at file level is not possible. Firebird requires exclusive access during times when it has the file open in a transaction. At other times, the file can be modified by other applications.

Syntax The CREATE TABLE statement for activating or creating an external file defines both the external file specification—local location and file name—and the typed Firebird columns represented by the structure of the contained records.

```
CREATE TABLE EXT_TBL
    EXTERNAL FILE filespec
      (columndef [,columndef,...],
      [line_delimiter_1 CHAR(1)
      [, line_delimiter_2 CHAR(1)]]);
```

`filespec` is the fully qualified local path and file specification for the external data file. The file need not exist at the time the table is created. However, from Firebird 1.5 forward, the CREATE statement will fail if the filespec refers to an unconfigured external file location—see the topic Securing external files, below, and the ExternalFileAccess configuration topic in Chapter 3.

`columndef` is an ordinary Firebird column definition. Non-character data types can be specified, provided every string extracted from the column's location in the external record is capable of being cast implicitly to that type

`line_delimiter` is an optional final column or pair of columns that can be defined to read the characters used by the file system to mark the end of a line of text. Although it makes reading the file easier for humans, it is not a requirement in a fixed format record unless programs that are going to read the data require it..

- on Linux/UNIX, this is the single character ASCII 10, the linefeed character
- on Windows, it is the ordered pair ASCII 13 (carriage return) followed by ASCII 10
- on Mac OS, it is ASCII 10 followed by ASCII 13
- other operating systems may use other variations or other characters

Restrictions and recommendations

Because the content of external files is beyond the control of the Firebird engine, certain restrictions and precautions are needed to ensure the integrity of both the data and the server when deploying them.

Securing external files

By default, access to external files is blocked by the ***ExternalFileAccess*** setting in `firebird.conf` being configured as NONE. A list of directories can be configured to restrict the locations where Firebird will search for or create external files. It is also possible to configure open access to anywhere in the file system. This is NOT recommended.

When deploying a database that uses this feature, make sure you set up a configuration for external files that cannot be compromised through either malicious or careless access.

For more information, refer to the parameter *ExternalFileAccess* in the companion volume to this, Vol. 3: ***Administering Firebird Servers and Databases*** or in Chapter 34 of ***The Firebird Book Second Edition***.

Format of external data

Firebird will create the external file itself if it does not find it in the location specified in the CREATE EXTERNAL TABLE `'<filespec>'` specification. If the file already exists, each record must be of fixed length, consisting of fixed-length fields that exactly match the declared maximum byte-length of the column specifications in the table definition. If the application that created the file uses hard line breaks, e.g. the two-byte carriage return and line break sequence in Windows text files, include a column to accommodate this sequence—see *End-of-line characters*, below.

BLOB and array data cannot be read from or written to an external file.

Most well-formed number data can be read directly from an external table and, in most cases, Firebird will be able to use its internal casting rules to interpret it correctly. However, it may be easier and more precise to read the numbers into character columns and, later, convert them using the CAST(..) function.

*Make sure you allow enough width to accommodate your data. For some guidelines on sizes, refer to the relevant chapter for the particular data type in Part Two, **Firebird Data Types and Domains**. In Chapter 6, the topic Valid Conversions contains a tabulated summary of the rules for data type conversions.*

CHAR vs VARCHAR

Using VARCHAR in the column definition of an external string field is not recommended because it is not a readily portable format:

```
<2-byte unsigned short><string of character bytes>
```

Varchar requires the initial 2-byte unsigned short to include the number of bytes in the actual string, and the string immediately follows. This is difficult or impossible for many external applications to achieve and it simply isn't worth the trouble. For this reason, favour CHAR over VARCHAR for string fields and ensure that the feeding application pads the strings to full length.

End-of-line characters

When you create the table that will be used to import the external data, you must define a column to contain the end-of-line (EOL) or new-line character if the application that created the file includes it. The size of this column must be exactly large enough to contain a particular system's EOL symbol (usually one or two bytes). For most versions of UNIX, it is 1 byte. For Windows and Macintosh, it is 2 bytes.

Tips for inserting non-printable characters

When inserting to an external file, the function `ASCII_CHAR(decimal_ASCII_code)` (or, for versions prior to v.2.1, the external function of the same name from the `ib_udf` function library) can be used to pass the non-printable characters as an expression to the line delimiter columns in the SQL statement. For example, to insert a carriage return and line feed into a column:

```
INSERT INTO MY_EXT_TABLE (
      <COLUMNS...>,
      CRLF)
VALUES (
      <column_values...>,
      ASCII_CHAR(13) || ASCII_CHAR(10));
```

An alternative is to create a table to store any non-printable characters your applications might need to store. Create a table for the purpose and create a regular text file on the same platform as the server, using an editor that "displays" non-printable characters. Open your NPC table using an interactive tool and copy-paste the characters from the file directly to the table. For statements performing inserts to the external file, the character can be subqueried from this NPC table.

Operations

Only INSERT and SELECT operations can be performed on the rows of an external table. Attempts to update or delete rows will return errors.

Because the data are outside the database, operations on an external table are not under Firebird's record version control. Inserts therefore take effect immediately and cannot be rolled back.

If you want your table to be under transaction control, create another, internal Firebird table, and insert the data from the external table into the internal one.

Importing external files to Firebird tables

To import an external file into a Firebird table, begin by making sure that you have set up the appropriate access conditions—refer to Chapter 37 regarding the server parameter ExternalFileAccess in the topic Server Configuration.

1 Create a table to view raw data

Create a Firebird table that allows you to view the external data. Declare all columns as CHAR. The text file containing the data must be on the server. In the following example, the external file exists on a UNIX system, so the EOL character is 1 byte.

```
CREATE TABLE EXT_TBL EXTERNAL FILE 'file.txt' (
      FNAME CHAR(10),
      LNAME CHAR(20),
      HDATE CHAR(10),
      NEWLINE CHAR(1));
COMMIT;
```

2 Create the working table

Create another Firebird table that will eventually be your working table. Include a column for the EOL character if you expect to export data from the internal table back to an external file later:

```
CREATE TABLE PERSONNEL (
      FIRST_NAME VARCHAR(10),
      LAST_NAME VARCHAR(20),
      HIRE_DATE DATE,
      NEW_LINE CHAR(1));
COMMIT;
```

3 Populate the file

Using a text editor, or an application that can output fixed-format text, create and populate the external file. Make each record the same length, pad the unused characters with blanks, and insert the EOL character(s) at the end of each record.

The number of characters in the EOL string is platform-specific—refer to the notes above.

The following example illustrates a fixed-length record with a length of 41 characters. "b" represents a blank space, and "n" represents the EOL:

```
12345678901234567890123456789012345678901
fname.....lname...............hdate.....n
CaitlinbbbCochranebbbbbbbbbbbb2014-12-10n
AlexanderbGalbraithbbbbbbbbbbb2013-10-01n
NicholasbbMailaubbbbbbbbbbbbbb2012-10-05n
RosebbbbbbGalbraithbbbbbbbbbbb2011-07-01n
MogginzbbbLeChatbbbbbbbbbbbbbb2011-09-21n
```

4 Test the file

A SELECT statement from table EXT_TBL returns the records from the external file:

```
SELECT FNAME, LNAME, HDATE FROM EXT_TBL;
```

```
FNAME     LNAME              HDATE
========= ================== ===========
Caitlin   Cochrane           2014-12-10
Alexander Galbraith          2013-10-01
Nicholas  Mailau             2012-10-05
Rose      Galbraith          2011-07-01
Mogginz   LeChat             2011-09-21
```

5 Complete the import

Insert the data into the destination table.

```
INSERT INTO PERSONNEL
  SELECT FNAME, LNAME, CAST(HDATE AS DATE),
  NEWLINE FROM EXT_TBL;
COMMIT;
```

If you try to access the external file whilst it is still opened by another application, the attempt will fail. The reverse is also true. Furthermore, in versions prior to v.2.0, once your application has opened the file as a table, it will be unavailable to other applications until your application disconnects from the database.

Now, when you perform a SELECT from PERSONNEL, the data from your external table will appear in converted form:

```
SELECT FIRST_NAME, LAST_NAME, HIRE_DATE
  FROM PERSONNEL;
FIRST_NAME LAST_NAME          HIRE_DATE
========== ================== ===========
Caitlin    Cochrane           10-DEC-2014
Alexander  Galbraith          01-OCT-2013
Nicholas   Mailau             05-OCT-2012
Rose       Galbraith          01-JUL-2011
Mogginz    LeChat             21-OCT-2011
```

Exporting Firebird tables to an external file

Carrying on with the example illustrated in the previous section, the steps for exporting data to our external table are similar:

1 Clear the external file

Open the external file in a text editor and remove everything from the file. Exit from the editor and again perform the SELECT query on EXT_TBL. It should be empty.

2 Pump out the data

Use an INSERT statement to copy the Firebird records from PERSONNEL into the external file, file.txt:

```
INSERT INTO EXT_TBL
  SELECT
    FIRST_NAME, LAST_NAME,
    cast(HIRE_DATE AS VARCHAR(11),
    ASCII_CHAR(10)
    FROM PERSONNEL
      WHERE FIRST_NAME LIKE 'Clau%';
```

3 Test the external table

Now, querying the external table:

```
SELECT FNAME, LNAME, HDATE FROM EXT_TBL;
```

```
FNAME      LNAME              HDATE
========== ================== ===========
Caitlin    Cochrane           10-DEC-2014
....
Mogginz    LeChat             21-OCT-2011
```

Converting external tables to internal tables

It is possible to convert the current data in external tables to an internal tables. The means to do this is to back up the database using the *gbak* utility with the `-convert` switch (abbreviation `-co`). All external tables defined in the database will be converted to internal tables by restoring the backup. Afterwards, the external table definition will be lost.

For more information, refer to the section *The gbak Utility* in the companion volume to this, Vol 3: ***Administering Firebird Servers and Databases***, or in ***The Firebird Book Second Edition***, in the chapter entitled ***Backing Up Databases.***

Dropped database

If you use DROP DATABASE to delete the database, you must also remove the external file—it will not be automatically deleted as a result of DROP DATABASE.

Altering Tables

The ALTER TABLE statement is used for changing the structure of a table: adding, changing or dropping columns or constraints. One statement can encompass several changes, if required. To submit an ALTER TABLE request, you need to be logged in as the table's creator (owner), SYSDBA or an equivalent superuser.

Alterations to each table, or to its triggers, are reference-counted. Any one table can be altered at most 255 times before you must back up and restore the database. However, the reference count is not affected by switching a trigger on and off using (and only this) syntax variant:

```
ALTER TRIGGER triggername ACTIVE | INACTIVE
```

*For more information about ALTER TRIGGER, consult the topic Changing Triggers in Chapter 30 of **The Firebird Book Second Edition** or Chapter 13 of the companion volume to this, **Developing with Firebird Data.***

Any data format conversions required by changes are not performed *in situ* by the engine. Firebird stores the new format description and delays the translation until the data are needed. It introduces a performance hit that could have an unanticipated impact on a user's work. Plan to perform a backup and restore after changes in table structures if the database contains any data.

Preparing to use ALTER TABLE

Before modifying or dropping columns or attributes in a table, you need to do three things:

1. Make sure you have the proper database privileges.
2. Save the existing data.
3. Drop any dependency constraints on the column.
4. Plan a backup and restore after changes in table structures if the database contains any data.

Altering Columns in a Table

Existing columns in tables can be modified in a few respects, viz.

- The name of the column can be changed to another name not already used in the table
- The column can be "moved" to a different position in the left-to-right column order
- Conversions from non-character to character data are allowed, with some restrictions

Syntax

```
ALTER TABLE table
  ALTER [COLUMN] simple_column_name alteration
alteration = new_col_name | new_col_type | new_col_pos
new_col_name = TO simple_column_name
new_col_type = TYPE datatype_or_domain
new_col_pos = POSITION integer
```

If you attempt to rename a column, you will bump into dependency problems if the column is referred to by a constraint or is used in a view, trigger or stored procedure.

Examples

Here we change the name of a column from EMP_NO to EMP_NUM:

```
ALTER TABLE EMPLOYEE
  ALTER COLUMN EMP_NO TO EMP_NUM; /* the keyword COLUMN is optional */
```

Next, the left-to-right position of the column—known as its degree—is moved:

```
ALTER TABLE EMPLOYEE
  ALTER COLUMN EMP_NUM POSITION 4;
```

This time, the data type of EMP_NUM is changed from INTEGER to VARCHAR(20):

```
ALTER TABLE EMPLOYEE
  ALTER COLUMN EMP_NUM TYPE VARCHAR(20);
```

Restrictions on altering data type

Firebird does not let you alter the data type of a column or domain in a way that might result in data loss.

- The new column definition must be able to accommodate the existing data. If, for example, the new data type has too few bytes or the datatype conversion is not supported, an error is returned and the change cannot proceed.
- When number types are converted to character types, each number type is subject to a minimum length in bytes, according to type. These are tabulated at the end of Chapter 8, in Table 8-4.
- Conversions from character data to non-character data are not allowed.
- Columns of BLOB and ARRAY types cannot be converted.

Attention

Any changes to the field definitions may require the indexes to be rebuilt.

Dropping columns

The owner of a table can use ALTER TABLE to drop (remove) a column definition and its data from a table. Dropping a column causes all data stored in it to be lost. The drop takes effect immediately unless another transaction is accessing the table. In this event, the other transaction continues uninterrupted and Firebird postpones the drop until the table is no longer in use.

Before attempting to drop a column, be aware of the dependencies that could prevent the operation from succeeding. It will fail if the column

- is part of a UNIQUE, PRIMARY, or FOREIGN KEY constraint.
- is involved in a CHECK constraint—there may be table-level CHECK constraints on the column in addition to any imposed by its domain.

- is used in a view, trigger, or stored procedure.

Dependencies must be removed before the column drop can proceed. Columns involved in PRIMARY KEY and UNIQUE constraints cannot be dropped if they are referenced by FOREIGN KEY constraints. In this event, drop the FOREIGN KEY constraint before dropping the PRIMARY KEY or UNIQUE key constraint and column it references. Finally, you can drop the column.

Syntax

```
ALTER TABLE name DROP colname [, DROP colname ...];
```

For example, the following statement drops the column JOB_GRADE from the EMPLOYEE table:

```
ALTER TABLE EMPLOYEE DROP JOB_GRADE;
```

To drop several columns with a single statement:

```
ALTER TABLE EMPLOYEE
  DROP JOB_GRADE,
  DROP FULL_NAME;
```

Dropping constraints

A correct sequence must be followed when dropping constraints, since both primary key and CHECK constraints are likely to have dependencies.

> *The isql command* `SHOW TABLE <table-name>` *lists out all the constraints and triggers for <table-name>. Alternatively, to find the names of constraints, it may be helpful to define and commit the four system views defined in the script* `system_views.sql` *provided in Appendix V.*

UNIQUE KEY and PRIMARY KEY constraints

When a primary key or unique constraint is to be dropped, it will be necessary first to find and drop any foreign key constraint (FK) that references it. If it is a unique key, the FK declaration actually names the columns of the unique constraint. For example,

```
...
FK_DATA_ID FOREIGN KEY DATA_ID
    REFERENCES  TEST_UQ(DATA_ID);
```

If the referenced key is the primary key, the name of the primary key column is optional in FK declarations and is often omitted. For example, looking at the `../examples/empbuild/employee.fdb` database:

```
...TABLE PROJECT (
...,
TEAM_CONSTRT FOREIGN KEY (TEAM_LEADER)
  REFERENCES EMPLOYEE );
```

Dropping a foreign key constraint is usually straightforward:

```
ALTER TABLE PROJECT
  DROP CONSTRAINT TEAM_CONSTRT;
COMMIT;
```

After that, it becomes possible to drop the primary key constraint (PK) on the EMP_NO column of the EMPLOYEE table:

```
ALTER TABLE EMPLOYEE
  DROP CONSTRAINT EMP_NO_CONSTRT;
```

CHECK constraints

Any CHECK conditions that were added during table definition can be removed without complications. CHECK conditions inherited from a domain are more problemmatical. To be free of the domain's constraints, it will be necessary to perform an `ALTER TABLE ALTER COLUMN ...TYPE` operation to change the column to another data type or domain.

Adding a column

One or more columns can be added to a table in a single statement, using the ADD clause. Each ADD clause includes a full column definition, which follows the same syntax as column definitions in CREATE TABLE. Multiple ADD clauses are separated with commas.

Syntax

```
ALTER TABLE table ADD <col_def>
<col_def> = col {<datatype> | [COMPUTED [BY] (<expr>) | domain}
[DEFAULT {literal |NULL |USER}]
[NOT NULL] [<col_constraint>]
[COLLATE collation]
<col_constraint> = [CONSTRAINT constraint] <constraint_def>
[<col_constraint>]
<constraint_def>=
PRIMARY KEY
| UNIQUE
| CHECK (<search_condition>)
| REFERENCES other_table [(other_col [, other_col ...])]
[ON DELETE {NO ACTION|CASCADE|SET DEFAULT|SET NULL}]
[ON UPDATE {NO ACTION|CASCADE|SET DEFAULT|SET NULL}]
```

The following statement adds a column, ALT_EMP_NO, to the EMPLOYEE table using the EMPNO domain:

```
ALTER TABLE EMPLOYEE
  ADD EMP_NO EMPNO NOT NULL;
```

Example Here we add two columns, EMAIL_ID and LEAVE_STATUS to the EMPLOYEE table:

```
ALTER TABLE EMPLOYEE
  ADD EMAIL_ID VARCHAR(10) NOT NULL,
  ADD LEAVE_STATUS DEFAULT 10 INTEGER NOT NULL;
```

Including integrity constraints

Integrity constraints can be included for columns that you add to the table. For example, a UNIQUE constraint could have been included for the EMAIL_ID column in the previous statement:

```
ALTER TABLE EMPLOYEE
  ADD EMAIL_ID VARCHAR(10) NOT NULL,
  ADD LEAVE_STATUS DEFAULT 10 INTEGER NOT NULL,
  ADD CONSTRAINT UQ_EMAIL_ID UNIQUE(EMAIL_ID);
```

or

```
ALTER TABLE EMPLOYEE
    ADD EMAIL_ID VARCHAR(10) NOT NULL UNIQUE,
    ADD LEAVE_STATUS DEFAULT 10 INTEGER NOT NULL;
```

Adding new table constraints

The ADD CONSTRAINT clause can be included to add table-level constraints relating to new or existing columns.

Syntax

```
ALTER TABLE name ADD [CONSTRAINT constraint] <tconstraint_opt>;
```

where `<tconstraint_opt>` can be a PRIMARY KEY, FOREIGN KEY, UNIQUE, or CHECK constraint. The CONSTRAINT constraint phrase is omitted if you don't care to name the constraint yourself.

Example

```
ALTER TABLE EMPLOYEE
  ADD CONSTRAINT UQ_PHONE_EXT UNIQUE(PHONE_EXT);
```

When ALTER TABLE is not enough

Sometimes, you need to make a change to a column that can not be achieved with ALTER TABLE. Examples might be where you need to change a column that is storing international language in character set NONE to another character set, to correct your design error; or to redefine a telephone number, originally defined by someone as an integer, as an 18-character column.

In the first case, it isn't possible to change the character set of a column—so you need a workaround that both preserves the data and makes it available in the correct character set. In the other case, simply changing the data type of the telephone number column won't work if we already have existing integer data in the column. We want to keep the actual numbers but we have to convert them to strings. That cannot be done in the current structure, because an integer column cannot store a string.

The workaround entails creating a temporary column in your table, with the correct attributes, and "parking" the data there whilst you drop and recreate the original column.

Steps

1 Add a temporary column to the table, having a definition with the new attributes you need.

```
ALTER TABLE PERSONNEL
    ADD TEMP_COL VARCHAR(18);
COMMIT;
```

2 Copy the data from the column to be changed to the temporary column, massaging it appropriately, e.g. applying a character set "introducer" to convert the text data to the correct character set or, in our example, casting it appropriately.

```
UPDATE PERSONNEL
    SET TEMP_COL = CAST(TEL_NUMBER AS VARCHAR(18))
    WHERE TEL_NUMBER IS NOT NULL;
COMMIT;
```

3 After verifying that the data in the temporary column have been changed as planned, drop the old column.

```
ALTER TABLE PERSONNEL
    DROP TEL_NUMBER;
COMMIT;
```

Rename the temporary column to be the name of the column just dropped:

```
ALTER TABLE PERSONNEL
    ALTER TEMP_COL TO TEL_NUMBER;
COMMIT;
```

Removing (Dropping) a Table

Use DROP TABLE to remove an entire table permanently from the database. This is permanent and, once committed, cannot be undone.

```
DROP TABLE name;
```

The following statement drops the table PERSONNEL:

```
DROP TABLE PERSONNEL;
```

The RECREATE TABLE statement

Sometimes, you may want to drop a table and create it again "from scratch". For these occasions, Firebird has RECREATE TABLE, which does the following:

- drops the existing table and all of the objects belonging to it
- commits the change
- creates the new table as specified in the clauses and sub-clauses

Data and ancillary objects such as constraints, indexes and triggers are not preserved. Make sure that you save the source of any of these ancillary definitions that you want to keep before submitting a RECREATE TABLE request!

Syntax

The syntax is identical to that of CREATE TABLE. Simply substitute the CREATE keyword with RECREATE and proceed.

Restrictions and recommendations

If the table is in use when you submit the DROP or RECREATE statement, the request will be denied, with an "Object xxxxx is in use" message.

Always take a backup before any activity that changes metadata.

Although it is possible to make metadata changes when users are on-line, it is not recommended, especially for radical changes like dropping and recreating tables. If necessary, force users off and get exclusive access. Instructions for getting exclusive access are in the companion volume to this, Vol. 3: ***Administering Firebird Servers and Databases*** and in ***The Firebird Book Second Edition***, in the topic *The gfix Tool Set*.

Temporary Tables

Firebird databases of on-disk structure (ODS) 11.1 and higher can store persistent definitions of tables that applications can use to store sets of temporary data during a run-time session. Instances of these temporary structures can be created by many session-users simultaneously—hence, they are known as *global temporary tables*, commonly abbreviated to "GTT".

Server versions lower than v.2.1 do not support GTTs. It is also not possible to create and use GTTs under a newer server if the ODS of the database is 11.0 or lower. Later, in the topic *Temporary Storage for Older Versions*, we look at the recommended way to emulate some of the features of GTTs for these lower versions.

Global Temporary Tables

The same structural features that you can apply to regular tables (indexes, triggers, field-level and table level constraints) can be applied to a global temporary table. However, a GTT cannot be linked in a referential relationship to a regular table nor to another GTT that has a different lifespan (see below), nor be referred to in a constraint or domain definition.

For obvious reasons, the EXTERNAL TABLE option is not possible for a GTT definition.

Each instance of a GTT gets its own "private" pages for data and indexes, laid out just like those for a regular table but inaccessible to any other instance. At the end of the lifetime of the GTT instance, those pages are released for immediate re-use, in much the same way as the data and index pages for regular tables are released when the table is dropped.

The private files containing the GTT instances are not subject to the Forced Writes setting of the database. They are always opened for asynchronous writes, i.e., Forced Writes is always OFF for GTT instances.

Lifespan of GTT Sets

An instance of a GTT—a set of data rows created by and visible within the given connection or transaction—is created when the GTT is referenced for the first time, usually at statement prepare time. The lifespan of a GTT "travels" with its definition and cannot be overridden, so make sure you define the right one for your requirements.

When defining a GTT, the options for specifying the lifespan of an instance are dictated by what you specify to happen ON COMMIT of the parent transaction:

- PRESERVE ROWS retains the set until the client session ends
- DELETE ROWS destroys the set when the parent transaction is committed or rolled back. Transaction lifespan is the default.

You can check the lifespan type of a GTT by querying the system table RDB$RELATIONS and looking at the RDB$RELATION_TYPE for the GTT. A value of 4 indicates a session-wide lifespan and 5 a transaction-level lifespan.

CREATE Syntax for a GTT

The pattern for the CREATE GLOBAL TEMPORARY TABLE statement is the same as for CREATE TABLE, with the addition of the lifespan clause and the exclusion of the EXTERNAL TABLE option, viz.,

```
CREATE GLOBAL TEMPORARY TABLE <table-identifier>(
  <column-definitions> [,
  <table-constraint-definitions])
  [ON COMMIT DELETE | PRESERVE ROWS]
```

Because transaction-level lifespan is the default, the ON COMMIT DELETE clause may be omitted if you want to specify this level.

Examples

The first example defines a GTT named GTT_S_01 whose instances will remain alive for the duration of the client session:

```
CREATE GLOBAL TEMPORARY TABLE GTT_S_01 (
    ID BIGINT NOT NULL,
    DESCRIPTION VARCHAR(100),
    UPDATE_TIME TIMESTAMP DEFAULT current_timestamp,
    CONSTRAINT PK_GTT_S_01 PRIMARY KEY (ID)
    )
    ON COMMIT PRESERVE ROWS;
    /* Remember to commit the DDL */
COMMIT;
```

Another example defines a GTT whose instance will be destroyed when the transaction in which it was invoked completes. It has a foreign key referencing the primary key of the GTT in our first example:

```
CREATE GLOBAL TEMPORARY TABLE GTT_T_02 (
    ID BIGINT NOT NULL PRIMARY KEY,
    DETAILS VARCHAR(200),
    UPDATE_TIME TIMESTAMP DEFAULT current_timestamp,
    MASTER_ID BIGINT NOT NULL
    REFERENCES GTT_S_01 (ID),
    CONSTRAINT PK_GTT_S_01 PRIMARY KEY (ID)
    ); -- ON COMMIT DELETE omitted because it is the default lifespan
    /* Remember to commit the DDL */
COMMIT;
```

When the GTT instances are destroyed, any DELETE triggers that are defined for the GTT will not fire.

Temporary Storage for Older Versions

While Firebird does not prevent end-user applications from executing DDL statements, such as CREATE TABLE and DROP TABLE, it is not recommended to write applications that do such things in the course of normal business. For versions prior to v.2.1 or databases of ODS 11.0 or lower, a popular model for storing temporary data is the "permanent temporary table".

The idea is to define a regular table structure in the permanent metadata that end-user applications will write to and read from in the course of a session or transaction. A batch identifier is included, written from a generator (sequence) for a session-wide lifespan or, for a transaction-wide lifespan, the CURRENT_TRANSACTION value.

Applications can insert, reprocess and delete rows in such a table during the course of a task—remember, Firebird does not put locks on tables in the normal course of events.

According to the conditions and needs of the application, it can itself be responsible for deleting the temporary rows when it is finished with the batch of rows it created, using the batch ID for a searched delete. Alternatively, the application could post a row containing the batch ID to a housekeeping table signalling "clean-up required" to a later, deferred operation that runs after hours, before a backup.

If you have the option of using GTTs for temporary storage, then do so. The "permanent temporary table" solution has no way to truly isolate the temporary data or to effect the garbage-free cleanup that GTTs provide.

Tree Structures

Table structures designed to store multi-layered hierarchical lists of nodes for "trees"—such as family trees, menus, classification systems and many others—are at cross-purposes with the design ideals of SQL databases, specifically normalization. We solve the problem by rigorously abstracting the inter-nodal relationship so that we store each node with its own unique identifier, along with a foreign key referencing the unique identifier of its immediate parent node. The "flattening" for use by applications requiring hierarchical sets is performed at run-time by data manipulation language (DML).

At the DDL level, the style of table to create—where every node of the notional tree structure has one and only one row and exactly one or no parent—is known as a "self-referencing table". The rationale and details for designing such tables can be found in Chapter 17, ***Referential Integrity***, in the topic *Self-Referencing Relationship*.

The DML side of the issue, tracking recursively through the nodes and building the flattened output, can be implemented using common table expressions (v.2.1 and above) or recursive stored procedures that return sets ("selectable stored procedures").

For more detail on this subject, refer to either the companion volume to this, Vol.2: ***Developing with Firebird Data*** or ***The Firebird Book Second Edition***, topics *Common Table Expressions* in the chapter entitled *Views and Other Run-time Sets* and *Recursive Procedures* in the *Stored Procedures* chapter.

CHAPTER

15

INDEXES

Indexes—sometimes pluralized as *indices*—are table attributes that can be placed on a column or a group of columns to accelerate the retrieval of rows.

An index serves as a logical pointer to the physical locations (addresses) of rows in a table, much as you search an index in a book to quickly locate the page numbers of topics that you want to read. In most cases, if the engine can fetch the requested rows directly by scanning an index instead of scanning all rows in the table, requests will complete faster.

A well-designed system of indexes plays a vital role in the tuning and optimization of your entire application environment. However, creating indexes should be considered largely as a tuning exercise that you will engage in once you have finalised the database structure and have a reasonable set of test data to play with.

Limits

Firebird allows up to 256 user-created indexes per table (although, in v.1.0.x, the limit is just 64). These are theoretical limits that are governed by both page size and the actual on-disk size of the index description data on the index root page. You could not store 256 indexes for a table in a database with a page size smaller than 16 Kb. On the index root page, each index needs 31 bytes for its identifier, space for descriptions of each segment (column) involved in the index and some bytes to store a pointer to the first page of the index. Even a 16 Kb page may not be able to accommodate 256 indexes if there are more than a few compound indexes in the table.

The total size (width) of an index cannot exceed one-quarter of the page size. In reality, the number of bytes may be significantly smaller than that figure. Factors that can reduce the number of actual "slots" available to store characters include:

- character sets that use multiple bytes per character
- international character sets with complex upper/lower case pairings and/or dictionary sorting rules
- use of non-binary collations
- multiple segments (composite indexes) which require the addition of padding bytes to retain the geometry of the index

In other words, using any character set except NONE will influence your decisions about index design—particularly whether to use composite indexes. That's the bad news. The good news is that Firebird makes good use of single-column indexes in multi-column searches and sorts, reducing the need for multi-column indexes that you might have considered essential from your experience with another DBMS.

Automatic vs User-defined Indexes

Firebird creates indexes to enforce various integrity constraints automatically—for more information, refer to Chapter 15, ***Tables*** and Chapter 17, ***Referential Integrity***. To delete these indexes, it is necessary to drop the constraints that use them.

Use of the constraint indexes is not restricted to their work supporting the integrity of keys and relationships. They are considered, along with all others, when queries are prepared.

When defining your own indexes, it is of utmost importance to avoid creating any index that duplicates an automatically-generated one. It puts the optimizer (see below) in the unhappy position of have to choose between equals. In many cases, it will solve the problem by not choosing either of them.

Importing legacy indexes

Do not import the "primary indexes" along with the tables you import from a migrating DBMS. There are two important reasons to abandon these indexes:

- Many legacy systems use hierarchical index structures to implement referential integrity. SQL databases do not use this logic to implement RI and these indexes usually interfere with Firebird's optimizer logic.
- Firebird creates its own indexes to support primary and foreign key constraints, regardless of any existing index. As noted above, duplicate indexes cause problems for the optimizer and should be avoided completely.

Directional indexes

The sort direction of indexes in Firebird is important. It is a mistake to assume that the same index can be used to sort or search "both ways", that, is lowest-to-highest and highest-to-lowest. As a rule of thumb, ASC (ascending) indexes will help searches where relatively low values are sought, whereas DESC (descending) indexes will help for maximum or high values .

If an automatic index is ASC (the default) there will be no problems if you need to define a DESC index using the same column(s). The reverse is also true: you can choose to have the automatic indexes for keys created in descending order. The optimizer will not be upset if you also create an ascending one on the same columns.

Query plans

Before a query is executed, a set of preparation routines—known as the optimizer—begins analyzing the columns and operations in the request, to calculate the fastest way to respond. It starts by looking for indexes on the tables and columns involved. Working its way through a sequence of cost-based decision paths, it develops a plan—a kind of "roadmap" for the route it will follow when it actually executes the query. The final plan it chooses reflects the cheapest route it can predict according to the indexes it can use.

The optimizer's plan can be viewed in an *isql* shell session in two ways:

1 By default, isql does not display the plan. Use SET PLAN ON to have the plan displayed at the top of the output from a SELECT query.

2 Use SET PLANONLY to submit queries and view the plans without actually running the queries. This enables you to inspect the plan for any query, not just SELECT queries.

For details about using *isql*, refer to the chapter entitled *Interactive SQL Utility (isql)*.

It is possible to override the optimizer's plan with one of your own, by including a PLAN clause in your query statement. Most third-party GUI tools provide the ability to view the plan, with or without running the query, and to override it.

Plans that seem to work faster on small, stable test sets will not necessarily satisfy on large, dynamic sets. Don't override the optimizer's plan unless you have tested your own and found it to be consistently faster on realistic data in well-simulated production conditions.

More about Query Plans

Query plans—particularly those generated by Firebird's optimizer engine—are discussed in greater detail in the chapter entitled ***DML Queries***, in the companion volume to this, Volume 2: ***Developing with Firebird Data*** or in ***The Firebird Book Second Edition***. See the topic *Query Plans and the Optimizer*.

How Indexes Can Help

If the optimizer decides to use an index, it searches the pages of the index to find the key values required and follows the pointers to locate the indicated rows in the table data pages. Data retrieval is fast because the values in the index are ordered. This allows the system to locate wanted values directly, by pointer, and avoid visiting unwanted rows at all. Using an index typically requires fewer page fetches than "walking through" every row in the table. The index is small, relative to the row size of the table, and, provided the index design is good, it occupies relatively fewer database pages than the row data.

Sorting and grouping

When the columns specified in an ORDER BY or GROUP BY clause are indexed, the optimizer can sequence the output by navigating the index(es) and assemble the ordered sets more directly than it can with non-indexed reads.

A DESCENDING index on the aggregated column can speed up the query for the aggregating function MAX(..), since the row with the maximum value will be the only one it visits.

For more information about using function expressions in queries, refer to Chapters 20, ***Expressions and Predicates*** and 23, ***Ordered and Aggregated Sets***.

Joins

For joins, the optimizer goes through a process of merging streams of data by matching the values specified in the implicit or explicit "ON" criteria. If an index is available for the column or columns on one side of the join, the optimizer builds its initial stream by using the index to match the join key with its correspondent from the table on the other side of the join. Without an index on either side, it must generate a map of the locations of the eligiblre rows of one side first and navigate that, in order to make the selections from the table on the other side of the join.

Comparisons

When an indexed column is evaluated to determine whether it is greater than, equal to or less than a constant, the value of the index is used for the comparison and non-matching rows are not fetched. Without an index, all of the candidate rows have to be fetched and compared in turn.

What to Index

The length of time it takes to search a whole table is directly proportional to the number of rows in the table. An index on a column can mean the difference between an immediate response to a query and a long wait. So— why not index every column?

The main drawbacks are that indexes consume additional disk space, and inserting, deleting, and updating rows takes longer on indexed columns than on non-indexed columns. The index must be updated each time a data item in the indexed column changes and each time a row is added to or deleted from the table.

Nevertheless, the boost in performance for data retrieval usually outweighs the overhead of maintaining a conservative but useful collection of indexes. You should create an index on a column when:

- Search conditions frequently reference the column. An index will help in date and numeric searches when direct comparisons or BETWEEN evaluations are wanted. Search indexes for character columns are useful when strings are to be evaluated for exact matches or against STARTING WITH and CONTAINING predicates. They are not useful with the LIKE predicate.
- The column does not carry an integrity constraint but is referenced frequently as a JOIN condition
- ORDER BY clauses frequently use the column to sort data.

  When sets must be ordered on multiple columns, composite indexes which reflect the output order specified in ORDER BY clauses can sometimes improve retrieval speed. Often, however, single-key indexes on each column that might be involved in sorting give better performance and thus are usually first choice on the test bed. Composite indexes should be tested thoroughly in a production simulation to verify whether they actually improve the sort.
- You need an index with special characteristics not provided by data or existing indexes, such as a non-binary collation or an ascending or descending direction
- Aggregations are to be performed on large sets. Single-column or suitably ordered complex indexes can improve the speed with which aggregations are formed in complex GROUP BY clauses

You should not create indexes for columns that

- are seldom referenced in search conditions
- are frequently updated non-key values, such as timestampers or user signatures
- have a small number of possible or actual values spread over a wide campus of rows
- are styled as two-phase (True/False) or three-phase (True/False/unknown) Boolean

When to index

Some indexes will suggest themselves to you during the initial design period—typically for requirements that you know will need particular sortings, groupings and evaluations. For the rest, it is very good practice to be conservative about creating indexes until it becomes clear that they might be beneficial. It is a rewarding strategy to defer the creation of doubtful indexes until after a point in development where you have good samplings of typical test data and an awareness of which operations are too slow.

The benefits of deferred index design include

- reduction of "performance fogging" that can interfere with the functional integrity testing
- faster identification of the real sources of bottlenecks
- avoidance of the overhead of maintaining unnecessary or inefficient indexes

Using CREATE INDEX

The DDL statement CREATE INDEX creates an index on one or more columns of a table. A single-column index enables indexed searching on only one column in response to a query, whereas multi-column index searches may facilitate searching one or more columns.

Syntax

```
CREATE [UNIQUE] [ASC[ENDING] | DESC[ENDING]] INDEX <index-name>
  ON <table-name> ( col [, col ...] | COMPUTED BY (<expr>);
```

Mandatory elements

CREATE INDEX <index-name>

—names the index. The identifier must be distinct from all other object identifiers in the database, apart from constraint and column identifiers. It is a good idea to use a systematic naming scheme, however, as an aid to self-documentation.

When designing your naming scheme, keep in mind that the supporting indexes automatically created by Firebird for integrity constraints can be given custom names and thus be integrated with the overall naming scheme.

<table-name>

—the name of the table to which the index applies

col [, col...]

—column name, or comma-separated list naming the columns which are to be the index keys. Column order is significant in indexes. For more information, see the topic below, *Multi-column Indexes*.

Example The following declaration, creates a non-unique, ascending index on a personal name column in a PERSON table. It may aid search conditions like WHERE LAST_NAME = 'Johnston' or WHERE LAST_NAME STARTING WITH 'Johns':

```
CREATE INDEX LAST_NAME_X ON PERSON(LAST_NAME);
```

Optional elements

UNIQUE

The UNIQUE keyword can be used on indexes for which you want to disallow duplicate entries. The column or group is checked for duplicate values when the index is created and for existing values each time a row is inserted or updated.

Unique indexes make sense only when you need to enforce uniqueness as an intrinsic characteristic of the data item or group. For example, you would not define a unique index on a column storing a person's name, because personal names are not intrinsically unique.

Conversely, a unique index is a good idea on a column containing a social security number, since a unique key violation on it would alert the user to an error that needed attention.

Example

In this example, a unique index is created on three columns of an inventory table to ensure that the system stores at most one row for each size and color of an item:

```
CREATE UNIQUE INDEX STK_SIZE_COLOR_UQX
    ON STOCK_ITEM (PRODUCT_ID, SIZE, COLOR);
```

Note that a unique index is not a key. If you require a unique key for referential purposes, apply a UNIQUE constraint to the column(s) instead. Refer to the topic *The UNIQUE constraint* in the previous chapter.

Finding duplicates

Of course, it won't be possible to create a unique index on a column that already contains duplicate values. Before defining a unique index, use a SELECT statement to find duplicate items in the table. For example, before putting a unique index on PRODUCT_NAME in this PRODUCT table, this check would reveal any duplicates in the column:

```
SELECT
  PRODUCT_ID,
  UPPER(PRODUCT_NAME)
FROM PRODUCT
  GROUP BY PRODUCT_ID, UPPER(PRODUCT_NAME)
    HAVING COUNT(*) > 1;
```

Upper-casing the column to make the search case-insensitive is not necessary from the point of view of data uniqueness. Still, if uniqueness has been "broken" by faulty data entry, we would want to find the offending records.

How you deal with duplicates depends on what they signify, according to your business rules, and the number of duplicates needing to be eliminated. Usually, a stored procedure will be the most efficient way to handle it. Stored procedures are discussed in detail in Chapters 28 and 29.

ASC[ENDING] or DESC[ENDING]

The keywords ASC[ENDING] and DESC[ENDING] determine the vertical sort order of the index. ASC specifies an index that sorts the values from lowest to highest. It is the default and can be omitted. DESC sorts the values from highest to lowest and must be specified if a descending index is wanted. A descending index may prove useful for queries that are likely to search for high values (oldest age, most recent, biggest, etc.) and for any ordered searches or outputs that will specify a sort order that is "highest first", ranked or in "newest-to-oldest" date order.

Example

The following definition creates a descending index on a table in the employee database:

```
CREATE DESCENDING INDEX DESC_X
  ON SALARY_HISTORY (CHANGE_DATE);
```

The optimizer will use this index in a query such as the following, which returns the employee numbers and salaries of the 10 employees who most recently had a raise:

```
SELECT FIRST 10 EMP_NO, NEW_SALARY
  FROM SALARY_HISTORY
ORDER BY CHANGE_DATE DESCENDING;
```

If you intend to use both ascending and descending sort orders on a particular column, define both an ascending and a descending index for the same column. For example, it will be fine to create the following index in addition to the one in the previous example:

```
CREATE INDEX ASCEND_X
  ON SALARY_HISTORY (CHANGE_DATE);
```

COMPUTED BY <expr>

From the "2" series forward, an index can be created using arbitrary expressions applied to columns in the table structure. The keywords COMPUTED BY preface the expression that is to define the index nodes. The index created is known as an *expression index*. Expression indexes have exactly the same features and limitations as regular indexes, except that, by definition, they cannot be composed of multiple segments.

In satisfying DML requests, the engine will use the expression index if the expression used in the search predicate matches exactly the expression used in the index declaration. The expression index will never be chosen otherwise.

Examples

This index provides the upper case value of a column , that would typically be useful for a case-insensitive search:

```
CREATE INDEX IDX1 ON T1
  COMPUTED BY ( UPPER(COL1 COLLATE PT_BR) );
COMMIT;
/**/
SELECT * FROM T1
  WHERE UPPER(COL1 COLLATE PT_BR) = 'ÔÛÂÀ'
-- PLAN (T1 INDEX (IDX1))
```

Indexing on a more complex expression:

```
CREATE INDEX IDX2 ON T2
  COMPUTED BY ( EXTRACT(YEAR FROM COL2) || EXTRACT(MONTH FROM COL2) );
COMMIT;
/**/
SELECT * FROM T2
  ORDER BY EXTRACT(YEAR FROM COL2) || EXTRACT(MONTH FROM COL2)
-- PLAN (T2 ORDER IDX2)
```

Multi-column Indexes

If your applications frequently need to search, order or group on the same group of multiple columns in a particular table, it might be of benefit to create a multi-column index (also known as a composite or complex index).

The optimizer is likely to use a subset of the segments of a multi-column index to optimize a query if the left-to-right order in which the query accesses the columns in an ORDER BY clause matches the left-to-right order of the column list defined in the index. However, queries do not need to be constructed with the exact column list that is defined in the index in order for it to be available to the optimizer. The index can also be used if the subset of columns used in the ORDER BY clause begins with the first columns in the multi-column index, *in the same order.*

Firebird can use a single element (or *segment*) of composite index to optimize a search if all of the elements to the left of that element are also used in the matching order. Consider a segmented index on three columns, Col_w, Col_x and Col_y, in that order:

Figure 15.1 Using a segmented index

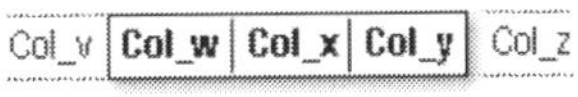

The index would be picked by the optimizer for this query:

```
SELECT <list of columns> FROM ATABLE
ORDER BY COL_w, COL_x;
```

It would not be picked for either of these queries:

```
SELECT <list of columns> FROM ATABLE
```

```
  ORDER BY COL_x, COL_y;
/**/
  SELECT <list of columns> FROM ATABLE
  ORDER BY COL_x, COL_w;
```

OR predicates in queries

If you expect to issue frequent queries against a table where the queries use the OR operator, it is better to create a single-column index for each condition. Since multi-column indexes are sorted hierarchically, a query that is looking for any one of two or more conditions must search the whole table, losing the advantage of an index.

For example, suppose the search requested

```
...
WHERE A > 10000 OR B < 300 OR C BETWEEN 40 AND 80
...
```

an index on (A,B,C) would be used to find rows containing eligible values of A but it could not be used for searching for B or C values because the OR operator works by testing each condition, beginning at the leftmost predication. The operation stops as soon as a condition is found to be true. By contrast, individual indexes on A, B and C would all be used. The direction of an index could be important here, too. For A, a descending index would be more useful than an ascending one if the search value is at the high end of range of stored values.

Search criteria

The same rules that apply to the ORDER BY clause also apply to queries containing a WHERE clause. The next example creates a multi-column index for the PROJECT table in `employee.fdb`:

```
CREATE UNIQUE INDEX PRODTYPEX
  ON PROJECT (PRODUCT, PROJ_NAME);
```

The optimizer will pick the PRODTYPEX index for this query, because the WHERE clause refers to the first segment of the index:

```
SELECT * FROM PROJECT
  WHERE PRODUCT ='software';
```

Conversely, it will ignore that index for the next query, because PROJ_NAME is not the first segment:

```
SELECT * FROM PROJECT
  WHERE PROJ_NAME STARTING WITH 'Firebird 1';
```

Inspecting Indexes

To inpect indexes defined in the current database, use the *isql* command SHOW INDEX:

- To see all indexes defined for a specific table, use the command
  `SHOW INDEX tablename`
- To view information about a specific index, use
  `SHOW INDEX indexname`

You can examine a great deal of useful information about populated indexes using the *gstat* tool. For details, refer to the section *Collecting Database Statistics—gstat* in the chapter entitled *Monitoring and Logging Features*, in either the companion volume to this, Vol. 3: ***Administering Firebird Servers and Databases***, or ***The Firebird Book Second Edition***.

Making an Index Inactive

The ALTER INDEX statement is used to switch the state of an index from active to inactive and vice versa. It can be used to switch off indexing before inserting or updating a large batch of rows, to avoid the overhead of maintaining the indexes during the long operation. After the operation, indexing can be reactivated and the indexes will be rebuilt.

Housekeeping

The other use for ALTER INDEX {ACTIVE | INACTIVE} is a housekeeping one. The distribution of values changes, gradually under normal conditions and, under some operating conditions, more frequently. The binary tree structures in which indexes are maintained are stored on index pages. As indexes grow and change, the nodes become progressively more spread across many linked pages, reducing the overall effectiveness of the index. Switching an index from active to inactive and back to active rebuilds it, equalising the distribution of nodes from page to page and, often, reducing the level of indirection, i.e., the depth of the "tree" of pages that have to be traversed when reading the nodes into the database cache. Every little bit helps when troubleshooting index performance problems.

Syntax

```
ALTER INDEX index-name INACTIVE | ACTIVE ;
```

ALTER INDEX cannot be used on any index that was auto-created to support a constraint.

For more information about ways to optimize the benefits of index use by Firebird's optimizer and to keep your indexes in good shape for continued efficiency, refer to the topic *Optimal Indexing* in the chapter entitled *DML Queries*, in either the companion volume to this, Vol. 2: ***Developing with Firebird Data***, or ***The Firebird Book Second Edition***.

'Index is in use' error

An index that is being used in a transaction cannot be altered or dropped until the transaction has finished using it. Attempts will have different results, according to the lock setting of the active transaction—

- In a WAIT transaction, the ALTER INDEX operation waits until the transaction completes
- In a NO WAIT transaction, Firebird returns an error.

For more information about transaction lock settings, refer to the topic *Locking Policy* in Chapter 26, ***Configuring Transactions***.

Altering the structure of an index

Unlike many ALTER statements, the ALTER INDEX syntax cannot be used to alter the structure or attributes of the object. You can either drop the index and define it afresh, using CREATE INDEX or you can create another index to use as an alternative.

Dropping an Index

The DROP INDEX statement removes a user-defined index from the database. No user can drop an index except the user who created it, or SYSDBA or another user with root/Administrator privileges.

Use DROP INDEX also when an index needs to have a change of structure: segments added, removed or reordered, sort order altered. First use a DROP INDEX statement to delete the index, then use a CREATE INDEX statement to recreate it, using the same name and the new characteristics.

Syntax

```
DROP INDEX name;
```

The following statement deletes an index from the JOB table in `employee.fdb`:

```
DROP INDEX MINSALX;
```

CHAPTER

16

REFERENTIAL INTEGRITY

The term referential integrity refers to the capability of a database to protect itself from receiving input that would result in an inconsistent relationship. Specifically, the referential integrity of a database exists according to its ability to enforce and protect a relationship between two tables.

Implementing formal referential constraints adds some extra work to the database designer's task, so—what is the payback? If you are new to the concept, then you are sure to find many reasons of your own to justify the additional time and attention, including the following:

BOMB-PROOFING Formal referential constraints—especially when used intelligently with other types of constraint—will bomb-proof the business rules of your databases against application bugs, regardless of their source. This becomes especially important when you deploy your systems to sites where unskilled or partly skilled staff have access to the database through third-party utilities.

QUERY SPEED Indexes automatically created for referential integrity constraints speed up join operations.

QUALITY CONTROL During development and testing, potential bugs tend to show up early because the database rejects operations that break the rules. Effectively, they eliminate the grief from proceeding with application development under false assumptions about data consistency.

SELF-DOCUMENTATION Integrity rules enforced by your database provide "free" documentation that eliminates the need for any descriptive documents apart from your schema scripts. The rules defined in the metadata correctly become the authoritative reference to the data model for new staff and future development.

Terminology

When a RDBMS provides the ability to declare the relationship between two tables, it is sometimes termed declarative referential integrity, a fuzzy term which seems to have been propagated by writers of magazine articles. Referential integrity is a design objective, a quality; the author prefers the term formal referential constraints when referring to the mechanisms for implementing the rules.

In a relational database management system—RDBMS—relationships between two tables are created by means of the foreign key constraint. The foreign key constraint enforces the rules of existence for the rows it represents, protecting the table against attempts to store rows that are inconsistent with the data model. However, this constraint does not need to work alone. Other integrity constraints—described in detail in the Chapter 15, ***Tables***—can work in combination with the referential constraint to protect the consistency of relationships.

The FOREIGN KEY Constraint

A foreign key is a column or set of columns in one table that corresponds in exact order to a column or set of columns defined as a PRIMARY KEY or as a UNIQUE constraint in another table. In its simplest form, it implements an optional *one-to-many* relationship.

An optional relationship exists when the relationship is made possible by the formal structure but is not required. That is to say, a parent instance may exist without any referencing child but, if both exist, both are constrained. The other side of the coin is a mandatory relationship. Mandatory relationships are discussed later in this chapter.

The standard entity-relationship model depicts a simple one-to-many relationship between two entities like this:

Figure 16.1 Entity-relationship model

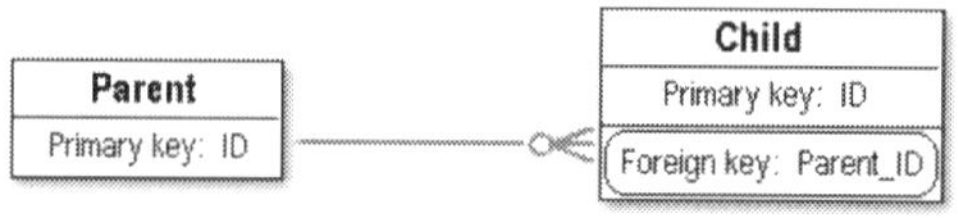

If we implement this model as two tables—PARENT and CHILD—then rows in the CHILD table are dependent on the existence of a linking row in PARENT. Firebird's FOREIGN KEY (FK) constraint enforces this relationship in the following ways:

- requires that the value presented in the FK column of the referencing table, CHILD (CHILD.PARENT_ID) must be able to be linked to a matching value present in the referenced unique key—in this case, the primary key—of PARENT (PARENT.ID)
- by default, disallows a row in PARENT to be deleted, or to have its linking unique key value changed to a different value, if dependent CHILD rows exist.
- must implement the relationship that was intended at the time the reference was created, or the last time it was updated
- by default, allows the FK column to be null. Since it is impossible to link null to anything, such child rows are orphans—they have no parent.

Implementing the constraint

In order to implement the referential constraint, certain prerequisites must be attended to. In this topic, we follow through a very simple example. If you are developing in an existing, complex environment, where SQL privileges are in effect, then you may need to be concerned about the REFERENCE privilege. It is introduced in a separate topic later in this chapter.

The parent structure

It is necessary to start with the parent table and implement a controlling unique key to which the dependent table will link. This is commonly the primary key of the parent table, although it need not be. A foreign key can link to a column or group which has been constrained using the UNIQUE constraint. For present purposes, we will use the primary key:

```
CREATE TABLE PARENT (
  ID BIGINT NOT NULL,
  DATA VARCHAR(20),
```

```
  CONSTRAINT PK_PARENT PRIMARY KEY(ID));
COMMIT;
```

The child structure

In the child structure, we need to include a column—PARENT_ID—that exactly matches the primary key of the parent in type and size (and also column order, if the linkage involves multiple columns):

```
CREATE TABLE CHILD (
ID BIGINT NOT NULL,
  CHILD_DATA VARCHAR(20),
  PARENT_ID BIGINT,
  CONSTRAINT PK_CHILD PRIMARY KEY(ID));
COMMIT;
```

The next thing to do is declare the relationship between the child and the parent by means of a FOREIGN KEY constraint.

Syntax for defining a FOREIGN KEY

```
...
FOREIGN KEY (column [, col ...])
REFERENCES (parent-table [, col ...])
[USING [ASC | DESC] INDEX index-name] /* v.1.5 and above */
[ON DELETE {NO ACTION | CASCADE | SET NULL  | SET DEFAULT}]
[ON UPDATE {NO ACTION | CASCADE | SET NULL  | SET DEFAULT}]
```

Defining our foreign key:

```
ALTER TABLE CHILD
  ADD CONSTRAINT FK_CHILD_PARENT
    FOREIGN KEY(PARENT_ID)
    REFERENCES PARENT(ID); /* REFERENCES PARENT is also valid,
    because ID is the primary key of PARENT */
```

Firebird stores the constraint FK_CHILD_PARENT and creates a non-unique index on the column(s) named in the FOREIGN KEY argument. The index will be named FK_CHILD_PARENT as well, unless you used the optional USING clause to assign a different name to the index.

V.1.0.x In Firebird 1.0.x, the index name will be INTEG_nn (where nn is a number).

If you specified a DESCENDING index for the referenced primary or unique constraint, you must be sure to specify USING DESC INDEX for any foreign keys that reference it.

The two tables are now engaged in a formal *referential integrity constraint.* We can add new rows to PARENT without restriction:

```
INSERT INTO PARENT (ID, DATA)
VALUES (1, 'Parent No. 1');
```

However, there are restrictions on CHILD. We can do this:

```
INSERT INTO CHILD (ID, CHILD_DATA)
  VALUES (1, 'Child No. 1');
```

Because the nullable column PARENT_ID was omitted from the column list, NULL is stored there. This is allowed under the default integrity rules. The row is an *orphan.*

However, we get a constraint error if we try to do this:

```
INSERT INTO CHILD (ID, CHILD_DATA, PARENT_ID)
  VALUES (2, 'Child No. 2', 2);
```

```
ISC ERROR CODE:335544466
ISC ERROR MESSAGE:
violation of FOREIGN KEY constraint "FK_CHILD_PARENT" on table "CHILD"
```

There is no row in PARENT having a PK value of 2, so the constraint disallows the insert.

Both of the following are allowed:

```
UPDATE CHILD
  SET PARENT_ID = 1
  WHERE ID = 1;
COMMIT;
/* */
INSERT INTO CHILD (ID, CHILD_DATA, PARENT_ID)
  VALUES (2, 'Child No.2', 1);
COMMIT;
```

Now, the PARENT row with ID=1 has two child rows. This is the classic master-detail structure—an uncomplicated implementation of the one-to-many relationship. To protect the integrity of the relationship, the default rules will disallow this because the parent has children:

```
DELETE FROM PARENT WHERE ID = 1;
```

Action triggers to vary integrity rules

Obviously, integrity rules take effect whenever some change in data occurs that affects the relationship. However, the default rules don't suit every requirement. We may want to override the rule that permits child rows to be created as orphan, or to be made orphans by having their foreign key set to null in an operation. If it is a problem for our business rules that a parent row cannot be deleted if it has dependent child rows, we may want Firebird to take care of the problem automatically.

Firebird's SQL language can oblige, through its optional automatic action triggers:

```
[ON DELETE {NO ACTION | CASCADE | SET NULL  | SET DEFAULT}]
[ON UPDATE {NO ACTION | CASCADE | SET NULL  | SET DEFAULT}]
```

Automatic action triggers

Firebird provides the optional standard DML events ON UPDATE and ON DELETE, along with a range of action options to vary the referential integrity rules. Together, the DML event and the automatic behavior specified by the action option form the action trigger—the action to be taken in this dependent table when modifying or deleting the referenced key in the parent. The actions defined include *cascading* the change to associated foreign table(s).

Action trigger semantics

```
NO ACTION
```

Because this is the default action trigger, the keyword can be—and usually is—omitted . The DML operation on the parent's PK leaves the foreign key unchanged and potentially blocks the operation on the parent.

```
ON UPDATE CASCADE
```

The cascade action directs that any changes in the parent key be passed down—cascaded—to the children. In the dependent table, the foreign key corresponding to the old value of the primary is updated to the new value of the primary key.

```
ON DELETE CASCADE
```

In the dependent table, the row with the corresponding key is deleted.

`SET NULL`

The foreign key corresponding to the old parent PK is set to NULL—the dependent rows become orphans. Clearly, this action trigger cannot be applied if the foreign key column is non-nullable.

`SET DEFAULT`

The foreign key corresponding to the old parent PK is set to its default value. There are some "gotchas" about the SET DEFAULT action that it is important to know about:

- the default value is the one that was in effect at the time the foreign key constraint was defined. If the column's default changes later, the original default for the FK's SET DEFAULT action does not follow the new default—it remains as the original.
- if no default was ever declared explicitly for the column, then its default is implicitly NULL. In this case, the SET DEFAULT behavior will be the same as SET NULL.
- if the default value for the foreign key column is a value that has no corresponding PK value in the parent, then the action trigger will cause a constraint violation.

Interaction of Constraints

By combining the formal referential constraint with other integrity constraints (see Chapter 15, ***Tables***) it is possible to implement most, if not all, of your business rules with a high degree of precision. For example, a NOT NULL column constraint will restrict the action options and prevent orphan rows, if required; whereas a foreign key column that is nullable can be used to implement special data structures such as trees (see below).

If you need to make a column of your foreign key non-nullable, then create a "dummy" parent row with an unused key value, such as 0 or –1. Use the SET DEFAULT action to emulate the SET NULL behavior by making the column default to the dummy key value.

Referential constraints can be assisted by CHECK constraints. In some cases, a CHECK constraint inherited from a domain could interfere or conflict with a referential constraint, too. It is worth spending a few minutes sketching out the effects of each constraint on paper or a whiteboard, to identify and eliminate any potential problems.

Custom Action Triggers

It is perfectly possible to write your own action triggers to customize or extend referential behavior. Although the automatic triggers are flexible enough to cover most requirements, there is one special case where custom triggers are generally called for. This is the case where creation of the mandatory enforcing index on the foreign key column is undesirable because the index would be of very low selectivity.

Broadly, indexes of low selectivity occur where a small number of possible values is spread over a large table, or where only a few possible values are ever used in the actual table data. The resulting massive duplication of values in the index—described as "long chains"—can impact query performance severely as the table grows.

Index selectivity is discussed in some detail in Chapters 19 and 21. If the topic is new to you, you are urged to digest it thoroughly before deciding to use formal integrity contstraints to implement every single one-to-many relationship in your data model "just because you can".

When writing custom referential triggers, you must make sure that your own triggers will preserve referential integrity when data in any key change. You might consider using your application code to achieve it but it is far from ideal. Triggers are much safer, since they centralise the data integrity rules in the database and enforce them for all types of access to the data, be it by program, utility tool, script or server application layer..

Without formal cascading update and delete actions, your custom solution must take care of rows in child tables that will be affected by changes to or deletions of parent keys. For example, if a row is to be deleted from the referenced table, your solution must first delete all rows in all tables that refer to it through foreign keys.

Refer to the topic *Referential Integrity Support* in the *Triggers* chapter of the companion volume, Volume2: ***Developing with Firebird Data*** for some discussion about implementing custom RI triggers.

Lookup Tables and Your Data Model

We often use lookup tables—also known as *control tables* or *definition tables*—to store static rows that can supply expanded text, conversion factors and the like to output sets and, often, directly to applications as selector lists. Examples are "type" tables that identify entities like account types or document types, "factor" tables used for currency conversion or tax calculation, and "code lookup" tables storing such items as color-matching codes. Dynamic tables are linked to these static tables by matching a foreign key with the primary key of the static table.

Data modeling tools cannot distinguish a lookup relationship from a master-detail relationship since, simplistically, one lookup row can supply values to many "user" rows. Tools represent it as a parent-child dependency and may erroneously recommend a foreign key on the "child" side.

Yet, in an implemented database, this relationship is not master-detail or parent-child, because the primary key value of the lookup set commands one and only one column. It has no effect on other relationships that this "pseudo-child" participates in.

It is tempting to apply a formal foreign key constraint to columns that reference lookup tables, with the argument that a cascading referential constraint will protect data consistency. The flaw here is that properly designed lookup tables will never change their keys—so there is no potential inconsistency to protect against.

Take a look at this example of a lookup relationship, inherited by converting a very poorly designed Access camping goods application to Firebird. Access client applications can do cute things with entire tables that allow amateurs to build "RAD" applications. This table was used in a visual control that could display a table and transplant a value into another table at the click of a button.

```
CREATE TABLE COLORS (COLOR CHARACTER(20) NOT NULL PRIMARY KEY);
```

Here is a DDL fragment from one of the tables that used COLORS for a lookup:

```
CREATE TABLE STOCK_ITEM (
...
  COLOR CHARACTER(20) DEFAULT 'NEUTRAL',
  ...,
  CONSTRAINT FK_COLOR FOREIGN KEY (COLOR)
    REFERENCES COLORS(COLOR)
    ON UPDATE CASCADE
    ON DELETE SET DEFAULT;
```

There were a lot of problems with this key. First, the COLORS table was available to the inventory buyers to edit as they saw fit. Updates cascaded all over the system whenever new items came into stock. Deletions frequently stripped the color information from the relatively few items where it mattered. Worst of all, the bulk of items in this system were one color—'NEUTRAL'—with the result that the foreign key's index was a real showstopper on inventory queries.

The "relational way" to avoid the unplanned breakage of consistency would have been to use a lookup key with no meaning as data (i.e. an atomic key):

```
CREATE TABLE COLORS (
```

```
  ID INTEGER NOT NULL PRIMARY KEY, /* or UNIQUE */
  COLOR CHARACTER(20));
COMMIT;
INSERT INTO COLORS (ID, COLOR)
  VALUES (0, 'NEUTRAL');
COMMIT;
CREATE TABLE STOCK_ITEM (
  ...
  COLOR INTEGER DEFAULT 0,
  ...);
```

Such a key need never change and it can (and should) be hidden from users entirely. Tables that use the lookup table store the stable key. Changes in available values are implemented as new lookup rows with new keys. Values already associated with keys do not change—they are preserved to ensure that history data are not compromised by subsequent changes.

In the event that, even with the higher distribution of key values, the foreign key would produce an index that was still poorly selective over a large table, the improvement to the stability of the table justifies avoiding a formal referential constraint. Existence can be easily enforced using custom triggers.

The REFERENCES Privilege

Firebird implements SQL security on all objects in the database. Every user—except the owner of the database and users with SYSDBA or system superuser privileges—must be GRANTed the necessary privileges to access an object. SQL privileges are discussed in great detail in Chapter 37, ***Database Security***.

However, one privilege may be of special significance in the design of your referential integrity infrastructure: the REFERENCES privilege. If the parent and child tables have different owners, a GRANT REFERENCES privilege may be needed to give users sufficient permission to enable referential constraint actions.

The REFERENCES privilege is granted on the referenced table in the relationship—that is, the table referenced by the foreign key—or, at least, on every column of the reference primary or unique key. The privilege needs to be granted to the owner of the referencing table (the child table) and also to any user who needs to write to the referencing table.

At run-time, REFERENCES kicks in whenever the database engine verifies that a value input to a foreign key is contained in the referenced table.

Because this privilege is also checked when a foreign key constraint is defined, it will be necessary for the appropriate permissions to be granted and committed beforehand. If you need to create a foreign key that refers to a table owned by someone else, that owner must first grant you REFERENCES privileges on that table. Alternatively, the owner can grant REFERENCES privileges to a role and then grant that role to you.

Don't make this harder than it needs to be. If there is no requirement to deny read privileges on the referenced table, then have the owner grant the REFERENCES privilege on it to your "general user" role or, if you are using it, to PUBLIC.

If you have these restrictions amongst your requirements, it may be necessary to maintain two separate permissions scripts—one for developers, that is run following table creation, and another for end-users, that is run on an otherwise completed schema.

Handling Other Forms of Relationship

Referential constraints can be applied to other forms of relationship apart from the optional one-to-many form described so far:

- One-to-one
- Many-to-many
- Self-referencing one-to-many (nested or tree relationships)
- Mandatory variants of any form of relationship

One-to-one relationship

Optional 1:1 structures can be valuable where an entity in your data model has a large number of distinct attributes, only some of which are accessed frequently. It can save storage and page reads dramatically to store occasional data in optional "peer" relations that share matching primary keys.

A 1:1 relationship is similar to a 1:many relationship, insofar as it links a foreign key to a unique key. The difference here is that the linking key needs to be unique to enforce the 1:1 relationship—to allow, at most, one dependent row per parent row.

It is usual to double up the use the primary key column(s) of the "peer" table as the foreign key to the parent.

```
CREATE TABLE PARENT_PEER (
  ID INTEGER NOT NULL,
  MORE_DATA VARCHAR(10),
  CONSTRAINT PK_PARENT_PEER PRIMARY KEY(ID),
  CONSTRAINT FK_PARENT_PEER_PARENT
  FOREIGN KEY (ID) REFERENCES PARENT);
```

The effect of this double usage is to cause two mandatory indexes to be created on the column that is the primary key of the peer table: one for the primary key and one for the foreign key. The FK index is stored as if it were non-unique but the PK index will enforce the uniqueness.

Sometimes, especially in older Firebird versions, the optimizer is quirky about this doubling up and could ignore the peer table's primary index. For example,

```
SELECT PARENT.ID, PARENT_PEER.ID,
  PARENT.DATA, PARENT_PEER.MORE_DATA
FROM PARENT JOIN PARENT_PEER
  ON PARENT.ID = PARENT_PEER.ID;
```

ignores the primary key index of the peer and produces this plan:

```
PLAN JOIN (PARENT_PEER NATURAL, PARENT INDEX (PK_PARENT))
```

With a "thin" key, such as the one used in the example, the impact on performance may not be severe. With a composite key, the effect may be serious, especially if there will be multiple joins involving several parent-to-peer 1:1 relations. It should at least make you want to test the plans and consider surrogating the primary keys of 1:1 structures.

It is not a bad thing if you choose to add a special column to a peer relation in order to implement distinct primary and foreign keys. It can be a useful aid to self-documentation.

Many-to-many relationship

In this interesting case, our data model shows us that each row in TableA may have relationships with multiple rows in TableB, while each row in TableB may have multiple relationships with rows in TableA:

Figure 16.2 Many-to-many relationship

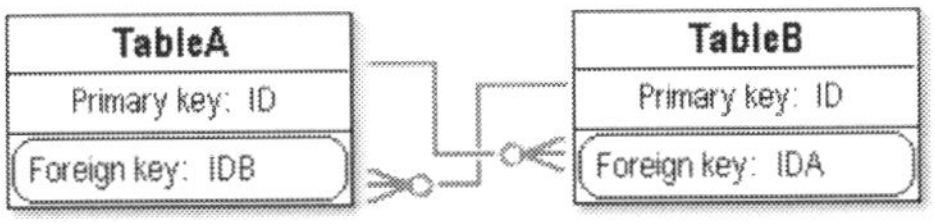

As modelled, this relationship gives rise to a condition known as a *circular reference*. The proposed foreign key in TableB references the primary key of TableA, which means that the TableB row cannot be created if there is no row in TableA with a matching primary key. However, for the same reason, the required row cannot be inserted into TableA if there is no matching primary key value in TableB.

Dealing with a circular reference

If your structural requirements dictate that such a circular reference must exist, it can be be worked around. Firebird allows a foreign key value to be NULL—provided the column is not made non-nullable by another constraint—because NULL, being a "non-value", does not violate the rule that the foreign key column must have a matching value in the referenced parent column. By making the FK on one table nullable, you can insert into that table and create the primary key that the other table requires:

```
CREATE TABLE TABLEA (
    ID INTEGER NOT NULL,
    ...,
  CONSTRAINT PK_TABLEA PRIMARY KEY (ID));
COMMIT;
--
CREATE TABLE TABLEB (
  ID INTEGER NOT NULL,
    ...,
    CONSTRAINT PK_TABLEB PRIMARY KEY (ID));
COMMIT;
--
ALTER TABLE TABLEA
  ADD CONSTRAINT FK_TABLEA_TABLEB
  FOREIGN KEY(IDB) REFERENCES TABLEB(ID);
COMMIT;
--
ALTER TABLE TABLEB
  ADD CONSTRAINT FK_TABLEB_TABLEA
  FOREIGN KEY(IDA) REFERENCES TABLEA(ID);
COMMIT;
```

The workaround:

```
INSERT INTO TABLEB(ID)
  VALUES(1);  /* creates a row with NULL in IDB */
COMMIT;
INSERT INTO TABLEA(ID, IDB)
  VALUES(22, 1);  /* links to the TABLEB row just created */
COMMIT;
UPDATE TABLEB
  SET IDA = 22 WHERE ID = 1;
COMMIT;
```

Clearly, this model is not without potential problems. In most systems, keys are generated, not supplied by applications. To ensure consistency, it becomes a job for all client applications inserting to these tables to know the value of both keys in both tables within a single transaction context. Performing the entire operation with a stored procedure would reduce the dependence of the relationship on application code.

In practice, tables with many:many relationships implemented circularly are very difficult to represent in GUI applications.

Using an intersection table

Generally, it is better practice to resolve many:many relationships by adding an *intersection table*. This special structure carries one foreign key for each table in the many:many relationship. Its own primary key (or a unique constraint) is a composite of the two foreign keys. The two related tables that are intersected by it do not have foreign keys relating to one another at all.

This implementation is easy to represent in applications. Before Insert and Before Update triggers on both tables take care of adding intersection rows when required.

Figure 16.3 Resolution of many:many relationship

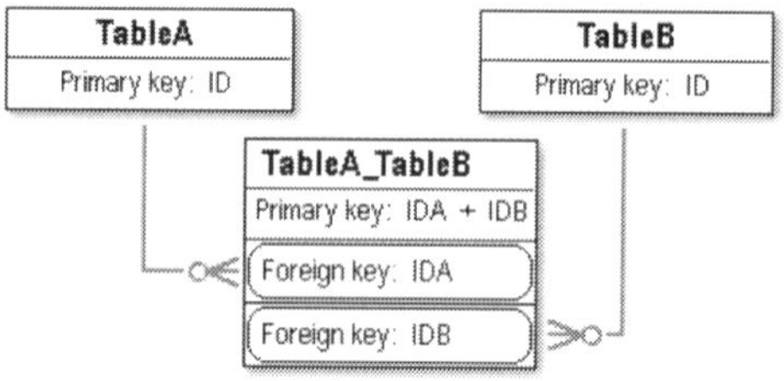

Implementing it:

```
CREATE TABLE TABLEA (
  ID INTEGER NOT NULL,
   ...,
  CONSTRAINT PK_TABLEA PRIMARY KEY (ID));
COMMIT;
--
CREATE TABLE TABLEB (
  ID INTEGER NOT NULL,
   ...,
  CONSTRAINT PK_TABLEB PRIMARY KEY (ID));
COMMIT;
--
CREATE TABLE TABLEA_TABLEB (
  IDA INTEGER NOT NULL,
  IDB INTEGER NOT NULL,
  CONSTRAINT PK_TABLEA_TABLEB
  PRIMARY KEY (IDA, IDB));
COMMIT;
--
ALTER TABLE TABLEA_TABLEB
  ADD CONSTRAINT FK_TABLEA FOREIGN KEY (IDA)
    REFERENCES TABLEA,
  ADD CONSTRAINT FK_TABLEB FOREIGN KEY (IDB)
    REFERENCES TABLEB;
COMMIT;
```

Self-Referencing Relationship

If your model has an entity whose primary key refers to a foreign key located in the same entity, you have a self-referencing relationship:

Figure 16.4 Self-referencing relationship

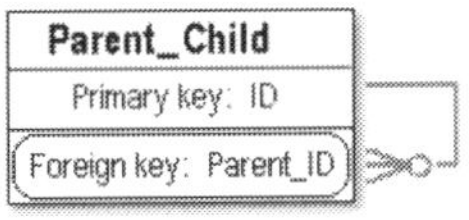

This is the classic *tree* hierarchy, where any row (member, node) can be both parent and child: that is, it can have children (or *branch*) rows dependent on it and, at the same time, it can be a child (branch) of another row (member, node). It needs a CHECK constraint or Before Insert and Before Update triggers to ensure that a PARENT_ID never points to itself.

If your business rules require that parents must exist before children can be added, you will want to use a value, e.g. –1, as the root node of the tree structure. The PARENT_ID should be made NOT NULL and defaulted to your chosen root value. The alternative is leave PARENT_ID as nullable, as in the example below, and use NULL as the root.

In general, custom triggers for Before Insert and Before Update will be required for trees that will be nested to more than two levels. For consistency in trees with a NULL root node, it is important to ensure that constraint actions do not create orphan children unintentionally.

```
CREATE TABLE PARENT_CHILD (
  ID INTEGER NOT NULL,
  PARENT_ID INTEGER
    CHECK (PARENT_ID <> ID));
COMMIT;
--
ALTER TABLE PARENT_CHILD
  ADD CONSTRAINT PK_PARENT
    PRIMARY KEY(ID);
COMMIT;
--
ALTER TABLE PARENT_CHILD
  ADD CONSTRAINT FK_CHILD_PARENT
    FOREIGN KEY(PARENT_ID)
      REFERENCES PARENT_CHILD(ID);
COMMIT;
```

About tree structures

Much more can be said about designing tree structures. It is a challenging topic in relational database design that stretches standard SQL to its boundaries. Unfortunately, it is beyond the scope of this Guide. For some interesting solutions, try ***SQL for Smarties*** by Joe Celko (Morgan Kaufmann, ISBN 1-55860-323-9).

Mandatory relationships

A mandatory—or obligatory—relationship is one which requires that a minimum of one referencing (child) row exist for each referenced (parent) row. For example, a delivery note structure—a header with customer and delivery address information—would be illogical if it were permitted to have header row without any referencing item lines.

It is a common beginner mistake to assume that a NOT NULL constraint on the child will make a one-to-many relationship mandatory. It does not, because the FOREIGN KEY constraint operates only in the context of an instantiated dependency. With no referencing row, the nullability of the foreign key is irrelevant to the issue.

A mandatory relationship is one place where user-defined trigger constraints must be added to extend referential integrity. Firebird SQL does not provide a "mandatoriness" constraint. It can take some fancy logic at both the client and the server to ensure that events will occur in the right sequence to meet both the referential constraint and the mandatoriness requirements. It will involve both insert and delete triggers, since the logic must enforce the 'minimum of one child' rule not only at creation time but when child rows are deleted.

For details about writing triggers and an example of a trigger solution for enforcing a mandatory relationship, refer to Chapter 30, ***Triggers***.

"Object is in Use" Error

It is worth mentioning this exception in the context of applying referential integrity constraints, since it is a regular source of frustration for new users. Firebird will not allow a referential constraint to be added or dropped if a transaction is using either of the participating tables. In versions 1.X, you will require exclusive access to avoid this error. In the later versions, you will be allowed to proceed but you can still expect an *Object in Use* exception if the tables affected by creating a FOREIGN KEY constraint are involved in an "interesting" transaction.

If you are yet to start getting your head around transactions (Part V of this book) then, for now, suffice it to say that everything you do potentially affects what someone else is doing and vice-versa. Everything is done in a transaction. Transactions isolate one piece of pending work from other pieces of pending work. At some point you can expect what you want to do to bump into what someone else is doing. When you want to alter the structures of objects, it's always best to operate in an exclusive bubble!

Sometimes it may be less than obvious to you just in what way the object is in use. Other dependencies—such as stored procedures or triggers that refer to your tables, or other referential constraints affecting one or both—can cause this exception to occur if they are in use by an uncommitted transaction. Metadata caches—blocks of server memory that hold metadata used to compile recent client requests and any recently-used stored procedure and trigger code—keep locks on the objects in their possession. Each connection has its own metadata cache, even on a Superserver, so the server could be holding locks on objects that no connection is actually using.

What this is all leading to recommend strongly that you get exclusive access to the database for any metadata changes, particularly those involving dependencies.

If you have exclusive access and the exception still occurs, don't overlook the possibility that you are using it yourself. If you are working in an admin utility with a data browser focused on one of your tables, then the object is in use!

CHAPTER

17

INTERACTIVE SQL UTILITY (ISQL)

The *isql* utility, installed in the `/bin` directory beneath your Firebird root, provides a non-graphical interface to Firebird databases that is consistent on all server and client platforms.

isql accepts both DDL and DML statements, as well as a subset of SQL-like console commands not available in DSQL. It can be used both for creating and maintaining metadata and for querying and changing data. It includes several admin tools and the option to perform some database operations directly from a command shell or through a shell script or batch file.

Several other database management systems have adopted the "isql" name for their interactive query programs. Always run Firebird's isql program from its own directory or provide the absolute file path if this is a problem on your server.

Interactive Mode

Interactive SQL (*isql*) is a command-line program, available on all platforms, that can be run locally or from a remote client.

- From a remote client, a valid user name and password are always required to run isql.
- If you are connecting locally, you can set the operating system variables ISC_USER and ISC_PASSWORD and avoid the need to enter them on commands. For more information about these variables, refer to ISC_USER and ISC_PASSWORD in the chapter entitled *Configuring Firebird and Its Environment* in the companion volume to this, Volume 3: ***Administering Firebird Servers and Databases*** or in ***The Firebird Book Second Edition***.

Some additional command-line switches can be used when invoking the interactive shell. They are noted later in this chapter, in Table 24.1, *Switches for isql command-line options*.

Default text editor

Some *isql* commands access your system's default text editor.

- On UNIX, Linux and some other POSIX platforms, the default editor is defined by one or the other of the two environment variables, EDITOR and VISUAL. The installation default is usually *vi*, *vim*, or *emacs* but you can set it to another preferred console (not X) text editor.

- On Windows, the default editor is *notepad.exe*. If you have another text editor that you prefer, you can define a system variable EDITOR for Firebird's use, that *isql* will recognise and try to use instead of the Windows default.

Use an editor that creates only plain text when invoked. Word processors and editors that open new files by default to anything but plain text are not suitable.

Starting isql

To start *isql*, open a command shell and cd to the /bin directory of your Firebird server or client installation. Use the following command pattern at the shell prompt and press the Enter key:

```
isql [<database_name>] [-u[ser] <user-name> -pas[sword] <password>]
```

- <database_name> is optional. If you include it, *isql* will open a connection to the database and start its shell already connected.

Use either the alias of the database or its absolute path. Include the hostname if you are invoking isql remotely, or locally using Superserver on POSIX.

- the switches -user <user-name> and -password <password> are optional when you are starting *isql* without a connection to the database and required if you are starting *isql* remotely. If the ISC_USER and ISC_PASSWORD environment variables are not set, they will also be required when you start *isql* locally.

Examples

On POSIX:

```
./isql
```

On Windows:

```
isql
```

starts the program.

```
./isql -user TEMPDBA -password osoweary [on POSIX]
isql -user TEMPDBA -password osoweary [on Windows]
```

starts the program and stores the supplied username and password without authenticating them.

```
isql hotchicken:/data/mydatabase.fdb -user TEMPDBA -password osoweary
```

starts the program on a Windows client and connects to the database on a POSIX server, provided the username and password are valid on the server.

```
./isql /data/mydatabase.fdb
```

starts the program locally on a POSIX Classic server and connects to the database, provided the environment variables ISC_USER and ISC_PASSWORD are set and are available to your Linux user profile.

You are in the *isql* shell if you can see the SQL> prompt, . If there were errors in the command string, or authentication problems, you might also see some error messages or you might be still at the command line.

If you are logged in to the database when *isql* starts up, you will see a console display similar to Figure 24.1. The appearance of the surrounding shell depends on the operating system. The *isql* shell is the same on all platforms:

Figure 17.1 Console display when isql starts logged-in

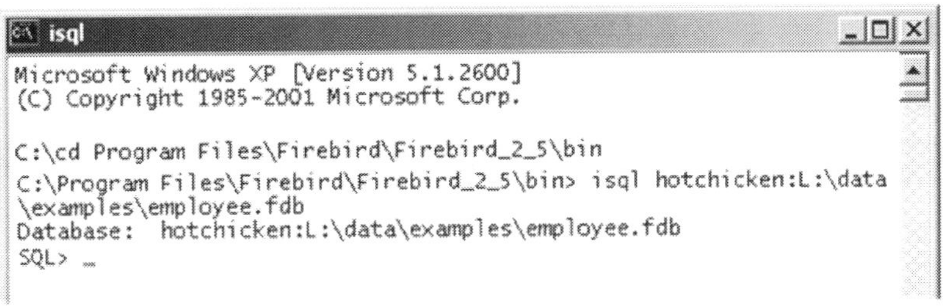

If you didn't enter a database path or alias or you used a username and password that are not defined on the server, you will see something similar to Figure 24.2:

Figure 17.2 Console display when isql starts not logged-in

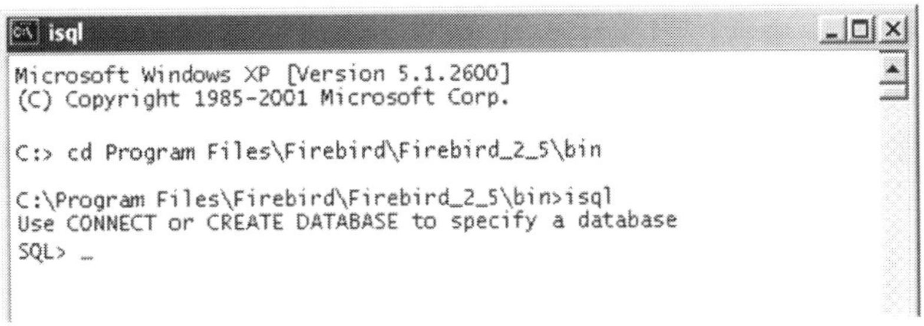

Connecting to a database

To connect to a database from the `SQL>` prompt in the *isql* shell, use the following examples as syntax patterns. Notice that the syntax and punctuation inside the *isql* shell are different to what are used when passing the connection parameters from the system shell:

```
CONNECT 'HOTCHICKEN:L:\DATA\EXAMPLES\EMPLOYEE.FDB'
  USER 'SYSDBA' PASSWORD 'masterkey';
```

connects to a remote or local server named HOTCHICKEN.

```
CONNECT 'L:\DATA\EXAMPLES\EMPLOYEE.FDB';
```

connects to a local server where *isql* already knows your Firebird username and password—either because you entered them correctly when you started *isql* or because *isql* is executing in a shell that can see the environment variables ISC_USER and ISC_PASSWORD.

```
CONNECT 'HOTCHICKEN:EMP3' USER 'SYSDBA' PASSWORD 'masterkey';
```

is equivalent to the first example, using an alias stored in `aliases.conf` on the server, that points to the path.

```
CONNECT 'L:/DATA/EXAMPLES/EMPLOYEE.FDB';
```

is equivalent to the second example—slashes may be forward or backward in *isql*.

Server (host) and path names

On Windows, don't confuse server names and shared disk resource names. The client/server network layer does not recognize mapped drives or shares. A drive identifier must always point to the actual drive-letter of a hard-drive or partition on the server host machine.

User authentication

Regardless of whether you log in directly from the command-line or do so when connecting inside the *isql* shell, authentication will fail if the server does not recognise the username or the password. For example, you will see this if your CONNECT statement fails:

Figure 17.3 Failed authentication

```
isql                                                    _ |□| x|
Microsoft Windows XP [Version 5.1.2600]
(C) Copyright 1985-2001 Microsoft Corp.

C:\cd Program Files\Firebird\Firebird_2_5\bin

C:\Program Files\Firebird\Firebird_2_5\bin>isql
Use CONNECT or CREATE DATABASE to specify a database
SQL> CONNECT 'L:\data\examples\employee.fdb'
CON> user 'SYSDBA' password 'monsterkey';
Statement failed, SQLCODE = -902
Your user name and password are not defined. Ask your
database administrator to set up a Firebird login.
SQL> _
```

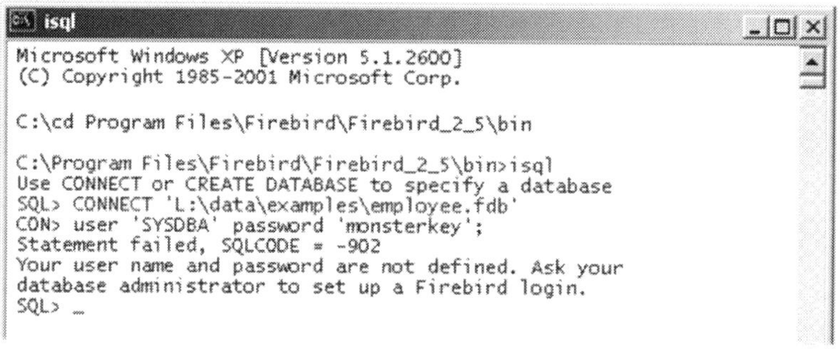

If this happens to you, double-check that you have spelt the username and password correctly; and that the password is correct for case. Passwords are case-sensitive; user names are not.

Using the Interface

Now you are logged in to a database, you can begin using *isql* to work with your data and metadata. Before getting into the work you can do with this utility, it will be useful to understand something about the interface and how it works with your work.

SET commands

Several commands are available inside isql that, in most cases, are not valid in any other environment. These are the commands using the SET verb, which can be used to set up various conditions within your *isql* session. We look at some of them in this section, while others are discussed a little later.

The continuation prompt

If you press Enter without remembering to finish a statement with a terminator, you will see the continuation prompt CON> instead of the isql prompt SQL>:

```
SQL> SHOW DATABASE
CON>
```

If it was a mistake, simply type the terminator character and press Enter again.

```
SQL> SHOW DATABASE
CON> ;
SQL>
```

However, you can use this feature to make your typing easier to read. For example:

```
SQL> CREATE TABLE ATABLE (
CON>    ID INTEGER NOT NULL,
CON>    DATA VARCHAR(20),
CON>    DATE_ENTERED DATE
CON>      DEFAULT CURRENT_DATE
CON> );
SQL>
```

One good reason to use the continuation feature at times is that you can use the OUTPUT command to pipe your isql input to a file (q.v.). Since the output is saved exactly as you type it, any blank-space indenting will be preserved. Many Firebird users use isql as their only script editor!

The terminator character

The default statement terminator is the semicolon (;), which is used for all of the examples in this chapter. You can change the terminator to any character or group of characters with the SET TERM[INATOR] command. For example, to change it to '!!', use this statement:

```
SQL> SET TERM !!;
SQL>
```

Now, if you try to use the semicolon as the terminator, *isql* will assume you have an unfinished statement:

```
SQL> SHOW DATABASE;
CON>
```

Then, if you supply the new terminator character to finish the statement, *isql* complains:

```
CON> !!
Command error: SHOW DATABASE;
SQL>
```

Transactions in isql

Transaction management in *isql* differs according to whether you issue a DDL statement, a SHOW command or other kinds of statements.

When *isql* starts, it starts a transaction in SNAPSHOT (concurrency) isolation with a lock resolution setting of WAIT. Unless you run DDL statements or SHOW commands, the transaction stays current—and thus uncommitted—until you issue a COMMIT or ROLLBACK statement.

You can start an explicit transaction by committing the current transaction and using a *SET TRANSACTION* statement to start a new one. For example, to start a READ COMMITTED NO WAIT transaction:

```
SQL> COMMIT;
SQL> SET TRANSACTION
CON> NO WAIT READ COMMITTED;
```

When you have finished your task, just issue a COMMIT statement as usual. The next statement will revert to the default configuration.

DDL statements

Each time you issue a DDL statement—those are the ones that define, modify or drop metadata objects— *isql* starts a special transaction for it and commits it immediately you press Enter. A new transaction is started immediately afterwards. You can change this automatic behavior by issuing the SET AUTODDL OFF command from the SQL prompt before you begin issuing your DDL statements:

```
SQL> SET AUTODDL OFF;
```

To switch back to autocommit mode for DDL statements:

```
SQL> SET AUTODDL ON;
```

For switching back and forth between autoddl *on* and *off*, a short version is available that simply sets autoddl off if it is on, and vice versa:

```
SQL> SET AUTO;
```

The autoddl feature works only with DDL statements.

SHOW commands

The SHOW commands query the system tables. Whenever you invoke a SHOW command, *isql* commits the existing transaction and starts a new one in READ COMMITTED isolation. This ensures that you always have an up-to-date view of metadata changes as soon as they occur.

Retrieving the line buffer

isql allows you to retrieve the line buffer, in a similar fashion to the way the *readline* feature works on POSIX platforms. Use the up and down arrow keys to "scroll through" the program's command buffer, a line at a time, to retrieve copies of lines you typed previously.

Using warnings

By default, *isql* issues warnings for certain conditions, for example:

* statements with no effect

* ambiguous join specifications in Firebird 1.0.x (in v.1.5 and higher, they will cause exceptions)

* expressions that produce different results in different versions of Firebird

* API calls that will be replaced in future versions

* when a database shutdown is pending

For toggling the display off and on during an interactive isql session, use SET WARNINGS or its shorthand counterpart, SET WNG.

Exception handling

SQL errors in are handled and delivered in much the same way as they are in any DSQL application—*isql* displays an error message consisting of the SQLSTATE code, the SQLCODE (SQL error code) and the text message from the Firebird status array:

Figure 17.4 Example of an error message in *isql*

```
isql                                          _ □ ×
SQL> select chocolate from customer;
Statement failed, SQLSTATE = 42S22
Dynamic SQL Error
-SQL error code = -206
-Column unknown
-chocolate
-At line 1, column 18

SQL>
```

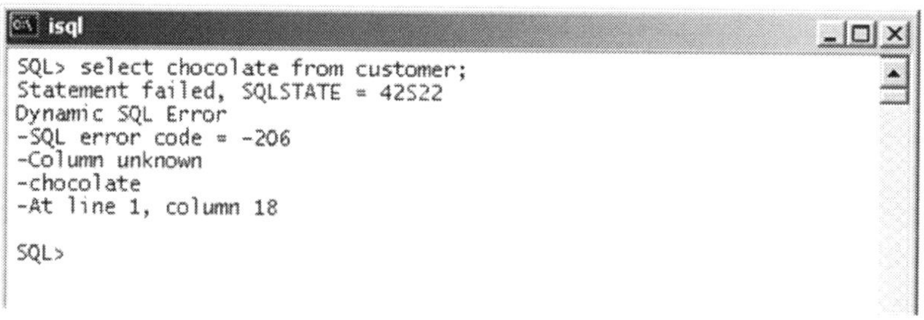

When an SQL error has occurred, all versions display the SQL error code. SQL errors with sub-zero SQLCODEs mean the statement has failed to execute. They are all listed in Appendix VII. You may also see one of the SQL warning or information messages, viz.

0 SUCCESS (successful execution).

+1—99 SQLWARNING (system warning or information message).

+100 NOT FOUND (indicates that no qualifying rows were found, or "end-of-file", i.e. the end of the current active set of rows was detected.

The SQLSTATE codes appear in isql versions 2.5 and higher. A reference listing for them is in Appendix VIII.

Dialect in *isql*

If you start the *isql* client program and attach to a database without specifying a dialect, *isql* takes on the dialect of the database.

You can set the *isql* dialect yourself, in the following ways:

* When starting isql:

```
bin] isql -s n
```

where n is 1, 2, or 3.

If you specify the dialect this way, isql retains that dialect after connection unless you explicitly change it.

- Within an isql session or in a SQL script

```
SET SQL DIALECT n;
```

isql continues to operate in that dialect unless it is explicitly changed.

The dialect can not be set as a parameter of a CREATE DATABASE statement.

When you create a database interactively using isql, the database will be in the dialect that is current in isql at the time the CREATE DATABASE statement is issued. You need to watch this if you had a dialect 1 database open previously, because isql stays in dialect 1 after it disconnects from the dialect 1 database.

Dialect effects

A dialect 1 client processes all commands according to the expectations of the ancient legacy InterBase 5 language and syntax, with certain variations. The effects may also show some variations according to which dialect is in force. For example, if you create a table that specifies a column of type DATE, you will see an info message telling you "DATE data type is now called TIMESTAMP".

- In a dialect 2 client, elements that have different interpretations in dialect 1 and 3 are all flagged with warnings or errors, to assist in migrating databases to dialect 3
- A dialect 3 client parses all statements according to native Firebird SQL semantics: double quotes are delimited identifiers and are not recognized as string delimiters, the DATE data type is date-only and exact numerics with precision greater than 9 are stored as BIGINT

v.1.0.x BIGINT=(NUMERIC(18,0)

SELECT statements

The console output from SELECT statements pours forth until there is no more data to be fetched. Columns are extended to the maximum defined width and there is no way to shorten or hide them. In practice, SELECT * queries with no WHERE clause will be not be much use to you.

Sometimes you will find it useful to use the *OUTPUT* command to pass the fetched data directly to a text file, where you can use a suitable editor to view it.

From the "2" series onward, isql displays CHAR and VARCHAR types defined in character set OCTETS (alias BINARY) in hexadecimal format.

BLOBs

By default, *isql* does not display the contents of BLOB columns, just their hexadecimal blob_ids. You can use the command *SET BLOBDISPLAY | SET BLOB* to change this behaviour.

You can use the blob_id with *BLOBDUMP* to dump the contents of a BLOB to a file and with *BLOBVIEW* to view (but not edit) a text BLOB in the default editor.

Stopping query output

From v.2.1 onward, output from a SELECT in an interactive *isql* session on any platform can be stopped using `Ctrl-C`. It does not cancel the query but it does stop the avalanche of data arriving on your screen or pouring into your output file.

Interactive Commands

You can enter three kinds of commands or statements interactively at the `SQL>` prompt:

- SQL data definition (DDL) statements, such as CREATE, ALTER, DROP, GRANT and REVOKE. These statements create, modify or remove metadata and objects, or control user access permission (privileges) to the database.
- SQL data manipulation (DML) statements such as SELECT, INSERT, UPDATE and DELETE. The output of SELECT statements can be displayed or directed to a file (see the OUTPUT command).
- *isql* commands, which fall into three main categories:
  - General commands (for example, commands to read an input file, write to an output file, or end an *isql* session)
  - SHOW commands (to display metadata or other database information)
  - SET commands (to modify the isql environment)

Scripts

While it is possible to build a database by submitting and committing a series of DDL statements during an interactive *isql* session, this is an ad hoc approach that leaves you with no documentation of what you did and potential holes in your QA review process.

It is very good practice to use a script to create your database and its objects. A script for creating and altering database objects is sometimes known as a *schema script*, a *data definition file* or just a *DDL script*.

In *isql* you will find utility commands both for creating scripts from your interactive command stream (OUTPUT) and for streaming one or a sequence of script files into the application (INPUT) through either the interactive interface or the command shell.

The topic of schema scripting is covered in detail later in this chapter, in the section *Creating and Running Scripts*.

General *isql* Commands

The general isql commands perform a variety of useful tasks, including reading, recording and processing schema scripts and executing shell commands. They are: BLOBDUMP, BLOBVIEW, EDIT, EXIT, HELP, INPUT, OUTPUT, QUIT and SHELL.

BLOBDUMP

stores BLOB data into a named file

```
BLOBDUMP blob_id filename ;
```

Arguments

blob_id	Identifier consisting of two hex numbers separated by a colon (:). The first number is the ID of the table containing the BLOB column, the second is a sequenced instance number. To get the blob_id, issue any SELECT statement that selects a column of BLOB data. The output will show the hex blob_id above or in place of the BLOB column data, depending on whether SET BLOB[DISPLAY] is ON or OFF.
filename	Fully qualified filesystem name of the file which is to receive the data.

Example

```
SQL> BLOBDUMP 32:d48 IMAGE.JPG ;
```

BLOBVIEW

displays BLOB data in the default text editor.

```
BLOBVIEW blob_id ;
```

Argument

blob_id	Identifier consisting of two hex numbers separated by a colon (:). See BLOBDUMP for instructions on how to determine the blob_id you are looking for. In current versions, BLOBVIEW does not support on-line editing of the BLOB. It may be introduced in a future release.

Example

```
SQL> BLOBVIEW 85:7 ;
```

BLOBVIEW may return an "Invalid transaction handle" error after you close the editor. It is a bug. To correct the situation, start a transaction manually, with

```
SQL> SET TRANSACTION;
```

EDIT

allows editing and re-execution of the previous isql command or of a batch of commands in a source file.

```
SQL> EDIT [filename];
```

Argument

filename	Optional, fully qualified filesystem name of file to edit.

Example

```
SQL> EDIT /usr/mystuff/batch.sql
```

EDIT can also be used to open the previous statements in your editor:

```
SQL> SELECT EMP_CODE, EMP_NAME FROM EMPLOYEE ;
SQL> EDIT ;
```

Press Enter to display the "scroll" from your *isql* session in your text editor. Edit it, save it if you wish, and exit. The edited batch of commands will be re-executed in your *isql* shell when you exit the editor.

EXIT

commits the current transaction without prompting, closes the database and ends the isql session. If you need to roll back the transaction instead of committing it, use QUIT instead.

```
SQL> EXIT ;
```

EXIT takes no arguments.

HELP

displays a list of *isql* commands with descriptions. You can combine it with OUTPUT to print the list to a file.

```
SQL> HELP ;
```

Example

```
SQL> OUTPUT HELPLIST.TXT ;
SQL> HELP ;
SQL> OUTPUT ; /* toggles output back to the monitor */
```

HELP takes no arguments.

INPUT

reads and executes a block of commands from a named text file (SQL script). Input files can embed other INPUT commands, thus providing the capability to designed chained or structured suites of DDL scripts. To create scripts, use a text editor or build them interactively, use the OUTPUT or EDIT commands.

```
SQL> INPUT filename ;
SQL> EDIT [filename];
```

Argument

filename	Fully qualified filesystem name of file containing SQL statements and commands to be opened executed, statement by statement.

Example

```
SQL> INPUT /data/schemascripts/myscript.sql ;
```

In a script:

```
...
CREATE EXCEPTION E010 'This is an exception.';
COMMIT;
-- TABLE DEFINITIONS
INPUT '/data/schemascripts/tabledefs.sql';
-- CONSTRAINT DEFINITIONS
INPUT 'data/schemascripts/constraintdefs.sql';
...
```

OUTPUT

redirects output to a disk file or (back) to the standard output device (monitor). Use SET ECHO commands to include or exclude commands:

- SET ECHO ON to output both commands and data
- SET ECHO OFF to output data only

```
SQL> OUTPUT [filename];
```

Argument

filename	Optional, fully qualified filesystem path to a file containing SQL statements and commands. If no file name is given, results appear on the standard monitor output, i.e., output-to-file is switched off

Example

```
SQL> OUTPUT d:\data\employees.dta ;
SQL> SELECT EMP_NO, EMP_NAME FROM EMPLOYEE ; /* output goes to file */
SQL> OUTPUT ; /* toggles output back to the monitor */
```

Tip *If you are using OUTPUT to build scripts, it will be necessary to edit them to remove any stray interactive isql commands. However, when you "replay" output in isql using INPUT, isql usually just ignores the echoed interactive commands.*

QUIT

Rolls back the current transaction and closes the isql shell.

```
SQL> QUIT ;
```

QUIT takes no arguments. If you need to commit the transaction instead of rolling it back, use EXIT instead.

SHELL

gives temporary access to a command-line shell without committing or rolling back any transaction.

```
SQL> SHELL [operating system command];
```

Argument

operating system command	Optional, a command or call that is valid in command shell from which *isql* was launched. The command will be executed and control returned to isql. If no command is specified, isql opens an interactive session in the command shell. Typing `exit` returns control to *isql*.

Example

```
SQL> SHELL dir /mydir | more ;
```

The example will display the contents of the directory `/mydir` and return control to *isql* when the display completes or if the *more* utility is terminated by Ctrl-C.

SHOW Commands

SHOW commands are used to display metadata, including tables, indexes, procedures, triggers and privileges. They can list the names of all objects of the specified type or supply detailed information about a particular object named in the command.

The SHOW commands are (approximately) the interactive equivalent of the command-line -extract, -x or -a options (q.v.). However, although you can use the OUTPUT command to send the output of the SHOW commands to a file, the saved text is not ready to use as a schema script without editing. Use the command-line options if obtaining a schema script is your goal.

Each SHOW command runs in its own READ COMMITTED statement, ensuring that each call returns the most up-to-date view of the state of the database.

SHOW CHECK

displays the names and sources for all user-defined CHECK constraints defined for a specified table.

```
SQL> SHOW CHECK tablename ;
```

Argument

tablename	Name of a table that exists in the attached database

Example

```
...
SQL> SHOW CHECK JOB ;
CONSTRAINT INTEG_12
  CHECK (min_salary < max_salary)
```

SHOW COLLATIONS

From v.2.1 onward, lists all the user-declared character set/collation pairs in the database.

Even if you have no user-declared character sets, you can still list out all of the installed character sets using

```
SELECT * FROM RDB$CHARACTER_SETS;
```

SHOW DATABASE

displays information about the attached database (file name, page size and allocation, sweep interval, transaction numbers, Forced Writes status, default character set). SHOW DB is a shorthand version of the command.

```
SQL> SHOW DATABASE | DB ;
```

SHOW DATABASE takes no arguments.

Figure 17.5 SHOW DATABASE output

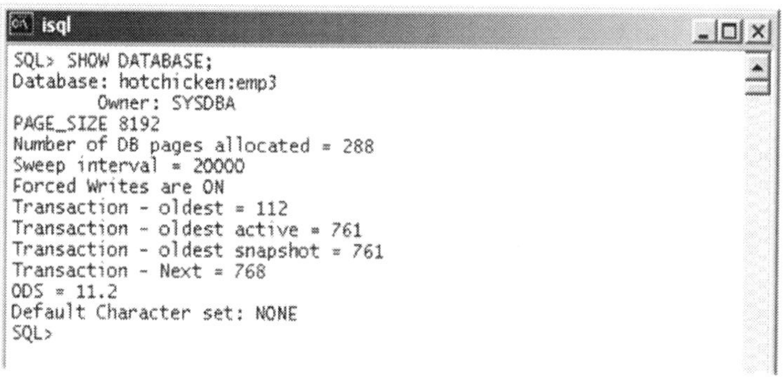

```
SQL> SHOW DATABASE;
Database: hotchicken:emp3
        Owner: SYSDBA
PAGE_SIZE 8192
Number of DB pages allocated = 288
Sweep interval = 20000
Forced Writes are ON
Transaction - oldest = 112
Transaction - oldest active = 761
Transaction - oldest snapshot = 761
Transaction - Next = 768
ODS = 11.2
Default Character set: NONE
SQL>
```

V.1.5.X *For the old versions, use SHOW VERSION to inspect the on-disk structure.*

SHOW DOMAIN[S]

displays domain information.

```
SQL> SHOW { DOMAINS | DOMAIN name };
```

Variations

SHOW DOMAINS	Lists the names of all the domains declared in the database
SHOW DOMAIN *name*	Displays definition of the named single domain

Examples

```
SQL> SHOW DOMAINS ;
D_CURRENCY D_NOTES
D_BOOLEAN D_PHONEFAX
... ...
SQL> SHOW DOMAIN D_BOOLEAN ;
D_BOOLEAN SMALLINT NOT NULL
DEFAULT 0
CHECK (VALUE IN (0,1)
```

SHOW EXCEPTION[S]

displays information about user-defined exceptions.

```
SQL> SHOW { EXCEPTIONS | EXCEPTION name };
```

Variations

SHOW EXCEPTIONS	Lists the names and texts of all exceptions declared in the database
SHOW EXCEPTION *name*	Displays text of the named single exception

Examples ...

```
SQL> SHOW EXCEPTIONS ;
Exception Name Used by, Type
=============== ============================
BAD_WIZ_TYPE UPD_FAVEFOOD, Stored procedure
Invalid Wiz type, check CAPS LOCK
...
SQL> SHOW EXCEPTION BAD_WIZ_TYPE ;
Exception Name Used by, Type
```

```
=============== ===========================
BAD_WIZ_TYPE UPD_FAVEFOOD, Stored procedure
Invalid Wiz type, check CAPS LOCK
```

SHOW FUNCTION[S]

displays information about external functions declared in the attached database.

```
SQL> SHOW { FUNCTIONS | FUNCTION name };
```

Variations

SHOW FUNCTIONS	Lists the names of all external functions declared in the database
SHOW FUNCTION *name*	Displays the declaration of the named external function

Examples ...

```
SQL> SHOW FUNCTIONS ;
ABS MAXNUM
LOWER SUBSTRLEN
... ...
SQL> SHOW FUNCTION maxnum ;
Function MAXNUM:
Function library is /usr/firebird/udf/ib_udf.so
Entry point is FN_MAX
Returns BY VALUE DOUBLE PRECISION
Argument 1: DOUBLE PRECISION
Argument 2: DOUBLE PRECISION
```

SHOW GENERATOR[S]

displays information about generators and sequences declared in the attached database.

```
SQL> SHOW { GENERATORS | GENERATOR name };
```

Variations

SHOW GENERATORS	Lists the names of all generators declared in the database, along with their current values
SHOW GENERATOR *name*	Displays the declaration of the named generator, along with its current value

Examples

```
...
SQL> SHOW GENERATORS ;
Generator GEN_EMPNO, Next value: 1234
Generator GEN_JOBNO, Next value: 56789
Generator GEN_ORDNO, Next value: 98765
... ...
SQL> SHOW GENERATOR gen_ordno ;
Generator GEN_ORDNO, Next value: 98765
```

SHOW GRANT

displays privileges and role ownership information about a named object in the attached database; or displays user membership within roles.

```
SQL> SHOW GRANT { object | rolename };
```

Argument Options

SHOW GRANT *object*	Takes the name of an existing table, view or procedure in the current database
SHOW GRANT *rolename*	Takes the name of an existing role in the current database. Use SHOW ROLES to list all the roles defined for this database.

Examples

```
...
SQL> SHOW GRANT JOB ;
GRANT SELECT ON JOB TO ALL
GRANT DELETE, INSERT, SELECT, UPDATE ON JOB TO MANAGER
SQL> SHOW GRANT DO_THIS ;
GRANT DO_THIS TO MAGICIAN
```

SHOW INDEX (SHOW INDICES)

displays information about a named index, about indices for a specified table or about indices for all tables in the attached database. The command can be abbreviated to SHOW IND.

```
SQL> SHOW {INDICES | INDEX [{ index | table }]};
```

Variations

SHOW INDEX	Prints details of all indexes in the database
SHOW INDEX *index*	Takes the name of an existing index in the current database and prints its details
SHOW INDICES *table*	Takes the name of an existing table in the current database and prints details of all its indexes

Examples

```
...
SQL> SHOW INDEX ;
RDB$PRIMARY1 UNIQUE INDEX ON COUNTRY(COUNTRY)
CUSTNAMEX INDEX ON CUSTOMER(CUSTOMER)
CUSTREGION INDEX ON CUSTOMER(COUNTRY, CITY)
RDB$FOREIGN23 INDEX ON CUSTOMER(COUNTRY)
...
SQL> SHOW IND COUNTRY ;
RDB$PRIMARY20 UNIQUE INDEX ON CUSTOMER(CUSTNO)
CUSTNAMEX INDEX ON CUSTOMER(CUSTOMER)
```

For information about the current states of indexes in the database, use gstat -i. Use of the gstat utility is described in the section Collecting Database Statistics—gstat in the chapter entitled Monitoring and Logging Features, in either the companion volume to this, Volume 3: ***Administering Firebird Servers and Databases*** *or* ***The Firebird Book Second Edition.***

SHOW PROCEDURE[S]

lists all procedures in the attached database,with their dependencies; or displays the text of the named procedure with the declarations and types (input/output) of any arguments. The command can be abbreviated to SHOW PROC.

```
SQL> SHOW {PROCEDURES | PROCEDURE name } ;
```

Variations

SHOW PROCEDURES	Lists out all procedures by name, together with their dependencies.
SHOW PROCEDURE *name*	For the named procedure, lists the source, dependencies and arguments.

Examples

```
SQL> SHOW PROCEDURES ;
Procedure Name Dependency Type
================ ======================== =======
ADD_EMP_PROJ EMPLOYEE_PROJECT Table
UNKNOWN_EMP_ID Exception
DELETE_EMPLOYEE DEPARTMENT Table
EMPLOYEE Table
EMPLOYEE_PROJECT Table
...
SQL> SHOW PROC ADD_EMP_PROJ ;
Procedure text:
===============================================================
BEGIN
BEGIN
INSERT INTO EMPLOYEE_PROJECT (
EMP_NO, PROJ_ID)
VALUES (
:emp_no, :proj_id) ;
WHEN SQLCODE -530 DO
EXCEPTION UNKNOWN_EMP_ID;
END
RETURN ;
END
===============================================================
Parameters:
EMP_NO INPUT SMALLINT
PROJ_ID INPUT CHAR(5)
```

SHOW ROLE[S]

displays the names of SQL roles for the attached database.

```
SQL> SHOW ROLES ;
```

SHOW ROLES takes no arguments.

Examples

```
...
SQL> SHOW ROLES ;
MAGICIAN MANAGER
PARIAH SLEEPER
...
```

To show user membership within roles, use `SHOW GRANT <rolename>`.

SHOW SQL DIALECT

displays the SQL dialects of the client and of the attached database, if there is one.

```
SQL> SHOW SQL DIALECT;
```

Example

```
...
SQL> SHOW SQL DIALECT;
```

```
Client SQL dialect is set: 3 and database SQL dialect is: 3
```

SHOW SYSTEM

displays the names of system tables, system views (if any) and, from V.2.0, pre-defined UDFs, for the attached database. It can be abbreviated to SHOW SYS.

```
SQL> SHOW SYS [ TABLES ] ;
```

The command takes no arguments. TABLES is an optional keyword that does not affect the behavior of the command.

Examples

```
...
SQL> SHOW SYS ;
RDB$CHARACTER_SETS RDB$CHECK_CONSTRAINTS
RDB$COLLATIONS RDB$DATABASE
...
```

For more detailed information about the system tables, see Appendix V.

SHOW TABLE[S]

lists all tables or views, or displays information about the named table or view.

```
SQL> SHOW { TABLES | TABLE name };
```

Variations

SHOW TABLES	Lists out names of all tables and views in alphabetical order, by name
SHOW TABLE *name*	Shows details about the named table or view. If the object is a table, the output contains column names and definitions, PRIMARY KEY, FOREIGN KEY and CHECK constraints, and triggers. If the object is a view, the output contains column names and the SELECT statement that the view is based on.

Examples

```
...
SQL> SHOW TABLES ;
COUNTRY CUSTOMER
DEPARTMENT EMPLOYEE
EMPLOYEE_PROJECT JOB
...
SQL> SHOW TABLE COUNTRY ;
COUNTRY COUNTRYNAME VARCHAR(15) NOT NULL
CURRENCY VARCHAR(10) NOT NULL
PRIMARY KEY (COUNTRY)
SQL> show table employee;
EMP_NO                  (EMPNO) SMALLINT Not Null
FIRST_NAME              (FIRSTNAME) VARCHAR(15) Not Null
LAST_NAME               (LASTNAME) VARCHAR(20) Not Null
PHONE_EXT               VARCHAR(4) Nullable
HIRE_DATE               TIMESTAMP Not Null DEFAULT 'NOW'
DEPT_NO                 (DEPTNO) CHAR(3) Not Null
                        CHECK (VALUE = '000' OR (VALUE > '0' AND VALUE <
= '999') OR VALUE IS NULL)
JOB_CODE                (JOBCODE) VARCHAR(5) Not Null
                        CHECK (VALUE > '99999')
```

```
JOB_GRADE                       (JOBGRADE) SMALLINT Not Null
                                CHECK (VALUE BETWEEN 0 AND 6)
JOB_COUNTRY                     (COUNTRYNAME) VARCHAR(15) Not Null
SALARY                          (SALARY) NUMERIC(10, 2) Not Null DEFAULT 0
                                CHECK (VALUE > 0)
FULL_NAME                       Computed by: (last_name || ', ' || first_name)
CONSTRAINT INTEG_28:
  Foreign key (DEPT_NO)    References DEPARTMENT (DEPT_NO)
CONSTRAINT INTEG_29:
  Foreign key (JOB_CODE, JOB_GRADE, JOB_COUNTRY)    References JOB (JOB_CODE, JO
B_GRADE, JOB_COUNTRY)
CONSTRAINT INTEG_27:
  Primary key (EMP_NO)
CONSTRAINT INTEG_30:
  CHECK ( salary >= (SELECT min_salary FROM job WHERE
                     job.job_code = employee.job_code AND
                     job.job_grade = employee.job_grade AND
                     job.job_country = employee.job_country) AND
          salary <= (SELECT max_salary FROM job WHERE
                     job.job_code = employee.job_code AND
                     job.job_grade = employee.job_grade AND
                     job.job_country = employee.job_country))

Triggers on Table EMPLOYEE:
SET_EMP_NO, Sequence: 0, Type: BEFORE INSERT, Active
SAVE_SALARY_CHANGE, Sequence: 0, Type: AFTER UPDATE, Active
SQL>
```

See also SHOW VIEWS (below).

SHOW TRIGGER[S]

displays all triggers defined in the database, along with the table they depend on; or, for the named trigger, displays its sequence, type, activity status (active/inactive) and PSQL definition. It can be abbreviated to SHOW TRIG.

```
SQL> SHOW {TRIGGERS | TRIGGER name } ;
```

Variations

SHOW TRIGGERS	Lists out all table names with their trigger names alphabetically
SHOW TRIGGER *name*	For the named trigger, identifies the table it belongs to, displays the header parameters, activity status and PSQL source of the body.

Examples

```
SQL> SHOW TRIGGERS ;
Table name Trigger name
================ ========================
EMPLOYEE SET_EMP_NO
EMPLOYEE SAVE_SALARY_CHANGE
CUSTOMER SET_CUST_NO
SALES POST_NEW_ORDER
SQL> SHOW TRIG SET_CUST_NO ;
Trigger:
SET_CUST_NO, Sequence: 0, Type: BEFORE INSERT, Active
```

```
AS
BEGIN
    new.custno = gen_id(cust_no_gen, 1);
END
```

SHOW VERSION

displays information about the software versions of *isql* and the Firebird server program, and the on-disk structure of the attached database. It can be abbreviated to SHOW VER.

```
SQL> SHOW VERSION ;
```

The command takes no arguments.

Example ...

```
SQL> SHOW VER ;
ISQL Version: WI-V2.5.0.26074 Firebird 2.5
Server version:
Firebird/x86/Windows NT (access method), version "WI-V2.5.0.26074 Firebird 2.5"
Firebird/x86/Windows NT (remote server), version "WI-V2.5.0.26074 Firebird 2.5/XNet
(DEV)/P12"
Firebird/x86/Windows NT (remote interface), version "WI-V2.5.0.26074 Firebird 2.5/XNet
(DEV)/P12"
on disk structure version 11.2
```

SHOW VIEW[S]

lists all views, or displays information about the named view.

See also SHOW TABLES.

```
SQL> SHOW { VIEWS | VIEW name } ;
```

Variations

SHOW VIEWS	Lists out the names of all views in alphabetical order
SHOW VIEW *name*	The output displays column names and the SELECT statement that the view is based on.

Example

```
SQL> SHOW VIEWS ;
PHONE_LIST CUSTOMER
...
SQL> SHOW VIEW PHONE_LIST;
EMP_NO                        (EMPNO) SMALLINT Not Null
FIRST_NAME                    (FIRSTNAME) VARCHAR(15) Not Null
LAST_NAME                     (LASTNAME) VARCHAR(20) Not Null
PHONE_EXT                     VARCHAR(4) Nullable
LOCATION                      VARCHAR(15) Nullable
PHONE_NO                      (PHONENUMBER) VARCHAR(20) Nullable
View Source:
==== ======
 SELECT
    emp_no, first_name, last_name, phone_ext, location, phone_no
    FROM employee, department
    WHERE employee.dept_no = department.dept_no
```

SET Commands

The SET commands enable you to view and change things about the *isql* environment. Some are available in scripts.

Many of the SET commands act as "toggles" that switch the feature on if it is off, or off if it is on. Using SET on its own will display the state of all the toggle settings.

SET AUTODDL | SET AUTO

specifies whether DDL statements are committed automatically after being executed, or committed only after an explicit COMMIT.

Available in scripts.

```
SQL> SET AUTODDL [ON | OFF] ; /* default is ON */
```

Options

SET AUTODDL ON	Toggles automatic commit on for DDL
SET AUTODDL OFF	Toggles automatic commit off for DDL
SET AUTO	With no argument, simply toggles AUTODDL on and off.

Example

```
...
SQL> SET AUTODDL OFF ;
SQL> CREATE TABLE WIZZO (x integer, y integer) ;
SQL> ROLLBACK; /* Table WIZZO is not created */
...
SQL>SET AUTO ON ;
SQL> CREATE TABLE WIZZO (x integer, y integer) ;
SQL> /* table WIZZO is created */
```

SET BAIL

When set ON, causes script execution to end and return on the first error encountered. It can be set either as a SET BAIL command in a script or passed as the –b[ail] switch when executing an input script from a command-line call to *isql*. If a "bail-out" occurs, script execution ends and a fail code—merely a non-zero number—is returned to the operating system. The error message will appear at the console or in the outupt file, according to other options passed and, in some cases, can return the line number where the error occurred.

- DML errors will be caught either at prepare time or at execution, according to the type of error that occurs.
- DDL errors will be caught at prepare time or at execution unless AUTODLL is off. In that case, the error will occur when the script issues an explicit COMMIT. In the latter case, it may be difficult to detect which statement actually triggers the bail-out.

Options

SET BAIL ON	Enables bail out on error
SET BAIL OFF	Disables bail out on error
SET BAIL	With no argument, simply toggles BAIL on and off.

Example

```
isql -b -i my_fb.sql -o results.log -m -m2
```

Note *isql will accept a SET BAIL command during an interactive session but it achieves nothing, even if the session is processing an INPUT script and encounters an error.*

SET BLOBDISPLAY | SET BLOB

specifies both sub_type of BLOB to display and whether BLOB data should be displayed.

```
SQL> SET BLOBDISPLAY [ n |ALL |OFF ];
```

SET BLOB is a shortened version of the same command.

Options and Arguments

n	BLOB SUB_TYPE to display. Default: *n*= 1 (text). Positive numbers are system-defined; negative numbers are user-defined.
SET BLOB[DISPLAY] ALL	Display BLOB data of any sub_type
SET BLOB[DISPLAY] OFF	Toggles display of BLOB data off. The output shows only the BlobID (two hex numbers separated by a colon (:). The first number is the ID of the table containing the BLOB column. The second is a sequenced instance number.

Example ...

```
SQL> SET BLOBDISPLAY OFF ;
SQL> SELECT PROJ_NAME, PROJ_DESC FROM PROJECT ;
SQL> /* rows show values for PROJ_NAME and Blob ID */
...
SQL>SET BLOB 1 ;
SQL> SELECT PROJ_NAME, PROJ_DESC FROM PROJECT ;
SQL> /* rows show values for PROJ_NAME and Blob ID */
SQL> /* and the blob text appears beneath each row */
```

SET COUNT

toggles off/on whether to display the number of rows retrieved by queries.

```
SQL> SET COUNT [ON | OFF] ;
```

Options

SET COUNT ON	Toggles on display of "rows returned" message
SET COUNT OFF	Toggles off display of "rows returned" message (default)

Example ...

```
SQL> SET COUNT ON ;
SQL> SELECT * FROM WIZZO WHERE FAVEFOOD = 'Pizza' ;
SQL> /* displays the data, followed by */
...
40 rows returned
```

SET ECHO

toggles off/on whether commands are displayed before being executed. Default is ON but you might want to toggle it to OFF if sending your output to a script file.

SQL> SET ECHO [ON | OFF] ; /* default is ON */

Options

SET ECHO ON	Toggles on command echoing (default)
SET ECHO OFF	Toggles off command echoing

Example Script `wizzo.sql`:

```
...
SET ECHO OFF;
SELECT * FROM WIZZO WHERE FAVEFOOD = 'Pizza' ;
SET ECHO ON ;
SELECT * FROM WIZZO WHERE FAVEFOOD = 'Sardines' ;
EXIT;
...
SQL > INPUT wizzo.sql ;
WIZTYPE FAVEFOOD
================ ====================
alpha Pizza
epsilon Pizza
SELECT * FROM WIZZO WHERE FAVEFOOD = 'Sardines' ;
WIZTYPE FAVEFOOD
================ ====================
gamma Sardines
lamda Sardines
```

SET HEAD[ING]

toggles off/on the displaying of column headers in output from SELECT statements, useful if you are passing the output to a file. By default, headings are ON. SET HEAD and SET HEADING are both valid. This command can be used in scripts.

SET NAMES

specifies the character set that is to be active in database transactions. This is very important if your database's default character set is not NONE. If the client and database character sets are mismatched, you risk transliteration errors and storing wrong data if you use isql for performing updates or inserts or for searches (including searched updates and deletes).

SET NAMES is available in scripts.

```
SQL> SET NAMES character-set ;
```

Argument

character-set	Name of the character set to activate. Default: NONE

Example In script:

```
...
SET NAMES ISO8859_1 ;
CONNECT 'HOTCHICKEN:/usr/firebird/examples/employee.gdb' ;
```

SET PLAN

specifies whether to display the optimizer's query plan.

```
SQL> SET PLAN [ON | OFF ];
```

Options

SET PLAN ON	Turns on display of the query plan (default)
SET PLAN OFF	Turns off display of the query plan.
SET PLAN	With no arguments, can be used as an ON/OFF toggle.

Example In a script:

```
...
  SET PLAN ON ;
  SELECT JOB_COUNTRY, MIN_SALARY
  FROM JOB
  WHERE MIN_SALARY > 50000
  AND JOB_COUNTRY = 'Sweden';
  ...
  SQL> INPUT iscript.sql
  PLAN (JOB INDEX (RDB$FOREIGN3,MINSALX,MAXSALX)
  JOB_COUNTRY MIN_SALARY
  =============== =====================
  Sweden 120550.00
```

SET PLANONLY

specifies to prepare SELECT queries and display just the plan, without executing the actual query.

```
SQL> SET PLANONLY ON | OFF;
```

The command works as a toggle switch. The argument is optional.

SET ROWCOUNT

specifies a limit to be the number of rows returned by a query .

The following statement will stop returning rows after the 100th row of any query in the session:

```
SQL> SET ROWCOUNT 100;
```

SET SQLDA_DISPLAY

Shows the information for raw SQLVARs in the input SQLDA parameters of INSERTs, UPDATEs and DELETEs. Each SQLVAR represents a field in the XSQLDA, the main structure used in the FB API to talk to clients transferring data into and out of the server.

Options

SET SQLDA_DISPLAY ON	Turns on display of the SQLVARs.
SET SQLDA_DISPLAY OFF	Turns off display of the SQLVARs (default).

In versions prior to v.2.0 it is available only in DEBUG builds.

SET SQL DIALECT

Sets the Firebird SQL dialect to which the client session is to be changed. If the session is currently attached to a database of a different dialect to the one specified in the command, a warning is displayed and you are asked whether you want to commit existing work (if any).

```
SQL> SET SQL DIALECT n ;
```

Argument

n	Dialect number. *n* = 1 for Dialect 1, 2 for Dialect 2, 3 for Dialect 3

Example

```
SQL> SET SQL DIALECT 3 ;
```

SET STATS

Specifies whether to display performance statistics following the output of a query.

```
SQL> SET STATS [ON |OFF];
```

Options

SET STATS ON	Turns on display of performance statistics.
SET STATS OFF	Turns off display of performance statistics. Default.
SET STATS	You can omit ON | OFF and use just SET STATS as a toggle.

Figure 17.6 SET STATS example

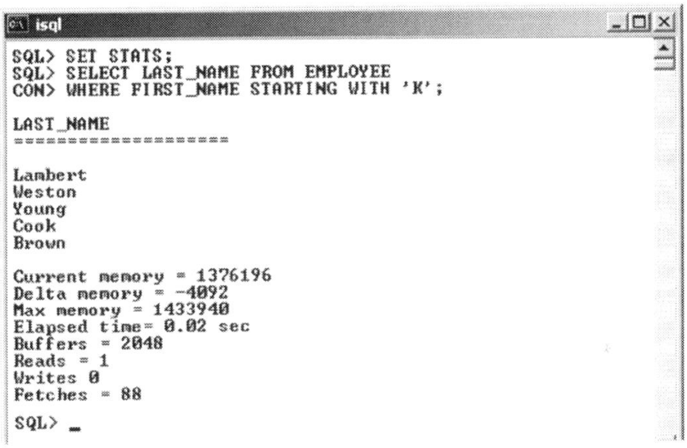

isql
SQL> SET STATS;
SQL> SELECT LAST_NAME FROM EMPLOYEE
CON> WHERE FIRST_NAME STARTING WITH 'K';
LAST_NAME
====================
Lambert
Weston
Young
Cook
Brown
Current memory = 1376196
Delta memory = -4092
Max memory = 1433940
Elapsed time= 0.02 sec
Buffers = 2048
Reads = 1
Writes 0
Fetches = 88
SQL> _

After issuing SET STATS ON, call COMMIT; to prompt isql to display the information about memory and buffer usage.

SET STATISTICS

SET STATISTICS is an SQL (not ISQL) command that you can use in *isql*—as well as in other programs—to recompute the selectivity of an index. It is mentioned here because, not surprisingly, people often get it confused with SET STATS. To find out why selectivity can be important in very dynamic tables, refer to the topic *Dropping an Index* in Chapter 16.

The syntax for the command, available only to the user that owns the index, is

```
SET STATISTICS index-name
```

SET TERM

Specifies the character which will be used as the command or statement terminator, from the next statement forward. Available in scripts. See the notes about this command earlier in this chapter.

```
SQL> SET TERM string ;
```

Argument

string	Character or characters which will be used as statement terminator. The default is ";"

Example

```
...
SET TERM ^^;
CREATE PROCEDURE ADD_WIZTYPE (WIZTYPE VARCHAR(16), FAVEFOOD VARCHAR(20))
AS
BEGIN
  INSERT INTO WIZZO(WIZTYPE, FAVEFOOD)
  VALUES ( :WIZTYPE, :FAVEFOOD) ;
END ^^
SET TERM ;^^
...
```

SET TRANSACTION

The command is used in some DSQL environments, including *isql*, to start a new transaction without using the specialised API call. The full range of parameters is available.

```
SET TRANSACTION [options];
```

Options

SET TRANSACTION	
read write| read only	Transactions are READ WRITE by default. Use READ ONLY to specify a read-only transaction.
wait | no wait	By default, a transaction will wait for access to a record if it encounters a lock conflict with another transaction. Specify NO WAIT to have the lock conflict raised immediately.
ignore limbo	From v.2.0, causes the records created by limbo transactions to be ignored. In general, it has little purpose in isql, being a facility intended for use by the *gfix* utility for resetting databases affected by an uncompleted two-phase transaction.
isolation level *xxx*	Can be READ COMMITTED, SNAPSHOT (the default) or SNAPSHOT TABLE STABILITY.
lock timeout *n*	From v.2.0, a timeout period of *n* seconds can be specified as the length of time the transaction is to wait for access to a record.
no auto undo	From v.2.0, prevents the transaction from building an undo log that would be used to undo work in the event of its being rolled back.
[no] record version	Only if isolation level is READ COMMITTED, specifies whether the transaction is to be allowed to prevail over other transactions that already have pending changes to a record (RECORD VERSION) or is to experience a conflict under those conditions (NO RECORD VERSION, the default).
reserving <*list of tables*>	Reserves locks on the tables in the comma-separated list

Example

```
SET TRANSACTION WAIT SNAPSHOT NO AUTO UNDO LOCK TIMEOUT 10
```

For more information about transactions and their configuration, refer to Part V.

SET TIME

Specifies whether to display the time portion of a DATE value (Dialect 1 only).

```
SQL> SET TIME [ON|OFF ];
```

Options

SET TIME ON	Toggles on time portion display in Dialect 1 DATE value. Default.
SET TIME OFF	Toggles off time portion display in Dialect 1 DATE value

Example

```
SQL> SELECT HIRE_DATE FROM EMPLOYEE WHERE EMP_NO = 145;
HIRE_DATE
------------------
16-MAY-2014
...
SQL>SET TIME ON ;
SQL> SELECT HIRE_DATE FROM EMPLOYEE WHERE EMP_NO = 145;
HIRE_DATE
------------------
16-MAY-2014 18:20:00
```

SET WARNINGS | SET WNG

Specifies whether warnings are to be output..

```
SQL> SET WARNINGS [ON |OFF ];
```

Options

SET WARNINGS ON	Switches on display of warnings if it was switched off, or if the session was started with the -nowarnings option.
SET WARNINGS OFF	Switches off display of warnings if it is currently on.
SET WNG	Alternative on/off toggle

Exiting an interactive *isql* session

To exit the *isql* utility and roll back all uncommitted work, enter:

```
SQL> QUIT;
```

To exit the isql utility and commit all work, enter:

```
SQL> EXIT;
```

Command Mode *isql*

Although *isql* has some handy interactive features, it is not restricted to being run in its own shell. Many of the interactive commands are available as command-line switches, making it potentially a powerful tool for automating and controlling changes. Some *isql* utilities—such as metadata extraction—are available only from the command shell. Operations on input and output files need not be interactive: in fact, calling *isql* with the -i[nput] and -o[utput] switches will not invoke the interactive shell.

Commands execute and, upon completion, return control automatically to the command shell. Calls to *isql* can also be batched inside shell scripts, cron scripts or batch files.

Operating isql in command mode

Open a command shell and change to the Firebird `/bin` directory of your Firebird server or client installation. Use the following syntax pattern for *isql* calls:

```
isql [options] [database_name] [-u[ser] <user-name> -pas[sword] <password>]
```

The `<options>` are noted in Table 24.1 below.

For SYSDBA operations, you can set the operating system variables ISC_USER and ISC_PASSWORD and avoid the need to enter them on commands. For non-SYSDBA activities, you will always need the owner credentials for operations on the database and/or objects.

The default statement terminator is the semicolon. You can change it to any character or group of characters with a command-line option (–t[erminator]).

If your command is connecting to a database for the purpose of running a script and its default character set is not NONE, you need to include the SET NAMES command in your script.

You can set the SQL dialect from the command line when invoking *isql*:

```
isql -s n ;
```

where *n* is 1, 2, or 3.

Quick help

If you call *isql* from the command line with an unknown switch—a question mark, for example—it will display a quick reference list of all its options and arguments:

```
opt/firebird/bin] isql -?
Unknown switch: ?
usage: isql [options] [<database>]
-a(all) extract metadata incl. legacy non-SQL tables
-b(ail) bail on errors (set bail on)
... etc.
```

Command-line switches

Only the initial characters in an option are required. You can also type any portion of the text shown here in square brackets, including the full option name. For example, specifying -n, -no, or -noauto have the same effect.

Table 17.1 Switches for isql command-line options

Option	Description
–a	Extracts all DDL for the named database, including non-DDL statements
–b[ail]	Since v.2.0, instructs *isql* to bail out on error, returning an error code (a non-zero integer) to the operating system. To understand how it works, please refer to the notes for *SET BAIL*.
–d[atabase] *name*	Used with the –x (extract) switch; changes the CREATE DATABASE statement that is extracted to a file. It should be a fully-qualified file path. Without the –d switch, CREATE DATABASE appears as a C-style comment, using the database name specified in the command line.
–c[ache]	Set number of cache pages used for this connection to the database. You can use this switch to override the cache size that is currently set for the database, for the duration.
–e[cho]	Displays (echoes) each statement before executing it

Option	Description
–ex[tract]	Extracts DDL for the named database; displays DDL to the screen unless output is redirected to a file
–i[nput] *file*	Reads commands from an input file instead of from keyboard input. The file argument must be a fully qualified file path. Input files can contain -input commands that call other files, enabling execution to branch and then return. isql commits work in the current file before opening the next.
–m[erge_stderr]	Merges `stderr` output with `stdout`. Useful for capturing output and errors to a single file when running *isql* in a shell script or batch file. It has no counterpart in interactive *isql*.
–m2	Since v2.0, sends the statistics and plans to the same output file as the other output, when an output file is in effect. It has no counterpart in interactive *isql*.
–n[oautocommit]	Turns off automatic committing of DDL statements. By default, DDL statements are committed automatically in a separate transaction
–now[arnings]	Displays warning messages if and only if an error occurs (by default, isql displays any message returned in a status vector, even if no error occurred).
–o[utput] *file*	Writes results to an output file instead of to standard output. The file argument must be a fully qualified file path.
–pas[sword] *password*	Used with –user to specify a password when connecting to a remote server or when required for a local operation. For access, both password and user must represent valid entries in the security database on the server.
–pag[elength] *n*	In query output, prints column headers every *n* lines instead of the default 20
–q[uiet]	Suppresses the "Use CONNECT or CREATE DATABASE..." message when the database path is not supplied on the command line.
–r[ole] *rolename*	Passes role *rolename*, case-insensitively, in upper case, along with user credentials on connection to the database
–r2 *rolename*	From v.2.0, passes a case-sensitive *rolename* (exactly as typed) along with user credentials on connection to the database
–s[ql_dialect] *n*	Interprets subsequent commands as dialect n until end of session or until dialect is changed by a SET SQL DIALECT statement. Refer to the topic Setting dialect in isql, earlier in this chapter.
–t[erminator] *x*	Changes the end-of-statement symbol from the default semicolon (;) to x, where x is a single character or any sequence of characters
–u[ser] user	Used with –password; specifies a user name when connecting to a remote server. For access, both password and user must represent a valid entry in the security database
–x	Same as –extract
–z	Displays the software versions of *isql*, server and client.

Extracting Metadata

From the command line, you can use the –extract option to output the DDL statements that define the metadata for a database. You can use the resulting text file to:

- Examine the current state of a database's system tables before planning alterations. This is especially useful when the database has changed significantly since its creation.
- Create a database with schema definitions that are identical to the extracted database.
- Open in your text editor to make changes to the database definition or create a new database source file.

All reserved words and objects are extracted into the file in uppercase unless the local language uses a character set that has no upper case. The output script is created with a COMMIT statement following each set of commands, so that tables can be referenced in subsequent definitions. The output file includes the name of the object and the owner, if one is defined.

The optional –output flag reroutes output to a named file.

Syntax pattern

```
isql [[-extract | -x][-a] [[-output | -o] outputfile]] database
```

The –x option can be used as an abbreviation for –extract. The –a flag directs *isql* to extract all database objects.

The output file specification, *outputfile*, must be a fully-qualified path placed after the -output switch directly. The path and name, or the alias, of the database being extracted can be at the end of the command.

The –extract function is not always as smart as it should be about dependencies. It is sometimes necessary to edit the output file to rectify creation order.

Using isql –extract

The following statement extracts the SQL schema from the database `employee.fdb` to a schema script file called `employee.sql`:

```
isql -extract -output /data/scripts/employee.sql /data/employee.fdb
```

This command is equivalent:

```
isql -x -output /data/scripts/employee.sql /data/employee.fdb
```

Objects and items not extracted

- System tables and views, system triggers
- External function and BLOB filter code—it's not part of the database.
- Object ownership attributes

Using isql –a

The -(e)x(tract) option extracts metadata for SQL objects only. If you wish to extract a schema script that includes declarations—such as DECLARE EXTERNAL FUNCTION and DECLARE FILTER—use the -a option.

For example, to extract DDL statements, external function declarations and BLOB filter declarations from database `employee.fdb` and store in the file `employee.sql`, enter:

```
isql -a -output /data/scripts/employee.sql /data/employee.fdb
```

Creating and Running Scripts

With Firebird, as with all true SQL database management systems, at some level you build your database and its objects—the metadata or schema of a database—using statements from a specialised subset of SQL statements known as Data Definition Language, or DDL. Even highly-featured graphical tools ultimately process your design in DDL statements.

Running a batch of DDL statements that has been scripted into in a text file is much closer to the "coal face". A script, or a set of scripts, can be processed by calling *isql* directly at the command line with an –input argument amongst its switches.

About Firebird scripts

A script for creating and altering database objects is sometimes referred to as a *data definition file* or, more commonly, a *DDL script*. A DDL script can contain certain *isql* statements, specifically some of the SET <parameter> commands. COMMIT is also a valid statement in a script.

Other scripts can be written for inserting basic or "control" data into tables, updating columns, performing data conversions and other maintenance tasks involving data manipulation. These are known as DML scripts (for Data Manipulation Language).

DDL and DML commands can be mixed in a script but, as a rule of thumb, good reason exist not to do it. Script processing allows "chaining" of scripts, linking one script file to another by means of the isql INPUT <filespec> statement. DDL and DML statements should be separated each into their own sequenced script files.

Script statements are executed in strict order. Use of the SET AUTODDL command enables you to control where statements or blocks of statements will be committed. It is also an option to defer committing the contents of a script until the entire script has been processed.

Why use scripts?

It is very good practice to use DDL scripts to create your database and its objects. Some of the reasons include

- Self-documentation. A script is a plain text file, easily handled in any development system, both for updating and reference. Scripts can—and should—include detailed comment text. Alterations to metadata can be signed and dated manually.
- Control of database development and change. Scripting all database definitions allows schema creation to be integrated closely with design tasks and code review cycles.
- Repeatable and traceable creation of metadata. A completely reconstructable schema is a requirement in the quality assurance and disaster recovery systems of many organizations.
- Orderly construction and reconstruction of database metadata. Experienced Firebird programmers often create a set of DDL scripts, designed to run and commit in a specific order, to make debugging easy and ensure that objects will exist when later, dependent objects refer to them.

What is in a DDL script?

A DDL script consists of one or more SQL statements to CREATE, ALTER, or DROP a database or any other object. It can include data manipulation language (DML) statements, although it is recommended to keep DDL and DML statements in separate scripts.

It is quite common to include (INPUT) one or more scripts amongst a chain of DDL scripts, containing INSERT statements to populate some tables with static control data. You might, for example, post statements to insert the initial rows in a table of Account Types.

The complex procedure language (PSQL) statements defining stored procedures and triggers can also be included. PSQL blocks get special treatment in scripts with regard to statement terminator symbols (see below).

Comments

A script can also contain comments, in two varieties.

Block comments

Block comments in DDL scripts use the C convention:

```
/* This comment can span multiple
lines in a script */
```

A block comment can occur on the same line as a SQL statement or *isql* command and can be of any length, as long as it is preceded by /* and followed by */.

In-line comments

The /* .... */ style of comment can also be embedded inside a statement as an in-line comment, e.g.

```
CREATE TABLE USERS1 (
USER_NAME VARCHAR( 128 ) /* security user name */
, GROUP_NAME VARCHAR( 128 ) /* not used on Windows */
, PASSWD VARCHAR( 32 ) /* will be stored encrypted */
, FIRST_NAME VARCHAR( 96 ) /* Defaulted */
, MIDDLE_NAME VARCHAR( 96 ) /* Defaulted */
, LAST_NAME VARCHAR( 96 ) /* Defaulted */
, FULL_NAME VARCHAR( 290 ) /* Computed */
) ;
```

One-line comments

In Firebird scripts you can use an alternative convention for commenting a single line: the double hyphen, e.g.,

```
-- don't change this!
```

The '--' commenting convention can be used anywhere on a line, to "comment out" everything from the marker to the end of the current line. For example:

```
CREATE TABLE MET_REPORT (ID BIGINT NOT NULL, -- COMMENT VARCHAR(40), invisible
WEATHER_CONDITIONS BLOB SUB_TYPE TEXT, LAST_REPORT TIMESTAMP);
```

v.1.0.x This double-hyphen style of comment is not implemented in the old v.1.0 series.

isql statements

The *isql* commands SET AUTODDL, SET SQL DIALECT, SET TERM, SET BAIL and INPUT are valid statements in a Firebird script.

Terminator symbols

All statements that are to be executed in the script must end with a terminator symbol.

- The default symbol is the semicolon (;).
- The default terminator can be overridden for all statements except procedure language statements (PSQL) by issuing a SET TERM command in the script.

Terminators and procedure language (PSQL)

For its internal statements, PSQL does not permit any terminator other than the default semi-colon (;). This restriction is necessary because CREATE PROCEDURE, RECREATE PROCEDURE, ALTER PROCEDURE, CREATE TRIGGER and ALTER TRIGGER, together with their subsequent PSQL statements, are complex statements in their own right—statements within a statement. The compiler needs to see semi-colons in order to recognize each distinct PSQL statement.

Thus, in scripts, it is necessary to override the terminator being used for script commands before commencing to issue the PSQL statements for a stored procedure or a trigger. After the last END statement of the procedure source has been terminated, the terminator should be reset to the default using another SET TERM statement.

Examples ...

```
CREATE GENERATOR GEN_MY_GEN ;
SET TERM ^^;
CREATE TRIGGER BI_TABLEA_0 FOR TABLEA
ACTIVE BEFORE INSERT POSITION 0
```

```
AS
BEGIN
  IF (NEW.PK IS NOT NULL) THEN
  NEW.PK = GEN_ID(GEN_MY_GEN, 1);
END ^^
SET TERM ;^^
```

...

Any string may be used as an alternative terminator, for example:

```
...
SET TERM @!#;
CREATE PROCEDURE...
AS
BEGIN
  ... ;
  ... ;
END @!#
SET TERM ;@!#
/**/
COMMIT;
/**/
SET TERM +;
CREATE PROCEDURE...
AS
BEGIN
  ... ;
  ... ;
END +
SET TERM ;+
/**/
COMMIT;
```

The SQL statement silently fails if significant text follows the terminator character on the same line. Whitespace and comments can safely follow the terminator, but other statements can not.

For example, in the following sequence, the COMMIT statement will not be executed:

```
ALTER TABLE ATABLE ADD F2 INTEGER; COMMIT;
```

whereas this one is fine:

```
ALTER TABLE ATABLE ADD F2 INTEGER;        /* counter for beans */
COMMIT;
```

Managing errors

Several options can help with pinpointing where an error occurs. The -o[utput] switch with its *file* argument enables *isql* to pass output to a log, while -e[cho] is the means of passing the commands and statements to your log and -m[erge] includes the error messages.

The *isql* script processor counts lines and can deliver the line number of the offending line and, if applicable, the position of the error in that line. What constitutes a "line", and therefore its number, can be variable, being governed by the underlying I/O layer. By and large, the start of a new line is recognised as the first non-whitespace character after a hard line-break, although *isql* itself will force a break if a line exceeds the limit of 32,767 bytes.

The line counting works correctly with nested scripts, using a separate line counter for each input file.

The position of the beginning of a keyword or phrase within the line that throws a DSQL parsing error is referred to as the "column". Thus, a message that reports "an error at line *m* column *n*" is referring to the *n*th character in the line. White space characters are counted.

Normal behaviour is for the script to continue executing whether errors occur or not. If you are echoing all the output, you can certainly discover what errors occurred but not always where they occurred.

Including the -b[ail] option causes script execution to stop as soon as an error occurs, which means you can finger your errors explicitly.

You can alternatively build your script to include a SET BAIL command and manage the bail-out behviour internally.

Basic steps

The basic steps for using script files are:

1 Create the script file

Use any suitable plain text editor. At the learning stage, you might wish to follow each DDL statement with a COMMIT statement, to ensure that an object will be visible to subsequent statements. As you become more practised, you will learn to commit statements in blocks, employing SET AUTODDL ON and SET AUTODDL OFF as a means of controlling interdependencies and testing/debugging scripts.

Ensure that every script ends with a carriage return and at least one blank line.

2 Execute the script

Use the INPUT command in an *isql* session or the Execute button (or equivalent) in your database management tool.

isql on POSIX:

```
SQL> INPUT /data/scripts/myscript.sql;
```

isql on Win32:

```
SQL> INPUT d:\data\scripts\myscript.sql;
```

3 View output and confirm database changes

External tools and Firebird *isql* versions vary in the information they return when a script trips up on a bad command and what they leave to you to put right. In an *isql* script, bear in mind that scripts containing SET AUTODDL commands and COMMIT statement will have accomplished work that cannot be rolled back.

Creating a script file

You can create DDL scripts in several ways, including:

- in an interactive isql session using the OUTPUT command to pass a series of DDL statements to a file
- in a plain ASCII text editor that formats line breaks according to the rules of the operating system shell in which the DDL script will be executed
- using one of the many specialized script editor tools that are available in third-party database design or administration tools for Firebird.
- using a CASE tool which can output DDL scripts according to the Firebird conventions

You can use any text editor to create a SQL script file, as long as the final file format is plain text (ASCII) and has lines terminated according to the rules of the operation system you intend to run the script on:

- on Windows the line terminator is carriage return + line feed (ASCII 13 followed by ASCII 10)

- on Linux/UNIX it is the solitary line feed or "new line" character (ASCII 10)
- on Mac OSX it is new line (ASCII 10) and on native Macintosh it is carriage return (ASCII 13)

Don't overlook the isql's metadata extract tools–they may prove useful for providing you with templates for your own scripts.

Some editing tools provide the capability to save in different text formats. It may prove useful to be able to save Linux-compatible scripts on a Windows machine, for example. However, take care that you use an editor that is capable of saving all characters in the character sets that will be used in the database. Also be sure to avoid an editor that saves text with any enhancements whatsoever.

A complete schema script file must begin with either a CREATE DATABASE statement or, if the database already exists, a CONNECT statement (including username and password in single quotes) that specifies the database on which the script file is to operate. The CONNECT or CREATE keyword must be followed by a complete, absolute database file name and directory path in single quotes or, if appropriate, an alias that has already been set up in `aliases.conf`.

!! **Do not use database aliases in scripts that create a database.**

For example:

```
SET SQL DIALECT 3 ;
CREATE DATABASE 'd:\databases\MyDatabase.fdb'
  PAGE_SIZE 8192
  DEFAULT CHARACTER SET ISO8859_1
  USER 'SYSDBA' PASSWORD 'masterkey';
```

or

```
CONNECT 'd:\databases\MyDatabase.gdb' USER 'SYSDBA' PASSWORD 'masterkey' ;
```

Committing work in scripts

Scripts do not run atomically. It is important to be aware of the effects of including commands and statements in your scripts that cause work to be committed. There is no hard and fast rule that says it is either "good" or "bad" to run scripts that cannot be reversed. Often, for example, you will have dependencies between DDL objects that will require committing in strict order. In script sequences where objects are created in one script and populated in another, errors will abound if commits are not carefully attended to.

DDL statements

Statements in DDL scripts can be committed in one or more of the following ways:

- by including COMMIT statements at appropriate points in the script to ensure that new database objects are available to all subsequent statements that depend on them.
- by including this statement at the beginning of the script:

```
SET AUTODDL ON ;
```

To turn off automatic commit of DDL in an isql script, use

```
SET AUTODDL OFF ;
```

The ON and OFF keywords are optional: the abbreviation SET AUTO can be used as a two-way switch. For clarity of self-documentation, it is recommended that you use SET AUTODDL with the explicit ON and OFF keywords.

Autocommit in isql

If you are running your script in *isql*, changes to the database from data definition (DDL) statements—for example, CREATE and ALTER statements—are automatically committed by default. This means that other users of the database see changes as soon as each DDL statement is executed.

Some scripting tools deliberately turn off this autocommitting behavior when running scripts, since it can make debugging difficult. Make sure you understand the behaviour of any third-party tool you use for scripts.

DML statements

Changes made to the database by data manipulation (DML) statements—INSERT, UPDATE and DELETE—are not permanent until they are committed. Explicitly include COMMIT statements in your script to commit DML changes.

To undo all database changes since the last COMMIT, use ROLLBACK. Committed changes cannot be rolled back.

Executing scripts

DDL scripts can be executed in an interactive isql session using the INPUT command, as described in the summary above. Many of the third-party tools have the ability to execute and even to intelligently debug scripts in a GUI environment.

Chaining scripts

A stable suite of scripts can be "chained" together using the isql INPUT statement as the last statement in the preceding script. For example, to chain a script named `leisurestore_02.sql` to the end of one named `leisurestore_01.sql`, end the script this way:

```
...
COMMIT;
    -- chain to CREATE TABLE statements
INPUT 'd:\scripts\leisurestore_02.sql' ;
    -- don't forget the carriage return!
```

The master script approach

The INPUT statement is not restricted to being the last in a script. Hence, another useful approach to maintaining script suites is to have one "master" script that inputs each of the subsidiary scripts in order. It has the benefit of making it easy to maintain large suites and you can include comments to indicate to others the contents of each input script.

Managing your schema scripts

Keeping a well-organised suite of scripts that precisely reflects the up-to-date state of your metadata is a valuable practice that admirably satisfies the most rigorous quality assurance system. The use of ample commentary within scripts is highly recommended, as is archiving all script versions in a version control system.

Disaster recovery

The most obvious purpose of such a practice is to provide a "fallback of last resort" for disaster recovery. If worst comes to worst—a database is ruined and backups are lost—metadata can be reconstructed from scripts. Surviving data from an otherwise unrecoverable database can be reconstituted by experts and pumped back.

A script alone will not save you. It is strongly recommended that a complete "recovery from basic ingredients" plan be tested and documented before a rollout.

Development control

Normally, more than one developer will work on the development of a database during its life cycle. Developers notoriously abhor writing system documentation! Keeping an annotated script record of every database change—including those applied interactively using *isql* or a third-party tool—is a painless and secure solution that works for everybody.

Metadata extraction

Several admin tools for Firebird, including *isql*, are capable of extracting metadata from a database for saving as a script file. For *isql* instructions, refer to the topic *Extracting Metadata* in this chapter. While metadata extraction is a handy adjunct to your scripting, there are good reasons to treat these tools as "helpers" and make a point of maintaining you main schema scripts manually:

- Metadata extraction tools generate only the current metadata. There is no history of changes—dates, reasons or authors.
- Some tools, including some versions of *isql*, are known to generate metadata in the wrong sequence for dependency, making the scripts useless for regenerating the database without editing. Such a task is between tedious and impossible, depending on how well the repairer knows the metadata.
- Even moderately-sized databases may have an enormous number of objects, especially where the system design makes intensive use of embedded code modules. Very large scripts are prone to failure due to various execution or resource limits. Large, poorly organized scripts are also confusing and annoying to work with as documentation.

Manual scripting

The author strongly advocates maintaining fully annotated schema scripts manually and splitting the mass into separate files. The following sample suite of scripts records and regenerates a database named `leisurestore.fdb`:

Table 17.2 Sample suite of schema scripts

File	Contents
leisurestore_01.sql	CREATE DATABASE statement, CREATE DOMAIN, CREATE GENERATOR and CREATE EXCEPTION definitions
leisturestore_02.sql	All CREATE TABLE statements, including UNIQUE constraints, ALTER TABLE statements adding all primary keys as named PRIMARY KEYconstraints
leisurestore_03.sql	ALTER TABLE statements adding FOREIGN KEY constraints
leisurestore_04.sql	CREATE INDEX statements
leisurestore_05.sql	CREATE TRIGGER statements
leisurestore_06.sql	CREATE PROCEDURE statements
leisurestore_07.sql	DML script that inserts rows into static (control) tables
leisurestore_08.sql	GRANT statements (security script)
leisurestore_09.sql	Recent changes, in correct sequence for dependency
leisurestore_10.sql	QA scripts (test data)

The Firebird Book
A Reference for Database Developers

SECOND EDITION

PART IV

Transactions

CHAPTER

18

OVERVIEW OF FIREBIRD TRANSACTIONS

In a client/server database such as Firebird, client applications never touch the data that are physically stored in the pages of the database. Instead, the client applications conduct conversations with the database management system—"the server"—by packaging requests and responses inside transactions. This topic visits some of the key concepts and issues of transaction management in Firebird.

- A data management system that is being updated by multiple users concurrently is vulnerable to a number of data integrity problems if work is allowed to overlap without any control. In summary, they are:
- Lost updates, that would occur when two users have the same view of a set and one performs changes, closely followed by the other, who overwrites the first user's work.
- Dirty reads, that permit one user to see the changes that another user is in the process of doing, with no guarantee that the other user's changes are final.
- Non-reproducible reads, that allow one user to selects rows continually while other users are updating and deleting. Whether this is a problem depends on the circumstances. For example, a month-end financials process or a snapshot inventory audit will be skewed under these conditions, whereas a ticketing application needs to keep all users' views synchronized to avoid double booking.
- Phantom rows, which arise when one user can select some but not all new rows written by another user. Again, this may be acceptable in some situations but will skew the outcomes of some processes.
- Interleaved transactions. These can arise when changes in one row by one user affect the data in other rows in the same table or in other tables being accessed by other users. They are usually timing-related, occurring when there is no way to control or predict the sequence in which users will perform the changes.

To solve these problems, Firebird applies a management model that isolates every task inside a unique context that prescribes the outcome if work within that task would be at risk of overlapping work being performed by other tasks. The state of the database can not change if there is any conflict.

Firebird does not permit dirty reads. In certain conditions, by design, it allows non-reproducible reads.

The ACID Properties

It is now more than 20 years since two researchers, Theo Haërder and Andreas Reuter, published a review paper describing requirements for maintaining the integrity of a database in a parallel updating environment. They distilled the requirements into four precepts defined as *atomicity*, *consistency*, *isolation* and *durability*—abbreviated in the acronym ACID[1]. Over the succeeding years, the ACID concept evolved as a benchmark for the implementation of transactions in database systems.

Atomicity

A transaction—also known as a *unit of work*—is described as consisting of a collection of data-transforming actions. To be "atomic", the transaction must be implemented in such a way that it provides the "all-or-nothing illusion that either all of these operations are performed or none of them is performed"[2]. The transaction either completes as a whole (commits) or aborts (rolls back).

Consistency

Transactions are assumed to perform correct transformations of the abstract system state—that is, the database must be left in a consistent state after a transaction completes, regardless of whether it commits or rolls back. The transaction concept assumes that programmers have mechanisms available to them for declaring points of consistency and validating them. In SQL, the standards provide for triggers, referential integrity constraints and check constraints to implement those mechanisms at the server.

Isolation

While a transaction is updating shared data, the system must give each transaction the illusion that it is running in isolation: it should appear that all other transactions ran either before it began or after it committed. While data are in transition from a starting consistent state to a final consistent state, they may be inconsistent with database state, but no data may be exposed to other transactions until the changes are committed.

The next chapter explores the three *levels of isolation* for transactions that Firebird implements, along with the options available to respond to conflicts and prevent the work of one transaction from interfering with the work of another.

Durability

Once a transaction commits, its updates must be "durable"—that is, the new state of all objects made visible to other transactions by the commit will be preserved and irreversible, regardless of events such as hardware failure or software crashing.

1. Theo Haërder and Andreas Reuter, *"Principles of Transaction-Oriented Database Recovery,"* ACM Computing Surveys 15(4) (1983): 287–317.
2. Andreas Reuter and Jim Gray, *"Transaction Processing Concepts and Techniques"* (San Francisco, CA: Morgan Kaufmann, 1993).

Context of a Transaction

A transaction encompasses a complete conversation between a client and the server. Each transaction has a unique context that causes it to be isolated it from all other transactions in a specific way. The rules for the transaction's context are specified by the client application program, by passing transaction *parameters*. A transaction starts when a client signals the beginning of the transaction and receives a transaction handle back from the server. It remains active until the client either commits the work (if it can) or rolls it back.

One transaction, many requests

In Firebird, every operation requested by a client must occur in the context of an active transaction. One transaction can entail one or many client requests and server responses within its bounds. A single transaction can span more than a single database, encompassing reads from and writes to multiple databases in the course of a task. Tasks that create databases or change their physical structure—single or batched DDL statements—entail transactions too.

The role of the client

Clients initiate all transactions. Once a transaction is under way, a client is responsible for submitting requests to read and write and also for completing—committing or rolling back—every transaction it starts.

A single client connection can have multiple transactions active.

The role of the server

It is the job of the server to account for each transaction uniquely and keep each transaction's view of database state consistent with its context. It has to manage all requests to change the database so that conflicts are handled appropriately and any risk of breaking the consistency of database state is pre-empted.

Figure 25.1 broadly illustrates a typical read-write transaction context from start to finish. It shows how the server manages many concurrent transactions independently of all others, even if the other transactions are active in the same client application.

Figure 18.1 Transaction context and independence

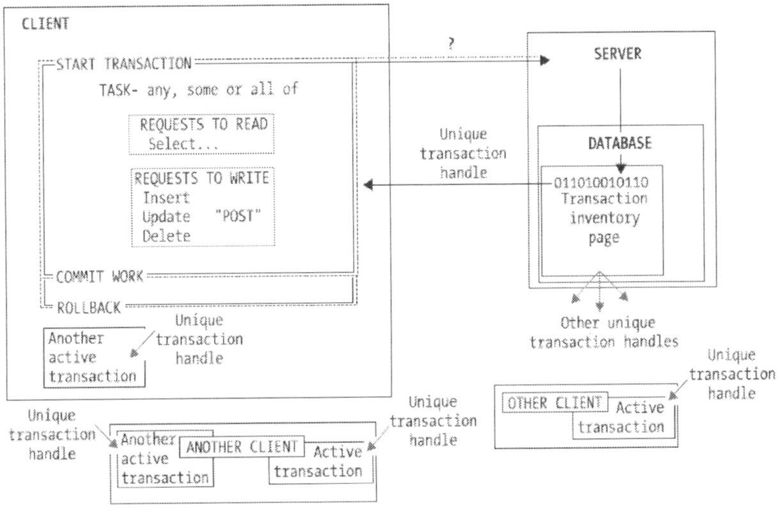

In this illustration, the application may use the transaction to select (read) sets of rows, any of which may be chosen by the user for updating or deleting. In the same transaction, new rows might be inserted. Update, insert or delete requests are "posted" to the server, one by one, as the user performs her task.

Atomicity of the model

The capability for a client application to issue multiple, reversible requests inside a single Firebird transaction has obvious advantages for tasks that need to execute a single statement many times with a variety of input parameters. It inherently provides atomicity for tasks where a group of statements must be executed and, finally, either committed as a single job or rolled back entirely if an exception occurs.

Transactions and the MGA

MGA—an acronym for multi-generational architecture—refers to the architectural model underlying state management in a Firebird database.

In the MGA model, each row stored in database holds the unique transaction ID of the transaction that writes it. If another transaction posts a change to the row, the server writes a new version of the row to disk, with the new transaction ID, and converts an image of the older version into reference (known as the delta) to this new version. The server now holds two "generations" of the same row.

Post vs COMMIT

The term "post" has probably been borrowed from older desktop accounting software, as an analogy to the posting of journals in accounting systems. The analogy is useful for distinguishing the two separate operations of writing a reversible change to the database (by executing a statement) and committing all of the changes executed by one or several statements. Posted changes are invisible beyond the boundaries of their transaction context and can be rolled back; committed changes are permanent and become visible to transactions that are subsequently started or updated.

If any conflict occurs upon posting, the server returns an exception message to the client and the commit fails. The application must then deal with the conflict according to its kind. The solution to an update conflict is often to roll back the transaction, causing all of the work to be "undone" as an atomic unit. If there is no conflict, the application can proceed to commit the work when it is ready.

Calls from the client to COMMIT or to ROLLBACK are the only possible ways to end a transaction. A failure to commit does not cause the server to roll back the transaction.

Rollback

Rollback never fails. It will undo any changes that were requested during the transaction: the change that caused the exception as well as any that would have succeeded had the exception not occurred.

Some rolled-back transactions do not leave row images on the disk. For example, any rollbacks instigated by the server to undo work performed by triggers simply vanish; and the record images created by inserts are normally expunged during rollback, with reference to an auto-undo log that is maintained for inserts. If a single transaction inserts a huge number of records, the auto-undo log is abandoned, with the result that a rollback will leave the images on disk. Other conditions that may cause inserted record images to remain on disk include server crashes during the operation or use of a transaction parameter that explicitly requests "no auto-undo".

Row locking

Under MGA, the existence of a pending new version of a row has the effect of locking it. In most conditions, the existence of a committed newer version blocks a request to update or delete the row as well—a *locking conflict*.

On receiving a request to update or delete, the server inspects the states of any transactions that own newer versions of the row. If the newest of those owner transactions is active or has been committed, the server responds to the requesting transaction according to the context—isolation level and lock resolution parameters—of the requesting transaction.

If the newest version's transaction is active, the requesting transaction will, by default, wait (parameter *WAIT*) for it to be completed (committed or rolled back) and then the server will allow it to proceed. However, if *NO WAIT* was specified, it returns a conflict exception to the requesting transaction.

If the newest version's transaction is committed and the requesting transaction is in *SNAPSHOT* (i.e. concurrency) isolation, the server refuses the request and reports a lock conflict. If the transaction is in *READ COMMITTED* isolation, with the default *RECORD_VERSION* setting, the server allows the request and writes a new record version on behalf of the transaction.

Other conditions are possible when the requesting transaction is in READ COMMITTED. The outcome of any transaction request may also be affected by unusual, pre-emptive conditions in the context of the transaction that owns the pending change. For more information about these variations, refer to the next chapter, where the transaction parameters are explored in detail.

Optimistic locking

Firebird does not use conventional two-phase locking at all for the most usual transaction contexts. Hence, all normal locking is at row-level and is said to be *optimistic*—each row is available to all read-write transactions until a writer creates a newer version of it.

On committing

Upon a successful commit, the old record version referenced by the delta image becomes an obsolete record.

- If the operation was an update, the new image becomes the latest committed version and the original image of the record, with the ID of the transaction that last updated it, is made available for garbage collection.
- If the operation was a deletion, a "stump" replaces the obsolete record. A sweep or a backup clears this stump and releases the physical space on disk that was occupied by the deleted row.

For detailed information about sweeping and garbage collection, refer to the section Management Tools in the chapter entitled Configuring and Managing Databases in either the companion volume to this, Volume 3: ***Administering Firebird Servers and Databases*** or ***The Firebird Book Second Edition***.

In summary, under normal conditions:

- any transaction can read any row that was committed before it started
- any read-write transaction can request to update or delete a row.
- a request (post) will usually succeed if no other read-write transaction has already posted or committed a change to a newer version of the record. Read-committed transactions are usually allowed to post changes overwriting versions committed by newer transactions.
- if a post succeeds, the transaction has a "lock" on the row. Other readers can still read the latest committed version but none will succeed in posting an update or delete statement for that row

Table-level locks

A transaction can be configured to lock whole tables. There are two acceptable ways to do this in DSQL: by isolating the transaction in *SNAPSHOT TABLE STABILITY* (a.k.a consistency) mode, forced repeatable read) or by *table reservation*. It should be emphasized that these configurations are for when unusually pre-emptive conditions are required. They are not recommended in Firebird for everyday use.

Pessimistic locking

An unacceptable way to impose a table-level lock is to apply a statement-level *pessimistic lock* that affects the whole table. A statement such as the following can do that:

```
SELECT * FROM ATABLE
[FOR UPDATE] WITH LOCK;
```

It is not, strictly speaking, an issue of transaction configuration. However, the configuration of the transaction that owns sets retrieved with this explicit pessimistic lock is important. The issue of pessimistic locking is discussed in Chapter 27, ***Programming with Transactions***.

Inserts

There are no deltas or locks for inserts. If another transaction has not pre-empted inserts by a table-level lock, an insert will always succeed if it does not violate any constraints or validation checks.

Transaction "Aging" and Statistics

When a client process secures a transaction handle, it acquires a unique internal identifier for the transaction and stores it on a transaction inventory page (TIP).

Transaction ID and age

Transaction IDs (TIDs) are 32-bit integers that are generated in a single-stepping series. A new or freshly-restored database begins the series at 1. Transaction age is determined from the TID: lowest is oldest.

TIDs and their associated state data are stored on *transaction inventory pages* (TIPs). On the database header page, system accounting maintains a set of fields containing TIDs that are of interest to it, viz. the oldest interesting (OIT), the oldest active (OAT) and the number to be used for the next transaction. A "snapshot" TID is also written each time the OAT increases, usually the same TID as the OAT, or close to it—or so you hope. It is a record of the OAT before the latest garbage collection began.

Getting the Transaction ID

The context variable CURRENT_TRANSACTION, supported since v.1.5, returns the TID of the transaction that requests it. It can be used in SQL wherever it is appropriate to use an expression. For example, to store the TID into a log table, you could use it like this:

```
INSERT INTO BOOK_OF_LIFE
  (TID, COMMENT, SIGNATURE)
  VALUES
  (CURRENT_TRANSACTION,
  'This has been a great day for transactions',
  CURRENT_USER);
```

It is important to remember that TIDs are cyclic. Because the numbering series will be reset after each restore, they should *never* be used for primary keys or unique constraints in persistent tables.

Transaction ID overflow

The transaction id is a 32-bit integer. If a series hit its 4 Gb limit and rolls over, bad things will happen. When the last transaction ends, the system transaction will not work and metadata updates will be impossible. Garbage collection will stop. User transactions will not start.

At 100 transactions per second, it takes one year, four months, eleven days, two hours, and roughly 30 minutes to roll over the TID.

Backing up and restoring into a fresh database resets the TID. Until recently, a neglected database would have had other trauma before the TID series exhausted itself. Now, with larger page sizes, larger disks and reduced need to watch the size of database files, the risk of blowing a transaction ID series is more apparent.

"Interesting transactions"

Server and client transaction accounting routines use TIDs to track the states of transactions. Housekeeping routines take the age of transactions into account when deciding which old record versions are "interesting" and which are not. Uninteresting transactions can be flagged for removal. The server remains interested in every transaction that not been hard-committed by a COMMIT statement.

Active, limbo, rolled back and dead transactions are all "interesting". Transactions that have been committed using COMMIT WITH RETAIN (a.k.a. soft commit or CommitRetaining) remain active until they are "hard-committed" and are thus stay interesting. Conditions can develop in which interesting transactions become "stuck" and progressively inhibit performance.

If neglected, stuck transactions will become the source of serious performance degradation. A stuck OIT will cause the number of transaction inventory pages to grow. The server maintains a bitmapped working table of the transactions stored in the TIPs. The table is copied and written to the database at the start of each transaction. As it becomes bloated by stuck transactions, it uses progressively more memory resources and memory becomes fragmented from constant reallocation of the resources.

Oldest Interesting Transaction (OIT)

The Oldest Interesting Transaction (OIT) is the lowest-numbered transaction in the TIPs (transaction inventory pages) that is in the state of having been involved with records that are in transactions which are as yet not hard-committed.

Oldest Active Transaction (OAT)

The Oldest Active Transaction (OAT is the lowest-numbered transaction in the TIPs that is active. A transaction is active as long as it is not hard-committed, not rolled back and not *in limbo*.

"Limbo transactions" cannot occur unless the application is running multi-database transactions.

Read-only transactions

A read-only transaction remains active (and interesting in some ways) until it is committed. However, an active read-only transaction that is in the recommended READ COMMITTED isolation level (see Chapter 26) never gets stuck and will not interfere with system housekeeping.

Don't confuse a read-only transaction with a read-write transaction that is in the process of passing output to a user interface from a SELECT statement. Even if the application makes the output set read-only, the underlying SELECT statement inside a read-write transaction can be—and often is—the cause of system slow-down.

Background garbage collection

Record versions from rolled back transactions are marked for purging from the database when they are found in the course of normal data processing—as a rule, if a row is accessed by a statement, any uninteresting old record versions that are eligible for removal will be tagged for collection by the garbage collector (GC).

*In the case of a Superserver installed with "native" or "mixed" GC enabled in the server's **GCPolicy** configuration parameter, the GC is a worker thread that works in the background. In all other cases, tagging and GC are performed cooperatively: that means that each client process or thread that touches a table will perform any outstanding GC before proceeding with the client request.*

Some corners of the database might not be visited for a long time by any statements, so there is no guarantee that that all of the record versions created by a rolled-back transaction will be tagged and, eventually, removed. As long as the record versions remain, the interesting transaction must remain "interesting", to preserve the state of the database.

A full database scan—by a backup, typically—will perform garbage collection but it can not change the state of transactions. That is the job of the full GC ritual that is performed by a sweep. A newly restored database has no garbage.

Rolled-back transactions

Transactions in the rolled-back state are not garbage-collected. They remain interesting until a database sweep tags them as "committed" and releases them for garbage collection. In systems with low contention, a periodic manual sweep may be all that's needed to deal with them.

Some systems that are not well-designed to deal with conflicts demonstrate high levels of rollback and tend to accumulate interesting transactions faster than the automatic database housekeeping procedures can cope. Such systems should be subjected to scheduled manual sweeps often if automatic sweeping seems not to manage well.

"Dead" transactions

Transactions are said to be "dead" if they are in an active state but there is no connection context associated with them. Transactions typically "die" in client applications that do not take care to end them before disconnecting users. Dead transactions are also part of the flotsam left behind when client applications crash or network connections are broken abnormally.

The server can not tell the difference between a genuinely active transaction and a dead one. As long as the cleanup following connection timeout is able to proceed and the regular garbage collection kicks in in a timely fashion, dead transactions need not be a problem. The timeout cleanup will roll them back and their garbage will eventually be dealt with normally.

Frequent, large accumulations of dead transactions can be a problem. Because they are rolled back, too many of them remain interesting for too long. In a system where user behavior, frequent crashes, power cuts or network faults generate huge numbers of dead transactions, dead-transaction garbage will become a big problem for performance.

Limbo transactions

Limbo transactions—which are discussed in more detail in Chapter 26—happen in the course of a failed two-phase COMMIT operation across multiple databases. The system recognizes them as a special case for human intervention, since the server itself cannot determine whether it is safe to either commit them or roll them back without causing inconsistency in a different database.

The only way to resolve a limbo transaction is to run the *gfix* tool over the database with the appropriate switches to achieve the desired outcome. Resolution changes the state of a limbo transaction to either "committed" or "rolled back". From that point, it is managed just like any other committed or rolled-back transaction.

Details for dealing with limbo transactions can be found in the chapter entitled *Configuring and Managing Databases* in the companion volume to this, Volume 3: ***Administering Firebird Servers and Databases*** or in ***The Firebird Book Second Edition***.

Keeping the OIT and the OAT moving

The admonition to "keep the OIT and OAT moving" is a catch-cry around all support solutions where performance is the problem. Time spent understanding the life-cycle of transactions in Firebird's multi-generational architecture will be one of your best investments for future work with Firebird and other open source databases that have MGA.

To begin understanding the interaction between the client processes that "own" the transactions, on the one hand, and the transaction inventory accounting maintained in the database, on the other, it is useful to be acquainted with the way the server and transactions interact in the mechanism.

The transaction state bitmap (TSB)

The internal *transaction state bitmap* (TSB) is a table of transaction IDs and their states, maintained by the server, that is initialized when an initial attachment is made to a database. In logical terms, the TSB tabulates each transaction found in the TIPs that is newer than the OIT. Whilst there are attachments to the database, the server process maintains the TSB dynamically, adding newer TIDs, updating states and sloughing off the TIDs that become uninteresting. It writes updates to the TIPs without reading them again from disk.

Figure 25.2 illustrates the steps. Each time the server processes a request for a transaction handle, it reads the database header page to acquire the TID for the next transaction. The TSB is updated and updates are written to the transaction inventory pages in the database.

Figure 18.2 Interaction of the client/server process and the TSB

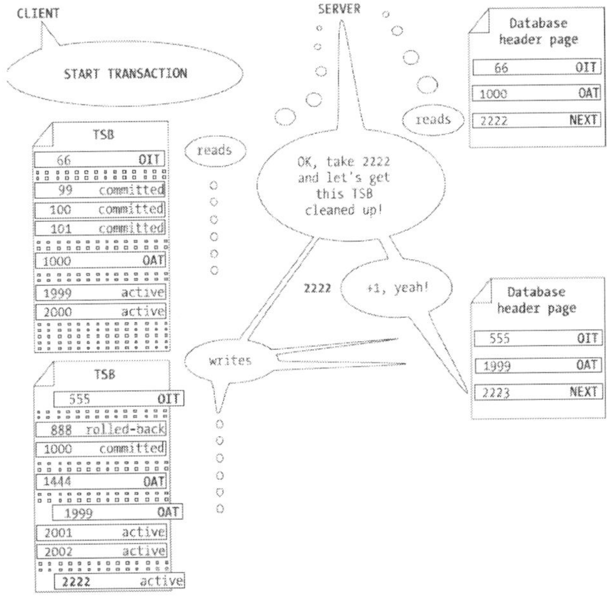

"Moving the OIT (and/or the OAT) forward" is Firebird-speak for the evolving increase in the values of the OIT and OAT in the bitmap and in the database header page as older transactions get committed and are eliminated from the TSB and newer transactions become identified as "oldest". Updating the database header page with the latest OIT, OAT and Next Transaction values is part of this dynamic ecology.

If the new transaction is a *SNAPSHOT* transaction, it will have its own copy of the TSB to maintain a consistent view of database state as it was when it began. A *READ COMMITTED* transaction always refers to the latest global TSB to get access to versions committed after it began.

Conditions for updating OIT and OAT

Each time the server starts another transaction, it tests the state of the TIDs it is holding in the TSB, eliminates those whose state has changed to "committed" and re-evaluates the OIT and OAT values. It compares them with those stored in the database page and, if necessary, includes them in the data accompanying the write of the new "Next transaction" ID it sends to the database header.

The OAT will keep moving forward if transactions are kept short enough to prevent active transactions and garbage from committed newer transactions from piling up too much. The OIT will keep moving forward as long as client processes are committing substantially more work than they are rolling back or losing as the result of crashes. Under these conditions, database performance will be in good shape.

A stuck OAT is worse than a stuck OIT. In a well-performing system, the difference between the OAT and the newest transaction should be a reasonably steady approximation of the (number of client processes running) times (the average number of transactions running per process). Sweep in off-work hours or keep automatic sweeping in force or do both.

In Chapter 27, ***Programming with Transactions***, you will find some client application strategies for optimizing the progress of the OIT and OAT.

The "gap"

The "gap" is another piece of Firebird-speak. It refers to the difference between the OIT and the OAT or, more specifically, the Oldest Snapshot. The gap will be small in comparison with overall transaction throughput or, ideally, zero. In these conditions, it can be a reasonable assumption that there are no transactions hanging around that are causing the TSB to bloat and the transaction inventory pages to proliferate outlandishly.

It is not the gap itself that impedes performance. The gap is an indicator of the volume of overhead that sub-optimal transaction management is adding to database activity—over-use and fragmentation of memory, excessive numbers of page-reads during searches and new page-allocations during updates and inserts. Solving and avoiding problems of degrading performance is all about controlling and reducing the gap.

Sweeping vs garbage collection

Garbage collection (GC) is a continual background process that is a function of the normal course of record retrieval and record version checking that is performed for each transaction. When obsolete record versions are found with TIDs lower than the OAT, one of two things will happen:

- on a Classic or Superclassic server they are removed immediately. This is referred to as *cooperative garbage collection*, because each transaction and each server instance participates in clearing garbage left behind by others.
- on Superserver they are "tagged" in an internal list of items for removal by the garbage collection thread. When a GC worker thread is woken up, it will deal with the items in this list and update it.

Sweeping performs this task, too, but, unlike GC, it can also deal with one category of interesting transactions: those that are in "rolled-back" state. It can also remove the stumps of deleted records and release the space for re-use.

The gap is important for automatic sweeping because the sweep interval setting of the database governs the maximum size the gap is allowed to be, before a sweep is triggered off. Automatic sweeping is a backstop that is rarely or never triggered in well-managed databases because the gap never reaches the threshold number.

By default, each database is created with a sweep interval—"maximum gap size"—of 20,000. It can be varied up or down, if necessary, or disabled altogether by setting the interval to 0.

It should be stressed that a gap that is consistently smaller than the sweep interval is not an indication that the database never needs sweeping! All databases must be swept—it is a question of human management whether they are swept automatically, or manually with *gfix*, or both, should the need arise. Think of automatic sweeping as a safety net, not as a substitute for sensible database management.

Transaction statistics

Firebird has some useful utilities for querying how well your database is managing the gap between OIT and OAT. You can use either to inspect the values on the database header page.

gstat

The command-line tool *gstat*, used with the `-header` switch, reveals a number of database statistics, including the current transaction IDs of OIT, OAT, Oldest Snapshot and the next new transaction. To use *gstat*, log in as SYSDBA on the host machine in a command shell and go to your Firebird bin directory. Type

Windows

```
gstat -h <path-to-database> -user sysdba -password whatever
```

POSIX

```
./gstat -h <path-to-database> -user sysdba -password whatever
```

Following is an extract from near the top of the output:

```
Oldest transaction 10075
Oldest active 100152
Oldest snapshot 100152
Next transaction 100153
```

- Oldest transaction is the OIT.
- Oldest active is obviously the OAT.
- Oldest snapshot is usually the same as OAT—it gets written when the OAT moves forward. It is the actual TID that the garbage collector reads as a signal that there is some garbage that it can handle.

For details of *gstat* usage, refer to the topic *Collecting Database Statistics—gstat* in the companion volume to this, Volume 3: ***Administering Firebird Servers and Databases*** or in Chapter 38 of ***The Firebird Book Second Edition***.

isql

You can get a similar view of the database header statistics in an isql session, using the SHOW DATABASE command. For details, see *SHOW DATABASE* in the previous chapter.

Many of the third-party Firebird admin tools provide equivalent reports.

What the statistics can tell you

It is a "given" that no garbage collection will ever be performed on obsolete record versions left behind by interesting transactions. However, the Oldest Snapshot marks the boundary where the GC stops looking for committed transactions. Any garbage from that transaction number upwards will be unattended, regardless of whether the newer transactions are interested or not.

If the gap between the OAT and the Next Transaction indicates a much higher number of transactions than you can account for by an enumeration of logged-in users and their tasks, you can be certain that a lot of garbage is missing the dustman. As that gap keeps growing, database performance becomes more and more sluggish. Servers have been known to throw an 'Out of memory' error or just crash because the TSB exhausted memory or caused too much fragmentation for the system's memory management services to handle. Low-end servers—especially those being used to deliver other services—may not even have enough resources left to record the evidence in the log.

If gaps—either between the OIT and the OAT or between the OAT and the Next transaction—seem to be a problem in your system, you can learn a lot about the effects of sweeping the database and improving your client applications if you keep logs of the statistics.

To obtain a text file of the simple statistics, simply pipe the output.of gstat -h to a text file according to the rules of your command shell. In the isql shell, use the output <filename> command to begin piping the output from the SHOW DATABASE command.

Trace logs

If you are running Firebird 2.5 or higher over a database of ODS 11.2 or higher, you may also gain insight into problem activity by running traces over a succession of sample periods. For details about running traces and setting up the trace logs, refer to the chapter entitled *Monitoring and Logging Features* in the companion volume to this, Volume 3: ***Administering Firebird Servers and Databases*** or in ***The Firebird Book Second Edition***.

mon$ tables

When you need to delve deeper to look for the sources of problem transactions, querying the monitoring tables can lead you where you want to go, if your database has an ODS of 11.1 or higher. For details of *mon$* tables usage, refer to the topic Monitoring Database Activity in the materials cited above.

CHAPTER

19

CONFIGURING TRANSACTIONS

A transaction is a "bubble" around any piece of work affecting the state of a database or, indeed, of more than one database. A user process starts a transaction and the same user process finishes it. Because user processes come in many shapes and sizes, every transaction is configurable. The mandatory and optional properties of a transaction are important parts of any transaction context.

Anatomy of a Transaction

A transaction starts inside the context of a client session. A DSQL statement—SET TRANSACTION—could be used by a suitable client application to start the default transaction once it has established a connection.

SET TRANSACTION is no longer used by most types of application, being most suited to applications written in the mostly disused ESQL (Embedded SQL) that provided a superset of SQL for old InterBase applications, that could be precompiled with a client application written in C. These days, virtually all client applications written for Firebird use instead the transaction-related API functions exposed by the Firebird client libraries, wrapped in one way or another in host language structures (classes, components, etc.). All of the parameters for SET TRANSACTION have counterparts in API functions and their argument structures—and more, since SET TRANSACTION comes with limitations.

One application that can use SET TRANSACTION dynamically is *isql* in its interactive mode, providing a useful environment for familiarising yourself with the various combinations of its parameters. It affects only the transactions in which DML statements run, since they use the default transaction. *isql* runs DDL in separate transactions.

The Default Transaction

In DSQL, the only transaction that can be started with SET TRANSACTION is the default one that is started automatically for the application if the application does not start It can only be a single-database transaction and it is not possible to start multiple transactions with SET TRANSACTION.

Syntax SET TRANSACTION has a few mandatory parameters and some optional ones. Used without any explicit parameters, it starts the transaction with default values in the mandatory parameters and no action for the optional ones.

Note *The syntax pattern describes the options for DSQL. Embedded SQL (ESQL) uses SET TRANSACTION differently and has a slightly different parameter set.*

Pattern:

```
SET TRANSACTION
[READ WRITE | READ ONLY]
[ [ISOLATION LEVEL] {
  SNAPSHOT [TABLE STABILITY] | READ COMMITTED [[NO] RECORD_VERSION]
  } ]
[WAIT | NO WAIT]
[LOCK TIMEOUT <seconds>]
[NO AUTO UNDO]
[IGNORE LIMBO]
[RESERVING table1 [, table2 ...]]
  [FOR [SHARED | PROTECTED] {READ | WRITE}]
```

Default settings

If SET TRANSACTION is requested without any parameters, the default transaction is configured with SNAPSHOT isolation in READ WRITE mode and the WAIT lock resolution policy and no lock timeout.

About Concurrency

The term *concurrency* broadly refers to the state in which two or more tasks are running inside the same database at the same time. In these conditions, the database is sometimes said to be supporting parallel tasks.

Inside a transaction's own "bubble", the owning process will be allowed to perform any operation that

1. is consistent with its own current view of the database and
2. would not, if committed, interfere with the consistency of any other active transaction's current view of the database

The engine's interpretation of consistency is governed by the transaction's configuration. That, in turn, is governed by the client application. Each transaction can be configured by means of a constellation of parameters that enable the client process to predict, with absolute assurance, how the database engine will respond if it detects a potential inconsistency.

Factors affecting concurrency

The four configurable parameters that affect concurrency are:

- isolation level
- lock resolution policy (a.k.a. blocking mode)
- access mode
- table reservation

For one level of isolation (READ COMMITTED) the current *states of the record versions* are also considered.

Isolation level

Firebird provides three outright levels of transaction isolation to define the depth of consistency the transaction requires. At one extreme, a transaction can get exclusive write access to an entire table whilst, at the other, the uncommitted transaction becomes current with every external change of database state.

No Firebird transaction will ever see any uncommitted changes pending for other transactions.

In Firebird, isolation level can be READ COMMITTED, SNAPSHOT or SNAPSHOT TABLE STABILITY. Within READ COMMITTED, two sub-levels are available: RECORD_VERSION and NO_RECORD_VERSION.

Standard levels of isolation

The SQL standard for transaction isolation is sympathetic to the two-phase locking mechanism that most RDBM systems use to implement isolation. As standards go, it is quite idiosyncratic in comparison with many of the other standards. It defines isolation not so much in terms of ideals as in terms of the phenomena each level allows (or denies). The phenomena with which the standard is concerned are:

Dirty read—occurs if the transaction is able to read the uncommitted (pending) changes of others.

Non-repeatable read—occurs if subsequent reads of the same set of rows during the course of the transaction could be different to what was read in those rows when the transaction began.

Phantom rows—phantoms occur if a subsequent set of rows read during the transaction differs from the set that was read when the transaction began. The phantom phenomenon happens if the subsequent read includes new rows inserted and/or excludes rows deleted that were committed since the first read.

Table 26.1 shows the four standard isolation levels recognized by the standard, with the phenomena that govern their definitions.

Table 19.1 SQL Standard isolation levels and governing phenomena

Isolation level	Dirty Read	Non-repeatable Read	Phantoms
READ UNCOMMITTED	Allowed	Allowed	Allowed
READ COMMITTED	Disallowed	Allowed	Allowed
REPEATABLE READ	Disallowed	Allowed	Allowed
SERIALIZABLE	Disallowed	Disallowed	Disallowed

READ UNCOMMITTED is not supported in Firebird at all.

READ COMMITTED conforms with the standard. At the two deeper levels, the nature of MGA prevails over the two-phase locking limitations implied by the standard. Mapping to the standard governance of REPEATABLE READ and SERIALIZABLE is not possible.

READ COMMITTED

The shallowest level of isolation is READ COMMITTED. It is the only level whose view of database state changes during the course of the transaction since, every time a commit version of a record it is accessing changes, the newly committed record version replaces the version the READ COMMITTED transaction began with. Inserts committed since this transaction began are made visible to it.

By design, READ COMMITTED isolation allows non-repeatable reads and does not prevent the phenomenon of phantom rows. It is the most useful level for high-volume, real-time data entry operations because it reduces data contention, but it is unsuitable for tasks that need a reproducible view.

Because of the transient nature of Read Committed isolation, the transaction ("ThisTransaction") can be configured to respond more conservatively to external commits and other pending transactions:

- with RECORD_VERSION (the default flag) the engine lets ThisTransaction read the latest committed version. If ThisTransaction is in READ WRITE mode, it will be allowed to overwrite the latest committed version, even if its own TID is newer than the TID on the latest committed version.
- with NO_RECORD_VERSION the engine effectively mimics the behavior of systems that use two-phase locking to control concurrency. It blocks ThisTransaction from writing a new version of the row if there is a pending update on the latest current version. Resolution depends on the lock resolution setting:
  - with WAIT, ThisTransaction waits until the other transaction either commits or rolls back its change. Its change will then be allowed if the other transaction rolled back or if its own TID is newer than the other transaction's TID. It will fail with a lock conflict if the other transaction's TID was newer.
  - with NOWAIT, ThisTransaction immediately receives a lock conflict notification.

The transaction can "see" all of the latest committed versions that its settings allow it to read, which is fine for insert, update, delete and execute operations. However, any output sets selected in the transaction must be requeried by the client application to get the updated view.

SNAPSHOT (Concurrency)

The "middle" level of isolation is SNAPSHOT, alternatively termed *Repeatable Read* or *Concurrency*. However, Firebird's SNAPSHOT isolation does not accord exactly with Repeatable Read as defined by the standard. It isolates the transaction's view from row-level changes to existing rows. However, because the MGA architecture, by nature, completely isolates snapshot transactions from new rows committed by other transactions, by denying SNAPSHOT transactions access to the global transaction state bitmap (TSB, see previous chapter), there is no possibility of SNAPSHOT transactions seeing phantom rows. Hence, a Firebird SNAPSHOT transaction provides a deeper level of isolation than the SQL's REPEATABLE READ.

Yet SNAPSHOT is not identical to SERIALIZABLE, because other transactions can update and delete rows that are in the purview of the snapshot transaction, provided they post first.

The transaction is guaranteed a non-volatile view of the database that will be unaffected by any changes committed by other transactions before it completes. It is a useful level for historical tasks like reporting and data export, which would be inaccurate if not performed over a completely reproducible view of the data.

SNAPSHOT is the default isolation level for the isql query tool and for many component and driver interfaces.

SNAPSHOT TABLE STABILITY (Consistency)

The "deepest" level of isolation is SNAPSHOT TABLE STABILITY, alternatively termed *Consistency* because it is guaranteed to fetch data in a non-volatile state which will remain externally consistent throughout the database as long as the transaction lasts. Read-write transactions can not even read tables that are locked by a transaction with this isolation level.

The table-level locking imposed by this isolation comprises all tables accessed by the transaction, including those with referential constraint dependencies.

This level constitutes an aggressive extension that guarantees serialization in the strict sense that no other transaction can insert or delete—or indeed, change—rows in the tables involved if any transaction succeeds in acquiring a handle with this isolation. Conversely, the TABLE STABILITY transaction will not be able to acquire a handle if any read-write transaction is currently reading any table that is in its intended purview. In terms of the standard, it is unnecessary, since SNAPSHOT isolation already protects transactions from all three of the phenomena governed by the SQL standard SERIALIZABLE level.

A consistency transaction is also referred to as a *blocking transaction* because it blocks access by any other read-write to any of the records that it is accesses and to any records that depend on those records.

Because of its potential to lock up portions of the database to other users needing to perform updates, SNAPSHOT TABLE STABILITY must be used with extreme care. Attend carefully to the size of the affected sets, the effects of joins and table dependencies and the likely duration of the transaction.

Locking Policy

Lock policy determines behaviour in the event the transaction ("ThisTransaction") tries to post a change that conflicts with a change already posted by another transaction. The options are WAIT and NO WAIT.

WAIT

WAIT (the default) causes the transaction to wait until rows locked by a pending transaction are released, before determining whether it can update them. At that point, if the other transaction has posted a higher record version, the waiting transaction will be notified that a lock conflict has occurred.

WAIT is often not the preferred blocking mode in high-volume, interactive environments because of its potential to slow down the busiest users and, in some conditions, to cause "livelocks" (see below).

WAIT is virtually pointless in SNAPSHOT isolation. Unless the blocking transaction eventually rolls back—the least likely scenario—the outcome of waiting is certain to be a lock conflict, anyway. In a READ COMMITTED transaction, the likelihood that the outcome of waiting would be a lock conflict is much reduced.

That is not to deny the usefulness of WAIT for some conditions. If the client application's exception handler handles conflicts arising from NO WAIT by continually retrying without pausing, the bottlenecking caused by repeated retries and failures is likely to be worse than if WAIT is specified, especially if the blocking transaction takes a long time to complete. By contrast, WAIT is potentially going to cause one exception, eventually handled by one rollback.

LOCK TIMEOUT

From the "2" series onward, a transaction can be optionally configured with a positive, non-zero integer value to specify how many seconds a WAIT should continue before excepting.

LOCK TIMEOUT and NO WAIT are mutually exclusive.

Where the likelihood of transactions colliding is high but transactions are short, WAIT is to be preferred because it guarantees that waiting requests will proceed in a FIFO sequence, rather than be required to take their chances with each repeated request. However, in user environments where a quick turnover can not be guaranteed, WAIT transactions are contraindicated because of their potential to hold back garbage collection.

NO WAIT

In a NO WAIT transaction, the server will notify the client immediately if it detects a new, uncommitted version of a row the transaction tries to change. In a reasonably busy multi-user environment, NO WAIT is sometimes preferable to the risk of creating bottle-necks of waiting transactions.

As a rule of thumb for SNAPSHOT transactions, throughput will be faster and interfaces more responsive if the client application chooses NO WAIT and handles lock conflicts through the use of rollback, timed retries or other appropriate techniques.

Access Mode

Access mode can be READ WRITE or READ ONLY. A READ WRITE transaction can select, insert, update and delete data. A READ ONLY transaction can only select data.

The default access mode is READ WRITE.

One of the benefits of a READ ONLY transaction is its ability to provide selection data for the user interface without tying up excessive resources on the server. Make sure your read-only transactions are configured with READ COMMITTED isolation, to ensure that garbage collection on the server can proceed past this transaction.

Table Reservation

Firebird supports a table locking mode to force full locks on one or more tables for the duration of a transaction. The optional RESERVING <list of tables> clause requests immediate full locks on all committed rows in the listed tables, enabling a transaction to guarantee itself exclusive access at the expense of any transactions that become concurrent with it.

Unlike the normal optimistic locking tactic, reservation (RESERVING clause with specified table arguments) locks all rows pessimistically— it takes effect at the start of the transaction, instead of waiting until the point at which an individual row lock is required.

You can reserve more than one table in a transaction.

Table reservation has three main purposes:

- to ensure that the tables are locked when the transaction begins, rather than when they are first accessed by a statement, as is the case when TABLE STABILITY isolation is used for table-level locking. The lock resolution mode (WAIT/NOWAIT) is applied during the transaction request and any conflict with other transactions having pending updates will result in a WAIT for the handle, or a denial of the handle in the NOWAIT case. This feature of table reservation is important because it greatly reduces the possibility of deadlocks.
- to provide dependency locking, i.e. the locking of tables which might be affected by triggers and integrity constraints. Dependency locking is not normally in Firebird. However, it will ensure that update conflicts arising from indirect dependency conflicts will be avoided.
- to strengthen the transaction's precedence with regard to one or more specific tables with which it will be involved. For example, a SNAPSHOT transaction that needs sole write access to all rows in a particular table could reserve it, while assuming normal precedence with regard to rows in other tables. This is a less aggressive way to apply table-level locking than the alternative, to use TABLE STABILITY isolation.

Uses for Table Reservation

When table-level locking is required, table reservation with SNAPSHOT or READ COMMITTED isolation is recommended in preference to using SNAPSHOT TABLE STABILITY when table-level locking is required. Table reservation is the less aggressive and more flexible way to lock tables pre-emptively. It is available for use with any isolation level. However, using it in combination with SNAPSHOT TABLE STABILITY is not recommended, because it has no effect in mitigating the tables that the transaction might access that are out of its scope.

Pre-emptive table locking is not for everyday use but it can be usefully employed for a task such as a pre-audit valuation or an "inventory freeze" report prior to a stocktake.

Parameters for table reservation

Each table reservation can be configured with distinct attributes to specify how multiple transactions should be treated when they request access to reserved table.

A SNAPSHOT TABLE STABILITY transaction can not get any access to ANY table that is reserved by table reservation.

The choices are:

```
[PROTECTED | SHARED] {READ | WRITE}
```

The PROTECTED attribute gives ThisTransaction an exclusive lock on the table it is reading and allows any other transaction that is in SNAPSHOT or READ COMMITTED isolation to read rows. Writes are restricted by one of the two modifers:

- PROTECTED WRITE allows ThisTransaction to write to the table.
- PROTECTED READ disallows writing to the table by any transaction, including ThisTransaction itself.

The SHARED attribute lets any SNAPSHOT or READ COMMITTED transaction read the table and provides two options for concurrent updating by other transactions:

- SHARED WRITE allows any SNAPSHOT read-write or READ COMMITTED read-write transaction to update rows in the set but no transaction as long as no transaction has or requests exclusive write
- SHARED READ is the most liberal reserving condition. It allows any other read-write transaction to update the table.

Summary

Any other transaction can read a table reserved by ThisTransaction, provided there is no aspect of the other transaction's configuration that gives it an exclusive WRITE right on the table, i.e. all can read if they are configured only to read and not to have any pre-emptive right to write. The following conditions will always block the other transaction from reading a table reserved by ThisTransaction:

- the other transaction is in SNAPSHOT TABLE STABILITY isolation
- the other transaction is configured to reserve the table PROTECTED WRITE (although it can read the table if ThisTransaction is reserving it with SHARED READ)
- the other transaction wants to reserve the table SHARED WRITE and ThisTransaction is reserving it with PROTECTED READ or PROTECTED WRITE

In case this is all too confusing still, in Figure 26.1, we'll let some configured transactions speak for themselves,

Figure 19.1 Configuring table reservation

Other Optional Parameters

IGNORE LIMBO, supported from the "2" series onward, tells the engine to ignore "in limbo" transactions that have been left behind by a failed multi-database transaction.

This parameter is available to applications via the API, for all versions of Firebird, as the member isc_tpb_ignore_limbo in the transaction parameter block (TPB).

NO AUTO UNDO, supported from the "2" series onward, tells the engine not to keep the internal "undo"log. By default, the server maintains this *internal savepoint log* of inserted and changed rows in memory. In the normal course of events, log entries are erased as each transaction commits or rolls back. However, under certain conditions, the system will abandon the log and refer directly to the global transaction state bitmap (TSB) instead. The transition is likely to happen when a huge insert is rolled back or a transaction using many repeated user savepoints (q.v.) has exhausted the capacity of the log.

This parameter is available to applications via the API, for all versions of Firebird, as the member isc_tpb_no_auto_undo in the transaction parameter block (TPB).

Record Versions

When an update request is successfully posted to the server, Firebird creates and writes to disk a reference linking the original row image as seen by the transaction—sometimes called a delta—and a new version of the row, incorporating the requested changes. The original and new row images are referred to as record versions.

When a new record version is created by a newer transaction than the one that created the "live" version, other transactions will not be able to update or delete the original unless the owner-transaction of the new version rolls back. The versioning process is described in detail in the previous chapter.

Until the transaction is eventually committed, it does not touch the "live" version again until the Commit occurs. Within its own context, it treats the posted version as if it were the latest committed version. Meanwhile, other transactions continue to "see" the latest committed version. In the case of SNAPSHOT transactions that started before ThisTransaction, the latest committed version that they see may be older than the one seen by our transaction and by other transactions that either started later or are in READ COMMITTED isolation.

Dependent rows

If the table that has an update posted to it has foreign keys linked to it, the server creates deltas of the rows from those tables that "belong to" the updated row. Those dependent rows—and any that are dependent on them through foreign keys—are thus made inaccessible for update by other transactions too, for the duration of the transaction.

Locking and Lock Conflicts

With Firebird, locking is governed by the relative ages of transactions and the records managed by Firebird's versioning engine. All locking applies at row level, except when a transaction is operating in SNAPSHOT TABLE STABILITY isolation or with a table reservation restriction that blocks write access.

Timing

The timing of the lock on the row in normal read-write activity is optimistic—no locking is in force on any row until the moment it is actually required. Until an update of the row is posted to the server, the row is free to be "won" by any read-write transaction.

Pessimistic locking

Pessimistic—or pre-emptive—locking can be applied to sets of rows or to entire tables. The table-locking options have already been explained (see *Table Reservation* and *SNAPSHOT TABLE STABILITY (Consistency)* isolation).

Row-level and set-level pessimistic locking is also an option where there is an application requirement to reserve a row or a small set in advance of actually posting an update or deletion. It is not a transaction setting.

Explicit row locking

Explicit pessimistic row locking is achieved with the optional WITH LOCK clause in the SELECT statement. It is restricted to "outer-level" SELECT statements that return output sets or define cursors. In cannot be applied to subqueries or virtual output sets that use SELECT expressions.

The abbreviated syntax for acquiring explicit pessimistic row locks is:

```
SELECT <output-list>
FROM <table-or-procedure-or-view>
[WHERE <search-conditions>]
[GROUP BY <grouping-specification>]
[UNION <select-expression> [ALL]]
[PLAN <plan-expression>]
[ORDER BY <column-list>]
[FOR UPDATE [OF col1 [,col2..]] [WITH LOCK]]
```

FOR UPDATE—which is not a locking instruction—requests that the output set be delivered to the client one row at a time, rather than as a batch. The optional phrase WITH LOCK is the element that forces the pre-emptive lock on a row as soon as the server outputs it from the server. Rows waiting to be output are not locked.

v.1.0.x Explicit row locking is not supported in v.1.0.x.

Dummy updates

The traditional way of achieving a pessimistic row lock with Firebird is the "dummy update". It is a hack that takes advantage of record versioning. Simply put, the client posts an update statement for the row that doesn't update anything: it just sets a column to its current value, causing the server to create a new record version and thus blocks other transactions from acquiring the row for updating or deletion.

The conditions where pessimistic locking might help and the recommended techniques are discussed in the next chapter, ***Programming with Transactions***.

Lock conflicts

A lock conflict is triggered when concurrent transactions try to update or delete the same row during a time when their views of database state overlap. Lock conflicts are the planned outcome of Firebird's transaction isolation and record versioning strategy, protecting volatile data from uncontrolled overwriting by parallel operations on the same data.

The strategy works so well that there are really only two conditions that can cause lock conflicts:

- Condition 1: one transaction—"ThisTransaction"—has posted an update or deletion for a row that another transaction, which started before ThisTransaction locked that row, attempts to update or delete. The other transaction encounters a lock conflict and has two choices: either
    - it can roll back its attempt and try again later against the newest committed version, or
    - it can wait until ThisTransaction either commits or rolls back.
- Condition 2: ThisTransaction is blocking the whole table against writes, because it has the table isolated in SNAPSHOT TABLE STABILITY or by a PROTECTED table reservation, and another transaction tries to update or delete a row or to insert a new row.

Suppose ThisTransaction posts a change to a row. Another transaction comes along and requests to change or delete the same row. In SNAPSHOT isolation with WAIT, the other transaction will keep waiting until ThisTransaction completes with either commit or rollback.

If ThisTransaction commits, then the other transaction will fail with an update conflict. The client that started the other transaction should have an exception handler that either rolls the transaction back and starts a new one to resubmit the request, or simply commits the transaction and exits.

Calling COMMIT in a lock conflict exception handler is not recommended, since it breaks the atomicity of the transaction—some work will complete, some will not and it will be impossible to predict database state afterwards. Rollback is almost always the right response to a lock conflict.

Unfortunately, Firebird tends to generalize all locking exceptions and report them as "deadlocks". The normal case just described is not a deadlock

What is a deadlock?

A deadlock is just a nickname, borrowed from the sport of wrestling, for the condition where two transactions are contending to update rows in overlapping sets and one transaction does not take any precedence over the other.

For example, ThisTransaction has an update pending on Row X and wants to update Row Y, while the other transaction has an update pending on Row Y and wants to update Row X and both transactions are in WAIT mode. As in wrestling, the deadlock can only be resolved if one contender withdraws its hold. One transaction must roll back and let the other commit its changes.

Firebird allows the application to resolve the deadlock by scanning for deadlocks every few seconds. It will arbitrarily pick one transaction from the deadlock and deliver a deadlock exception.

Developers should not dread deadlock messages. On the contrary, they are the essence of isolating the work of multiple users in transaction contexts. You should anticipate them and handle them effectively in your client application.

When ThisTransaction is selected to resolve the deadlock, the application's exception handler should roll it back to allow the other transaction to resume and complete its work. The alternative—committing ThisTransaction in the exception handler—is not recommended, since ThisTransaction becomes non-atomic and the other transaction will fail with a lock conflict.

"Deadly embrace"

In rare cases, more than two transactions could be deadlocked in contention for the same overlapping sets. It is sometimes called "the deadly embrace". The deadlock scan will fail one transaction (ThisTransaction), handing it over to the client for exception resolution, as before. However, this time, even if the client rolls back ThisTransaction, those other transactions are still deadlocked out there.

"Livelock"

The client might start a new transaction and retry, but the other contenders are still deadlocked, waiting for the next deadlock scan to extricate another of the contenders with a deadlock exception. As long as the retrying application keeps retrying with a WAIT transaction, it is just going to wait for some indefinite time for the other transactions to resolve the deadly embrace. For those futile retries, the transactions are said to be in a "livelock".

In short, it is important in the first place to avoid transaction contexts that make it possible for a deadly embrace to occur. As added protection, exception handlers should be made capable of quickly dealing with deadlocks and ensuring that problem transactions finish cleanly and without delay.

In the "2" series clients, you have the option of setting a LOCK TIMEOUT in seconds. If your applications are getting deadlocks too often, experiment with a few low values first—say 1 to 5 seconds—and see whether it improves the situation.

PART V

Appendices

APPENDIX

I

INTERNAL AND EXTERNAL FUNCTIONS

In this Appendix are summarised descriptions of the internal and external functions available in Firebird.

At the end of this Appendix, for your convenience, we provide the guidelines for *Building regular expressions* extracted from the ***Firebird 2.5 Language Reference Update***, published by the Firebird Project and usually included in the binary download kits. Regular expressions are used with the SIMILAR TO comparison predicate which is supported in Firebird 2.5+ versions.

Internal Functions

At version 2.1, a large number of functions that had previously been implemented as external (UDFs) were coded internally and, in many cases, made compliant with the ISO standards with respect to input arguments. Some new functions were added also.

Conditional Logic Functions

COALESCE

```
COALESCE (<value1>, <value2> [, <valueN> ... ]) -- return type depends on input
```

Takes a comma-separated list of two or more arguments (columns, expressions, constants, etc.) that resolve to values of the same type and returns the value of the first argument that evaluates to a non-null value. If all the input arguments resolve as NULL, the result is NULL.

Example

This example tries to create an identifying description for a vehicle by running through a list of descriptive fields until it finds one that has a value in it. If all fields are NULL, it returns 'Unknown'.

```
select
  coalesce (Make, Model, Series, 'Unknown') as Listing
from Catalog;
```

Comment

Available from v.1.5+. In Firebird 1.0.x, to accomplish the same effect, refer to the external functions iNVL and sNVL.

DECODE

```
DECODE( <expression>, <search>, <result> [ , <search>, <result> ... ] [, <default> ]
```

DECODE is a shortcut for a CASE ... WHEN ...ELSE expression.

Example

```
select
  decode(state, 0, 'deleted', 1, 'active', 'unknown') as retval
from things;
```

IIF `IIF (<condition>, <value_if_true>, <value_if_false>)`

Returns `<value_if_true>` if condition is met, otherwise returns `<value_if_false>`. Arguments `<value_if_true>` and `<value_if_false>` can be columns, constants, variables or expressions and must be of compatible types. The `<condition>` argument must be a valid predication that returns a logical result.

Example The following statement returns PACKAGE_SIZE as 'LARGE' if the value in the Qty field is 100 or greater; otherwise, it returns 'SMALL'.

```
SELECT
  PRODUCT,
  IIF ((Qty >= 100), 'LARGE', 'SMALL') AS PACKAGE_SIZE
FROM INVENTORY;
```

Comment *Available from Firebird 1.5 onward. Its usage is somewhat limited. From v.2.0 on, it is recommended to use a CASE expression instead.*

NULLIF `NULLIF (value1, value2)`

Returns NULL if `value1` and `value2` resolve to a match; if there is no match, then `value1` is returned. Arguments `value1` and `value2` can be columns, constants, variables or expressions.

Example This statement will cause the STOCK value in the PRODUCTS table to be set to NULL on all rows where it is currently stored as 0:

```
UPDATE PRODUCTS
  SET STOCK = NULLIF(STOCK, 0)
```

Comment *Available from Firebird 1.5 onward.*

Date and Time Functions

DATEADD

```
DATEADD( <number> <timestamp_part> TO <date_time> )
DATEADD( <timestamp_part>, <number>, <date_time> )

timestamp_part ::= { YEAR | MONTH | | WEEK | DAY | HOUR | MINUTE | SECOND | MILLISECOND }
```

Returns a date, time or timestamp value incremented (or decrementsed, when negative) by the specified amount of time.

Examples

```
select dateadd(day, -1, current_date) as yesterday from rdb$database;
```

or (expanded syntax)

```
select dateadd(-1 day to current_date) as yesterday from rdb$database;
```

Comments

1. *WEEK was added at v.2.5.*
2. *YEAR, MONTH, WEEK and DAY cannot be used with time values.*
3. *In versions prior to v.2.5, HOUR, MINUTE, SECOND and MILLISECOND cannot be used with date values.*
4. *All timestamp_part values can be used with timestamp values.*

DATEDIFF

```
DATEDIFF( <timestamp_part> FROM <date_time> TO <date_time> )
DATEDIFF( <timestamp_part>, <date_time>, <date_time> )
timestamp_part ::= { YEAR | MONTH | WEEK | DAY | HOUR | MINUTE | SECOND | MILLISECOND }
```

Returns an exact numeric value representing the interval of time from the first date, time or timestamp value to the second one.

Example

```
select
  datediff(DAY, (cast('TOMORROW' as date) -10), current_date)
as datediffresult from rdb$database;
```

Comments

1. WEEK was added at v.2.5.

2. Returns a positive value if the second value is greater than the first one, negative when the first one is greater, or zero when they are equal.

3. Comparison of date with time values is invalid.

4. YEAR, MONTH,, WEEK and DAY cannot be used with time values. In versions prior to v.2.5, HOUR, MINUTE, SECOND and MILLISECOND cannot be used with date values.

5. All timestamp_part values can be used with timestamp values.

EXTRACT

```
EXTRACT (<time_part> FROM <datetime>) -- returns a SMALLINT or DECIMAL(6,4)
```

Extracts and returns an element from a DATE, TIME or TIMESTAMP expression as a numerical value. The return value will be a SMALLINT or DECIMAL(6,4), depending on which <time_part> is requested.

The <datetime> argument is a column or expression that resolves to a DATE, TIME or TIMESTAMP. Valid values for the <time_part> argument are:

<time_part>	Description	Type and Range
YEAR	The year represented by a DATE or TIMESTAMP input. Not valid for a TIME input.	SMALLINT in the range 1-9999
MONTH	The month represented by a DATE or TIMESTAMP input. Not valid for a TIME input.	SMALLINT in the range 1-12
DAY	The day of the month represented by a DATE or TIMESTAMP input. Not valid for a TIME input.	SMALLINT in the range 1-31
WEEKDAY	The day of the week represented by a DATE or TIMESTAMP input. Not valid for a TIME input.	SMALLINT in the range 0-6, where 0 is Sunday.
YEARDAY	The day of the year represented by a DATE or TIMESTAMP input. Not valid for a TIME input.	SMALLINT in the range 0-365, where 0 is January 1.
HOUR	The hour of the day represented by a TIME or TIMESTAMP input. Returns zero if the input is a DATE type.	SMALLINT in the range 0-23

<time_part>	Description	Type and Range
MINUTE	The minutes part of a TIME or TIMESTAMP input. Returns zero if the input is a DATE type.	SMALLINT in the range 0-59
SECOND	The seconds and sub-seconds parts of a TIME or TIMESTAMP input. Returns zero if the input is a DATE type.	DECIMAL(6,4) in the range 0.0000–59.999

Example In this trigger fragment, a document code based on the current year and a generator value is created from elements of a TIMESTAMP value:

```
...
if (new.DocCode is NULL) then
begin
  varDocCode = CAST (EXTRACT(YEAR FROM CURRENT_DATE AS CHAR(4)));
  varDocCode = varDocCode ||'-'|| CAST (GEN_ID (GenDocID,1) as VARCHAR (18));
  new.DocCode = varDocCode;
end
...
```

Comment *Available in all versions.*

String and Character Functions

ASCII_CHAR

```
ASCII_CHAR( <number> )
```

Returns the ASCII character with the specified decimal code. The argument to ASCII_CHAR must be in the range 0 to 255. The result is returned in character set NONE.

Example

```
select ascii_char(x) from y;
```

ASCII_VAL

```
ASCII_VAL( <string> )
```

Returns the decimal ASCII code of the first character of the specified string.

- Returns 0 if the string is empty
- Throws an error if the first character is multi-byte
- The argument may be a text BLOB of 32,767 bytes or less

Example

```
select ascii_val(x) from y;
```

BIT_LENGTH

```
BIT_LENGTH( <string> | <string_expr> )
```

Returns the length of a string in bits.

Example

```
select
  rdb$relation_name,
  bit_length(rdb$relation_name),
  bit_length(trim(rdb$relation_name))
from rdb$relations;
```

CHAR_LENGTH interchangeable with ***CHARACTER_LENGTH***

```
CHAR_LENGTH( <string> | <string_expr> )
```

Returns the number of characters in a string or expression result.

Examples

```
select
    rdb$relation_name,
    character_length(rdb$relation_name),
    char_length(trim(rdb$relation_name))
from rdb$relations;
```

Comment *See also OCTET_LENGTH*

GEN_UUID

```
GEN_UUID() -- no arguments
```

Returns a universal unique number.

Example

```
insert into records (id)
  value (gen_uuid());
```

HASH

```
HASH( <string> )
```

Returns a HASH of a string.

Example

```
select hash(x) from y;
```

LEFT

```
LEFT( <string>, <number> )
```

Returns the substring of a specified length that appears at the start of a left-to-right string.

Example

```
select left(name, char_length(name) - 10)
from people
where name like '% OLIVEIRA';
```

Comments

1. The first position in a string is 1, not 0.
2. If the <number> argument evaluates to a non-integer, banker's rounding is applied.
See also RIGHT.

LOWER

```
LOWER( <string> )
```

Returns the input argument converted to all lower-case characters.

Example

```
isql -q -ch dos850

SQL> create database 'test.fdb';
SQL> create table t (c char(1) character set dos850);
SQL> insert into t values ('A');
SQL> insert into t values ('E');
SQL> insert into t values ('Á');;
SQL> insert into t values ('É');
SQL> select c, lower(c) from t;
C      LOWER
====== ======
A      a
```

```
E    e
Á    á
É    é
```

Comments *Available in v.2.0.x*

The misrepresentation of the accute accent on the upper case 'A' in our example is a shortcoming of the rendering of this font.

LPAD `LPAD( <string1>, <n> [, <string2> ] )`

A "left-padding" function—prepends `<string2>` to the beginning of `<string1>` until the length of the result string becomes equal to `<n>`.

Example

```
select lpad(x, 10) from y;
```

Comment *See also RPAD*

OCTET_LENGTH `OCTET_LENGTH( <string> | <string_expr> )`

Returns the length of a string or expression result in bytes.

Examples

```
select
  rdb$relation_name,
  octet_length(rdb$relation_name),
  octet_length(trim(rdb$relation_name))
from rdb$relations;
```

Comment *See also CHARACTER_LENGTH | CHAR_LENGTH*

OVERLAY `OVERLAY( <string1> PLACING <string2> FROM <startpos> [ FOR <length> ] )`

Returns `<string1>` modified so that the substring that occupied the `<length>` positions FROM `<startpos>` are replaced by `<string2>`.

If `<length>` is not specified, CHAR_LENGTH(`<string2>`) is implied.

Example

```
SELECT
  OVERLAY('Today is Tuesday'
  PLACING ' not ' FROM 9 FOR 1
  AS DENIAL
FROM RDB$DATABASE
-- returns 'Today is not Tuesday'
```

Comments

1. The first position in a string is 1, not 0.

2. If the <startpos> and/or <length > argument evaluates to a non-integer, banker's rounding is applied.

3. The function will fail with text BLOBs of a multi-byte character set if the length of the result would be greater than 1024 bytes.

PI `PI() -- no arguments`

Returns the Pi constant (3.1459...).

Example

```
val = PI();
```

POSITION

```
POSITION(<string2> IN <string1>)
POSITION( <string2>, <string1> [, <offset-position>] )
```

Returns the start position of the <string2> inside <string1>, relative to the beginning of <string1>. In the second form, an offset position may be supplied so that the function will ignore any matches occuring before the offset position and return the first match following that.

Examples

```
select rdb$relation_name from rdb$relations
where position('RDB$' IN rdb$relation_name) = 1;
/* */
position ('be', 'To be or not to be', 10)
```

returns 17. The first occurrence of 'be' occurs within the offset and is ignored.

```
position ('be', 'To buy or not to buy', 10)
```

returns 0 because the searched substring was not found.

REPLACE

```
REPLACE( <stringtosearch>, <findstring>, <replstring> )
```

Replaces all occurrences of <findstring> in <stringtosearch> with <replstring>.

Example

```
select replace(x, ' ', ',') from y;
```

REVERSE

```
REVERSE( <value> )
```

Returns a string in reverse order—useful for creating an expression index that indexes strings from right to left.

Examples

```
create index people_email on people
  computed by (reverse(email));
select * from people
  where reverse(email) starting with reverse('.br');
```

RIGHT

```
RIGHT( <string>, <number> )
```

Returns the substring, of the specified length, from the right-hand end of a string.

Example

```
select
  right(rdb$relation_name,
  char_length(rdb$relation_name) - 4)
from rdb$relations
where rdb$relation_name like 'RDB$%';
```

Comment

See also LEFT

RPAD

```
RPAD( <string1>, <length> [, <string2> ] )
```

"Right-padding" function for strings—appends <string2> to the end of <string1> until the length of the result string becomes equal to <length>.

Example

```
select rpad(x, 10) from y;
```

Comments

1. *If <string2> is omitted the default value is one space.*
2. *If the result string would exceed the length, the final application of <string2> is truncated.*

See also LPAD

SUBSTRING `SUBSTRING(<str> FROM startpos [FOR <n>]) -- returns a CHAR(n) or a text BLOB`

Extracts a substring from a string `<str>`, starting at the position indicated by `startpos` and ending at the end of `<str>`. If the optional FOR `<n>` argument is supplied, the extracted substring will end when its length is equal to `<n>` if the end of `<str>` has not been reached already.

The arguments `startpos` and `<n>` (length for the substring) must resolve to integer types, while `<str>` can be any expression that evaluates to a string of 32,767 bytes or less or a BLOB not exceeding that byte-length limit. The first byte in the input string is at position 1.

Up to and including v.2.0, the return value is a string, regardless of whether the input `<str>` is a string or a BLOB. From v.2.1 forward, a text BLOB is returned if the input is a text or binary BLOB.

Important *Prior to v.2.1, a SUBSTRING of a text BLOB does not work if the BLOB is stored in a multi-byte character set.*

Examples

```
insert into Abbreviations(PID, Abbreviation)
select
  PID,
  substring(Surname from 1 for 3)
from PERSON;
```

Comment *Available in versions 1.5+.*

TRIM

```
TRIM <left paren> [ [ <trim specification> ] [ <trim character> ]
  FROM ] <value expression> <right paren>
<trim specification> ::= LEADING | TRAILING | BOTH
<trim character> ::= <value expression>
```

Trims characters (default: blanks) from the left and/or right of a string.

Rules

1 If <trim specification> is not specified, BOTH is assumed.

2 If <trim character> is not specified, ' ' is assumed.

3 If <trim specification> and/or <trim character> is specified, FROM should be specified.

4 .If <trim specification> and <trim character> is not specified, FROM should not be specified.

5 If a text BLOB substring is specified as <value expres- sion>, the value returned must not exceed 32,767 bytes.

Examples

```
select
  rdb$relation_name,
  trim(leading 'RDB$' from rdb$relation_name)
from rdb$relations
where rdb$relation_name starting with 'RDB$';
/* */
select
trim(rdb$relation_name) || ' is a system table' from rdb$relations
where rdb$system_flag = 1;
```

Comment *Available in v.2.0.x*

BLOB Functions

Virtually all internal functions that are available to character types are also available to BLOBS of sub_type 1 (TEXT). Care should be taken always to ensure that string inputs and outputs never exceed the maximum length limit of the VARCHAR type, which is 32,765 bytes.

Mathematical Functions

ABS

```
ABS( <number> )
```

Returns the absolute value of a number.

Example

```
select abs(amount) from transactions;
```

CEIL / CEILING

```
{ CEIL | CEILING }( <number> )
```

Returns a value representing the smallest integer that is greater than or equal to the input argument.

Examples

```
1) select ceil(val) from x;
2) select ceil(2.1), ceil(-2.1) from rdb$database;-- returns 3, -2
```

Comment *See also FLOOR*

EXP

```
EXP( <number> )
```

Returns the exponential *e* to the argument.

Example

```
select exp(x) from y;
```

FLOOR

```
FLOOR( <number> )
```

Returns a value representing the largest integer that is less than or equal to the input argument.

Examples

```
1) select floor(val) from x;

2) select floor(2.1), floor(-2.1) from rdb$database; -- returns 2, -3
```

Comment *See also CEILING*

LN

```
LN( <number> )
```

Returns the natural logarithm of a number.

Example

```
select ln(x) from y;
```

LOG

```
LOG( <number>, <number> )
```

LOG (x, y) returns the logarithm base x of y.

Example

```
select log(x, 10) from y;
```

LOG10 `LOG10( <number> )`

Returns the logarithm base ten of a number.

Example `select log10(x) from y;`

MAXVALUE `MAXVALUE( <value> [, <value> ...] )`

Returns the maximum value of a list of values.

Example `select maxvalue(v1, v2, 10) from x;`

MINVALUE `MINVALUE( <value> [, <value> ...] )`

Returns the minimum value of a list of values.

Example `select minvalue(v1, v2, 10) from x;`

MOD `MOD( <number>, <number> )`

Modulo: MOD(X, Y) returns the 'remainder' part of the division of X by Y.

Example `select mod(x, 10) from y;`

POWER `POWER( <number>, <number> )`

POWER(X, Y) returns X to the power of Y.

Example `select power(x, 10) from y;`

RAND `RAND() -- no argument`

Returns a random number between 0 and 1.

Examples `select * from x order by rand();`

ROUND `ROUND( <number>, [<number>] )`

Returns a number rounded to the specified scale.

Example `select round(salary * 1.1, 0) from people;`

Comment *If the scale (second parameter) is negative or is omitted, the integer part of the value is rounded. E.g., ROUND(123.456, -1) returns 120.000.*

SIGN `SIGN( <number> )`

Returns 1, 0, or -1 depending on whether the input value is positive, zero or negative, respectively.

Example `select sign(x) from y;`

SQRT `SQRT( <number> )`

Returns the square root of a number.

Example `select sqrt(x) from y;`

TRUNC `TRUNC( <number> [, <number> ] )`

Returns the integral part (up to the specified scale) of a number.

Examples

```
1) select trunc(x) from y;
2) select trunc(-2.8), trunc(2.8)
from rdb$database;-- returns -2, 2
3) select trunc(987.65, 1), trunc(987.65, -1)
from rdb$database;-- returns 987.60, 980.00
```

Trigonometrical Functions

ACOS `ACOS( <number> )`

Returns the arc cosine of a number. Argument to ACOS must be in the range -1 to 1. Returns a value in the range 0 to Pi.

Example

```
select acos(x) from y;
```

ASIN `ASIN( <number> )`

Returns the arc sine of a number. The argument to ASIN must be in the range -1 to 1. It returns a result in the range -Pi/2 to Pi/2.

Example

```
select asin(x) from y;
```

ATAN `ATAN( <number> )`

Returns the arc tangent of a number. Returns a value in the range -Pi/2 to Pi/2.

Example

```
select atan(x) from y;
```

ATAN2 `ATAN2( <number1>, <number2> )`

Returns the arctangent of (<number1>/<number2>). Returns a value in the range -Pi to Pi.

Example

```
select atan2(x, y) from z;
```

COS `COS( <number> )`

Returns the cosine of a number. The angle is specified in radians and returns a value in the range -1 to 1.

Example

```
select cos(x) from y;
```

COSH `COSH( <number> )`

Returns the hyperbolic cosine of a number.

Example

```
select cosh(x) from y;
```

COT `COT( <number> )`

Returns the reciprocal of the tangent of <number>.

Example `select cot(x) from y;`

SIN `SIN( <number> )`

Returns the sine of an input number that is expressed in radians.

Example `select sin(x) from y;`

SINH `SINH( <number> )`

Returns the hyperbolic sine of a number.

Example `select sinh(x) from y;`

TAN `TAN( <number> )`

Returns the tangent of an input number that is expressed in radians.

Example `select tan(x) from y;`

TANH `TANH( <number> )`

Returns the hyperbolic tangent of a number.

Example `select tanh(x) from y;`

Binary Functions

BIN_AND `BIN_AND( <number> [, <number> ...] )`

Returns the result of a binary AND operation performed on all arguments.

Example `select bin_and(flags, 1) from x;`

BIN_NOT `BIN_NOT( <number> )`

v.2.5+ Returns the result of a binary NOT operation performed on the argument.

Example `select bin_not(flags) from x;`

BIN_OR `BIN_OR( <number> [, <number> ...] )`

Returns the result of a binary OR operation performed on all arguments.

Example `select bin_or(flags1, flags2) from x;`

BIN_SHL `BIN_SHL( <number>, <number> )`

Returns the result of a binary shift left operation performed on the arguments (first << second).

Example `select bin_shl(flags1, 1) from x;`

BIN_SHR `BIN_SHR( <number>, <number> )`

Returns the result of a binary shift right operation performed on the arguments (first >> second).

Example

```
select bin_shr(flags1, 1) from x;
```

BIN_XOR

```
BIN_XOR( <number> [, <number> ...] )
```

Returns the result of a binary XOR operation performed on all arguments.

Example

```
select bin_xor(flags1, flags2) from x;
```

Miscellaneous Functions

GEN_ID

```
GEN_ID( <generator-name>, <step> )
```

Returns a value from the named generator. The number returned depends on the <step> argument (a SMALLINT):

- a step of 0 returns the last-generated value
- a step of 1 returns a unique, new number that is 1 greater than the last generated
- a step of 10 returns a unique, new number that is 10 greater than the last generated
- a step of -1 returns a number that is 1 less than the last generated and ALSO decrements the last-generated value—usually a recipe for disaster

Example

```
select gen_id (MY_GENERATOR, 1) from RDB$DATABASE;
```

Comment From v.2.0 forward, you might prefer to use the alternative method for retrieving the next value from a generator, alias SEQUENCE in standard SQL. Refer to the NEXT VALUE FOR syntax for sequences.

External Functions

This summary covers the external function libraries that are distributed officially with the Firebird binary kits, viz., `fbudf[.dll]` and `ib_udf[.dll]`.

The popular, original 32-bit Windows-only *FreeUDFLib* created by Gregory Deatz in Delphi in the 1990s is not strenuously maintained any more and, at the time of writing, a 64-bit version was not known to exist.

Many of the functions contained in it have been taken up and improved as *FreeAdHocUDF*, an open source project led by Christoph Theuring. *FreeAdHocUDF* is actively maintained and is available for multiple OS platforms in both 64-bit and 32-bit versions. Many of the string functions support multi-byte character sets, including UTF8. For more information, including documentation, visit http://freeadhocudf.org.

Conditional Logic Functions

The external functions in this group should be considered deprecated for Firebird versions 1.5 and higher.

INULLIF (fbudf)

```
INULLIF (value1, value2) -- returns a NUMERIC or NULL
```

Arguments `value1` and `value2` can be columns, constants, variables or expressions. The function returns NULL if `value1` and `value2` resolve to a match; if there is no match, then `value1` is returned.

Applicable to fixed numeric types only and should be used only with Firebird 1.0.x. With Firebird 1.5 and higher, use the internal function NULLIF( ).

Example This statement will cause the STOCK value in the PRODUCTS table to be set to NULL on all rows where it is currently stored as 0:

```
UPDATE PRODUCTS
SET STOCK = iNULLIF(STOCK, 0)
```

Comment *See also sNullIf( ), internal function NULLIF( )*

INVL (fbudf)

```
INVL(value1, value2) -- return a NUMERIC or NULL
```

This function attempts to mimic the NVL( ) function of Oracle, for fixed numeric types only. It will cause `value2` to be output if `value1` resolves to NULL, otherwise it returns `value1`. If both `value1` and `value2` resolve to NULL, then NULL is returned.

The `value1` argument is a column or an expression involving a column. Floating-point types are not supported. If necessary, use CAST( ) in your expression to transform the value to a numeric type. `value2` is an expression or constant that will resolve to the value which is to be output if `value1` resolves to NULL.

Example The following query outputs 0 if STOCK is NULL:

```
SELECT PRODUCT_ID, PRODUCT_NAME, INVL(STOCK, 0) FROM PRODUCTS;
```

Comment *See also sNVL( ), iNullIf( ), internal function COALESCE( ).*

SNULLIF (fbudf)

```
SNULLIF (value1, value2) -- returns a string or NULL
```

Arguments `value1` and `value2` can be columns, constants, variables or expressions. The function returns NULL if `value1` and `value2` resolve to a match; if there is no match, then `value1` is returned.

Applicable to character types only and should be used only with Firebird 1.0.x. With Firebird 1.5 and higher, use the internal function NULLIF( ).

Example This query will set the column IS_REGISTERED to NULL in all rows where its value is 'T' and REGISTRATION_DATE is NULL:

```
UPDATE ATABLE
  SET IS_REGISTERED = SNULLIF(IS_REGISTERED, 'T')
WHERE REGISTRATION_DATE IS NULL;
```

Comment *Deprecated for versions 1.5 onward.*

The string length limit of 32,765 bytes applies.

See also iNullIf( ). For Firebird 1.5 and higher, see internal function NULLIF( ).

SNVL (fbudf)

```
SNVL(value1, value2) -- returns a string or NULL
```

This function attempts to mimic the NVL( ) function of Oracle, for character types only. It will cause `value2` to be output if `value1` resolves to NULL, otherwise it returns `value1`. If both `value1` and `value2` resolve to NULL, then NULL is returned.

The `value1` argument is a column or an expression involving a column. `value2` is an expression or constant that will resolve to the value which is to be output if `value1` resolves to NULL.

Example The following query calculates and outputs a runtime column, BIRTH_YEAR, for each student. Where this value resolves to NULL, the string "Not known" is output instead:

```
SELECT FIRST_NAME, LAST_NAME, SNVL(CAST(EXTRACT(YEAR FROM BIRTH_DATE) AS VARCHAR(9)),
'Not known') AS BIRTH_YEAR FROM STUDENT_REGISTER;
```

Comment *See also iNVL( ), sNullIf( ), internal function COALESCE( ).*

Mathematical Functions

In many, if not all cases, external math functions have been superseded by inbuilt (internal) functions from v.2.1 onward.

ABS (ib_udf)

```
ABS(value) -- returns DOUBLE PRECISION
```

Returns the absolute value of a number. The argument **value** is a column or expression that is compatible with a signed or unsigned DOUBLE PRECISION number.

Example This statement will calculate a total of values that are negative and return it as a positive value:

```
SELECT ABS(SUM(ASSET_VALUE)) AS LIABILITY FROM ASSET_REGISTER
WHERE ASSET_VALUE < 0;
```

Comment *See the inbuilt function ABS().*

BIN_AND (ib_udf)

```
BIN_AND(value1, value2) -- returns INTEGER
```

Returns the result of a binary (bitwis)e AND operation performed on the two input values, **value1** and **value2**, which are columns or expressions that evaluate to SMALLINT or INTEGER type.

Example

```
SELECT BIN_AND(128,24) AS ANDED_RESULT FROM RDB$DATABASE;
```

BIN_OR (ib_udf)

```
BIN_OR (value1, value2) -- returns INTEGER
```

Returns the result of a binary (bitwise) OR operation performed on the two input values, **value1** and **value2**, which are columns or expressions that evaluate to SMALLINT or INTEGER type.

Example

```
SELECT BIN_AND(128,24) AS ORED_RESULT FROM RDB$DATABASE;
```

BIN_XOR (ib_udf)

```
BIN_XOR (value1, value2) -- returns INTEGER
```

Returns the result of a binary (bitwise) XOR operation performed on the two input values, **value1** and **value2**, which are columns or expressions that evaluate to SMALLINT or INTEGER type.

Example

```
SELECT BIN_XOR(128,24) AS EXORED_RESULT FROM RDB$DATABASE;
```

CEILING (ib_udf)

```
CEILING (value) -- returns DOUBLE PRECISION
```

Returns the smallest integer that is greater than or equal to the input value, a column or expression that evaluates to a number of DOUBLE PRECISION type.

Example

```
SELECT CEILING(LAST_TOTAL) AS ROUND_UP_NEAREST
  FROM SALES_HISTORY;
```

Comment *Return value is a DOUBLE PRECISION number with a zero decimal part.*

DIV (ib_udf)

```
DIV (value1, value2) -- returns DOUBLE PRECISION
```

Divides the two integer inputs and returns the quotient, discarding the decimal part. Arguments `value1` and `value2` are columns or expressions that evaluate to numbers of SMALLINT or INTEGER type. The function behaves almost like integer-by-integer division in databases created in dialect 3—the distinction being that the division returns a double.

Example

```
SELECT DIV(TERM, (CURRENT_DATE - START_DATE)/365) AS YEARS_REMAINING
  FROM MORTGAGE_ACCOUNT
WHERE ACCOUNT_ID = 12345;
```

Comment *Return value is a DOUBLE PRECISION number with a zero decimal part.*

DPOWER (fbudf)

```
DPOWER (value, exponent) -- returns DOUBLE PRECISION
```

Takes a number value or expression and an exponent and returns to exponential value.

Example

```
SELECT DPOWER(2.64575,2) AS NEARLY_7 FROM RDB$DATABASE;
```

Comment *See also SQRT( ).*

FLOOR (ib_udf)

```
FLOOR(value) -- returns DOUBLE PRECISION
```

Returns a floating-point value representing the largest integer that is less than or equal to value. The `value` argument is a column or expression that evaluates to a number of DOUBLE PRECISION type.

Example

```
SELECT FLOOR(CURRENT_DATE - START_DATE) AS DAYS_ELAPSED
FROM DVD_LOANS;
```

Comment *Return value is a DOUBLE PRECISION number with a zero decimal part.*

LN (ib_udf)

```
LN (value) -- returns DOUBLE PRECISION
```

Returns the natural logarithm of a number. The argument `value` is a column or expression that evaluates to a number of DOUBLE PRECISION type.

Example

```
SELECT LN((CURRENT_TIMESTAMP - LEASE_DATE)/7) AS NLOG_WEEKS
FROM LEASE_ACCOUNT;
```

Comment *For v.2.1 +, see internal function LN( ).*

LOG (ib_udf)

```
LOG(value1, value2) -- returns DOUBLE PRECISION
```

Returns the logarithm base x=`value1` of number y=`value2`.

Argument `value1` (the logarithm base) and `value2` (the number to be operated on) are columns or expressions that evaluate to numbers of DOUBLE PRECISION type.

Example

```
SELECT LOG(8, (CURRENT_TIMESTAMP - LEASE_DATE)/7)) AS LOG_WEEKS
FROM LEASE_ACCOUNT;
```

Comment *The Firebird 1.0.x version of this function has a bug that was inherited from InterBase: LOG(x,y) erroneously inverts the arguments and returns the log base y of number x. It was corrected in the v.1.5 library. Be aware that very oldstored procedures and application code may incorporate workaround code for the bug.*

For v.2.1 +, see internal function LOG( ).

LOG10
(ib_udf)

```
LOG10 (value) -- returns DOUBLE PRECISION
```

Returns the logarithm base 10 of the input **value**, a column or expression that evaluates to a number of DOUBLE PRECISION type.

Example

```
SELECT LOG10((CURRENT_TIMESTAMP - LEASE_DATE)/7) AS LOG10_WEEKS
FROM LEASE_ACCOUNT;
```

Comment *For v.2.1 +, see internal function LOG10( ).*

MODULO
(ib_udf)

```
MODULO (value1, value2) -- returns DOUBLE PRECISION
```

Modulo function—returns the remainder from a division between two integers. Arguments **value1** and **value2** are columns or expressions that evaluate to numbers of SMALLINT or INTEGER type.

Example A snippet from a trigger:

```
...IF (MODULO(NEW.HOURS * 100, 775) > 25.0) THEN
    NEW.OVERTIME_HOURS = MODULO(NEW.HOURS * 100, 775) / 100;
```

Comment *For v.2.1 +, see internal function MOD( ).*

PI
(ib_udf)

```
PI() -- returns DOUBLE PRECISION
```

Returns the value of Pi = 3.14159 . . . This function takes no arguments but the parentheses are required.

Example

```
SELECT PI() AS PI_VALUE
FROM RDB$DATABASE;
```

Comment *For v.2.1 +, see internal function PI( ).*

RAND
(ib_udf)

```
RAND() -- returns FLOAT
```

Returns a random number between 0 and 1. Function takes no arguments, but parentheses are required.

Until Firebird 2.0, the current time is used to seed the random number generator. The older implementation can cause identical numbers to be generated if the function is called more than once in a second.

From Firebird 2.0, seeding is itself random and the problem of duplicate numbers is avoided. If you want to retain the old behaviour on a v.2.0 or higher server version, use SRAND( ) instead.

Example

```
SELECT RAND() AS RANDOM_NUMBER FROM RDB$DATABASE;
```

Comment *Note that this function does not work in early sub-releases of Firebird 1.5.*

For v.2.1 +, see internal function RAND( ).

ROUND
(fbudf)

```
ROUND (value) -- returns a number of an integer type
```

Rounds a fixed numeric number up or down to the nearest integer.

The **value** argument is a column or expression that evaluates to a fixed numeric type with a scale > 0.

This is plain rounding—if the digit immediately to the right of the decimal is equal to or greater than 5, it adds 1 to the digit at the left of the decimal point, and then truncates any digits to the right. Otherwise, it truncates all digits to the right of decimal point.

Example The following statement calculates an estimate based on the result of rounding the product of two NUMERIC(11,2) numbers up or down:

```
SELECT
  JOB_NO,
  ROUND(RATE * HOURS) + 1 AS ESTIMATE
FROM QUOTATION
WHERE RATE IS NOT NULL AND HOURS IS NOT NULL;
```

Comment *See also TRUNCATE( ). For v.2.1 +, see internal function ROUND( ).*

SIGN
(ib_udf)

```
SIGN(value) -- returns SMALLINT (1=positive | 0=zer0 | -1=negative)
```

Returns 1, 0, or -1 depending on whether the input value is positive, zero, or negative, respectively. The **value** argument is a column or expression that evaluates to a number of DOUBLE PRECISION type.

Example A snippet from a trigger:

```
e...IF (SIGN(NEW.CURRENT_VALUE) < 1) THEN ...
```

Comment *For v.2.1 +, see internal function SIGN( ).*

SQRT
(ib_udf)

```
SQRT (value) -- returns DOUBLE PRECISION
```

Returns the square root of a number, **value**, that is a column or expression resolving to a number of DOUBLE PRECISION type.

~TSR

Example A snippet from a trigger:

```
...
IF (SQRT(NEW.HYPOTENUSE) = SQRT(NEW.SIDE1) + SQRT(NEW.SIDE2)) THEN
  NEW.RIGHT_ANGLED_TRIANGLE = 'T';
```

Comment *For v.2.1 +, see internal function SQRT().*

SRAND
(ib_udf)

```
SRAND() -- returns FLOAT
```

Returns a random number between 0 and 1. Function takes no arguments, but parentheses are required. The current time is used to seed the random number generator.

Example

```
SELECT SRAND() AS RANDOM_NUMBER FROM RDB$DATABASE;
```

Comment *Note that this function was introduced at v.2.0 to retain the original seeding mechanism that was used by RAND( ) in older versions.*

For v.2.1 +, see internal function RAND( ).

TRUNCATE
(fbudf)

```
TRUNCATE (value) -- returns a number of an integer type
```

Truncates a fixed numeric type, **value**, to the next lowest integer. The value argument is a column or expression that resolves to a fixed numeric type with a scale > 0.

As with some other functions in this library, you need to make two declarations to get "coverage" for both 32-bit and 64-bit inputs. Check the declarations in the script `fdudf.sql` for *truncate* and *i64truncate*.

Example The following statement calculates an estimate based on the result of truncating the product of two NUMERIC(11,2) numbers:

```
SELECT
  JOB_NO,
  TRUNCATE(RATE * HOURS) + 1 AS ESTIMATE
FROM QUOTATION
WHERE RATE IS NOT NULL AND HOURS IS NOT NULL;
```

Comment *For v.2.1 +, see internal function TRUNCATE().*

Date and Time Functions

***DOW* (fbudf)** `DOW (value) -- returns a string`

Takes a TIMESTAMP and returns the day of the week (in English) as a mixed-case string. The **value** argument is a column or expression that evaluates to a TIMESTAMP type.

Return values 'Monday', 'Tuesday', 'Wednesday', 'Thursday', 'Friday', 'Saturday', or 'Sunday'.

Example This statement adds four days and returns the day of the week for that adjusted date:

```
SELECT DOW(CURRENT_DATE + 4)
FROM RDB$DATABASE;
```

Comment *See also SDOW( ), internal function EXTRACT( ).*

***SDOW* (fbudf)** `SDOW (value) -- returns a string`

Takes a TIMESTAMP and returns the abbreviated day of the week (in English) as a mixed-case string. The **value** argument is a column or expression that evaluates to a TIMESTAMP type.

Return values 'Mon', 'Tue', 'Wed', 'Thu', 'Fri', 'Sat', or 'Sun'.

Example This statement adds four days and returns the day of the week for that adjusted date:

```
SELECT SDOW(CURRENT_DATE + 4)
FROM RDB$DATABASE;
```

Comment *See also DOW( ), also internal function EXTRACT( ).*

***ADDDAY* (fbudf)** `ADDDAY (value1, value2) -- returns a TIMESTAMP`

Adds a whole number of days to a date or time type value and returns the adjusted date as a TIMESTAMP. The argument value1 is a column or expression that evaluates to a date or time type, value2 is the number of days to add (integer) or an integer expression.

If the input is a TIME type, the days are added to that time of day on the current date. If it is a DATE type, the time of day will be midnight.

Example This statement adds 4 days and returns the adjusted date and time as midnight, 4 days later:

```
SELECT ADDDAY(CURRENT_DATE, 4)
FROM RDB$DATABASE;
```

Comment *See also ADDHOUR( ), ADDMINUTE( ), etc. For v.2.1 +, see internal function DATEADD( ).*

ADDHOUR (fbudf)

```
ADDHOUR (value1, value2) -- returns a TIMESTAMP
```

Adds a whole number of hours to a date or time type value and returns the adjusted date as a TIMESTAMP. The argument value1 is a column or expression that evaluates to a date or time type, value2 is the number of hours to add (integer) or an integer expression.

If the input is a TIME type, the hours are added to that time of day on the current date. If it is a DATE type, they are added to midnight of the current date. The adjusted TIMESTAMP is equivalent to `value1 + (value2/12)`).

Example This statement adds 10 hours and returns the adjusted date and time:

```
SELECT ADDHOUR(CURRENT_TIMESTAMP, 10)
FROM RDB$DATABASE;
```

Comment *See also ADDDAY( ), ADDMINUTE( ), etc. For v.2.1 +, see internal function DATEADD( ).*

ADDMILLISECOND (fbudf)

```
ADDMILLISECOND (value1, value2) -- returns a TIMESTAMP
```

Adds a whole number of milliseconds to a date or time type value and returns the adjusted date as a TIMESTAMP. The argument value1 is a column or expression that evaluates to a date or time type, value2 is the number of hours to add (integer) or an integer expression.

If the input is a TIME type, the milliseconds are added to that time of day on the current date. If it is a DATE type, the input time of day will be midnight.

Example This statement adds 61,234 milliseconds to the current system time. It effectively adds the milliseconds to the current system timestamp:

```
SELECT ADDMILLISECOND(CURRENT_TIME, 61234)
FROM RDB$DATABASE;
```

Comment *See also ADDDAY( ), ADDHOUR( ), etc. For v.2.1 +, see internal function DATEADD( ).*

ADDMINUTE (fbudf)

```
ADDMINUTE(value1, value2) -- returns a TIMESTAMP
```

Adds a whole number of minutes to a date or time type value and returns the adjusted date as a TIMESTAMP. The argument value1 is a column or expression that evaluates to a date or time type, value2 is the number of hours to add (integer) or an integer expression.

If the input is a TIME type, the minutes are added to that time of day on the current date. If it is a DATE type, the input time of day will be midnight.

Example This statement adds 45 minutes to the current system time. It effectively adds the minutes to the current system timestamp:

```
SELECT ADDMINUTE(CURRENT_TIME, 45)
FROM RDB$DATABASE;
```

Comment *See also ADDDAY( ), ADDHOUR( ), etc. For v.2.1 +, see internal function DATEADD( ).*

ADDMONTH (fbudf)

```
ADDMONTH(value1, value2) -- returns a TIMESTAMP
```

Adds a whole number of months to a date or time type value and returns the adjusted date as a TIMESTAMP. The argument value1 is a column or expression that evaluates to a date or time type, value2 is the number of hours to add (integer) or an integer expression.

The result is an adjusted TIMESTAMP that is (`value2`) calendar months later than `value1` .If the input is a TIME type, the months are added to that time of day on the current date. If it is a DATE type, the input time of day will be midnight.

Example This statement uses ADDMONTH( ) to calculate the term for a contract:

```
UPDATE CONTRACT SET FINAL_DATE =
  CASE CONTRACT_TERM
    WHEN 'HALF-YEARLY' THEN ADDMONTH(START_DATE, 6)
    --- (Cont.)
    WHEN 'YEARLY' THEN ADDMONTH(START_DATE, 12)
  ELSE
    ADDWEEK(START_DATE, TRUNCATE(CONTRACT_AMT/WEEKLY_FEE))
  END
WHERE START_DATE IS NOT NULL
  AND AMT_PAID IS NOT NULL
  AND WEEKLY_FEE IS NOT NULL
  AND CONTRACT_ID = 12345;
```

Comment *See also ADDDAY( ), ADDHOUR( ), etc. For v.2.1 +, see internal function DATEADD( ).*

ADDSECOND (fbudf) `ADDSECOND (value1, value2) -- returns a TIMESTAMP`

Adds a whole number of seconds to a date or time type value and returns the adjusted date as a TIMESTAMP. The argument `value1` is a column or expression that evaluates to a date or time type, `value2` is the number of seconds to add (integer) or an integer expression.

If the input is a TIME type, the seconds are added to that time of day on the current date. If it is a DATE type, the input time of day will be midnight.

Example This statement adds 120 seconds to the current system date. It effectively adds the seconds to midnight of the current system date:

```
SELECT ADDSECOND(CURRENT_DATE, 120) FROM RDB$DATABASE;
```

Comment *See also ADDDAY( ), ADDHOUR( ), etc. For v.2.1 +, see internal function DATEADD( ).*

ADDWEEK (fbudf) `ADDWEEK (value1, value2) -- returns a TIMESTAMP`

Adds a whole number of weeks to a date or time type value and returns the adjusted date as a TIMESTAMP. The argument `value1` is a column or expression that evaluates to a date or time type, `value2` is the number of weeks to add (integer) or an integer expression.

The returned value is an adjusted TIMESTAMP, equivalent to `(value1 + (7 * value2))`. If the input is a TIME type, the weeks are added to that time of day on the current date. If it is a DATE type, the input time of day will be midnight.

Example This statement calculates how many weeks' fees were paid, and uses it with ADDWEEK( ) to calculate the final date of a contract:

```
UPDATE CONTRACT
  SET FINAL_DATE = ADDWEEK(START_DATE, TRUNCATE(CONTRACT_AMT/WEEKLY_FEE))
  WHERE START_DATE IS NOT NULL
    AND AMT_PAID IS NOT NULL
    AND WEEKLY_FEE IS NOT NULL
    AND CONTRACT_ID = 12345;
```

Comment *See also ADDDAY( ), ADDHOUR( ), etc. For v.2.1 +, see internal function DATEADD( ).*

ADDYEAR (fbudf)

```
ADDYEAR (value1, value2) -- returns a TIMESTAMP
```

Adds a whole number of years to a date or time type value and returns the adjusted date as a TIMESTAMP. The argument `value1` is a column or expression that evaluates to a date or time type, `value2` is the number of years to add (integer) or an integer expression.

If the input is a TIME type, the years are added to that time of day on the current date. If it is a DATE type, the input time of day will be midnight.

Example This statement calculates the final date of a lease, given the starting date:

```
UPDATE LEASE
  SET FINAL_DATE = ADDYEAR(START_DATE, 5)
  WHERE START_DATE IS NOT NULL AND LEASE_ID = 12345;
```

Comment *See also ADDDAY( ), ADDHOUR( ), etc. For v.2.1 +, see internal function DATEADD( ).*

GetExactTimestamp (fbudf)

```
GETEXACTTIMESTAMP( ) -- returns a TIMESTAMP
```

Returns the system time as a TIMESTAMP, to the nearest millisecond. It takes no arguments.

In versions prior to v.2.1, the date and time context variable CURRENT_TIMESTAMP and the predefined date literal 'NOW' return system time only to the nearest second. For the older versions, GETEXACTTIMESTAMP() is the only way to get the exact system time.

Example

```
SELECT GETEXACTTIMESTAMP() AS TSTAMP FROM RDB$DATABASE;
```

String and Character Functions

If you are upgrading to Firebird 2.0 or higher, you should note that a number of the string functions in the *ib_udf* library have been enhanced to accept NULL inputs. The affected functions are ASCII_CHAR, LOWER, "LOWER", LPAD, LTRIM, RPAD, RTRIM, SUBSTR and SUBSTRLEN.

To behave correctly when passing NULL, these functions must be declared as in this example for ASCII_CHAR():

```
DECLARE EXTERNAL FUNCTION ascii_char
INTEGER NULL
RETURNS CSTRING(1) FREE_IT
ENTRY_POINT 'IB_UDF_ascii_char' MODULE_NAME 'ib_udf';
```

ASCII_CHAR (ib_udf)

```
ASCII_CHAR (value) -- returns a string
```

Returns the single-byte printable or non-printable ASCII character corresponding to the decimal value passed in `value`, which can be a column, constant, or expression of type SMALLINT or INTEGER.

Example This statement will insert a carriage return and a line feed into a column on every row of an external table:

```
UPDATE EXT_FILE SET EOL= ASCII_CHAR(13) || ASCII_CHAR(10);
```

Comment *Firebird 2.1 +, see internal function ASCII_CHAR( ).*

To ensure correct behaviour with the NULL signal enhancement for the input parameters of this function under v.2.0+ servers, refer to the note at the head of this section. If upgrading from an older server version, the declaration must be dropped and the function redeclared to include the NULL signal.

ASCII_VAL (ib_udf)

```
ASCII_VAL(value) -- returns an integer type
```

Returns the decimal ASCII value of the character passed in. The arguments **value** is a column, constant, or expression of type CHAR.

Example

```
SELECT ASCII_VAL('&') AS ASC_NUM FROM RDB$DATABASE;
```

Comment

Firebird 2.1 +, see internal function ASCII_VAL( )

LOWER (ib_udf)

```
LOWER (value) -- returns a string
```

Returns the input string converted to lower case characters. It works only with ASCII characters. The argument **value** is a column or expression that evaluates to an ASCII string of 32,765 bytes or less. The return value is a CHAR(n) or VARCHAR(n) of the same size as the input string.

Example

The following statement will return the string 'come and sit at my table':

```
SELECT LOWER('Come and Sit at MY TABLE') AS L_STRING
FROM RDB$DATABASE;
```

Comment

This function can receive and return up to 32,767 characters, the limit for a Firebird character string. Treat the limit as 32,765 characters unless you are certain that the result will never be returned into a VARCHAR( ) column or variable.

To ensure correct behaviour with the NULL signal enhancement for the input parameters of this function under v.2.0+ servers, refer to the note at the head of this section. If upgrading from an older server version, the declaration must be dropped and the function redeclared to include the NULL signal.

In Firebird 2.0, it is recommended you drop the old declaration of LOWER( ) and use the internal function LOWER( ) instead.

If you must continue to use the external function under Firebird 2.0 or later, drop the old declaration and redeclare it as "LOWER" (with the double quotes, see below).

"LOWER" (ib_udf)

```
"LOWER" (value) -- returns a string
```

In Firebird 2.0+, the redeclaration of the external function LOWER( ) with a double-quoted identifier is strongly recommended if you must keep using an external function for lower-casing a string, to avoid conflicting with the internally implemented LOWER( ) function.

It is an identifier change only: the function itself works exactly like the LOWER( ) ecternal function as described above. It is a case of dropping the function declaration and declaring it afresh with the surrounding double quotes.

Tip

The file `ib_sql2.sql` *in the /UDF/ directory of v.2+ installations has a script for this redeclaration.*

Comment

To ensure correct behaviour with the NULL signal enhancement for the input parameters of this function under v.2.0+ servers, refer to the note at the head of this section. If upgrading from an older server version, the declaration must be dropped and the function redeclared to include the NULL signal.

If you have a choice, use the internal function LOWER( ).

LPAD (ib_udf)

```
LPAD(value, length, in_char) -- returns a string
```

Prepends the given character **in_char** to the beginning of the input string, **value**, until the length of the result string becomes equal to the given number, **length**.

The **value** argument should be a column or expression that evaluates to a string not longer than (32767 - **length**) bytes.

The **length** argument should be an integer type or expression.

The **in_char** argument should be a single character, to be used as the padding character.

The result is A CHAR(n) OR VARCHAR(n), where n is the supplied length argument.

Example The following statement will return the string '##########RHUBARB':

```
SELECT LPAD('RHUBARB, 17, '#') AS LPADDED_STRING FROM RDB$DATABASE;
```

Comment *This function can receive and return up to 32,767 characters, the limit for a Firebird character string. Treat the limit as 32,765 characters unless you are certain that the result will never be returned into a VARCHAR( ) column or variable.*

To ensure correct behaviour with the NULL signal enhancement for the input parameters of this function under v.2.0+ servers, refer to the note at the head of this section. If upgrading from an older server version, the declaration must be dropped and the function redeclared to include the NULL signal.

See also RPAD( ). For v.2.1 +, see the internal function LPAD( ).

LTRIM (ib_udf)

```
LTRIM (value) -- returns a string
```

Removes leading spaces from the input string. The input argument `value` is a column or expression that evaluates to a string not longer than 32,767 bytes. The string returns a CHAR(n) OR VARCHAR(n) with no leading space characters.

This function can accept up to 32,765 bytes, including space characters, the limit for a Firebird VARCHAR.

Example The following Before Insert trigger fragment will trim any leading spaces from the input:

```
NEW.CHARACTER_COLUMN = LTRIM(NEW.CHARACTER_COLUMN);
```

Comment *To ensure correct behaviour with the NULL signal enhancement for the input parameters of this function under v.2.0+ servers, refer to the note at the head of this section. If upgrading from an older server version, the declaration must be dropped and the function redeclared to include the NULL signal.*

See also RTRIM( ) and, for v.2.0+, the internal function TRIM( ).

RPAD (ib_udf)

```
RPAD(value, length, in_char) -- returns a string
```

Appends the given character `in_char` to the end of the input string, `value`, until the length of the result string becomes equal to the given number, `length`.

The `value` argument should be a column or expression that evaluates to a string not longer than (32767 - `length`) bytes.

The `length` argument should be an integer type or expression.

The `in_char` argument should be a single character, to be used as the padding character.

The result is A CHAR(n) OR VARCHAR(n), where n is the supplied length argument.

Example The following statement will return the string 'Framboise***********'

```
TSRSELECT RPAD('Framboise, 20, '*') AS RPADDED_STRING
FROM RDB$DATABASE;
```

Comment *This function can receive and return up to 32,767 characters, the limit for a Firebird character string. Treat the limit as 32,765 characters unless you are certain that the result will never be returned into a VARCHAR( ) column or variable.*

To ensure correct behaviour with the NULL signal enhancement for the input parameters of this function under v.2.0+ servers, refer to the note at the head of this section. If upgrading from an older server version, the declaration must be dropped and the function redeclared to include the NULL signal.

See also LPAD( ). For v.2.1 +, see the internal function RPAD( ).

RTRIM* *(ib_udf)

```
RTRIM (value) -- returns a string
```

Removes trailing spaces from the input string. The input argument **value** is a column or expression that evaluates to a string not longer than 32,767 bytes. The string returns a CHAR(n) OR VARCHAR(n) with no trailing space characters.

This function can accept up to 32,765 bytes, including space characters, the limit for a Firebird VARCHAR.

Example The following Before Insert trigger fragment will trim anytrailing spaces from the input:

```
NEW.CHARACTER_COLUMN = RTRIM(NEW.CHARACTER_COLUMN);
```

Comment *To ensure correct behaviour with the NULL signal enhancement for the input parameters of this function under v.2.0+ servers, refer to the note at the head of this section. If upgrading from an older server version, the declaration must be dropped and the function redeclared to include the NULL signal.*

See also LTRIM( ) and, for v.2.0+, the internal function TRIM( ).

SRIGHT* *(fbudf)

```
SRIGHT (value, length) -- returns a string
```

Returns a substring from the supplied **value**, being the rightmost **length** characters in **value**. The **value** argument is a column or expression that evaluates to a string not longer than 32,767 bytes; **length** is an integer type or expression.

This function can accept up to 32,765 bytes, the limit for a Firebird VARCHAR.

Example The following statement will return the string 'fox jumps over the lazy dog.':

```
SELECT SRIGHT('The quick brown fox jumps over the lazy dog.', 28) AS R_STRING
FROM RDB$DATABASE;
```

Comment *See also SUBSTR( ), SUBSTRLEN( ), internal function SUBSTRING( ).*

STRLEN* *(ib_udf)

```
STRLEN (value) -- returns INTEGER
```

Returns the length of a string. The argument **value** is a column or expression that evaluates to a string not longer than 32,765 bytes. The integer return value is the count of characters in the string.

This function can accept up to 32,765 bytes, including space characters, the limit for a Firebird VARCHAR.

Example The following PSQL fragment returns the length of a column to a local variable:

```
...
DECLARE VARIABLE LEN INTEGER;
...
SELECT COL1, COL2, COL3 FROM ATABLE
INTO :V1, :V2, :V3;
LEN = STRLEN(V3);
...;
```

Comment *See also SUBSTRLEN( ). For v.2.1+, see the internal function CHARACTER_LENGTH( ).*

SUBSTR* *(ib_udf)

```
SUBSTR (value, pos1, pos2) -- returns a string
```

Returns a string consisting of the characters from **pos1** to **pos2** inclusively If **pos2** is past the end of the string, the function will return all characters from **pos1** to the end of the string.

The **value** argument is a column or expression that evaluates to a string. **pos1** and **pos2** are columns or expressions that evaluate to integer types. The function can accept up to 32,765 bytes, including space characters, the limit for a Firebird VARCHAR.

Example The following statement strips the first three characters from the string in COLUMNB and sets its value to be the string starting at position 4 and ending at position 100. If the string ends before position 100, the result will be all of the characters from position 4 to the end of the string:

```
UPDATE ATABLE
  SET COLUMNB = SUBSTR(COLUMNB, 4, 100)
WHERE...
```

Comment *If you are porting a legacy application written for InterBase, be aware that this implementation of SUBSTR( ) differs from that of SUBSTR( ) in the Borland distributions of the ib_udf library, which returns NULL when pos2 is past the end of the input string.*

To ensure correct behaviour with the NULL signal enhancement for the input parameters of this function under v.2.0+ servers, refer to the note at the head of this section. If upgrading from an older server version, the declaration must be dropped and the function redeclared to include the NULL signal.

This function is deprecated from v.1.5 forward, in favour of the internal function SUBSTRING( ).

See also SUBSTRLEN( ), RTRIM( ).

SUBSTRLEN (ib_udf)

```
SUBSTRLEN(value, startpos, length) -- returns a string
```

This function, deprecated by the internal function SUBSTRING( ) from v.1.5 forward, does not (as its name implies) return the length of anything. It returns a string of size `length` starting at startpos. The actual length of the string will be the lesser of the `length` argument and the number of characters from `startpos` to the end of the input `value`. The argument value is a column or expression that evaluates to a string not longer than 32,765 bytes; the other two arguments are integer constants or expressions.

Example The following statement takes the value of a column and updates it by removing the first three characters and, after that, removing any trailing characters if the remaining string is longer than 20 characters:

```
UPDATE ATABLE
  SET COLUMNB = SUBSTRLEN(COLUMNB, 4, 20)
WHERE...
```

Comment *To ensure correct behaviour with the NULL signal enhancement for the input parameters of this function under v.2.0+ servers, refer to the note at the head of this section. If upgrading from an older server version, the declaration must be dropped and the function redeclared to include the NULL signal.*

See also SUBSTR( ), RTRIM( ), and the internal functions SUBSTRING( ) (v.1.5+) and TRIM() (v.2.0+).

BLOB Functions

STRING2BLOB (fbudf)

```
STRING2BLOB (value) -- returns a BLOB of sub_type 1 (TEXT)
```

Takes a string field (column, variable, expression) and returns a text BLOB.The value argument is a column or expression that evaluates to a VARCHAR type of 300 characters or less.

Under most conditions in Firebird 1.5+, it will not be necessary to call this function. Firebird will accept a string that is within the byte-length limit of a VARCHAR directly as input to a BLOB.

Example This PSQL fragment concatenates two strings and converts the result to a text BLOB:

```
...
```

```
DECLARE VARIABLE V_COMMENT1 VARCHAR(250);
DECLARE VARIABLE V_COMMENT2 VARCHAR(45);
DECLARE VARIABLE V_MEMO VARCHAR(296) = '';
...
-- (Cont.)
SELECT <..other fields...>, COMMENT1, COMMENT2 FROM APPLICATION
WHERE APPLICATION_ID = :APP_ID
INTO <..other variables..>, :V_COMMENT1, V_COMMENT2;
IF (V_COMMENT1 IS NOT NULL) THEN
  V_MEMO = V_COMMENT1;
IF (V_COMMENT2 IS NOT NULL) THEN
BEGIN
  IF (V_MEMO = '') THEN
    V_MEMO = V_COMMENT2;
  ELSE
    V_MEMO = V_MEMO ||' '|| V_COMMENT2;
END
IF (V_MEMO <> '') THEN
  INSERT INTO MEMBERSHIP (FIRST_NAME, LAST_NAME, APP_ID, BLOB_MEMO)
  VALUES (
    :FIRST_NAME, :LAST_NAME, :APP_ID, STRING2BLOB(:V_MEMO));
...
```

Trigonometrical Functions

ACOS
(ib_udf)

```
ACOS (value) -- returns DOUBLE PRECISION
```

Calculates the arccosine (inverse of cosine) of a number between –1 and 1. If the number is out of bounds, it returns *NaN*. The **value** argument is a column or expression that is compatible with a signed or unsigned DOUBLE PRECISION number, evaluating to a valid cosine value. The return value is a DOUBLE PRECISION number, in degrees.

Example This snippet from a trigger converts a raw cosine value to degrees:

```
...
IF (NEW.RAW_VALUE IS NOT NULL) THEN
  NEW.READING1 = ACOS(NEW.RAW_VALUE);
```

Comment *See also COS( ), COSH( ), and other trigonometric functions. For v.2.1+, refer to the internal function of the same name.*

ASIN
(ib_udf)

```
ASIN (value) -- returns DOUBLE PRECISION
```

Calculates the arcsine (inverse of sine) of a number between –1 and 1. If the number is out of range, it returns *NaN*. The **value** argument is a column or expression that is compatible with a signed or unsigned DOUBLE PRECISION number, evaluating to a valid sine value. The return value is a DOUBLE PRECISION number, in degrees.

Example This snippet from a trigger converts a raw cosine value to degrees:

```
...
IF (NEW.RAW_VALUE IS NOT NULL) THEN
  NEW.READING1 = ASIN(NEW.RAW_VALUE);
```

Comment *See also SIN( ), SINH( ), and other trigonometric functions. For v.2.1+, refer to the internal function of the same name.*

ATAN (ib_udf)

```
ATAN (value) -- returns DOUBLE PRECISION
```

Returns the arctangent (inverse of tangent) of the input argument **value**, which is a column or expression resolving to a valid tan(gent) value compatible with a signed or unsigned DOUBLE PRECISION number. The return value is a DOUBLE PRECISION number, in degrees.

Example This snippet from a trigger converts a raw tan(gent) value to an arc, in degrees:

```
...
IF (NEW.RAW_VALUE IS NOT NULL) THEN
  NEW.READING1 = ATAN(NEW.RAW_VALUE);
```

Comment *See also ATAN2( ), TAN( ), TANH( ), and other trigonometric functions. For v.2.1+, refer to the internal function of the same name.*

ATAN2 (ib_udf)

```
ATAN2 (value1, value2) -- returns DOUBLE PRECISION
```

Returns a value that is an arc, in degrees, calculated as the arctangent of the result of dividing one tangent by another. The arguments **value1** and **value2** are both numeric columns or expressions evaluating as DOUBLE PRECISION numbers that are valid tan(gent) values. The return value is a DOUBLE PRECISION number, the result the arctangent of (value1/value2) in degrees.

Example This PSQL snippet stores a value that is an arc, in degrees, calculated as the arctangent of the result of dividing one tangent by another:

```
...
UPDATE HEAVENLY_HAPPENINGS
  SET INCREASE_RATIO = ATAN2(INITIAL_TAN, FINAL_TAN)
WHERE HAPPENING_ID = :happening_id;
```

Comment *See also ATAN( ), TAN( ), TANH( ). For v.2.1+, refer to the internal function of the same name.*

COS (ib_udf)

```
COS (value) -- returns DOUBLE PRECISION
```

Returns the cosine of value. The **value** argument is a column or expression that is compatible with a signed or unsigned DOUBLE PRECISION number, evaluating to a value (in degrees) between –263 and 263. The return value is a DOUBLE PRECISION number, or 0 if the input is out of range.

Important *If value is greater than or equal to 263, or less than or equal to -263, there is a loss of significance in the result of the call, and the function generates a _TLOSS error and returns a 0.*

Example This snippet from a trigger calculates and stores the cosine of an angular measurement input in degrees:

```
...
IF (NEW.READING1 IS NOT NULL) THEN
  NEW.RDG_COSINE = COS(NEW.READING1);
```

Comment *See also SIN( ), COS( ), ACOS( ), COSH( ). For v.2.1+, refer to the internal function of the same name.*

COSH (ib_udf)

```
COSH (value) -- returns DOUBLE PRECISION
```

Returns the hyperbolic cosine of value. The value argument is a column or expression that is compatible with a signed or unsigned DOUBLE PRECISION number, evaluating to a value (in degrees) between –263 and 263. The return value is a DOUBLE PRECISION number, or 0 if the input is out of range.

Important *If value is greater than or equal to 263, or less than or equal to -263, there is a loss of significance in the result of the call, and the function generates a _TLOSS error and returns a 0.*

Example This snippet from a trigger calculates and stores the hyperbolic cosine of an angular measurement input in degrees:

```
...
IF (NEW.READING1 IS NOT NULL) THEN
  NEW.RDG_COS_HYP = COSH(NEW.READING1);
```

Comment *See also SINH( ), TANH( ), and other trigonometric functions. For v.2.1+, refer to the internal function of the same name.*

COT* *(ib_udf) `COT (value) -- returns DOUBLE PRECISION`

Returns the cotangent of `value`. The `value` argument is a column or expression that is compatible with a signed or unsigned DOUBLE PRECISION number, evaluating to a value (in degrees) between –263 and 263. The return value is a DOUBLE PRECISION number, or 0 if the input is out of range.

Important *If value is greater than or equal to 263, or less than or equal to -263, there is a loss of significance in the result of the call, and the function generates a _TLOSS error and returns a 0 ("a quiet NaN").*

Example This snippet from a trigger calculates and stores the cotangent of an angular measurement input in degrees:

```
...
IF (NEW.READING1 IS NOT NULL) THEN
  NEW.RDG_COTAN = COT(NEW.READING1);
```

Comment *See also TAN( ), ATAN( ), TANH( ). For v.2.1+, refer to the internal function of the same name.*

SIN* *(ib_udf) `SIN (value) -- returns DOUBLE PRECISION`

Returns the sine of `value`. The value argument is a column or expression that is compatible with a signed or unsigned DOUBLE PRECISION number, evaluating to a value (in degrees) between –263 and 263. The return value is a DOUBLE PRECISION number, or 0 if the input is out of range.

Important *If value is greater than or equal to 263, or less than or equal to -263, there is a loss of significance in the result of the call, and the function generates a _TLOSS error and returns a 0 ("a quiet NaN").*

Example This snippet from a trigger calculates and stores the sine of an angular measurement input in degrees:

```
...
IF (NEW.READING1 IS NOT NULL) THEN
  NEW.RDG_SINE = SIN(NEW.READING1);
```

Comment *See also COS( ), ASIN( ), SINH( ). For v.2.1+, refer to the internal function of the same name.*

SINH* *(ib_udf) `SINH (value) -- returns DOUBLE PRECISION`

Returns the hyperbolic sine of `value`. The value argument is a column or expression that is compatible with a signed or unsigned DOUBLE PRECISION number, evaluating to a value (in degrees) between –263 and 263. The return value is a DOUBLE PRECISION number, or 0 if the input is out of range.

NotesIf value is greater than or equal to 263, or less than or equal to ?263, there is a loss of significance in the result of the call, and the function generates a _TLOSS error and returns a 0.

Important *If value is greater than or equal to 263, or less than or equal to -263, there is a loss of significance in the result of the call, and the function generates a _TLOSS error and returns a 0 ("a quiet NaN").*

Example This snippet from a trigger calculates and stores the hyperbolic sine of an angular measurement input in degrees:

```
...
IF (NEW.READING1 IS NOT NULL) THEN
    NEW.RDG_SIN_HYP = SINH(NEW.READING1);
```

Comment *See also SIN( ), TANH( ), COSH( ). For v.2.1+, refer to the internal function of the same name.*

TAN (ib_udf)

```
TAN (value) -- returns DOUBLE PRECISION
```

Returns the tangent of `value`. The `value` argument is a column or expression that is compatible with a signed or unsigned DOUBLE PRECISION number, evaluating to a value (in degrees) between –263 and 263. The return value is a DOUBLE PRECISION number, or 0 if the input is out of range.

Important *If value is greater than or equal to 263, or less than or equal to -263, there is a loss of significance in the result of the call, and the function generates a _TLOSS error and returns a 0 ("a quiet NaN").*

Example This snippet from a trigger calculates and stores the tangent of an angular measurement input in degrees:

```
...
IF (NEW.READING1 IS NOT NULL) THEN
  NEW.RDG_TAN = TAN(NEW.READING1);
```

Comment *See also COT( ), ATAN( ), TANH( ). For v.2.1+, refer to the internal function of the same name.*

TANH (ib_udf)

```
TANH (value) -- returns DOUBLE PRECISION
```

Returns the hyperbolic tangent of `value`. The `value` argument is a column or expression that is compatible with a signed or unsigned DOUBLE PRECISION number, evaluating to a value (in degrees) between –263 and 263. The return value is a DOUBLE PRECISION number, or 0 if the input is out of range.

Important *If value is greater than or equal to 263, or less than or equal to -263, there is a loss of significance in the result of the call, and the function generates a _TLOSS error and returns a 0.*

Example This snippet from a trigger calculates and stores the hyperbolic tangent of an angular measurement input in degrees:

```
...
IF (NEW.READING1 IS NOT NULL) THEN
  NEW.RDG_TAN_HYP = TANH(NEW.READING1);
```

Comment *See also TAN( ), ATAN( ). For v.2.1+, refer to the internal function of the same name.*

Building regular expressions

These guidelines are extracted from the ***Firebird 2.5 Language Reference Update***, by Paul Vinkenoog and other Firebird Project authors.

Characters

Within regular expressions, most characters represent themselves. The only exceptions are the special characters below:

```
[ ] ( ) | ^ - + * % _ ? {
```

...and the escape character, if it is defined.

A regular expression that doesn't contain any special or escape characters only matches strings that are identical to itself (subject to the collation in use). That is, it functions just like the "=" operator:

```
'Apple' similar to 'Apple' -- true
'Apples' similar to 'Apple' -- false
'Apple' similar to 'Apples' -- false
'APPLE' similar to 'Apple' -- depends on collation
```

Wildcards

The known SQL wildcards _ and % match any single character and a string of any length, respectively:

```
'Birne' similar to 'B_rne' -- true
'Birne' similar to 'B_ne' -- false
'Birne' similar to 'B%ne' -- true
'Birne' similar to 'Bir%ne%' -- true
'Birne' similar to 'Birr%ne' -- false
```

Notice how % also matches the empty string.

Character classes

A bunch of characters enclosed in brackets define a character class. A character in the string matches a class in the pattern if the character is a member of the class:

```
'Citroen' similar to 'Cit[arju]oen' -- true
'Citroen' similar to 'Ci[tr]oen' -- false
'Citroen' similar to 'Ci[tr][tr]oen' -- true
```

As can be seen from the second line, the class only matches a single character, not a sequence.

Within a class definition, two characters connected by a hyphen define a range. A range comprises the two endpoints and all the characters that lie between them in the active collation. Ranges can be placed anywhere in the class definition without special delimiters to keep them apart from the other elements.

```
'Datte' similar to 'Dat[q-u]e' -- true
'Datte' similar to 'Dat[abq-uy]e' -- true
'Datte' similar to 'Dat[bcg-km-pwz]e' -- false
```

The following predefined character classes can also be used in a class definition:

`[:ALPHA:]`

Latin letters a..z and A..Z. With an accent-insensitive collation, this class also matches accented forms of these characters.

`[:DIGIT:]`

Decimal digits 0..9.

`[:ALNUM:]`
Union of [:ALPHA:] and [:DIGIT:].

`[:UPPER:]`
Uppercase Latin letters A..Z. Also matches lowercase with case-insensitive collation and accented forms with accent-insensitive collation.

`[:LOWER:]`
Lowercase Latin letters a..z. Also matches uppercase with case-insensitive collation and accented forms with accent-insensitive collation.

`[:SPACE:]`
Matches the space character (ASCII 32).

`[:WHITESPACE:]`
Matches vertical tab (ASCII 9), linefeed (ASCII 10), horizontal tab (ASCII 11), formfeed (ASCII 12), carriage return (ASCII 13) and space (ASCII 32).

Including a predefined class has the same effect as including all its members. Predefined classes are only allowed within class definitions. If you need to match against a predefined class and nothing more, place an extra pair of brackets around it.

```
'Erdbeere' similar to 'Erd[[:ALNUM:]]eere' -- true
'Erdbeere' similar to 'Erd[[:DIGIT:]]eere' -- false
'Erdbeere' similar to 'Erd[a[:SPACE:]b]eere' -- true
'Erdbeere' similar to [[:ALPHA:]] -- false
'E' similar to [[:ALPHA:]] -- true
```

If a class definition starts with a caret, everything that follows is excluded from the class. All other characters match:

```
'Framboise' similar to 'Fra[^ck-p]boise' -- false
'Framboise' similar to 'Fr[^a][^a]boise' -- false
'Framboise' similar to 'Fra[^[:DIGIT:]]boise' -- true
```

If the caret is not placed at the start of the sequence, the class contains everything before the caret, except for the elements that also occur after the caret:

```
'Grapefruit' similar to 'Grap[a-m^f-i]fruit' -- true
'Grapefruit' similar to 'Grap[abc^xyz]fruit' -- false
'Grapefruit' similar to 'Grap[abc^de]fruit' -- false
'Grapefruit' similar to 'Grap[abe^de]fruit' -- false
'3' similar to '[[:DIGIT:]^4-8]' -- true
'6' similar to '[[:DIGIT:]^4-8]' -- false
```

Lastly, the already mentioned wildcard "_" is a character class of its own, matching any single character.

Quantifiers

A question mark immediately following a character or class indicates that the preceding item may occur 0 or 1 times in order to match:

```
'Hallon' similar to 'Hal?on' -- false
'Hallon' similar to 'Hal?lon' -- true
'Hallon' similar to 'Halll?on' -- true
'Hallon' similar to 'Hallll?on' -- false
'Hallon' similar to 'Halx?lon' -- true
'Hallon' similar to 'H[a-c]?llon[x-z]?' -- true
```

An asterisk immediately following a character or class indicates that the preceding item may occur 0 or more times in order to match:

```
'Icaque' similar to 'Ica*que' -- true
'Icaque' similar to 'Icar*que' -- true
```

```
'Icaque' similar to 'I[a-c]*que' -- true
'Icaque' similar to '_*' -- true
'Icaque' similar to '[[:ALPHA:]]*' -- true
'Icaque' similar to 'Ica[xyz]*e' -- false
```

A plus sign immediately following a character or class indicates that the preceding item must occur 1 or more times in order to match:

```
'Jujube' similar to 'Ju_+' -- true
'Jujube' similar to 'Ju+jube' -- true
'Jujube' similar to 'Jujuber+' -- false
'Jujube' similar to 'J[jux]+be' -- true
'Jujube' sililar to 'J[[:DIGIT:]]+ujube' -- false
```

If a character or class is followed by a number enclosed in braces, it must be repeated exactly that number of times in order to match:

```
'Kiwi' similar to 'Ki{2}wi' -- false
'Kiwi' similar to 'K[ipw]{2}i' -- true
'Kiwi' similar to 'K[ipw]{2}' -- false
'Kiwi' similar to 'K[ipw]{3}' -- true
```

If the number is followed by a comma, the item must be repeated at least that number of times in order to match:

```
'Limone' similar to 'Li{2,}mone' -- false
'Limone' similar to 'Li{1,}mone' -- true
'Limone' similar to 'Li[nezom]{2,}' -- true
```

If the braces contain two numbers separated by a comma, the second number not smaller than the first, then the item must be repeated at least the first number and at most the second number of times in order to match:

```
'Mandarijn' similar to 'M[a-p]{2,5}rijn' -- true
'Mandarijn' similar to 'M[a-p]{2,3}rijn' -- false
'Mandarijn' similar to 'M[a-p]{2,3}arijn' -- true
```

The quantifiers ?, * and + are shorthand for {0,1}, {0,} and {1,}, respectively.

OR-ing terms

Regular expression terms can be OR'ed with the | operator. A match is made when the argument string matches at least one of the terms:

```
'Nektarin' similar to 'Nek|tarin' -- false
'Nektarin' similar to 'Nektarin|Persika' -- true
'Nektarin' similar to 'M_+|N_+|P_+' -- true
```

Sub-expressions

One or more parts of the regular expression can be grouped into sub-expressions (also called sub-patterns) by placing them between parentheses. A sub-expression is a regular expression in its own right. It can contain all the elements allowed in a regular expression, and can also have quantifiers added to it.

```
'Orange' similar to 'O(ra|ri|ro)nge' -- true
'Orange' similar to 'O(r[a-e])+nge' -- true
'Orange' similar to 'O(ra){2,4}nge' -- false
'Orange' similar to 'O(r(an|in)g|rong)?e' -- true
```

Escaping special characters

In order to match against a character that is special in regular expressions, that character has to be escaped. There is no default escape character; rather, the user specifies one when needed:

```
'Peer (Poire)' similar to 'P[^ ]+ \(P[^ ]+\)' escape '\' -- true
'Pera [Pear]' similar to 'P[^ ]+ #[P[^ ]+#]' escape '#' -- true
'Päron-Äppledryck' similar to 'P%$-Ä%' escape '$' -- true
'Pärondryck' similar to 'P%--Ä%' escape '-' -- false
```

The last line demonstrates that the escape character can also escape itself, if needed.

APPENDIX

II

Reserved and Non-Reserved Keywords

Table II.1 contains keywords that are, or have been, reserved in some way in Firebird.

Not all keywords used in Firebird are covered by the SQL standards. The standard keywords are shown in **bold**.

Of those that are non-standard, most that were formerly reserved have been made non-reserved as releases have progressed. You can recognise them in the table by the designation "Y, NR" which translates as "Yes, it is a keyword but No, it is not reserved".

In some cases, you will notice a designation that includes the abbreviation "cont." That means the keyword is reserved in some contexts. What rules their "reservedness" is whether they are used as identifiers in a context where they conflict with language elements used in that context.

Keywords shown in square brackets, e.g. [BOOLEAN] are generally reserved words in the standards that Firebird has not implemented yet. It is not wise to use them as identifiers, since they are likely to be implemented in Firebird at some point. For example, it would be unwise to create a domain called BOOLEAN, since it is very likely that Firebird will have a native type of that name in future.

Keywords

Table II.1 Keywords Reserved and Not Reserved in Firebird SQL

Keyword	Firebird 2.5	2.1	2.0	1.5	1.0
A					
ABS	Y, NR	Y, NR	-	-	-
ACCENT	Y, NR	Y, NR	-	-	-
ACOS	Y, NR	Y, NR	-	-	-
ACTION	Y, NR	Y, NR	Y, NR	Y	Y
ACTIVE	Y	Y	Y	Y	Y
ADD	Y	Y	Y	Y	Y
ADMIN	Y	Y	Y	Y	Y

Keyword	Firebird 2.5	2.1	2.0	1.5	1.0
AFTER	Y	Y	Y	Y	Y
ALL	Y	Y	Y	Y	Y
ALTER	Y	Y	Y	Y	Y
ALWAYS	Y, NR	Y, NR	-	-	-
AND	Y	Y	Y	Y	Y
ANY	Y	Y	Y	Y	Y
ARE	Y	Y	Y	Y	Y
AS	Y	Y	Y	Y	Y
ASC | ASCENDING	Y	Y	Y	Y	Y
AT	Y	Y	Y	Y	Y
ASCII_CHAR	Y, NR	Y, NR	-	-	-
ASCII_VAL	Y, NR	Y, NR	-	-	-
ASIN	Y, NR	Y, NR	-	-	-
ATAN	Y, NR	Y, NR	-	-	-
ATAN2	Y, NR	Y, NR	-	-	-
AUTO	Y (cont.)	Y (cont.)	Y	Y	Y
AUTONOMOUS	Y, NR	-	-	-	-
AUTODDL	Y (cont.)	Y (cont.)	Y (cont.)	Y	Y
AVG	Y	Y	Y	Y	Y
B					
BACKUP	Y, NR	Y, NR	Y, NR	-	-
BASE	?	?	?	Y	Y
BASENAME	N	N	N	Y	Y
BASE_NAME	-	-	-	Y	Y
BEFORE	Y	Y	Y	Y	Y
BEGIN	Y	Y	Y	Y	Y
BETWEEN	Y	Y	Y	Y	Y
BIGINT	Y, NR	Y	Y	Y	Y
BIN_AND	Y, NR	Y, NR	-	-	-
BIN_NOT	Y, NR	Y, NR (v.2.1.1)	-	-	-
BIN_OR	Y, NR	Y, NR	-	-	-
BIN_SHL	Y, NR	Y, NR	-	-	-
BIN_SHR	Y, NR	Y, NR	-	-	-
BIN_XOR	Y, NR	Y, NR	-	-	-
BIT_LENGTH	Y	Y	Y	-	-
BLOB				Y	Y
BLOBEDIT				Y	Y
BLOCK	Y, NR	Y, NR	Y, NR	-	-
[BOOLEAN	-	-	-	-	-
BOTH	Y, NR	Y, NR	Y	-	-
BREAK				Y, NR	Y
BUFFER				Y	Y
BY				Y	Y

Keyword	Firebird 2.5	2.1	2.0	1.5	1.0
C					
CACHE	N	N	N	Y	Y
CALLER	Y, NR	-	-	-	-
CASCADE	Y, NR	Y, NR	Y, NR	Y	Y
CASE	Y	Y	Y	Y	-
CAST				Y	Y
CEIL | CEILING	Y, NR	Y, NR	-	-	-
CHAR | CHARACTER				Y	Y
CHAR_LENGTH	Y	Y	Y	-	-
CHARACTER_LENGTH	Y	Y	Y	-	-
CHAR_TO_UUID	Y, NR	-	-	-	-
CHECK	Y	Y	Y	Y	Y
CHECK_POINT_LEN	N	N	N	Y	Y
CHECK_POINT_LENGTH				Y	Y
CLOSE	Y	Y	Y	-	-
COALESCE	Y(con.)	Y(con.)	Y (con.)	Y	Y
COLLATE				Y	Y
COLLATION	Y, NR	Y, NR	Y, NR	-	-
COLUMN				Y	Y
COMMENT	Y, NR	Y, NR	Y, NR	-	-
COMMIT				Y	Y
COMMITTED				Y	Y
COMMON	Y, NR				
COMPILETIME				Y	Y
COMPUTED				Y	Y
CONDITIONAL				Y	Y
CONNECT	Y	Y	-	-	-
CONSTRAINT				Y	Y
CONTAINING				Y	Y
CONTINUE				Y	Y
COS	Y, NR	Y, NR	-	-	-
COSH	Y, NR	Y, NR	-	-	-
COT	Y, NR	Y, NR	-	-	-
COUNT	Y	Y	Y	Y	Y
CREATE	Y	Y	Y	Y	Y
CROSS	Y	Y	-	-	-
CSTRING	N	N	N	Y	Y
CURRENT	Y	Y	Y	Y	Y
CURRENT_CONNECTION	Y, NR	Y	Y	Y	Y
CURRENT_DATE	Y	Y	Y	Y	Y
CURRENT_ROLE	Y, NR	Y	Y	Y	Y
CURRENT_TIME	Y	Y	Y	Y	Y
CURRENT_TIMESTAMP	Y	Y	Y	Y	Y

Keyword	**Firebird 2.5**	**2.1**	**2.0**	**1.5**	**1.0**
CURRENT_TRANSACTION	Y, NR	Y	Y	Y	Y
CURRENT_USER	Y	Y	Y	Y	Y
CURSOR	Y	Y	Y	Y	Y
D					
DATA	Y, NR	-	-	-	-
DATABASE	Y, NR	Y	Y	Y	Y
DATE	Y	Y	Y	Y	Y
DATEADD	Y, NR	Y, NR	-	-	-
DATEDIFF	Y, NR	Y, NR	-	-	-
DAY	Y	Y	Y	Y	Y
DB_KEY	Y	Y	Y	Y	Y
DEBUG	Y, NR	Y	Y	Y	Y
DEC	Y	Y	Y	Y	Y
DECIMAL	Y	Y	Y	Y	Y
DECLARE	Y	Y	Y	Y	Y
DECODE	Y, NR	Y, NR	-	-	-
DEFAULT	Y	Y	Y	Y	Y
[DEFERRED]	-	-	-	N	N
DELETE	Y	Y	Y	Y	Y
DELETING (con.)	Y (con.)	Y (con.)	Y (con.)	Y	-
DESC | DESCENDING				Y	Y
DIFFERENCE	Y, NR	Y, NR	Y, NR	-	-
DESCRIBE	Y	Y	Y	Y	Y
DESCRIPTOR	Y, NR	Y, NR	Y, NR	Y, NR	Y
DISCONNECT	Y	Y	-	-	-
DISPLAY	N	N	N	Y	Y
DISTINCT	Y	Y	Y	Y	Y
DO	Y	Y	Y	Y	Y
DOMAIN	Y	Y	Y	Y	Y
DOUBLE	Y	Y	Y	Y	Y
DROP	Y	Y	Y	Y	Y
E					
ECHO	Y, NR	Y, NR	Y	Y	Y
EDIT	Y, NR	Y, NR	Y	Y	Y
ELSE	Y	Y	Y	Y	Y
END	Y	Y	Y	Y	Y
ENTRY_POINT	Y, NR	Y, NR	Y	Y	Y
ESCAPE	Y	Y	Y	Y	Y
EVENT	Y, NR	Y, NR	Y	Y	Y
EXCEPTION	Y	Y	Y	Y	Y
EXECUTE	Y	Y	Y	Y	Y
EXISTS	Y	Y	Y	Y	Y
EXIT	Y	Y	Y	Y	Y

Keyword	Firebird 2.5	2.1	2.0	1.5	1.0
EXP	Y, NR	Y, NR	-	-	-
EXTERN	?	?	?	Y	Y
EXTERNAL	Y	Y	Y	Y	Y
EXTRACT	Y	Y	Y	Y	Y
F					
[FALSE]	-	-	-	-	-
FETCH	Y	Y	Y	Y	Y
FILE				Y	Y
FILTER				Y	Y
FIRST	Y, NR	Y, NR	Y, NR	Y, NR	Y
FIRSTNAME	Y, NR	-	-	-	-
FLOAT	Y	Y	Y	Y	Y
FLOOR	Y, NR	Y, NR	-	-	-
FOR	Y	Y	Y	Y	Y
FOREIGN	Y	Y	Y	Y	Y
FOUND	Y	Y	Y	Y	Y
FREE_IT	Y, NR	Y, NR	Y	Y	Y
FROM	Y	Y	Y	Y	Y
FULL	Y	Y	Y	Y	Y
FUNCTION	Y	Y	Y	Y	Y
G					
GDSCODE	Y	Y	Y	Y	Y
GENERATED	Y, NR	Y, NR	-	-	-
GENERATOR	Y, NR	Y, NR	Y, NR	Y	Y
GEN_ID	Y	Y	Y	Y	Y
GEN_UUID	Y, NR	Y, NR	-	-	-
GLOBAL	Y	Y	N	N	N
GOTO	Y, NR	Y, NR	Y, NR	Y	Y
GRANT	Y	Y	Y	Y	Y
GRANTED	Y, NR	-	-	-	-
GROUP	Y	Y	Y	Y	Y
GROUP_COMMIT_WAIT	N	N	N	Y	Y
GROUP_COMMIT_WAIT_TIME	?	?	?	Y	Y
H					
HASH	Y, NR	Y, NR	-	-	-
HAVING	Y	Y	Y	Y	Y
HEADING	?	?	?	Y	Y
HELP	?	?	?	Y	Y
HOUR	Y	Y	Y	Y	Y
I					
IF	Y	Y	Y	Y	Y
IIF	Y, NR	Y, NR	Y, NR	N	Y
IMMEDIATE	Y	Y	Y	Y	Y

Keyword	Firebird 2.5	2.1	2.0	1.5	1.0
IN	Y	Y	Y	Y	Y
INACTIVE	Y (con.)	Y (con.)	Y	Y	Y
INDEX	Y	Y	Y	Y	Y
INDICATOR	Y	Y	Y	Y	Y
INIT	Y, NR	Y, NR	Y, NR	Y	Y
INNER	Y	Y	Y	Y	Y
INPUT	Y	Y	Y	Y	Y
INPUT_TYPE	?	?	?	Y	Y
INSENSITIVE	Y	Y	-	-	-
INSERT	Y	Y	Y	Y	Y
INSERTING	Y (con.)	Y (con.)	Y (con.)	Y	-
INT	Y	Y	Y	Y	Y
INTEGER	Y	Y	Y	Y	Y
INTO	Y	Y	Y	Y	Y
IS	Y	Y	Y	Y	Y
ISOLATION	Y	Y	Y	Y	Y
ISQL	?	?	?	Y	Y
J					
JOIN	Y	Y	Y	Y	Y
K					
KEY	Y	Y	Y	Y	Y
L					
LAST	Y (con.)	Y (con.)	Y (con.)	Y	-
LASTNAME	Y, NR	-	-	-	-
LC_MESSAGES	?	?	?	Y	Y
LC_TYPE	?	?	?	Y	Y
LEADING	Y	Y	-	-	-
LEAVE	Y (con.)	Y (con.)	Y (con.)	Y	-
LEFT	Y	Y	Y	Y	Y
LENGTH	Y, NR	Y, NR	Y, NR	Y	Y
LEV	?	?	?	Y	Y
LEVEL	Y	Y	Y	Y	Y
LIKE	Y	Y	Y	Y	Y
LIST	Y, NR	Y, NR	-	-	-
LN	Y, NR	Y, NR	-	-	-
LOCK	Y (con.)	Y (con.)	Y (con.)	Y	-
LOG	Y, NR	Y, NR	-	-	-
LOG10	Y, NR	Y, NR	-	-	-
LOGFILE	N	N	N	Y	Y
LOG_BUFFER_SIZE	?	?	?	Y	Y
LOG_BUF_SIZE	N	N	N	Y	Y
LONG	Y	Y	Y	Y	Y

Keyword	Firebird 2.5	2.1	2.0	1.5	1.0
LOWER	Y	Y	Y	-	-
LPAD	Y, NR	Y, NR	-	-	-
M					
MANUAL	?	?	?	Y	Y
MAPPING	Y, NR	-	-	-	-
MATCHED	Y, NR	Y, NR	-	-	-
MATCHING	Y, NR	Y, NR	-	-	-
MAX	Y	Y	Y	Y	Y
MAXIMUM	?	?	?	Y	Y
MAXIMUM_SEGMENT	?	?	?	Y	Y
MAX_SEGMENT	?	?	?	Y	Y
MAXVALUE	Y, NR	Y, NR	-	-	-
MERGE	Y	Y	Y	Y	Y
MESSAGE	?	?	?	Y	Y
MIDDLENAME	Y, NR	-	-	-	-
MIN	Y	Y	Y	Y	Y
MINIMUM	?	?	?	Y	Y
MINUTE	Y	Y	Y	Y	Y
MINVALUE	Y, NR	Y, NR	-	-	-
MOD	Y, NR	Y, NR	-	-	-
MODULE_NAME	?	?	?	Y	Y
MONTH	Y	Y	Y	Y	Y
N					
NAMES	Y	Y	Y	Y	Y
NATIONAL	Y	Y	Y	Y	Y
NATURAL	Y	Y	Y	Y	Y
NCHAR	Y	Y	Y	Y	Y
NEXT	Y, NR	Y, NR	Y, NR	-	-
NO	Y	Y	Y	Y	Y
NOAUTO	?	?	?	Y	Y
NOT	Y	Y	Y	Y	Y
NULL	Y	Y	Y	Y	Y
NULLIF	Y (con.)	Y (con.)	Y (con.)	Y	-
NULLS	Y (con.)	Y (con.)	Y (con.)	Y	-
NUM_LOG_BUFS	N	N	N	Y	Y
NUM_LOG_BUFFERS	?	?	?	Y	Y
NUMERIC	Y	Y	Y	Y	Y
O					
OCTET_LENGTH	Y	Y	Y	-	-
OF	Y	Y	Y	Y	Y
ON	Y	Y	Y	Y	Y
ONLY	Y	Y	Y	Y	Y
OPEN	Y	Y	Y	-	-

Keyword	Firebird 2.5	2.1	2.0	1.5	1.0
OPTION	Y	Y	Y	Y	Y
OR	Y	Y	Y	Y	Y
ORDER	Y	Y	Y	Y	Y
OS_NAME	Y, NR	-	-	-	-
OUTER	Y	Y	Y	Y	Y
OUTPUT	Y	Y	Y	Y	Y
OUTPUT_TYPE	?	?	?	Y	Y
OVERFLOW	?	?	?	Y	Y
OVERLAY	Y, NR	Y, NR	-	-	-
P					
PAD	Y, NR	Y, NR	-	-	-
PAGE	?	?	?	Y	Y
PAGELENGTH	?	?	?	Y	Y
PAGES	?	?	?	Y	Y
PAGE_SIZE	?	?	?	Y	Y
PARAMETER	Y	Y	Y	Y	Y
PASSWORD	?	?	?	Y	Y
PI	Y, NR	Y, NR	-	-	-
PLACING	Y, NR	Y, NR	-	-	-
PLAN	Y	Y	Y	Y	Y
POSITION	Y	Y	Y	Y	Y
POST_EVENT	Y	Y	Y	Y	Y
POWER	Y, NR	Y, NR	-	-	-
PRECISION	Y	Y	Y	Y	Y
PREPARE	Y	Y	Y	Y	Y
PRESERVE	Y, NR	Y, NR	-	-	-
PRIMARY	Y	Y	Y	Y	Y
PRIVILEGES	Y	Y	Y	Y	Y
PROCEDURE	Y	Y	Y	Y	Y
PUBLIC	Y	Y	Y	Y	Y
Q					
QUIT	Y (cont.)	Y (cont.)	Y (cont.)	Y	Y
R					
RAND	Y, NR	Y, NR	-	-	-
RAW_PARTITIONS	N	N	N	Y	Y
RDB$DB_KEY	?	?	?	Y	Y
READ	Y	Y	Y	Y	Y
REAL	Y	Y	Y	Y	Y
RECORD_VERSION	Y	Y	Y	Y	Y
RECREATE	Y	Y	Y	Y	Y
RECURSIVE	Y	Y	-	-	-
REFERENCES	Y	Y	Y	Y	Y

Keyword	Firebird 2.5	2.1	2.0	1.5	1.0
RELEASE	Y	Y	Y	Y	Y
REPLACE	Y, NR	Y, NR	-	-	-
RESERVE	Y	Y	Y	Y	Y
RESERVING	Y	Y	Y	Y	Y
RESTART	Y, NR	Y, NR	Y, NR	-	-
RESTRICT	-	-	-	Y	Y
RETAIN	Y	Y	Y	Y	Y
RETURN	?	?	?	Y	Y
RETURNING	Y, NR	Y, NR	Y, NR	-	-
RETURNING_VALUES	Y	Y	Y	Y	Y
RETURNS	Y	Y	Y	Y	Y
REVERSE	Y, NR	Y, NR	-	-	-
REVOKE	Y	Y	Y	Y	Y
RIGHT	Y	Y	Y	Y	Y
ROLE	Y, NR	Y, NR	Y, NR	Y	Y
ROLLBACK	Y	Y	Y	Y	Y
ROUND	Y, NR	Y, NR	-	-	-
ROW_COUNT	Y	Y	Y	Y	-
ROWS	Y	Y	Y	-	-
RPAD	Y, NR	Y, NR	-	-	-
RUNTIME	?	?	?	Y	Y
S					
SAVEPOINT	Y	Y	Y	Y	-
SCALAR_ARRAY	Y, NR	Y, NR	Y, NR	-	-
SCHEMA	[Y]	[Y]	[Y]	[Y]	[Y]
SECOND	Y	Y	Y	Y	Y
SELECT	Y	Y	Y	Y	Y
SENSITIVE	Y	Y	-	-	-
SEQUENCE	Y, NR	Y, NR	Y, NR	-	-
SET	Y	Y	Y	Y	Y
SHADOW	Y, NR	Y, NR	Y	Y	Y
SHARED	?	?	?	Y	Y
SHELL	?	?	?	Y	Y
SHOW	?	?	?	Y	Y
SIGN	Y, NR	Y, NR	-	-	-
SIMILAR	Y	-	-	-	-
SIN	Y, NR	Y, NR	-	-	-
SINGULAR	Y	Y	Y	Y	Y
SIZE	Y	Y	Y	Y	Y
SKIP	Y, NR	Y, NR	Y, NR	Y, NR	Y
SMALLINT	Y	Y	Y	Y	Y
SNAPSHOT	Y, NR	Y, NR	Y	Y	Y
SOME	Y	Y	Y	Y	Y

Keyword	Firebird 2.5	2.1	2.0	1.5	1.0
SORT	?	?	?	Y	Y
SOURCE	Y, NR	-	-	-	-
SPACE	Y, NR	Y, NR	-	-	-
SQL	Y, NR	Y, NR	Y, NR	Y	Y
SQRT	Y, NR	Y, NR	-	-	-
SQLCODE	Y	Y	Y	Y	Y
SQLERROR	Y	Y	Y	Y	Y
SQLWARNING	Y	Y	Y	Y	Y
SQLSTATE	Y	-	-	-	-
STABILITY	Y	Y	Y	Y	Y
START	Y	Y	-	-	-
STARTING	Y	Y	Y	Y	Y
STARTS	Y	Y	Y	Y	Y
STATEMENT	Y (con.)	Y (con.)	Y (con.)	Y	-
STATIC	?	?	?	Y	Y
STATISTICS	Y, NR	Y, NR	Y, NR	Y	Y
SUB_TYPE				Y	Y
SUBSTRING	Y, NR	Y, NR	Y, NR	Y, NR	Y
SUM	Y	Y	Y	Y	Y
SUSPEND	Y (con.)	Y (con.)	Y	Y	Y
T					
TABLE	Y	Y	Y	Y	Y
TAN	Y, NR	Y, NR	-	-	-
TANH	Y, NR	Y, NR	-	-	-
TEMPORARY	Y, NR	Y, NR	-	-	-
TERM	Y (con.)	Y (con.)	Y (con.)	Y	Y
TERMINATOR	Y (con.)	Y (con.)	Y (con.)	Y	Y
THEN	Y	Y	Y	Y	Y
TIME	Y	Y	Y	Y	Y
TIMESTAMP	Y	Y	Y	Y	Y
TO	Y	Y	Y	Y	Y
TRAILING	Y	Y	Y	-	-
TRANSACTION	Y	Y	Y	Y	Y
TRANSLATE	Y	Y	Y	Y	Y
TRANSLATION	Y	Y	Y	Y	Y
TRIGGER	Y	Y	Y	Y	Y
TRIM	Y	Y	Y	-	-
[TRUE]	-	-	-	-	-
TRUNC	Y, NR	Y, NR	-	-	-
TWO_PHASE	Y, NR	-	-	-	-
TYPE	N	N	N	Y	Y
U					
UNCOMMITTED	?	?	?	Y	Y

Keyword	Firebird 2.5	2.1	2.0	1.5	1.0
UNION	Y	Y	Y	Y	Y
UNIQUE	Y	Y	Y	Y	Y
[UNKNOWN]	-	-	-	-	-
UPDATE	Y	Y	Y	Y	Y
UPDATING	Y (con.)	Y (con.)	Y (con.)	Y	-
UPPER	Y	Y	Y	Y	Y
USER	Y	Y	Y	Y	Y
USING	Y	Y (con.)	Y (con.)	N	-
UUID_TO_CHAR	Y, NR	-	-	-	-
V					
VALUE	Y	Y	Y	Y	Y
VALUES	?	?	?	Y	Y
VARCHAR	Y	Y	Y	Y	Y
VARIABLE	Y	Y	Y	Y	Y
VARYING	Y	Y	Y	Y	Y
VERSION	?	?	?	Y	Y
VIEW	Y	Y	Y	Y	Y
W					
WAIT	Y, NR	Y	Y	Y	Y
WEEK	Y, NR	Y, NR	-	-	-
WEEKDAY	Y, NR	Y, NR	Y, NR	Y	Y
WHEN	Y	Y	Y	Y	Y
WHENEVER	Y	Y	Y	Y	Y
WHERE	Y	Y	Y	Y	Y
WHILE	Y	Y	Y	Y	Y
WITH	Y	Y	Y	Y	Y
WORK	Y	Y	Y	Y	Y
WRITE	Y	Y	Y	Y	Y
Y					
YEAR	Y	Y	Y	Y	Y
YEARDAY	Y, NR	Y, NR	Y, NR	Y	Y

APPENDIX

III

CONTEXT VARIABLES

Context variables are system-maintained variable values in the context of the current client connection and its activity.

About Context Variables

The context variables listed below in Table III.1, ***Available context variables***, are available for use in DDL, DML and PSQL. Some are available only in PSQL and most are available only in Dialect 3 databases.

Table III.1 Available context variables

Context variable	Data type	Description	Availability
CURRENT_CONNECTION	INTEGER	System ID of the connection that is making this query	Firebird 1.5 onward, DSQL and PSQL
CURRENT_DATE	DATE	Current date on the host server's clock	All versions, all SQL environments
CURRENT_ROLE	VARCHAR(31)	The ROLE name under which the CURRENT_USER is logged in, returns empty string if the current log-in isn't using a role.	All versions, all SQL environments
CURRENT_TIME	TIME	Current time on the server's clock, expressed as seconds since midnight	All versions, all SQL environments, Dialect 3 only
CURRENT_TIMESTAMP	TIMESTAMP	Current date and time on the host server's clock to the nearest second	All versions, all SQL environments
CURRENT_TRANSACTION	INTEGER	System ID of the transaction in which this query is being requested	Firebird 1.5 onward, DSQL and PSQL
CURRENT_USER	VARCHAR(128)	User name that is communicating through this instance of the client library	All versions, all SQL environments

Context variable	Data type	Description	Availability
ROW_COUNT	INTEGER	Count of rows changed/deleted/added by a DML statement, available when the operation is complete	Firebird 1.5 onward, stored procedure language (PSQL) only
UPDATING	BOOLEAN	Returns true if an UPDATE statement is executing	Firebird 1.5 onward, trigger dialect of PSQL only
INSERTING	BOOLEAN	Returns true if an INSERT statement is executing	Firebird 1.5 onward, trigger dialect of PSQL only
DELETING	BOOLEAN	Returns true if a DELETE statement is executing	Firebird 1.5 onward, trigger dialect of PSQL only
SQLCODE	INTEGER	Returns the SQLCODE inside a WHEN exception block. For usage see Chapter 32, Handling and Events	Firebird 1.5 onward, procedure language (PSQL) only
GDSCODE	INTEGER NOTE: use the symbolic name to test.	Returns the GDSCODE inside a WHEN exception block. For usage see Chapter 32, Error Handling and Events	Firebird 1.5 onward, procedure language (PSQL) only
USER	VARCHAR(128)	User name that is communicating through this instance of the client library	All versions, all SQL environments. Available in Dialects 1 and 3.

APPENDIX

IV

FIREBIRD LIMITS

Most of the actual limits on a Firebird database are practical rather than defined by the software. For example, you can define up to 32,767 columns in a table, but why would you want to? Listed in Table IV.1 are a number of theoretical and practical limits applicable to the various versions of Firebird. Limits do change as on-disk structure versions progress, so make a point of studying release notes to track changes.

Table IV.1 Firebird Limits

Object	Item	Version	Limit	Comments
Identifiers	Maximum length	All	31 characters for almost all object types	Cannot use characters outside the range of US ASCII (ASCIIZ) unless double-quoted. Double-quoted identifiers cannot be used in dialect 1 databases.
		ODS < 11	27 characters for constraint names	As above
Dates	Earliest date	All	January 1, 100 A.D.	
	Latest date	All	December 31, 9999 A.D	It is believed that the engine is susceptible to crashing if the system date of the server is set higher than the year 2039.
Server	Maximum connected clients: TCP/IP	All	1,024	Work on a base maximum of about 150 concurrent Superserver clients for a normal interactive application on a server of low-to-medium specification, with low-to-moderate contention, before performance might make you consider upgrading. For Classic server, the numbers may be lower because each client consumes more resources.
Server (cont.)	Maximum connected clients: NetBEUI	All	930 approx.	

Object	Item	Version	Limit	Comments
	Maximum number of databases open in one transaction	All		The number of databases opened during a transaction started by isc_start_multiple() is limited only by available system resources. A transaction started by isc_start_transaction() limits concurrent database attachments to 16.
Database	Number of tables	All	32,767	
	Maximum size	All	7 TB approx.	Theoretical limit, approximate. There is no known record of a Firebird database as large as 7TB.
	Maximum file size	All		Depends on the file system. FAT32 and ext2 are 2GB. Older NTFS and some ext3 are usually 4GB. Many 64-bit file systems place no limit on the size of a shared-access file.
	Maximum number of files per database	All	Theoretically, 216 (65,536), including shadow files)	The limitation is more likely to be imposed by the operating system's limit on the number of files that can be opened simultaneously by one process. Some permit the limit to be raised.
	Maximum page_size	v.1.5+ (ODS 10.1+)	16,384 bytes	Other sizes are 1,024, 2,048, 4,096 (default), and 8192 bytes. V.2.0 and higher will not create databases with page_size smaller than 4,094 bytes.
		ODS 10.0	8,192 bytes	
	Maximum cache buffers	ODS 11+	128,000 pages	Practical limit depends on available RAM. The total size (cache pages * page_size on Superserver; cache pages * page_size * no. of concurrent users on Classic server) should never be more than half of the available RAM. Consider 10,000 pages as a practical limit and tweak backward or forward from there as performance dictates.
		ODS 10.x	65,536 pages	...
Tables	Maximum versions per table	All	255	Firebird keeps account of up to 255 formats for each table. The format version steps up by 1 each time a metadata change is done. When any table reaches the limit, the whole database becomes unavailable—it must be backed up and then work resumed on the restored version.
Tables (cont.)	Maximum row size: user tables	All	64 KB	Count bytes. BLOB and ARRAY columns each cost 8 bytes to store the ID; VARCHARs, byte length + 2; CHARs, byte-length; SMALLINT, 2; INTEGER, FLOAT, DATE and TIME, 4; BIGINT, DOUBLE PRECISION and TIMESTAMP, 8; NUMERIC and DECIMAL, 4 or 8, depending on precision.
	Maximum row size: system tables	All	128 KB	

Object	Item	Version	Limit	Comments
	Maximum number of rows	ODS 11+	2^{63} - 1	Rows are enumerated with a 32-bit unsigned integer per table and a 32-bit row slot index. A table with long rows—either a lot of fields or very long fields—will store fewer records than a table with very short rows. All rows—including deleted ones—use up numbers; BLOBs and BLOB fragments stored on table data pages use up numbers, too.
		ODS 10.x	2^{32} rows, more or less, to a maximum table size of 30GB	
	Maximum number of columns	All		Depends on data types used (see Maximum row size).
	Maximum indexes per table	ODS 10.1+		256
		ODS 10.0		64
	Maximum size of external file			4GB on Windows NTFS, 2GB on Windows FAT32, Linux ext2 and ext3, and Solaris.
Indexes	Theoretical maximum size: applies to a single-column index, where the character set is single-byte and uses the default (binary) collation sequence.	ODS 11+	One quarter of the page_size	Count bytes, not characters. The practical maximum is reduced by compound indexing, multi-byte character sets, and complex collation sequences. A single-column index using 3-byte UNICODE_FSS characters, for example, can have a maximum of (2048/3) = 682 characters on a database with a page_size of 8192. Some ISO8859 collation sequences consume up to 4 bytes per character just for the sorting attributes.
		ODS 10.x	252 bytes	...
	Maximum number of segments	All	16	
Queries	Maximum joined tables	All	Theoretically, 256	Other factors come to bear, such as the number of Boolean evaluations required by the joins. From the point of view of resources and performance, the largest practicable number of table references is probably around 16. Always test with realistic volumes and kinds of data.
	Maximum nesting level	Any	No theoretical limit	Deep nesting of subqueries is sub-optimal for performance. Performance and resource consumption will determine your practical limit, on a query-by-query basis.
	Maximum size of ORDER BY key-set data	All	32KB	...

Object	Item	Version	Limit	Comments
PSQL modules	Maximum size of BLR	All	48KB	Stored procedure and trigger sources are compiled into BLR bytecode, which is more dense than the PSQL source. Still, if you hit this limit, try to break up your monumental procedure into a "master" procedure with callable chunks.
	Maximum number of events per module	Any	No limit	Practical limit is related to the length limit for BLR byte code (above).
	Levels of embedded calls: POSIX	All	1,000	...
	Levels of embedded calls: Windows	All	750	...
BLOBs	Maximum BLOB size	Any	Depends on page_size	For a 2KB page size, the BLOB size maximum is 512MB. For a 4KB page size, the BLOB size maximum is 4GB. For a 8KB page size, it is 32GB, and for a 16KB page size, it is 256GB.
	Maximum segment size	Any	Theoretically, 64KB	BLOBs are stored in segments. However, in DSQL, it is not essential to define a non-default segment size, since client settings cause BLOB data to be segmented for transport according to network packet size. Server economics determine the actual size of segments in storage.

APPENDIX

V

SYSTEM TABLES AND VIEWS

When you create a database, Firebird begins by building its own tables in which to store the metadata for all database objects—not just your user-defined objects but also its own internal objects, whose identifiers are prefixed with 'RDB$'. All versions have the metadata tables.

From version 2.1 forward, databases also contain the definitions for the monitoring tables, prefixed with the characters "MON$". See ***Monitoring Tables*** on page 392.

Metadata Tables

The descriptions in this section are intended to assist with designing queries that you can use to help you understand and administer your databases.

> *There are DDL statements (CREATE, ALTER, etc.) for changing metadata. It is not recommended at all to use DML statements to update system tables. The risk of corruption from doing so is extreme.*
>
> *In a future release—probably v.3.0—the system tables will be made read-only.*

Following the metadata definitions for the system tables, you will find DDL listings for a number of views over the system that you might find useful.

The following abbreviations are used in the tables:

- IDX: Indexed
- UQ: Unique

Where there are compound indexes, numbers are given to indicate the precedence of the index segments.

RDB$BACKUP_HISTORY

Stores history of *nBackup* backups (from v.2.0 onward).

Table V.1 RDB$BACKUP_HISTORY

rdb$backup_history.column	Data Type	IDX	UQ	Description
RDB$BACKUP_ID	INTEGER	Y(1)	Y	Unique ID of one backup
RDB$BACKUP_LEVEL	INTEGER	Y(2)	(compound)	Indicates which backup level this backup file applies to
RDB$FILE_NAME	VARCHAR(255)	—	—	Name of file where backup is stored. Character set=NONE
RDB$GUID	VARCHAR(38)	—	—	?. Character set=NONE
RDB$SCN	INTEGER	—	—	Scan identifier
RDB$TIMESTAMP	TIMESTAMP	—	—	Timestamp of backup start

RDB$CHARACTER_SETS

Stores records for character sets available to the database

Table V.2 RDB$CHARACTER_SETS.

rdb$character_sets.column	Data Type	IDX	UQ	Description
RDB$CHARACTER_SET_NAME	CHAR(31)	Y	Y	Name of a character set known to Firebird.
RDB$FORM_OF_USE	CHAR(31)	—	—	Not used
RDB$NUMBER_OF_CHARACTERS	INTEGER	—	—	Number of characters in the set (not used for the available character sets).
RDB$DEFAULT_COLLATE_NAME	CHAR(31)	—	—	Name of the binary collation sequence for the character set. It is always the same as the character set name.
RDB$CHARACTER_SET_ID	SMALLINT	Y	Y	Unique identifier for this character set, wherever it is used.
RDB$SYSTEM_FLAG	SMALLINT	—	—	Will be 1 if the character set is defined by the system at database create; 0 for a user-defined character set.
RDB$DESCRIPTION	BLOB TEXT	—	—	For storing documentation.
RDB$FUNCTION_NAME	CHAR(31)	—	—	Not used, but may become available for user-defined character sets that are accessed via an external function.
RDB$BYTES_PER_CHARACTER	SMALLINT	—	—	Size of characters in the set, in bytes. For example, UNICODE_FSS uses 3 bytes per character.

RDB$CHECK_CONSTRAINTS

Cross-references names and triggers for CHECK and NOT NULL constraints.

Table V.3 RDB$CHECK_CONSTRAINTS.

rdb$check_constraints.column	Data Type	IDX	UQ	Description
RDB$CONSTRAINT_NAME	CHAR(31)	Y	—	Name of a constraint.
RDB$TRIGGER_NAME	CHAR(31)	Y	—	For a CHECK constraint, this is the name of the trigger that enforces the constraint. For a NOT NULL constraint, this is the name of the column to which the constraint applies—the table name can be found through the constraint name.

RDB$COLLATIONS

Stores definitions of collation sequences for character sets

Table V.4 RDB$COLLATIONS.

rdb$collations.column	Data Type	IDX	UQ	Description
RDB$COLLATION_NAME	VARCHAR(31)	Y	Y	Name of the collation sequence
RDB$COLLATION_ID	SMALLINT	Y(1)	Y(1)	With the character set ID, unique collation identifier
RDB$BASE_COLLATION_NAME	VARCHAR(31)			Name of collation that is extended by this collation
RDB$CHARACTER_SET_ID	SMALLINT	Y(2)	Y(2)	With the collation ID, unique collation identifier
RDB$COLLATION_ATTRIBUTES	SMALLINT	—	—	Not used externally
RDB$SPECIFIC_ATTRIBUTES	TEXT BLOB			Holds attributes added to or modified from base collation. Character set UNICODE_FSS
RDB$SYSTEM_FLAG	SMALLINT	—	—	User-defined=0; system-defined=1 or higher
RDB$DESCRIPTION	BLOB TEXT	—	—	For storing documentation
RDB$FUNCTION_NAME	CHAR(31)	—	—	Not currently used

RDB$DATABASE

A single-record table containing basic information about the database.

Table V.5 RDB$DATABASE

rdb$database.column	Data Type	IDX	UQ	Description
RDB$DESCRIPTION	BLOB TEXT	—	—	Comment text included with the CREATE DATABASE/CREATE SCHEMA statement is supposed to be written here. It doesn't happen. However, you can add any amount of text to it by way of documentation and it will survive a gbak and restore.
RDB$RELATION_ID	SMALLINT	—	—	A number that steps up by 1 each time a new table or view is added to the database.
RDB$SECURITY_CLASS	CHAR(31)	—	—	Can refer to a security class defined in RDB$SECURITY_CLASSES, to apply database-wide access control limits.
RDB$CHARACTER_SET_NAME	CHAR(31)	—	—	Default character set of the database. NULL if the character set is NONE.

RDB$DEPENDENCIES

Stores dependencies between database objects.

Table V.6 RDB$DEPENDENCIES

rdb$dependencies.column	Data Type	IDX	UQ	Description
RDB$DEPENDENT_NAME	CHAR(31)	Y	—	Names the view, procedure, trigger, or computed column tracked by this record.
RDB$DEPENDED_ON_NAME	CHAR(31)	Y	—	The table that the view, procedure, trigger, or computed column refers to.
RDB$FIELD_NAME	VARCHAR(31)	—	—	Names one column in the depended-on table that the view, procedure, trigger, or computed column refers to.
RDB$DEPENDENT_TYPE	SMALLINT	—	—	Identifies the object type (view, procedure, trigger, computed column). The number comes from the table RDB$TYPES—objects are enumerated where RDB$FIELD_NAME = 'RDB$OBJECT_TYPE'.
RDB$DEPENDED_ON_TYPE	SMALLINT	—	—	Identifies the type of the object depended on (same object paradigm as for RDB$DEPENDENT_TYPE).

RDB$EXCEPTIONS

Stores custom exceptions, i.e., created with CREATE EXCEPTION.

Table V.7 RDB$EXCEPTIONS

rdb$exceptions.column	Data Type	IDX	UQ	Description
RDB$EXCEPTION_NAME	CHAR(31)	Y	Y	Name of the custom exception
RDB$EXCEPTION_NUMBER	INTEGER	Y	Y	System-assigned unique exception number
RDB$MESSAGE	VARCHAR(78)	—	—	Custom message text
RDB$DESCRIPTION	BLOB TEXT	—	—	Can be used for documentation
RDB$SYSTEM_FLAG	SMALLINT	—	—	User-defined=0; system-defined=1 or higher

RDB$FIELD_DIMENSIONS

Stores information about dimensions of array columns.

Table V.8 RDB$FIELD_DIMENSIONS

rdb$field_dimensions.column	Data Type	IDX	UQ	Description
RDB$FIELD_NAME	CHAR(31)	Y	—	Name of the array column. It must be a RDB$FIELD_NAME in the table RDB$FIELDS.
RDB$DIMENSION	SMALLINT	—	—	Identifies one dimension in the array column. The first has the identifier 0.
RDB$LOWER_BOUND	INTEGER	—	—	Lower bound of this dimension.
RDB$UPPER_BOUND	INTEGER	—	—	Upper bound of this dimension.

RDB$FIELDS

Stores definitions of domains and of column names for tables and views. Each row for a non-domain column has a corresponding row in RDB$RELATION_FIELDS. In reality, every instance of RDB$FIELDS is a domain. You can, for example, do this:

```
CREATE TABLE ATABLE (
  EXAMPLE VARCHAR(10) CHARACTER SET ISO8859_1);
COMMIT;
SELECT RDB$FIELD_SOURCE FROM RDB$RELATION_FIELDS
  WHERE RDB$RELATION_NAME = 'ATABLE'
  AND RDB$FIELD_NAME = 'EXAMPLE';
RDB$FIELD_SOURCE
=============================
SQL$99
/* */
ALTER TABLE ATABLE
  ADD EXAMPLE2 SQL$99;
COMMIT;
```

The new column is added, having the same attributes as the original.

Table V.9 RDB$FIELDS

rdb$fields.column	Data Type	IDX	UQ	Description
RDB$FIELD_NAME	CHAR(31)	Y	Y	For domains, it is the domain name. For table and view columns, it is the internal, database-unique field name, linking to RDB$FIELD_SOURCE in RDB$RELATION_FIELDS. NB Firebird creates a domain in this table for every column definition that is not derived from a user-defined domain.
RDB$QUERY_NAME	CHAR(31)			Not used in Firebird.
RDB$VALIDATION_BLR	BLOB BLR			Not used in Firebird.
RDB$VALIDATION_SOURCE	BLOB TEXT			Not used in Firebird.

rdb$fields.column	Data Type	IDX	UQ	Description
RDB$COMPUTED_BLR	BLOB BLR	—	—	Binary language representation of the SQL expression that Firebird evaluates when a COMPUTED BY column is accessed.
RDB$COMPUTED_SOURCE	BLOB TEXT	—	—	Original source text of the expression that defines a COMPUTED BY column.
RDB$DEFAULT_VALUE	BLOB BLR	—	—	Default rule for the default value, in binary language representation.
RDB$DEFAULT_SOURCE	BLOB TEXT	—	—	Ditto; in original form.
RDB$FIELD_LENGTH	SMALLINT	—	—	Length of the column in bytes. Float, date, time, and integer are 4 bytes. Double precision, BigInt, timestamp, and blob_id are 8 bytes.
RDB$FIELD_SCALE	SMALLINT	—	—	Negative number representing the scale of a NUMERIC or DECIMAL column.
RDB$FIELD_TYPE	SMALLINT	—	—	Number code of the data type defined for the column: 7=smallint, 8=integer, 12=date, 13=time, 14=char, 16=bigint, 27=double precision, 35=timestamp, 37=varchar, 261=blob. Codes for numeric and decimal are the same as that of the integer-type that is used to store it.
RDB$FIELD_SUB_TYPE	SMALLINT	—	—	BLOB subtype, namely 0=untyped, 1=text, 2=BLR (binary language representation), 3=ACL (access control list), 5=encoded table metadata, 6=description of a cross-database transaction that didn't complete normally.
RDB$MISSING_VALUE	BLOB BLR			Not used in Firebird.
RDB$MISSING_SOURCE	BLOB TEXT			Not used in Firebird.
RDB$DESCRIPTION	BLOB TEXT	—	—	Available to use for documentation.
RDB$SYSTEM_FLAG	SMALLINT	—	—	1=system table; anything else, user-defined table.
RDB$QUERY_HEADER	BLOB TEXT			Not used in Firebird.
RDB$SEGMENT_LENGTH	SMALLINT	—	—	For BLOB columns, a suggested length for BLOB buffers. Not relevant in Firebird.
RDB$EDIT_STRING	VARCHAR(125)			Not used in Firebird.

rdb$fields.column	Data Type	IDX	UQ	Description
RDB$EXTERNAL_LENGTH	SMALLINT	—	—	Length of the field as it is in an external table. Always 0 for regular tables.
RDB$EXTERNAL_SCALE	SMALLINT	—	—	Scale factor of an integer field in an external table; represents the power of 10 by which the integer is multiplied.
RDB$EXTERNAL_TYPE	SMALLINT	—	—	Data type of the field as it is in an external table. Data types are the same as for regular tables, but include 40=null-terminated text (CSTRING).
RDB$DIMENSIONS	SMALLINT	—	—	Number of dimensions defined, if column is an array type. Always 0 for non-array columns.
RDB$NULL_FLAG	SMALLINT	—	—	Indicates whether column is nullable (empty) or non-nullable (1).
RDB$CHARACTER_LENGTH	SMALLINT	—	—	Length of a CHAR or VARCHAR column, in characters (not bytes).
RDB$COLLATION_ID	SMALLINT	—	—	Number ID of the collation sequence (if defined) for a character column or domain.
RDB$CHARACTER_SET_ID	SMALLINT	—	—	Number ID of the character set for character columns, BLOB columns, or domains. Links to RDB$CHARACTER_SET_ID column in RDB$CHARACTER_SETS.
RDB$FIELD_PRECISION	SMALLINT	—	—	Indicates the number of digits of precision available to the data type of the column.

RDB$FILES

Stores volume details of database secondary files and shadow files.

Table V.10 RDB$FILES

rdb$files.column	Data Type	IDX	UQ	Description
RDB$FILE_NAME	VARCHAR(253)	—	—	Name of a database secondary file (volume) in a multi-volume database, or a shadow file.
RDB$FILE_SEQUENCE	SMALLINT	—	—	Sequence in the volume order of database secondary files, or sequence in the shadow file set.
RDB$FILE_START	INTEGER	—	—	Starting page number.
RDB$FILE_LENGTH	INTEGER	—	—	File length, in database pages.

rdb$files.column	Data Type	IDX	UQ	Description
RDB$FILE_FLAGS	SMALLINT	—	—	Internal use.
RDB$SHADOW_NUMBER	SMALLINT	—	—	Shadow set number. Required to identify the file as a member of a shadow set. If it is null or 0, Firebird assumes the file is a secondary database volume.

RDB$FILTERS

Stores and keeps track of information about BLOB filters.

Table V.11 RDB$FILTERS

rdb$filters.column	Data Type	IDX	UQ	Description
RDB$FUNCTION_NAME	CHAR(31)	—	—	Unique name of the BLOB filter
RDB$DESCRIPTION	BLOB TEXT	—	—	User-written documentation about the BLOB filter and the two subtypes it is meant to operate on
RDB$MODULE_NAME	VARCHAR(253)	—	—	The name of the dynamic library/shared object where the BLOB filter code is located
RDB$ENTRYPOINT	CHAR(31)	—	—	The entry point in the filter library for this BLOB filter
RDB$INPUT_SUB_TYPE	SMALLINT	Y(1)	Y(1)	The BLOB subtype of the data to be transformed.
RDB$OUTPUT_SUB_TYPE	SMALLINT	Y(2)	Y(2)	The BLOB subtype that the input data is to be transformed to.
RDB$SYSTEM_FLAG	SMALLINT	—	—	Externally defined (i.e., user-defined=0, internally defined=1 or greater)

RDB$FORMATS

Keeps account of the number of metadata changes performed on tables. Each time a table or view gets a change, it gets a new format number. The purpose is to allow applications to access a changed table without the need to recompile. When the format number of any table reaches 255, the whole database becomes inaccessible for querying. It is then necessary to back up the database, restore it, and resume work in the newly built database.

Table V.12 RDB$FORMATS

rdb$formats.column	Data Type	IDX	UQ	Description
RDB$RELATION_ID	SMALLINT	Y(1)	Y(1)	Number ID of a table or view in RDB$RELATIONS.
RDB$FORMAT	SMALLINT	Y(2)	Y(2)	Identifier of the table format. There can be up to 255 such rows for any particular table
RDB$DESCRIPTOR	BLOB FORMAT	—	—	BLOB listing the columns and data attributes at the time the format record was created.

RDB$FUNCTION_ARGUMENTS

Stores the attributes of arguments (parameters) of external functions.

Table V.13 RDB$FUNCTION_ARGUMENTS

rdb$functions_arguments.column	Data Type	IDX	UQ	Description
RDB$FUNCTION_NAME	CHAR(31)	Y	—	Unique name of the external function, matching a function name in RDB$FUNCTIONS.
RDB$ARGUMENT_POSITION	SMALLINT	—	—	Position of the argument in the argument list: 1=first, 2=second, etc.
RDB$MECHANISM	SMALLINT	—	—	Whether the argument is passed by value (0), by reference (1), by descriptor (2), or by BLOB descriptor (3).
RDB$FIELD_TYPE	SMALLINT	—	—	Number code of the data type defined for the column: 7=smallint, 8=integer, 12=date, 13=time, 14=char, 16=bigint, 27=double precision, 35=timestamp, 37=varchar, 40=cstring (null-terminated string), 261=blob.
RDB$FIELD_SCALE	SMALLINT	—	—	Scale of an integer or fixed numeric argument.
RDB$FIELD_LENGTH	SMALLINT	—	—	Length of the argument in bytes. For lengths of non-character types, refer to `RDB$FIELDS.RDB$FIELD_LENGTH`.
RDB$FIELD_SUB_TYPE	SMALLINT	—	—	For BLOB arguments, BLOB subtype.
RDB$CHARACTER_SET_ID	SMALLINT	—	—	Numeric ID for the character set, for a character argument, if applicable.
RDB$FIELD_PRECISION	SMALLINT	—	—	Digits of precision available to the data type of the argument.
RDB$CHARACTER_LENGTH	SMALLINT	—	—	Length of a CHAR or VARCHAR argument, in characters (not bytes).

RDB$FUNCTIONS

Stores information about external functions.

Table V.14 RDB$FUNCTIONS

rdb$functions.column	Data Type	IDX	UQ	Description
RDB$FUNCTION_NAME	CHAR(31)	Y	Y	Unique name of an external function.
RDB$FUNCTION_TYPE	SMALLINT			Not currently used.
RDB$QUERY_NAME	CHAR(31)	—	—	This is meant to be an alternative name for the function, for use in isql queries. It doesn't work.
RDB$DESCRIPTION	BLOB TEXT	—	—	Available for documentation.
RDB$MODULE_NAME	VARCHAR(253)	—	—	Name of the dynamic library/shared object where the code for the function is located.
RDB$ENTRYPOINT	CHAR(31)	—	—	Name of the entry point in the library where this function is to be found.
RDB$RETURN_ARGUMENT	SMALLINT	—	—	Ordinal position of the return argument in the parameter list, relative to the input arguments.
RDB$SYSTEM_FLAG	SMALLINT	—	—	Externally defined (user-defined)=1; system-defined=0.

RDB$GENERATORS

Stores names and IDs of generators and sequences.

Table V.15 RDB$GENERATORS

rdb$generators.column	Data Type	IDX	UQ	Description
RDB$GENERATOR_NAME	CHAR(31)	Y	Y	Name of generator.
RDB$GENERATOR_ID	BIGINT	—	—	System-assigned unique ID for the generator.
RDB$SYSTEM_FLAG	SMALLINT	—	—	0=user-defined; 1 or greater=system-defined. Firebird uses a number of generators internally.
RDB$DESCRIPTION	BLOB TEXT	—	—	For storing documentation.

RDB$INDEX_SEGMENTS

Stores the segments and positions of multi-segment indexes.

Table V.16 RDB$INDEX_SEGMENTS

rdb$index_segments.column	Data Type	IDX	UQ	Description
RDB$INDEX_NAME	CHAR(31)	Y	—	Name of the index. Must be kept consistent with the corresponding master record in RDB$INDICES.
RDB$FIELD_NAME	CHAR(31)	—	—	Name of a key column in the index. Matches the RDB$FIELD_NAME of the database column, in RDB$RELATION_FIELDS.
RDB$FIELD_POSITION	SMALLINT	—	—	Ordinal position of the column in the index (left to right).
RDB$STATISTICS	DOUBLE PRECISION	—	—	Stores per-segment selectivity statistics (v.2+)

RDB$INDICES

Stores definitions of all indexes.

Table V.17 RDB$INDICES

rdb$indices.column	Data Type	IDX	UQ	Description
RDB$INDEX_NAME	CHAR(31)	Y	Y	Unique name of the index.
RDB$RELATION_NAME	CHAR(31)	Y	—	Name of the table the index applies to. Matches a RDB$RELATION_NAME in a record in RDB$RELATIONS.
RDB$INDEX_ID	SMALLINT	—	—	Internal number ID of the index. Writing to this column from an application will break the index.
RDB$UNIQUE_FLAG	SMALLINT	—	—	Indicates whether the index is unique (1=unique, 0=not unique).
RDB$DESCRIPTION	BLOB TEXT	—	—	Available for documentation.
RDB$SEGMENT_COUNT	SMALLINT	—	—	Number of segments (columns) in the index.
RDB$INDEX_INACTIVE	SMALLINT	—	—	Indicates whether the index is currently inactive (1=inactive, 0=active).
RDB$INDEX_TYPE	SMALLINT	—	—	Distinguish regular indexes (0) from expression indexes (1). Not used in versions older than v.2.0.
RDB$FOREIGN_KEY	VARCHAR(31)	Y	—	Name of the associated foreign key constraint, if any.
RDB$SYSTEM_FLAG	SMALLINT	—	—	Indicates whether the index is system-defined (1 or greater) or user-defined (0).

rdb$indices.column	Data Type	IDX	UQ	Description
RDB$EXPRESSION_BLR	BLOB BLR	—	—	Binary language representation of an expression, used for runtime evaluation for expression indexes. Not used in versions older than v.2.0.
RDB$EXPRESSION_SOURCE	BLOB TEXT	—	—	Source of an expression used for an expression index. Not used in versions older than v.2.0.
RDB$STATISTICS	DOUBLE PRECISION	—	—	Stores the latest selectivity of the index, as calculated at start-up or by SET STATISTICS.

RDB$LOG_FILES

An obsolete system table.

RDB$PAGES

Stores information about database pages.

Table V.18 RDB$PAGES

rdb$pages.column	Data Type	IDX	UQ	Description
RDB$PAGE_NUMBER	INTEGER	—	—	Unique number of a database page that has been physically allocated.
RDB$RELATION_ID	SMALLINT	—	—	ID of table whose data are stored on the page
RDB$PAGE_SEQUENCE	INTEGER	—	—	Sequence number of this page, relative to other pages allocated for this table.
RDB$PAGE_TYPE	SMALLINT	—	—	Identifies the type of data stored on the page (table data, index, etc.)

RDB$PROCEDURE_PARAMETERS

Stores the parameters for stored procedures.

Table V.19 RDB$PROCEDURE_PARAMETERS

rdb$procedure_parameters.column	Data Type	IDX	UQ	Description
RDB$PARAMETER_NAME	CHAR(31)	Y(2)	Y(2)	Name of the parameter.
RDB$PROCEDURE_NAME	CHAR(31)	Y(1)	Y(1)	Name of the procedure
RDB$PARAMETER_NUMBER	SMALLINT	—	—	Sequence number of parameter.
RDB$PARAMETER_TYPE	SMALLINT	—	—	Indicates whether parameter is input (0) or output (1).
RDB$FIELD_SOURCE	CHAR(31)	—	—	System-generated unique column name
RDB$DESCRIPTION	BLOB TEXT	—	—	Available for documentation.
RDB$SYSTEM_FLAG	SMALLINT	—	—	Indicates whether the parameter is system-defined (1 or greater) or user-defined (0).
RDB$COLLATION_ID	SMALLINT	—	—	

rdb$procedure_parameters.column	Data Type	IDX	UQ	Description
RDB$DEFAULT_SOURCE	BLOB TEXT	—	—	Character set UNICODE_FSS
RDB$DEFAULT_VALUE	BLOB BLR	—	—	
RDB$NULL_FLAG	SMALLINT			Indicates whether the parameter is non-nullable (1 or greater) or nullable (0).
RDB$PARAMETER_MECHANISM	SMALLINT			
RDB$FIELD_NAME	NCHAR(31)			Character set UNICODE_FSS
RDB$RELATION_NAME	NCHAR(31)			Character set UNICODE_FSS

RDB$PROCEDURES

Stores definitions of stored procedures.

Table V.20 RDB$PROCEDURES

rdb$procedures.column	Data Type	IDX	UQ	Description
RDB$PROCEDURE_NAME	CHAR(31)	Y	Y	Name of procedure.
RDB$PROCEDURE_ID	SMALLINT	Y	—	System-defined unique ID of procedure.
RDB$PROCEDURE_INPUTS	SMALLINT	—	—	Indicates whether there are input parameters (1) or not (0)
RDB$PROCEDURE_OUTPUTS	SMALLINT	—	—	Indicates whether there are output parameters (1) or not (0)
RDB$DESCRIPTION	BLOB TEXT	—	—	Available for documentation.
RDB$PROCEDURE_SOURCE	BLOB TEXT	—	—	Source code of the procedure
RDB$PROCEDURE_BLR	BLOB BLR	—	—	Binary language representation (BLR) of the procedure code.
RDB$SECURITY_CLASS	CHAR(31)	—	—	Can refer to a security class defined in RDB$SECURITY_CLASSES, to apply access control limits.
RDB$OWNER_NAME	VARCHAR(31)	—	—	User name of the procedure's owner.
RDB$RUNTIME	BLOB SUMMARY	—	—	Description of metadata of procedure, internal use for optimization
RDB$SYSTEM_FLAG	SMALLINT	—	—	User-defined (0) or system-defined (1 or greater)
RDB$PROCEDURE_TYPE	SMALLINT			
RDB$DEBUG_INFO	BLOB BINARY			
RDB$VALID_BLR	SMALLINT			

RDB$REF_CONSTRAINTS

Stores actions for referential constraints.

Table V.21 RDB$REF_CONSTRAINTS

rdb$ref_constraints.column	Data Type	IDX	UQ	Description
RDB$CONSTRAINT_NAME	CHAR(31)	Y	Y	Name of a referential constraint.
RDB$CONST_NAME_UQ	CHAR(31)	—	—	Name of the primary key or unique constraint referred to in the REFERENCES clause of this constraint.
RDB$MATCH_OPTION	CHAR(7)	—	—	Current value is FULL in all cases; reserved for future use.
RDB$UPDATE_RULE	CHAR(11)	—	—	Referential integrity action applicable to this foreign key when the primary key is updated: `NO ACTION | CASCADE | SET NULL | SET DEFAULT`.
RDB$DELETE_RULE	CHAR(11)	—	—	Referential integrity action applicable to this foreign key when the primary key is deleted. Rule options as defined in the column RDB$UPDATE_RULE

RDB$RELATION_CONSTRAINTS

Stores information about table-level integrity constraints.

Table V.22 RDB$RELATION_CONSTRAINTS

rdb$relation_constraints.column	Data Type	IDX	UQ	Description
RDB$CONSTRAINT_NAME	CHAR(31)	Y	Y	Name of a table-level constraint.
RDB$CONSTRAINT_TYPE	CHAR(11)	Y(2)	—	Primary key/unique/foreign key/pcheck/not null
RDB$RELATION_NAME	CHAR(31)	Y(1)	—	Name of the table this constraint applies to.
RDB$DEFERRABLE	CHAR(3)	—	—	Currently NO in all cases; reserved for future implementation of deferred constraint.
RDB$INITIALLY_DEFERRED	CHAR(3)	—	—	Ditto.
RDB$INDEX_NAME	CHAR(31)	Y	—	Name of the index that enforces the constraint (applicable if constraint is PRIMARY KEY, UNIQUE, or FOREIGN KEY).

RDB$RELATION_FIELDS

Stores the definitions of columns.

Table V.23 RDB$RELATION_FIELDS

rdb$relation_fields.column	Data Type	IDX	UQ	Description
RDB$FIELD_NAME	CHAR(31)	Y(1)	Y(1)	Name of the column, unique in table or view.
RDB$RELATION_NAME	CHAR(31)	Y(2)	Y(2)	Name of table or view.
		Y	—	(Another index)
RDB$FIELD_SOURCE	CHAR(31)	Y	—	The system-generated name (SQL$nn) for this column, correlated in RDB$FIELDS. If the column is based on a domain, the two correlated RDB$FIELD_SOURCE columns store the domain name.
RDB$QUERY_NAME	CHAR(31)			Not used currently.
RDB$BASE_FIELD	CHAR(31)	—	—	For a view only, the column name from the base table. The base table is identified by an internal ID in the column RDB$VIEW_CONTEXT.
RDB$EDIT_STRING	VARCHAR(125)			Not used in Firebird.
RDB$FIELD_POSITION	SMALLINT	—	—	Position of column in table or view in relation to the other columns. Note that for tables, you can alter this using ALTER TABLE ALTER COLUMN POSITION n, where n is the new field_position.
RDB$QUERY_HEADER	BLOB TEXT			Not used in Firebird.
RDB$UPDATE_FLAG	SMALLINT			Not used in Firebird.
RDB$FIELD_ID	SMALLINT	—	—	Transient number ID, used internally. It changes after backup and restore, so don't rely on it for queries in applications and don't change it.
RDB$VIEW_CONTEXT	SMALLINT	—	—	For a view column, internal number ID for the base table where the field comes from. Don't modify this column.
RDB$DESCRIPTION	BLOB TEXT	—	—	Can store documentation about the column.
RDB$DEFAULT_VALUE	BLOB BLR	—	—	Binary language representation of the DEFAULT clause, if any.
RDB$SYSTEM_FLAG	SMALLINT	—	—	User-defined (0) or system-defined (1 or greater).
RDB$SECURITY_CLASS	CHAR(31)	—	—	Can refer to a security class defined in RDB$SECURITY_CLASSES, to apply access control limits to all users of this column.
RDB$COMPLEX_NAME	CHAR(31)	—	—	Reserved for future implementation.

rdb$relation_fields.column	Data Type	IDX	UQ	Description
RDB$NULL_FLAG	SMALLINT	—	—	Indicates whether column is nullable (empty) or non-nullable (1).
RDB$DEFAULT_SOURCE	BLOB TEXT	—	—	Original source text of the DEFAULT clause, if any.
RDB$COLLATION_ID	SMALLINT	—	—	ID of non-default collation sequence (if any) for column.

RDB$RELATIONS

Stores tables and view definition header information.

Table V.24 RDB$RELATIONS

rdb$relations.column	Data Type	IDX	UQ	Description
RDB$VIEW_BLR	BLOB BLR	—	—	Binary language representation of the query specification for a view; null on tables.
RDB$VIEW_SOURCE	BLOB TEXT	—	—	The query specification for a view.
RDB$DESCRIPTION	BLOB TEXT	—	—	Optional documentation.
RDB$RELATION_ID	SMALLINT	Y	—	Internal number ID for the table. Don't modify this column.
RDB$SYSTEM_FLAG	SMALLINT	—	—	Indicates whether the table is user-created (0) or system-created (1 or greater). Don't modify this flag on user-defined or system tables.
RDB$DBKEY_LENGTH	SMALLINT	—	—	For views, aggregated length of the DB_KEY. It is 8 bytes for tables. For views, it is 8 * number of tables the view definition refers to. Don't modify this column.
RDB$FORMAT	SMALLINT	—	—	Internal use—don't modify.
RDB$FIELD_ID	SMALLINT	—	—	Internal use—don't modify. It stores the number of columns in the table or view.
RDB$RELATION_NAME	CHAR(31)	Y	Y	Name of the table or view.
RDB$SECURITY_CLASS	CHAR(31)	—	—	Can refer to a security class defined in RDB$SECURITY_CLASSES, to apply access control limits to all users of this table.
RDB$EXTERNAL_FILE	VARCHAR(253)	—	—	Full path to the external data file, if any.
RDB$RUNTIME	BLOB SUMMARY	—	—	Description of table's metadata. Internal use for optimization.

rdb$relations.column	Data Type	IDX	UQ	Description
RDB$EXTERNAL_DESCRIPTION	BLOB EFD	—	—	BLOB of sub_type external_file_description, a text BLOB type that can be used for documentation.
RDB$OWNER_NAME	VARCHAR(31)	—	—	User name of table's or view's owner (creator), for SQL security purposes.
RDB$DEFAULT_CLASS	CHAR(31)	—	—	Default security class, applied when new columns are added to a table.
RDB$FLAGS	SMALLINT	—	—	Internal flags.
RDB$RELATION_TYPE	SMALLINT			(V.2.5+) To distinguish GTTs from regular relations?

RDB$ROLES

Stores role definitions.

Table V.25 RDB$ROLES

rdb$roles.column	Data Type	IDX	UQ	Description
RDB$ROLE_NAME	VARCHAR(31)	Y	Y	Role name.
RDB$OWNER_NAME	VARCHAR(31)	—	—	User name of role owner
RDB$DESCRIPTION				
RDB$SYSTEM_FLAG				

RDB$SECURITY_CLASSES

Stores and tracks access control lists.

Table V.26 RDB$SECURITY_CLASSESRDB$TRANSACTIONS

rdb$security_class.column	Data Type	IDX	UQ	Description
RDB$SECURITY_CLASS	CHAR(31)	Y	Y	Name of security class. This name must stay consistent in all places where it is used (RDB$DATABASE, RDB$RELATIONS, RDB$RELATION_FIELDS).
RDB$ACL	BLOB ACL	—	—	Access control list associated with the security class. It enumerates users and their permissions.
RDB$DESCRIPTION	BLOB TEXT	—	—	Documentation of the security class here defined.

RDB$TRANSACTIONS

Tracks cross-database transactions.

Table V.27 RDB$TRANSACTIONS

rdb$transactions.column	Data Type	IDX	UQ	Description
RDB$TRANSACTION_ID	INTEGER	Y	Y	Unique ID of the transaction being tracked
RDB$TRANSACTION_STATE	SMALLINT	—	—	State of the transaction: limbo(0), committed(1), rolled back (2)
RDB$TIMESTAMP	TIMESTAM P			For future implementation.
RDB$TRANSACTION_DESCRIPTION	BLOB TD	—	—	BLOB of sub_type transaction_description, describing a prepared multi-database transaction, available in case a lost connection cannot be restored

RDB$TRIGGER_MESSAGES

Stores trigger message definitions (system use).

Table V.28 RDB$TRIGGER_MESSAGES

rdb$trigger_messages.column	Data Type	IDX	UQ	Description
RDB$TRIGGER_NAME	CHAR(31)	Y	—	Name of the trigger the message is associated with.
RDB$MESSAGE_NUMBER	SMALLINT	—	—	Message number (1 to a maximum of 32767)
RDB$MESSAGE	VARCHAR(78)	—	—	Trigger message text

RDB$TRIGGERS

Stores definitions of all triggers.

Table V.29 RDB$TRIGGERS

rdb$triggers.column	Data Type	IDX	UQ	Description
RDB$TRIGGER_NAME	CHAR(31)	Y	Y	Name of the trigger.
RDB$RELATION_NAME	CHAR(31)	Y	—	Name of the table or view that the trigger is for.
RDB$TRIGGER_SEQUENCE	SMALLINT	—	—	Sequence (position) of trigger. Zero usually means no sequence was defined.
RDB$TRIGGER_SOURCE	BLOB TEXT	—	—	Stores the PSQL source code for the trigger.

rdb$triggers.column	Data Type	IDX	UQ	Description
RDB$TRIGGER_BLR	BLOB BLR	—	—	Stores the binary language representation of the trigger.
RDB$TRIGGER_INACTIVE	SMALLINT	—	—	Whether the trigger is currently inactive (1=inactive, 0=active).
RDB$TRIGGER_TYPE	SMALLINT	—	—	1=before insert, 2=after insert, 3=before update, 4=after update, 5=before delete, 6=after delete. Multi-event triggers (Firebird 1.5 and onward) have various trigger types using higher numbers. The actual type code depends on which events are covered and the order in which the events are presented. (NB: There is no apparent reason that the order of events should make a difference to the trigger_type code.)
RDB$DESCRIPTION	BLOB TEXT	—	—	Optional documentation.
RDB$SYSTEM_FLAG	SMALLINT	—	—	User-defined (0) or system-defined (1 or greater).
RDB$FLAGS	SMALLINT	—	—	Internal use.
RDB$DEBUG_INFO	BLOB BINARY			V.2.0+
RDB$VALID_BLR	SMALLINT			(V.2.1+) Will be flagged (1) if an object on which the trigger depends is altered

RDB$TYPES

Stores definitions of enumerated types used around Firebird.

Table V.30 RDB$TYPES

rdb$types.column	Data Type	IDX	UQ	Description
RDB$FIELD_NAME	CHAR(31)	—	—	Column name for which this enumeration is defined. Note that the same column name appears consistently in multiple system tables.
RDB$TYPE	SMALLINT	—	—	Enumeration ID for type that RDB$TYPE_NAME identifies. The series of number is unique within a single enumerated type (e.g., 0=table, 1=view, 2=trigger, 3=computed column, 4=validation, 5=procedure are all types of RDB$OBJECT_TYPE).

rdb$types.column	Data Type	IDX	UQ	Description
RDB$TYPE_NAME	CHAR(31)	Y	—	The text representation of the type identified by the RDB$FIELD_NAME value and the RDB$TYPE value.
RDB$DESCRIPTION	BLOB TEXT	—	—	Optional documentation.
RDB$SYSTEM_FLAG	SMALLINT			User-defined (0) or system-defined (1 or greater).

RDB$USER_PRIVILEGES

Stores SQL permissions.

Table V.31 RDB$USER_PRIVILEGES

rdb$user_privileges.column	Data Type	IDX	UQ	Description
RDB$USER	CHAR(31)	Y	—	User who has been granted the permission.
RDB$GRANTOR	CHAR(31)	—	—	Name of user who granted the permission.
RDB$PRIVILEGE	CHAR(6)	—	—	The privilege that is granted by the permission.
RDB$GRANT_OPTION	SMALLINT	—	—	Whether the permission carries WITH GRANT OPTION authority. 1=Yes, 0=No.
RDB$RELATION_NAME	CHAR(31)	Y	—	The object on which the permission has been granted.
RDB$FIELD_NAME	CHAR(31)	—	—	Name of a column to which a column-level privilege applies (UPDATE or REFERENCES privileges only).
RDB$USER_TYPE	SMALLINT	—	—	Identifies the type of user that was granted the permission (e.g., a user, procedure, view, etc.)
RDB$OBJECT_TYPE	SMALLINT	—	—	Identifies the type of object on which the privilege was granted.

RDB$VIEW_RELATIONS

An obsolete table.

System Views

The following system views are a subset of those defined in the SQL-92 standard. They can provide useful information about your data. You might like to copy the listings into a script and install the views in all your databases.

CHECK_CONSTRAINTS

Lists all of the CHECK constraints defined in the database, with the source code of the constraint definition.

```
CREATE VIEW CHECK_CONSTRAINTS (
  CONSTRAINT_NAME,
  CHECK_CLAUSE )
AS
  SELECT RC.RDB$CONSTRAINT_NAME,
  RT.RDB$TRIGGER_SOURCE
  FROM RDB$CHECK_CONSTRAINTS RC
  JOIN RDB$TRIGGERS RT
    ON RT.RDB$TRIGGER_NAME = RC.RDB$TRIGGER_NAME;
```

CONSTRAINTS_COLUMN_USAGE

Lists columns used by PRIMARY KEY and UNIQUE constraints and those defining FOREIGN KEY constraints.

```
CREATE VIEW CONSTRAINTS_COLUMN_USAGE (
TABLE_NAME,
COLUMN_NAME,
CONSTRAINT_NAME )
AS
  SELECT RC.RDB$RELATION_NAME, RI.RDB$FIELD_NAME, RC.RDB$CONSTRAINT_NAME
  FROM RDB$RELATION_CONSTRAINTS RC
JOIN RDB$INDEX_SEGMENTS RI
    ON RI.RDB$INDEX_NAME = RC.RDB$INDEX_NAME;
```

REFERENTIAL_CONSTRAINTS

Lists all the referential constraints defined in a database.

```
CREATE VIEW REFERENTIAL_CONSTRAINTS (
  CONSTRAINT_NAME,
  UNIQUE_CONSTRAINT_NAME,
  MATCH_OPTION,
  UPDATE_RULE,
  DELETE_RULE )
AS
  SELECT RDB$CONSTRAINT_NAME, RDB$CONST_NAME_UQ, RDB$MATCH_OPTION,
  RDB$UPDATE_RULE, RDB$DELETE_RULE
  FROM RDB$REF_CONSTRAINTS;
```

TABLE_CONSTRAINTS

Lists the table-level constraints.

```
CREATE VIEW TABLE_CONSTRAINTS (
  CONSTRAINT_NAME,
  TABLE_NAME,
  CONSTRAINT_TYPE,
  IS_DEFERRABLE,
  INITIALLY_DEFERRED )
AS
  SELECT RDB$CONSTRAINT_NAME, RDB$RELATION_NAME,
  RDB$CONSTRAINT_TYPE, RDB$DEFERRABLE, RDB$INITIALLY_DEFERRED
  FROM RDB$RELATION_CONSTRAINTS;
```

Monitoring Tables

v.2.1 and higher

Database monitoring was introduced at Firebird 2.1 and enhanced at v.2.5. It works on databases of ODS 11.1 and higher.

The changes in v.2.5 for handling of file specifications and other character parameter items in the DPB are reflected in a change to the character set of the related columns in the MON$ tables, which are defined by the system domain RDB$FILE_NAME2. The character set of that domain definition changes at v.2.5, from NONE to UNICODE_FSS.

The columns affected by the character set change are MON$DATABASE_NAME, MON$ATTACHMENT_NAME and MON$REMOTE_PROCESS.

MON$CONTEXT_VARIABLES

Retrieves known context variables

Table V.32 MON$CONTEXT_VARIABLES

mon$context_variables.column	Data Type	Description	Vers.
MON$ATTACHMENT_ID	INTEGER	Attachment ID. Contains a valid ID only for session-level context variables. Transaction-level variables have this field set to NULL.	V.2.5
MON$TRANSACTION_ID	INTEGER	Transaction ID. Contains a valid ID only for transaction-level context variables. Session-level variables have this field set to NULL.	V.2.5
MON$VARIABLE_NAME	VARCHAR(31)	Name of context variable	V.2.5
MON$VARIABLE_VALUE	(Varies)	Value of context variable	V.2.5

MON$DATABASE

Retrieves properties of the connected database

Table V.33 MON$DATABASE

mon$database.column	Data Type	Description	Vers.
MON$DATABASE_NAME	VARCHAR(253)	Database pathname or alias. Character set is NONE in v.2.1, UNICODE_FSS from v.2.5 onward.	v.2.1
MON$PAGE_SIZE	SMALLINT	Page size	v.2.1
MON$ODS_MAJOR	SMALLINT	Major ODS version	v.2.1
MON$ODS_MINOR	SMALLINT	Minor ODS version	v.2.1
MON$OLDEST_TRANSACTION	INTEGER	Transaction ID of the oldest [interesting] transaction (OIT)	v.2.1
MON$OLDEST_ACTIVE	INTEGER	Transaction ID of the oldest active transaction (OAT)	v.2.1
MON$OLDEST_SNAPSHOT	INTEGER	Transaction ID of the Oldest Snapshot (OST), i.e., the number of the OAT when the last garbage collection was done)	v.2.1
MON$NEXT_TRANSACTION	INTEGER	Transaction ID of the next transaction that will be started	v.2.1

mon$database.column	Data Type	Description	Vers.
MON$PAGE_BUFFERS	INTEGER	Number of pages allocated in the page cache	v.2.1
MON$SQL_DIALECT	SMALLINT	SQL dialect of the database	v.2.1
MON$SHUTDOWN_MODE	SMALLINT	Current shutdown mode: 0: online 1: multi-user shutdown 2: single-user shutdown 3: full shutdown	v.2.1
MON$SWEEP_INTERVAL	INTEGER	The sweep interval configured in the database header. Value 0 indicates that sweeping is disabled.	v.2.1
MON$READ_ONLY	SMALLINT	Read-only/Read-write flag	v.2.1
MON$FORCED_WRITES	SMALLINT	Synchronous/asynchronous writes flag	v.2.1
MON$RESERVE_SPACE	SMALLINT	Reserve space/Use-all-space flag	v.2.1
MON$CREATION_DATE	TIMESTAMP	Creation date and time, i.e., when the database was created or last restored.	v.2.1
MON$PAGES	BIGINT	Number of pages allocated on disk. Multiply by page size to estimate the on-disk size of the database at snapshot time. Note that a database on a raw device always returns 0	v.2.1
MON$BACKUP_STATE	SMALLINT	Current state of database with respect to *nbackup* physical backup: 0: normal 1: stalled 2: merge	v.2.1
MON$STAT_ID	INTEGER	Statistics ID	v.2.1

MON$ATTACHMENTS

Retrieves attachments connected to the connected database

Table V.34 MON$ATTACHMENTS

mon$attachments.column	Data Type	Description	Vers.
MON$ATTACHMENT_ID	INTEGER	Attachment ID	v.2.1
MON$SERVER_PID	INTEGER	Server Process ID	v.2.1
MON$STATE	SMALLINT	Attachment state 0: idle 1: active	v.2.1
MON$ATTACHMENT_NAME	VARCHAR(253)	Connection string. Character set is NONE in v.2.1, UNICODE_FSS from v.2.5 onward.	v.2.1
MON$USER	CHAR(93)	User name	v.2.1
MON$ROLE	CHAR(93)	Role name	v.2.1
MON$REMOTE_PROTOCOL	VARCHAR(8)	Remote protocol name	v.2.1
MON$REMOTE_ADDRESS	VARCHAR(253)	Remote address	v.2.1

mon$attachments.column	Data Type	Description	Vers.
MON$REMOTE_PID	INTEGER	Remote client process ID, contains non-NULL values only if the client library is version 2.1 or higher	v.2.1
MON$REMOTE_PROCESS	VARCHAR(253)	Remote client process pathname. Contains non-NULL values only if the client library is version 2.1 or higher. Can contain a non-pathname value if an application has specified a custom process name via the DPB. Character set is NONE in v.2.1, UNICODE_FSS from v.2.5 onward.	v.2.1
MON$CHARACTER_SET_ID	SMALLINT	Attachment character set	v.2.1
MON$TIMESTAMP	TIMESTAMP	Connection date and time	v.2.1
MON$GARBAGE_COLLECTION	SMALLINT	Garbage collection flag, indicates whether GC is allowed for this attachment (as specified via the DPB in isc_attach_database)	v.2.1
MON$STAT_ID	INTEGER	Statistics ID	v.2.1

MON$TRANSACTIONS

Retrieves transactions started in the connected database

Table V.35 MON$TRANSACTIONS

mon$transactions.column	Data Type	Description	Vers.
MON$TRANSACTION_ID	INTEGER	Transaction ID	v.2.1
MON$ATTACHMENT_ID	INTEGER	Attachment ID	v.2.1
MON$STATE	SMALLINT	Transaction state 0: Idle (transaction has one or more statements that are prepared and waiting to execute and no statements with open cursors) 1: Active (transaction has one or more statements executing or fetching or with pending inserts, updates or deletes)	v.2.1
MON$TIMESTAMP	TIMESTAMP	Transaction start date and time	v.2.1
MON$TOP_TRANSACTION	INTEGER	ID of Top transaction, the upper limit used by the sweeper transaction when advancing the global OIT. All transactions above this threshold are considered active. It is normally equivalent to the MON$TRANSACTION_ID but COMMIT RETAINING or ROLLBACK RETAINING will cause MON$TOP_TRANSACTION to remain unchanged ("stuck") when the transaction ID is incremented.	v.2.1

mon$transactions.column	Data Type	Description	Vers.
MON$OLDEST_TRANSACTION	INTEGER	Local OIT ID (i.e., the OIT as known within the transaction's own isolation context)	v.2.1
MON$OLDEST_ACTIVE	INTEGER	Local OAT ID (i.e., the OAT as known within the transaction's own isolation context)	v.2.1
MON$ISOLATION_MODE	SMALLINT	Isolation level 0: consistency 1: concurrency 2: read committed record version 3: read committed no record version	v.2.1
MON$LOCK_TIMEOUT	SMALLINT	Lock timeout -1: infinite wait 0: no wait N: timeout configured as N seconds	v.2.1
MON$READ_ONLY	SMALLINT	Read-only flag	v.2.1
MON$AUTO_COMMIT	SMALLINT	Auto-commit flag	
MON$AUTO_UNDO	SMALLINT	Auto-undo flag, indicates the auto-undo status set for the transaction, i.e., whether a transaction-level savepoint was created. The existence of the transaction-level savepoint allows changes to be undone if ROLLBACK is called and the transaction is then just committed. If this savepoint does not exist, or it does exist but the number of changes is very large, then an actual ROLLBACK is executed and the the transaction is marked in the transaction inventory (TIP) as "dead".	
MON$STAT_ID	INTEGER	Statistics ID	v.2.1

MON$STATEMENTS

Retrieved prepared statements in the connected database

Table V.36 MON$STATEMENTS

mon$statements.column	Data Type	Description	Vers.
MON$STATEMENT_ID	INTEGER	Statement ID	v.2.1
MON$ATTACHMENT_ID	INTEGER	Attachment ID	v.2.1
MON$TRANSACTION_ID	INTEGER	Transaction ID—contains valid values for active statements only	v.2.1

mon$statements.column	Data Type	Description	Vers.
MON$STATE	SMALLINT	Statement state 0: Idle (state after prepare, until execution begins) 1: Active (state during execution and fetch. Idle state (0) returns after cursor is closed) 2: Stalled, i.e., in the interval between client fetches from the open cursor. CPU time is not used during this state.[1]	v.2.1
MON$TIMESTAMP	TIMESTAMP	Statement start date and time. Values are valid for active statements only.	v.2.1
MON$SQL_TEXT	BLOB TEXT	Statement text, if applicable. Contains NULL for GDML statements.	v.2.1
MON$STAT_ID	INTEGER	Statistics ID	v.2.1

1. The *Stalled* state was introduced in Firebird 2.5.1. Priorly, statements in this state were rolled in with *Active*.

Note *The execution plan and the values of parameters are not available.*

MON$CALL_STACK

Retrieves call stacks of active PSQL requests in the connected database

Table V.37 MON$CALL_STACK

mon$call_stack.column	Data Type	Description	Vers.
MON$CALL_ID	INTEGER	Call ID	v.2.1
MON$STATEMENT_ID	INTEGER	Top-level DSQL statement ID, groups call stacks by the top-level DSQL statement that initiated the call chain. This ID represents an active statement record in the table MON$STATEMENTS.	v.2.1
MON$CALLER_ID	INTEGER	Caller request ID	v.2.1
MON$OBJECT_NAME	CHAR(93)	PSQL object name (Trigger name, procedure name)	v.2.1
MON$OBJECT_TYPE	SMALLINT	PSQL object type 2: trigger 5: procedure	v.2.1
MON$TIMESTAMP	TIMESTAMP	Date and time of start of request.	v.2.1
MON$SOURCE_LINE	INTEGER	SQL source line number, contains line and column information related to the PSQL statement currently being executed	v.2.1
MON$SOURCE_COLUMN	INTEGER	SQL source column number, containz line and column information related to the PSQL statement currently being executed	v.2.1
MON$STAT_ID	INTEGER	Statistics ID	v.2.1

MON$IO_STATS

Retrieves disk input/output statistics

Table V.38 MON$IO_STATS

mon$iostats.column	Data Type	Description	Vers.
MON$STAT_ID	INTEGER	Statistics ID	v.2.1
MON$STAT_GROUP	SMALLINT	Statistics group ID 0: database 1: attachment 2: transaction 3: statement 4: call	v.2.1
MON$PAGE_READS	BIGINT	Number of page reads	v.2.1
MON$PAGE_WRITES	BIGINT	Number of page writes	v.2.1
MON$PAGE_FETCHES	BIGINT	Number of page fetches	v.2.1
MON$PAGE_MARKS	BIGINT	Number of pages with changes pending	v.2.1

MON$MEMORY_USAGE

Retrieves current memory usage on the host of the connected database

Table V.39 MON$MEMORY_USAGE.

mon$memory_usage.column	Data Type	Description	Vers.
MON$STAT_ID	INTEGER	Statistics ID	v.2.5
MON$STAT_GROUP		Statistics group 0: database 1: attachment 2: transaction 3: statement 4: call Memory usage statistics in MON$STATEMENTS and MON$STATE represent actual CPU consumption	v.2.5
MON$MEMORY_USED	BIGINT	Number of bytes currently in use. High-level memory allocations performed by the engine from its pools. Can be useful for tracing memory leaks and for investigating unusual memory consumption and the attachments, procedures, etc. that might be responsible for it.	v.2.5
MON$MEMORY_ALLOCATED	BIGINT	Number of bytes currently allocated at the OS level. Low-level memory allocations performed by the Firebird memory manager. These are bytes actually allocated by the operating system, so it enables the physical memory consumption to be monitored. On the whole, only MON$DATABASE and memory-bound objects point to non-zero "allocated" values. Small allocations are not allocated at this level, being redirected to the database memory pool instead.	v.2.5
MON$MAX_MEMORY_USED	BIGINT	Maximum number of bytes used by this object.	v.2.5
MON$MAX_MEMORY_ALLOCATED	BIGINT	Maximum number of bytes allocated from the operating system by this object	v.2.5

MON$RECORD_STATS

Retrieves record-level statistics

Table V.40 MON$RECORD_STATS

mon$record_state.column	Data Type	Description	Vers.
MON$STAT_ID	INTEGER	Statistics ID	v.2.1
MON$STAT_GROUP	SMALLINT	Statistics group ID 0: database 1: attachment 2: transaction 3: statement 4: call	v.2.1
MON$RECORD_SEQ_READS	BIGINT	Number of records read sequentially	v.2.1
MON$RECORD_IDX_READS	BIGINT	Number of records read via an index	v.2.1
MON$RECORD_INSERTS	BIGINT	Number of inserted records	v.2.1
MON$RECORD_UPDATES	BIGINT	Number of updated records	v.2.1
MON$RECORD_DELETES	BIGINT	Number of deleted records	v.2.1
MON$RECORD_BACKOUTS	BIGINT	Number of records where a new primary record version or a change to an existing primary record version is backed out due to rollback or savepoint undo	v.2.1
MON$RECORD_PURGES	BIGINT	Number of records where the record version chain is being purged of versions no longer needed by OAT or younger transactions	v.2.1
MON$RECORD_EXPUNGES	BIGINT	Number of records where record version chain is being deleted due to deletions by transactions older than OAT	v.2.1

APPENDIX

VI

CHARACTER SETS AND COLLATIONS

If you have installed a later version and the character set or collation sequence you want is not listed here, read the release notes of your version and any other versions since v.2.5 to see whether it has been added.

Implemented and Activated Character Sets

Table VI.1 lists the character sets and collations available to databases when Firebird 2.5 was released. Some of those listed are not available in earlier Firebird versions.

Table VI.1 Character Sets and Collations, Firebird 2.5

ID	Name	Bytes per Character	Collation	Language	Aliases
2	**ASCII**	1	ASCII	English	ASCII7, USASCII
56	**BIG_5**	2	BIG_5	Chinese, Vietnamese, Korean	BIG5, DOS_950, WIN_950
68	**CP943C**	4	CP943C_UNICODE	Japanese (V.2.1+)	–
50	**CYRL**	1	CYRL	Russian	–
			DB_RUS	dBase Russian	–
			PDOX_CYRL	Paradox Russian	–
10	**DOS437**	1	DOS437	English—USA	DOS_437
			DB_DEU437	dBase German	–
			DB_ESP437	dBase Spanish	–
			DB_FRA437	dBase French	–
			DB_FIN437	dBase Finnish	–
			DB_ITA437	dBase Italian	–
			DB_NLD437	dBase Dutch	–
10	DOS437	1	DB_SVE437	dBase Swedish	–
			DB_UK437	dBase English—UK	–
			DB_US437	dBase English—USA	–
			PDOX_ASCII	Paradox ASCII code page	–

ID	Name	Bytes per Character	Collation	Language	Aliases
			PDOX_SWEDFIN	Paradox Swedish/Finnish code pages	–
			PDOX_INTL	Paradox International English code page	–
9	**DOS737**	**1**	DOS737	Greek	DOS_737
15	**DOS775**	**1**	DOS775	Baltic	DOS_775
11	**DOS850**	**1**	DOS850	Latin I (no Euro symbol)	DOS_850
			DB_DEU850	German	–
			DB_ESP850	Spanish	–
			DB_FRA850	French	–
			DB_FRC850	French—Canada	–
			DB_ITA850	Italian	–
			DB_NLD850	Dutch	–
			DB_PTB850	Portuguese—Brazil	–
			DB_SVE850	Swedish	–
			DB_UK850	English—UK	–
			DB_US850	English—USA	–
45	**DOS852**	**1**	DOS852	Latin II	DOS_852
			DB_CSY	dBase Czech	–
			DB_PLK	dBase Polish	–
			DB_SLO	dBase Slovakian	–
			PDOX_PLK	Paradox Polish	–
			PDOX_HUN	Paradox Hungarian	–
			PDOX_SLO	Paradox Slovakian	–
			PDOX_CSY	Paradox Czech	–
46	**DOS857**	**1**	DOS857	Turkish	DOS_857
			DB_TRK	dBase Turkish	–
16	**DOS858**	**1**	DOS858	Latin I + Euro symbol	DOS_858
13	**DOS860**	**1**	DOS860	Portuguese	DOS_860
			DB_PTG860	dBase Portuguese	–
47	**DOS861**	**1**	DOS861	Icelandic	DOS_861
			PDOX_ISL	Paradox Icelandic	–
17	**DOS862**	**1**	DOS862	Hebrew	DOS_862
14	**DOS863**	**1**	DOS863	French—Canada	DOS_863
			DB_FRC863	dBase French—Canada	–
18	**DOS864**	**1**	DOS864	Arabic	DOS_864
12	**DOS865**	**1**	DOS865	Nordic	DOS_865
			DB_DAN865	dBase Danish	–
			DB_NOR865	dBase Norwegian	–
12	DOS865	1	PDOX_NORDAN4	Paradox Norwegian and Danish	–
48	**DOS866**	**1**	DOS866	Russian	DOS_866
49	**DOS869**	**1**	DOS869	Modern Greek	DOS_869

ID	Name	Bytes per Character	Collation	Language	Aliases
6	**EUCJ_0208**	**2**	EUCJ_0208	EUC Japanese	EUCJ
57	**GB_2312**	**2**	GB_2312	Simplified Chinese (Hong Kong, PRC)	DOS_936, GB2312, WIN_936
69	**GB18030**	**4**		Chinese national standard describing the required language and character support necessary for software in China. Activated from ICU in V.2.5+	–
67	**GBK**	**2**		Chinese, sub-set of GB18030 and super-set of GB_2312	–
21	**ISO8859_1**	**1**	ISO8859_1	Latin 1	ANSI, ISO88591, LATIN1
			FR_CA	French—Canada	–
			DA_DA	Danish	–
			DE_DE	German	–
			ES_ES	Spanish	–
			ES_ES_CI_AI (v.2.0 +)	Spanish case- and accent-insensitive	–
			FI_FI	Finnish	–
			FR_FR	French	–
			FR_FR_CI_AI	French—case-insensitive and accent-insensitive (V.2.1+)	–
			IS_IS	Icelandic	–
			IT_IT	Italian	–
			NO_NO	Norwegian	–
			DU_NL	Dutch	–
			PT_PT	Portuguese	–
			PT_BR	Portuguese—Brazil (V.2.0+)	–
			SV_SV	Swedish	–
21	ISO8859_1	1	EN_UK	English—UK	–
			EN_US	English—USA	–
22	**ISO8859_2**	**1**	ISO8859_2	Latin 2—Central European (Croatian, Czech, Hungarian, Polish, Romanian, Serbian, Slovakian, Slovenian)	ISO-8859-2, ISO88592, LATIN2
22	ISO8859_2		CS_CZ	Czech	–
			ISO_HUN	Hungarian	–
			ISO_PLK	Polish (V.2.0+)	–
23	**ISO8859_3**	**1**	ISO8859_3	Latin3—Southern European (Maltese, Esperanto)	ISO-8859-3, ISO88593, LATIN3

ID	Name	Bytes per Character	Collation	Language	Aliases
34	**ISO8859_4**	1	ISO8859_4	Latin 4—Northern European (Estonian, Latvian, Lithuanian, Greenlandic, Lappish)	ISO-8859-4, ISO88594, LATIN4
35	**ISO8859_5**	1	ISO8859_5	Cyrillic (Russian)	ISO-8859-5, ISO88595
36	**ISO8859_6**	1	ISO8859_6	Arabic	ISO-8859-6, ISO88596
37	**ISO8859_7**	1	ISO8859_7	Greek	ISO-8859-7, ISO88597
38	**ISO8859_8**	1	ISO8859_8	Hebrew	ISO-8859-8, ISO88598
39	**ISO8859_9**	1	ISO8859_9	Latin 5	ISO-8859-9, ISO88599, LATIN5
40	**ISO8859_13**	1	ISO8859_13	Latin 7—Baltic Rim	ISO-8859-13, ISO885913, LATIN7
63	**KOI8R**		KOI8-RU	Russian character set and dictionary collation (v.2.0+)	–
64	**KOI8U**		KOI8-UA	Ukrainian character set and dictionary collation (v.2.0+)	–
44	**KSC_5601**	2	KSC_5601	Korean (Unified Hangeul)	DOS_949, KSC5601, WIN_949
			KSC_DICTIONARY	Korean—dictionary order collation	–
19	**NEXT**	1	NEXT	NeXTSTEP encoding	–
			NXT_US	English—USA	–
			NXT_FRA	French	–
			NXT_ITA	Italian	–
19	NEXT	1	NXT_ESP	Spanish	–
			NXT_DEU	German	–
0	**NONE**	1	NONE	Code-page neutral; uppercasing limited to ASCII codes 97–122	–
1	**OCTETS**	1	OCTETS	Binary character	BINARY
5	**SJIS_0208**	2	SJIS_0208	Japanese	SJIS
66	**TIS620**	1	TIS620_UNICODE	Thai (V.2.1+)	
3	**UNICODE_FSS**	3	UNICODE_FSS	Specialised set of UNICODE UTF8	SQL_TEXT, UTF-8 (v.1.X only), UTF8 (v. 1.X only), UTF_FSS
4	**UTF8**	1-4	UCS_BASIC	Universal, UNICODE 4 (V.2.0+)	UTF_8, UTF-8
			UNICODE	UNICODE collation (V.2.0+)	–

ID	Name	Bytes per Character	Collation	Language	Aliases
			UNICODE_CI	UNICODE case-insensitive (V.2.1+)	–
			UNICODE_CI_AI	UNICODE case-insensitive, accent-insensitive (V.2.5+)	–
51	**WIN1250**	**1**	WIN1250	ANSI—Central European	WIN_1250
			BS_BA	Bosnian (V.2.0+)	–
			WIN_CZ	Czech (V.2.0+)	–
			WIN_CZ_AI	Czech—accent-insensitive (V.2.0+)	–
			WIN_CZ_CI_AI	Czech—case-insensitive, accent-insensitive (V.2.0+)	–
			PXW_CSY	Czech	–
			PXW_PLK	Polish	–
			PXW_HUN	Hungarian	–
			PXW_HUNDC	Hungarian—dictionary sort	–
			PXW_SLOV	Slovakian	–
52	**WIN1251**	**1**	WIN1251	ANSI—Cyrillic	WIN_1251
			WIN1251_UA	Ukrainian	–
			PXW_CYRL	Paradox Cyrillic (Russian)	–
53	**WIN1252**	**1**	WIN1252	ANSI—Latin I	WIN_1252
			PXW_SWEDFIN	Swedish and Finnish	–
			PXW_NORDAN4	Norwegian and Danish	–
			PXW_INTL	English—International	–
53	WIN1252	1	PXW_INTL850	Paradox Multi-lingual Latin I	–
			WIN_PTBR	Portuguese—Brazil (V.2.0+)	–
			PXW_SPAN	Paradox Spanish	–
54	**WIN1253**	**1**	WIN1253	ANSI Greek	WIN_1253
			PXW_GREEK	Paradox Greek	–
55	**WIN1254**	**1**	WIN1254	ANSI Turkish	WIN_1254
			PXW_TURK	Paradox Turkish	–
58	**WIN1255**	**1**	WIN1255	ANSI Hebrew	WIN_1255
59	**WIN1256**	**1**	WIN1256	ANSI Arabic	WIN_1256
60	**WIN1257**	**1**	WIN1257	ANSI Baltic	WIN_1257
			WIN1257_EE	Estonian dictionary collation (v.2.0+)	–
			WIN1257_LT	Lithuanian dictionary collation (v.2.0+)	–
			WIN1257_LV	Latvian dictionary collation (v.2.0+)	–
65	**WIN1258**	**1**	WIN1258	Vietnamese (v.2.0+)	WIN_1258 (V.2.5+)

APPENDIX

VII

RESOURCES

In this Appendix is an eclectic collection of resources that you might not know about if you've only recently discovered Firebird.

Use the alphabetical Glossary at the end of the book to look up any unfamiliar terms.

Free Documentation

The *Language Reference* volume of the original InterBase 6 beta documentation set from 2000 is your starting point. Still available from archives as a PDF book, it comprehensively covers all of the SQL elements that were implemented at the point where Firebird began.

Since then, members of the Firebird open source project, most notably Paul Vinkenoog, have written updates covering changes and new implementations in Firebird's SQL language over the many versions. There is one update book for each major version from v.1.5 onward, each accumulating onto the previous update. That means, for example, that if you are working with Firebird 2.5, you need only the original InterBase 6 ***Language Reference*** and the ***Firebird 2.5 Language Reference Update*** to have the complete language documentation.

Links for downloading these and many other useful documents can be found at *http://www.firebirdsql.org/en/reference-manuals/*

Books

If your previous contact with SQL has been minimal, a good book on SQL basics is invaluable. The following list—not exhaustive—may be helpful.

Joe Celko writes SQL books aimed at problem-solving. The SQL is mostly standard, with perhaps a bias toward Oracle. Titles:

SQL For Smarties: Advanced SQL Programming

Classic book of magic spells for SQL programming.

Data and Databases: Concepts in Practice

SQL Puzzles and Answers

The Essence of SQL by ***David Rozenshtein and Tom Bondur***: Very concise, very much a beginner book.

SQL For Dummies, 7th Edition by ***Allen G. Taylor***. Approachable and standards-friendly introduction to basic language elements, with usable examples.

The Practical SQL Handbook by ***Judith S. Bowman*** et al.: How-to and desktop reference for standard SQL, well-reviewed.

Free help

The Firebird community is known for its free peer support. The Firebird Project itself manages a number of mail lists where resident experts can answer questions at all levels. Some run from the Sourceforge list servers while others run as Yahoo groups.

You can subscribe to any of these lists directly from the page *http://www.firebirdsql.org/en/mailing-lists/* at the Firebird web site. At that page, you will also find links to servers that have the list archives available with keyword searching.

SQL and Firebird server support

For all Firebird SQL-related questions, join the firebird-support forum at *http://tech.groups.yahoo.com/group/firebird-support/*. This is a volunteer email list where long-time and new Firebird users share experience. You can also subscribe from the link at the top of this topic.

Client interface support

Separate lists exist for most of the application language interfaces that wrap the Firebird client API. At the page linked at the top of this topic you can find lists for Java (firebird-java), ADO.NET (firebird-net-provider), ODBC (firebird-odbc-devel), PHP (firebird-php) and Python (firebird-python). For Delphi and Lazarus developers, the owners of IBObjects (*www.ibobjects.com*), FIBPlus (*www.devrace.com*) and UIB Components (*www.progdigy.com/forums/*) all run free support lists or newsgroups with registration available at their websites.

A fuller range of connectivity options can be found through links at *http://www.ibphoenix.com/download/connectivity/*

Third-Party Tools

The following is a selection of established tools that developers and DBAs are likely to find useful. It is far from exhaustive—the field is huge. Many more options can be found at a links section at the IBPhoenix web-site: start at *http://www.ibphoenix.com/download/tools/*.

Table VII.1 Third-party tools for use with Firebird

Tool	Vendor	Description
dbBackup	IBPhoenix	Multi-faceted administration front-end for configuring, managing and logging *gbak* backups locally or remotely for one or many databases on multiple platforms. Includes scheduling, optional zip compression, automatic restart after an interruption and many more DBA-friendly features. Commercial:one-off lifetime license fee, free trial available .
dbFile	IBPhoenix	A cross-platform command-line tool for importing and exporting data between Firebird databases and a range of external data file formats. The supported formats are delimited data-sensitive, fixed position data-sensitive and fixed format text (fixed field position and record size). Available for Linux, MacOSX and Windows. IBPhoenix can build *dbFile* to order for other platforms. Commercial:one-off lifetime license fee, free trial available.
FBDataGuard	IBSurgeon Ltd	Monitors databases and the server environment, captures statistics and sends alerts when possible problems appear; performs backups. Acts as an automatic administrative assistant and has tools for recovering data from seriously corrupted databases.
FBFirstAID	IBSurgeon Ltd	Automatic diagnosis and repair of corrupted databases that Firebird's own tools cannot handle. Commercial. Free trial of analysis tool available.
FBScanner	IBSurgeon Ltd	Profiler for database applications using TCP/IP networks, monitoring user activity, managing database connections and troubleshooting network "Connection reset by peer" errors directly through Firebird's network layer. Can audit applications and tune performance, audit applications, tune performance and log SQL queries, transactions and connections.
FB TraceManager	Upscene Productions	A commercial product to ease the use of the new Firebird 2.5 Trace API in various levels. The integrated parser processes the Trace API raw output and optional storage of parsed trace data in the FB TraceManager database enables further reporting and analysis. The Event Processing Engine allows to define customizable script-based event rules to spot user-defined conditions in near real-time. Additionally, beside the Trace API, per-database monitoring capabilities makes the product an integrated toolset for database and server monitoring.

Tool	Vendor	Description
IBAnalyst	IBSurgeon Ltd	Administrator's graphical toolset for analysing detailed database statistics and identifying possible problems with database performance, maintenance and interaction with applications. Outputs improvement suggestions automatically, according to state of statistics.
IB LogManager Product Family	Upscene Productions	Commercial set of tools to integrate a trigger-based, server-side auditing mechanism into a Firebird database to keep track of data changes. The additional addons *IBLMPump* and *IBLMRedo_cmd* can help to set up and maintain a master-to-many-slave database standby environment .
IB Replication Suite	IBPhoenix	A tool set for implementing and controlling database replication in all Firebird versions. Replicator integrates with databases, allowing users to replicate data seamlessly and transparently between databases on both local and remote sites. The Server component runs as a service (or a daemon) on Windows and Linux 32-bit and 64-bit servers, as a 32-bit application. A 64-bit version is available for Linux. Versions for InterBase v.5+ and Oracle v.9+ are also available. The graphical admnistrative component, Replication Manager, is a Windows client application that can interact with Server components running on any host platform. A database that is configured as a participant in replication is called a "replicant". Any "source" or "target" database may be a replicant, including InterBase 5+ and Oracle 9+ databases, even a specially-formatted text file, provided the Server component can find the required replicant licences installed and available. A wide variety of replication topographies is achievable and multiple configurations can be defined for running at different times or simultaneously. Commercial: Server and Replicant licences are purchased according to the configuration (or configurations) of servers and replicants.

Commercial Help and Support

The most prominent commercial provider of support and consultancy related to Firebird is *IBPhoenix*. It offers a variety of support plans and operates, via the Internet, in most countries world-wide.

IBSurgeon Ltd specialises in recovering severely corrupted databases, a service it can provide either by working on a file copy sent by international courier or, if urgency or security restraints require it, by remote-connecting directly to your system.

Its other prime service is *optimization* of the structure of a poorly-performing database and its physical environment.

Index

GLOSSARY

THE FIREBIRD BOOK SECOND EDITION

Glossary

ADO
Acronym for ActiveX Data Objects, a high-level application-to-data source interface introduced by Microsoft in 1996. Earlier versions could only access relational databases with fixed columns and data types but later versions could interface also with other DBMS models, filesystems, data files, email messages, tree structures and heterogeneous data structures.

Aggregate (function)
An aggregate function returns a result derived from a calculation that aggregates (collects together) values from a set of rows that is grouped in some fashion by the syntax of the SQL statement.

For example, the internal function SUM() operates on a non-null numerical column to return the result of adding all of the values in that column together for all of the rows cited by a WHERE or GROUP BY clause. Output which is aggregated by a WHERE clause returns one row of output, whereas that aggregated by a GROUP BY clause potentially returns multiple rows.

Alerter (events)
A term coined to represent a client routine or class which is capable of "listening" for specific database EVENTs generated from triggers or stored procedures running on the server.

'ALICE'
Internal name for the source code for the *gfix* utilities - a corruption of the words "all else".

Alternative key ('alternate key')
This is a term used for a unique key that is not the primary key. A unique key is created by applying the UNIQUE constraint to a column or group of columns. A foreign key in a formal referential integrity relationship can link its REFERENCES clause to an alternative key.

API
See *Application Programming Interface.*

Application Programming Interface (API)
An application programming interface (API) provides a set of formal structures through which application programs can communicate with functions internal to another software. The Firebird API surfaces such an interface as a dynamically-loaded client library compiled specifically for each supported platform. The Firebird API structures are C structures, designed to be translatable to virtually any host application language. Translations can be found for Java, Pascal, Perl and, to some degree, PHP 4, Python and others.

Argument
An argument is a value of a prescribed data type and size which is passed to a function or stored procedure to be operated upon. Stored procedures can be designed to both accept input arguments and return output arguments. For the returned values of functions (both internal and user-defined) the term result is more commonly used than argument

The terms *parameter* and *argument* are often used interchangeably with regard to stored procedures, thanks to Borland's adoption of the term *parameter* in its Delphi data access classes to name the properties to which stored procedure arguments are assigned..

Array slice
A contiguous range of elements from a Firebird array is known as a *slice.* A slice can consist of any contiguous block of data from an array, from a single element of one dimension to the maximum number of elements of all defined dimensions.

Atomicity
In the context of transactions, *atomicity* refers to the character of the transaction mechanism that wraps a grouping of changes to rows in one or more tables to form a single unit of work that is either committed entirely or rolled back entirely.

In the context of a key, a key is said to be *atomic* if its value has no meaning as data.

AutoCommit

When a change is posted to the database, it will not become permanent until the transaction in which it was posted is committed by the client application. If the client rolls back the transaction, instead of committing it, the posted changes will be cancelled.

Some client development tools provide a mechanism by which posting any change to any table invokes a follow-up call to commit the transaction, without further action by the user. This mechanism is usually called *AutoCommit*, or some similar term. It is not a Firebird mechanism—Firebird never commits transactions started by clients.

Autonomous transaction

A transaction that can be started inside a trigger or stored procedure to execute some operation separately from the "main" transaction in which the module itself is running. Autonomous transactions are supported in Firebird PSQL from v.2.5 onward.

Backup/restore (Firebird-style)

Backup is an external process initiated by a user—usually SYSDBA—to decompose a database into a collection of compressed disk structures comprising metadata and data which are separated for storage. *Restore* is another external process—also user-initiated—which completely reconstructs the original database from these stored elements. The backup process also performs a number of housecleaning tasks on a database whilst reading it for backing up; and a restored database will be completely free of "garbage". See also *gbak* and *nBackup*.

BDE

Borland Database Engine. Originally designed as the database engine of Paradox and, later, dBase, it was extended to provide a generic middleware connectivity layer between a variety of relational database engines and Borland application development tools for the Microsoft DOS and Windows platforms. The vendor-specific rules applicable to each RDBMS are encapsulated in a set of driver libraries known as SQL Links. The SQL Links drivers are version-specific.

By 2000, when Borland released the codebase from which Firebird 1.0 was developed, it had already deprecated the BDE in favour of lighter, more modern driver technologies. The last known version of the BDE (v.5.2) shipped with Borland Delphi 6 in 2000. An InterBase driver in this distribution only partly supports Firebird.

Binary tree

A logical tree structure in which a node can subtend a maximum of two branches. Firebird indexes are formed in binary tree structures.

BLOB

Mnemonic for *Binary Large Object.* This is a data item of unlimited size, in any format, which is streamed into the database byte-by-byte and stored without any format modification. Firebird allows BLOBs of different types to be classed by means of sub-types. Firebird's ancestor, InterBase, was the first relational database to support storage of BLOBs. See also *CLOB.*

BLOB Control Structure

A C language structure, declared in an external function module as a *typedef*, through which a blob function call accesses a blob. An external BLOB function cannot refer to actual BLOB data: it refers to a pointer to a blob control structure instead.

BLOB Filter

A BLOB Filter is a specialized external function (UDF) that transforms BLOB data from one subtype to another. Firebird includes a set of internal BLOB filters which it uses in the process of storing and retrieving metadata. One internal filter converts text data transparently between SUB_TYPE 0 (none) and SUB_TYPE 1 (text, sometimes referred to as 'Memo'). Developers can write BLOB filters to transform the contents of BLOBs. They are declared to individual databases, as other kinds of external functions are.

BLR

Binary Language Representation, an internal relational language with a binary notation that is a super set of the "human-readable" languages that can be used with Firebird, viz.. SQL and GDML. Firebird's DSQL interface to the server translates queries into BLR. The BLR versions of compiled triggers and stored procedures, check constraints, defaults and views are stored in BLOBs. Some client tools, for example IB_SQL and the command-line tool isql, have facilities to inspect this BLR code. In *isql*, execute the command SET BLOB ALL, perform SELECT statements to get the appropriate BLR fields from the system tables.

Buffer

A buffer is a block of memory for caching copies of pages read from the database. The term buffer is synonymous with cache page. See also *Page* and *Cache.*

'BURP'

Internal name for the *gbak* code—a mnemonic for "Backup [and] Restore Program".

Cache

When a page is read from disk it is is copied into a block of memory known as the database cache or, simply, the cache. The cache consists of buffers, each the size of a database page, determined by the page_size parameter declared when the database is created.

The word buffer in this context means a block of memory exactly the same size as one database page. The cache size is configurable, as a number of pages (or buffers). Hence, to calculate the size of the cache, multiply the *page_size* by the number of cache pages (*buffers*).

Cardinality (of a set)

The number of rows in a physical or specified set. The cardinality of a row refers to its position in the top-to-bottom order of the set.

Case-insensitive index

This is an index using a collation sequence in which lower-case characters are treated as though they were the same as their upper-case equivalents. Firebird 1.0 does not support case-insensitive indexes. Case-insensitive collation sequences have been appearing regularly from Firebird 1.5 forward.

Cascading integrity constraints

Firebird provides the optional capability to prescribe specific behaviors and restrictions in response to requests to update or delete rows in tables which are pointed to by the REFERENCES sub-clause of a FOREIGN KEY constraint. The CASCADE keyword causes changes performed on the "parent" row to flow on to rows in tables having the FOREIGN KEY dependencies. ON DELETE CASCADE, for example, will cause dependent rows to be deleted when the parent is deleted.

Casting

Casting is a mechanism for converting output or variable values of one data type into another data type by means of an expression. Firebird SQL provides the CAST() function for use in both dynamic SQL (DSQL) and procedural SQL (PSQL) expressions. From the "2" series forward, casting to the type of a *domain* is possible.

Character set

Two super-sets of printable character images and control sequences are in general use today in software environments—ASCII/ANSI and UNICODE. ASCII characters, represented by one byte, have 256 possible variants whilst UNICODE, of two, three or four bytes, can accommodate tens of thousands of possibilities. Because databases need to avoid the prohibitive overhead of making available every possible printable and control character used for programming anywhere in the world, the super-sets are divided up into code pages, also known as code tables. Each code page defines a subset of required characters for a specific language, or family of languages, mapping each character image to a number. The images and control sequences within each code page are referred to collectively as a character set. A character image might be mapped to different numbers in different characters sets.

Firebird supports a default character set for a database and definition of an explicit character set for any character, varchar or BLOB SUB_TYPE 1 (text BLOB) column. If no character set is defined for a database, its character set defaults to NONE, causing all character data to be stored exactly as presented, with no attempt to convert characters (transliterate) to any particular character set.

Classic architecture

The term "Classic architecture" refers to the original InterBase model where a separate server process is started for each client connection. It predated the "Superserver" model which threads all client processes from a single server process. SuperClassic, a variant of Classic that superintends threaded Classic instances, was developed to take advantage of multiple processors and larger RAM configurations on 64-bit hosts.

CLOB

Mnemonic for 'Character Large OBject'. This term has crept into use recently, as other RDBMSs have mimicked Firebird's support for storing large objects in databases and have made up their own names for them. A CLOB is equivalent to Firebird's BLOB SUB_TYPE 1 (TEXT). See also BLOB.

Coercing data types

In the Firebird API's XSQLDA structures, converting a data item of one SQL type to another, compatible SQL type is known as data type coercion.

Collation order

Defines how a sort operation orders character columns in output sets, the pairing of lower case and upper case characters for the UPPER() function and how characters in character columns are compared in searches. A collation order applies to a specific character set. If multiple collation orders are available for a particular character set, one collation order will be treated as the default. By convention, the default collation order has the same name as the character set and is binary, ordering items only by their numerical codes without recourse to specific rules.

Column In SQL databases, data are stored in structures which can be retrieved as tables or, more correctly, sets. A set consists of one or more rows each identical in the horizontal arrangement of distinctly defined items of data. One distinct item of data considered vertically for the length of the set is known as a column. Application developers often refer to columns as fields.

Commit When applications post changes affecting rows in database tables, new versions of those rows are created in temporary storage blocks. Although the work is visible to the transaction in which it occurred, it cannot be seen by other users of the database. The client program must instruct the server to commit the work in order for it to be made permanent. If a transaction is not committed, it must be rolled back in order to undo the work.

CommitRetaining Also known as "soft Commit", this is a transaction setting that implements the COMMIT WITH RETAIN attribute of a transaction. With this attribute, a transaction's context is kept active on the server until the client application finally calls Commit (a "hard Commit") and allows the transaction inventory management processes to pass it through for garbage collection. The widespread use CommitRetaining in applications is a common cause of performance degradation. See also Oldest Interesting Transaction.

Common table expression (CTE) A non-persistent e set object that is set up by a client application at run-time with a "preamble" to define a complex set to interact with one or more other sets within a single DSQL statement. A CTE is highly optimized and usually performs faster than a stored procedure that could do the equivalent processing. A CTE can be self-referencing, providing an efficient way to perform a recursive operation on a set.

Concurrency The term *concurrency* broadly refers to multiple users accessing the same data simultaneously. It is also widely used in documentation and support lists to refer to the particular set of attributes that apply to a transaction—isolation level, locking policy and others. For example, someone may ask you "What are your concurrency settings?"

Even more specifically, the word *concurrency* is often used as a synonym for the SNAPSHOT *isolation level.*

Constraint Firebird makes many provisions for defining formal rules which are to be applied to data. Such formal rules are known as constraints. For example, a PRIMARY KEY is a constraint which marks a column or group of columns as a database-wide pointer to all of the other columns in the row defined by it. A CHECK constraint sets one or more rules to limit the values which a column can accept.

Contention When two transactions attempt to update the same row of a table simultaneously, they are said to be in contention—they are contending (or competing).

Correlated Subquery A query specification can define output columns that are derived from expressions. A subquery is a special kind of expression that returns a single value which is itself the output of a SELECT statement. In a correlated sub-query, the WHERE clause contains one or more search keys that are relationally linked to (and matched to) columns in the main query.

Crash A slang term for abormal termination of the server or a client application.

Crash recovery Processes or procedures that are implemented to restore the server and/or client applications into running condition following an abnormal termination of either the server or the application, or both.

CTE See *Common table expression.*

CVS Acronym for Concurrent Versions System, an open-source program that allows developers to keep track of different development versions of source code. CVS is widely used for open source projects, including some sub-projects of Firebird. The Firebird core code's version control system is *Subversion.*

Cyclic links In a database context, this is a term for an inter-table dependency where a foreign key in one table(TableA) refers to a unique key in another table (TableB) which contains a foreign key which points back, either directly, or through a reference to another table, to a unique key in TableA.

Database In its broadest sense, the term *database* applies to any persistent file structure which stores data in some format which permits it to be retrieved and manipulated by applications.

Firebird is not a database. It is a system that manages databases.

Database trigger A PSQL module that is defined to run automatically when a client session opens or closes or when a transaction starts, commits or rolls back. First supported in Firebird "2" series.

DB_KEY See *RDB$DB_KEY*.

DDL Mnemonic for *Data Definition Language*—the subset of SQL that is used for defining and managing the structure of data objects. Any SQL statement starting with the keywords CREATE, ALTER, RECREATE, CREATE OR REPLACE, or DROP is a DDL statement. In Firebird, some DDL statements start with the keyword DECLARE, although not all DECLARE statements are DDL.

Deadlock When two transactions are in contention to update the same version of a row, the transactions are said to be ***in deadlock*** when one transaction (T1), having a lock on row A, requests to update row B, which is locked by another transaction (T2) and T2 wants to update row A. Normally, genuine deadlocks are rare, because the server can detects most deadlocks and resolves them itself without raising a deadlock exception. The Firebird server unfortunately generalizes all lock conflict exceptions into a single error code that reports a "deadlock", regardless of the actual source of the conflict. Client application code must resolve a lock conflict by having one transaction roll back in order to allow the other to commit its work.

Degree (of a set) The number of columns in a tabular set. The degree of a column refers to its position in the left-to-right sequence of columns, starting at 1.

Deployment The process of distributing and installing software components for production use.

Derived table A non-persistent set object that is defined in a SELECT expression by the client application at run-time, to provide a set intended to interact with other sets inside a single statement.

Dialect A term that distinguishes Firebird's native SQL language set from an older language set that was implemented in Firebird's predecessor, InterBase® 5. The older language set remains available to Firebird for near-compatibility with legacy databases, as "dialect 1". The native Firebird set is "dialect 3".

DML Mnemonic for *Data Manipulation Language*, the major subset of SQL statements, which perform operations on sets of data.

Domain A Firebird SQL feature whereby you can assign an identifying name to a set of data characteristics and constraints (CREATE DOMAIN) and then use this name in lieu of a data type when defining columns in tables and, under some conditions, in CAST() expressions and when defining arguments and variable in PSQL modules (stored procedures, triggers and executable blocks).

DPB Mnemonic for *Database Parameter Buffer*, a character array defined by Firebird's application programming interface (API). It used by applications to convey the parameters that specify the characteristics of a client connection request, along with their specific item values, across the API.

DSQL *Dynamic SQL*— refers to statements that an application submits in run-time, with or without parameters, as contrasted with "static SQL" statements which are coded directly into special code blocks of a host language program and are subsequently preprocessed for compilation within older-style embedded SQL applications. Applications which use Firebird API calls, either "raw" or through a class library which encapsulates the Firebird API, are using DSQL.

DSQL can also be executed inside a PSQL module by way of the EXECUTE STATEMENT syntax.

DTP Desktop publishing, the activity of using computer methods to prepare documents for publication in print or on the Web.

'DUDLEY' Internal name for the source-code for the deprecated metadata utility, gdef. The name derives from the mnemonic "DDL" (*Database Definition Language*).

dyn, also DYN A byte–encoded language for describing data definition statements. Firebird's DSQL subsystem parses data definition language (DDL) statements and passes them to a component that outputs DYN for interpretation by the Y-Valve, another subsystem which is responsible for updating the system tables.

Error A condition in which a requested SQL operation cannot be performed because something is wrong with the data supplied to a statement or procedure or with the syntax of the statement itself. When Firebird encounters an error, it does not proceed with the request but returns an *exception message* to the client application. See also *Exception.*

Error Code An integer constant returned to the client or to a calling procedure when Firebird encounters an error condition. See also *Error, Exception.*

ESQL Mnemonic for *Embedded SQL*, the mostly outmoded subset of SQL provided for embedding static SQL in special blocks within a host application, usually written in C.

Event An event implements Firebird's capability to pass a notification to a "listening" client application if requested to do so by a POST_EVENT call in a trigger or stored procedure.

Executable block A block of executable code, written in PSQL, that is submitted from a client application at run-time, using the syntax implemented as EXECUTE BLOCK. Supported in Firebird versions from the "2" series onward.

Executable string A string variable composed as a DSQL statement, that is passed to EXECUTE STATEMENT inside a PSQL module, for execution outside the module. From v.2.5, syntax is available to use replaceable parameters in the string and to execute the statement in a separate transaction, in the same database or another database..

Exception An exception is the Firebird server's response to an error condition that occurs during a database operation. Several hundred exception conditions are realized as error codes, in a variety of categories, which are passed back to the client in the *Error Status Vector (Array).* Exceptions are also available to stored procedures and triggers, where they can be handled by a custom routine.

Firebird supports user-defined exceptions as well.

External function Until v.2.1, Firebird has but a few built-in, SQL-standard functions. To extend the range of functions available for use in expressions, the Firebird engine can access custom functions, written in a host language such as C/C++ or Delphi, as if they were built-in. Several free libraries of ready-made external functions—also known as "UDFs" ("user-defined functions") exist among the Firebird community, including two that are included with the Firebird binary release distributions. New UDFs can be written easily in languages that support the C calling conventions.

Executable stored procedure Stored procedure that is called using EXECUTE PROCEDURE and does not return a multi-row result set. *c.f. Selectable stored procedure.*

Execute In a client application, *execute* is commonly used as a verb which means "perform my request" when a data manipulation statement or stored procedure call has been prepared by the client application.

In DSQL and PSQL, the phrase EXECUTE PROCEDURE is used with a stored procedure identifier and its input arguments, to invoke executable stored procedures. PSQL also supports EXECUTE STATEMENT, whereby a DSQL statement is taken as a string argument and executed from within the PSQL module.

fdb or FDB By convention, the suffix used for a Firebird primary database file. It is no more than a convention: Firebird works with any other file suffix, or none at all.

FIBPlus Trade name of the extended, commerical version of the older *FreeIBComponents* of Greg Deatz, data access components encapsulating the Firebird and InterBase APIs, for use with the Embarcadero RAD development products.

Foreign Key A foreign key is a formal constraint on a column or group of columns in one table that links that table to another table's corresponding primary or unique key. If the foreign key is non-unique and the table itself has a primary key, the table is capable of being the "many" side of a 1:Many relationship.

Firebird supports the declaration of a formal foreign key constraint which will enforce referential integrity automatically. When such a constraint is declared, Firebird automatically creates a non-unique index on the column or columns to which the constraint applies and also records the dependencies between the tables that are linked by the constraint.

Garbage collection

General term for the cleanup process that goes in the database during normal use to remove obsolete back-versions of rows that have been updated. In Superserver, garbage collection runs as a background thread to the main server process. Garbage collection can also be performed by sweeping and by backing up the database.

gbak

The command-line utility (found in the /bin directory of your Firebird installation) that backs up and restores databases. It is not a file-copy program: its backup operation decomposes the metadata and data and stores them separately, in a compressed binary format, in a filesystem file. By convention, backup files are often given the filename suffix "gbk" or "fbk".. Restoring decompresses this file and reconstructs the database as a new database file, before feeding the data into the database objects and rebuilding the indexes.

Apart from normal data security tasks expected of a backup utility, gbak performs important roles in the regular maintenance of "database hygiene" and in the recovery of corrupted databases. See also *nBackup*.

gdb or GDB

By convention, this is the file extension traditionally used for InterBase databases. However, a Firebird database file can have any extension, or none at all. Many Firebird developers use ".fdb" instead, to distinguish their Firebird databases from their InterBase databases, or as part of a solution to a performance-crippling "safety feature" introduced by Microsoft Corporation into their XP and Server 2003 operating systems, targeted at files having the ".gdb" extension.

Why "GDB"? It is a mnemonic artifact of the name of the company that created the original InterBase, Groton Database Systems.

GDML

Mnemonic for Groton Data Manipulation Language, a high-level relational language similar to SQL. GDML was the original data manipulation language of InterBase, functionally equivalent to DML in Firebird SQL but with some data definition capabilities. It is still supported through the interactive query utility, qli.

gdef

gdef was an older InterBase utility for creating and manipulating metadata. Since isql and the dynamic SQL interface can handle DDL, gdef is virtually redundant now. However, because it can output DYN language statements for several host programming languages including C and C++, Pascal, COBOL, ANSI COBOL, Fortran, BASIC, PLI and ADA, it still has its uses in the development of embedded SQL applications.

Generator

A number-generating engine for producing unique numbers in series. The statement CREATE GENERATOR generator_name seeds a distinct series of signed 64-bit integer numbers. SET GENERATOR TO n sets the first number in the series. The function GEN_ID (generator_name, m) causes a new number to be generated, which is m higher than the last generated number. See also *Sequence*.

gfix

gfix is a collection of command-line utilities, including database repair tools of limited capability. It includes tools to activate database shadows, to put the database into single-user (exclusive access) mode (shutdown) and to restore it to multi-user access (restart). It can resolve limbo transactions left behind by multiple-database transactions, set the database cache, enable or disable forced (synchronous) writes to disk, perform sweeping and set the sweep interval, switch a Firebird database from read/write to read-only or vice versa and set the database dialect.

Global temporary table (GTT)

A table definition that can be set up, much like a regular table, and available for any client or transaction to instantiate and populate. Each instantiation has a limited scope, either transaction "life" or the life of the client session. The instantiation is stored in a private file not visible to other connections or (if transaction-scoped) other transactions.

gpre

In ESQL application development ("embedded applications" that do not use the API), *gpre* is the preprocessor for static SQL language blocks in host language source code, translating them to BLR format in preparation for compiling. It can preprocess C, C++, COBOL, Pascal and ADA host code, on selected platforms.

Grant/Revoke

SQL commands GRANT and REVOKE, which are used for setting up user privileges for accessing the objects in a database.

Groton — *Groton Data Systems*, the name of the original company that designed and developed the relational database system that was named "InterBase". From InterBase, eventually, evolved Firebird. Two of the original Groton directors, Jim Starkey and Ann Harrison, were actively involved in aspects of Firebird development in its early years. Ann is still a regular contributor to the Firebird peer support forums.

gsec — *gsec* is Firebird's command-line security utility for managing the server-level user/password database (security2.fdb for v.2.0+, security.fdb for v.1.5, isc4.gdb for v.1.0), which applies to all users and all databases. This utility cannot be used to create or modify roles, since roles exist within a database.

gstat — *gstat* is the command-line utility with which to gather statistics about a Firebird database. It analyzes the internal layout, like the fill factor, header page, index pages, log page and system relations. Table-by-table information about record versions (usually lengthy) can be optionally obtained, using the -r and –t tablename switches together.

GTT — See *Global temporary table.*

Hierarchical database — An old design concept for implementing table-to-table relationships in databases by building up tree structures of inherited indexes.

Host-language — General term referring to the language in which application code is written.

Identity attribute — Some RDBM systems—MSSQL for example—support a table attribute which automatically implements a surrogate primary key integer column for a table and causes a new value to be generated automatically for each new row inserted. Firebird does not support this attribute directly. A similar mechanism can be achieved by explicitly defining an integer field of adequate size, creating a generator to populate it and defining a Before Insert trigger that calls the GEN_ID() function to get the next value of the generator.

IBO — Mnemonic for IB Objects, data access components and data-aware controls encapsulating the Firebird and InterBase APIs, for use with the Embarcadero RAD products on Windows and, latterly, Lazarus and FreePascal for cross-platform development.

IBX — Mnemonic for *InterBaseXpress*, data access components encapsulating the InterBase API, distributed previously by Borland for interfacing InterBase with the Delphi and C++ Builder products of which they were once proprietors.

Index — A specialized data structure, maintained by the Firebird engine, providing a compact system of data pointers to the rows of a table.

INET error — In the firebird.log, marks an error received by the Firebird network layer from a TCP/IP client/server connection.

Installation — Refers to the procedure and process of copying the software to a computer and configuring it for use. Often also used to refer to the file system layout of the Firebird components on the server.

InterBase — A relational database management system that was the ancestor of Firebird. Developed originally by a company named Groton Data Systems, it passed into the ownership of the Borland Software company early in the 1990s. InterBase version 6 was released into open source in 2000 under the InterBase Public License. Firebird was developed by independent developers from this open source code base and immediately became a forked development when the IB6 source code tree was made read-only.

Closed, proprietary versions of InterBase are still developed and marketed by the Embarcadero company that acquired it in 2008.

InterClient — Obsolete JDBC Type 2 Java client for the original InterBase 6 open source server. In Firebird, it is superseded by Jaybird, a family of open source JDBC/JCA compliant Java drivers (Type 4 and Type 2).

InterServer — Obsolete, Java-driven server-based communication layer originally distributed with the InterBase 6 open source code release. Neither InterServer nor its companion InterClient have ever been developed by the Firebird Project, having been superseded by a more modern and open Java interface, named Jaybird.

ISC, isc, etc.

Error messages, some environment variables and many identifiers in the Firebird API have the prefix "ISC" or "isc". As a matter of purely historical interest, these initials are derived from the initial letters of "InterBase Software Corporation", the name of a subsidiary company of Borland that existed during some periods of Borland's life as a software producer.

Isolation level

This attribute of a transaction prescribes the way one transaction shall interact with other transactions accessing the same database, in terms of visibility and locking behavior. Firebird supports three levels of isolation: Read Committed, Repeatable Read (also known as "Snapshot" or "Concurrency") and Snapshot Table Stability (also known as "Consistency"). Although Read Committed is the default for most relational engines, Firebird's default level is Repeatable Read, thanks to optimistic, row-level locking.

See also *Transaction Isolation.*

isql

Name of Firebird's console-mode interactive query utility, which can connect to one database at a time. It has a powerful set of commands, including its own subset of SQL-like commands, supplementary to the regular dynamic SQL command set. It has a large set of embedded macros for obtaining metadata information. isql can output batches of commands, including embedded comments, to a file; and it can "run" such a file as a script—the recommended way to create and alter database objects.

JDBC

Java Database Connectivity, a set of standards for constructing drivers for connecting Java applications to SQL databases.

Join

JOIN is the SQL keyword for specifying to the engine that the output of the SELECT statement involves merging columns from multiple tables, linked by matching one or more pairs of keys.

jrd

The internal name of the Firebird database engine kernel. It is a mnemonic for *Jim's Relational Database*, an artifact of the original engine, invented by Jim Starkey, which became InterBase and, later, Firebird.

Key

A key is a constraint on a table which is applied to a column or group of columns in the table's row structure. A *primary key* or a *unique key* points to the unique row in which it exists; while a *foreign key* points to a unique row in another table by linking to its primary key or another unique key.

Kill (shadows)

When a database shadow is created using the MANUAL keyword, and the shadow becomes unavailable, further attachments to the database are blocked. In order to re-enable attachments to the database, it is necessary to issue a –kill database command from the *gfix* utility to delete references to the shadow.

Leaf bucket

In a binary index tree, the data item in the last index on a node of the tree is known as a leaf bucket. The leaf buckets figure reported in *gstat* index statistics provides an approximate count of the number of rows in the table.

Limbo (transaction)

A *limbo transaction* can occur where a transaction spans more than one database. Multi-database transactions are protected by *two-phase commit* which guarantees that, unless the portions of the transaction residing in each database get committed, all portions will be rolled back. If one or more of the databases involved in the transaction becomes unavailable before the completion of the two-phase commit, the transaction remains unresolved and is said to be *in limbo.*

Locking conflict

Under Firebird's optimistic locking scheme, a row becomes locked against update from other transactions as soon as its transaction posts an update request for it. Where the isolation level of the transaction is SNAPSHOT TABLE STABILITY (also known as *consistency*), the lock occurs as soon as the transaction reads the row. A locking conflict occurs when another transaction attempts to post its own update to that row. Locking conflicts have various causes, characteristics and resolutions according to the specific settings of the transactions involved.

Lock resolution (policy)

As a general term, refers to the measures taken in application code to resolve the conditions that occur when other transactions attempt to update a row that is locked by a transaction because of an update request. As a specific term, *lock resolution policy* refers to the WAIT/NO WAIT parameter setting of a transaction, that specifies how a transaction should react if a locking conflict arises.

Metadata — A generic quantity noun referring to the structure of all the objects that comprise a database. Because Firebird stores the definitions of its objects right inside the database, using its own native tables, data types and triggers, the term "metadata" also refers to the data stored in these system tables.

Monitoring tables (MON$ tables) — A suite of read-only tables, system-defined at database-create time, for use by clients on demand, for system and database monitoring.

Multi-generational architecture (MGA) — Term used for the engine mechanism of Firebird, that enables *optimistic row locking* and a high level of *transaction isolation* that protects a transaction's dynamic view of the database and its changes to rows in that view, without blocking other readers. It is achieved by the engine's capability to store multiple versions of rows concurrently and to "age" these versions with respect to the original view. See also *Versioning architecture.*

Natural (scan) — Seen sometimes in the query plans created by the optimizer, indicating that the associated table will be scanned in "natural order", i.e. in no particular order and without reference to an index.

nBackup — Multi-level incremental backup utility first available in the Firebird "2" series. Unlike *gbak*, it is "data-unaware", backing up snapshot page images while storing active work in files known as *deltas*.

Non-standard SQL — A term often heard with reference to relational database management systems that have a low degree of conformance with the ISO language and syntax standards for SQL. It is often used to describe or refer to idiomatic SQL implementations n Firebird. See also *Standard SQL*.

Non-unique key — This is a column or group of columns that can act as a pointer to a grouping of rows in a set. A foreign key constraint to implement a 1:Many relationship is typically formed by matching a non-unique column or group in a "child" or "detail" set to a unique key in a "parent" or "master" set.

Normalization — A technique commonly used during the analysis of data preceding database design to abstract repeating groups of data out of multiple tables and eliminate the potential to duplicate the same "facts" in related tables.

Null — Sometimes wrongly referred to as a "null value", null is the *state* of a data item which has no known value. Logically it is interpreted as unknown and is thus unable to be evaluated in expressions.

Null is never equivalent to zero, blank, an empty (zero length) string and it does not represent either infinity or NaN. It represents the state of a data item which either has never been assigned a value or has been set NULL by an operation.

"NULL is a state, not a value." (Now, where is that T-shirt?)

ODBC — Mnemonic for Open Database Connectivity. It is a call-level interface standard that allows applications to access data in any database which has a driver supporting this standard. Several ODBC drivers are available that support Firebird, including an open source one developed within the Firebird Project that is internally consistent with the JDBC (Java Database Connectivity) standard.

ODS — Mnemonic for On-Disk Structure. It is a number that refers to the version of the internal structure and layout of a Firebird or InterBase database. Firebird 1 creates ODS 10, v.1.5 creates ODS 10.1, v.2.0 creates ODS 11.0, v.2.1 creates ODS 11.1 and v.2.5 creates ODS 11.2. A Firebird server can work with a database of a lower ODS than it creates but not with one higher than it creates; nor can it create a database of a higher or lower ODS.

A database can be raised to a higher ODS by backing it up with the *gbak* -b[ackup] -t[ransportable] option using the old version's *gbak* program, and restoring from that *gbak* file using the new version's *gbak*.. If migrating from v.2.0 or lower to v.2.1 or higher, be sure to check the *Migration Notes* (Ch. 5) before you start.

OLAP — Mnemonic for On-Line Analytical Processing, a technology that is applied to databases that have grown to such a volume that it is impracticable for them to be queried directly as the basis of business decisions. Typically, OLAP systems are designed to analyze and graph trends, identify and capture historical milestones or anomalies, manufacture projections and hypothetical scenarios, crunch large volumes of data for reports, and so on, in reasonable time.

OS — Abbreviation for "operating system".

Oldest active transaction (OAT) A statistic maintained by the Firebird engine, global to a database, the oldest transaction still in the database that has not been either committed or rolled back.

Oldest interesting transaction (OIT) A statistic maintained by the Firebird engine, global to a database, it is the ID of the oldest transaction that has not been committed. It is sometimes the same transaction as OAT but it may not be, since any transaction that is still active, has been rolled back, committed using COMMIT WITH RETAIN (CommitRetaining) or left in limbo by a failed two-phase commit remains "interesting". When the OIT gets "stuck" at a much lower transaction ID than the newest transactions, garbage collection (cleanup of old record versions) can not proceed past it (to higher-numbered transactions) and database operations slow down and, eventually hang completely. OIT can be retrieved as OIT can be retrieved using the -header switch of the *gstat* command-line utility.

OLE-DB Mnemonic for *Object Linking and Embedding for Databases.* OLE is a Microsoft standard developed and promoted for incorporating binary objects of many diverse types (images, documents, etc.) into Windows applications, along with application-level linking to the software engines that create and modify them. OLE-DB was added in an attempt to provide developers with the means to supply a more vendor-specific support for database connectivity—especially relational databases—than can be achieved with "open" standards such as ODBC. More recently, Microsoft layered the ADO (Access Data Objects) technology on top of OLE-DB.

OLTP Mnemonic for *On-line Transaction Processing*, recognized as one of the essential requirements for a database engine.Broadly speaking, OLTP refers to support for clients performing operations that read, alter or create data in real time.

Optimization Generally, optimization refers to techniques for making the database and application software perform as responsively as possible. As a specific term, it is often applied to the techniques used by the Firebird engine to analyze SELECT statements and construct efficient plans for retrieving data. The routines in the Firebird engine which calculate these plans are known collectively as *the Firebird optimizer.*

Page A Firebird database is made up of fixed-sized blocks of disk space called *pages.* The Firebird engine allocates pages as it needs to. Once it stores data, a page could be any one of 10 different *types* of pages, all of equal size—the size defined in the PAGE_SIZE attribute during database creation. The type of page the engine stores to disk depends on the type of data object being stored on the page—data, index, blob, etc.

Page_size The size of each fixed block on disk is determined by the page_size specified for the database when the database is created or restored. Chunks of cache memory are also allocated in page_size units.

Parameter A widespread term in many Firebird contexts, it can refer to the values that are passed as arguments to and returned from stored procedures (input parameters, output parameters). The term can aslso refer to the data items that are passed to the function blocks of the Firebird API (database parameter block,transaction parameter block, service parameter block) or to the attributes, as seen from an application, of a connection instance (connection parameters) or a transaction (transaction parameters).

In client applications, placeholder tokens that are accepted for passing into WHERE clauses of SQL statements, for substitution by constant values at run-time are often implemented as "parameters"—hence the term *parameterized queries.*

PHP Short for *PHP: Hypertext Preprocessor*, an open source embedded HTML scripting language used to create web applications, especially those with database back-ends. It has good support for a number of network protocols. Its strength lies in its compatibility with many types of database engines. Also, PHP can talk across networks using IMAP, SNMP, NNTP, POP3, or HTTP. PHP's originator, in 1994, was Rasmus Lerdorf. Since 1997, it has been in the hands of a large open source community.

Plan See *Query Plan*

Platform Term loosely used to refer to the combination of hardware and operating system software, or operating system software alone. For example, "the Windows Server 2011 platform", "the Linux platform", "UNIX platforms". "Cross-platform" usually means "applicable to multiple platforms" or "portable to other platforms".

Prepare An API function that is called before a query request is submitted for the first time, requesting validation of the statement, construction of a query plan and several items of information about the data expected by the server.

Primary Key A table-level constraint that marks one column or a group of columns as the key which must identify each row as unique within the table. Although a table may have more than one unique key, only one of those keys may be the primary key. When you apply the PRIMARY KEY constraint to columns in a Firebird table, uniqueness is enforced by the automatic creation of a unique index that is, by default, ascending, and named according to a convention.

PSQL Mnemonic for *Procedural SQL*, the subset of SQL extensions implemented for writing stored procedures and triggers. There are minor differences between the subsets of PSQL allowed for stored procedures and for triggers.

qli Query Language Interpreter, an interactive query client tool for Firebird. It can process DDL and DML statements in both SQL and GDML, the pre-SQL query language of Firebird's ancestor, InterBase 3. Although largely succeeded by *isql* and a number of third-party GUI tools, *qli* has some value for its capability to realize some engine features not so far implemented in Firebird SQL. Unlike its successor, *isql*, *qli* can connect to more than one database at the same time and can simulate multi-database joins.

Query A general term for any SQL request made to the server by a client application.

Query Plan A strategy for the use of indexes and access methods for sorting and searching in queries. The Firebird optimizer always computes a plan for every SELECT query, including subqueries. It is possible to specify a custom plan using the PLAN clause syntax.

RDB$— Prefix seen in the identifiers of many system-created objects in Firebird, a relic from "Relational DataBase", abbreviated as "RDB", the name of an early relational database developed by DEC. The design of RDB was the precursor to Firebird's ancestor, InterBase.

RDB$DB_KEY The hidden, volatile, unique key that is calculated internally for every row in a table, from the physical address of the page on which the row starts and its offset from the beginning of the page. It is directly related to the cardinality of tables and sets and can change without trace or warning. It will always change when the database is restored from a backup. RDB$DB_KEY should never be treated as persistent. With care, it can be used dependably within an atomic operation to speed up certain operations in DSQL and PSQL dramatically.

RDBMS *Relational Database Management System.* Generically, it is a concept for storing data according to an abstract model that uses matching keys to link a formal group of data to another formal group of data, thereby representing a relationship between the two groups.

Read Committed The least restrictive *isolation level* for any Firebird transaction, Read Committed permits the transaction to update its view of the database to reflect work committed by other transactions since the transaction began. The isolation levels SNAPSHOT and SNAPSHOT TABLE STABILITY do not permit the original view to change.

Read Uncommitted A theoretical isolation level in which one transaction can see the uncommitted work of another: also known as "Dirty Read". Firebird does not support this isolation level at all.

Redundancy A condition in a database where the same "fact" is stored in two unrelated places. Ideally, redundancy should be avoided by attention to normalization during analysis. However, there are circumstances where a certain amount of redundancy is justified. For example, accounting transactions often contain data items which arguably could be derived by joining, looking up or calculation from other structures. However, a legal requirement to store a permanent record that will not be altered if database relationships subsequently change would overrule the case for eliminating redundancy.

Redundant Indexes Redundant indexes often arise when existing databases are imported to Firebird from another RDBMS. When a PRIMARY KEY, UNIQUE or FOREIGN KEY constraint is applied to a column or columns, Firebird automatically creates an index to enforce the constraint. In so doing, Firebird ignores any existing indexes that duplicate its automatic index. Having duplicate indexes on keys or any other columns can defeat the query optimizer, causing it to create plans that are inherently slow.

Referential integrity

Generally, referential integrity is a term that refers to the way an RDBMS implements mechanisms that formally support and protect the dependencies between tables. Referential integrity support refers to the language and syntax elements available to provide these capabilities.

Firebird provides formal mechanisms for supporting referential integrity, including cascading constraints for foreign key relationships. It is sometimes referred to as *declarative* referential integrity.

Regular expression

In the simplest terms, a regular expression (also known as a *regex* or a *regexp*) is a pattern that is matched against an operand string expression from left to right. A regex is composed of alphanumeric characters and various wildcards and can be very complex and exacting about the string patterns it seeks to match. In Firebird, a regex is used with the SIMILAR TO operator.

Relation

In relational database theory, a self-contained body of data formally arranged in columns and rows. The term is almost interchangeable with 'table'—except that a relation cannot have duplicate rows, whereas a table can. In Firebird, the terminology persists in the names of some system tables, e.g. RDB$RELATIONS, which contains an entry for each table in the database.

A view is considered by some documentation writers to be a relation. The author disagrees, since view cannot participate in relationships.

Relationship

An abstract term referring to the way relations (or tables) are linked to one another through matching keys. For example, an Order Detail table is said to be in a dependency relationship or a Foreign Key relationship with an Order Header table.

Replication

Replication is a systematic process whereby data are copied from one database to another on a regular basis, according to predictable rules, in order to bring two or more databases into a synchronized state.

Result table

A result table is the set of rows output from a SQL SELECT query. More correctly, *result set*. Synonymous with *output set*.

Role

A standard SQL mechanism for defining a set of permissions to use objects in a database. Once a role is created, permissions are assigned to it, using GRANT statements, as if it were a user. The role is then GRANTed to individual users as if it were itself a privilege, thus simplifying the maintenance of user permissions in a database.

Rollback

In general, rollback is the act or process of undoing all of the work that has been posted during the course of a transaction. As long as a transaction has work pending that is posted but not committed, it remains unresolved and its effects are invisible to other transactions. If the client application calls for a ROLLBACK, all of the posted work is cancelled and the changes are lost. Once a transaction is committed, its work cannot be rolled back.

Schema

A term for the formal description of a database, usually realized as a script, or set of scripts, containing the SQL statements defining each and every object in the database. The term schema is often interchangeable with the term metadata.

Schema cache

A mechanism whereby some descriptive elements of a database are stored on a client's local disk or in its local memory for quick reference at run-time, to avoid the need for constantly requerying the database to obtain schema (metadata) attributes.

Scrollable cursor

A cursor is a pointer to a row in a database table or output set. A cursor's position in the database is determined from the cardinality of the row to which it is currently pointing, i.e. its offset from the first row in the set. Repositioning the cursor requires returning the pointer to the first row in order to find the new position. A scrollable cursor is one which is capable of locating itself at a specified new position (upward or downward) relative to its current position. It is not supported in Firebird. Several connectivity interfaces simulate a scrollable cursor at the client side.

Selectivity of an index

As a general term, refers to the spread of possible values for the index column throughout the table. The fewer the possible values, the lower the selectivity. Low selectivity can also occur where an index with a higher number of possible values is represented in actual data by a very high rate of duplication of a few values. Low selectivity is bad, high is good. . A unique index has the highest possible selectivity.

Selectable stored procedure

Stored procedure that is written using special PSQL syntax to output a multi-row result set to the caller. It is called using a SELECT statement. cf *Executable stored procedure*.

Sequence
A standards-compliant number-generating engine for producing unique numbers in series. The statement CREATE SEQUENCE *sequence_name* seeds a distinct series of signed 64-bit integer numbers. The NEXT VALUE FOR *sequence_name* function causes a new number to be generated, which is 1 higher than the last generated number. See also *Generator.*

Services API
An application programming interface to the functions accessed by several of the Firebird command-line server utilities, providing a function-driven interface to backup, statistics, housekeeping, user management and other utilities. The Services API, or parts of it, may be inaccecible to some early Classic server versions.

Sets
In relational database terms, collections of data are managed in sets consisting of one or more rows made up of one or more columns of data, each column containing one data item of a specific size and type. For example, a SELECT query specification or a view defines a set for output to a client application or PSQL module, while an UPDATE query specification defines a set upon which the specified operation is to be performed.

Shadowing and shadows
Shadowing is an optional process available on a Firebird server, whereby an exact copy of a database is maintained, warts and all, in real time, on a separate hard-disk on the same server machine where the database resides. The copy is known as a *database shadow.* The purpose is to provide a way for a database to quickly resume operation after physical damage to the hard-drive where the original database resides. A shadow is not a useful substitute for either replication or backup.

SMP
Acronym for *Symmetric Multiprocessing*, a computer architecture that makes multiple CPUs available to a single operating system, to execute individual processes simultaneously. In theory, any idle processor can be assigned any task and, the more CPUs on the system, the better performance and load capacity.

Snapshot
SNAPSHOT is one of the three *transaction isolation levels* supported by Firebird. It provides a stable view of the database which remains current to the user of the transaction throughout the life of that transaction. It is also known as *concurrency level* isolation. See also *Read Committed, Snapshot Table Stability.*

Snapshot Table Stability
SNAPSHOT TABLE STABILITY is the most protective of the three transaction isolation levels supported by Firebird. It enforces a consistent view of the database for the user of the transaction, by preventing any other transaction from updating any row which it has selected, even if the STS transaction has not yet posted any change. It is also known as *consistency level* isolation. See also *Read Committed, Snapshot.*

SQL
The name of a query language designed to extract meaningful sets of data from a relational database and write data to it in a completely predictable fashion. Its correct pronunciation is "ess-cue-ell", not "sequel" as some people believe. ("Sequel" was the name of another query language, in medieval times.) It is also not an acronym for "Structured Query Language".

Standard SQL, SQL Standard
Refers to the syntax and implementation of SQL language elements as published by the International Standards Organization (ISO). This very complex standard prescribes definitions across an exhaustive range of syntax and functionality, at a number of levels.

Stored Procedure
Stored procedures are compiled modules of code which are stored in the database for invocation by applications and by other server-based code modules (triggers, other procedures). They are defined to the database in a source language—procedural SQL, or PSQL—consisting of regular SQL statements as well as special SQL language extensions which supply structure, looping, conditional logic, local variables, input and output arguments, exception handling and more.

Subquery
A query specification can define output columns that are derived from expressions. A subquery is a special kind of expression that returns a result which is itself the output of a SELECT statement. Also known as a *sub-select* or *embedded query.*

Sub-select, subselect
See *Sub-query.* A *sub-selected column* is one which is specified or output from a sub-query. Such columns are not updatable.

Subversion
An open-source version control system that allows developers to keep track of different development versions of source code. The Firebird core code's version control system is Subversion although, for many years, it was CVS, another version control software system.

Superclassic architecture

Implemented in Firebird 2.5, it is a process-threading model that superintends multiple Classic instances as threads. It is recommended for well-resourced 64-bit hosts as it makes effective use of multiple CPUs and large RAM installations. Not recommended for 32-bit host machines with more than a handful of users.

Superclassic is the model implemented as the embedded engine on all platforms from v.2.5 onwards.

Superserver architecture

SuperServer is the name originally given to the process-threading multi-user model, to distinguish it from the original InterBase model that instantiates one server process for each client connection. The original model is referred to as *Classic.*

Surrogate key

In defining a unique key, e.g. a primary key, it may occur that no column, or combination of columns, can be guaranteed to provide a unique identifier for each and every row. In that case, a column can be added and populated by values that are certain to be unique. Such a key is known as a *surrogate key*.

In Firebird, surrogate keys are most commonly implemented using generators (sequences). Surrogate keys are also frequently used as a matter of good design principle, to conform with rules of *atomicity*. See also *atomic.*

Sweeping

Sweeping is the process that collects and frees obsolete versions of each record in a database when a threshold number is reached. This number, which defaults to 20,000 and is known as the sweep interval, is calculated on the difference between the *oldest interesting transaction* and the *oldest snapshot transaction.* Automatic sweeping can be disabled by setting a sweep interval of zero. A manual sweep can be invoked ad hoc, using the *gfix* utility. Sweeping is not a feature of RDBM systems that do not store multiple obsolete record versions.

SYSDBA

SYStem DataBase Administrator, i.e. a person with responsibility for administering databases.

System tables

Because relational database engines are self-contained, all of the metadata, or schema—data that describe the structure and attributes of database objects—are maintained within the database, in a suite of pre-defined tables which is created by the CREATE DATABASE command. These tables which store "data about data" are known as system tables. Firebird system tables all have identifiers that begin with the prefix 'RDB$' and actually include data about themselves, as well as every other object in the database.

Firebird versions 2.1+ also store definitions for *Monitoring Tables* that are instantiated and populated on demand by a user request.

Table

A term borrowed from desktop database technology and entrenched perpetually in SQL, depicting a logical structure that stores sets of data in a tabulated format, as records (rows) of fields, each record being, by definition, identical from left to right in the number and relative placement of fields and their data types and sizes. In reality, Firebird does not store data in a physically tabulated form at all, but in contiguous blocks of disk space known as pages.

Transaction

A logical unit of work, which can involve one or many statements or executions of statements. A transaction begins when the client application starts it and ends when it either commits the transaction or rolls it back. A transaction is an *atomic* action: a commit must be able to commit every piece of pending work, otherwise all of its work is abandoned. A rollback, similarly, will cancel every piece of pending work that was posted since the start of the transaction.

Transaction isolation

A mechanism by which each transaction is provided with an environment that makes it appear (to itself and its owner) that it is running alone in the database. When multiple transactions are running concurrently, the effects of all of the other transactions are invisible to each transaction, from when it starts until it is committed. Firebird supports not just one but three levels of isolation, including one level which can see the effects of other transactions as they are committed. See *Read Committed*, also *Snapshot*, *Snapshot Table Stability*.

Transitively-dependent

A constraint or condition where one table (C) is dependent on another table (A), because table C is dependent on another table (B) which is dependent on A. Such a dependency would arise, for example, if table B had a foreign key referencing table A's primary key and table C had a foreign key referencing table B's primary key. The term is also used in data modeling to refer to a condition where, during normalization, an attribute in one entity has a partial (but incomplete) dependency on a unique attribute set in another entity.

Table-level trigger A table-level trigger is a module of compiled code belonging to a table, that performs an action when a DML event happens to a row in that table. Any number of event actions can be coded to occur in a prescribed sequence, before and/or after an insert, update or delete operation on a table's row, with virtually the full range of procedural SQL (PSQL) being available.

See also *Database trigger.*

Tuple In relational database terminology, the "strictly correct" name for a row in a table, or a group of columns that is a subset of a row. Purists would say that *row* is the SQL name for a tuple.

UDF Mnemonic for *User Defined Function*, more correctly named external function. See *External Function.*

Unbalanced index Firebird indexes are maintained as binary tree structures. These structures are said to be unbalanced when new nodes are added continually in a manner that causes major branching on one "side" of the binary tree. Typically, this could occur when a process inserts hundreds of thousands of new rows inside a single transaction. For this reason, it is recommended that indexes be deactivated during massive inserts. Subsequent re-activation will rebuild fully balanced indexes.

Uninstallation An ugly, back-formed word, confusing to non-English speakers, since it is not found in any self-respecting dictionary—yet! Its approximate meaning is 'a process that is the reverse of installation', i.e. removing a previously installed software product from a computer system.. It usually doesn't mean "deletion of component files" as installation often loads or creates artefacts in odd locations, that could cause trouble if left "installed".

Union A clause in a SELECT query specification that enables the output rows of two or more SELECT statements to be combined into one final output set, as long as each of the UNIONed sets matches all of the others by the degree, data type and size of its output columns. The sets may be selected from different tables.

Updatable view A view is said to be updatable if it is constructed from a regular query on a single table and all of its columns exist in the underlying table. Some non-updatable views can be made updatable by the creation of triggers. See also *View.*

Validation Validation is a mechanism whereby new data applied to a column in a table are checked by some means to determine whether they fit a required format, value or range of values. Two ways to implement validation in the database are CHECK constraints and triggers. A CHECK constraint will throw an exception if the input data fail to test true against the given expression or constant. With triggers, the new.value can be tested more thoroughly and, if it fails, can be passed to a custom exception.

Versioning architecture Also known as multi-generational architecture (MGA), the feature, until recently unique to Firebird and InterBase, of storing a new version of a changed row, or an inserted row on disk for the duration of a transaction, where it remains visible to that transaction even though it is not yet committed to the database. When the commit occurs, the new version becomes permanent in the database and the old version is flagged as obsolete. When considering contenders for a concurrent update in a conflict situation, the engine also uses attributes of the pending record versions concerned to determine precedence, if any.

View A view is a standard SQL object which is a stored query specification that can behave in many ways like a physical table. A view does not provide physical storage for user data: it acts as a predefined container for a set of output data that exist in one or more tables.

WNET The deprecated "Windows Networking" protocol, also known as Named Pipes and (erroneously) NetBEUI. (NetBEUI is a transport layer, not a protocol.)

WNET error In the firebird.log, marks an error received by the Firebird network layer from a Windows Named Pipes ("Windows networking") client/server connection.

XNET An improved implementation of the Windows serverless connection mechanism—referred to as the "local protocol" and *ipserver*—that was introduced in Firebird 2.0.

XSQLDA Mnemonic for "eXtended SQL Descriptor Area". It is a host-language data structure in the API which is used to transport data between a client application and the server's dynamic SQL parser module. XSQLDAs come in two types: input descriptors and output descriptors.

XSQLVAR Structure for defining *sqlvar*, an important field in the XSQLDA structure, used in the API for passing and returning input and output parameters.

Y valve Name given to the Firebird subsystem that determines which of Firebird's several "internal engines" should be used when attaching to a database. For example, one decision is whether to attach locally or as a remote client; another is to determine whether the attachment is being attempted to a database with an incompatible on-disk structure (ODS)

3652813R00259

Printed in Great Britain
by Amazon.co.uk, Ltd.,
Marston Gate.